Employer's Guide to Health Care Reform
2012–2013 Edition

by Brian M. Pinheiro, Jean C. Hemphill, Clifford J. Schoner,
Jonathan M. Calpas, and Kurt R. Anderson

The *Employer's Guide to Health Care Reform* is designed to assist employers in updating their health and welfare benefit plans to comply with the Patient Protection and Affordable Care Act and the Health Care and Education Reconciliation Act of 2010 (which are collectively referred to in this *Guide* as the Affordable Care Act). Along the way, the book identifies opportunities created by the Affordable Care Act for employers to control or reduce their overall health benefit spending. It touches on the national debate that continues to rage regarding the fundamental principles, culminating in the U.S. Supreme Court's decision in *National Federation of Independent Business v. Sebelius*, as well as the details of health care reform, but it is not intended to be a partisan treatise. Rather, *Employer's Guide to Health Care Reform* is a step-by-step practical guide for employers struggling to keep up with the rapid pace of changes affecting their health benefit plans.

Highlights of the 2012–2013 Edition

The Affordable Care Act reflects lawmakers' ambitious goal of transforming the delivery of health care in the United States. Notwithstanding its length, the Act leaves many of the details of health care reform in the hands of the federal agencies, including the United States Departments of Health and Human Services, Labor, and Treasury. Since enactment of the Affordable Care Act on March 23, 2010, federal regulators have been churning out reams of new regulations, procedures, and sub-regulatory guidance to implement the new law. In this edition, you will find discussion of the latest health care reform developments and detailed explanations of these important topics:

- A review of the landmark U.S. Supreme Court decision in *National Federation of Independent Business v. Sebelius*, which upholds the constitutionality of the Affordable Care Act (see Chapter 3)

- When is a plan a "grandfathered" health plan—and how to keep it that way (see Sections 5.01 and 5.02)

- Whether an employer-sponsored health plan covering solely retirees is subject to the Affordable Care Act design changes, such as the requirement to cover children through age 26 (see Section 5.03)

- What types of subsidies and tax credits are available right now to employers that provide health coverage to employees (see Sections 7.01 and 7.03)

- Which health plans and benefits are currently subject to new prohibitions on annual and lifetime limits, and what exemptions are available (see Section 8.01)

- How and when the Affordable Care Act restricts preexisting-condition exclusions (see Sections 8.02 and 9.01)

- When must an employer-sponsored health plan provide full coverage for preventive health services without cost-sharing (see Section 8.03)

- What are the consequences of offering health plan coverage to children up to age 26 (see Section 8.04)

- What are the new claims and appeals processes mandated by the Affordable Care Act for health plans (see Section 8.05)

Law & Business

- What additional changes to health plan design are going to be required beginning in 2014 (see Chapter 9)
- How will employer-sponsored health plans need to change their employee communications to address the Affordable Care Act requirements (see Section 10.01)
- What new types of reporting will be required for health plans (see Sections 10.01–10.07)
- What is the "individual mandate" to enroll in health coverage (see Section 11.01)
- Which employers will have to pay a penalty if they do not provide adequate and affordable health plan coverage (see Section 11.02)
- How employers can determine whether their coverage is adequate and affordable (see Section 11.02)
- What is a health care Exchange, and how will it affect the U.S. health care system (see Section 11.04)
- What states will need to do to set up a health care Exchange (see Section 11.04)
- How the Affordable Care Act affects retiree prescription drug coverage under Medicare Part D and how the changes create new opportunities for employers (see Section 12.01)
- How and when the new nondiscrimination rules apply to insured health benefits, and what are the consequences of discriminatory coverage (see Section 12.02)
- Which employer-sponsored health plans are subject to auto-enrollment and when do the rules go into effect (see Section 12.03)
- What are the new Form W-2 reporting requirements for employer-sponsored health plans and when do they go into effect (see Section 12.06)
- When health care flexible spending accounts (Health FSAs) and health savings accounts (HSAs) may and may not pay reimbursements for over-the-counter medicines and drugs (see Sections 13.02 and 13.03)
- What is the purpose of the transitional reinsurance fee to be assessed from 2014 through 2016 (see Sections 13.04[A] and 13.04[F])

The 2012–2013 Edition also provides numerous examples, new charts and appendices with important guidance, useful acronyms, and an updated Index.

11/12

For questions concerning this shipment, billing, or other customer service matters, call our Customer Service Department at 1-800-234-1660.

For toll-free ordering, please call 1-800-638-8437.

EMPLOYER'S GUIDE TO HEALTH CARE REFORM

2012–2013 Edition

Brian M. Pinheiro
Jean C. Hemphill
Clifford J. Schoner
Jonathan M. Calpas
Kurt R. Anderson

Ballard Spahr LLP

Wolters Kluwer
Law & Business

This publication is designed to provide accurate and authoritative information in regard to the subject matter covered. It is sold with the understanding that the publisher and the author(s) are not engaged in rendering legal, accounting, or other professional services. If legal advice or other professional assistance is required, the services of a competent professional should be sought.

—From a *Declaration of Principles* jointly adopted by
a Committee of the American Bar Association and
a Committee of Publishers and Associations.

Published by Wolters Kluwer Law & Business in New York.

Wolters Kluwer Law & Business serves customers worldwide with CCH, Aspen Publishers and Kluwer Law International products.

Printed in the United States of America

ISBN 978-1-4548-1032-2

1 2 3 4 5 6 7 8 9 0

FSC
MIX
FSC® C103993

About Wolters Kluwer Law & Business

Wolters Kluwer Law & Business is a leading global provider of intelligent information and digital solutions for legal and business professionals in key specialty areas, and respected educational resources for professors and law students. Wolters Kluwer Law & Business connects legal and business professionals as well as those in the education market with timely, specialized authoritative content and information-enabled solutions to support success through productivity, accuracy and mobility.

Serving customers worldwide, Wolters Kluwer Law & Business products include those under the Aspen Publishers, CCH, Kluwer Law International, Loislaw, Best Case, ftwilliam.com and MediRegs family of products.

CCH products have been a trusted resource since 1913, and are highly regarded resources for legal, securities, antitrust and trade regulation, government contracting, banking, pension, payroll, employment and labor, and healthcare reimbursement and compliance professionals.

Aspen Publishers products provide essential information to attorneys, business professionals and law students. Written by preeminent authorities, the product line offers analytical and practical information in a range of specialty practice areas from securities law and intellectual property to mergers and acquisitions and pension/benefits. Aspen's trusted legal education resources provide professors and students with high-quality, up-to-date and effective resources for successful instruction and study in all areas of the law.

Kluwer Law International products provide the global business community with reliable international legal information in English. Legal practitioners, corporate counsel and business executives around the world rely on Kluwer Law journals, looseleafs, books, and electronic products for comprehensive information in many areas of international legal practice.

Loislaw is a comprehensive online legal research product providing legal content to law firm practitioners of various specializations. Loislaw provides attorneys with the ability to quickly and efficiently find the necessary legal information they need, when and where they need it, by facilitating access to primary law as well as state-specific law, records, forms and treatises.

Best Case Solutions is the leading bankruptcy software product to the bankruptcy industry. It provides software and workflow tools to flawlessly streamline petition preparation and the electronic filing process, while timely incorporating ever-changing court requirements.

ftwilliam.com offers employee benefits professionals the highest quality plan documents (retirement, welfare and non-qualified) and government forms (5500/PBGC, 1099 and IRS) software at highly competitive prices.

MediRegs products provide integrated health care compliance content and software solutions for professionals in healthcare, higher education and life sciences, including professionals in accounting, law and consulting.

Wolters Kluwer Law & Business, a division of Wolters Kluwer, is headquartered in New York. Wolters Kluwer is a market-leading global information services company focused on professionals.

WOLTERS KLUWER LAW & BUSINESS
SUPPLEMENT NOTICE

This product is updated on a periodic basis with supplements to reflect important changes in the subject matter. If you have purchased this product directly from Wolters Kluwer Law & Business, we have already recorded your subscription for the update service.

If, however, you purchased this product from a bookstore and wish to receive future updates and revised or related volumes billed separately with a 30-day examination review, please contact our Customer Service Department at 1-800-234-1660 or send your name, company name (if applicable), address, and the title of the product to:

Wolters Kluwer Law & Business
Distribution Center
7201 McKinney Circle
Frederick, MD 21704

Important Contact Information

- To order any title, go to *www.aspenpublishers.com* or call 1-800-638-8437.

- To reinstate your manual update service, call 1-800-638-8437.

- To contact Customer Service, e-mail *customer.service@wolterskluwer.com*, call 1-800-234-1660, fax 1-800-901-9075, or mail correspondence to: Order Department—Aspen Publishers, Wolters Kluwer Law & Business, PO Box 990, Frederick, MD 21705.

- To review your account history or pay an invoice online, visit *www.aspenpublishers.com/payinvoices*.

ABOUT THE AUTHORS

Brian M. Pinheiro is the chair of the Employee Benefits and Executive Compensation Group at Ballard Spahr LLP and a member of the Health Care Group and the Health Care Reform Initiative. Mr. Pinheiro represents clients on matters relating to employer-sponsored health and welfare benefit plans; executive compensation, including Section 409A and the Section 280G golden parachute rules; and tax-qualified retirement plans, including cash balance pension plans and section 401(k) plans and section 403(b) tax-sheltered annuity programs. Prior to joining Ballard, he was a tax law specialist for the Employee Plans Division of the Internal Revenue Service (National Office).

Mr. Pinheiro is a frequent lecturer on employee benefits and executive compensation issues and an adjunct professor of law at Temple University James F. Beasley School of Law. *Chambers USA: America's Leading Lawyers for Business* named Mr. Pinheiro a leader in the field of benefits and compensation law in the 2006 through 2010 editions. He also is co-editor of *ERISA: A Comprehensive Guide, Fourth Edition* and co-author of the forthcoming *Employee Stock Ownership Plan Answer Book, Fourth Edition* (both published by Wolters Kluwer Law & Business).

Mr. Pinheiro graduated with distinction from Georgetown University Law Center with an LL.M. in tax law and a Certificate in Employee Benefits. He is also a graduate of Boston College (B.A.), and Catholic University of America Columbus School of Law (J.D., *magna cum laude*), where he served as Production Editor for the Catholic University Law Review.

Jean C. Hemphill is a partner in the Business and Finance Department of Ballard Spahr LLP. She is the chair of the Health Care Group and a member of the Employee Benefits and Executive Compensation, Mergers and Acquisitions/Private Equity, Nonprofit Organizations, and Higher Education Groups. She concentrates her practice in the areas of general corporate, health care, employee benefits, and nonprofit, health care, and church plan laws.

Before joining Ballard Spahr in 1997, Ms. Hemphill was Vice President and General Counsel of the Board of Pensions of the Presbyterian Church (U.S.A.). She continues to serve as General Counsel for the Board and legal counsel to numerous other denominational benefits programs. She is a director of the National Health Law Project and a frequent lecturer on health care and nonprofit law subjects.

Ms. Hemphill is a graduate of the University of Pennsylvania and Temple University's James E. Beasley School of Law. She has an AV Peer Review Rating from Martindale-Hubbell.

Clifford J. Schoner is of counsel in the Employee Benefits and Executive Compensation Group at Ballard Spahr LLP. He concentrates his practice in employee benefits law, including the treatment of executive compensation and benefits in mergers and acquisitions and all fiduciary aspects of plan operation and investment.

Before joining Ballard Spahr, Mr. Schoner worked with Union Pacific Railroad Company as ERISA counsel for more than 17 years. He serves on the Executive Committee and Board of Directors of the ERISA Industry Committee (ERIC) and also chairs ERIC's Legal Committee.

Mr. Schoner is a graduate of Syracuse University (B.A.), Rutgers School of Law—Camden (J.D.), and New York University School of Law, Graduate Division (LL.M.).

Jonathan M. Calpas is an associate in the Employee Benefits and Executive Compensation Group at Ballard Spahr LLP. Mr. Calpas represents for-profit, tax-exempt, church, and government employers on matters related to tax-qualified retirement plans and employer-sponsored health and welfare plans. He focuses on compliance with the statutory and regulatory rules relating to such plans, including rules arising out of the Internal Revenue Code, ERISA, and HIPAA.

Before joining Ballard Spahr, Mr. Calpas worked for a large cable communications company as a financial accountant, and also worked for a major public accounting firm assisting clients with corporate and partnership tax compliance issues. Mr. Calpas is a Certified Public Accountant in the Commonwealth of Pennsylvania.

Mr. Calpas is a graduate of Pennsylvania State University (B.S., *with distinction*) and Temple University James E. Beasley School of Law (J.D.), where he was a member of the Temple Journal of Science, Technology & Environmental Law.

Kurt R. Anderson is counsel in the Employee Benefits and Executive Compensation Group at Ballard Spahr LLP. Mr. Anderson's practice encompasses a full range of services with respect to the creation, administration and termination of employee benefit plans, including both retirement and health and welfare plans. He has substantial experience in advising public- and private-sector clients regarding operational compliance and communication of employee benefit plans.

Mr. Anderson is a graduate of Yale College (B.A., *cum laude*) and the University of Pennsylvania Law School (J.D., *cum laude*).

ACKNOWLEDGMENTS

Putting together a comprehensive review of health care reform from an employer's point of view is not an easy task. We could not have produced this text without a tremendous amount of assistance and support. We wish to thank the Employee Benefits and Executive Compensation Group and the Labor and Employment Group at Ballard Spahr LLP, with particular thanks to Marla Roshkoff, Ed Leeds, Samantha McMillan, Josh Bobrin, Brian Pedrow, John Langel, Dan Johns, Shannon Farmer, Steve Suflas, Denise Keyser, Pat Harvey, John McLaughlin, Bob Krauss, Maggie Devitt, Robin Ireland, Eileen Kenney, Maryanne Barrett, Barbara Stokes, and Randee Borasky.

For editorial guidance, encouragement, and support from the inception of this project, we thank May Wu, Senior Managing Editor at Wolters Kluwer Law & Business. For copyediting and indexing, we thank Susan M. Junkin.

We also wish to thank our families and friends who have tolerated interminable discussions about health care reform during the past months.

TABLE OF CONTENTS

CHAPTER 14 ANALYZING THE IMPACT OF HEALTH CARE REFORM

APPENDICES

INDEX

PREFACE

"What does health care reform really mean?" This is the question we have heard over and over again since the summer of 2009 from clients, friends, neighbors and family members, and even from total strangers calling and e-mailing in to television and radio shows. Media reports focused on some of the more scandalous rumors, including the now infamous "death panel" debate among national politicians. Somehow, new legislation that meant so much for so many seemed to be understood by so few.

We undertook an effort, beginning in the summer of 2009 and continuing through 2012, to educate ourselves and to explain to our clients (many of whom are employers) exactly how and why health care reform is relevant. Along the way, we discovered that health care reform will have a significant impact on virtually every employer, and even presents some cost-savings opportunities upon which employers who are paying attention can capitalize. Debate over health care reform rages on in Congress (in the form of amending legislation), in the courts and among the states, which will play a significant role in implementation. In the summer of 2012, the focus for challengers to health care reform has shifted from the courts to the national political arena. While the landmark 2010 legislation created a blueprint for health care reform in the United States, we are certain that the specifics will continue to evolve in 2013 and future years.

We wrote this book as a guide to health care reform for employers. We tried to be comprehensive while still providing practical pointers. We hope you find this book to be as helpful as we found the process of writing it to be interesting.

Brian Pinheiro
Jean Hemphill
Cliff Schoner
Jonathan Calpas
Kurt Anderson

LIST OF ACRONYMS

ACA	Affordable Care Act
ACIP	Advisory Committee on Immunization Practices
ACO	Accountable care organizations
AD&D	Accidental death & dismemberment insurance
AHRQ	HHS Agency for Healthcare Research and Quality
AMT	Alternative minimum tax
AWP Statutes	Any willing provider statutes
CABG	Coronary artery bypass graft surgery
CBO	Congressional Budget Office
CDC	Centers for Disease Control
CHIP	Children's Health Insurance Program
CLAS	Culturally and linguistically appropriate services
CMS	HHS Centers of Medicare and Medicaid Services
COBRA	Consolidated Omnibus Budget Reconciliation Act of 1985
CPI-U	Consumer Price Index for All Urban Customers
DOL	U.S. Department of Labor
DRG	Diagnostic related group
EGWP	Employer group waiver plan
EMTALA	Emergency Medical Treatment and Labor Act
EPSDT	Early and Periodic Screening, Diagnostic and Treatment
ERISA	Employee Retirement Income Security Act of 1974
ERL	Early retiree list (for ERRP)
ERRP	Early Retiree Reinsurance Program
FEHBP	Federal Health Benefits Program
FDA	Food and Drug Administration
FICA	Federal Insurance Contributions Act
FLSA	Fair Labor Standards Act of 1938
FMLA	Family and Medical Leave Act of 1993
FPL	Federal poverty level
FSA	Flexible spending account
FTE	Full-time equivalent employee
FUTA	Federal Unemployment Tax Act
GDP	Gross domestic product
HCERA*	Health Care and Education Reconciliation Act of 2010
HDHP	High-deductible health plan
HELP	U.S. Senate Health, Education, Labor and Pension Committee
HHS	U.S. Department of Health and Human Services
HI	Hospital Insurance (portion of FICA)
HIPAA	Health Insurance Portability and Accountability Act of 1996

HMO	Health maintenance organization
HRA	Health reimbursement account
HRSA	Health Resources and Services Administration
HSA	Health savings account
IPPS	Inpatient Prospective Payment System
IRO	Independent review organization
IRS	Internal Revenue Service
LEP	Limited English proficiency
MEWA	Multiple employer welfare arrangement
MHPAEA	Mental Health Parity and Addiction Equity Act of 2008
MLR	Medical loss ratio
MMA	Medicare Prescription Drug, Improvement and Modernization Act of 2003
MSA	Medical savings account
NAIC	National Association of Insurance Commissioners
NCQA	National Committee for Quality Assurance
OBRA	Omnibus Budget Reconciliation Act
OTC	Over the counter
PHSA	Public Health Service Act
POS	Point of service
PPA	Pension Protection Act of 2006
PPACA*	Patient Protection and Affordable Care Act of 2010
PPO	Preferred provider organization
QHP	Qualified health plan
RDS	Retiree drug subsidy
SAFRA	Student Aid and Fiscal Responsibility Act
SBC	Summary of benefits and coverage
SECA	Self-Employment Contribution Act
SMM	Summary of material modifications
SPD	Summary plan description
SSA	Social Security Act
SWS	ERRP Secure Web site
TPA	Third-party administrator
TRICARE	TRICARE military service plans
UCR	Usual, customary, and reasonable
URAC	Utilization Review Accreditation Commission (formerly)
VBID	Value-Based Insurance Design
VEBA	Voluntary Employees' Beneficiary Association

*For convenience, when we intend to refer to both the PPACA and the HCERA, we refer to the "Affordable Care Act" (ACA) or simply the "Act."

CHAPTER 1

INTRODUCTION

What does health care reform mean for employers? That is the simple and straightforward question which this book, the *Employer's Guide to Health Care Reform,* attempts to address. While the question may be simple and straightforward, the answer is not. Health care reform presents different opportunities and challenges for different types of employers. How an employer will be affected by, and need to prepare for, health care reform depends on a number of variables, including:

- The size and composition (e.g., full time vs. part time) of the employer's workforce;

- The average income level of employees;

- The extent to which the employer's workforce is unionized;

- Whether the employer provides coverage to pre- and/or post-Medicare retirees, in addition to active employees;

- The types of group health plans provided to employees, including traditional indemnity, preferred provider organizations (PPOs), point-of-service (POS) arrangements, health maintenance organizations (HMOs), high-deductible and consumer-driven health plans, health reimbursement accounts (HRAs), health flexible spending accounts (Health FSAs), and health savings accounts (HSAs);

- Whether the costs incurred under those plans are "self-funded" by the employer out of its operating assets, or funded through insurance (or a combination of both);

- The design of the employer's group health plan and the terms and conditions of coverage;

- Whether the employer is for-profit or nonprofit; and

- The degree to which health benefits continue to be viewed as an important benefit for the recruiting and retention of employees in the employer's industry.

The health care reform effort is a once-in-a-generation overhaul of about one-sixth of the United States economy.[1] In a landmark decision, the U.S. Supreme Court has determined that the Patient Protection and Affordable Care Act, the legislative vehicle for health care reform, is constitutional and, barring repeal, is here to stay.[2] Health care reform could fundamentally alter the manner in which health care benefits are provided to Americans, potentially shifting from an employment-based system to an individual-based system run through "Exchange" marketplaces organized at the state level. Shortly after signing the health care reform law on March 23, 2010, President Obama said:

---

[1] *See* Patient Protection and Affordable Care Act of 2010 § 1501(a)(2)(B) (finding that "[n]ational health spending is projected to increase from [\$2.5 trillion], or 17.6 percent of the economy, in 2009 to [\$4.7 trillion] in 2019"). *See also* Executive Office of the President, Council of Economic Advisors, *The Economic Case for Health Care Reform,* http://www.whitehouse.gov/assets/documents/ CEA_Health_Care_Report.pdf, p. 1 (June 2009) (providing that health care expenditures represent almost 18% of GDP in 2009 and are projected to rise to 34% of GDP by 2040); Congressional Budget Office, *The Long Term Outlook for Health Care Spending,* http:// www.cbo.gov/ftpdocs/87xx/doc8758/MainText.3.1.shtml, p. 3 (indicating the total spending on health care for 2007 equaled about 16% of the United States gross domestic product for that year).

[2] National Fed'n of Indep. Bus. v. Sebelius, 132 S. Ct. 1133 (2012).

I said this once or twice, but it bears repeating: If you like your current insurance, you will keep your current insurance. No government takeover; nobody is changing what you've got if you're happy with it. If you like your doctor, you will be able to keep your doctor. In fact, more people will keep their doctors because your coverage will be more secure and more stable than it was before I signed this legislation.[3]

While the new law does not force individuals to drop or change their coverage, it remains to be seen whether employers, through which many individuals currently have health insurance coverage, decide to continue to provide the same type of coverage in light of the health care reform changes. Because health care reform will be implemented in pieces over the next decade, subject to several intervening federal and state election cycles, it is difficult to predict what the health care system will look like in future years. Legislative changes, regulatory interpretations, court decisions, and market-place reactions all will shape the manner in which health care reform is implemented.

The breadth and depth of the changes, along with the protracted and divisive political process that led to the changes, have created substantial confusion among the employers who will be affected by health care reform. This guide addresses issues that are important to employers as follows:

- Chapter 2 provides the context for health care reform by describing the relevant aspects of the United States health care system prior to reform and explaining the objectives that health care reform is intended to address. It also discusses the legislative process that resulted in health care reform, the structure of the new law and how it relates to other laws affecting human resources and employee benefits, and how the changes in the new law will be enforced.

- Chapter 3 discusses the U.S. Supreme Court's decision in *National Federation of Independent Business v. Sebelius*, and describes how the Court addressed the various constitutional challenges to health care reform.

- Chapter 4 introduces some of the basic concepts of the new law and defines key terms used throughout the statute. Among other things, this chapter explains the subtle yet important differences between a "group health plan" and "health insurance coverage."

- Chapter 5 describes in detail certain exemptions from the health care reform requirements. Grandfathered health plans will allow an employer to avoid some, but not all, of the health care reform changes. Plans that only cover retirees or that only provide certain "excepted" benefits, on the other hand, can be exempt from all health care reform requirements. Employers will need to carefully consider whether they can or should take advantage of these exemptions.

- Chapter 6 summarizes the provisions in the Affordable Care Act that are intended to make health care coverage more accessible and more affordable to Americans and reviews the timeline for their implementation.

- Chapter 7 addresses the temporary programs that have already been established to preserve, extend, or expand coverage to the demographic groups most likely to be uninsured: high-risk individuals, early retirees, employees of small business, and young adults. Among the changes are an immediate opportunity for employers to receive reimbursements from the federal government for providing certain health coverage to retirees and a tax credit for small businesses that provide health insurance to their employees.

- Chapter 8 discusses the basic changes to health plan design that must be implemented prior to 2014 under the new law. Most of the design changes were effective for 2011 (or earlier),

---

[3] President Obama, remarks at the U.S. Department of the Interior (Mar. 23, 2010), http://www.whitehouse.gov/blog/2010/03?page=3.

and employers will need to amend their plan documents and communications materials to reflect the changes.

- Chapter 9 discusses additional changes to health plan design that must be implemented beginning with the 2014 plan year. Employers will have a bit more time to determine how to update their plan documents and communications materials to reflect these changes.

- Chapter 10 summarizes the transparency and accountability reporting that the Affordable Care Act imposes on group health plans and health insurance issuers as well as the information that will become available to individuals about their health coverage options either directly from their employer plan sponsor or through a United States Department of Health and Human Services (HHS) Web portal.

- Chapter 11 focuses on the "meat and potatoes" of the health care reform law, explaining the obligation of individuals to enroll in certain health coverage or pay a penalty, as well as the obligation of employers to provide certain health coverage or pay a penalty. It also describes the "Exchanges" created by the new law, and how certain individuals can obtain subsidized health insurance coverage through an Exchange.

- Chapter 12 explains operational changes in the new law that will have a direct or indirect effect on employers, including a series of changes that will affect the Medicare Part D retiree drug subsidy (RDS) payable to employers that offer certain retiree prescription drug coverage.

- Chapter 13 examines some of the new taxes and revenue-raisers that will have a direct or indirect impact on employers. Employers will need to amend certain plans, including Health FSAs, to reflect these changes.

- Chapter 14 summarizes the most relevant changes from different points of view. For example, it identifies which changes large employers should be considering and compares them to the changes in which small employers would be most interested. It also discusses the changes that are most significant for full-time and part-time employees, union and non-union groups, modest- and high-income employees, and self-funded and insured group health plans.

The appendices in the *Employer's Guide to Health Care Reform* provide handy references to primary source guidance issued by the regulatory agencies, relevant forms and instructions, and model notices.

CHAPTER 2

EVOLUTION OF HEALTH CARE REFORM

§ 2.01   Reasons for Health Care Reform

While there has been widespread debate and disagreement about how to reform the health care system in the United States, there does not seem to be much of a dispute about the basic problems that need to be addressed:

- Improving access to and the quality of care,

- Reining in the ever-increasing cost of health care, and

- Finding a way to pay for any reforms that are enacted.

Improving access to and quality of care. For 2008, the U.S. Census Bureau determined that 46.3 million people in the United States, or more than 15 percent of the total population, did not have health insurance coverage.[1] An estimated 87 million people were uninsured at some point in 2007 or 2008.[2] Young adults represented approximately 33 percent of the uninsured population.[3] People who do not have insurance tend not to receive preventive care and often fail to treat minor health problems before they turn into chronic or high-cost problems. Failure to receive timely and proper care leads to lost workplace productivity and higher rates of serious illness and death.[4]

Reining in the ever-increasing cost of health care. Employers certainly do not need to be reminded of the need to address increasing health care costs. Premiums for health coverage have more than doubled in the last decade, which is more than three times the rate of wage increases over the same period.[5] Many employers have faced double-digit increases in the cost of health coverage in recent years, even as they have seen their revenues shrink in a recessionary economy.

Finding a way to pay for any reforms that are enacted. Nearly everyone involved in the health care reform debate seemed to agree that if any reforms were enacted, they needed to be accompanied by enough tax increases and other revenue raisers to have a net positive effect on the federal budget. On March 20, 2010, the Congressional Budget Office released its final cost estimate on the new health care reform law, in which it projected that the law would produce a net $143 billion reduction in federal deficits over the 2010-2019 period.[6] Much of the savings comes from provisions in the new law to address Medicare fraud, waste, and abuse, and to otherwise streamline the health care system. However, the law also includes tax increases for certain high earners, as well as an array of fees and penalties on individuals, employers, and other constituents in the health care system.[7]

After more than a year of intense political debate about how to solve the problems of the United States health system, Congress passed and President Obama signed two bills: the Patient Protection

---

[1] U.S. Census Bureau, Income, Poverty and Health Insurance Coverage in the United States: 2008, http://www.census.gov/prod/2009pubs/p60-236.pdf, p. 20 (Sept. 2009); *see also* Peter R. Orszag, Director of Office of Management & Budget, Counting the Uninsured: 46 Million or "More Than 30 Million?," http://www.whitehouse.gov/omb/blog/09/09/10/CountingtheUninsured46MillionorMorethan30Million/ (explaining that the 46.3 million figure includes about 10 million illegal aliens).

[2] Meena Seshamani, M.D., Ph.D., The Costs of Inaction, the Urgent Need for Health Reform, http://www.healthreform.gov/reports/inaction/diminishing/index.html.

[3] Meena Seshamani, M.D., Ph.D., Young Americans and Health Insurance Reform: Giving Young Americans the Security and Stability They Need, http://www.healthreform.gov/reports/youngadults/youngamericans.pdf.pdf.

[4] Meena Seshamani, M.D., Ph.D., The Costs of Inaction, the Urgent Need for Health Reform, http://www.healthreform.gov/reports/inaction/diminishing/index.html.

[5] Lower Premiums, Stronger Businesses: How Health Insurance Reform Will Bring Down Costs for Small Businesses, http://www.healthreform.gov/reports/smallbusiness2/index.html (citing Kaiser Family Foundation, Employer Health Benefit Survey (Menlo Park, CA: Kaiser Family Foundation, 2009), http://ehbs.kff.org/).

[6] Letter from Douglas W. Elmendorf, Director of the Congressional Budget Office, to the Honorable Nancy Pelosi, Speaker of the United States House of Representatives, dated March 20, 2010, http://www.cbo.gov/ftpdocs/113xx/doc11379/Manager's AmendmenttoReconciliationProposal.pdf.

[7] See **Chapter 13**, *infra*, for a discussion of the new taxes and revenue raisers.

and Affordable Care Act (enacted on March 23, 2010)[8] and the Health Care and Education Reconciliation Act of 2010 (enacted on March 31, 2010).[9] We refer to the laws throughout this book as the "PPACA" and the "HCERA," or together as the "Affordable Care Act" (ACA) or "the Act."

§ 2.02   The Employer-Based Health Care Coverage Landscape Prior to Health Care Reform

Approximately 177 million Americans (59 percent of the total population) obtain their health care coverage through an employer-based arrangement.[10] Ninety-six percent of employers with 50 or more employees offer health care coverage; 43 percent of employers with fewer than 50 employees offer coverage.[11] Under an employer-based arrangement, an individual may potentially be covered as an employee; a former employee (either under COBRA coverage or as a retiree under an active or retiree plan); a spouse of a current or former employee; a child or stepchild of a current or former employee, including adopted children, a grandchild being raised by an employee, a legal ward or a foster child of the employee; a domestic partner; or a child of a domestic partner.

[A]   Group Health Plans

When an employer offers coverage to more than one employee, a "group health plan" is established.[12] A group health plan may be insured, self-funded (sometimes referred to as self-insurance), or both.

An "insured" group health plan is one that is funded through the purchase of insurance. The employer (and possibly the current and former employees) pays a premium to an insurance company, and any benefits payable under the plan are paid by the insurance company out of its assets. A "self-funded" group health plan is one that is funded out of the employer's general assets. The employer may hire an insurance company or other third party to decide and pay claims, but the benefits payable under the plan are paid out of the employer's general assets. Self-funded plans tend to be less expensive, because employers do not have to pay premium taxes or fund insurance company reserves, but the costs may be more volatile depending on the experience of covered employees and their dependents. Some employers that sponsor self-funded plans purchase stop-loss insurance to cap their individual or aggregate claims exposure. Approximately 55 percent of workers are covered by self-funded employer-based plans.[13]

While most small employers offer coverage through the group health insurance market, smaller employers sometimes join together in various arrangements to obtain better rates for coverage as a group or an association. Employers with a unionized labor workforce may, as an alternative to offering coverage directly, contribute on behalf of their union employees to health plans sponsored or operated by a union, including Taft-Hartley trust arrangements. As discussed in more detail in Chapter 11, the Affordable Care Act maintains existing employer-based group health plan coverage principles. At the same time, it creates a new independent infrastructure for individuals and their dependents to access affordable, quality health care coverage outside of their employment.

---

[8] Pub. L. No. 111-148, 124 Stat. 119.

[9] Pub. L. No. 111-152, 124 Stat. 1029.

[10] U.S. Census Bureau, Income, Poverty and Health Insurance Coverage in the United States (2007).

[11] Executive Office of the President, Council of Economic Advisors, The Economic Case for Health Care Reform, http://www.whitehouse.gov/assets/documents/CEA_Health_Care_Report.pdf, p. 8 (June 2009).

[12] 42 U.S.C. § 300gg-91(a)(1); I.R.C. § 5000(b)(1).

[13] Kaiser/HRET Survey of Employer-Sponsored Health Benefits, 1999–2007.

[B] Plan Design

There are many different types of health plan designs offered by employers in their group health plans. Different coverage offerings may include, for example, traditional indemnity plans; managed care plans such as health maintenance organizations (HMOs); preferred provider organizations (PPOs) and point-of-service (POS) arrangements; high-deductible and consumer-driven arrangements; and account-based arrangements, such as health reimbursement arrangements (HRAs), health savings accounts (HSAs), health flexible spending accounts (Health FSAs), and Archer medical spending accounts (Archer MSAs).

Some employers offer a single health plan that provides medical, behavioral health, and prescription drug benefits through a single insurance carrier or third-party administrator (TPA). Other employer plans carve out basic medical coverage from care or services offered by specialty providers, such as a separate prescription drug plan or a separate behavioral health benefits plan that provides mental health and substance abuse benefits. To cover out-of-pocket expenses that may not otherwise be covered by the plan, an employer may offer a supplemental HRA, HSA, or Health FSA so that its employees can pay those costs with pretax dollars.

An employer may provide a single health care coverage package or a variety of options from which employees can choose through a cafeteria plan (sometimes referred to as a "Section 125 plan" or a "flexible benefits plan") offered by an employer.[14] The employee's choice of coverage may result in a higher contribution amount toward the premium for the coverage or different levels of deductibles, copays, and cost-sharing. In some cafeteria plans, employees may opt out of coverage altogether and receive the amounts they otherwise would have paid as pretax premiums for health coverage as additional cash compensation.

Under the Affordable Care Act, these plan designs may continue but they may not qualify as health care coverage in which an individual must enroll or that an employer must offer to avoid paying a tax or penalty. Many will qualify if their benefit coverage provisions are amended to conform with the requirements for qualified coverage.

[C] Regulation of Health Care Plans

Most, but not all, employer-sponsored health plans are subject to regulation by the United States Department of Labor (DOL) under the Employee Retirement Income Security Act of 1974, as amended (ERISA).[15] Also, since most employer-sponsored health plans are provided on a pretax basis to employees and former employees and their spouses and dependents, the plans are subject to rules set forth in the Internal Revenue Code of 1986, as amended (Code) and corresponding U.S. Treasury regulations.[16] Health plans sponsored by government and church employers are exempt from ERISA,[17] but are subject to the tax laws as well as federal health care laws and regulations in the Code and the Public Health Service Act (PHSA)[18] that are administered by the United States Department of Health and Human Services (HHS).

Insurance companies, often referred to as health insurance carriers or issuers, are licensed by the individual states and regulated by the state departments of insurance. An employment-based group health plan that is insured (as opposed to self-funded) may be subject to federal mandates under ERISA and state law mandates that govern the insurance industry.

---

[14] *See* I.R.C. § 125 (providing the cafeteria plan design requirements).

[15] Pub. L. No. 93-406, 88 Stat. 829.

[16] I.R.C. §§ 105, 106.

[17] 29 U.S.C. § 1003(b). A church plan may elect to be subject to ERISA, and such an election is irrevocable. I.R.C. § 410(d).

[18] PHSA, 42 U.S.C. Ch. 6A.

Most self-funded plans are not subject to regulation by the states. If the self-funded plan is subject to ERISA, the plan will be exempt from most state regulation under the ERISA preemption clause.[19]

Under the Affordable Care Act, the same regulatory entities continue to preside over the provision of health coverage by employers and insurance companies. However, HHS, the administrative agency currently responsible for Medicare, Medicaid, and other federal government health care programs, takes on a new and vastly expanded role with respect to employment-based and individual health care coverage and becomes the predominant regulatory agency. Currently, the DOL and state insurance departments are the primary regulators of employer-based health care coverage.

[D] Coverage Other Than Employment-Based Coverage

Those who do not receive their health coverage through their employers may be covered by one of the existing government health care programs—for example, Medicare, a state Medicaid plan under Title XIX of the Social Security Act, a state children's health insurance program (CHIP), active military and veterans' coverage under TRICARE, or the Indian Health Service. Those who do not have access to coverage through an employer or a government program may purchase coverage in the private individual insurance market. There are also some states that offer coverage under Medicaid or other programs to individuals who have income in excess of the federal government's income eligibility guidelines or who are unable to obtain affordable insurance through the private market due to a preexisting condition or serious health issue. Two states, Utah and Massachusetts, have already established and implemented a model "exchange" where individuals can purchase health insurance offered through a state-regulated marketplace.[20] These exchanges are precursors to the exchange provisions that form one of the central elements of the Affordable Care Act.

[E] Taxation of Employment-Based Health Care Coverage

Most employment-based health care coverage is a tax-free benefit for employees and their eligible dependents. Under the Code, a taxpayer may exclude from gross income employer-provided health coverage for the employee, the employee's spouse, or the employee's qualified dependents[21] or direct or indirect reimbursement for medical care.[22]

For these purposes (and prior to the Affordable Care Act), each dependent child must have met certain relationship, residency, support, and age requirements set forth in Section 152 of the Code.[23] A dependent child includes an individual who is the son, daughter, stepson, or stepdaughter of the employee, and a child includes both an individual who is legally adopted by the employee and an individual who is lawfully placed with the employee for legal adoption by the employee.[24] A child also includes an eligible foster child, defined as an individual who is placed with the employee by an authorized placement agency or by judgment, decree, or other court order.[25] A married child is not a dependent beginning with the calendar year in which the individual files a joint income tax return.[26] To be an eligible dependent, the dependent child (1) must have the same principal place of residence as the

---

[19] 29 U.S.C. § 1144(a) (preempting any and all state laws insofar as they relate to any employee benefits plan covered by ERISA).

[20] *See* John R. Graham, Debating the Wisdom of Creating Health Exchanges (Mar. 3, 2011) *available at* http://healthreformreport .com/2011/03/debating-the-wisdom-of-creating-health-exchanges.php.

[21] I.R.C. § 106.

[22] I.R.C. § 105(b).

[23] I.R.C. § 105.

[24] I.R.C. § 152.

[25] I.R.C. § 152(f)(1).

[26] I.R.C. § 152(b)(2).

taxpayer for at least half the year, (2) must have not provided more than one-half of his or her own support in the calendar year, and (3) must have not attained age 19 (age 24 if a student) as of the close of the calendar year.[27]

Most employment-based group health plans have adopted dependent eligibility requirements that are consistent with the requirements of the Code for tax-free benefits for the employee. The exception is coverage provided to a domestic partner (and the domestic partner's dependent children). To the extent that an employer provides coverage for domestic partners who do not otherwise qualify as dependents for tax purposes, the value of the coverage is subject to federal income tax. The Affordable Care Act eliminates the dependent child residency and support requirements and raises the age limit for tax-free health care benefits from employers.[28]

§ 2.03 The Legislative Process: Making Sausage

The unusual two-law structure of the Affordable Care Act is the result of a tortured legislative process spanning almost a full calendar year.

[A] Legislative History

In the U.S. House of Representatives, the health care reform legislation was originally set forth in different versions of H.R. 3200, the "America's Affordable Health Care Choices Act," that were adopted by the House Ways and Means Committee and the House Education and Labor Committee on July 17, 2009. The House Energy and Commerce Committee released its markup of H.R. 3200 on this same date. The result of these bills was H.R. 3962, the "Affordable Health Care for America Act," which the House passed on November 7, 2009.

The first congressional committee to propose legislation was the United States Senate's Health, Education, Labor, and Pension (HELP) Committee, which reported out its bill (S. 1679, the Affordable Health Choices Act) on July 15, 2009. Two months later, on September 16, 2009, Senate Finance Committee Chairman Max Baucus (D-Mont.) released his chairman's mark for health care reform legislation. After eight days of meetings during which 135 amendments were considered and 79 roll call votes were held, the Senate Finance Committee issued a report.[29] This bill then went through a reconciliation process with the HELP Committee bill that resulted in the Senate's passage of H.R. 3950, the "Patient Protection and Affordable Care Act," on December 24, 2009. Although this is the bill that ultimately became the basis for the PPACA, as described below, the final legislation differs from the bill passed by the Senate on December 24, 2009.

Once the House and the Senate had passed different versions of the health care reform legislation, the Senate used its budget reconciliation process as the vehicle for reconciling the two versions. The first step in this cumbersome process required the House of Representatives to adopt verbatim the Senate's version of the legislation contained in H.R. 3590 and then separately adopt provisions (H.R. 4872) amending this law to reflect the desires of the House, which the House did in successive votes taken on March 21, 2009. H.R. 3590, now having been passed by both the House and the Senate, went to President Obama for signature. President Obama signed the PPACA on March 23, 2010.

The Senate then took up for consideration H.R. 4872 under its budget reconciliation process, which is a process not subject to filibuster under the rules of the Senate and thus permits the Senate

---

[27] I.R.C. § 152(c).

[28] See *infra* **Section 8.04[A]–[B][2]** notes 60–98 and accompanying text (discussing the extended coverage requirement for adult children and the broadened tax exclusion for child coverage).

[29] S. Rep. No. 111-89, Report to Accompany S. 1796 on Providing Affordable, Quality Health Care for All Americans and Reducing the Growth in Health Care Spending and for Other Purposes, together with Additional and Minority Views.

to pass legislation by a majority vote. Because the Senate parliamentarian ruled that two provisions in H.R. 4872 concerning student loans were not eligible for the budget reconciliation process, the Senate passed H.R. 4872, without these two provisions, on March 25, 2010. On the same day, the House passed the Senate's amended version of H.R. 4872, which is the version of the HCERA signed by President Obama on March 30, 2010.

To a large extent the provisions set forth in the two laws reflect measures on which the House and Senate were in agreement in principle. At the time, both congressional chambers seemed to agree on the importance of an individual mandate, mechanisms to encourage employers to continue providing health benefits to their employees, the need to subsidize coverage for low-income individuals and families, market reforms (e.g., the elimination of preexisting conditions, guaranteed issue and renewal, limits on lifetime and annual maximums, restrictions on waiting periods, understandable and consistent explanations of coverage), and benefit improvements (e.g., expansion of dependent coverage, first-dollar availability of preventive care, wellness incentives).

Two fault lines that emerged at the end of the legislative process concerned the major health care policy issue of whether there should be a public option and the equally, if not more, prominent social policy issue about the use of federal funds to pay for abortions.[30] The House ultimately backed away from its insistence on a public option and, after President Obama agreed to issue a Presidential Order reaffirming the administration's commitment to not using federal funds to pay for abortions,[31] enough House members overcame their reservations on the abortion issue to ensure the passage of H.R. 3950 by the House.

[B] Laws Affected by the Affordable Care Act

The Affordable Care Act amends a variety of federal laws, including the PHSA, the Code, ERISA, the Fair Labor Standards Act of 1938 (the FLSA),[32] the Social Security Amendments Act,[33] and the Indian Health Care Improvement Act.[34] The Affordable Care Act also enacts a number of new laws, such as the Catalyst to Better Diabetes Care Act of 2009,[35] the Cures Acceleration Network Act of 2009,[36] the Establishing a Network of Health-Advancing National Centers of Excellence for Depression Act of 2009,[37] the Congenital Heart Futures Act,[38] and the Young Women's Breast Health Education and Awareness Requires Learning Young Act of 2009.[39] Finally, in what may be a first, the Affordable Care Act amends itself.[40]

As if the foregoing were not overwhelming enough, HCERA, in turn, amends parts of provisions set forth in PPACA as if such amendments were included in PPACA in the first place,[41] adds new provisions to PPACA,[42] independently amends the provisions of federal laws,[43] and enacts at least one new law of its own—the Student Aid and Fiscal Responsibility Act (SAFRA).[44]

---

[30] *See* Lois Montgomery & Paul Kane, House health-care vote Sunday may hinge on abortion issues, http://www.washingtonpost.com (Mar. 21, 2010).

[31] *Id.*

[32] Pub. L. No. 75-718, 52 Stat. 1060.

[33] Pub. L. No. 98-21, 97 Stat. 65.

[34] Pub. L. No. 94-437, 90 Stat. 400.

[35] PPACA § 10407.

[36] PPACA § 10409.

[37] PPACA § 10410.

[38] PPACA § 10411.

[39] PPACA § 10413.

[40] PPACA, tit. X, pt. 1.

[41] *See, e.g.,* HCERA § 1001.

[42] HCERA § 1102.

[43] *See, e.g.,* HCERA § 1103.

[44] HCERA § 2001.

The end result of the legislative process is an Act that is broad in scope and uniquely complex. This should not be surprising, given the difficulty of the subject matter, the competing governing philosophies of the two major political parties, the myriad interest groups affected, the lack of any consensus for reform among the public, and the fact that three committees of the House and two committees of the Senate were involved in developing the legislative proposals.

[C] Architecture of the Affordable Care Act

The Affordable Care Act is made up of ten titles.[45] A crucial building block for understanding the Act's impact on employment-based group health plans is understanding the architecture of Title I of the Act, which is captioned "Quality, Affordable Health Care for All Americans." In broad brush, the relevant portions of Title I of the Act, which will be discussed in substantial detail in this guide, are:

- Subtitle A of Title I of the Act[46] and Part 1 of Subtitle C of Title I of the Act,[47] which impose new substantive and reporting requirements on employment-based group health plans through amendments to the PHSA;

- Section 1251 of Part 2 of Subtitle C of Title I of the Act, which modifies the application of Subtitles A and C of Title I of the Act for employment-based group health plans that are grandfathered health plans;[48]

- Subtitle F of Title I of the Act, which imposes the individual enroll-or-pay rules[49] and the pay-or-play penalty on large employers that do not provide their full-time employees with minimum essential coverage;[50] and

- The "conforming amendments" contained in Subtitle G of Title I of the Act, which, along with existing provisions of the PHSA,[51] allocate responsibility for enforcing Part A of the PHSA among the DOL,[52] the IRS,[53] and the HHS.[54]

---

[45] They are: Title I—Quality, Affordable Health Care For All Americans; Title II—Role of Public Programs; Title III—Improving the Quality and Efficiency of Health Care; Title IV—Prevention of Chronic Disease and Improving Public Health; Title V—Health Care Workforce; Title VI—Transparency and Program Integrity; Title VII—Improving Access to Innovative Medical Therapies; Title VIII—CLASS Act; Title IX—Revenue Provisions; and Title X—Strengthening Quality, Affordable Health Care for All Americans.

[46] Section 1001(5) of Subtitle A of Title I of the Act adds the following new sections to Part A of the PHSA (42 U.S.C. §§ 300gg et seq.): No Lifetime or Annual Limits (PHSA § 2711); Prohibition on Rescission (PHSA § 2712); Coverage of Preventive Health Services (PHSA § 2713); Extension of Dependent Coverage (PHSA § 2714); Development and Utilization of Uniform Explanations of Coverage Documents and Standardized Definitions (PHSA § 2715); Provision of Additional Information (PHSA § 2715A); Prohibition on Discrimination in Favor of Highly Compensated Individuals (PHSA § 2717); Ensuring the Quality of Care (PHSA § 2717); Bringing Down the Cost of Health Care Coverage (PHSA § 2718); Appeals Process (PHSA § 2719); Patient Protections (PHSA § 2719A).

[47] Section 1201(4) of Part 1 of Subtitle C of Title I of the Act adds the following new sections to Part A of the PHSA: Prohibition of Preexisting Condition Exclusions or other Discrimination Based on Health Status (PHSA § 2704); Fair Health Insurance Premiums (PHSA § 2701); Guaranteed Availability of Coverage (PHSA § 2702); Guaranteed Renewability of Coverage (PSA § 2703); Prohibiting Discrimination Against Individual Participants and Beneficiaries Based on Health Status (PHSA § 2705); Non-Discrimination in Health Care (PHSA § 2706); Comprehensive Health Insurance Coverage (PHSA § 2707); Prohibition on Excessive Waiting Periods (PHSA § 2708); and Coverage for Individuals Participating in Approved Clinical Trials (PSA § 2709).

[48] PPACA § 1251(a).

[49] PPACA § 1501.

[50] PPACA § 1513.

[51] 42 U.S.C. § 300gg-22.

[52] PPACA § 1562(e).

[53] PPACA § 1562(f).

[54] PPACA § 1562(c)(14).

§ 2.04   Enforcement Responsibility

The Affordable Care Act's new substantive requirements incorporated into the PHSA apply to health coverage provided on an insured and self-funded basis and on an individual and group basis.[55] The three agencies of the federal government historically involved in administering laws applying to such coverage—the DOL, IRS, and HHS—will all be involved in enforcing these requirements.

The Affordable Care Act incorporates the PHSA enforcement provisions, which authorize HHS to enforce the terms of the PHSA with respect to individual health insurance coverage and employment-based group health plans sponsored by government employers (other than the federal government), into ERISA and the Code.[56] However, the incorporation of the PHSA enforcement provisions is limited to their application to "group health plans" and "health insurance issuers providing health insurance coverage in connection with group health plans."

Thus, it appears that the DOL and the IRS are responsible for enforcing Part A of the PHSA with respect to group health plans that provide coverage on a self-funded or insured basis, other than with respect to such coverage provided by an employment-based group health plan sponsored by a government employer (other than the federal government). HHS retains enforcement authority over non–federal government employment-based group health plans and health insurance issued to individuals by insurance companies. States have primary authority to enforce the Affordable Care Act's group and individual market provisions over issuers of group and individual health insurance.[57]

---

[55] 42 U.S.C. §§ 300gg *et seq.*

[56] PPACA §§ 1562(e), (f). The provisions of the PHSA are incorporated into Subpart B of Part 7 of Subtitle A of Title I of ERISA, which generally includes portability, access, and renewability requirements applicable to group health plans. The provisions of the PHSA are incorporated into Subchapter B of Chapter 100 of the Code, which generally includes portability, access, and renewability requirements applicable to group health plans.

[57] PHSA § 2723(a)(2).

CHAPTER 3

CONSTITUTIONAL CHALLENGES TO HEALTH CARE REFORM

§ 3.01 Introduction

The role of the federal government in regulating the affairs of the nation is limited to discharging the powers assigned to it under the United States Constitution.[1] Any action of the federal government that is not authorized by these "enumerated powers" is unconstitutional. In *National Federation of Independent Business v. Sebelius*,[2] the United States Supreme Court determined that the individual enroll-or-pay requirement of the Affordable Care Act[3] (the so-called individual mandate) is within these enumerated powers.[4] For purposes of this discussion, it is sufficient to understand that, beginning in 2014, this mandate will generally require most individuals to purchase health insurance coverage or pay a dollar amount to the federal government.

The Court considered whether the individual enroll-or-pay requirement represents an exercise of the federal government's constitutional authority to impose taxes,[5] regulate interstate commerce under what is commonly referred to as the "Commerce Clause,"[6] or impose any requirements necessary and proper to perform any power of the federal government under the Constitution.[7] By a vote of 5-4, with Chief Justice Roberts in the majority, the Court held that the individual enroll-or-pay requirement is a constitutional exercise of the federal government's power to impose taxes.[8] By an identical 5-4 vote, again with Chief Justice Roberts in the majority, but with four different justices dissenting, the Court held that the enroll-or-pay requirement could not be imposed by the federal government under the Commerce Clause or under the federal government's power to impose regulations that are necessary and proper for the performance of any power of the federal government under the Constitution.[9]

Separately, the Court considered whether the federal government's ability to withhold all Medicaid funding to a state if the state declines to adopt the Affordable Care Act's expanded Medicaid eligibility program was constitutional.[10] The Court ultimately decided that the federal government did not have the ability to withhold all Medicaid funding from such a state.[11] While the federal government is authorized under the Spending Clause of the Constitution[12] to spend money and to attach conditions to its expenditures, it may not "conscript state [agencies] into the national bureaucratic

---

[1] United States v. Lopez, 514 U.S. 514, 552 (1995) ("The Constitution creates a Federal Government of enumerated powers. [citations omitted] As James Madison wrote, '[t]he powers delegated by the proposed Constitution to the federal government are few and defined. Those which are to remain in the State governments are numerous and indefinite.' [citations omitted]").

[2] No. 11-393 (U.S. June 28, 2012).

[3] The individual enroll-or-pay requirement is discussed in **Chapter 11**.

[4] Accordingly, the Court reversed this part of the judgment of the Eleventh Circuit in *Seven-Sky v. Holder*, 648 F.3d 1235 (11th Cir. 2011). The other appellate court decisions involving constitutional challenges to the individual enroll-or-pay requirement are *Liberty University v. Geither*, 671 F.3d 391 (4th Cir. 2011), *Thomas More Law Center v. Obama*, 651 F.3d 529 (6th Cir. 2011), and *Seven-Sky v. Holder*, 661 F.3d 391 (D.C. Cir. 2011).

[5] U.S. Const. art. I, § 8, cl. 1 ("Congress shall have the Power to lay and collect Taxes . . . to . . . provide for . . . the general Welfare of the United States.").

[6] U.S. Const. art. I, § 8, cl. 3 ("To regulate Commerce with foreign Nations, and among the several States, and with the Indian Tribes.").

[7] U.S. Const. art. I, § 8, cl. 18 ("To make all Laws which shall be necessary and proper for carrying into Execution the foregoing powers, and all other Powers vested by this Constitution in the Government of the United States, or in any Department or Officer thereof.").

[8] Chief Justice Roberts's opinion of the Court on this issue was joined by Justices Ginsburg, Sotomayor, Breyer, and Kagan. Chief Justice Roberts's opinion is hereafter cited to as the "Roberts Opinion." The separate opinion authored by Justice Ginsburg is hereafter cited to as the "Ginsburg Opinion."

[9] Chief Justice Roberts reached this conclusion in his opinion, and Justices Scalia, Kennedy, Thomas, and Alito reached the same conclusion in a separate opinion jointly issued by them, which is hereafter cited to as the "Joint Opinion."

[10] *Roberts Opinion* at 45–59.

[11] *Roberts Opinion* at 58.

[12] U.S. Const. art. I, § 8, cl. 1 ("[T]o pay the Debts and provide for the . . . general Welfare of the United States.").

army."[13] In other words, the Court felt that the federal government overstepped its authority by imposing such a draconian penalty on states that did not adopt the new Medicaid eligibility program. The Court, citing an existing severability provision in the Medicaid statute, concluded that the remainder of the Affordable Care Act would stand, provided that the federal government is only able to withhold the incremental additional Medicaid funding contemplated by the Affordable Care Act for states that do not adopt the expanded Medicaid eligibility program.[14]

The following discussion summarizes the Court's analysis of the constitutionality of the individual enroll-or-pay requirement under these constitutional powers of the federal government.

§ 3.02   Federal Government's Taxing Power[15]

All members of the Court agreed that a payment to the federal government from a person due to the person's commission of an unlawful act is not a tax that can be imposed under the federal government's power to impose taxes.[16] The Justices disagreed over whether a failure to purchase health insurance, which results in a person's making a payment to the federal government under the individual enroll-or-pay requirement, is an unlawful act.

[A]   The Majority

A majority of the Justices agree that it is "fairly possible" to characterize the requirement as imposing a tax, even though payment is described in the law as a penalty.[17] In support of this conclusion they note that the requirement resembles a tax because it raises revenue for the federal government, is paid when federal tax returns are filed, results in different amounts being paid by individuals based on factors such as taxable income, number of dependents, and filing status, is part of the Internal Revenue Code, and is enforced by the Internal Revenue Service.[18] Further, the individual enroll-or pay requirement mandates a payment whether or not a person intentionally violates the law, while a punitive law typically imposes its sanction only on those who intentionally violate the law.[19] For the members of the majority, the label affixed by the federal government to a payment is not determinative of whether the payment is a tax for constitutional purposes.[20] Instead, the relevant inquiry is what negative legal consequences flow from a person's failure to obtain health insurance coverage.[21] If the only such consequence is a payment to the federal government, which is not punitive in amount,[22] the payment is a tax that the federal government can impose under its constitutional power to impose taxes.[23]

---

[13] *Roberts Opinion* at 55 (citing FERC v. Mississippi, 456 U.S. 742, 775 (1982)).

[14] *Roberts Opinion* at 56 (citing 42 U.S.C. § 1396(c)).

[15] As a preliminary matter, Chief Justice Roberts determined that the Anti-Injunction Act, 26 I.R.C. § 7421, did not prevent the Court from addressing the constitutional issue at this time. This statute generally prohibits litigation regarding taxes before they are paid. Justice Roberts found that the Anti-Injunction Act is inapplicable to the individual enroll-or-pay requirement because the federal government's decision to call the requirement a penalty should be respected when determining whether the requirement imposes a tax or a penalty. *See Roberts Opinion* at 11–15.

[16] *Roberts Opinion* at 37; *Joint Dissent* at 18.

[17] *Roberts Opinion* at 32.

[18] *Roberts Opinion* at 33.

[19] *Roberts Opinion* at 35–36.

[20] *Roberts Opinion* at 33–35.

[21] *Roberts Opinion* at 37.

[22] *Roberts Opinion* at 42. A punitive tax is considered a penalty.

[23] *Roberts Opinion* at 15 and 37. Having concluded that the individual enroll-or-pay requirement is a tax for constitutional purposes, Chief Justice Roberts went on to rule that it is not a "direct tax" prohibited by Article 1, § 9, clause 4 of the Constitution, which provides: "No Capitation, or other direct, Tax shall be laid, unless in Proportion to the Census or Enumeration herein before directed to be

[B] The Dissent

The dissenting Justices argue that the individual enroll-or-pay requirement must either be a tax or a penalty.[24] If it is a penalty, the requirement can only be imposed by the federal government under the Commerce Clause.[25] According to the dissenting Justices, the individual enroll-or-pay requirement imposes a monetary penalty, because the amount is payable for violation of a law.[26] Additionally, and independent of this fact, the law's characterization of the payment as a penalty means the individual enroll-or-play requirement is not a tax for constitutional purposes.[27] Thus, the dissenters assert that only by rewriting the requirement could one conclude that it imposes a tax for constitutional purposes.[28]

§ 3.03 Federal Government's Commerce Clause Power

The Justices initially considered whether the Commerce Clause by itself authorizes the federal government to impose the individual enroll-or-pay requirement. Additionally, they considered whether the requirement is authorized by what is commonly referred to as the "Necessary and Proper Clause" of the Constitution, which permits the federal government to impose any requirements necessary and proper to perform any power of the federal government under the Constitution.[29]

[A] Commerce Clause

Chief Justice Roberts's opinion and the joint opinion of Justices Scalia, Kennedy, Thomas, and Alito (the "Joint Opinion"), which determines that the individual enroll-or-pay requirement is not authorized by the Commerce Clause, express the relevant power under the Commerce Clause as one that permits the federal government to regulate activities having a substantial relation to or effect on interstate commerce.[30] The portion of Justice Ginsburg's opinion finding that the individual enroll-or-pay requirement is authorized by the Commerce Clause, which was joined by Justices Sotomayor, Breyer, and Kagan (the "Ginsburg Opinion"), similarly describes the relevant power under the Commerce Clause.[31] Justice Thomas also filed a separate opinion in which he reaffirms his position that the Commerce Clause does not authorize the federal government to regulate activities that have a substantial effect on interstate commerce, and urges the Court to abandon the "substantial effect" test.[32]

[1] The Majority

Chief Justice Roberts and the Justices issuing the Joint Opinion conclude that the individual enroll-or-pay requirement is not authorized by the Commerce Clause because the requirement does

---

taken." This is because a direct tax is either a capitation tax ("head tax") or a tax on real or personal property. The individual enroll-or-pay requirement is not a capitation tax because it is payable only when a person fails to have health insurance coverage and is not a tax on real or personal property. *See Roberts Opinion* at 40–41.

[24] *Joint Opinion* at 17.

[25] *Joint Opinion* at 16–17.

[26] *Joint Opinion* at 19.

[27] *Joint Opinion* at 20.

[28] *Joint Opinion* at 24.

[29] U.S. Const. art. I, § 8, cl. 18, *supra* note 7.

[30] *Roberts Opinion* at 17; *Joint Opinion* at 10.

[31] *Ginsburg Opinion* at 15.

[32] *See* separate opinion issued by Justice Thomas. The Commerce Clause additionally authorizes the federal government to regulate the channels of interstate commerce and the instrumentalities of and persons or things in interstate commerce. *See* United States v. Lopez, 514 U.S. 558–59 (1995).

not regulate any commercial activity in which a person engages.[33] That is to say, the requirement only regulates a person who has not engaged in the commercial activity of obtaining health insurance coverage by requiring the person to pay an amount to the federal government.[34] Limiting the scope of the federal government's power under the Commerce Clause to activities in which persons actually engage is critical from a constitutional perspective, according to these Justices, because it ensures that the regulatory power of the federal government remains more limited than that of the individual states.[35]

The Justices in the majority find additional support for limiting this aspect of the federal government's power under the Commerce Clause from the text of the Commerce Clause, which gives the federal government the power to regulate interstate commerce.[36] Absent an affirmative action by a person, the federal government has nothing to regulate.[37] The activity being regulated is the purchase of health insurance coverage, and the individual enroll-or-pay requirement does not regulate this activity.[38] Instead, it compels a person to engage in this activity or pay an amount to the federal government.[39]

[2] The Dissent

The Ginsburg Opinion, emphasizing that a purpose of the Commerce Clause is to permit the federal government to regulate economic activity for the general benefit of the country in situations where the states acting separately have insufficient power to act,[40] rejects the majority view that a failure to have health insurance coverage is not an economic activity within the scope of the federal government's power to regulate. According to these Justices, the decision whether to purchase health insurance coverage is the economic activity that is the subject of the individual enroll-or-pay requirement,[41] and this decision has a substantial effect on the interstate market for health

---

[33] See *Roberts Opinion* at 20; *Joint Opinion* at 12–13. The Ginsburg Opinion argues that drawing a distinction between activity that can be regulated by the federal government and inactivity that cannot be regulated by the federal government repeats the mistake the Court made in the past in trying to apply the Commerce Clause in a formalistic way based on a determination whether a commercial activity was commerce or not commerce or had a direct or indirect effect on interstate commerce. See *Ginsburg Opinion* at 25. Instead, Justice Ginsburg argues that the Court's precedent instructs that the scope of the federal government's authority should be based on practical considerations that are informed by actual experience. See *Ginsburg Opinion* at 14–15.

[34] See *Roberts Opinion* at 18 and 24; *Joint Opinion* at 11–12. Both Justice Roberts and the Justices issuing the Joint Opinion describe the relevant market as the one within which health insurance contracts are bought and sold. See *Roberts Opinion* at 27; *Joint Opinion* at 5. The Ginsburg Opinion faults the majority for describing in this way the market that is being regulated. In Justice Ginsburg's opinion, the federal government legitimately could define this market as the market for health care over a longer term, such as a decade. Statistical evidence indicates an uninsured person is virtually certain to consume health care within this period. See *Ginsburg Opinion* at 18–20. Therefore, the individual enroll-or-pay requirement establishes that payments for products acquired in the health care market will be made through insurance. See *Ginsburg Opinion* at 22.

[35] See *Roberts Opinion* at 1–4, 23–24, and 26; *Joint Opinion* at 2, 12–13, and 14–15. The Ginsburg Opinion argues that limiting the scope of the Commerce Clause to activities substantially affecting interstate commerce will not result in this power's having no limits. The limits Justice Ginsburg identifies include the unique feature of the health care market under which those who do not pay for health care are subsidized by those who do pay for such care. See *Ginsburg Opinion* at 27–31.

[36] See *Roberts Opinion* at 18–19; *Joint Opinion* at 13.

[37] See *Roberts Opinion* at 18–19; *Joint Opinion* at 13.

[38] See *Roberts Opinion* at 20 and 25; *Joint Opinion* at 11 and 12–13.

[39] See *Roberts Opinion* at 18, 20, 23, and 24; *Joint Opinion* at 13 and 15.

[40] See *Ginsburg Opinion* at 12–14.

[41] See *Ginsburg Opinion* at 16–17. Justice Roberts opines that characterizing the decision not to obtain health care coverage as an economic activity is something that only might make sense to an economist, because its economic effect on commerce is measurable. The Framers of the Constitution, on the other hand, were practical men who understood that the power to regulate commerce does not encompass the power to compel it. See *Roberts Opinion* at 24. The Joint Opinion rejects the argument set forth in the Ginsburg Opinion, because the Commerce Clause permits the federal government to regulate commerce, which is everything affecting commerce, unless there is a difference between activity and inactivity. See *Joint Opinion* at 13.

care.[42] A person's lack of such coverage has an effect on this market because sooner or later nearly every person seeks a health care service or good,[43] which is provided regardless of whether the person has health insurance coverage. Providers of health care services and goods increase the price of their products to account for those provided at no cost to persons who do not have health insurance coverage.[44]

[B] Necessary and Proper Clause

[1] The Majority

Chief Justice Roberts and the Justices issuing the Joint Opinion conclude that the Necessary and Proper Clause does not permit the federal government to regulate inactivity.[45] Doing so would enable Congress to "create the necessary predicate to the exercise of an enumerated power."[46] The Constitution does not permit this sort of bootstrapping. Accordingly, the notion that the individual enroll-or-pay requirement is necessary in order for the guaranteed-issue and community-rating requirements imposed on insurance companies to accomplish their objectives does not justify from a constitutional perspective any federal regulation of a person's inactivity.[47] The Constitution's limitation of the federal government's powers to those enumerated in the Constitution would be undermined if the federal government is permitted to regulate inactivity as a result of the Necessary and Proper Clause, when such inactivity cannot be constitutionally regulated under the Commerce Clause.[48]

[2] The Dissent

The Ginsburg Opinion initially cites several prior Supreme Court cases in which a federal regulation is found to satisfy the necessary prong of the Necessary and Proper Clause if, among other formulations, the federal regulation effectuates the federal government's power under the Commerce Clause.[49] Justice Ginsburg notes that it is not in dispute that the Commerce Clause permits the federal government to impose the guaranteed-issue and community-rating requirements on insurance companies.[50] Because these requirements standing alone will result in an "adverse-selection death-spiral in the health-insurance market,"[51] the individual enroll-or-pay requirement effectuates these regulations by preventing the death spiral from occurring.[52] Thus, according to the Ginsburg Opinion, the individual enroll-or-pay requirement falls within the power granted to the federal government by the Necessary and Proper Clause.[53]

---

[42] *See Ginsburg Opinion* at 16–17. Justice Roberts disagrees with the assertion that everyone is active in the health care market because of the inevitable need for health care. A person who does not have health insurance coverage and is not consuming health care products is not engaged in any commercial activity. *See Roberts Opinion* at 25. The mere fact that such a person will eventually need health care means only that such person at some point in the future will become active in the health care market. The Commerce Clause permits the federal government to regulate a person who is active in this market, not someone who will become active in the market at a future date. *See Roberts Opinion* at 26. The Joint Opinion voices the same disagreement. *See Joint Opinion* at 10–11.

[43] *Ginsburg Opinion* at 3–4.

[44] *Ginsburg Opinion* at 16.

[45] *Roberts Opinion* at 28–30; *Joint Opinion* at 8–9.

[46] *Roberts Opinion* at 29.

[47] *Roberts Opinion* at 29–30; *Joint Opinion* at 5–9.

[48] *Roberts Opinion* at 29–30; *Joint Opinion* at 9.

[49] *Ginsburg Opinion* at 31–32.

[50] *Ginsburg Opinion* at 32.

[51] *Ginsburg Opinion* at 33.

[52] *Ginsburg Opinion* at 33.

[53] *Ginsburg Opinion* at 31–33.

The Ginsburg Opinion challenges the majority's assertion that the individual enroll-or-pay requirement undermines any limitation on the power of the federal government inherent in the Commerce Clause.[54] The Court cases otherwise limiting the scope of the federal government's power under the Necessary and Proper Clause address situations in which the federal government is seeking through regulation to compel the states to enforce federal regulations.[55] Compelling the states to enforce federal regulations is not permissible under the Necessary and Proper Clause because such compulsion violates state sovereignty.[56] Because the individual enroll-or-pay requirement is imposed directly on individuals, it does not implicate the constitutional concern of protecting the sovereignty of the states.[57]

---

[54] *Ginsburg Opinion* at 33–36.

[55] *Ginsburg Opinion* at 33–34.

[56] *Ginsburg Opinion* at 34.

[57] *Ginsburg Opinion* at 34.

Chapter 4

HEALTH CARE COVERAGE KEY TERMS

The Affordable Care Act's coverage reforms address both employment-based group health plans and individual insurance coverage. When considering a health care reform provision, it is critically important to carefully identify the entity or type of coverage that is subject to the provision. The applicability of each provision may vary depending on whether the plan is insured or self-funded, large or small market, and so forth. To assist employers and human resource professionals in understanding these important differences, we define the key terms as follows:

A *health plan* means both health insurance coverage and a group health plan.[1] The term "health plan" does not include a group health plan or multiple-employer welfare arrangement (MEWA) if the plan or the MEWA is not subject to state insurance regulation under the ERISA preemption provision.[2] In other words, a health plan does not include a self-funded employment-based group health plan. The term "health plan" generally is used in the Affordable Care Act when referring to Exchange-provided coverage.[3]

Health insurance coverage is defined as "benefits consisting of medical care (provided directly through insurance or reimbursement or otherwise and including items and services paid for as medical care) under any hospital or medical service policy or certificate, hospital or medical service plan contract, or health maintenance organization contract offered by a health insurance issuer."[4]

A *group health plan* is an employee welfare benefit plan (as defined in Section 3(1) of ERISA) that provides medical care services and supplies for employees or their dependents (as defined under the terms of the plan) directly or through insurance, reimbursement, or otherwise.[5] A group health plan includes both insured and self-funded arrangements.

A *health insurance issuer* (also referred to as an "issuer") is an entity that is licensed to engage in the business of insurance in a state and that is subject to state law that regulates insurance.[6]

The *group health insurance market* is health insurance coverage sold to group health plans.[7] The market is divided into the large-group market and the small-group market. For purposes of an insurance market, a small employer is defined as an employer that employed, on average, at least one but no more than 100 employees on business days during the preceding calendar year.[8] A state may elect the option of defining a small employer as an employer that employed on average at least one but not more than 50 employees beginning on January 1, 2016.[9]

Individual health insurance coverage is health insurance coverage offered to individuals in the individual market, but does not include short-term limited-duration insurance.[10]

The *individual market* means the market for health insurance coverage offered to individuals other than in connection with a group health plan.[11]

---

[1] PPACA § 1301(b)(1).

[2] PPACA § 1301(b)(1)(B) (referencing 29 U.S.C. § 1144).

[3] See *infra* **Section 11.04** notes 60–148 and accompanying text (discussing Exchanges).

[4] PPACA § 1301(b)(2) (referencing 42 U.S.C. § 300gg-91(b)(1)).

[5] PPACA § 1301(b)(3) (referencing 42 U.S.C. § 300gg-91(a)(1)).

[6] PPACA § 1301(b)(2) (referencing 42 U.S.C. § 300gg-91(b)(1)).

[7] PPACA §§ 1304, 1551 (referencing 42 U.S.C. § 300gg-91(e)).

[8] PPACA §§ 1304(b)(1), 1562(c)(16) (amending 42 U.S.C. § 300gg-91(e)(2)).

[9] PPACA § 1304(b)(2).

[10] PPACA §§ 1304, 1551 (referencing 42 U.S.C. § 300gg-91(b)(5)).

[11] PPACA §§ 1304, 1551 (referencing 42 U.S.C. § 300gg-91(e)(1)(A)).

A *health insurance product* is not defined in the Act, but HHS defines it as a package of benefits that an issuer offers that is reported to state regulators in an insurance filing.[12]

A *grandfathered health plan* is a group health plan or individual health insurance coverage in existence on March 23, 2010, that continues to satisfy certain requirements.[13] The requirements for grandfathered health plans are described at length in **Chapter 5**.

Essential health benefits consist of coverage for items and services in a comprehensive list of categories set forth in the Affordable Care Act under such terms and conditions as shall be determined by HHS pursuant to guidelines set forth in the Act.[14] HHS has not formally defined what will comprise "essential health benefits," but it has published a bulletin and a set of FAQs, which further expand on issues addressed in the bulletin, that provide some insight into how this term is likely to be defined.[15]

A. *Definitional Approach*

HHS has indicated that in defining "essential health benefits" (EHB) it will pursue an approach that will (1) encompass the ten categories of services identified in the statute; (2) reflect typical employer health benefit plans; (3) reflect balance among the categories; (4) account for diverse health needs across many populations; (5) ensure that there are no incentives for coverage decisions, cost sharing, or reimbursement rates to discriminate impermissibly against individuals because of their age, disability, or expected length of life; (6) ensure compliance with the Mental Health Parity and Addiction Equity Act of 2008 (MHPAEA);[16] (7) provide states a role in defining EHB; and (8) balance comprehensiveness and affordability for those purchasing coverage.

B. *Benchmarking*

HHS intends to propose that EHB be defined by a benchmark plan selected by each state. The selected benchmark plan would serve as a reference plan, reflecting both the scope of services and any limits offered by a typical employer plan in that state as required by Section 1302(b)(2)(A) of the Affordable Care Act. This approach is based on the approach established by Congress for the Children's Health Insurance Program (CHIP), created in 1997, and for certain Medicaid populations.

C. *Benchmarking Options*

HHS's analysis of offerings that exist today suggests that the following four benchmark plan types for 2014 and 2015 best reflect the statutory standards for EHB in the Affordable Care Act:

1. The largest plan by enrollment in any of the three largest small group insurance products in the state's small group market;

2. Any of the largest three state employee health benefit plans by enrollment;

3. Any of the largest three national Federal Employees Health Benefits Program (FEHBP) plan options by enrollment; or

4. The largest insured commercial non-Medicaid Health Maintenance Organization (HMO) operating in the state.

---

[12] 45 C.F.R. § 159.110.

[13] PPACA § 1251. See *infra* **Section 5.01**, for a detailed discussion of grandfathered plans.

[14] PPACA § 1302(b).

[15] *See* Center for Consumer Info. & Ins. Oversight, Essential Health Benefits Bull. (Dec. 16, 2011), *available at* http://cciio.cms.gov/resources/files/Files2/12162011/esssential_health_benefits_bulletin.pdf; and Frequently Asked Questions on Essential Health Benefits Bull., *available at* http://cciio.cms.gov/resources/files/Files2/02172012/ehb-faq-508.pdf (setting forth the corresponding FAQs). The HHS Bulletin and FAQs are reproduced in **Appendix R**.

[16] Pub. L. No. 110-343, 122 Stat. 3765 (the MHPAEA was enacted as part of the Emergency Economic Stabilization Act of 2008, which also established the Troubled Asset Relief Program).

To preserve state flexibility, HHS intends to propose that states be permitted to select a single benchmark to serve as the standard for qualified health plans inside the Exchange operating within the state and plans offered in the individual and small group markets in the state. To determine enrollment in plans for specifying the benchmark options, HHS intends to propose to use enrollment data from the first quarter two years prior to the coverage year and that states select a benchmark in the third quarter two years prior to the coverage year. If a state does not exercise the option to select a benchmark health plan, HHS intends to propose that the default benchmark plan for that state would be the largest plan by enrollment in the largest product in the state's small group market.

D. *Coverage Gaps in Benchmark Plans*

HHS understands that not every benchmark plan will include coverage of all ten categories of benefits identified in the Affordable Care Act (e.g., some of the benchmark plans do not routinely cover habilitative services or pediatric oral or vision services). If a category is missing in the benchmark plan, it must nevertheless be covered by health plans required to offer EHB. In selecting a benchmark plan, a state may need to supplement the benchmark plan to cover each of the ten categories. HHS intends to propose that if a benchmark is missing other categories of benefits, the state must supplement the missing categories using the benefits from any other benchmark option. In a state with a default benchmark with missing categories, the benchmark plan would be supplemented using the largest plan in the benchmark type (e.g., small group plans or state employee plans or FEHBP) by enrollment offering the benefit. If none of the benchmark options in that benchmark type offer the benefit, the benefit will be supplemented using the FEHBP plan with the largest enrollment.

E. *Benefit Design Flexibility*

To meet the EHB coverage standard, HHS intends to require that a health plan offer benefits that are "substantially equal" to the benefits of the benchmark plan selected by the state and modified as necessary to reflect the ten coverage categories. This is the same equivalency standard that applies to plans under CHIP. Similar to the flexibility provided under CHIP, HHS intends to propose that a health insurance issuer have some flexibility to adjust benefits, including both the specific services covered and any quantitative limits provided they continue to offer coverage for all ten statutory EHB categories. Any flexibility provided would be subject to a baseline set of relevant benefits, reflected in the benchmark plan as modified. HHS indicated that permitting flexibility would provide greater choice to consumers, promoting plan innovation through coverage and design options, while ensuring that plans providing EHB offer a certain level of benefits.

See **Section 11.04[C][1]** for more information regarding EHB.

Minimum essential coverage includes (1) coverage under specified government programs; (2) health insurance coverage obtained in the individual market that provides for essential health benefits; (3) health insurance coverage obtained in the small group market that provides for essential health benefits; (4) health insurance coverage obtained in the large group market; (5) grandfathered health plan coverage, whether or not it is provided through health insurance coverage; and (6) coverage under a governmental plan, whether or not it is provided through health insurance coverage.[17] It appears that the latter three types of coverage provide minimum essential coverage as long as they provide any coverage that is not an excepted benefit.[18] Absent from the list is coverage provided on a self-funded basis through a group health plan.[19] This may, and should, be remedied by HHS exercising its authority to designate other health benefits coverage as minimum essential coverage. HHS could limit its designation to self-funded coverage that provides essential health benefits.

An *exchange plan* is a "qualified health plan," which is described at length in **Chapter 11**.

---

[17] PPACA § 1401(a) (adding Section 36B to the Code and referencing I.R.C. §§ 5000A(f)(1), (2), and PHSA § 2707).

[18] I.R.C. § 5000A(f)(3).

[19] I.R.C. § 5000A(f)(2)(B). The term "large group market" as used in this provision is defined in Section 1304 of the Act as "the health insurance market under which individuals obtain health insurance coverage." "Health insurance coverage" is coverage purchased through a health insurance issuer that is subject to state insurance law (i.e., not a self-funded plan).

Retiree-only plans are defined after the enactment of the Affordable Care Act in the Code and ERISA as any group health plan covering fewer than two active employees on the first day of the plan year.[20] The Affordable Care Act deletes the subsection of the PHSA that contained a comparable exclusion for such plans subject to the provisions of the PHSA. This curious deletion is discussed in the preamble to the interim final regulations for group health plans and health insurance coverage relating to grandfathered health plan status under the Affordable Care Act jointly issued by HHS, DOL, and IRS on June 14, 2010.[21] The preamble affirms that the deletion of the provision from the PHSA does not affect group health plans subject to the Code and ERISA, which means such plans are not subject to Parts A and C of Title I of the Affordable Care Act. For group health plans subject to the PHSA (i.e., group health plans that provide their benefits through health insurance and nonfederal government group health plans that provide their benefits on a self-funded basis), the preamble announces a no-enforcement policy at the federal level. Recognizing that the states have independent authority to regulate group health insurance issuers, the preamble "encourages" the states to adopt the same position. As a result, it is currently unclear if retiree-only plans that provide benefits through health insurance or that are offered on a self-funded basis by nonfederal governmental employers will be required by one or more states to conform such coverage to the requirements of Parts A and C of Title I of the Affordable Care Act.

The *Uniform Glossary* provides standard definitions of certain health-coverage-related terms and medical terms in accordance with Section 2715(g)(2) of the PHSA. The uniform glossary was developed by HHS and related agencies, in consultation with the National Association of Insurance Commissioners (NAIC), to provide generalized plain-English definitions to help consumers understand the basics of insurance.[22] At the same time, the uniform glossary, which was published as part of the final regulations on the summary of benefits and coverage in the Federal Register on February 14, 2012, specifically cautions that it is intended to be a general educational tool and that individual plan terms may differ (and refers consumers to the summary of benefits and coverage for information on how to obtain an accurate description of their actual plan or policy terms). The final regulations direct a plan or issuer to make the Uniform Glossary available upon request within seven business days. A plan or issuer satisfies this requirement by providing, in the summary of benefits and coverage, an Internet address where an individual may review and obtain the uniform glossary, a telephone number to obtain a paper copy of the uniform glossary, and a disclosure that paper copies are available upon request.[23]

---

[20] The Act deletes the current subsection of the PHSA that excludes from the scope of the portion of the PHSA amended by Parts A and C of Title I of the Act any group health plan covering fewer than two active employees on the first day of its plan year. The Act does not delete the comparable exclusions in the Code (Section 9832(a)(2)) and ERISA (Section 732(a)), which laws have also been amended by the Act to include these provisions of the PHSA. PPACA §§ 1562(e), (f).

[21] Group Health Plans and Health Insurance Coverage Relating to Status as a Grandfathered Health Plan Under the Patient Protection and Affordable Care Act, Interim Final Rule and Proposed Rule, 75 Fed. Reg. 34,538–70, amending 26 C.F.R. pts. 54 and 602, 29 C.F.R. pt. 2590, and 45 C.F.R. pt. 147. The relevant discussion appears at 75 Fed. Reg. 34,539–40.

[22] Preamble to the final rule of Summary of Benefits and Coverage and Uniform Glossary, 45 C.F.R. § 147.200 (2012).

[23] Final rule of Summary of Benefits and Coverage and Uniform Glossary, 45 C.F.R. § 147.200 (2012).

CHAPTER 5

HEALTH CARE REFORM EXEMPTIONS

§ 5.01 Grandfathered Health Plans: "If You Like Your Current Insurance, You Will Keep Your Current Insurance"

In March 2010, at the time health care reform became a reality, close to 85 percent of Americans had some form of health care coverage either through their employer, a government program like Medicare, Medicaid, or military coverage, or private health care insurance.[1] While the cost of coverage has steadily increased, perhaps unsustainably, for most employees, employers, or other plan sponsors, many individuals were satisfied with the terms and conditions of their coverage. President Obama and the congressional leadership promised those individuals that nothing in the law would prohibit them from continuing their existing coverage arrangements.[2]

That promise was incorporated into the Affordable Care Act, which provides in part that "[n]othing in this Act (or an amendment made by the Act) shall be construed to require that an individual terminate coverage under a group health plan or health insurance coverage in which such individual was enrolled on the date of enactment of the Act."[3] Further, the individual may continue to renew the existing coverage for subsequent periods.[4] These existing group health plans and individual health insurance coverages are defined in the law as "grandfathered health plans."[5] The government estimated that there would be approximately 2.2 million grandfathered health plans in 2011.[6]

Grandfathered health plans are exempt from some, but not all, of the coverage improvements and market reforms that the Affordable Care Act imposes on group health plans and individual insurance issuers and, after January 1, 2014, plans offered through the Exchange option.[7] A chart listing the PPACA group health plan coverage improvement provisions and their applicability to grandfathered health plans is shown in **Appendix A.**

The Affordable Care Act restricts changes to grandfathered health plans after the date of enactment but allows for new entrants into the plan. The law limits enrollment in a grandfathered health plan to individuals enrolled on March 23, 2010, family members of those individuals,[8] and new employees (and their families).[9]

Based on the language of the statute, many employers and plans were hesitant to make any change to their plans, lest their coverage be de-grandfathered. Such fears were alleviated in part on June 14, 2010, when HHS, Treasury, and the DOL jointly published interim final regulations for group health plans and health insurance coverage relating to grandfathered health plan status under the Affordable Care Act.[10] Attempting to balance the objective of preserving the ability of employers and

---

[1] See **Section 2.01** notes 3–5 (providing statistics on access to health coverage).

[2] See **Chapter 1** note 2 and accompanying text (quoting President Obama).

[3] PPACA § 1251(a). The date of enactment of the PPACA is March 23, 2010.

[4] PPACA § 1251(b).

[5] PPACA § 1251(e).

[6] 75 Fed. Reg. 34,555.

[7] When the grandfathered health plan provision (PPACA § 1251) was drafted and approved by the Senate HELP Committee, grandfathered health plans were exempted from Subtitles A (the coverage improvement provisions) and C (the market reforms that begin in January 2014). The Senate Finance Committee's sections of the bill, Titles IX and X, amended the provision to subject grandfathered health plans to Sections 2715 and 2718. PPACA § 10103(d). In the HCERA, Section 1251(a) was further amended to extend certain of the insurance market reforms to grandfathered health plans, including the provisions relating to excessive waiting periods (PHSA § 2708), the prohibitions on lifetime and annual limits (PHSA § 2711), the extension of dependent coverage (PHSA § 2714), and preexisting-condition exclusions (PHSA § 2704). HCERA § 2301. Also, the dependent coverage provisions application to grandfathered health plans was clarified. HCERA § 2301.

[8] PPACA § 1251(b).

[9] PPACA § 1251(c).

[10] 75 Fed. Reg. 34,538–70, amending 26 C.F.R. pts. 54 and 602, 29 C.F.R. pt. 2590, and 45 C.F.R. § 147. See **Appendix B** for grandfathered health plan regulations.

individuals to maintain existing coverage with the goal of expanding access to quality health coverage, the regulations delineate very broadly at what point changes to an existing plan are significant enough to cause the plan or health insurance coverage to cease to be a grandfathered health plan.

It is important to note that the regulations are written as "negative rules," which, according to officials in the Obama administration, means that changes that are not expressly prohibited are permitted, subject to the anti-abuse provisions in the regulations. In general, a material reduction in benefits, a substantial increase in the employee's financial responsibility for costs through cost-sharing and/or premium contribution increases, or a change in the insurance issuer[11] will cause a plan to lose its grandfathered health plan status. Plan changes that improve benefits or reduce costs for employees and beneficiaries are permitted without cessation of grandfathered health plan status.

[A] Grandfathered Health Plan Defined

A *grandfathered health plan* is coverage provided by a group health plan (self-funded or insured) or a health insurance issuer in which an individual was enrolled on March 23, 2010 (for as long as it maintains its status under the grandfather rules).[12] A grandfathered health plan does not cease to be such a plan merely because one or more (or even all) of the individuals enrolled as of March 23, 2010, are no longer enrolled, provided that someone has been enrolled continuously in the plan since March 23, 2010.

The grandfathered health plan determination must be made for each separate benefit package made available under the plan.[13] Thus, it is possible for a single group health plan to have both grandfathered and non-grandfathered benefit options.

[B] New Enrollees in Grandfathered Health Plans After March 23, 2010

The Affordable Care Act permits a grandfathered health plan to enroll "new employees" and "family members" of existing and new enrolled employees.[14] However, the terms "new employee" and "family member" are not defined in the Act.

[1] New Employees

The regulations clarify that new employees include both newly hired and newly enrolled employees and their families.[15] By clarifying that "new employees" includes "newly enrolled employees," the regulations accommodate routine employer plan enrollment practices, as well as legally required enrollments. For example, under current law employers permit existing employees who deferred enrollment because they had other coverage available through another source (typically through a spouse or other employer on more favorable terms) to enroll in the employer's coverage when they lose the other coverage. When an employee loses the other coverage for reasons specified in the law

---

[11] If the issuer of group health insurance coverage is changed on or after November 15, 2010, the group health insurance coverage is still eligible to retain its grandfathered health plan status. For this purpose, the date the new coverage becomes effective—not the date a contract for a new policy is entered into—is the operative date. If an issuer was changed after March 23, 2010, but before November 15, 2010, the group health insurance coverage is no longer eligible to retain grandfathered health plan status. 26 C.F.R. § 54.9815-1251T(a)(1)(ii); 29 C.F.R. § 2590.715-1251(a)(1)(ii); 45 C.F.R. § 147.140(a)(1)(ii); *see* 75 Fed. Reg. 70,116 (Nov. 17, 2010) (explaining the interest in treating changes in insurers in a manner that is consistent with treatment of changes in administrators of self-funded plans).

[12] 26 C.F.R. § 54.9815-1251T; 29 C.F.R. § 2590.715-1251; 45 C.F.R. § 147.140.

[13] 26 C.F.R. § 54.9815-1251T; 29 C.F.R. § 2590.715-1251; 45 C.F.R. § 147.140(a)(1)(i).

[14] PPACA §§ 1251(b), (c).

[15] 26 C.F.R. § 54.9815-1251(b); 29 C.F.R. § 2590.715-1251(b); 45 C.F.R. § 147.140.

and regulations, the employer is required under the Health Insurance Portability and Accountability Act of 1996 (HIPAA) to maintain a special enrollment period for that employee.[16] The grandfathered health plan regulations permit the enrollment, after March 23, 2010, of any employee entitled under the HIPAA special enrollment rules to enroll in the employment-based plan.[17]

Likewise, an existing employee who did not enroll in a group health plan offered by an employer prior to March 23, 2010, because he or she was working in an employment classification that was ineligible for coverage under the plan may be enrolled in the plan without loss of grandfathered health plan status.[18] For example, the employee may have been working on a part-time basis prior to March 23, 2010, and is now working in a full-time position with eligibility for health care benefits. When the employment classification changes and renders the employee eligible to enroll, the employee will be deemed a "new employee" for purposes of enrolling in a grandfathered health plan.

The regulations also address new employees who became employed in connection with a merger or acquisition. Existing employees of the newly acquired company are "new employees" for purposes of health care coverage in a grandfathered health plan.

There are two anti-abuse provisions in the regulations relating to the definition of new employee. First, if the principal purpose of the merger, acquisition, or business restructuring is to cover new individuals under the grandfathered health plan, the plan ceases to be a grandfathered health plan.[19] This anti-abuse rule is to prevent grandfather status from being bought and sold as a commodity in commercial transactions.

The second anti-abuse rule relates to employees transferred into the plan or health insurance coverage (transferee plan) from a plan or health insurance coverage under which the employees were covered on March 23, 2010 (the transferor plan).[20] Under the second rule, one must first compare the terms of the transferee plan with those of the transferor plan (as in effect on March 23, 2010), then consider the terms of the transferee plan as an amendment to the transferor plan. If the amendment would have caused the transferor plan to lose grandfathered health plan status and there was no bona fide employment-based reason for the transfer of the employees into the transferee plan, then the enrollment of the transferee plan employees into the transferor plan would cause the plan to cease being a grandfathered health plan. Bona fide employment-based reasons for purposes of a transfer include the elimination of a benefit package because (1) the issuer is exiting the market; (2) the issuer no longer offers the product to the employer; (3) there has been a change in a collective bargaining agreement; (4) low or declining participation makes it impractical for a plan sponsor to continue to offer the benefit package; and (5) multiple benefit packages covering a significant portion of other employees remain available to the employees being transferred.[21] Changing the terms or cost of coverage is not a bona fide employment-based reason.

[2] Family Members

Who is a "family member" for purposes of the grandfathered health plan provision? Neither the Affordable Care Act nor the interim final regulations answer that question. Many employment-based group health plans define eligible family members as the spouse and the dependent children of the employee. Some plans incorporate by reference the Code's definition of a dependent child.[22] Other plans define the term more broadly and include coverage for domestic partners.

---

[16] 29 U.S.C. § 1181(f).

[17] 26 C.F.R. § 54.9815-1251T(b)(1); 29 C.F.R. § 2590.715-1251(b)(1); 45 C.F.R. § 147.140(b)(1).

[18] 26 C.F.R. § 54.9815-1251T(b)(1); 29 C.F.R. § 2590.715-1251(b)(1); 45 C.F.R. § 147.140(b)(1).

[19] 26 C.F.R. § 54.9815-1251T(b)(2)(i); 29 C.F.R. § 2590.715-1251(b)(2)(i); 45 C.F.R. § 147.140(b)(2)(i).

[20] 26 C.F.R. § 54.9815-1251T(b)(2)(ii); 29 C.F.R. § 2590.715-1251(b)(2)(ii); 45 C.F.R. § 146.140(b)(2)(ii).

[21] FAQs About Affordable Care Act Implementation Part VI (Apr. 1, 2011), *available at* http://www.dol.gov/ebsa/pdf/faq-aca6.pdf.

[22] *See* I.R.C. § 152 (defining "dependent" for tax purposes).

Notwithstanding the absence of express guidance in the regulations, representatives of HHS and the DOL have explained at various briefings following the release of the grandfather regulations that, subject to the anti-abuse rules, any changes to a group health plan or health insurance coverage that are not prohibited in the regulations would be permissible. When asked expressly whether an amendment to a plan after March 23, 2010, to provide coverage for domestic partners and their families as dependents would result in the loss of grandfathered health plan status, a representative of President Obama's administration responded that an expansion of access to or an increase in benefits for employees would not result in the loss of a plan's grandfathered health plan status.[23]

[C]   Reforms Imposed on Grandfathered Health Plans

When the Affordable Care Act was originally drafted, grandfathered health plans were exempt from all of the coverage improvement requirements imposed on group health plans and individual insurance coverage. However, as the bills moved through Congress, amendments were made that subjected grandfathered health plans to most of the key immediate coverage improvement requirements.[24]

Effective for the first plan year[25] that began on or after September 23, 2010 (except as otherwise noted), grandfathered health plans are subject to the following coverage improvements and additional requirements described in more detail in Chapters 8 and 9:

- Extended dependent coverage;[26]

- Preexisting-condition exclusion prohibitions (beginning with the first plan year on or after September 23, 2010, for children under age 19, and in 2014 for older individuals);

- Prohibitions on lifetime maximum dollar limits on benefits;

- Prohibitions on annual dollar limits for essential medical benefits;

- Prohibitions on eligibility waiting periods in excess of 90 days (beginning in 2014);

- Prohibitions on rescission or non-renewal of coverage, except for fraud or intentional misrepresentations of material fact;

- Provision of uniform benefit summaries to all eligible enrollees and participants; and

- Requirements for insured plans to spend at least 85 percent of their premium revenues on medical claims costs for large-employer plans and 80 percent for small-employer plans, or rebate a portion of the premium revenues.[27]

By contrast, grandfathered health plans are exempt from the following coverage improvements and additional requirements described in more detail in Chapters 8 and 9:

---

[23] 26 C.F.R. § 54.9815-1251T(g); 29 C.F.R. § 2590.715- 1251(g); 45 C.F.R. § 147.140(g) (setting forth the "negative" nature of the rules).

[24] See note 7.

[25] The term "plan year" means the year that is designated as the plan year in the plan document of an employment-based group health plan. If the plan document does not designate a plan year, if the plan year is not a 12-month plan year, or if there is no plan document, the plan year is: (1) the deductible or limit year used under the plan; (2) the policy year, if the plan does not impose deductibles or limits on a 12-month basis; (3) the sponsor's taxable year, if the plan does not impose deductibles or limits on a 12-month basis, and either the plan is not insured or the insurance policy is not renewed on a 12-month basis; or (4) the calendar year, in any other case. 45 C.F.R. § 149.2.

[26] Grandfathered health plans can exclude adult children who are eligible for other employment-based group health plan coverage. See **Section 8.04[A]–[B][2]** notes 59–98 and accompanying text (discussing the extended dependent coverage provision).

[27] PPACA § 1251(a).

- Coverage of preventive health services with no cost-sharing;

- Provision of information on plan design to HHS;

- Prohibition on discriminating in favor of highly paid employees in insured plans;

- Reporting to HHS on quality-of-care and wellness programs;

- Requirement to implement a claims appeals process, including external review;

- For insured plans, limits on variances in premium costs, guaranteed availability and renewability, and provision of essential health benefits (beginning in 2014);

- Prohibition against discrimination among health care providers (beginning in 2014); and

- Limits on annual cost-sharing (beginning in 2014).[28]

[D] Maintenance of Grandfather Status

The grandfathered health plan regulations identify specific types of changes the adoption of that will cause a grandfathered health plan to forfeit its "grandfather" status.[29] These changes are:

- The elimination of substantially all benefits to diagnose or treat a particular condition;

- Any increase in a percentage cost-sharing requirement;

- Any increase in a fixed-amount cost-sharing requirement, other than a copayment, in excess of the maximum percentage increase permitted under the regulation;

- Any increase in a fixed-amount copayment in excess of the greater of the allowable maximum percentage or a fixed-dollar-amount increase established by the regulation;

- Certain decreases in the premium contribution rate by employers; and

- Certain additions or modifications of overall annual or lifetime limits on the dollar value of benefits.

HHS, Treasury, and the DOL have made it clear that a plan will cease to be a grandfathered health plan when one of the aforementioned changes becomes effective, regardless of when the amendment is adopted. Therefore, if an amendment was adopted on September 1, 2012, and the change is effective beginning January 1, 2013, the plan would cease to be a grandfathered health plan on January 1, 2013.[30]

[1] Elimination of Coverage for a Particular Condition

If a grandfathered health plan or health insurance coverage is amended to eliminate all or substantially all benefits to diagnose or treat a particular condition, the plan will cease to be a grandfathered plan.[31] For example, if a plan is amended to eliminate benefits for cystic fibrosis, the plan will cease to be a grandfathered health plan (even if the number of participants with the condition is small).

---

[28] PPACA § 1251(a).

[29] 26 C.F.R. § 54.9815-1251T(g); 29 C.F.R. § 2590.715-1251(g); 45 C.F.R. § 147.140(g).

[30] FAQs About Affordable Care Act Implementation Part VI (Apr. 1, 2011), *available at* http://www.dol.gov/ebsa/pdf/faq-aca6.pdf.

[31] 26 C.F.R. § 54.9815-1251T(g)(1)(i); 29 C.F.R. § 2590.715-1251(g)(1)(i); 45 C.F.R. § 147.140(g)(1)(i).

Likewise, the elimination of any necessary element to diagnose or treat a condition is considered the elimination of all or substantially all benefits. For example, if a plan covered a mental health condition, the accepted treatment plan for which is prescription medication and counseling, and the plan eliminates the counseling benefit, the elimination would trigger the loss of grandfathered health plan status.

[2]   Increasing Cost-Sharing Requirements

The regulations limit the amount that a participant's cost-sharing requirements may be increased without causing the grandfathered health plan or health insurance coverage to cease being a grandfathered health plan. Cost-sharing requirements include deductibles, copayments, or co-insurance amounts.

[a]   *Increases in Percentage Cost-Sharing Requirements Prohibited*

The rules prohibit any increase, measured from March 23, 2010, in a percentage cost-sharing requirement.[32]

The regulations include the following example:

Example. On March 23, 2010, a grandfathered health plan has a co-insurance requirement of 20 percent for inpatient surgery. The plan is subsequently amended to increase the co-insurance requirement to 25 percent.

In this example, the increase in the co-insurance requirement from 20 percent to 25 percent causes the plan to cease to be a grandfathered health plan.

This restriction may preclude certain plan changes that have become fairly routine. For example, if a plan's prescription drug plan has a copayment of 20 percent for each generic drug, 30 percent for each brand-name formulary drug, and 40 percent for any non-formulary prescription drug, the copayment percentages may not be increased if the plan wants to maintain its grandfather status.

[b]   *Limits on Fixed-Amount Cost-Sharing Increases (Other Than a Copayment)*

Any increase in a fixed-amount cost-sharing requirement (other than copayments) in excess of a maximum percentage increase, determined as of the effective date of the increase, will cause the plan to cease being a grandfathered health plan.[33] The "maximum percentage increase" is defined as medical inflation, expressed as a percentage, plus 15 percentage points.[34] The 15-percentage-point increase is a one-time aggregate addition, not an annual allowance.

"Medical inflation" means the increase since March 2010 in the overall medical care component of the Consumer Price Index for All Urban Consumers (CPI-U) (unadjusted) published by the DOL using the 1982–1984 base of 100. The March 2010 CPI-U is 387.142.[35] For purposes of determining the medical inflation percentage at a future date, identify the index amount for any month in the 12 months before the new change is to take effect, subtract 387.142 from that number, and then divide that amount by 387.142.

---

[32] 26 C.F.R. § 54.9815-1251T(g)(1)(ii); 29 C.F.R. § 2590.715-1251(g)(1)(ii); 45 C.F.R. § 147.140(g)(1)(ii).

[33] 26 C.F.R. § 54.9815-1251T(g)(1)(iii); 29 C.F.R. § 2590.715-1251(g)(1)(iii); 45 C.F.R. § 147.140(g)(1)(iii).

[34] 26 C.F.R. § 54.9815-1251T(g)(3)(ii); 29 C.F.R. § 2590.715-1251(g)(3)(ii); 45 C.F.R. § 147.140(g)(3)(ii).

[35] 26 C.F.R. § 54.9815-1251T(g)(3)(i); 29 C.F.R. § 2590.715-1251(g)(3)(i); 45 C.F.R. § 147.140(g)(3)(i).

However, HHS, Treasury, and the DOL have determined that if a plan has a fixed-amount cost-sharing requirement other than a copayment (e.g., a deductible or out-of-pocket limit) that is based on a percentage-of-compensation formula, that cost-sharing arrangement will not cause the plan or coverage to cease to be a grandfathered health plan as long as the formula remains the same as that which was in effect on March 23, 2010. Accordingly, if the percentage-of-compensation formula for determining an out-of-pocket limit is unchanged and an employee's compensation increases, then the employee could face a higher out-of-pocket limit, but that change would not cause the plan to relinquish grandfather status.[36]

[c] Limits on Fixed-Amount Copayment

Fixed-amount copayments are limited to a total increase in the copayment measured from March 23, 2010, of no more than the greater of (1) $5.00 (adjusted by medical inflation) or (2) the maximum percentage increase described above in **Section 5.01[D][2][b]**.[37] If an employer plan sponsor raises the copayment level for a category of services (such as outpatient or primary care) by an amount that exceeds this limit but retains the copayment level for other categories of services (such as inpatient care or specialty care), such a change will cause the plan to relinquish grandfather status because each change in cost-sharing is separately tested against the limit.

The regulations provide a number of examples.[38]

Example 1. On March 23, 2010, a grandfathered health plan has a copayment requirement of $30 per office visit for specialists. The plan is subsequently amended to increase the copayment requirement to $40. Within the 12-month period before the $40 copayment takes effect, the greatest value of the overall medical care component of the CPI-U (unadjusted) is 475.

In this [example], the increase in the copayment from $30 to $40, expressed as a percentage, is 33.33%[.] Medical inflation []from March 2010 is 0.2269 (475 − 387.142 = 87.858; 87.858 ÷ 387.142 = 0.2269). The maximum percentage increase permitted is 37.69% (0.2269 = 22.69%; 22.69% [+] 15% = 37.69%). Because 33.33% does not exceed 37.69%, the change in the copayment requirement at that time does not cause the plan to cease to be a grandfathered health plan.

Example 2. [The facts are the same as those in Example 1], except the grandfathered health plan subsequently increases the $40 copayment requirement to $45 for a later plan year. Within the 12-month period before the $45 copayment takes effect, the greatest value of the overall medical care component of the CPI-U (unadjusted) is 485.

[T]he increase in the copayment from $30 (the copayment that was in effect on March 23, 2010) to $45, expressed as a percentage, is 50%. Medical inflation [] from March 2010 is 0.2527 (485 − 387.142 = 97.858; 97.858 ÷ 387.142 = 0.2527). The increase that would cause a plan to cease to be a grandfathered health plan [] is the greater of the maximum percentage increase of 40.27% (0.2527 = 25.27%; 25.27% [+] 15% = 40.27%), or $6.26 ($5 × 0.2527 = $1.26; $1.26 [+] $5 = $6.26).

Because 50% exceeds 40.27% and $15 exceeds $6.26, the change in the copayment requirement at that time causes the plan to cease to be a grandfathered health plan.

---

[36] FAQs About Affordable Care Act Implementation Part V (Dec. 22, 2010), *available at* http://www.dol.gov/ebsa/pdf/faq-aca5.pdf.

[37] 26 C.F.R. § 54.9815-1251T(g)(1)(iv); 29 C.F.R. § 2590.715-1251(g)(1)(iv); 45 C.F.R. § 147.140(g)(1)(iv).

[38] 26 C.F.R. § 54.9815-1215T(g)(4); 29 C.F.R. § 2590.715-1251(g)(4); 45 C.F.R. § 147.140(g)(4).

Example 3. On March 23, 2010, a grandfathered health plan has a copayment of $10 per office visit for primary care providers. The plan is subsequently amended to increase the copayment requirement to $15. Within the 12-month period before the $15 copayment takes effect, the greatest value of the overall medical care component of the CPI-U (unadjusted) is 415.

[T]he increase in the copayment, expressed as a percentage, is 50%[.] Medical inflation [] from March 2010 is 0.0720 (415.0 − 387.142 = 27.858; 27.858 ÷ 387.142 = 0.0720. The increase that would cause a plan to cease to be a grandfathered health plan is the greater of the maximum percentage increase of 22.20% (0.0720 = 7.20%; 7.20% [+] 15% = 22.20%), or $5.36 ($5 × 0.0720 = $0.36; $0.36 [+] $5 = $5.36). The $5 increase in copayment [] would not cause the plan to cease to be a grandfathered health plan [], which would permit an increase in the copayment of up to $5.36.

Example 4. The same facts as Example [3], except on March 23, 2010, the grandfathered health plan has no copayment ($0) for office visits for primary care providers. The plan is subsequently amended to increase the copayment requirement to $5.

In this [example], medical inflation [] from March 2010 is 0.0720 (415.0 − 387.142 = 27.858; 27.858 ÷ 387.142 = 0.0720)[.] The increase that would cause a plan to cease to be a grandfathered health plan [] is $5.36 ($5 × 0.0720 = $0.36; $0.36 [+] $5.00 = $5.36). The $5 increase in copayment in this [example] is less than $5.36. Thus, the $5 increase in copayment does not cause the plan to cease to be a grandfathered health plan.

[d] Changes in Level of Cost-Sharing for Brand-Name Prescription Drugs

HHS, Treasury, and the DOL issued the following Q&A to illustrate that the movement of the brand-name drug into a higher cost-sharing tier does not cause a plan to relinquish grandfather status.

Q2: My plan bases the level of cost sharing for brand-name prescription drugs on the classification of the drugs under the plan as having or not having generic alternatives. The classification of a drug that had no generic alternative changes because a generic alternative becomes available and is added to the formulary, with a resulting increase in the cost-sharing level for the brand-name drug. Does that increase cause my plan to relinquish its grandfather status?

A2: No. For example, if, on March 23, 2010, the terms of the plan included prescription drug benefits with different cost sharing divided into tiers as follows:

- Tier 1 includes generic drugs only;
- Tier 2 includes brand name drugs with no generic available;
- Tier 3 includes brand name drugs with a generic available in Tier 1; and
- Tier 4 includes IV chemotherapy drugs.

A drug was previously classified in Tier 2 as a brand name drug with no generic available. However, a generic alternative for the drug has just been released and is added to the formulary. Since the generic is now available, the plan moves the brand name drug into Tier 3 and adds the generic to Tier 1. This movement of the brand name drug into a higher cost-sharing tier does not cause the plan to relinquish grandfather status.[39]

---

[39] FAQs About Affordable Care Act Implementation Part VI (Apr. 1, 2011), *available at* http://www.dol.gov/ebsa/pdf/faq-aca6.pdf.

[3] Increasing Employees' Contribution Rate for Premiums

A plan or health insurance coverage will lose its grandfather status if the employer decreases its contribution rate based on the cost of coverage more than five percentage points below the contribution rate for the coverage period that includes March 23, 2010.[40] Cost of coverage equals the applicable premium for the coverage for COBRA purposes.

Likewise, an employer may not decrease its contribution rate based on a formula by more than 5 percent below the contribution rate for coverage as of March 23, 2010.[41]

The regulations include the following examples:

Example 1. On March 23, 2010, a self-funded group health plan provides two tiers of coverage—self-only and family. The employer contributes 80 percent of the total cost of coverage for self-only and 60 percent of the total cost of coverage for family. Subsequently, the employer reduces the contribution to 50 percent for family coverage, but keeps the same contribution rate for self-only coverage.

The decrease of 10 percentage points for family coverage in the contribution rate based on cost of coverage causes the plan to cease to be a grandfathered health plan. The fact that the contribution rate for self-only coverage remains the same does not change the result.

Example 2. On March 23, 2010, a self-funded grandfathered health plan has an annual COBRA premium for the 2010 plan year of $5,000 for self-only coverage and $12,000 for family coverage. The required employee contribution for the coverage is $1,000 for self-only coverage and $4,000 for family coverage. Thus, the employer's contribution rate based on cost of coverage for 2010 is 80 percent (($5,000 − $1,000) ÷ $5,000) for self-only coverage and 67 percent (($12,000 − $4,000) ÷ $12,000) for family coverage. For a subsequent plan year, the COBRA premium is $6,000 for self-only coverage and $15,000 for family coverage. The employee contributions for that plan year are $1,200 for self-only coverage and $5,000 for family coverage. Thus, the contribution rate based on cost of coverage is 80 percent (($6,000 − $1,200) ÷ $6,000) for self-only coverage and 67 percent (($15,000 − $5,000) ÷ $15,000) for family coverage.

Because there is no change in the contribution rate based on cost of coverage, the plan retains its status as a grandfathered health plan. The result would be the same if all or part of the employee contribution was made on a pretax basis through a cafeteria plan under Code Section 125.

[4] Changes in Limits on the Dollar Value of Benefits

If a plan or health insurance coverage did not impose an overall annual or lifetime limit on the dollar value of all benefits as of March 23, 2010, it may not add such a limit and continue to maintain grandfathered health plan status.[42]

If a plan or health insurance coverage had an overall lifetime limit on the dollar value of all benefits but no overall annual limit as of March 23, 2010, it will lose its grandfathered health plan status if it adopts an overall annual limit at a dollar value that is lower than the dollar value of the lifetime limit as of March 23, 2010.[43]

---

[40] 26 C.F.R. § 54.9815-1251T(g)(1)(v)(A); 29 C.F.R. § 2590.715-1251(g)(1)(v)(A); 45 C.F.R. § 147.140(g)(1)(v)(A).

[41] 26 C.F.R. § 54.9815-1251T(g)(1)(v)(A); 29 C.F.R. § 2590.715-1251(g)(1)(v)(A); 45 C.F.R. § 147.140(g)(1)(v)(A).

[42] 26 C.F.R. § 54.9815-1251T(g)(1)(vi)(A); 29 C.F.R. § 2590.715-1251(g)(1)(vi)(A); 45 C.F.R. § 147.140(g)(1)(vi)(A).

[43] 26 C.F.R. § 54.9815-1251T(g)(1)(vi)(B); 29 C.F.R. § 2590.715-1251(g)(1)(vi)(B); 45 C.F.R. § 147.140(g)(1)(vi)(B).

Finally, if a plan or health insurance coverage imposed an overall annual limit on the dollar value of all benefits as of March 23, 2010, it may not decrease the dollar value of the annual limit (regardless of whether the plan or coverage also imposed an overall lifetime limit on March 23, 2010) and continue to maintain its grandfathered health plan status.[44]

[E] Plan Design Changes That Will Not Result in Forfeiture of Grandfather Status

The preamble to the grandfathered health plan regulations sheds some light on the rationale of HHS, Treasury, and the DOL for the negative rule approach to the regulations and provides some broad guidance for plan administrators. Generally, the regulations are designed to take into account "reasonable changes routinely made by plan sponsors or issuers without the plan or health insurance coverage relinquishing its grandfather status."[45]

The agencies acknowledged that "plan sponsors and issuers of grandfathered health plans should be permitted to take steps within the boundaries of the grandfather definition to control costs, including limited increases in cost-sharing and other plan changes not prohibited by these interim final regulations."[46]

Premiums can be raised as long as the contribution rate of the employees is not increased disproportionately in relation to the employer's share as described in **Section 5.01[D]** above.

In addition, changes other than the prohibited changes described in the regulation "will not cause a plan or coverage to cease to be a grandfathered health plan. Examples include changes to premiums, changes to comply with federal or state legal requirements, changes to voluntarily comply with provisions of the Affordable Care Act, and changing third-party administrators, provided these changes are made without exceeding the standards described in **Section 5.01[D]** above).[47]

A change in a third-party administrator by a self-funded plan would not necessarily cause the plan to be so different from the plan in effect on March 23, 2010, that it should forfeit its grandfather status.[48] Similarly, on and after November 15, 2010, the change of an insurance issuer in an insured plan does not result in the loss of grandfather status for the employer's plan.[49]

The seemingly broad license to make any changes other than those that are specifically prohibited may not continue indefinitely. In the preamble to the regulations, the agencies invite comments as to whether other changes should be added to the list of prohibited changes. Specifically, they ask whether the following actions should result in cessation of grandfathered health plan status:

1. Any changes to plan structure (such as switching from a health reimbursement arrangement to major medical coverage);

2. Changes in a network plan's provider network, and if so, what magnitude of change would be prohibited;

3. Changes to a prescription drug formulary, and if so, what magnitude of changes would be prohibited; or

4. Any other substantial change to the overall benefit design.[50]

---

[44] 26 C.F.R. § 54.9815-1251T(g)(1)(vi)(C); 29 C.F.R. § 2590.715-1251(g)(1)(vi)(C); 45 C.F.R. § 147.140(g)(1)(vi)(C).

[45] 75 Fed. Reg. 34,546.

[46] 75 Fed. Reg. 34,547.

[47] 75 Fed. Reg. 34,544.

[48] *See* Fed. Reg. 34,544 (providing examples of changes that would not affect grandfathered health plan status).

[49] 26 C.F.R. § 54.9815-1251T(a)(1)(ii); 29 C.F.R. § 2590.715-1251(a)(1)(ii); 45 C.F.R. § 146.140(a)(1)(ii); 75 Fed. Reg. 70,116 (Nov. 17, 2010) (explaining the need to amend the regulation to make changes in insurers consistent with changes in third-party administrators of self-funded plans).

[50] 75 Fed. Reg. 34,544. See **Appendix C** for the amendment to grandfathered health plan regulations.

Importantly, the agencies indicate that any new standards published in the final regulations that are more restrictive than the final interim regulations would only apply prospectively after the publication of the final rules.[51]

[F] Document Retention and Disclosure Requirements

A plan or health insurance issuer must maintain records that document the plan or policy terms in effect on March 23, 2010, and any other documents that are necessary to verify the continuing status of the grandfathered health plan. The records must be made available for examination by participants, beneficiaries, individual policy subscribers, or state or federal agency officials.[52]

Grandfathered health plans and health insurance coverage must include a statement in any plan materials provided to participants or beneficiaries describing the benefits provided under the plan or coverage that discloses that the plan is a grandfathered health plan and provides contact information for questions and complaints.[53] A grandfathered health plan will comply with this disclosure requirement if it includes the following model disclosure language (or a similar statement) whenever a summary of the benefits under the plan is provided to participants and beneficiaries.

> This [group health plan or health insurance issuer] believes this [plan or coverage] is a "grandfathered health plan" under the Patient Protection and Affordable Care Act (the Affordable Care Act). As permitted by the Affordable Care Act, a grandfathered health plan can preserve certain basic health coverage that was already in effect when that law was enacted. Being a grandfathered health plan means that your [plan or policy] may not include certain consumer protections of the Affordable Care Act that apply to other plans, for example, the requirement for the provision of preventive health services without any cost sharing. However, grandfathered health plans must comply with certain other consumer protections in the Affordable Care Act, for example, the elimination of lifetime limits on benefits.
>
> Questions regarding which protections apply and which protections do not apply to a grandfathered health plan and what might cause a plan to change from grandfathered health plan status can be directed to the plan administrator at [insert contact information]. [For ERISA plans, insert: You may also contact the Employee Benefits Security Administration, U.S. Department of Labor at 1-866-444-3272 or www.dol.gov/ebsa/healthreform. This website has a table summarizing which protections do and do not apply to grandfathered health plans.] [For individual market policies and nonfederal governmental plans, insert: You may also contact the U.S. Department of Health and Human Services at www.healthreform.gov.]

While it is not necessary to include the disclosure statement with each plan or issuer communication to participants and beneficiaries (such as an explanation of benefits (EOB)), plan sponsors and issuers are encouraged to identify other communications in which disclosure of grandfathered health plan status would be appropriate and consistent with the goal of providing participants and beneficiaries with the information needed to understand, and make informed choices about, health coverage.

[G] Analyzing the Benefits of Maintaining a Grandfathered Health Plan

Weighing the benefits versus the burdens of maintaining a grandfathered health plan is a plan-specific exercise. Each plan or employer must consider both the Affordable Care Act coverage reform exemptions available to grandfathered health plans and the restrictions imposed on reductions in benefits and cost-shifting to plan participants.

---

[51] 75 Fed. Reg. 34,545.

[52] 26 C.F.R. § 54.9815-1251T(a)(3); 29 C.F.R. § 2590.715-1251(a)(3); 45 C.F.R. § 147.140(a)(3).

[53] 26 C.F.R. § 54.9815-1251T(a)(2); 29 C.F.R. § 2590.715-1251(a)(2); 45 C.F.R. § 147.140(a)(2).

With respect to the exemptions from the coverage and insurance market reforms, the most substantial exemption for insured plans may be the exemption from the Act's rating restrictions. While the Affordable Care Act rating rules will not apply to insured grandfathered health plans, state rating rules (if any) will still apply. For an employer with a younger workforce (typically a lower-risk group under conventional rating rules), remaining a grandfathered health plan may mean lower premiums than entering the larger, high-risk non-grandfathered risk pool. The converse may be true for a plan with a demographic profile of older or more high-risk individuals.

For those employers that have already imposed substantial cost-sharing and premium contribution obligations on employees, the regulatory restrictions on cost increases may not be a major concern because the permitted medical inflation maximum increases may be acceptable from a cost standpoint. If a plan has not yet adopted an employee contribution amount or has very limited cost-sharing provisions, the inability to adopt those changes now may outweigh the benefits of remaining a grandfathered health plan. Many cost-sharing benefit structures are designed to modify plan members' utilization of high-cost drugs, providers, or facilities. In addition to the first-dollar financial savings that such provisions produce for the plan, the additional costs saved by changing utilization patterns may be even more substantial. Weighing the benefits of being a grandfathered health plan versus capturing those cost savings may lead an employer to elect to forgo the grandfather status. Plan changes to promote utilization improvements and quality care initiatives, particularly in disease management programs, can still be implemented but may need to be restructured to provide positive incentives for plan members rather than financial penalties in the form of increased copays or co-insurance.

Aside from the economic and regulatory impact on an employer-based group health plan, there are likely to be human resources considerations, such as the value that the employees place on the benefit and the competition for labor in the industry, which an employer must factor into the decision.

[H] Transitional Rules

Certain changes to the terms of the plan or health insurance coverage that are not effective until after March 23, 2010, are deemed to be considered part of the plan as of March 23, 2010. Namely:

- Changes effective after March 23, 2010, pursuant to a legally binding contract entered into on or before March 23, 2010;

- Changes effective after March 23, 2010, pursuant to a filing on or before March 23, 2010, with a state insurance department; and

- Changes effective after March 23, 2010, pursuant to written amendments to a plan that were adopted on or before March 23, 2010.[54]

If a plan or health insurance issuer made changes to the terms of the plan or coverage that were adopted prior to June 17, 2010, the plan or coverage will not cease to be a grandfathered health plan under the rules if the changes are revoked or modified to conform with the regulations effective as of the first day of the first plan year that began on or after September 23, 2010.[55]

The preamble also indicates that for purposes of enforcement, "the Departments will take into account good-faith efforts to comply with a reasonable interpretation of the statutory requirements and may disregard changes to plan and policy terms that only modestly exceed those changes described in [the grandfathered health plan regulations] and are adopted before the date the regulations were made publicly available."[56]

---

[54] 26 C.F.R. § 54.9815-1251T(g)(2)(i); 29 C.F.R. § 2590.715-1251(g)(2)(i); 45 C.F.R. § 147.140(g)(2)(i).

[55] 26 C.F.R. § 54.9815-1251T(g)(2)(ii); 29 C.F.R. § 2590.715-1251(g)(2)(ii); 45 C.F.R. § 147.140(g)(2)(ii).

[56] 75 Fed. Reg. 34,544.

§ 5.02 Collectively Bargained Insured Plans

The Affordable Care Act contains a special rule applicable to certain insured employment-based group health plans that are subject to collective bargaining. The special rule applies to "health insurance coverage maintained pursuant to one or more collective bargaining agreements . . . ratified before [March 23, 2010]."[57] For purposes of determining whether a collective bargaining agreement ratified before the enactment of the Affordable Care Act has been terminated, the Act disregards any amendments that implement the Act's coverage improvement requirements.

If such insured coverage exists, "the provisions of [Subtitles A and C] (and the amendments made by such subtitles) shall not apply until the date on which the last of the collective bargaining agreements relating to the coverage terminates."[58] The interim final regulations on grandfathered health plans limit the effect of this seemingly broad language to the preservation of grandfathered health plan status for such plans when they enter into new insurance arrangements while the special rule is applicable to the group health plan.[59]

Interpretational challenges presented by the special rule for collectively bargained insured plans not resolved by the interim final regulations are as follows:

- *When is a plan "maintained" pursuant to one or more collective bargaining agreements?*
  This issue arises when a plan covers both union and non-union employees. The traditional rule applied to this situation is that a plan is maintained pursuant to a collective bargaining agreement if at least 25 percent of the covered group is participating in the plan pursuant to a collective bargaining agreement.[60] It is unclear whether the 25 percent rule will apply for purposes of the special rule.

- *If a plan provides coverage on both an insured and a self-funded basis, how does one determine if the plan provides insured or self-funded coverage for purposes of the special rule?*
  For example, if a plan provides medical benefits on an insured basis and prescription drug benefits on a self-funded basis, will the whole plan (medical plus prescription) be treated as an insured plan no matter what percentage of its total benefits are provided on an insured basis, or will the benefits provided by the respective portions of the plan be considered different benefit packages?

- *When does a collective bargaining agreement "terminate" for purposes of this section?*
  Under the Railway Labor Act and certain state laws governing collective bargaining between a public-sector employer and labor unions representing employees, an employer cannot unilaterally change the status quo at the expiration of a collective bargaining agreement.[61] Instead, the terms of the expired agreement remain in effect. It is not clear in these circumstances on which date the collective bargaining agreement would terminate for purposes of the temporary exemption.

---

[57] PPACA § 1251(d). The interim final regulations confirm that the special rule only applies to health insurance maintained under one or more collective bargaining agreements. 26 C.F.R. § 54.9815-1251T(f)(1); 29 C.F.R. § 2590.715-1251(f)(1); 45 C.F.R. § 147.140(f)(1).

[58] PPACA § 1251(d).

[59] 26 C.F.R. § 54.9815-1251T(a)(1)(ii); 29 C.F.R. § 2590.715-1251(a)(1)(ii), 45 C.F.R. § 147.140(a)(1)(ii).

[60] *See, e.g.,* I.R.S. Priv. Ltr. Ruls. 9610025 (Mar. 8, 1996), 8618043 (Feb. 4, 1986), 8605032 (Nov. 5, 1985) (applying the 25% rule).

[61] *See, e.g.,* Detroit & Toledo Shore Line R.R. v. United Transp. Union, 396 U.S. 142 (1969) (regarding the Railway Labor Act); Philadelphia Hous. Auth. v. PLRB, 620 A.2d 594 (Pa. Commw. Ct. 2003) (applying Pennsylvania public sector labor law).

§ 5.03   Exemption for Retiree-Only Plans

The preamble to the grandfathered health plan regulations indicates that "retiree-only plans" are not subject to Parts A and C of Title I of the Affordable Care Act, which set forth various plan design and operational changes for employment-based group health plans and group health insurance coverage.[62] A *retiree-only plan* is defined after the enactment of the Affordable Care Act in the Code and ERISA as any group health plan covering fewer than two active employees on the first day of the plan year.[63]

Complications can arise when determining whether a health plan covers two or more active employees on the first day of the plan year, especially for employers that offer multiple benefit packages. In general, all health benefits made available by an employer are considered to constitute one group health plan unless it is clear from the instruments governing the arrangements that the benefits are being provided under separate plans and the arrangements are operated pursuant to the instruments as separate plans. Employers that wish to take advantage of the retiree-only exemption should review their group health plan documents to ensure that the documents reflect the employer's intent to have separate plans for active employees and retirees. Also, employers that rehire former employees must make sure that the rehired employees are covered under the active employee plan.

The Affordable Care Act deletes the subsection of the PHSA that contained a comparable exclusion for such plans subject to the provisions of the PHSA (i.e., group health plans that provide their benefits through health insurance, and state and local government group health plans that provide their benefits on a self-funded basis). Thus, for the plans subject to the PHSA, the preamble announces a no-enforcement policy at the federal level.[64] Recognizing that the states have independent authority to regulate group health insurance issuers, the preamble "encourages" the states to adopt the same position. As a result, it is currently unclear whether retiree-only plans that provide benefits through health insurance or that provide benefits on a self-funded basis to employees of nonfederal governmental employers will be required by one or more states to conform such coverage to the requirements of Parts A and C of Title I of the Affordable Care Act.

§ 5.04   Exemption for Excepted Benefits

Along the same lines as the exemption for retiree-only plans, the preamble to the grandfathered health plan regulations provides that "excepted benefits" generally are not subject to Parts A and C of Title I of the Affordable Care Act.[65] Excepted benefits generally include dental-only and vision-only plans, Health FSAs, Medigap policies, and AD&D coverage.[66]

To the extent that dental and/or vision coverage is integrated as part of a group health plan, it is unlikely to be considered an "excepted benefit[]" and would be subject to Parts A and C of Title I of the Affordable Care Act. Some key factors to analyze when deciding whether dental and/or vision coverage is an excepted benefit include: (1) whether such coverage is offered pursuant to a separate plan, policy, certificate, or contract of insurance; (2) whether a participant may elect not to receive the coverage; and (3) whether a participant who elects the coverage must pay an additional contribution or premium.

---

[62] 75 Fed. Reg. 34,539–40.

[63] The Act deletes the current subsection of the PHSA that excludes from the scope of the portion of the PHSA amended by Parts A and C of Title I of the Act any group health plan covering fewer than two active employees on the first day of its plan year. The Act does not delete the comparable exclusions in the Code (Section 9832(a)(2)) and (ERISA (Section 732(a)), which laws have also been amended by the Act to include these provisions of the PHSA. PPACA §§ 1562(e), (f).

[64] 75 Fed. Reg. 34,539–40.

[65] 75 Fed. Reg. 34,539–40.

[66] 26 C.F.R. § 54.9831-1; 29 C.F.R. § 2590.732; 45 C.F.R. §§ 146.145, 148.220.

Again, the Affordable Care Act deletes the subsection of the PHSA that contained a comparable exclusion for excepted benefits subject to the provisions of the PHSA (i.e., group health plans that provide their benefits through health insurance and state and local government group health plans that provide their benefits on a self-funded basis), and the preamble announces a similar non-enforcement position.[67]

---

[67] 75 Fed. Reg. 34,539–40.

CHAPTER 6

QUALITY, AFFORDABILITY, AND ACCESSIBILITY

Congress recognized that while universal access to affordable, quality health care coverage could not be implemented immediately, preliminary measures could be adopted to begin the transition and improve access to coverage. The major reforms, such as prohibitions on preexisting-condition exclusions for adults,[1] guaranteed availability and renewability of individual insurance coverage, and the state Exchanges, do not begin until January 1, 2014. The period from the date of enactment of the Affordable Care Act, March 23, 2010, through January 1, 2014, is sometimes referred to as the "transition period."

The changes that become effective during the transition period generally are interim measures intended to preserve or improve access to affordable coverage by demographic groups that currently represent significant portions of the underinsured—young adults, early retirees, and high-risk individuals. The Affordable Care Act also imposes a number of immediate coverage and reporting requirements on existing group health plans and individual insurance coverage. Premiums charged by insurance issuers begin to be regulated and limited. Finally, new reporting requirements are providing more consumer information about available options and costs, premium transparency, and quality information. Each of these measures is described in detail in subsequent chapters. A quick list of the reforms that begin during the transition period follows.

§ 6.01 Immediate Steps to Expand and Preserve Coverage[2]

Effective as of March 23, 2010, the Affordable Care Act directs HHS to take steps immediately to establish the following programs and activities:

- A high-risk health insurance pool program to provide health insurance coverage for eligible individuals beginning no later than June 21, 2010 (90 days after enactment), and ending on January 1, 2014;[3]

- A temporary reinsurance program to provide reimbursement for employer-sponsored group health plans for a portion of the cost of providing health insurance coverage to early retirees (including their eligible spouses, surviving spouses, and dependents) for the period June 21, 2010, through January 1, 2014;[4]

- A small-employer tax credit to subsidize part of a small employer's cost of coverage for employees;[5]

- An Internet portal through which a resident of any state may identify affordable health insurance options in that state, including Medicaid coverage, any high-risk pool offered by a state, and the new federal high-risk pool described above (beginning July 1, 2010).[6]

In 2010, HHS implemented these programs in a timely fashion (see **Chapter 7**).

---

[1] Prohibitions on preexisting-condition exclusions for children under age 19 apply for the first plan year beginning on or after September 23, 2010. PPACA § 1255(2) (amending PHSA § 2704).

[2] These steps are found primarily in Subtitle B of Title I of the Act.

[3] PPACA § 1101.

[4] PPACA § 1102.

[5] PPACA § 1421.

[6] PPACA § 1103.

§ 6.02   Transition Period Coverage Improvements Applicable to Group Health Plans[7]

Effective for plan years beginning on or after September 23, 2010 (six months after the date of enactment), the Affordable Care Act amends the PHSA to prohibit certain practices and add new coverage requirements for group health plans and health insurance issuers offering group or individual health insurance coverage, including:

- A prohibition on lifetime or annual limits on the dollar value of certain benefits;[8]

- A prohibition on preexisting-condition exclusion provisions for children under age 19;[9]

- Minimum preventive health services coverage requirements without cost-sharing by the enrollee;[10]

- The extension of coverage for children until age 26;[11]

- Requirements for an appeals process of coverage determinations and claims that must include, at a minimum, an internal process and an external review process that is binding on the plan;[12]

- Restrictions on rescissions of plan coverage of an enrollee, other than for fraud or an intentional misrepresentation of material fact, and subject to notice of cancellation;[13]

- A required standardized summary of benefits and coverage to be provided to applicants, enrollees, and policy holders prior to enrollment and upon renewal of coverage;[14] and

- A prohibition on eligibility rules for insured group health plans that have the effect of discriminating in favor of higher-wage employees.[15]

HHS, the DOL, and the IRS issued regulations and guidance for each of these requirements. These are reviewed in detail in **Chapter 8.**

§ 6.03   Coverage Improvements Applicable to Employment-Based Coverage Effective January 1, 2014[16]

Some coverage improvements are deferred until January 1, 2014, when the Exchanges begin and the insurance issuer market reforms become effective. These include:

- Prohibitions on preexisting-coverage exclusions for adults;[17]

- Underwriting of premiums for insured coverage limited to certain ratios for age and tobacco use;[18]

---

[7] The immediate changes applicable to health plans are found primarily in Subtitle A of Title I of the Act. Also, these requirements are subject to the discussion of grandfathered health plans and collectively bargained plans in **Chapter 5.**

[8] PPACA § 1001 (adding PHSA § 2711).

[9] PPACA §§ 1201 (adding PHSA § 2704), 1255(2).

[10] PPACA § 1001 (adding PHSA § 2713).

[11] PPACA § 1001 (adding PHSA § 2714).

[12] PPACA § 1001 (adding PHSA § 2719).

[13] PPACA § 1001 (adding PHSA § 2712).

[14] PPACA § 1001 (adding PHSA § 2715).

[15] PPACA § 1001 (adding PHSA § 2716).

[16] These provisions are found primarily in Subtitle C of Title I of the Act.

[17] PPACA § 1201 (adding PHSA § 2704).

[18] PPACA § 1201 (adding PHSA § 2701).

- Guaranteed availability and renewability of coverage by all insured plans;[19]

- Prohibitions on discrimination in benefits against individual participants and beneficiaries based on health status;[20]

- Annual cost-sharing limits for comprehensive benefits;[21]

- Prohibitions on discrimination against health care provider participation;[22]

- No waiting periods in excess of 90 days;[23] and

- Coverage of medical services in clinical trials.[24]

More guidance is expected (and needed) prior to the effective date of these requirements. The IRS has already requested comments on how the employer pay-or-play requirements (which it refers to as the "shared-responsibility" provisions) should be coordinated with the 90-day waiting period rule and the automatic enrollment provisions.[25] The law and existing standards and guidance are reviewed in **Chapter 9.**

§ 6.04 New Reporting Obligations

Insurers and group health plans will be subject to various new reporting obligations to HHS:

- To facilitate the introduction of the Web portal for consumers as of July 1, 2010 (described in **Section 6.01**), insurers were required to submit plan background information to HHS and more specific pricing and benefit information.[26]

- Beginning in 2012, insurers will be required to report on the percentage of total premium revenue that is expended on clinical service, health care quality improvement, and non-claims costs.[27] Insurers will be required to provide an annual rebate to each enrollee, on a pro rata basis, if the non-claims costs exceed 20 percent of the premium for the large group market and 25 percent of the premium for the small group and individual markets.[28]

- Group health plans and insurance coverage will be required to report on their benefits and reimbursement provisions that improve health outcomes, prevent medical errors and improve patient safety, and implement wellness and health promotion activities.[29]

- Group health plans and health insurance issuers must submit certain information regarding plan design to HHS.[30]

- Employers will be required to report on employer-sponsored insured and self-insured coverage to the IRS, and to furnish related statements to employees, effective for years beginning after December 31, 2013.[31]

---

[19] PPACA § 1201 (adding PHSA §§ 2702, 2703).
[20] PPACA § 1201 (adding PHSA § 2705).
[21] PPACA § 1201 (adding PHSA § 2707(b)).
[22] PPACA § 1201 (adding PHSA § 2706).
[23] PPACA § 1201 (adding PHSA § 2708).
[24] PPACA § 1201 (adding PHSA § 2709).
[25] I.R.S. Notice 2011-36, 2011-21 I.R.B. 792 (May 23, 2011).
[26] 45 C.F.R. § 159.120. See **Appendix D.**
[27] PPACA § 1001 (adding PHSA § 2718(a)).
[28] PPACA § 1001 (adding PHSA § 2718(b)).
[29] PPACA § 1001 (adding PHSA § 2717).
[30] PPACA § 1001 (adding PHSA § 2715A).
[31] PPACA § 1514(a) (adding I.R.C. §§ 6055 and 6056).

- Each hospital must publish annually a list of its standard charges for items and services it provides.[32]

These reporting requirements are further explained in **Chapter 10.**

§ 6.05   Additional Electronic Transaction Standards

To advance the financial transactions that will be necessary to implement and operate the Exchanges, HHS also is charged with the adoption of additional uniform standards and business operating rules under HIPAA for the electronic exchange of information by health plans with respect to eligibility, electronic funds transfers, enrollment and disenrollment, health care premium payments, and claims-related transactions.[33]

---

[32] PPACA § 1001 (adding PHSA § 2718(c)).
[33] PPACA § 1104.

CHAPTER 7

PRESERVING AND EXPANDING IMMEDIATE ACCESS TO COVERAGE

The immediate changes that become effective during the transition period (i.e., the period between March 23, 2010, and January 1, 2014) generally are interim measures intended to preserve or improve access to affordable coverage by demographic groups that currently represent significant portions of the underinsured—young adults, early retirees, employees of small employers, and high-risk individuals. This chapter reviews the immediate transition period reforms and subsidies relating to preserving and expanding coverage and discusses their implications for employment-based group health plans.

§ 7.01 Temporary Reinsurance Program for Early Retirees

[A] Background

The Affordable Care Act directed HHS to establish a temporary Early Retiree Reinsurance Program (ERRP) no later than June 21, 2010, for reimbursement of expenses relating to the provision of employment-based health coverage to early retirees.[1] HHS indicated, in the form of interim final regulations, that to better align the ERRP with plan years, the ERRP and the regulations would become effective on June 1, 2010.[2] Funding is limited, and the Program is scheduled to end on January 1, 2014, to coincide with the commencement of the Exchanges.

The ERRP is designed to encourage employers to continue providing retiree health coverage to pre-Medicare retirees.[3] According to the White House, employer-provided retiree health coverage is a valuable benefit because early retirees, as compared to the general population, have greater health risk, incur greater health costs, and have relatively less access to adequate and affordable health coverage.[4]

If an employer wishes to seek reimbursement under the ERRP, it must act quickly. The Affordable Care Act allocates only $5 billion to the program, and that amount is likely to be used up before the ERRP's scheduled ending date in 2013. Both applications for the ERRP and claims submitted under the ERRP are evaluated on a first-come, first-served basis.[5] As of February 17, 2012, HHS had paid $4.73 billion in reimbursements to more than 2,800 approved ERRP applicants across the nation.[6] The average cumulative reimbursement per plan sponsor is approximately $189,700, but some plan sponsors have well in excess of the average, including the UAW Retiree Medical Trust, AT&T, Verizon Communications, and California Public Employees' Retirement System, which each received through February 2012 more than $387 million, $213 million, $162 million, and $131 million, respectively.[7]

CMS has indicated that plan sponsors participating in the ERRP are expected to use ERRP reimbursement funds as soon as possible, but not later than December 31, 2014.[8]

---

[1] PPACA § 1102.

[2] Preamble to 45 C.F.R. pt. 149 § III.B (p. 49).

[3] Preamble to 45 C.F.R. pt. 149 § I.A (p. 5). *See* HHS Regulations on Early Retirement Reinsurance Program, 75 Fed. Reg. 24,450–70 (May 5, 2010).

[4] The White House, Fact Sheet: Early Benefits from the Affordable Care Act of 2010—Reinsurance Program for Early Retirees (May 4, 2010), http://www.whitehouse.gov/the-press-office/fact-sheet-early-retiree-reinsurance-program.

[5] 45 C.F.R. §§ 149.310, 149.315. Denied claims may be appealed to HHS within 15 days of the claim denial, and only one level of appeal is permitted. 45 C.F.R. § 149.500.

[6] Early Retiree Reinsurance Program Status Update (Feb. 2012), *available at* http://cciio.cms.gov/resources/files/Files2/02172012/errp_progress_report.pdf.

[7] Early Retiree Reinsurance Program: Reimbursement Update, *available at* http://cciio.cms.gov/resources/files/Files2/02172012/errp-posting_feb2012.pdf

[8] *See* CMS Notice on Early Retirement Reinsurance Program, 77 Fed. Reg. 16,551 (Mar. 21, 2012).

[B] Applying for the ERRP

The window to submit an application for reimbursement under the ERRP closed on May 5, 2011.[9]

Prior to May 5, 2011, an employer that maintained a retiree health plan for early retirees could have applied to HHS under the ERRP to receive reinsurance payments for certain costs incurred.[10] The Affordable Care Act defines an "early retiree" as an individual age 55 or older who is not Medicare-eligible (either by reason of attaining age 65 or being disabled), and is not an active employee of the employer that has made substantial contributions to fund the employment-based retiree health plan.[11]

[C] Participating in the ERRP

[1] Reimbursement of Costs

Once approved, HHS is authorized to reimburse up to 80 percent of the costs associated with the provision of retiree health coverage between $15,000 and $90,000 per year.[12] Both dollar amounts are adjusted each year based on the percentage increase in the Medical Care Component of the Consumer Price Index for all urban consumers (rounded to the nearest multiple of $1,000).[13] The costs subject to reinsurance include costs incurred with respect to the early retiree, his or her spouse, surviving spouse, and dependents, net of discounts, and other negotiated price concessions.[14] Significantly, such costs may include costs actually paid by the early retiree, spouse, surviving spouse, or dependent in the form of deductibles, copayments, and co-insurance.[15] If the group health plan is insured, the actual net costs incurred by the insurer and the early retiree may be counted, but the premium costs paid by the plan sponsor or the early retiree are excluded.[16]

Because the ERRP started on June 1, 2010, plan sponsors are eligible for reinsurance for only part of their 2010 plan year. Only costs incurred on or after June 1, 2010, can be reimbursed under the ERRP.[17] However, HHS allows plan sponsors to count costs incurred prior to June 1, 2010 (but during the 2010 plan year), against both the $15,000 threshold and the $90,000 maximum limit.[18] Thus, if at least $15,000 in costs has been incurred with respect to an early retiree in the 2010 plan year prior to June 1, 80 percent of costs incurred from June 1, 2010, through the end of the 2010 plan year are eligible for reinsurance (subject to the $90,000 limit).

---

[9] See CMS Notice on Early Retirement Reinsurance Program, 76 Fed. Reg. 18,766–67 (Apr. 5, 2011).

[10] The application process is intended to be consistent with the process for applying for Medicare Part D RDS payments. See **Section 12.01[C]** notes 22–31 and accompanying text (discussing the RDS payment process). One significant difference, however, is that only one application is required under the ERRP for all years (through the end of 2013). 45 C.F.R. § 149.40(d). Application for RDS payments under Medicare Part D must be made annually. See http://www.rds.cms.hhs.gov/app_deadline.htm (providing information about RDS application deadlines).

[11] PPACA § 1102(a)(2)(C).

[12] PPACA § 1102(c); 45 C.F.R. § 149.100. Coverage for which reinsurance is available under the ERRP includes costs for medical, surgical, hospital prescription drug, and other types of health coverage, but not for "excepted benefits" (such as long-term care) as described in HIPAA. 45 C.F.R. § 149.2 (defining "claim" or "medical claim"). Also, a "dependent" means an individual covered as a dependent under the plan, regardless of whether such individual is a dependent for tax purposes under Section 152 of the Code. 45 C.F.R. § 149.2.

[13] PPACA § 1102(c); 45 C.F.R. § 149.115(c).

[14] Spouses, surviving spouses, and dependents are not subject to the age 55, non–Medicare eligible, and retired conditions applicable to early retirees. 45 C.F.R. § 149.2 (definition of "early retiree"). Negotiated price concessions include any direct or indirect remuneration offered to a plan sponsor, health insurer, or plan that would serve to decrease the costs incurred under the plan. 45 C.F.R. § 149.2 (definition of "negotiated price concession").

[15] PPACA § 1102(c)(1).

[16] 45 C.F.R. § 149.100.

[17] 45 C.F.R. § 149.105.

[18] 45 C.F.R. § 149.105.

The reinsurance payments received under the ERRP are not treated as income to the employer maintaining the employment-based retiree health plan.[19] Thus, the reinsurance payments appear to create a double tax benefit for employers that can deduct the cost of providing retiree health benefits and receive tax-free reimbursements for those same costs under the ERRP. Ironically, this is the same type of inequitable double tax benefit that the Affordable Care Act unwinds with respect to the retiree drug subsidy (RDS) payments under Medicare Part D.[20]

As of February 2012, the ERRP had disbursed nearly all of its allocated funding to a variety of entities, including for-profit companies, schools and educational institutions, unions, state and local governments, religious organizations, and other not-for-profit plan sponsors, to help reduce their health plan benefit costs and those of their plan participants, including early retirees and their spouses, surviving spouses, dependents, and active workers.[21] Because the $5 billion funding limit is almost exhausted, CMS communicated on December 9, 2011, that any claim submitted with an incurred date of service after December 31, 2011, will be rejected.[22] Plan sponsors must not include in their claim lists any claims for which the incurred date is after December 31, 2011.[23] If health benefit items or services with later incurred dates are submitted, the *entire* claim list will be deemed invalid.[24] However, CMS continues to accept ERRP reimbursement requests for claims incurred on or before December 31, 2011.[25]

If there are not sufficient funds to pay in its entirety the last reimbursement request that causes the initial exhaustion of the $5 billion, CMS will use available funds to partially honor that reimbursement request, and will pay the balance of that reimbursement request if additional funds become available.[26] Reimbursement requests received after the $5 billion funding has been fully exhausted will be held in the order of receipt, pending the availability of funds. Plan sponsors with reimbursement requests on hold can expect to:

- Receive an email notifying them that their reimbursement requests have been placed on hold pending the availability of funds;

- Have access to information about the position of their requests in the list of held reimbursement requests; and

- Be paid in the order in which reimbursement requests were received, if additional funds become available.[27]

At this point, the federal government has not indicated an intent to provide any additional funds for the ERRP.

---

[19] PPACA § 1102(c)(5).

[20] See **Section 12.01[C]** notes 22–31 and accompanying text (discussing the Act provision that eliminates the employer's deduction for retiree prescription drug costs that are reimbursed through RDS payments).

[21] Early Retiree Reinsurance Program Status Update (Feb. 2012), *available at* http://cciio.cms.gov/resources/files/Files2/02172012/errp_progress_report.pdf.

[22] Press Release, Update on ERRP Payment Processing and Announcement of End Date for Newly Incurred Claims (Dec. 9, 2011), http://www.errp.gov/newspages/20111209-updated-payment-processing-new-incurred-date.shtml

[23] *See* CMS Notice on Early Retirement Reinsurance Program, 76 Fed. Reg. 77,537 (Dec. 13, 2011).

[24] *See* CMS Notice on Early Retirement Reinsurance Program, 76 Fed. Reg. 77,537 (Dec. 13, 2011).

[25] Press Release, Update on ERRP Payment Processing and Announcement of End Date for Newly Incurred Claims (Dec. 9, 2011), http://www.errp.gov/newspages/20111209-updated-payment-processing-new-incurred-date.shtml.

[26] Press Release, Update on ERRP Payment Processing and Announcement of End Date for Newly Incurred Claims (Dec. 9, 2011), http://www.errp.gov/newspages/20111209-updated-payment-processing-new-incurred-date.shtml.

[27] Press Release, Update on ERRP Payment Processing and Announcement of End Date for Newly Incurred Claims (Dec. 9, 2011), http://www.errp.gov/newspages/20111209-updated-payment-processing-new-incurred-date.shtml.

[2] Process for Requesting Reimbursement Under the ERRP

In order to request reimbursement under the ERRP, a plan sponsor must adhere to the following process instituted by HHS. Additional details on the following steps are available in the "Training Presentations and Videos" section of the ERRP's Web site at *http://www.errp.gov*.

Step 1. Receive confirmation from HHS that an application for the ERRP has been approved.

Step 2. Register an "Authorized Representative" and "Account Manager" on the ERRP's secure Web site (SWS) maintained by HHS. A plan sponsor may assign designees to assist with the duties generally performed by an Authorized Representative and/or Account Manager, such as (i) editing the early retiree list setup; (ii) reporting cost data; (iii) requesting reimbursement; (iv) changing banking information; and (v) viewing, sending, and receiving early retiree data.

Step 3. Identify early retirees.

Step 4. Set up the early retiree list (ERL) through the ERRP's SWS.

Step 5. Submit the ERL by uploading it through the ERRP's SWS or by transmitting it via a mainframe connection to the ERRP's mainframe. Plan sponsors are required to submit an ERL prior to submitting summary cost data to determine which individuals are eligible for the ERRP. Plan sponsors should only submit individuals who have reached the $15,000 cost threshold. However, if a subscriber's dependent meets the cost threshold and the subscriber does not, the subscriber record must still be submitted along with the dependent record on the ERL. There is no limit to the number of times a plan sponsor may submit an ERL.

Step 6. Review the ERL response file from HHS, which communicates the periods of each individual's ERRP eligibility. The plan sponsor must use the approved periods contained in the file to query claims data for the purpose of ensuring that only eligible costs are submitted with each reimbursement request.

Step 7. Enlist a single party to collect and aggregate cost data to ensure that (i) only early retirees with $15,000 or more in health benefit costs are included in the ERL; (ii) each early retiree's threshold reduction and limit reduction are calculated accurately; (iii) price concessions (e.g., rebates, discounts, charge-backs, etc.) are allocated appropriately to all early retirees; and (iv) only costs for the eligible time periods in the ERL response file are included in cost submissions. All information will be reported by plan for each plan year. Cost data is cumulative, and each new cost data submission will be a complete replacement of prior submissions.

Step 8. Create the ERRP claim list. The claim list must include both the claim items or services for which the plan sponsor is currently requesting reimbursement, and the items or services upon which the plan sponsor has based the sponsor's previous reimbursement requests for that plan year. The detailed claims data must be cumulative, and each claim list replaces the previously submitted claim list for the plan year.

Step 9. Send the claim list to the ERRP Center.

Step 10. Review the ERRP Center claim list response file.

Step 11. Submit summary cost data through the ERRP's SWS. While summary cost data may be entered and saved at any time, reimbursement requests may only be submitted once per calendar quarter for a given plan year. Only the costs associated with ERRP-eligible individuals may be submitted. To protect the integrity of the ERRP against fraud and abuse, a separation of duties prohibits the individual who reports summary cost data from requesting reimbursement.

Step 12. Build and submit a reimbursement request, allowing at least 30 days between reimbursement requests.

[3] Notice to Plan Participants

A form notice must be delivered to all individuals who are plan participants (not just early retirees) notifying them that, because the plan sponsor is participating in the ERRP with respect to the plan, the plan sponsor may use the reimbursements to reduce plan participants' premium contributions, copayments, deductibles, co-insurance, or other out-of-pocket costs, and therefore plan participants may experience such changes in the terms and conditions of their plan participation. Such notice must be distributed no later than a reasonable time after the plan sponsor receives its first ERRP reimbursement. The form notice may be delivered by U.S. mail or by courier service to each plan participant's last known address. Alternatively, for those plan participants who are actively working, plan sponsors may send the notices electronically, provided the participants have the ability to access documents at their regular place of work and have access to the plan sponsor's electronic information system on a daily basis as part of their work duties.

§ 7.02 Pre-Existing Condition Insurance Plans

As described above, the most far-reaching health care reforms, relating to the establishment of Exchanges and the implementation of the individual "enroll or pay" and the employer "pay or play" requirements, are not scheduled to occur until 2014.[28] In order to implement the policy goal of providing universal access to health coverage, the Affordable Care Act calls for the prompt establishment of temporary high-risk insurance pools to provide health insurance coverage to uninsured eligible individuals who have preexisting conditions.[29] The Act indicates that these "temporary high-risk pools" will operate through 2013, at which point the individuals receiving health insurance coverage through the pools would be able to enroll in health insurance coverage through the Exchanges.[30]

The Affordable Care Reform Act directed HHS to establish the temporary high-risk pools directly, or to work with states and nonprofit entities to set up the pools. On April 5, 2010, HHS Secretary Kathleen Sebelius sent a letter to each state seeking expressions of state interest in participating in the establishment of temporary high-risk pools.[31] In the letter, the Secretary outlined five possible options for states:

- Operate a new high-risk pool alongside an existing high-risk pool maintained by the state;

- Establish a new high-risk pool, where the state does not currently offer such a pool;

- Build upon existing coverage programs designed to cover high-risk individuals;

---

[28] See **Chapter 11** for a discussion of Exchanges, individual "enroll or pay," and employer "pay or play."
[29] PPACA § 1101. Only U.S. citizens and nationals are eligible for the temporary high-risk pools. PPACA § 1101(d)(1).
[30] PPACA § 1101(a).
[31] *See* http://www.hhs.gov/news/press/2010pres/04/20100402b.html.

- Contract with an insurance carrier to provide subsidized coverage for uninsured individuals with preexisting conditions; or

- Do nothing, in which case HHS would establish the temporary high-risk pool for the state.[32]

The Affordable Care Act appropriates $5 billion in funding for the state-based temporary high-risk pools.[33] HHS will allocate the funding among the states using a formula similar to what it uses to allocate Children's Health Insurance Program (CHIP) funds.[34] To avoid abuse, the Act provides that states entering into an arrangement with HHS to provide temporary high-risk pools cannot reduce the annual amount expended by the state on existing state high-risk pools during the year prior to the year in which the arrangement is established.[35] The temporary high-risk pools must provide coverage to eligible individuals that (1) does not impose any preexisting-condition exclusions; (2) covers at least 65 percent of eligible costs; (3) has out-of-pocket expense limits that do not exceed, for 2012, $6,050 for self-only coverage or $12,100 for family coverage; (4) meets certain premium limitations (including a limitation that premiums cannot vary based on age by a ratio of more than four to one); and (5) satisfies any other requirements imposed by HHS.[36]

According to the HHS Web site (http://www.healthcare.gov), as of April 2012, 23 states and the District of Columbia have adopted the federal temporary high-risk pool, called the Pre-Existing Condition Insurance Plan (PCIP).[37] Enrollment in the PCIP and the state-based temporary high-risk pools has been significantly lower than initially forecasted, with only 48,879 individuals enrolled in the programs nationwide as of December 31, 2011 (as compared to an initial forecast of 375,000 covered individuals by the end of 2010).[38] It is unclear whether premium costs for the programs remain too high, and/or whether the existence of the programs has not been properly communicated to the general population.

While the establishment of the PCIP and state-based temporary high-risk pools does not directly affect employment-based group health plans, employers need to be aware of the rules prohibiting the dumping of risk on the temporary high-risk pools. The Affordable Care Act directs HHS to establish criteria for determining whether insurers and employment-based group health plans have discouraged individuals from remaining in prior coverage based on that individual's health status (the "anti-dumping rule").[39] The determination will be based in part on whether the employer, the plan, or the insurer provided money or other financial incentives to the individual to disenroll from the employment-based group health plan. The sanction for violating the anti-dumping rule is to reimburse the medical expenses incurred by the temporary high-risk pool.[40]

Many employers offer "opt-out" arrangements pursuant to which employees may elect to decline coverage under the employer's group health plan in exchange for some monetary or other incentive. Such arrangements usually are offered to all employees or broad-based portions of the total employee

---

[32] *See* http://www.hhs.gov/news/press/2010pres/04/20100402b.html.

[33] PPACA § 1101(g).

[34] *See* Fact Sheet—Temporary High Risk Pool Program, http://www.hhs.gov/cciio/initiative/hi_risk_pool_facts.html. California, the most populous state, would receive the most funding—approximately $761 million.

[35] PPACA § 1101(e).

[36] PPACA § 1101(c); *see also* I.R.S. Rev. Proc. 2011-32, 2011-22 I.R.B. 835 (providing the out-of-pocket expense limits for 2012).

[37] See http://www.healthcare.gov/law/features/choices/pre-existing-condition-insurance-plan/index.html#state. The 23 states that have adopted the PCIP are Alabama, Arizona, Delaware, Florida, Georgia, Hawaii, Idaho, Indiana, Kentucky, Louisiana, Massachusetts, Minnesota, Mississippi, Nebraska, Nevada, North Dakota, South Carolina, Tennessee, Texas, Vermont, Virginia, West Virginia, and Wyoming.

[38] *See* http://www.healthcare.gov/news/factsheets/2012/02/pcip02232012a.html; Amy Goldstein, *Enrollment in High-Risk Insurance Pools Lagging Behind Predictions,* Wash. Post (Feb. 10, 2011), *available at* http://www.washingtonpost.com/wp-dyn/content/article/2011/02/10/AR 2011021004184.html.

[39] PPACA § 1101(e).

[40] PPACA § 1101(e)(2).

population. So long as such arrangements are broad-based, it would seem that they would not run afoul of the anti-dumping rule because they would not be basing eligibility for the opt-out payment on an individual's health status.

§ 7.03 Small-Employer Incentives

[A] Employer Eligibility

Because employees of small employers make up a substantial portion of the ranks of the uninsured, the Affordable Care Act includes incentives for small employers to make health insurance coverage available to employees. For tax years beginning after December 31, 2009, employers that employ fewer than 25 full-time equivalent employees (FTEs) and have average annual wages of less than $50,000[41] per FTE became eligible for tax credits if they maintain a "qualifying arrangement"[42] for their employees.[43] Most tax-exempt employers[44] are also eligible for the credit, but special rules apply in calculating the amount of the credit and the annual wages (if any employees are members of the clergy). For tax years 2010 through 2013, a household employer that otherwise satisfies the requirements is also eligible for the credit.

The tax credits only apply to eligible small employers that provide medical benefits through health insurance coverage (i.e., the tax credits are not available to self-funded plans[45]) prior to January 1, 2014, at which point the Exchanges become operational.[46] Once the Exchanges become operational, the tax credits are available only to eligible small employers that provide medical benefits through a QHP (a qualified health plan—i.e., a plan offered through the Exchange).

[B] Employer Limitations

Employers may not treat any premiums paid pursuant to a salary reduction arrangement under a Section 125 cafeteria plan as an employer contribution.[47] An additional limitation for employers is that the controlled group rules under Code Sections 414(b), (c), (m), and (o) will apply when determining the size of an employer.[48] Thus, all employees of a controlled group or affiliated service group and all wages paid to, and premiums paid for, employees by the members of the controlled group or affiliated service group generally are taken into account in determining who is an eligible small employer.[49]

---

[41] The $50,000 wage limit will be adjusted for inflation beginning in 2014. I.R.C. § 45R(d)(3)(B)(ii).

[42] A "qualifying arrangement" is an arrangement under which the employer non-electively pays premiums for each employee enrolled in health insurance coverage offered by the employer in an amount equal to a uniform percentage (but not less than 50 percent) of the premium cost of the coverage. I.R.S. Notice 2010-44 § II(A), 2010-22 I.R.B. 717.

[43] PPACA § 1421 (adding I.R.C. § 45R(d)). Although the term "eligible small employer" is defined in Section 45R(d)(1) to include employers with "no more than" 25 FTEs and average annual wages that "do not exceed" $50,000, the phase-out of the credit amount under Section 45R(c) operates in such a way that an employer with exactly 25 FTEs or with average annual wages exactly equal to $50,000 is not in fact eligible for the credit. I.R.S. Notice 2010-44 § II(A), 2010-22 I.R.B. 717.

[44] This refers to any tax-exempt organization described in Code Section 501(c) that is exempt from taxation under Section 501(a). Agencies or instrumentalities of the federal government, or of state, local, or Indian tribal governments, are not eligible employers.

[45] Qualifying small employers providing coverage through a self-funded church plan may be eligible for a credit on the health care coverage costs under those plans.

[46] I.R.C. § 45R(b).

[47] I.R.C. § 45R(e)(3).

[48] I.R.C. § 45R(e)(5).

[49] See **Section 7.03[E]** for an explanation of which employees are excluded from the tax-credit calculation.

[C] Form and Amount of Credit

These tax credits will come in the form of general business tax credits for for-profit employers.[50] The credit offsets only an employer's actual income tax liability or its alternative minimum tax (AMT) for the year. The tax credits may be carried forward if the for-profit entity does not have enough tax liability in a given year to use the full amount of the tax credit.[51] For the 2010 through 2013 taxable years, the credit amount is equal to 35 percent (25 percent for tax-exempt entities) of the aggregate amount of non-elective employer contributions made on behalf of employees to an insured health plan.[52] Tax-exempt employers are entitled to a refundable credit that may not exceed the total amount of the income and Medicare taxes the employer withholds for the year plus the employer's share of the Medicare tax on employees' wages.[53] For taxable years beginning on or after January 1, 2014, the amount of the credit increases to 50 percent (35 percent for tax-exempt entities) of the aggregate amount of non-elective employer contributions made on behalf of employees to a QHP.[54]

[D] Proration of Credit

The credit is prorated based on the number of employees and the average salary base. If the number of FTEs exceeds ten, the reduction is determined by multiplying the otherwise applicable credit amount by a fraction, the numerator of which is the number of FTEs in excess of ten and the denominator of which is 15. If average annual wages exceed $25,000, the reduction is determined by multiplying the otherwise applicable credit amount by a fraction, the numerator of which is the amount by which average annual wages exceed $25,000 and the denominator of which is $25,000.[55] In both cases, the result of the calculation is subtracted from the otherwise applicable credit to determine the credit to which the employer is entitled.[56] See the following tables for specific detail on credit proration.

---

[50] I.R.C. § 38(b)(36).

[51] I.R.S. Notice 2010-44 § IV, 2010-22 I.R.B. 717.

[52] I.R.C. § 45R(g).

[53] I.R.C. § 45R(f).

[54] I.R.C. § 45R(b).

[55] I.R.S. Notice 2010-44 § III(C), 2010-22 I.R.B. 717.

[56] I.R.S. Notice 2010-44 § III(C), 2010-22 I.R.B. 717.

TABLE 7-1. Small Employer Tax Credit as a Percent (Maximum of 35%) of Employer Contribution to Premiums, For-Profit Firms in 2010–2013 and Nonprofit Firms in 2014 and Beyond[57]

# of employees	Average Wage					
	Up to $25,000	$30,000	$35,000	$40,000	$45,000	$50,000
Up to 10	35%	28%	21%	14%	7%	0%
11	33%	26%	19%	12%	5%	0%
12	30%	23%	16%	9%	2%	0%
13	28%	21%	14%	7%	0%	0%
14	26%	19%	12%	5%	0%	0%
15	23%	16%	9%	2%	0%	0%
16	21%	14%	7%	0%	0%	0%
17	19%	12%	5%	0%	0%	0%
18	16%	9%	2%	0%	0%	0%
19	14%	7%	0%	0%	0%	0%
20	12%	5%	0%	0%	0%	0%
21	9%	2%	0%	0%	0%	0%
22	7%	0%	0%	0%	0%	0%
23	5%	0%	0%	0%	0%	0%
24	2%	0%	0%	0%	0%	0%
25	0%	0%	0%	0%	0%	0%

---

[57] Congressional Research Serv., Summary of Small Business Health Insurance Tax Credit Under PPACA (P.L. 111-148) (Apr. 5, 2010), *available at* http://www.ncsl.org/documents/health/SBtaxCredits.pdf.

TABLE 7-2. Small Employer Tax Credit as a Percent (Maximum of 50%) of Employer Contribution to Premiums, For-Profit Firms in 2014 and Beyond[58]

# of employees	Average Wage					
	Up to $25,000	$30,000	$35,000	$40,000	$45,000	$50,000
Up to 10	50%	40%	30%	20%	10%	0%
11	47%	37%	27%	17%	7%	0%
12	43%	33%	23%	13%	3%	0%
13	40%	30%	20%	10%	0%	0%
14	37%	27%	17%	7%	0%	0%
15	33%	23%	13%	3%	0%	0%
16	30%	20%	10%	0%	0%	0%
17	27%	17%	7%	0%	0%	0%
18	23%	13%	3%	0%	0%	0%
19	20%	10%	0%	0%	0%	0%
20	17%	7%	0%	0%	0%	0%
21	13%	3%	0%	0%	0%	0%
22	10%	0%	0%	0%	0%	0%
23	7%	0%	0%	0%	0%	0%
24	3%	0%	0%	0%	0%	0%
25	0%	0%	0%	0%	0%	0%

---

[58] Congressional Research Serv., Summary of Small Business Health Insurance Tax Credit Under PPACA (P.L. 111-148) (Apr. 5, 2010), *available at* http://www.ncsl.org/documents/health/SBtaxCredits.pdf.

TABLE 7-3. Small Employer Tax Credit as a Percent (Maximum of 25%) of Employer Contribution to Premiums, Nonprofit Firms in 2010–2013[59]

# of employees	Average Wage					
	Up to $25,000	$30,000	$35,000	$40,000	$45,000	$50,000
Up to 10	25%	20%	15%	10%	5%	0%
11	23%	18%	13%	8%	3%	0%
12	22%	17%	12%	7%	2%	0%
13	20%	15%	10%	5%	0%	0%
14	18%	13%	8%	3%	0%	0%
15	17%	12%	7%	2%	0%	0%
16	15%	10%	5%	0%	0%	0%
17	13%	8%	3%	0%	0%	0%
18	12%	7%	2%	0%	0%	0%
19	10%	5%	0%	0%	0%	0%
20	8%	3%	0%	0%	0%	0%
21	7%	2%	0%	0%	0%	0%
22	5%	0%	0%	0%	0%	0%
23	3%	0%	0%	0%	0%	0%
24	2%	0%	0%	0%	0%	0%
25	0%	0%	0%	0%	0%	0%

[E] Calculation of Employees

The calculation to determine the number of FTEs for the tax credit is different from similar calculations used for other purposes under the Affordable Care Act. For this purpose, FTEs are determined by dividing the total number of hours of service[60] for which wages were paid by the employer to employees, including leased employees, during the taxable year, by 2,080.[61] The resulting number

---

[59] Congressional Research Serv., Summary of Small Business Health Insurance Tax Credit Under PPACA (P.L. 111-148) (Apr. 5, 2010), *available at* http://www.ncsl.org/documents/health/SBtaxCredits.pdf.

[60] An employee's hours of service for a year include the following: (1) each hour for which an employee is paid, or entitled to payment, for the performance of duties for the employer during the employer's taxable year; and (2) each hour for which an employee is paid, or entitled to payment, by the employer on account of a period of time during which no duties are performed due to vacation, holiday, illness, incapacity (including disability), layoff, jury duty, military duty, or leave of absence (except that no more than 160 hours of service are required to be counted for an employee on account of any single continuous period during which the employee performs no duties). In calculating the total number of hours of service, the employer may use any of the following methods: (1) determine actual hours of service; (2) use a days-worked equivalency whereby the employee is credited with 8 hours of service for each day for which the employee would be required to be credited with at least one hour of service; or (3) use a weeks-worked equivalency whereby the employee is credited with 40 hours of service for each week for which the employee would be required to be credited with at least one hour of service. I.R.S. Notice 2010-44 § II(C), 2010-22 I.R.B. 717.

[61] I.R.C. § 45R(d)(2)(A).

is then rounded to the next lowest whole number. If an employee works more than 2,080 hours of service during any taxable year, any hours over 2,080 are not included.[62] All FTEs are considered in this analysis, not just the ones who are enrolled in the health insurance coverage or QHP.[63]

Certain employees are excluded from consideration, including:[64]

- Employee-owners, their spouses, and their family members, including sole proprietors, shareholders owning more than 2 percent of a Subchapter S corporation, and any owners of more than 5 percent of other businesses;

- An individual who satisfies the dependent eligibility criteria under Section 152 of the Code; and

- Seasonal workers, unless the seasonal worker works for the employer for at least 121 days during the taxable year.

Ministers who are employees under the common-law test for determining worker status are counted for purposes of determining an employer's FTEs and premiums paid for coverage.[65]

[F] Calculation of Average Annual Wages

Average annual wages are determined by dividing (1) the aggregate amount of wages that were paid to *all* employees (other than clergy)[66] (not just FTEs) by the employer during the taxable year, by (2) the number of FTEs of the employer (including employed clergy)[67] for the taxable year.[68] This amount is rounded to the next lowest multiple of $1,000.[69] While the hours worked by an employee in excess of 2,080 hours are not taken into consideration for the purpose of calculating FTEs, the wages paid to an employee who works in excess of 2,080 hours per year are taken into consideration.[70] Therefore, if an employee works 2,200 hours and earns $10 per hour, only 2,080 of the 2,200 hours are considered for determining employer size, but all wages paid ($22,200) are factored into the calculation for average annual wages.

[G] Qualifying Arrangements

To be eligible for the tax credit, an employer must pay premiums for health insurance coverage under a qualifying arrangement.[71] A qualifying arrangement is an arrangement under which the

---

[62] I.R.C. § 45R(d)(2)(B).

[63] I.R.S. Notice 2010-44 § II(D) Ex. 4, 2010-22 I.R.B. 717.

[64] I.R.C. §§ 45R(d)(5), 45R(e)(1).

[65] The worker status of a minister must be determined by the employer for wage-reporting purposes. An employer must report a minister's wages on a Form W-2 if the minister is an employee under the common-law test. If self-employed, the minister should receive a Form 1099 from any employer from whom he or she received more than $600.

[66] A minister employee's wages are not included in the average annual wages determination. A minister's wages are not subject to Social Security or Medicare tax under FICA. As a result, a minister has no wages as defined under Section 3121(a) for purposes of the average wages. I.R.S. Notice 2010-82 § III(B), 2010-51 I.R.B. 857.

[67] As drafted, the Act provides "the full number of full-time equivalent employees of the employee," which is clearly a typographical error and will likely be corrected via a technical correction. I.R.C. § 45R(d)(3)(A)(ii).

[68] I.R.C. § 45R(d)(3)(A).

[69] I.R.C. § 45R(d)(3)(A).

[70] I.R.S. Notice 2010-44 § II(E), 2010-22 I.R.B. 717.

[71] A special transitional rule for the 2010 taxable year provides that in the case of an employer who pays a non-elective amount equal to at least 50% of the premium for single (employee-only) coverage for each enrolled employee, such employer will be deemed to satisfy the uniformity requirement for a qualifying arrangement, even if the employer does not pay the same percentage of the premium for each such employee who has more expensive coverage (e.g., family coverage). I.R.S. Notice 2010-44 § V, 2010-22 I.R.B. 717.

employer pays premiums for each employee enrolled in health insurance coverage offered by the employer in an amount equal to a uniform percentage (not less than 50 percent) of the premium cost of the coverage for single (employee-only) coverage.

Each benefits package is considered a separate health insurance plan, and each plan must satisfy the uniformity requirement. The amount or percentage of employer contribution need not be identical for each plan.[72] In states where tax credits or premium subsidies are available to small employers that provide health insurance to their employees, the amount of premium paid by the employer is not reduced by the premium subsidy or credit for purposes of determining whether the employer paid a uniform amount or percentage of the premium. Generally, the premium payments made by the state are treated as an employer contribution for purposes of the tax credit.

For purposes of this credit prior to January 1, 2014, health insurance coverage includes, but is not limited to, limited-scope dental or vision, long-term care, nursing home care, home health care, community-based care, coverage for specific diseases, hospital indemnity or other fixed indemnity insurance, Medicare supplements, and other supplemental coverage. Premium payments made pursuant to any of these plans can be counted as being paid under a qualifying arrangement.[73] However, different types of health insurance plans cannot be aggregated to satisfy the requirements for a qualifying arrangement.[74] Each type of coverage must separately satisfy the uniformity requirements for a qualifying arrangement.[75] Therefore, if an eligible small employer paid 60 percent of the premium cost for medical coverage but only 40 percent of the premium cost for dental coverage, the employer would be eligible for the tax credit only with respect to the medical coverage since it did not pay at or above the 50 percent threshold for dental coverage.

The uniformity requirement applies to premiums paid for those employees enrolled in a plan; it is not a coverage requirement.

[H] Employer Premiums

The amount of an employer's premium payments that are considered for purposes of the credit is limited to the lesser of (1) the actual premiums contributed by the employer or (2) the average premium for the small group market in the state in which the employer offers coverage. The state average premiums are listed in *Instructions to Form 8941*. A copy of Form 8941 and the Instructions are included in **Appendix E**.

For 2010, premiums that were paid during the 2010 taxable year but prior to the date of enactment of the Affordable Care Act may be included for purposes of the credit.[76]

[I] Claiming the Tax Credit

A taxable employer claims the tax credit on its annual income tax return by attaching a Form 8941 showing the calculation of the credit. A tax-exempt employer claims the refundable credit by filing a Form 990-T with an attached Form 8941.[77]

An employer should take the following steps to determine if it is eligible for a tax credit under Section 45R of the Code:

---

[72] *See* I.R.S. Notice 2010-82 § III.G.2, 2010-51 I.R.B. 857, for more information and examples on the application of the uniformity requirements to varying types of premiums and benefits packages.

[73] I.R.S. Notice 2010-44 § II.G, 2010-22 I.R.B. 717.

[74] I.R.S. Notice 2010-44 § II.G, 2010-22 I.R.B. 717.

[75] I.R.S. Notice 2010-44 § II.G, 2010-22 I.R.B. 717.

[76] I.R.S. Notice 2010-44 § II.F, 2010-22 I.R.B. 717.

[77] I.R.S. Notice 2010-22 § II.A, 2010-22 I.R.B. 717.

Step 1.   Determine the employees who are taken into account for purposes of the tax credit.

Step 2.   Determine the number of hours of service performed by the employees in Step 1.

Step 3.   Calculate the number of FTEs. If there are fewer than 25, continue. If there are 25 or more FTEs, the employer does not qualify for the tax credit.

Step 4.   Determine the average annual wages paid per FTE. If the average wages are less than $50,000, continue. If the average annual wages are $50,000 or more, the employer does not qualify for the tax credit.

Step 5.   Go to the charts in **Section 7.03[D]** and determine the applicable percentage credit.

Step 6.   Determine the total premiums contributed by the employer that are taken into account for purposes of the credit (i.e., paid under a qualifying arrangement).

Step 7.   Determine the amount of credit-eligible taxes paid by the employer (general income tax or alternative minimum tax for taxable employers; employee withholding and Medicare taxes for tax-exempt entities).

Step 8.   Multiply the total premiums determined in Step 6 by the applicable percentage credit determined in Step 5.

Generally, the employer is eligible for a tax credit equal to the lesser of the amount in Step 7 or Step 8. The amount may be subject to certain additional adjustments listed in Form 8941 for some employers.

See **Appendix E** for Form 8941 and the corresponding instructions, which include worksheets that may be helpful in making these determinations.

CHAPTER 8

COVERAGE IMPROVEMENTS DURING THE TRANSITION PERIOD

This chapter discusses coverage improvements that become effective during the transition period, subject to the discussion in Chapter 5 of grandfathered health plans and other exemptions.

§ 8.01   Prohibitions on Lifetime and Annual Dollar Limits on Benefits

Group health plans and health insurers offering group health or individual insurance coverage are prohibited from imposing lifetime limits on the dollar value of benefits for any participant or beneficiary, and from imposing most annual limits on essential health benefits.[1] The ban on lifetime and annual dollar benefits starts for plan years beginning on after September 23, 2010.[2] HHS, Treasury, and the DOL issued interim final regulations published in the *Federal Register* on June 28, 2010, further explaining these restrictions.[3]

The elimination of lifetime dollar limits, and the restriction and elimination (by 2014) of annual dollar limits, apply to both grandfathered and non-grandfathered health plans.

There are a few exceptions:

- A plan may exclude all benefits for a condition. A condition-based exclusion is not considered an annual or lifetime limit. However, if any benefits are provided for a condition, the rules regarding lifetime and annual limits apply.[4] (Notwithstanding the foregoing, other requirements of federal or state law could require coverage of certain conditions.) Also, under the grandfather rules, the elimination of all benefits for a condition could result in the forfeiture of the plan's grandfather status.[5]

- A plan or issuer can still place annual or lifetime dollar limits with respect to specific covered benefits that are not "essential health benefits," to the extent such limits are otherwise lawful under federal or state law.[6]

- It remains lawful to impose limits on benefits that are not dollar limits. Examples include limits on a per-visit or per-treatment basis, or a per-procedure dollar limit. Such limits should, of course, be reviewed to ensure they are otherwise lawful under applicable federal or state law.

- The restrictions on annual dollar limits do not apply to health flexible spending accounts.[7]

- The restrictions on annual dollar limits do not apply to health reimbursement accounts (HRAs) that were in effect prior to September 23, 2010.[8]

The elimination of lifetime dollar limits and restrictions on annual limits will place a premium on a plan's medical necessity and case management activities to avoid ineffective and costly over-utilization of services by providers and plan participants.

---

[1] PPACA § 1001 (adding PHSA § 2711).

[2] PPACA § 1001 (adding PHSA § 2711).

[3] 75 Fed. Reg. 37,188–241 and 37,242–43, amending 26 C.F.R. pts. 54 and 602; 29 C.F.R. § 2590; 45 C.F.R. pts. 144, 146, and 147. *See* Tri-Agency Regulations on Preexisting Condition Exclusions, Lifetime and Annual Limits, Rescissions and Patient Protections, 75 Fed. Reg. 37,188–241 (June 28, 2010), *available at* http://webapps.dol.gov/FederalRegister/PdfDisplay.aspx?DocId=23983.

[4] 26 C.F.R. § 54.9815-2711T(b)(2); 29 C.F.R. § 2590.715-2711(b)(2); 45 C.F.R. § 147.126(b)(2).

[5] See **Section 5.01**.

[6] 26 C.F.R. § 54.9815-2711T(b)(1); 29 C.F.R. § 2590.715-2711(b)(1); 45 C.F.R. § 147.126(b)(1).

[7] 26 C.F.R. § 54.9815-2711T(a)(2)(ii); 29 C.F.R. § 2590.715-2711(a)(2)(ii); 45 C.F.R. § 147.126(a)(1)(ii). See also **Section 8.01[D]**.

[8] Center for Consumer Info. & Ins. Oversight, Center for Medicare & Medicaid Servs., Department of Health & Human Servs., CCIIO Supplemental Guidance (CCIIO 2011-1E): Exemption for Health Reimbursement Arrangements that are Subject to PHS Act Section 2711 (Aug. 19, 2011), *available at* http://cciio.cms.gov/resources/files/final_hra_guidance_20110819.pdf.

[A] Lifetime Limits

Effective for plan years beginning on or after September 23, 2010, a group health plan and health insurance issuer offering group or individual health insurance coverage may not establish lifetime limits on the dollar value of benefits for a participant or beneficiary.[9] If an employee or beneficiary lost coverage due to a lifetime maximum dollar limit prior to the effective date of the regulations but is still otherwise eligible for the coverage, the plan must notify the individual in writing that the lifetime limit on the dollar value of all benefits no longer applies and that the individual, if covered, is once again eligible for benefits. If the individual is not enrolled in the plan, the individual must be given an opportunity to enroll for at least 30 days (including written notice).[10] Notice to the employee, on behalf of a dependent, satisfies the notice obligation. The previously covered individual re-enrolls into the plan as a special enrollee.[11] This means that the enrollee must be offered all of the benefit packages available to similarly situated individuals who did not lose coverage by reason of reaching the lifetime limit. The enrollee cannot be required to pay more for coverage than similarly situated individuals.

[B] Annual Limits

[1] Restricted Annual Limits on Essential Benefits

During the transition period prior to January 1, 2014, group health plans and health insurers offering group health or individual insurance coverage may impose restricted annual limits with respect to the scope of benefits that are essential health benefits to the extent permitted by HHS.[12] The regulations impose a three-year phased-in approach to the annual limit restriction:

- For plan years beginning after September 23, 2010, and before September 23, 2011, the minimum annual limit on benefits is $750,000.

- For plan years beginning after September 23, 2011, and before September 23, 2012, the minimum annual limit on benefits is $1,250,000.

- For plan years beginning after September 23, 2012, and before December 31, 2013, the minimum annual limit on benefits is $2,000,000.[13]

Only essential benefits are to be taken into account in determining whether an individual has received the applicable amount.[14] The regulations define "essential health benefits" by cross-reference to Section 1302(b) of the Affordable Care Act and note that further regulations will be forthcoming. Section 1302(b) defines "essential health benefits" as including at least the following ten general categories: (1) ambulatory patient services; (2) emergency services; (3) hospitalization; (4) maternity and newborn care; (5) mental health and substance use disorder services, including behavioral health treatment; (6) prescription drugs; (7) rehabilitative and habilitative services[15] and devices; (8) laboratory

---

[9] PHSA § 2711.

[10] 26 C.F.R. § 54.9815-2711T(e); 29 C.F.R. § 2590.715-2711(e); 45 C.F.R. § 147.126(e).

[11] 26 C.F.R. § 54.9815-2711T(e)(4); 29 C.F.R. § 2590.715-2711(e)(4); 45 C.F.R. § 147.126(e)(4).

[12] 26 C.F.R. 54.9815-2711T(a)(2); 29 C.F.R. § 2590.715-2711(a)(2); 45 C.F.R. § 147.126(a)(2).

[13] 26 C.F.R. 54.9815-2711T(d)(1); 29 C.F.R. § 2590.715-2711(d)(1); 45 C.F.R. § 147.126(d)(1).

[14] 26 C.F.R. 54.9815-2711T(d)(2); 29 C.F.R. § 2590.715-2711(d)(2); 45 C.F.R. § 147.126(d)(2).

[15] "Habilitative services" includes various therapies used to treat autism. Numerous state laws currently mandate coverage of such services, but several state laws allow annual dollar limits on those benefits. Unless HHS clarifies this provision in the essential benefit regulations, the state law annual limits may not be permissible under PPACA.

services; (9) preventive and wellness services and chronic disease management; and (10) pediatric services, including oral and vision care.[16] Until further regulations are issued, group health plans are subject to a "good faith" standard in determining which benefits they provide are "essential" and "non-essential."[17]

The regulations restrict the impact of annual *dollar* limits with respect to essential health benefits. They are silent with respect to limits based on the number of visits or treatments, or per-procedure dollar limits, so it appears that such limits remain lawful, and will likely serve as a basis for the redesign of plans to address rising costs (although replacing annual dollar limits with limits on the number of treatments or per-procedure dollar limits may cause a grandfathered health plan to lose its grandfather status).

The annual dollar limit restrictions in the Affordable Care Act at first appeared to seal the fate of limited benefit or so-called "mini-Med" plans that typically provide benefits that are capped at relatively low annual amounts. However, the regulations provide that HHS may establish a program (for years prior to 2014) to permit individual limited benefit plans or mini-Med plans to apply for a waiver of the restricted annual dollar limit if such a plan can demonstrate that the compliance with the annual dollar limit rules would result in either a significant decrease in access to benefits or a significant increase in premiums for the plan or policy.[18]

On September 3, 2010, HHS issued sub-regulatory guidance in the form of a memorandum that outlines the process for obtaining a waiver of the annual dollar limit restriction prior to 2014. To qualify for a waiver, the plan or coverage must have been offered prior to September 23, 2010. By subsequent guidance issued on June 17, 2011, HHS significantly changed the procedural requirements for obtaining a waiver, and ceased accepting new applications for waivers effective September 22, 2011. All plans, therefore, that wished to obtain a waiver must have filed an application prior to September 23, 2011.

Originally, a waiver, if granted, only applied to the plan or policy year beginning between September 23, 2010, and September 23, 2011, thereby requiring plans and issuers to reapply for the waiver for subsequent plan or policy years prior to January 1, 2014. Waiver applications had to be submitted at least 30 days before the start of the plan or policy year, although the practical deadline for many plans was at least 30 days before the start of the plan's open enrollment period. No specific waiver application form was mandated, but the application had to include:

- A description of the terms of the plan or policy for which the waiver was sought (a certificate of coverage or summary plan description appears to be sufficient for this purpose);

- The number of individuals covered by the plan or policy form(s) submitted;

- The annual limit(s) and rates applicable to the plan or policy form(s) submitted;

- A brief description of why compliance with the interim final regulations would result in a significant decrease in access to benefits for those currently covered, or a significant increase in premiums paid by those covered, together with any supporting documentation; and

- An attestation, signed by the plan administrator or CEO of the insurance issuer, certifying that the plan or policy form was in place prior to September 23, 2010, and that the application of restricted annual limits to the plan or policy would result in a significant decrease in access to benefits or a significant increase in premium cost.

---

[16] *See* PPACA § 1302(b) (defining essential health benefits).
[17] See **Section 11.04[C][1]** for a discussion of essential health benefits.
[18] 26 C.F.R. § 54.9815-2711T(d)(3); 29 C.F.R. § 2590.715-2711(d)(3); 45 C.F.R. § 147.126(d)(3).

A plan or issuer that applied for a waiver should retain documents in support of the application for potential examination by HHS.[19]

Under HHS's revised procedure, any plan or issuer that received a waiver of the restricted annual limit of $750,000 for a plan or policy year beginning on or after September 23, 2010, but before September 23, 2011, does not need to reapply for future years. Instead, it can elect to extend its waiver by completing and filing a waiver extension form, a streamlined process by which the plan or issuer would, in conjunction with its election to extend the waiver, provide "annual update" information, including any updated contact information, updated enrollment information, the plan or policy's current annual limit, and signed attestations that the plan or policy was in existence prior to September 23, 2010, that compliance with the Affordable Care Act's annual dollar limit requirement would result in a "significant decrease in access to benefits" or a "significant increase in premiums," and that it will comply with the annual notice requirement described below.

Each waiver recipient will be required to distribute an updated annual notice to eligible plan participants and subscribers (the "Annual Notice"). The updated Annual Notice must be provided together with the plan or policy materials for each plan or policy year for which the waiver applies (e.g., with the summary plan description or open enrollment materials). The revised HHS procedures set forth the required text of the Annual Notice, which must be "prominently displayed in clear, conspicuous 14-point bold type on the front of the materials." Written permission must be obtained to use different language to satisfy the Annual Notice requirement.[20]

[2] Non-Essential Benefits

A group health plan or health insurance issuer offering group health or individual insurance coverage may impose lifetime or annual limits on coverage of specific benefits that are not essential health benefits, or exclude all benefits for a condition.[21]

---

[19] Memorandum from Steve Larsen, Director, Officer of Oversight, Department of Health & Human Services (Sept. 3, 2010).

[20] CCIIO Supplemental Guidance (CCIIO 2011-1D): Concluding the Annual Limit Waiver Application Process (June 17, 2011), *available at* http://cciio.cms.gov/resources/files/06162011_annual_limit_guidance_2011-2012_final.pdf. The required text of the Annual Notice is as follows:

> The Affordable Care Act prohibits health plans from applying dollar limits below a specific amount on coverage for certain benefits. This year, if a plan applies a dollar limit on the coverage it provides for certain benefits in a year, that limit must be at least [$750,000/$1.25 million/$2 million, as applicable].
>
> Your health coverage, offered by [name of group health plan or health insurance issuer], does not meet the minimum standards required by the Affordable Care Act described above. Your coverage has an annual limit of:
>
> [dollar amount] on [all covered benefits]
> and/or
> [dollar amount(s)] on [which covered benefits — notice should describe all annual limits that apply].
>
> This means that your health coverage might not pay for all of the health care expenses you incur. For example, a stay in a hospital costs around $1,853 per day. At this cost, your insurance would only pay for [insert amount] days.
>
> Your health plan has requested that the U.S. Department of Health and Human Services waive the requirement to provide coverage for certain key benefits of at least [$750,000/$1.25 million/$2 million, as applicable] this year. Your health plan has stated that meeting this minimum dollar limit this year would result in a significant increase in your premiums or a significant decrease in your access to benefits. Based on this representation, the U.S. Department of Health and Human Services has waived the requirement for your plan until [the ending date of the plan or policy year beginning before January 1, 2014].
>
> If you are concerned about your plan's lower dollar limits on key benefits, you and your family may have other options for health care coverage. For more information, go to www.HealthCare.gov.
>
> If you have any questions or concerns about this notice, contact [provide contact information for plan administrator or health insurance issuer]. [For plans offered in states with a Consumer Assistance Program:] In addition, you can contact [contact information for consumer assistance program].

[21] 26 C.F.R. § 54.9815-2711T(b); 29 C.F.R. § 2590.715-2711(b); 45 C.F.R. § 147.126(b).

[C] Student Health Plans

On March 21, 2012, HHS released a final regulation, addressing insured student health plans at colleges and universities.[22] The regulation treats a student health plan as *individual* health insurance coverage, and considers such individual coverage sufficient to satisfy the individual coverage mandate if the plan meets certain conditions. These conditions include the following:

- The student health plan must be provided by a college or university through an insurance contract with a health insurance company. It appears that a self-funded plan would not fall within the scope of the proposed regulations.

- Coverage availability must be limited to enrolled students and their dependents.

- Students (or their dependents) cannot be excluded on the basis of a preexisting condition or other health status factor.

- Preventive care must be provided without cost-sharing (e.g., copayments). However, a college or university can continue to charge a student health fee to help offset the cost of operating a student health clinic.

- There can be no lifetime limits on essential health benefits. An annual limit on essential health benefits can be imposed, but cannot be less than (1) $100,000 for policy years beginning before September 23, 2012, and (2) $500,000 for policy years beginning on or after September 23, 2012, but before January 1, 2014.

The issuer with respect to a student health plan that does not satisfy the above requirements must notify enrolled students to that effect. The following model language can be used:

> Your student health insurance coverage, offered by [*name of health insurance issuer*] may not meet the minimum standards required by the health care reform law for the restrictions on annual dollar limits. The annual dollar limits ensure that consumers have sufficient access to medical benefits throughout the annual term of the policy. Restrictions for annual dollar limits for group and individual health insurance coverage are $1.25 million for policy years before September 23, 2012; and $2 million for policy years beginning on or after September 23, 2012, but before January 1, 2014. Restrictions for annual dollar limits for student health insurance coverage are $100,000 for policy years before September 23, 2012, and $500,000 for policy years beginning on or after September 23, 2012, but before January 1, 2014. Your student health insurance coverage put an annual limit of: [Dollar amount] on [which covered benefits—notice should describe all annual limits that apply]. If you have any questions or concerns about this notice, contact [provide contact information for the health insurance issuer]. Be advised that you may be eligible for coverage under a group health plan of a parent's employer or under a parent's individual health insurance policy if you are under age 26. Contact the plan administrator of the parent's employer plan or the parent's individual health insurance issuer for more information.[23]

[D] Account-Based Plans

The prohibition on annual dollar limits for benefits under a group health plan does not apply to account-based plans, including Health Flexible Spending Accounts (Health FSAs), Medical Savings

---

[22] 45 C.F.R. § 147.145. The proposed regulation was released February 11, 2011, and can be found at 76 Fed. Reg. 7767–82. The final regulation, including preambles, is at 77 Fed. Reg. 16,453–70.

[23] 45 C.F.R. § 147.145(d)(2).

Accounts (MSAs) established under Section 220 of the Code, Health Savings Accounts (HSAs) established under Section 223 of the Code, and certain Health Reimbursement Accounts (HRAs).[24]

In the preamble to the regulations, it is noted that the annual limits do not apply to MSAs and HSAs because they are not group health plans. Amounts in those arrangements are available for medical and non-medical expenses.

An HRA is a self-insured medical expense reimbursement account plan funded solely by employer contributions, under which unused amounts can be carried forward to future years.[25] HRAs have generated interest as a means by which employers may provide health benefits to employees under a "defined contribution" approach, with fixed employer contributions that are predictable and promote cost certainty. Some HRAs stand alone and others are offered in tandem with conventional group health coverage, providing a source of employer-provided funds to help employees pay non-covered expenses such as copays and deductibles. The preamble to the interim final regulation that implements the Affordable Care Act's annual dollar limit restrictions provides that the annual limit prohibition will not apply if the HRA is integrated with a group health plan and the group health plan complies with the regulations.[26]

In response to requests that the exemption for HRAs be expanded, HHS issued supplemental guidance on August 19, 2011,[27] which exempts as a class all HRAs that would otherwise be subject to the annual dollar limit restriction, provided the HRA arrangement was in effect prior to September 23, 2010. This class exemption recognizes that HRAs by design limit benefits to the amount of the participant's then-current account balance, and that applying the annual dollar limit restriction to an HRA would destroy its utility. Nevertheless, because the guidance only applies to HRAs in effect prior to September 23, 2010, employers will be effectively prohibited from establishing new HRA plans for their active employees, unless such HRAs operate in tandem with the employer's conventional group health plan to assist employees in paying for noncovered medical costs and services. An HRA, therefore, can no longer be established on a stand-alone basis as a "defined contribution" solution to medical care cost inflation.[28]

Stand-alone HRAs remain viable, it appears, only in contexts where the Affordable Care Act does not apply. Significantly, stand-alone HRAs remain viable for retirees, because the Affordable Care Act does not apply to a retiree-only plan.[29] Many public and private sector employers are establishing stand-alone HRAs to replace existing "defined benefit" retiree medical commitments with an alternative that provides the employer with cost certainty based on fixed contribution commitments and no risk for unfunded future benefit liabilities. HRAs also should remain viable as a "defined contribution" alternative to a conventional dental-only or vision-only plan.[30]

---

[24] 26 C.F.R. § 54.9815-2711T(a)(2)(ii); 29 C.F.R. § 2590.715-2711(a)(2)(ii); 45 C.F.R. § 147.126(a)(2)(ii).

[25] *See, e.g.*, I.R.S. Notice 2002-45, 2002-2 C.B. 93; Rev. Rul. 2002-41, 2002-2 C.B. 75.

[26] 75 Fed. Reg. 37,190–91.

[27] CCIIO Supplemental Guidance (CCIIO) 2011-1E: Exemption for Health Reimbursement Arrangements that are Subject to PHS Act Section 2711 (Aug. 19, 2011), *available at* http://cciio.cms.gov/resources/files/final_hra_guidance_20110819.pdf.

[28] For this reason, employers that elect to drop their health coverage, pay the pay-or-play penalty described in **Section 11.02,** and send employees to an Exchange to purchase their own individual health insurance coverage (as described in **Section 11.04**) will have limited flexibility in supplementing the cost of employee coverage. Absent this policy choice to apply the annual limit prohibition to HRAs, such employers may have been able to set up HRAs to reimburse employees for a portion of their health insurance costs.

[29] See **Section 5.03**.

[30] Dental-only plans and vision-only plans may qualify as "excepted benefits" not subject to the Affordable Care Act. See **Section 5.04**.

§ 8.02 Prohibition on Preexisting-Condition Exclusion Provisions for Children Under Age 19

The Affordable Care Act generally extends the group health plan prohibition on preexisting-condition exclusion provisions to the individual insurance market as one of the market reforms that begins on January 1, 2014.[31] However, the Act accelerates the prohibition for enrollees who are under age 19 for plan or coverage years beginning on and after September 23, 2010.[32] No coverage or enrollment limitations may be imposed, regardless of the child's previous coverage status. The terms and conditions applicable to preexisting-condition provisions are explained in detail in **Section 9.01.**

§ 8.03 Coverage of Preventive Health Services

The Affordable Care Act requires any group health plan or health insurance company offering group or individual health insurance coverage to provide, at a minimum and without the imposition of any cost-sharing requirements, coverage for specific items or services in four separate and distinct areas.[33] This coverage mandate does not, however, apply to grandfathered health plans.[34]

First, the preventive health benefit must cover all evidence-based items or services that have in effect a rating of "A" or "B" in the current recommendations of the United States Preventive Services Task Force (Task Force).[35] Second, the preventive health benefit must cover immunizations for routine use in children, adolescents, and adults that have in effect a recommendation by the Advisory Committee on Immunization Practices (ACIP) of the Centers for Disease Control and Prevention (CDC) with respect to the individual involved.[36]

Third, preventive health benefits for infants, children, and adolescents must include preventive care and screenings set forth in comprehensive guidelines supported by the Health Resources and Services Administration (HRSA). The Early and Periodic Screening, Diagnostic, and Treatment (EPSDT) service is Medicaid's comprehensive and preventive child health program for individuals under age 21. EPSDT includes periodic screening, vision, dental, and hearing services.[37] In addition, the Social Security Act (SSA) requires that any medically necessary health care service (as defined in the SSA) be provided to an EPSDT recipient even if the service is not available under the state's Medicaid plan to the rest of the Medicaid population.[38] The goal of the EPSDT program is to assess the child's health needs through initial and periodic examinations and evaluations, and to ensure that the health problems found are diagnosed and treated early, before they become more complex and their treatment more costly.

Fourth, for women, in addition to the preventive care and screenings identified by the Task Force, the preventive health benefit must also include any other preventive care and screenings set forth in comprehensive guidelines supported by the HRSA. The Affordable Care Act provides that while the current recommendations of the Task Force regarding breast cancer screening, mammography, and

---

[31] PPACA § 1201 (adding PHSA § 2704); 26 C.F.R. § 54.9815-2704T; 29 C.F.R. § 2590.715-2704; 45 C.F.R. § 147.108.

[32] 26 C.F.R. § 54.9815-2704T(b)(2); 29 C.F.R. § 2590.715-2704(b)(2); 45 C.F.R. § 147.108(b)(2). *See* Tri-Agency Regulations on Preexisting Condition Exclusions, Lifetime and Annual Limits, Rescissions and Patient Protections, 75 Fed. Reg. 37,188–241 (June 28, 2010), *available at* http://webapps.dol.gov/FederalRegister/PdfDisplay.aspx?DocId=23983.

[33] PPACA § 1001 (adding PHSA § 2718). See **Appendix F** for tri-agency regulations on preventive care.

[34] 29 C.F.R. § 2590.715-1251(c).

[35] The 2010–2011 Guide to Clinical Preventive Services can be accessed at http://www.ahrq.gov/clinic/pocketgd.htm.

[36] A recommendation is considered to be for routine use if it is listed on the Immunization Schedules of the CDC. The schedules are available from the CDC's Web site at http://www.cdc.gov/vaccines/recs/schedules/default.htm. Copies of the 2012 schedules for children, adolescents, and adults are reprinted in **Appendix G.**

[37] Adopted in the Omnibus Budget Reconciliation Act of 1989, Pub. L. No. 101-239, 103 Stat. 2106.

[38] 42 U.S.C. § 1396d(r)(5) (referencing 42 U.S.C. § 1396d(a) for the definition of health care service).

prevention apply, the controversial Task Force recommendations regarding the recommended frequency of screening mammographies released in November 2009 are to be disregarded.[39] The Task Force, the CDC, and the HRSA update their recommendations from time to time. The Affordable Care Act provides that HHS may establish a minimum interval between the date on which a recommendation or guideline is issued and the plan year with respect to which the requirement must be adopted. The minimum interval is to be at least one year.[40]

HHS also may develop guidelines that permit a group health plan or health insurance issuer offering group individual health insurance coverage to utilize value-based insurance designs (VBIDs).[41] VBID programs adjust the plan participant's cost-sharing to correlate it with the clinical benefit that the particular item or service may have for the individual. Thus, the more clinically beneficial the therapy for the patient, the lower that patient's cost-sharing obligation. Higher cost-sharing obligations apply to interventions with little or no proven benefit.[42]

The University of Michigan Center for Value-Based Insurance Design, established in 2005 to develop, evaluate, and promote value-based insurance initiatives, has a list of papers and other resources on this subject available on its Web site (*http://www.sph.umich.edu/vbidcenter/index.htm*).

HHS, Treasury, and the DOL issued interim final regulations, effective September 17, 2010, seeking to clarify the manner in which certain preventive care benefits should be provided under group health plans without cost-sharing:

- For plans with both in-network and out-of-network benefits, there is no requirement that free coverage for preventive care benefits be extended to benefits provided out-of-network. Participants can be required to utilize an in-network provider to receive such benefits without cost-sharing, and cost-sharing requirements can be imposed on care received for out-of-network providers.[43]

- If an item of preventive care service, which is required to be covered without cost-sharing (an "applicable preventive care service"), is billed separately (or is tracked as individual encounter data separately) from an office visit, then the plan or issuer can impose cost-sharing with respect to office visits.

- If an applicable preventive care service is not billed separately (or is not tracked as individual encounter data separately) from an office visit *and* the primary purpose of the office visit is the delivery or administration of the applicable preventive care service, then the plan or issuer cannot impose cost-sharing with respect to the office visit.

- If an applicable preventive care service is not billed separately (or is not tracked as individual encounter data separately) from an office visit *and* the primary purpose of the office visit is *not* the delivery or administration of the applicable preventive care service, then the plan or issuer can impose cost-sharing with respect to the office visit.[44]

- A plan or issuer is free to impose cost-sharing with respect to other preventive care services that are not applicable preventive care services, and may also impose cost-sharing in the event that a covered preventive care service is no longer an applicable preventive care service.[45] However, any such change that permits cost-sharing to be re-imposed must be administered

---

[39] PHSA § 2713(a)(5).
[40] PHSA § 2713(b).
[41] PHSA § 2713(c).
[42] Health Affairs, Feb. 2010.
[43] 26 C.F.R. § 54.9815-2713T(a)(3); 29 C.F.R. § 2590.715-2713(a)(3); 45 C.F.R. § 147.130(a)(3).
[44] 26 C.F.R. § 54.9815-2713T(a)(2); 29 C.F.R. § 2590.715-2713(a)(2); 45 C.F.R. § 147.130(a)(2).
[45] 26 C.F.R. §§ 54.9815-2713T(a)(5)(3), (b)(2); 29 C.F.R. §§ 2590.715-2713(a)(5), (b)(2); 45 C.F.R. §§ 147.130(a)(5), (b)(2).

consistent with the general requirement that a material modification in coverage must be preceded by 60 days' advance notice.

- Finally, a plan or issuer may impose cost-sharing with respect to a treatment that is not an applicable preventive care service, even if the treatment results from an applicable preventive care service.

One of the most controversial regulations under PPACA requires, with very limited exceptions, any non-grandfathered group health plan or health insurer offering group or individual health insurance to provide coverage for women's contraceptive services as a no-cost preventive health benefit.[46]

The HRSA was charged with developing comprehensive guidelines for preventive care and screenings for women that would be covered under PPACA-compliant non-grandfathered health care plans and policies without cost-sharing (the HRSA Guidelines).[47]

The HRSA Guidelines require no-cost coverage under all non-grandfathered plans and policies in the areas of (1) well-woman visits; (2) screening for gestational diabetes; (3) human papilloma virus testing; (4) counseling for sexually transmitted infections; (5) counseling and screening for human immune-deficiency virus; (6) breastfeeding support, supplies, and counseling; (7) screening and counseling for interpersonal and domestic violence; and (8) contraceptive services (with an exception for plans maintained for employees of "religious employers"). Required to be covered are:

> all Food and Drug Administration approved contraception methods, sterilization procedures, and patient education and counseling, for women with reproductive capacity as prescribed by a provider.[48]

The interim final regulations implementing the preventive health benefit rules were amended on August 1, 2011, to provide the HRSA with the discretion to establish an exemption from the contraceptive services requirement for group health plans (and associated group health insurance coverage) established or maintained by certain religious employers.[49] For purposes of this exemption only, a "religious employer" is narrowly defined as an organization that:

- Has the inculcation of religious values as its purpose;
- Primarily employs persons who share the religious tenets of the organization;
- Serves primarily persons who share the religious tenets of the organization; and
- Is a nonprofit organization as describe in the Internal Revenue Code.[50]

The twin requirements that an exempted "religious employer" both employ and serve primarily persons who share the organization's religious tenets effectively limits the exemption to houses of worship. It does not include most religious-institution-affiliated hospitals, educational institutions, and charities that commonly employ individuals without regard to religious affiliation or that serve the general public.

This proposed rule-making triggered a tremendous number of comments, from both women's health advocates who wanted even a narrow religious employer exemption eliminated, and advocates for religiously affiliated employers who sought an expanded exemption for hospitals, schools, and other service organizations affiliated with a church.

In response, HHS, Treasury, and the DOL have jointly decided to retain the narrow religious employer exemption, reasoning that a broader exemption would deny no-cost contraceptives services

---

[46] *See* 26 C.F.R. § 54.9815-2713 and 45 C.F.R. § 147.130(a)(1)(iv).

[47] The HRSA Guidelines, issued August 1, 2011, can be found at http://www.hrsa.gov/womensguidelines.

[48] *Id.* Excluded are contraceptive-related items and services for men such as vasectomies and condoms.

[49] 26 C.F.R § 54.9815-2713T; 29 C.F.R. § 2590.715-2713; 45 C.F.R. § 147.130, 76 Fed. Reg. 46,621. The amendments to the interim final regulations are set forth in **Appendix H**.

[50] *Id.*

to many employees who do not share the religious tenets of their employer or have no religious objection to the use of contraception and therefore are likely to use contraceptives:

> Including these employers within the scope of the exemption would subject their employees to the religious views of the employer, limiting access to contraception, and thereby inhibiting the use of contraceptive services and the benefits of preventive care.[51]

Access to no-cost contraceptives is viewed by HHS, Treasury, and the DOL as broadly supporting the "unique health needs of women," which create a "disparity" that "places women in the workplace at a disadvantage compared to their male coworkers":

> [A]ccess to contraception improves the social and economic status of women. Contraceptive usage, by reducing the number of unintended and potentially unhealthy pregnancies, furthers the good of eliminating this disparity by allowing women to achieve equal status as healthy and productive members of the job force.[52]

While maintaining the narrow religious employer exception, HHS issued on February 10, 2012, a bulletin establishing a one-year temporary enforcement safe harbor for group health plans sponsored by nonprofit organizations that do not provide some or all of the contraceptive coverage otherwise required because of the organization's religious beliefs.[53] The enforcement safe harbor is in effect until the first plan year that begins on or after August 1, 2013 (e.g., until January 1, 2014, for a calendar year plan). None of HHS, Treasury, or the DOL will take any enforcement action against an employer, group health plan, or health insurance issuer that complies with the conditions of the temporary enforcement safe harbor described in the bulletin. The basic requirements are:

- The plan sponsor must be organized and operated as a nonprofit entity

- Contraceptive coverage has not been provided, on and after February 10, 2012, by the group health plan because of the religious beliefs of the organization[54]

- The following notice is provided to plan participants, in any application materials distributed in connection with enrollment or re-enrollment of coverage that is effective for plan years beginning on or after August 1, 2012:

NOTICE TO PLAN PARTICIPANTS
The organization that sponsors your group health plan has certified that it qualifies for a temporary enforcement safe harbor with regard to the Federal requirement to cover contraceptive services without cost-sharing. During this one-year period, coverage under your group health plan will not include coverage of contraceptive services.

- The organization self-certifies that it satisfies the above-described criteria, and files a certification in accordance with procedures set forth in the bulletin.

Before the end of the temporary enforcement safe harbor, HHS, Treasury, and the DOL intend to amend the tri-agency regulations to better "accommodate" religious organizations' religious

---

[51] 77 Fed. Reg. 8728. *See* **Appendix H.**

[52] 77 Fed. Reg. 8728. *See* **Appendix H.**

[53] Guidance on the Temporary Enforcement Safe Harbor for Certain Employers, Group Health Plans and Group Health Insurance Issuers with Respect to the Requirement to Cover Contraceptive Services Without Cost Sharing Under Section 2713 of the Public Health Service Act, Section 715(a)(1) of the Employee Retirement Income Security Act, and Section 9815(a)(1) of the Internal Revenue Code (Feb. 10, 2012), *available at* http://cciio.cms.gov/resources/files/Files2/02102012/20120210-Preventive-Services-Bulletin.pdf. The Bulletin is reprinted in **Appendix I.**

[54] The temporary enforcement safe harbor also applies to student health insurance plans arranged by nonprofit educational institutions.

objections to providing contraceptive services while assuring that employees of such organizations still have access to no-cost contraceptive services.

The intended approach is to maintain no-cost contraceptive services while protecting religious organizations with religious objections to contraceptive coverage from having to contract, arrange, or pay for contraceptive coverage. According to the tri-agency Advance Notice of Proposed Rulemaking published in the *Federal Register* on March 21, 2012,[55] the agencies intend to propose a requirement whereby the health insurance issuer for such a religious organization's group health plan will "assume the responsibility for the provision of contraceptive coverage without cost sharing to participants and beneficiaries covered under the plan, independent of the religious organization."[56] For self-insured plans, the agencies intend to propose that the plan's third-party administrator (or other independent entity) assume responsibility for providing no-cost coverage for contraceptive services.[57]

Still unanswered is how broadly a "religious organization" eligible for this religious accommodation rule will be defined. One approach under consideration is to include hospitals, educational institutions, and charities that are tax-exempt and that are controlled or associated with a church or association of churches. Comments have been solicited regarding the breadth of the definition, including whether a religious accommodation rule should apply to church-affiliated for-profit entities as well. Whatever the final definition, it is likely that religious organizations will be required to satisfy a periodic self-certification process to qualify for the accommodation, which will be subject to examination.

The probable terms of the accommodation with respect to insured plans may include the following:

- A health insurance issuer will not include contraceptive services under the religious organization's insured coverage. Contraceptive services would not be included in the plan document, contract, or premium charged to the religious organization.

  - Instead, the health insurance issuer would provide "separate" coverage for contraceptive services to the plan's participants and beneficiaries, and notify plan participants and beneficiaries of its availability. Under this approach, no notice obligation would be imposed on the religious organization.

- Health insurance issuers would be unable to charge the religious organization for the cost of separately provided contraceptive services. The anticipated accommodations will similarly seek to shield religious organizations that sponsor self-funded health plans from contracting, arranging, and paying for contraceptive services, by requiring the plan's third-party administrator to administer and pay for, or arrange for the administration and payment of, coverage for such services. Comments have been sought regarding possible options for funding the third-party administrator's contraceptive coverage without using funds provided by the religious organization.[58]

§ 8.04   Extension of Coverage for Children Up to Age 26

[A]   General Rules

As noted in **Chapter 2,** young adults represent a significant portion (30 percent) of the Americans who lacked health insurance coverage prior to health care reform. Young adults have the lowest

---

[55] 77 Fed. Reg. 16,501–08. See **Appendix J** for the Advance Notice of Proposed Rulemaking regarding contraceptive services.
[56] 77 Fed. Reg. 16,503.
[57] 77 Fed. Reg. 16,503.
[58] A number of these possible options are discussed at 77 Fed. Reg. 16,505–07.

rate of access to employer-based coverage and lack the financial resources to cover health care bills when and if they should be incurred. While young adults generally are healthier than most other age groups, they still need coverage; one in six young adults has a chronic illness like cancer, diabetes, or asthma.[59] The Affordable Care Act addresses that need in several ways. First, it requires all group health plans and all health insurance issuers offering group or individual health insurance coverage that provide coverage for dependent children to continue to make that coverage available to adult children (regardless of the child's marital status) until the child attains age 26.[60] Second, the Act amends the Code to make the extended dependent coverage a pretax benefit for an employee or a deductible benefit for self-employed taxpayers.[61] Third, the Act provides for a high-deductible catastrophic coverage option for adults under age 30 participating in the Exchanges beginning in 2014. This section will discuss the extension of coverage requirements for group health plans and the corresponding tax implications. The Exchange plan for adults under age 30 is covered in **Chapter 11**.[62]

Effective for the first plan year beginning on or after September 23, 2010, any group health plan (insured or self-funded), including grandfathered health plans, and any individual insurance coverage that offers dependent coverage for children must make such coverage available to the employee or individual until the child attains age 26.[63] The Affordable Care Act does not require a plan or policy to provide coverage for dependents, but, if coverage is available to dependents, the coverage must also be extended to older children.[64] Thus, if a group health plan or individual insurance policy does not offer coverage for anyone other than the employee or the individual, the requirement does not apply. This provision applies to all employment-based coverage, including grandfathered health plans, but it does not apply to retiree-only plans or plans providing only excepted benefits such as limited-scope dental or vision coverage plans.[65]

HHS, Treasury, and the DOL have jointly issued interim final regulations interpreting the extended coverage requirement.[66] The agencies announced that surcharges for coverage of children under age 26 are not allowed except where the surcharges apply regardless of the age of the child. Plans cannot vary benefits or other terms of the plan or insurance coverage based on the age of the child.[67]

The tri-agency regulations also confirm that plans and issuers cannot limit dependent coverage to unmarried children.[68] However, a plan or issuer is not required to cover the spouse or the child of a covered child.[69] The regulations provide that conditioning coverage on whether a child is a tax dependent or a student, or resides with or receives financial support from the parent or is married, is no longer an appropriate factor for a child at any age under age 26 and plans or coverage may not use those requirements to deny coverage to children.[70] However, these traditional criteria for defining a plan's coverage of children can be retained for separately offered dental or vision coverage that constitutes "excepted benefits" under Section 733 of ERISA.

---

[59] Young Adults and the Affordable Care Act: Protecting Young Adults and Eliminating Burdens on Families and Businesses, DOL briefing paper released with Dependent Coverage Interim Final Rules on May 9, 2010.

[60] PPACA § 1001 (adding PHSA § 2714), *as amended by* PPACA § 10103(d) and HCERA § 2301(b).

[61] HCERA § 1004(d) (amending I.R.C. §§ 105(b), 163(*l*), 501(c)(9), 401(h)).

[62] See **Section 11.04[D]**.

[63] PHSA § 2714.

[64] PHSA § 2714(a).

[65] PPACA § 1251(a), *as amended by* HCERA § 2301(a).

[66] 45 C.F.R. §§ 147.000 *et seq.*; Treas. Reg. §§ 54.9815-2714T *et seq.* (Treasury regulations); 29 C.F.R. §§ 2590.715-2714 *et seq.* (DOL regulations). See **Appendix K**.

[67] 45 C.F.R. § 147.120(d); Treas. Reg. § 54.9815-2714T(d); 29 C.F.R. § 2590.715-2714(d).

[68] 45 C.F.R. § 147.120(b); Treas. Reg. § 54.9815-2714T(b); 29 C.F.R. § 2590.715-2714(b).

[69] 45 C.F.R. § 147.120(c); Treas. Reg. § 54.9815-2714T(c); 29 C.F.R. § 2590.715-2714(c).

[70] 45 C.F.R. § 147.120(b); Treas. Reg. § 54.9815-2714T(b); 29 C.F.R. § 2590.715-2714(b).

The value of medical coverage or reimbursement of medical expenses provided by an employer to its employees and their spouses and dependent children is treated as tax-free compensation for employees for federal income tax purposes.[71] The Affordable Care Act amends the Code to extend pre-tax treatment for employment-based health coverage provided to adult children of an employee up to the calendar year in which the child reaches age 27.[72] The amendments to the Code, which are effective immediately, now base the tax-free treatment of dependent health coverage solely on relationship and age.

Under Section 105(b) of the Code,[73] an employee may exclude from gross income the amounts paid to reimburse the employee for qualified medical expenses of the taxpayer, his spouse, and his dependents as defined in Section 152 of the Code.[74] To be a dependent for purposes of receiving tax-free health benefits, the individual must meet both a relationship and age test. The individual must be

---

[71] I.R.C. § 105(b).

[72] HCERA § 1004(d); see I.R.S. Notice 2010-38, 2010-20 I.R.B. 682 (addressing the tax treatment of extended coverage for dependents).

[73] Section 105(b) provides as follows:

> (b) Amounts expended for medical care. Except in the case of amounts attributable to (and not in excess of) deductions allowed under section 213 (relating to medical, etc., expenses) for any prior taxable year, gross income does not include amounts referred to in subsection (a) if such amounts are paid, directly or indirectly, to the taxpayer to reimburse the taxpayer for expenses incurred by him for the medical care (as defined in section 213(d)) of the taxpayer, his spouse, and his dependents (as defined in section 152, determined without regard to subsections (b)(1), (b)(2), and (d)(1)(B) thereof). Any child to whom section 152(e) applies shall be treated as a dependent of both parents for purposes of this subsection.

[74] Section 152 of the Code provides, in relevant part:

> (c) Qualifying Child.—For purposes of this section—(1) In general.—The term "qualifying child" means, with respect to any taxpayer for any taxable year, an individual—(A) who bears a relationship to the taxpayer described in paragraph (2), (B) who has the same principal place of abode as the taxpayer for more than one-half of such taxable year, (C) who meets the age requirements of paragraph (3), (D) who has not provided over one-half of such individual's own support for the calendar year in which the taxable year of the taxpayer begins, and (E) who has not filed a joint return (other than only for a claim of refund with the individual's spouse under section 6013 for the taxable year beginning in the calendar year in which the taxable year of the taxpayer begins.
> (2) Relationship.—For purposes of paragraph (1)(A), an individual bears a relationship to the taxpayer described in this paragraph if such individual is—(A) a child of the taxpayer or a descendant of such a child, or (B) a brother, sister, stepbrother, or stepsister of the taxpayer or a descendant of any such relative.
> (3) Age requirements.—(A) In general.—For purposes of paragraph (1)(C), an individual meets the requirements of this paragraph if such individual is younger than the taxpayer claiming such individual as a qualifying child and—(i) has not attained the age of 19 as of the close of the calendar year in which the taxable year of the taxpayer begins, or (ii) is a student who has not attained the age of 24 as of the close of such calendar year. (B) Special rule for disabled.—In the case of an individual who is permanently and totally disabled (as defined in section 22(e)(3)) at any time during such calendar year, the requirements of subparagraph (A) shall be treated as met with respect to such individual."

I.R.C. §§ 152(c)(1), (2), (3).

> Section 152(f) defines "child" as follows:
> (f) Other Definitions and Rules.—For purposes of this section—(1) Child defined.—(A) In general.—The term "child" means an individual who is—(i) a son, daughter, stepson, or stepdaughter of the taxpayer, or (ii) an eligible foster child of the taxpayer. (B) Adopted child.—In determining whether any of the relationships specified in subparagraph (A)(i) or paragraph (4) exists, a legally adopted individual of the taxpayer, or an individual who is lawfully placed with the taxpayer for legal adoption by the taxpayer, shall be treated as a child of such individual by blood. (C) Eligible foster child.—For purposes of subparagraph (A)(ii), the term "eligible foster child" means an individual who is placed with the taxpayer by an authorized placement agency or by judgment, decree, or other order of any court of competent jurisdiction. (2) Student defined.—The term "student" means an individual who during each of 5 calendar months during the calendar year in which the taxable year of the taxpayer begins—(A) is a full-time student at an educational organization described in section 170(b)(1)(A)(ii), or (B) is pursuing a full-time course of institutional on-farm training under the supervision of an accredited agent of an educational organization described in section 170(b)(1)(A)(ii) or of a State or political subdivision of a State.

I.R.C. § 152(f).

a child or descendant of such a child or a brother, sister, stepbrother, or stepsister of the taxpayer or a descendant of any such relative.[75] An adopted child stands in the same position as a natural child of the taxpayer.[76] The age test, prior to the enactment of the Affordable Care Act, was under age 19, or for students, under age 24 as of the close of such calendar year.[77]

The Affordable Care Act adds a new category of individuals eligible for tax-free employment-based coverage—"any child of the taxpayer who as of the end of the taxable year has not attained age 27."[78] Parallel amendments were also made to provide an equivalent deduction for self-employed tax-payers under Section 162(*l*)(1) of the Code.[79] The Act does not limit the tax-advantaged treatment of employment-based health coverage to "dependent" children, i.e., the residency and support requirements no longer apply.

To further address the tax issues associated with extended coverage for adult children, the Internal Revenue Service issued guidance, in the form of Notice 2010-38, on the tax treatment of health coverage for children up to age 27.[80] The IRS guidance indicates that, effective March 30, 2010, employment-based health coverage for an employee's child who has not attained age 27 as of the end of the employee's taxable year is excluded from the employee's gross income for federal income tax purposes.[81] The IRS guidance provides five examples illustrating the new rule, including the following:

> **Example 1.** Employer X provides health care coverage for its employees and their spouses and dependents and for any employee's child (as defined in § 152(f)(1)) who has not attained age 26. For the 2010 taxable year, Employer X provides coverage to Employee A and to A's son, C. C will attain age 26 on November 15, 2010. During the 2010 taxable year, C is not a full-time student. C has never worked for Employer X. C is not a dependent of A because prior to the close of the 2010 taxable year C had attained age 19 (and was also not a student who had not attained age 24).
>
> C is a child of A within the meaning of § 152(f)(1). Accordingly, and because C will not attain age 27 during the 2010 taxable year, the health care coverage and reimbursements provided to him under the terms of Employer X's plan are excludable from A's gross income under §§ 106 and 105(b) for the period on and after March 30, 2010, through November 15, 2010 (when C attains age 26 and loses coverage under the terms of the plan).[82]

The examples affirm that status as a tax dependent (as defined in Section 152 of the Code) is not required to qualify for the tax exemption. Note that unless states make conforming changes to state tax laws, the extended coverage provided to children over age 19 (or age 23) may be subject to state income taxes.[83]

A grandfathered health plan is subject to the requirement to extend coverage to adult children up to age 26.[84] However, for plan years prior to January 1, 2014, grandfathered health plans may exclude an adult child from coverage if the adult child is eligible to enroll in another employer-sponsored

---

[75] I.R.C. § 152(c)(2).

[76] I.R.C. § 152(f)(1)(B).

[77] I.R.C. § 152(c)(3).

[78] HCERA § 1004(d) (amending I.R.C. §§ 105(b), 162(*l*), 501(c)(9), 401(h) to include children of the taxpayer who had not attained age 27 before the close of the tax year).

[79] HCERA § 1004(d)(2).

[80] I.R.S. Notice 2010-38, 2010-20 I.R.B. 682. See **Appendix L.**

[81] I.R.S. Notice 2010-38 § II.

[82] I.R.S. Notice 2010-38 § 11, Ex. 1.

[83] *See, e.g.,* Cal. A.B. 36 (enacted Apr. 7, 2011) (conforming tax treatment of extended coverage for children to federal law).

[84] PPACA § 1251(a)(4)(A)(iv).

health plan.[85] This special exclusion does not apply where the child is eligible for coverage under the plans of the employers of both parents to avoid a situation where each plan excludes the child based on eligibility for the other.[86] For plan years beginning on or after January 1, 2014, a grandfathered health plan can no longer use this special exclusion and must comply with all requirements of the extended coverage provision.[87] Employers will need to weigh whether the benefits of the special exclusion from the extended coverage requirement and other grandfathered health plan advantages outweigh the limited flexibility that employers will have to make changes to grandfathered health plans.

[B] Transitional Relief

When President Obama signed the Affordable Care Act, many individuals with children graduating from school or reaching the current age limits of their plans in 2010 were surprised to learn that the extended coverage provision did not take effect until the first plan year beginning on or after September 23, 2010. While coverage was available for these children under COBRA or private health insurance, the cost was prohibitive for many. Due to overwhelming demand from the administration, HHS, and plan members, many insurance carriers announced that they would voluntarily provide extended coverage for adult children as of May 1, 2010.[88]

Other children whose coverage had expired previously, but who are under age 26, may want to re-enroll in their parents' coverage. The tri-agency regulations published on May 10, 2010, formalize the transitional procedures for children to return to coverage under the plan.[89] The transitional rules apply to individuals whose coverage ended or was denied and never started because their eligibility for dependent coverage ended before age 26. The coverage availability is required to be effective on the first day of the first plan year beginning on or after September 23, 2010.[90] For calendar year plans, this means no later than January 1, 2011.

[1] Notice of Enrollment Opportunity

Under the transitional rules, the plan or issuer is required to give the child a special opportunity to enroll that continues for at least 30 days.[91] The opportunity (including a written notice describing the enrollment opportunity) must be provided beginning not later than the first day of the first plan year beginning on or after September 23, 2010.[92] The written notice must include a statement that children whose coverage ended or who were denied coverage because the availability of the dependent coverage ended before the child attained age 26 are eligible to enroll for coverage.[93] It is unclear whether a child who was previously dropped from coverage for reasons other than expiration of eligibility is entitled to the special enrollment opportunity. The obligation to provide the notice of enrollment opportunity can be satisfied for both the plan and the issuer if the notice is provided to the employee or the individual on behalf of the child.[94] The notice may be included with other enrollment materials that a plan distributes to its employees, as long as the statement is prominent.[95]

---

[85] PPACA § 1251(a)(4)(B)(ii).

[86] Preamble to tri-agency regulations on extended dependent coverage, pp. 11–12.

[87] PPACA § 1251(a)(4)(B)(ii).

[88] For a list of the insurance companies, *see* http://www.hhs.gov/cciio/regulations/adult_child_faq.html.

[89] 45 C.F.R. § 147.120(f); Treas. Reg. § 54.9815-2714T(f); 29 C.F.R. § 2590.715-2714(f).

[90] PHSA § 2714.

[91] 45 C.F.R. § 147.120(f)(2); Treas. Reg. § 54.9815-2714T(f)(2); 29 C.F.R. § 2590.715-2714(f)(2).

[92] 45 C.F.R. § 147.120(f)(2); Treas. Reg. § 54.9815-2714T(f)(2); 29 C.F.R. § 2590.715-2714(f)(2).

[93] 45 C.F.R. § 147.120(f)(2)(ii); Treas. Reg. § 54.9815-2714T(f)(2)(ii); 29 C.F.R. § 2590.715-2714(f)(2)(ii).

[94] 45 C.F.R. § 147.120(f)(2)(ii); Treas. Reg. § 54.9815-2714T(f)(2)(ii); 29 C.F.R. § 2590.715-2714(f)(2)(ii).

[95] 45 C.F.R. § 147.120(f)(2)(ii); Treas. Reg. § 54.9815-2714T(f)(2)(ii); 29 C.F.R. § 2590.715-2714(f)(2)(ii).

[2]   Terms of Enrollment

Any child who enrolls through the special enrollment opportunity must be treated as if enrolled under the HIPAA special enrollment rules, which means that the child will not be treated as a late enrollee.[96] The child must be offered all the benefit packages available to similarly situated individuals who did not lose coverage by reason of loss of dependent eligibility status.[97] There can be no difference in benefits or cost-sharing requirements, and the child cannot be required to pay more for coverage than similarly situated individuals who did not lose coverage by reason of cessation of dependent status.[98]

§ 8.05   Mandated Claim and Appeal Process

Group health plans and health insurance issuers offering group or individual health insurance coverage, other than grandfathered health plans, are required to implement appeals processes that comply with the Affordable Care Act no later than the first day of the first plan year beginning on or after September 23, 2010.[99] The Act requires the process to provide:

- An internal claim appeal process during which an enrollee may review his or her file, present evidence and testimony, and continue receiving coverage during the pendency of the internal appeals process.[100]

- An external claim appeal process during which an enrollee may review his or her file, present evidence and testimony, and continue receiving coverage during the pendency of the external appeals process.[101]

- Notice of the appeal process and the availability of any office of health insurance consumer assistance or ombudsman established under the Affordable Care Act to assist enrollees with the appeal process, in a manner that is culturally and linguistically appropriate.[102]

HHS, Treasury, and the DOL issued interim final regulations[103] and amendments to these regulations[104] implementing these requirements. On August 23, 2010, the agencies issued interim guidance for self-funded group health plans in the form of Technical Release 2010-01,[105] which was modified by Technical Release 2011-02.[106] On September 20, 2010, the three agencies issued Technical Release 2010-02, which provided an interim enforcement grace period until July 1, 2011,

---

[96] 45 C.F.R. § 147.120(f)(4); Treas. Reg. § 54.9815-2714T(f)(4); 29 C.F.R. § 2590.715-2714(f)(4).

[97] 26 C.F.R. § 54.9815-2714T(f)(4), 29 C.F.R. § 2590.715-2714(f)(4), 45 C.F.R. § 147.120(f)(4).

[98] 26 C.F.R. § 54.9815-2714T(f)(4), 29 C.F.R. § 2590.715-2714(f)(4), 45 C.F.R. § 147.120(f)(4).

[99] PPACA § 1001 (adding PHSA § 2719), *as amended by* PPACA § 10101(g).

[100] PHSA § 2719(a).

[101] PHSA § 2719(b).

[102] PHSA § 2719(a) (referencing PPACA § 1002, which adds PHSA § 2793, to award grants to states to establish offices of health insurance consumer assistance or health insurance ombudsman programs); see **Section 8.05[C]** notes 228–230 and accompanying text (addressing the consumer assistance and ombudsman provisions).

[103] 75 Fed. Reg. 43,330–64 (July 23, 2010), *amending* 26 C.F.R. pts. 54 and 602; 29 C.F.R. pt. 2590; 45 C.F.R. pt. 147 in **Appendix M.**

[104] 76 Fed. Reg. 37,208–34 (June 24, 2011), *amending* 26 C.F.R. pt. 54; 29 C.F.R. pt. 147; 45 C.F.R. pt. 147 in **Appendix N.**

[105] Technical Release 2010-01 (Federal External Appeal Process), *available at* http://www.dol.gov/ebsa/pdf/ACATechnicalRelease2010.01.pdf.

[106] Technical Release 2011-02 (Guidance on External Review), *available at* http://www.dol.gov/ebsa/newsroom/tr11-02.html.

for certain of the requirements relating to the internal appeal process,[107] and subsequently extended this grace period to January 1, 2012, in Technical Release 2011-01[108] for all but one of the requirements identified in Technical Release 2010-02.

The requirements for an internal claim and appeal process and external appeal process are discussed separately below. Because these requirements do not apply to grandfathered health plans, the avoidance of these requirements may be a key consideration for employers seeking to maintain grandfathered health plan status.

[A] Internal Claim Appeal Process

The interim final regulations, as amended, describe the internal claim and appeal process required of a group health plan or health insurance issuer of group health coverage, whether or not covered by ERISA.[109] The plan or the issuer must comply with the DOL's existing regulations[110] on the internal claim and appeal process,[111] as modified by the interim final regulation, as amended.[112]

The interim final regulation modifies the DOL's existing regulation on the internal claim and appeal process in the following ways, some of which were subject to the enforcement grace period and subsequently modified by the amendment to the interim final regulation:

- An adverse benefit determination eligible for review under the internal claim and appeal process is expanded to include a rescission of coverage, whether or not it results in any denial of coverage.[113]

- A claimant must be notified about the decision regarding a claim for urgent care no later than 24 hours (rather than 72 hours) after receipt of the claim.[114] Compliance with this requirement is subject to the interim enforcement grace period until plan years beginning on and after January 1, 2012,[115] and thereafter the amended interim regulation restores the original rule's response period but requires that the group health plan defer to an attending provider's determination that the claim relates to urgent care.[116]

- A claimant must be able to review the claim file and provide evidence and testimony in connection with an appeal of a denied claim under the internal claim and appeal process.[117] Additionally, in connection with such an appeal, the claimant must receive any new or additional evidence considered, relied upon, or generated during the appeal sufficiently in advance of the date as of which the appeal is to be decided to give the claimant a reasonable chance to

---

[107] Technical Release 2010-02 (Enforcement Grace Period), *available at* http://www.dol.gov/ebsa/pdf/ACATechnicalRelease 2010-02.pdf. The grace period is available to a group health plan that "is working in good faith to implement the standards." Tech. Rel. 2010-02, at 4.

[108] Technical Release 2011-01 (Extension of Non-Enforcement Period), *available at* http://www.dol.gov/ebsa/newsroom/ tr11-02.html. This Technical Release also made the interim enforcement grace period available to plans not working in good faith to implement these requirements during either the original or the extended grace period. Tech. Rel. 2011-01, at 4.

[109] 26 C.F.R. § 54.9815-2719T(b)(1); 29 C.F.R. § 2590.715-2719(b)(1); 45 C.F.R. § 147.136(b)(1).

[110] 29 C.F.R. § 2560.503-1.

[111] 26 C.F.R. § 54.9815-2719T(b)(2)(i); 29 C.F.R. § 2590.715-2719(b)(2)(i); 45 C.F.R. § 147.136(b)(2)(i).

[112] 26 C.F.R. § 54.9815-2719T(b)(2)(ii); 29 C.F.R. § 2590.715-2719(b)(2)(ii); 45 C.F.R. § 147.136(b)(2)(ii).

[113] 26 C.F.R. § 54.9815-2719T(b)(2)(ii)(A); 29 C.F.R. § 2590.715-2719(b)(2)(ii)(A); 45 C.F.R. § 147.136(b)(2)(ii)(A). See **Section 8.06** for a discussion of the prohibition on rescissions.

[114] 26 C.F.R. § 54.9815-2719T(b)(2)(ii)(B); 29 C.F.R. § 2590.715-2719(b)(2)(ii)(B); 45 C.F.R. § 147.136(b)(2)(ii)(B).

[115] Tech. Rel. 2010-02, at 3.

[116] 26 C.F.R. § 54.9815-2719T(b)(2)(ii)(B); 29 C.F.R. § 2590.715-2719(b)(2)(ii)(B); 45 C.F.R. § 147.136(b)(2)(ii)(B). The term "urgent care" is defined in 29 C.F.R. § 2560.503-1(m)(1).

[117] 26 C.F.R. § 54.9815-2719T(b)(2)(ii)(C); 29 C.F.R. § 2590.715-2719(b)(2)(ii)(C); 45 C.F.R. § 147.136(b)(2)(ii)(C). It does not appear that a claimant must be provided with an opportunity to provide testimony in person.

respond prior to such date[118] and, if the adverse decision on appeal is based on a new or additional rationale, the claimant must be notified of the rationale sufficiently in advance of the date as of which the appeal is to be decided to give the claimant a reasonable chance to respond prior to such date.[119]

- An internal claim and appeal must be adjudicated in an independent and impartial manner by persons who are independent and impartial.[120]

- Certain plans may have to communicate in a non-English language with some of their participants. Compliance with this requirement is subject to the interim enforcement grace period until plan years beginning on and after January 1, 2012.[121] The requirement set forth in the interim final regulation[122] was modified by the amendment of the interim final regulation.[123] Under the amendment of the interim final regulation, the requirement applies to notices sent to any address in a county that the DOL, HHS, and IRS identify as a county in which 10 percent or more of the population is literate only in a non-English language.[124] These notices must include a statement in the non-English language(s) indicating how to access oral language services in the applicable non-English language that will answer questions and provide assistance with filing claims and appeals, which includes claims and appeals under the external review process. Further, pursuant to a request, a plan must provide a notice in any applicable non-English language.

- The interim final regulation requires that an adverse benefit determination[125] or final adverse benefit determination[126] include information identifying the claim,[127] the reason or reasons for the adverse determination,[128] and a description of any standard used to deny the

---

[118] 26 C.F.R. § 54.9815-2719T(b)(2)(ii)(C)(1); 29 C.F.R. § 2590.715-2719(b)(2)(ii)(C)(1); 45 C.F.R. § 147.136(b)(2)(ii)(C)(1). However, the period within which the appeal must be decided is not altered by the need for a plan or issuer to comply with this requirement.

[119] 26 C.F.R. § 54.9815-2719T(b)(2)(ii)(C)(2); 29 C.F.R. § 2590.715-2719(b)(2)(ii)(C)(2); 45 C.F.R. § 147.136(b)(2)(ii)(C)(2). The period within which the appeal must be decided is not altered by the need for a plan or issuer to comply with this requirement.

[120] 26 C.F.R. § 54.9815-2719T(b)(2)(ii)(D); 29 C.F.R. § 2590.715-2719(b)(2)(ii)(D); 45 C.F.R. § 147.136(b)(2)(ii)(D). For example, a medical expert must not be chosen because the expert has a reputation for favoring a plan's position, and the adjudicators of claims cannot have a financial incentive to deny claims.

[121] Tech. Rel. 2011-01, at 4–5.

[122] The interim final regulation applied this requirement to a plan covering fewer than 100 participants at the beginning of its plan year if at least 25% of its participants were literate in the same non-English language. If a plan covered 100 or more participants at the beginning of its plan year, the requirement applied if the lesser of 500 or 10% of participants were literate in the same non-English language. Any notices provided by a plan that met the applicable threshold relating to participants not literate in one or more non-English languages had to include a statement in the non-English language or languages offering to provide such notice in the applicable non-English language. If the offer was accepted by a participant, all subsequent notices to the participant had to be in the applicable non-English language. 26 C.F.R. § 54.9815-2719T(b)(2)(ii)(E); 29 C.F.R. § 2590.715-2719(b)(2)(ii)(E); 45 C.F.R. § 147.136(b)(2)(ii)(E); 75 Fed. Reg. 43,330–64 (July 23, 2010).

[123] 26 C.F.R. § 54.9815-2719T(e); 29 C.F.R. § 2590.715-2719(e); 45 C.F.R. § 147.136(e).

[124] A list of these counties for 2012 is available at http://www.cms.gov/resources/fact sheets/clas-data.html.

[125] An "adverse benefit determination" is "any . . . denial, reduction, or termination of, or a failure to provide or make payment (in whole or in part) for a benefit" and any rescission of coverage. 26 C.F.R. § 54.9815-2719T(a)(2)(i); 29 C.F.R. § 2590.715-2719(a)(2)(i); 45 C.F.R. § 147.136(a)(2)(i).

[126] A "final adverse benefit determination" is "an adverse benefit determination that has been upheld by a plan or issuer at the completion of the internal appeals process." 26 C.F.R. § 54.9815-2719T(a)(2)(v); 29 C.F.R. § 2590.715-2719(a)(2)(v); 45 C.F.R. § 147.136(a)(2)(v).

[127] The information must include "the date of service, the health care provider, the claim amount (if applicable), the diagnosis code and its corresponding meaning, and the treatment code and its corresponding meaning." 26 C.F.R. § 54.9815-2719T(b)(2)(ii)(E)(1); 29 C.F.R. § 2590.715-2719(b)(2)(ii)(E)(1); 45 C.F.R. § 147.136(b)(2)(ii)(E)(1); 75 Fed. Reg. 43,330–64 (July 23, 2010).

[128] The information must include "the denial code and its corresponding meaning, as well as a description of the plan's or issuer's standard, if any, that was used in denying the claim." 26 C.F.R. § 54.9815-2719T(b)(2)(ii)(E)(2); 29 C.F.R. § 2590.715-2719(b)(2)(ii)(E)(2); 45 C.F.R. § 147.136(b)(2)(ii)(E)(2); 75 Fed. Reg. 43,330–64 (July 23, 2010).

claim.[129] Additionally, a final adverse benefit determination must contain a "discussion" of the determination.[130] Compliance with these requirements is subject to the interim enforcement grace period until July 1, 2011.[131] On and after July 1, 2012, the interim enforcement grace period is extended to the first plan year beginning on and after July 1, 2011,[132] and the amendment of the interim final regulation then replaces the requirement that information identifying the claim include diagnosis and treatment codes and their respective meanings with a requirement that a plan include a statement in the determination that this information is available upon request and comply with a request for such information by a claimant as soon as practicable.[133]

- An adverse benefit determination or final adverse benefit determination[134] must further describe the appeal process (both internal and external),[135] how to make an appeal,[136] the contact information for the office of health insurance consumer assistance or ombudsman,[137] and the fact that such office is available to assist the claimants.[138] Compliance with this requirement is subject to the interim enforcement grace period until the first plan year beginning on and after July 1, 2011.[139]

- If a plan or issuer fails to "strictly" comply with the requirements for an internal claim and appeal process, the claimant is entitled to start the external appeal process or institute litigation under ERISA, except if any violation is de minimis, non-prejudicial, attributable to a plan's good cause or matters beyond the plan's control, and not part of a pattern of ongoing noncompliance by the plan.[140] A claimant has the right to request a written explanation from the plan making plain why the plan meets this standard.[141] The ultimate determination as to whether the standard is met is made by the external reviewer or a court and, if the external reviewer or court accepts the plan's explanation, the plan must advise the claimant within ten days that the claim may be resubmitted for consideration under the internal appeal claim process.[142] If a court agrees to hear the claim, under ERISA,[143] the deferential standard of review

---

[129] 26 C.F.R. § 54.9815-2719T(b)(2)(ii)(E)(2); 29 C.F.R. § 2590.715-2719(b)(2)(ii)(E)(2); 45 C.F.R. § 147.136(b)(2)(ii)(E)(2); 75 Fed. Reg. 43,330–64 (July 23, 2010).

[130] 26 C.F.R. § 54.9815-2719T(b)(2)(ii)(E)(2); 29 C.F.R. § 2590.715-2719(b)(2)(ii)(E)(2); 45 C.F.R. § 147.136(b)(2)(ii)(E)(2); 75 Fed. Reg. 43,330–64 (July 23, 2010).

[131] Tech. Rel. 2011-01, at 4–5.

[132] Tech. Rel. 2011-01, at 5. Accordingly, for a calendar year plan the grace period for this requirement expires on January 1, 2012, while the grace period for a plan using any other plan year expires on the first day of the plan's next following plan year (e.g., the grace period expires on July 1, 2012, for a plan using a July 1 to June 30 plan year.)

[133] 26 C.F.R. § 54.9815-2719T(b)(2)(ii)(E); 29 C.F.R. § 2590.715-2719(b)(2)(ii)(E); 45 C.F.R. § 147.136(b)(2)(ii)(E).

[134] Although the interim final regulations do not expressly provide that the following information must be included in an adverse benefit determination or final adverse benefit determination, the model notices provided for these determinations include this information. These model notices can be accessed at http://www.dol.gov/ebsa and in **Appendix O.** Thus, the requirements described in the text in connection with notes 127–130 apply to the explanations of benefits typically provided to participants.

[135] 26 C.F.R. § 54.9815-2719T(b)(2)(ii)(E)(3); 29 C.F.R. § 2590.715-2719(b)(2)(ii)(E)(3); 45 C.F.R. § 147.136(b)(2)(ii)(E)(3).

[136] 26 C.F.R. § 54.9815-2719T(b)(2)(ii)(E)(3); 29 C.F.R. § 2590.715-2719(b)(2)(ii)(E)(3); 45 C.F.R. § 147.136(b)(2)(ii)(E)(3).

[137] 26 C.F.R. § 54.9815-2719T(b)(2)(ii)(E)(4); 29 C.F.R. § 2590.715-2719(b)(2)(ii)(E)(4); 45 C.F.R. § 147.136(b)(2)(ii)(E)(4). See **Section 8.05[C]** for a discussion of the office of health insurance consumer assistance or ombudsman.

[138] 26 C.F.R. § 54.9815-2719T(b)(2)(ii)(E)(4); 29 C.F.R. § 2590.715-2719(b)(2)(ii)(E)(4); 45 C.F.R. § 147.136(b)(2)(ii)(E)(4).

[139] Tech. Rel. 2011-01, at 4–5.

[140] 26 C.F.R. § 54.9815-2719T(b)(2)(ii)(F)(2); 29 C.F.R. § 2590.715-2719(b)(2)(ii)(F)(2); 45 C.F.R. § 147.136(b)(2)(ii)(F)(2). The interim final regulation prior to its amendment did not contain this exception. 26 C.F.R. § 54.9815-2719T(b)(2)(ii)(F); 29 C.F.R. § 2590.715-2719(b)(2)(ii)(F); 45 C.F.R. § 147.136(b)(2)(ii)(F); 75 Fed. Reg. 43,330–64 (July 23, 2010).

[141] 26 C.F.R. § 54.9815-2719T(b)(2)(ii)(F)(2); 29 C.F.R. § 2590.715-2719(b)(2)(ii)(F)(2); 45 C.F.R. § 147.136(b)(2)(ii)(F)(2).

[142] 26 C.F.R. § 54.9815-2719T(b)(2)(ii)(F)(2); 29 C.F.R. § 2590.715-2719(b)(2)(ii)(F)(2); 45 C.F.R. § 147.136(b)(2)(ii)(F)(2).

[143] *See* ERISA § 502(a)(1)(B).

set forth in *Firestone v. Bruch*[144] is inapplicable.[145] Compliance with this requirement is subject to the interim enforcement grace period until the first plan year beginning on and after January 1, 2012.[146]

- During the pendency of an appeal, a plan or issuer must continue to provide coverage to the extent set forth in the DOL's existing regulation,[147] which generally provides that reimbursements for an authorized course of treatment cannot be reduced or terminated without providing advance notice and an opportunity for review before their reduction or termination.[148]

[B] External Claim Appeal Process

A health insurance issuer is solely responsible for complying with the Affordable Care Act's external claim appeal procedure[149] if (1) the issuer offers group health insurance that is subject to regulation by a state, (2) the state requires the issuer to comply with an external review process, and (3) the external review process satisfies the consumer protections contained in the Uniform Health Carrier External Review Model Act issued by the National Association of Insurance Commissioners (NAIC External Review Act).[150] A group health plan is solely responsible for complying with the Affordable Care Act's external claim appeal procedure[151] if (1) it is subject to regulation by the state (and it does not provide insured coverage),[152] (2) the state requires the plan to comply with an external review process, and (3) the external review process satisfies the consumer protections contained in the NAIC External Review Act. In all other situations responsibility for complying with the Affordable Care Act's external claim appeal process falls on both the group health plan and the health insurance issuer.[153]

The following section explains how a group health plan subject to state law determines whether the state law contains an external review process that satisfies the consumer protections contained in the NAIC External Review Act. It then describes how a group health plan not subject to such a state law can comply with the Affordable Care Act's external claim appeal process.

[1] Group Health Plan Subject to Acceptable State External Review Law

The interim final regulations, as amended, set forth the standards that HHS will apply to determine whether a state external review law satisfies the consumer protections contained in the NAIC External Review Act.[154] The preamble to the interim final regulations indicates that it does not appear that all existing state external review laws comply with these standards.[155] Accordingly, the interim

---

[144] 489 U.S. 101 (1989) (if plan gives fiduciary discretion to determine eligibility and make interpretations, the fiduciary's exercise of discretion is reviewed by a court using an arbitrary and capricious standard).

[145] 26 C.F.R. § 54.9815-2719T(b)(2)(ii)(F)(1); 29 C.F.R. § 2590.715-2719(b)(2)(ii)(F)(1); 45 C.F.R. § 147.136(b)(2)(ii)(F)(1). In the case law decided prior to the Affordable Care Act, courts generally apply the *Firestone* standard of review, unless procedural irregularities taint the fiduciary's decision. *See* Alliant Techsystems Inc. v. Marks, 465 F.3d 864 (8th Cir. 2006); Abatie v. Alta Health & Life Ins., 458 F.3d 955 (9th Cir. 2006).

[146] Tech. Rel. 2011-01, at 4–5.

[147] 29 C.F.R. § 2560.503-1(f)(2)(ii).

[148] 26 C.F.R. § 54.9815-2719T(b)(2)(iii); 29 C.F.R. § 2590.715-2719(b)(2)(iii); 45 C.F.R. § 147.136(b)(2)(iii).

[149] 26 C.F.R. § 54.9815-2719T(c)(1)(i); 29 C.F.R. § 2590.715-2719(c)(1)(i); 45 C.F.R. § 147.136(c)(1)(i).

[150] The NAIC External Review Act can be accessed at http://www.dol.gov/ebsa/pdf/externalreviewmodelact.pdf.

[151] 26 C.F.R. § 54.9815-2719T(c)(1)(ii); 29 C.F.R. § 2590.715-2719(c)(1)(ii); 45 C.F.R. § 147.136(c)(1)(ii).

[152] State and local government plans and non-electing church plans fall within this category because they are not covered by ERISA. *See* ERISA §§ 4(b)(1), (2).

[153] 26 C.F.R. § 54.9815-2719T(c)(1)(iii); 29 C.F.R. § 2590.715-2719(c)(1)(iii); 45 C.F.R. § 147.136(c)(1)(iii).

[154] 26 C.F.R. § 54.9815-2719T(c)(2); 29 C.F.R. § 2590.715-2719(c)(2); 45 C.F.R. § 147.136(c)(2).

[155] 75 Fed. Reg. 43,330, 43,336.

final regulations provide a transition rule under which a state external review law applicable to a group health plan will be deemed to meet the standards.[156]

The transition rule, which originally applied only to plan years beginning before July 1, 2011,[157] was extended by the amendment to the interim final regulations until January 1, 2012.[158] On and after January 1, 2012, and before January 1, 2014, a health insurance issuer or a group health plan that is otherwise subject to state law will have to comply with the federal external review requirement[159] unless HHS has determined that the applicable state law meets the standards set forth in the interim final regulations or temporary standards set forth in Technical Release 2011-02.[160] On and after January 1, 2014, a health insurance issuer or a group health plan that is otherwise subject to state law will have to comply with the federal external review requirement unless HHS has determined that the applicable state law meets the standards set forth in the interim final regulations, as amended.[161]

Before January 1, 2012, an insurer subject to a state external review law must comply with that law.[162] If no such law applies to an insurer, the insurer must comply with an external review process administered by the Office of Personnel Management under an agreement with HHS.[163] A self-insured group health plan that is subject to state law and not subject to any state external review law can either comply with the federal review process or use the external review process applicable to group health plans subject to ERISA.[164] A health insurance issuer or a group health plan that is subject to state law, which does not meet the standards set forth in the interim regulations, as amended, complies with the federal external review requirement on and after January 1, 2012,[165] by electing[166] to either participate in an external review process administered by the Office of Personnel Management[167] or use the external review process applicable to group health plans subject to ERISA.[168]

---

[156] 26 C.F.R. § 54.9815-2719T(c)(3); 29 C.F.R. § 2590.715-2719(c)(3); 45 C.F.R. § 147.136(c)(3); 75 Fed. Reg. 43,330–64 (July 23, 2010).

[157] 26 C.F.R. § 54.9815-2719T(c)(3); 29 C.F.R. § 2590.715-2719(c)(3); 45 C.F.R. § 147.136(c)(3); 75 Fed. Reg. 43,330–64 (July 23, 2010).

[158] 26 C.F.R. § 54.9815-2719T(c)(3)(i); 29 C.F.R. § 2590.715-2719(c)(3)(i); 45 C.F.R. § 147.136(c)(3)(i).

[159] The federal external review process is administered by the Office of Personnel Management and is described in Technical Guidance for Interim Procedures for Federal External Review Relating to Internal Claims and Appeals and External Review for Health Insurance Issuers in the Group and Individual Markets Under the Patient Protection and Affordable Care Act (Aug. 26, 2010), available at http://cciio.cms.gov/resources/files/interim_appeals_guidance.pdf.

[160] Tech. Rel. 2011-02, at 5–6. A list of the states that satisfy either of these requirements is available at http://cciio.cms.gov/resources/files/external-appeals.html. Accordingly, any final adverse benefit determination on or after January 1, 2012, is subject to the federal external review requirement unless HHS has determined that the applicable state law meets these standards. 26 C.F.R. § 54.9815-2719T(c)(3)(ii); 29 C.F.R. § 2590.715-2719(c)(3)(ii); 45 C.F.R. § 147.136(c)(3)(ii).

[161] Tech. Rel. 2011-02, at 5–6. The external review process applicable to group health plans is discussed in the text accompanying notes 169–227.

[162] 26 C.F.R. § 54.9815-2719T(c)(3); 29 C.F.R. § 2590.715-2719(c)(3); 45 C.F.R. § 147.136(c)(3); 75 Fed. Reg. 43,330–64 (July 23, 2010).

[163] See Technical Guidance for Interim Procedures for Federal External Review Relating to Internal Claims and Appeals and External Review for Health Insurance Issuers in the Group and Individual Markets (Aug. 26, 2010), available at http://cciio.cms.gov/resources/files/interim_appeals.

[164] See Interim Procedures for Federal External Review Relating to Internal Claims and Appeals and External Review Under the Patient Protection and Affordable Care Act for Self-Insured Non-Federal Governmental Health Plans (Sept. 23, 2010), available at http://cciio.cms.gov/resources/files/technical_guidance_for_self_funded_non_federal_plans.pdf.

[165] Tech. Rel. 2011-02, at 7–8.

[166] The election process is described in Instructions for Self-Insured Nonfederal Government Health Plans and Health Insurance Issuers Offering Group and Individual Health Coverage on How to Elect a Federal External Review Process (June 22, 2011), available at http://cciio.cms.gov/resources/files/hhs_srg_election.

[167] See Technical Guidance for Interim Procedures for Federal External Review Relating to Internal Claims and Appeals and External Review for Health Insurance Issuers in the Group and Individual Markets under the Patient Protection and Affordable Care Act (Aug. 26, 2010), available at http://cciio.cms.gov/resources/file/interim_appeals.

[168] Tech. Rel. 2011-02, at 7–8.

[2] Group Health Plan Subject to Federal External Review Requirement

The interim final regulations, as amended, set forth the requirements that will be used to establish the standards for an external review process to satisfy the federal external review requirement.[169] The preamble to the interim final regulations indicates that these standards will be provided in future guidance.[170] Technical Release 2010-01 provides alternative interim enforcement safe harbors[171] that a group health plan subject to the federal external review requirement can use to satisfy the requirement, pending the issuance of further guidance.[172]

Initially, a group health plan can comply with the federal external review requirement by voluntarily complying with the external review process of any state that permits self-funded plans to access the state's external review process for insured plans.[173] Alternatively, a group health plan can comply with the federal external review requirement by complying with the procedures of Technical Release 2010-01,[174] as modified by Technical Release 2011-02.

[a] Federal External Review—Request Not Eligible for Expedited External Review

The applicable procedures for a request for external review that is not eligible for expedited external review are summarized below. The discussion indicates when a different rule applies for a request for expedited external review.[175]

- A claimant must have the right to file a request for external review within four months after receiving a notice of adverse benefit determination or final internal adverse benefit determination.[176] Effective for claims for which external review has not been initiated prior to September 20, 2011, and until revoked by the DOL and Treasury, external review is available only for adverse benefit determinations or final adverse benefit determinations involving medical judgment or a rescission of coverage.[177] The external reviewer determines the availability of external review.[178]

- The group health plan must complete a preliminary review of an external review request within five days of its receipt,[179] unless the request is eligible for expedited external review.[180] If the group health plan determines that the claimant is or was covered by the group health plan at the time the health care item or service is requested or was provided and that the claimant has exhausted the internal appeal process or is not required to exhaust such

---

[169] 26 C.F.R. § 54.9815-2719T(d)(1); 29 C.F.R. § 2590.715-2719(d)(1); 45 C.F.R. § 147.136(d)(1).

[170] 75 Fed. Reg. 43,330, 43,336–37.

[171] A group health plan can comply with the federal external review requirement in other ways. Compliance will be determined on a case-by-case basis. *See* FAQs About the Affordable Care Act Implementation Part 1, FAQ 8, http://www.dol.gov.ebsa/faqs/faq-aca.html.

[172] Tech. Rel. 2010-01, at 2. *See* DOL Tech. Rel. 2010-01 (External Review Process), *available at* http://www.dol.gov/ebsa/pdf/ACATechnicalRelease2010-01.pdf.

[173] Tech. Rel. 2010-01, at 3.

[174] Tech. Rel. 2010-01, at 3.

[175] See **Section 8.05[B][2][b]** for a discussion of the procedures for expedited external review.

[176] Tech. Rel. 2010-01, at 3. If there is no corresponding date four months after receipt of such a notice, the claimant must file an appeal by the first day of the fifth month after receipt of the notice. If the last day of the appeal period is a Saturday, Sunday, or federal holiday, the last day becomes the next day that is not a Saturday, Sunday, or federal holiday.

[177] 26 C.F.R. § 54.9815-2719T(d)(1)(ii); 29 C.F.R. § 2590.715-2719(d)(1)(ii). The term "medical judgment" includes "medical necessity, appropriateness, health care setting, level of care, or effectiveness of a covered benefit; or [a] determination that a treatment is experimental or investigational." 26 C.F.R. § 54.9815-2719T(d)(1)(ii)(A); 29 C.F.R. § 2590.715-2719(d)(1)(ii)(A).

[178] 26 C.F.R. § 54.9815-2719T(d)(1)(ii)(A); 29 C.F.R. § 2590.715-2719(d)(1)(ii)(A).

[179] Tech. Rel. 2010-01, at 3.

[180] See **Section 8.05[B][2][b]**.

appeal process,[181] the group health plan must notify the claimant in writing within one business day thereafter and assign an independent review organization (IRO), which is accredited by URAC (formerly known as the Utilization Review Accreditation Commission) or a similar nationally recognized accrediting organization, to handle the external review.[182] If the group health plan determines that the claimant is not or was not covered by the group health plan at the time the health care item or service is requested or was provided, or that the claimant has not exhausted any mandatory internal appeal process, the group health plan must state the applicable determination(s) and provide contact information for the U.S. Department of Labor's Employee Benefits Security Administration in a written notice to the claimant within one business day thereafter; in this case, no IRO is assigned by the group health plan.[183] If the group health plan determines that the claimant has not provided all of the information and forms required to process the request for external review, the group health plan must identify the missing information in a written notice to the claimant within one business day thereafter and permit the claimant to provide such information by the later of the end of the external appeal filing period or 48 hours after the claimant's receipt of the notice.[184]

- A group health plan must contract with at least three IROs to conduct external reviews.[185] External reviews must be assigned by a group health plan on a rotating or some other basis that preserves each IRO's independence and protects against bias.[186] An IRO cannot have any financial incentive to uphold the denial of benefits.[187] The Affordable Care Act Implementation FAQs Part 1 issued on September 20, 2010, indicate that a group health plan does not automatically violate this requirement if it does not contract with at least three IROs.[188] As of January 1, 2012, this relief was available only if the group health plan contracted with at least two IROs.[189] A group health plan must contract with at least three IROs as of July 1, 2012, to meet this requirement.[190]

- The contract under which the IRO conducts external reviews must:

  — indicate that the IRO will use legal experts in appropriate circumstances;[191]
  — require that the IRO will timely notify a claimant that the claimant's request for external review is accepted;[192]
  — obligate the IRO to inform the claimant that the IRO will consider additional information submitted by the claimant within ten business days after the claimant receives the notice;[193]
  — except for a request for expedited external review,[194] require that the group health plan provide the IRO with the documents and information the group health plan considered in

---

[181] See discussion of expedited review accompanying notes 222–227 *infra*.

[182] Tech. Rel. 2010-01, at 3–4.

[183] Tech. Rel. 2010-01, at 3–4.

[184] Tech. Rel. 2010-01, at 3–4.

[185] Tech. Rel. 2010-01, at 4. A group health plan does not have to directly contract with the IROs if the group health plan contracts with a third-party administrator that contracts with the IROs. *See* FAQs, *supra* note 171, at FAQ 9.

[186] Tech. Rel. 2010-01, at 4.

[187] Tech. Rel. 2010-01, at 4.

[188] FAQs, *supra* note 171, at FAQ 8.

[189] Tech Rel. 2011-02, at 8–9.

[190] Tech. Rel. 2011-02, at 8–9.

[191] Tech. Rel. 2010-01, at 4.

[192] Tech. Rel. 2010-01, at 4.

[193] Tech. Rel. 2010-01, at 4. The IRO *may* consider other material submitted by the claimant after the expiration of the ten-day period.

[194] See discussion of expedited review accompanying notes 222–227 *infra*.

making the adverse benefit determination or final internal adverse benefit determination within five business days after assigning the external review to the IRO;[195]

— obligate the IRO to transmit any information submitted by the claimant to the group health plan within one business day of its receipt by the IRO[196] (the group health plan *may* reverse its adverse benefit determination or final internal adverse benefit determination based on such information,[197] in which case the group health plan must provide the claimant and the IRO with written notice of its reversal within one business day[198] and the IRO must terminate the external review);[199]

— require the IRO to review all the materials timely provided by the claimant and the group health plan,[200] review the claim anew,[201] and not be bound by anything occurring during the group health plan's internal claim and appeal process;[202]

— require the IRO to consider, to the extent available and considered appropriate by the IRO, even if not provided by the group health plan or the claimant:[203] the claimant's medical records;[204] the attending health care professional's recommendation;[205] reports of health care professionals and other documents submitted by a health insurance issuer or the claimant's treating provider;[206] the terms of the group health plan, unless inconsistent with applicable law;[207] appropriate practice guidelines; clinical review criteria developed and used by the group health plan, except if inconsistent with the terms of the group health plan or applicable law;[208] and the opinion of the IRO's clinical reviewer(s) regarding the appropriate and available information or documents;[209]

— except for a request for expedited external review,[210] require that the IRO's final external review decision be provided in writing[211] to the claimant and the group health plan within 45 days after the IRO is assigned the external review;[212]

— require the IRO's final external review decision to contain: a general description of the reason for the external review;[213] the date the IRO was assigned the external review and

---

[195] Tech. Rel. 2010-01, at 4. If the plan fails to comply with this requirement, the IRO *may* decide to reverse the determination made by the group health plan, which determination, if made, must be communicated in writing to the group health plan and claimant within one business day. Thus, it appears that the IRO has discretion to decide the claim based on such documents and information provided by the group health plan within the five-day period, even if incomplete. No provision is made in the interim enforcement safe harbor for the group health plan to provide such documents or information to the IRO after the expiration of the five-day period or any other documents or information. Thus, it is not clear whether the IRO is precluded from considering anything submitted by the group health plan that is not among the documents and information considered by the group health plan in making the adverse determination, which is provided to the IRO within the five-day period.

[196] Tech. Rel. 2010-01, at 5.

[197] Tech. Rel. 2010-01, at 5.

[198] Tech. Rel. 2010-01, at 5.

[199] Tech. Rel. 2010-01, at 5.

[200] Tech. Rel. 2010-01, at 5.

[201] Tech. Rel. 2010-01, at 5.

[202] Tech. Rel. 2010-01, at 5.

[203] Tech. Rel. 2010-01, at 5.

[204] Tech. Rel. 2010-01, at 5.

[205] Tech. Rel. 2010-01, at 5.

[206] Tech. Rel. 2010-01, at 5.

[207] Tech. Rel. 2010-01, at 5.

[208] Tech. Rel. 2010-01, at 5.

[209] Tech. Rel. 2010-01, at 5.

[210] See discussion of the strict timing deadlines in an expedited review accompanying notes 226 and 227 *infra*.

[211] A Model Notice of Final External Review Decision is available at http://www.dol.gov/ebsa/healthreform/.

[212] Tech. Rel. 2010-01, at 5.

[213] Tech. Rel. 2010-01, at 6. The description must include "information sufficient to identify the claim (including the date or dates of service, the health care provider, the claim amount (if applicable), the diagnosis code and the corresponding meaning, the treatment code and its corresponding meaning, and the reason for the previous denial)."

the date on which the IRO made its decision;[214] identification of evidence considered by the IRO in making its decision;[215] a discussion of the principal reason(s) for the IRO's decision;[216] a statement that the determination is binding except to the extent that the claimant or group health plan may have other remedies available under state or federal law;[217] a statement that the claimant may have a right to judicial review;[218] and the current contact information for the applicable office of health insurance consumer assistance or ombudsman;[219] and

— if the IRO reverses the group health plan's adverse benefit determination or final adverse benefit determination, require the IRO to maintain records associated with the external review for six years and make them available, subject to state and federal privacy laws, to the claimant, the group health plan, and any state or federal oversight agency.[220]

- If the IRO reverses the group health plan's adverse benefit determination or final adverse benefit determination, the group health plan must immediately provide the coverage or reimburse the expense that was the subject of the IRO's reversal.[221]

[b] Federal External Review—Request Eligible for Expedited External Review

A request for external review is eligible for expedited external review in the following circumstances:

- A claimant has received an adverse benefit determination, the claimant has filed a request for an expedited internal appeal of the adverse benefit determination, and the time frame for completion of the expedited internal appeal would seriously jeopardize the life or health of the claimant or the claimant's ability to regain maximum function.[222]

- A claimant has received a final internal adverse benefit determination and the time frame for completion of the external appeal would seriously jeopardize the life or health of the claimant or the claimant's ability to regain maximum function, or involves a final internal adverse benefit determination for a claimant who has received emergency care at a facility from which the claimant has not been discharged and concerns a health care item or service, admission, availability of care, or continued stay.[223]

Except to the extent described below, an expedited external review is subject to the same requirements as a regular external review.

- The group health plan's preliminary review must occur immediately, and the group health plan must provide all necessary documents and information to the IRO using an expeditious method.[224]

---

[214] Tech. Rel. 2010-01, at 6.

[215] Tech. Rel. 2010-01, at 6. Any specific coverage provisions or evidence-based standards must be identified.

[216] Tech. Rel. 2010-01, at 6. This must include the rationale for the decision and any evidence-based standards relied upon in making the decision.

[217] Tech. Rel. 2010-01, at 6.

[218] Tech. Rel. 2010-01, at 6.

[219] Tech. Rel. 2010-01, at 6. See **Section 8.05[C]** for a discussion of the office of health insurance consumer assistance or ombudsman.

[220] Tech. Rel. 2010-01, at 6.

[221] Tech. Rel. 2010-01, at 6.

[222] Tech. Rel. 2010-01, at 6–7.

[223] Tech. Rel. 2010-01, at 7.

[224] Tech. Rel. 2010-01, at 7.

• The group health plan must assign an IRO when the group health plan determines the request for external review is eligible for expedited external review.[225]

The IRO must notify the claimant and the group health plan of the IRO's final external review decision as expeditiously as required by the claimant's medical condition or circumstances and in no event more than 72 hours after the expedited external review is assigned to the IRO.[226] If such notice is initially provided orally, the IRO must confirm its decision in writing to the claimant and the plan within 48 hours.[227]

[C]   Office of Health Insurance Consumer Assistance or Ombudsman Established

The Affordable Care Act provides funding for states to establish offices of health insurance consumer assistance or ombudsman.[228] To receive such funding, a state must create an independent position that deals with issues concerning "health insurance coverage with respect to federal health insurance requirements and under state law."[229] The Act generally uses the term "health insurance coverage" when referring to health insurance offered by insurance carriers.[230] One of this position's duties is to provide assistance to enrollees filing internal appeals with group health plans or health insurance issuers.

§ 8.06   Prohibitions on Rescissions

Another coverage improvement added by the Affordable Care Act is a prohibition on the cancellation or rescission of coverage by a group health plan or a health insurance issuer offering group or individual health insurance coverage of an enrollee once the enrollee is covered under the plan or coverage.[231]

Rescission is permitted, however, where a covered individual has performed an act, practice, or omission that constitutes fraud, or where the individual makes an intentional misrepresentation of material fact.[232]

The plan or issuer must provide at least 30 days' advance written notice to the participant or subscriber before coverage can be rescinded.[233] For purposes of these rules, a "rescission" is a cancellation or termination of coverage that has retroactive effect (for example, a cancellation that treats coverage as void from the outset), or a cancellation that voids benefits paid up to a year before the cancellation.[234] This 30-day advance notice requirement is intended to provide the individual with an effective opportunity to challenge or question the rescission before it goes into effect.

Coverage cannot be rescinded for an inadvertent omission. The regulations include the example of an individual who enrolled for coverage by completing a questionnaire regarding prior medical history. The questionnaire included a general question asking, "Is there anything else relevant to your health that we should know?" The individual inadvertently failed to list that he visited a psychologist

---

[225] Tech. Rel. 2010-01, at 7.

[226] Tech. Rel. 2010-01, at 7.

[227] Tech. Rel. 2010-01, at 7.

[228] PPACA § 1002 (adding PHSA § 2793).

[229] PHSA § 2793.

[230] See **Chapter 4** note 4 and accompanying text (defining health insurance coverage).

[231] PPACA § 1001 (adding PHSA § 2712).

[232] PHSA § 2712; 26 C.F.R. § 54.9815-2712T(a)(1); 29 C.F.R. § 2590.715-2712(a)(1); 45 C.F.R. § 147.128(a)(1).

[233] 26 C.F.R. § 54.9815-2712T(a)(1); 29 C.F.R. § 2590.715-2712(a)(1); 45 C.F.R. § 147.128(a)(1). *See* Tri-Agency Regulations on Preexisting Condition Exclusions, Lifetime and Annual Limits, Rescissions and Patient Protections, 75 Fed. Reg. 37,188–241 (June 28, 2010), *available at* http://webapps.dol.gov/FederalRegister/PdfDisplay.aspx?DocId=23983.

[234] 26 C.F.R. § 54.9815-2712T(a)(2); 29 C.F.R. § 2590.715-2712(a)(2); 45 C.F.R. § 147.128(a)(2).

on two occasions, six years previously. The individual is later diagnosed with breast cancer and seeks benefits. The plan cannot rescind coverage on the basis of the individual's failure to disclose the psychologist visits, because the omission was inadvertent and was neither fraudulent nor the intentional misrepresentation of material fact.[235]

Coverage under a group health plan or health insurance generally may be cancelled only with notice and only as permitted under the law.[236] Generally, coverage may only be nonrenewed or discontinued by a health insurance issuer for the following reasons:[237]

- Nonpayment of premiums;

- Fraud;

- Termination of the plan, where the issuer is ceasing to offer coverage in the individual market in accordance with applicable state law;

- Movement outside the service area—where an individual no longer resides, lives, or works in the service area (or in an area for which the issuer is authorized to do business), but only if such coverage is terminated uniformly without regard to any health status–related factor of covered individuals; or

- Association membership ceases—in the case of health insurance coverage that is made available in the individual market only through one or more bona fide associations, the membership of the individual in the association (on the basis of which the coverage is provided) ceases, but only if such coverage is terminated uniformly without regard to any health status–related factor of covered individuals.[238]

The last provision will affect mostly individual health insurance coverage, as most group health plans are already subject to such prohibitions under HIPAA.[239]

§ 8.07 Patient Protections

[A] Designation of Primary Care Physician

The Affordable Care Act imposes on group health plans (self-funded and insured), and on individual health insurance coverage offered through an issuer, new requirements relating to a participant's choice of health care professional.[240] Three requirements relate to plans with network designs. A fourth requirement, relating to emergency services, applies to any type of plan. None of these requirements applies to grandfathered health plans.[241]

If a plan or policy requires a participant or beneficiary to designate a primary care provider, then the plan or issuer must permit each participant or beneficiary to designate any participating primary care provider who is available to accept such individual. The interim final regulations expand upon

---

[235] 26 C.F.R. § 54.9815-2712T(a)(3); 29 C.F.R. § 2590.715-2712(a)(3); 45 C.F.R. § 147.128(a)(3).

[236] PHSA § 2702.

[237] PHSA § 2742.

[238] PHSA § 2712 (citing PHSA § 2742(b) for cancellation with notice provisions); 26 C.F.R. § 54.9815-2712T; 29 C.F.R. § 2590.715-2712; 45 C.F.R. § 147.128.

[239] PHSA §§ 2731 (as renumbered by PPACA § 1001(3)) (guaranteeing availability of insurance coverage in the small-group market), 2702 (guaranteeing availability of insurance coverage for certain individuals).

[240] PHSA § 2719A.

[241] 26 C.F.R. § 54.9815-2719AT; 29 C.F.R. § 2590.715-2719A; 45 C.F.R. § 147.138.

the statutory provision and provide that a plan or issuer must permit the designation of a primary care physician specializing in pediatrics if the covered person is a child.[242]

In addition, if a plan or policy provides coverage for obstetrical or gynecological care, a female participant or beneficiary seeking such care cannot be required to first obtain an authorization from the primary care physician in order to see an in-network specialist for obstetrical or gynecological care. This provision is not intended to preclude a plan or issuer from requiring the obstetrician or gynecologist to comply with the plan's or policy's rules and procedures relating to pre-authorizations or referrals for certain items and services. The regulations also make it clear that these patient rights apply to health care professionals, a definition that includes any individual who is authorized under applicable state law to provide obstetrical or gynecological care, and not limited to a physician.[243]

Notice must be provided to each participant or beneficiary describing each of their rights with respect to the designation of a physician. The regulation includes model language:[244]

(A)   For plans and issuers that require or allow for the designation of primary care providers by participants or beneficiaries:

> *[Name of group health plan or health insurance issuer] generally [requires/allows] the designation of a primary care provider. You have the right to designate any primary care provider who participates in our network and who is available to accept you or your family members. [If the plan or health insurance coverage designates a primary care provider automatically, insert: Until you make this designation, [name of group health plan or health insurance issuer] designates one for you.] For information on how to select a primary care provider, and for a list of the participating primary care providers, contact the [plan administrator or issuer] at [insert contact information].*

(B)   For plans and issuers that require or allow for the designation of a primary care provider for a child, add:

> *For children, you may designate a pediatrician as the primary care provider.*

(C)   For plans and issuers that provide coverage for obstetric or gynecological care and require the designation by a participant or beneficiary of a primary care provider, add:

> *You do not need prior authorization from [name of group health plan or issuer] or from any other person (including a primary care provider) in order to obtain access to obstetrical or gynecological care from a health care professional in our network who specializes in obstetrics or gynecology. The health care professional, however, may be required to comply with certain procedures, including obtaining prior authorization for certain services, following a pre-approved treatment plan, or procedures for making referrals. For a list of participating health care professionals who specialize in obstetrics or gynecology, contact the [plan administrator or issuer] at [insert contact information].*

[B]   Coverage of Emergency Services

If a group health plan (self-funded or insured) provides any benefits with respect to services in the emergency department of a hospital, coverage must be provided:

---

[242] 26 C.F.R. § 54.9815-2719AT(a)(2); 29 C.F.R. § 2590.715-2719A(a)(2); 45 C.F.R. § 147.138(a)(2). *See* Tri-Agency Regulations on Preexisting Condition Exclusions, Lifetime and Annual Limits, Rescissions and Patient Protections, 75 Fed. Reg. 37,188–241 (June 28, 2010), *available at* http://webapps.dol.gov/FederalRegister/PdfDisplay.aspx?DocId=23983.

[243] 26 C.F.R. § 54.9815-2719AT(a)(3)(i)(B); 29 C.F.R. § 2590.715-2719A(a)(3)(i)(B); 45 C.F.R. § 147.138(a)(3)(i)(B).

[244] 26 C.F.R. § 54.9815-2719AT(a)(4)(iii); 29 C.F.R. § 2590.715-2719A(a)(4)(iii); 45 C.F.R. § 147.138(a)(4)(iii).

- Without the need for any prior authorization determination, even if provided on an out-of-network basis;

- Without regard to whether the health care provider furnishing the emergency services is a participating provider;

- If emergency services are provided out-of-network, without imposing any administrative requirement or limitation on coverage that is more restrictive than the requirements that apply to an in-network provider;

- If emergency services are provided out-of-network, without imposing cost-sharing requirements (copayments and co-insurance amounts) that exceed the cost-sharing requirements applicable to an in-network provider (although the participant may be required to pay the excess of charges over the amount the plan or policy pays the out-of-network provider based on, e.g., its determination of reasonable and customary charges, i.e., balance billing is permitted); and

- Without regard to any other term or condition of coverage other than the exclusion of or coordination of benefits, and applicable waiting period and cost-sharing.

The regulations require a plan or policy to pay an out-of-network provider of emergency services a reasonable amount for its services. A plan or issuer satisfies the copayment and co-insurance provisions if it pays an out-of-network provider an amount equal to the greatest of (1) the negotiated contract rate with in-network providers (or the median thereof), (2) the amount calculated using the same method that the plan generally uses to determine payments for out-of-network services (e.g., the plan can continue to limit benefits to amounts not in excess of reasonable and customary charges) but substituting the in-network cost-sharing provisions for the out-of-network cost-sharing provisions, or (3) the amount Medicare would pay for the service.[245]

The regulations define the terms *emergency medical condition, emergency services,* and *stabilize* consistent with the definitions found in the Emergency Medical Treatment and Labor Act (EMTALA),[246] except that the definition of an emergency medical condition is based on the judgment of a prudent layperson, whereas the standard in EMTALA is based on the judgment of qualified hospital medical personnel. "Emergency medical condition" is defined as a medical condition manifesting itself by acute symptoms of sufficient severity (including severe pain) so that a prudent layperson who possesses an average knowledge of health and medicine could reasonably expect the absence of immediate medical attention to place his or her health in serious jeopardy, or to result in serious impairment of bodily functions or serious dysfunction of any bodily organ or part.[247] "Emergency services" includes emergency screening and treatment sufficient to stabilize the patient.

---

[245] 26 C.F.R. § 54.9815-2719AT(b)(3); 29 C.F.R. § 2590.715-2719A(b)(3); 45 C.F.R. § 147.138(b)(3).
[246] Section 1867 of the Social Security Act, 42 U.S.C. § 1395dd.
[247] 26 C.F.R. § 54.9815-2719AT(b)(4)(i); 29 C.F.R. § 2590.715-2719A(b)(4)(i); 45 C.F.R. § 147.138(b)(4)(i).

CHAPTER 9

IMPROVEMENTS EFFECTIVE JANUARY 1, 2014

A number of the most important coverage reforms become effective as of January 1, 2014,[1] when the Exchanges become available for individuals and certain small employers, and the employer and individual coverage mandates also become effective.[2] These reforms include prohibitions on preexisting conditions for individuals age 19 and older, guaranteed issue and renewability, fair insurance premium pricing requirements, health status discrimination prohibitions, and limitations on annual cost-sharing and deductible requirements. In coordinating the timing of the reforms with the mandates, Congress acknowledged that without the mandates, the insurance market reforms may lead to unsustainable adverse selection, particularly for the individual insurance market. If you prohibit preexisting-condition exclusion provisions and require guaranteed eligibility for enrollment in the individual insurance market, but do not mandate continuous coverage, individuals may only buy coverage when they need it. This is contrary to sound insurance principles and financing of risk. As described in detail in **Chapter 3**, the individual mandate has survived constitutional challenge and has been upheld by the United States Supreme Court as an exercise of the federal government's taxing power.

Most of the market reforms discussed in this chapter apply to coverage offered by health insurance issuers, either in individual or group health plan coverage. The Health Insurance Portability and Accountability Act (HIPAA) imposed many of those reforms on employer group health plans in the late 1990s. There are a few new reforms that also apply to self-funded group health plans and a few of the reforms apply to grandfathered health plans. The sections that follow describe in detail the types of plans subject to the requirements.

§ 9.01 Prohibitions on Preexisting-Coverage Exclusions or Other Discrimination Based on Health Status

The Affordable Care Act prohibits all preexisting-condition exclusions by group health plans and individual health coverage offered by health insurance issuers beginning on January 1, 2014.[3] Health insurers as well as group health plans will be prohibited from imposing certain preexisting-condition exclusions and establishing eligibility based on health status–related factors of the individual or a dependent of an individual. These provisions apply to grandfathered health plans.

[A] Prohibition on Preexisting-Condition Exclusions

Preexisting-condition exclusions generally have been limited for employment-based health care coverage since the adoption of HIPAA in 1996.[4] Under HIPAA, employer group health plans subject to the Employee Retirement Income Security Act of 1974 (ERISA) are prohibited from excluding an employee or eligible dependent from health care coverage on the basis of a preexisting condition as long the individual maintained "creditable coverage" without a gap of more than 63 days. If the individual did not have the required continuous coverage, an employer health plan could limit coverage for the condition for up to one year.

Under the Affordable Care Act, effective January 1, 2014, no preexisting-condition exclusions will be permitted for group health plans or individual health insurance policies, regardless of whether continuous coverage has been maintained.

---

[1] These reforms are found in Subtitle C of Title I of the Act.

[2] See **Chapter 11** for a discussion of the Exchanges and the individual and employer coverage mandates.

[3] PPACA § 1201 (adding PHSA § 2704).

[4] 42 U.S.C. § 300gg(a).

As previously discussed, no preexisting-condition exclusion limitation is applicable to enrollees under age 19 in the individual or group insurance markets for plan years beginning on or after September 23, 2010.[5] The elimination of *all* preexisting-condition exclusions from employer group and individual insurance markets is one of the most significant health insurance reforms.

[B] Prohibitions on Discrimination Based on Health Status

The Affordable Care Act extends health status discrimination prohibitions to the individual health insurance coverage market beginning in 2014.[6] This change imposes on issuers of individual health insurance coverage the health status discrimination, premium contribution restrictions, genetic information discrimination, genetic testing limitations, and genetic data collection prohibitions currently applicable to employer group health plans.[7]

The following factors related to health status are specified currently in the PHSA:

- Health status;
- Medical condition;
- Claims experience;
- Receipt of health care;
- Medical history;
- Genetic information;
- Evidence of insurability (including conditions arising out of acts of domestic violence); and
- Disability.

The Affordable Care Act authorizes HHS to add any other health status factor determined to be appropriate.

[C] Employer Health and Wellness Programs

The Affordable Care Act provides that health promotion and disease prevention programs offered by an employer that meet certain requirements will not violate the prohibition on discrimination on the basis of health status.[8]

An employer may offer a premium discount, rebate, or other reward for participation in a wellness program if the reward is not conditioned upon an individual's satisfying a standard that is related to a health status factor.[9] A reward may be in the form of a discount or rebate of a premium or contribution, a waiver of all or part of a cost-sharing obligation (such as deductibles, copayments, or co-insurance), the absence of a surcharge, or the value of a benefit that would otherwise not be provided by the plan.[10] If the employer desires to condition the reward upon an individual's satisfying a standard that is related to a health status factor, additional requirements are imposed. They include:

---

[5] See **Section 8.02**.
[6] PPACA § 1201 (adding PHSA § 2705).
[7] 42 U.S.C. § 300gg-1.
[8] PPACA § 1201 (adding PHSA § 2705(j)).
[9] PHSA § 2705(j)(2).
[10] PHSA § 2705(j)(2).

- The reward may not exceed 30 percent of the cost of employee-only coverage or, if dependents are fully eligible for the wellness program, 30 percent of the cost of such coverage (the total of the employer and employee contributions) under the plan;

- The program must be reasonably designed to promote health or prevent disease (i.e., has a reasonable chance of improving health or preventing disease and is not a subterfuge for discriminating based on health status);

- Eligible individuals must be given the opportunity to qualify for the reward at least once each year;

- The full reward must be made available to all similarly situated individuals; and

- The plan or issuer involved must describe the availability of the reasonable alternative (or possibility of a waiver) in any plan materials that describe the terms of the wellness program.[11]

To be available to all similarly situated individuals, the reward program must include a reasonable alternative standard (or waiver of the applicable standard) for obtaining the reward for any individual for whom it is unreasonably difficult or medically inadvisable, due to a medical condition, to satisfy the conditions of the reward.[12] The plan or issuer may seek verification from the individual's physician to substantiate the unreasonableness or medical inadvisability of the condition.[13] Existing employer wellness programs that meet all applicable regulations may continue for as long as the regulations remain in effect.

[D] Wellness Program Demonstration Projects for Health Insurance Issuers

HHS is directed to establish a ten-state demonstration project by July 1, 2014, under which states may apply the employer wellness program provisions to insured plans.[14]

§ 9.02 Fair Health Insurance Premiums

To make coverage more affordable for everyone, the Affordable Care Act includes prohibitions on "discriminatory premium rates" charged by health insurance issuers for health insurance issued in the individual or small-group market and defines certain underwriting restrictions on the rate-setting of premiums.[15] These requirements apply to any coverage offered through a state Exchange to the large group market (defined as more than 100 employees unless a state elects to define the small-group market as no more than 50 employees, in which case the large-group market would be more than 50 employees).[16]

Under the Affordable Care Act, the premium rates for individual and small group health insurance coverage may vary with respect to a particular plan or coverage only by:

- Whether such plan covers an individual or family;

- Geographical rating areas to be established by each state;

- Permissible age bands to be established by HHS in consultation with the NAIC (except that the rate may not vary by more than 3 to 1 for adults); and

---

[11] PHSA § 2705(j)(3).
[12] PHSA § 2705(j)(3)(D).
[13] PHSA § 2705(j)(3)(D).
[14] PPACA § 1201 (adding PHSA § 2705(l)).
[15] PPACA § 1201 (adding PHSA § 2701).
[16] PHSA § 2701; see **Chapter 4** notes 7–9 (defining large- and small-group markets).

- Tobacco use (except that the rate may not vary by more than 1.5 to 1).[17]

Underwriting of premiums cannot be based on any other factor, including the claims experience of a small group.

The impact of these reforms on small employers' insured group health plans will depend on the demographics and claims experience of the group. If the group is younger and healthier than the average small group, the cost of coverage may increase. On the other hand, a small group of older participants with more medical needs or a small group with one or more individuals with substantial claims experience should be able to purchase coverage on a more affordable and stable premium basis. These provisions do not apply to grandfathered health plans.

§ 9.03 Guaranteed Issue and Renewability

Throughout the course of the health care reform debate, terrible stories were featured in the media about individuals losing their jobs and being uninsurable thereafter or having their coverage cancelled when the insurance company learned that the participant or a dependent now had a chronic or serious medical condition. The insurance market reforms are designed to end those insurance practices.

Beginning in 2014, each health insurance issuer that offers health insurance in the individual or group market in a state must accept every employer and every individual who applies for coverage.[18] The issuer may restrict enrollment to open or special enrollment periods as described in regulations to be published by HHS. Likewise, the Affordable Care Act requires each issuer to renew or continue in force the coverage at the option of the employer or the individual.[19] These provisions apply to grandfathered health plans.

§ 9.04 Prohibiting Discrimination Against Health Care Providers

Another provision of the Affordable Care Act that applies to both group health plans and health insurance issuers offering group or individual health insurance coverage, other than grandfathered health plans, prohibits discrimination against any health care provider who is acting within the scope of the provider's license or certification under applicable state law.[20] An example of the application of this provision is benefits coverage that covers acupuncture services only if provided by a licensed physician. If the state where the coverage is offered licenses acupuncturists and the services that are covered under the plan if provided by a physician are within the scope of the acupuncturist's license, the coverage would have to include services performed by the acupuncturist as well as the physician. This is a significant change for employment-based group health plans because they can no longer limit reimbursements to only certain types of providers (e.g., doctor vs. chiropractor).

This is not an "any willing provider" provision;[21] the Affordable Care Act specifies that a group health plan or insurance issuer shall not be required to contract with any health care provider willing to abide by the terms and conditions for participation established by the plan.[22] Thus, a plan can limit the number of participating providers in the network. A plan or issuer may also establish varying reimbursement rates based on quality or performance measures.

---

[17] PHSA § 2701(a).

[18] PPACA § 1201 (adding PHSA § 2702).

[19] PPACA § 1201 (adding PHSA § 2703).

[20] PPACA § 1201 (adding PHSA § 2706).

[21] *See* Kentucky Ass'n of Health Plans v. Nichols, 227 F.3d 352 (6th Cir. 2000) (considering ERISA preemption of the Kentucky AWP statute).

[22] PHSA § 2706.

§ 9.05   Quality Coverage Provisions

[A]   Comprehensive Benefits Coverage in Individual and Small-Group Markets

The Affordable Care Act's market reforms also require a health insurance issuer that offers health insurance coverage in the individual or small-group market to ensure that the coverage includes the essential health benefits package required for Exchange plans.[23] For a full description of those requirements, see **Section 11.04.**

[B]   Cost-Sharing Limits on Group Health Plans

Group health plans, other than grandfathered health plans, are required to ensure that any annual cost-sharing imposed under the plan does not exceed the limits imposed on Exchange plans.[24] Beginning in 2014, the cost-sharing limit is $2,000 for single coverage and $4,000 for family coverage.[25] See **Section 11.04[E]** for a more complete description of the annual cost-sharing limitations.

§ 9.06   Limits on Waiting Periods

Group health plans and health insurers offering group health insurance coverage may not impose any time-based waiting period for coverage in excess of 90 days.[26] According to IRS Notice 2012-59 (Aug. 30, 2012), a waiting period is the period of time that must pass before coverage for an otherwise eligible employee or dependent can become effective, and delays caused by the employee or dependent (e.g., lateness in filing forms) does not count against the waiting period. The impact of this requirement will be felt most acutely by employers with high-turnover workforces, which may currently have longer waiting periods to avoid the cost of coverage for short-term employees. In addition to increasing the cost of coverage for the employer, it may also increase the administrative burden on a group health plan with respect to COBRA continuation administration and elections by short-term employees to opt out of coverage initiated under the large-employer automatic enrollment provisions. See **Section 12.03** for more information on large-employer automatic enrollment requirements. In IRS Notice 2012-58 (Aug. 31, 2012), the IRS published guidance on a series of safe harbors that employers may use in determining how the waiting period applies to newly hired, variable-hour, and seasonal employees.

The Affordable Care Act's limitation on time-based waiting periods does not affect an employer's ability to impose other eligibility conditions on participation in its group health plan. For example, an employer is still permitted to limit group health plan participation to full-time employees. Any time-based waiting period measurement is expected to start on the date that the employee would otherwise be eligible for the group health plan (but for the waiting period).[27]

§ 9.07   Coverage for Individuals Participating in Approved Clinical Trials

Coverage for medical services provided to a participant in a clinical trial has long been a subject of debate and dispute. The Affordable Care Act clarifies the obligation of a group health plan or a

---

[23] PPACA § 1201 (adding PHSA § 2702(a)).

[24] PPACA § 1201 (adding PHSA § 2707(b)).

[25] PHSA § 2707(b) (referencing the deductible limit for HSAs, as set forth in Section 223(c)(2)(A)(ii) of the Code).

[26] PPACA § 1201 (adding PHSA § 2708).

[27] *See* I.R.S. Notice 2012-17, 2012-9 I.R.B. 430 (Feb. 9, 2012) (describing anticipated guidance on waiting periods).

health insurance issuer, other than grandfathered health plans, offering group or individual health coverage to cover routine patient costs that would be covered if the participant were not in a study.[28] The requirements are effective beginning January 1, 2014.

The clinical trial must be an approved phase I, II, III, or IV clinical trial that is a federally funded trial, an investigational new drug application subject to FDA review, or a drug trial that is exempt from having an investigational new drug application.[29] The clinical trial must be conducted in relation to the prevention, detection, or treatment of cancer or other life-threatening disease or condition, i.e., any disease or condition from which the likelihood of death is probable unless the course of the disease or condition is interrupted.[30]

A plan or insurance policy may not deny or impose additional conditions upon coverage of a qualified individual's routine patient costs for items or services furnished in connection with a study.[31] The individual must be eligible according to the trial protocol, and either the individual must be referred to the clinical trial by a participating health care provider or the participant or beneficiary must provide medical and scientific information establishing that the individual's participation in the study would be appropriate.[32] The plan is not required to cover the cost of the investigational item, device, or service itself, items that are provided solely to satisfy data collection and analysis needs and that are not used in direct clinical management of the patient, or any service that is clearly inconsistent with widely accepted standards of care.[33]

If a participating provider is participating in a clinical trial, a plan or issuer may require the participant to participate through a participating provider, if the provider will accept the participant in the study. If the study is conducted outside the state in which the participant resides, the plan or issuer must provide the coverage. If a plan or issuer does not provide coverage for out-of-network benefits, the plan or issuer is not obligated to provide benefits provided outside the coverage's health care provider network.[34]

---

[28] PPACA § 10103(c) (adding PHSA § 2709).

[29] PHSA § 2709(d).

[30] PHSA § 2709(e).

[31] PHSA § 2708(a)(2).

[32] PHSA § 2709(b).

[33] PHSA § 2709(b)(2)(B).

[34] PHSA § 2709(c).

CHAPTER 10

TRANSPARENCY AND ACCOUNTABILITY

The Affordable Care Act imposes numerous reporting and disclosure requirements on group health plans and health insurance issuers to make information about coverage options available to consumers. It also directs HHS to make most of that information available to the public on Web sites and a portal established for this purpose. Many of the data reporting and communication requirements begin during the transition period (March 23, 2010–January 1, 2014).

Since the law's enactment, a remarkable amount of information has been gathered and posted on Web sites established by HHS and related agencies. Thus far, the Health Care Reform portal (*http://www.healthcare.gov*) has been up and running in accordance with the ambitious timelines set forth in the Act. A wealth of information—including consumer-focused information, employer information, all of the proposed and final regulations and comments filed thereto, FAQs, listening sessions, press releases, forms, and guidance—is available on the Web site. The consumer information is very easy to navigate. The HHS regulations and other legal guidance materials are available at the Center for Consumer Information and Insurance Oversight (CCIIO) Web site (*http://cciio.cms.gov*). The health care coverage information and data that will be compiled from all the new reporting obligations of insurers and employers also will be posted. The Affordable Care Act's reporting requirements are imposed initially on insurers[1] but also imposed on employment-based group health plans. The goal is to have robust benefits information about available health insurance coverage and pricing of plans readily obtainable from the Web site before 2014.

§ 10.01   Uniform Summary of Benefits and Coverage

While the government has placed emphasis on making information available publicly on a Web site, the Web is not its exclusive method of communication. The law also prescribes the distribution of more traditional benefit summaries (available in electronic or hard copy) to employees and subscribers. The Affordable Care Act sets forth, in great detail, the standards for the summary, which must not exceed four double-sided pages in length nor include print smaller than 12-point type.[2] The requirement to provide a summary of benefits and coverage and a uniform glossary under Section 2715 of the PHSA and the final regulations applies for disclosures to participants and beneficiaries who enroll or re-enroll in group health coverage (through an open enrollment period if applicable or otherwise, including re-enrollees and late enrollees or those who are newly eligible or special enrollees), beginning on the first day of the first enrollment period if applicable, or if no enrollment period, the first day of the first plan year, that begins on or after September 23, 2012.[3] The purpose is to have each plan uniformly summarized so that an individual consumer can use the summary to compare health insurance coverage and understand the terms of his or her coverage.

[A]   Culturally and Linguistically Appropriate Communication

Each summary must be presented in a culturally and linguistically appropriate manner and utilize terminology understandable by the average plan enrollee.[4] HHS has issued national standards for culturally and linguistically appropriate services (CLAS) in health care.[5] CMS commissioned a paper on the subject, which defines these terms as follows.[6]

---

[1] The data reporting obligations on insurers beginning as early as the summer of 2010 are summarized at http://www.hhs.gov/cciio/gatheringinfo/index.html.

[2] PHSA § 2715(b)(1); Final Rule, Summary of Benefits and Coverage, 45 C.F.R. § 147.200 (2012).

[3] Preamble to Final Rule, Summary of Benefits and Coverage, 45 C.F.R. § 147.200 (2012).

[4] PHSA § 2715(b)(2).

[5] *See* http://minorityhealth.hhs.gov/templates/browse.aspx?lvl=2&lvlID=15 (for health care organizations) and www.ahrq.gov/about/cods/planclas.htm (for managed care plans).

[6] Agency for Healthcare Research & Quality, What Is Cultural and Linguistic Competence? (Rockville, Md. Feb. 2003), http://www.ahrq.gov/about/cods/cultcompdef.htm.

Linguistic Competence: Providing readily available, culturally appropriate oral and written language services to limited English proficiency (LEP) members through such means as bilingual/bicultural staff, trained medical interpreters, and qualified translators.

Cultural Competence: A set of congruent behaviors, attitudes, and policies that come together in a system or agency or among professionals that enables effective interactions in a cross-cultural framework.

Cultural and Linguistic Competence: The ability of health care providers and health care organizations to understand and respond effectively to the cultural and linguistic needs brought by the patient to the health care encounter.

Cultural competence requires organizations and their personnel to:

- Value diversity;

- Assess themselves;

- Manage the dynamics of difference;

- Acquire and institutionalize cultural knowledge; and

- Adapt to diversity and the cultural contexts of individuals and communities served.

There are currently 14 CLAS standards, of which four are mandated standards for all health care organizations and other recipients of federal funds.[7] The mandated standards include providing competent language assistance services, including interpreter services, at no cost to each patient/consumer with limited English proficiency at all points of contact in a timely manner during all hours of operation; verbal offers and written notices in the preferred language of the patients/consumers informing them of their right to receive language assistance; and providing patients/consumers with easily understood patient-related materials and signage in the languages of commonly encountered groups.[8] While these standards are applicable to health care providers, they are instructive to health plans as well. In order to satisfy the requirement that the summary be provided in a culturally and linguistically appropriate manner, a group health plan must follow the rules for providing notices with respect to claims and appeals set forth in the regulations. These rules generally require that for plans covering 100 or more participants at the beginning of the plan year:

- The plan must provide oral language services (such as a telephone customer assistance hotline) that include answering questions in any applicable non-English language;

- The plan must provide, upon request, a summary in any applicable non-English language; and

- The plan must include in the English versions of all summaries, a statement prominently displayed in any applicable non-English language clearly indicating how to access the language services provided by the plan.[9]

---

[7] *See* http://minorityhealth.hhs.gov/templates/browse.aspx?lvl=2&lvlID=15.

[8] *See* http://minorityhealth.hhs.gov/templates/browse.aspx?lvl=2&lvlID=15. *See also* Henry J. Kaiser Family Found., *Compendium of Cultural Competence*, Initiatives in Health Care (Jan. 2003), *at* http://www.kff.org/uninsured/loader.cfm?url=/commonspot/security/getfile.cfm&PageID=14365.

[9] 45 C.F.R. § 147.136(e). Sample statements in applicable non-English languages may be found at http://cciio.cms.gov/resources/files/sbc-template-doc.DOC.

A non-English language is an applicable non-English language if 10 percent or more of the population residing in the county is literate only in the same non-English language as determined in guidance published by HHS.[10]

The foregoing requirements also apply to plans covering fewer than 100 participants at the beginning of the plan year, if the plan provides notices upon request in a non-English language in which 25 percent or more of all plan participants are literate only in the same non-English language.[11]

[B] Use of Uniform Definitions of Standard Insurance Terms and Medical Terms

The Act directs HHS, in consultation with the National Association of Insurance Commissioners (NAIC), to issue, within 12 months of the enactment of the law, standard definitions of insurance-related and medical terms to be used in the summary and other communications with individuals.[12] On February 14, 2012, HHS and the related agencies published final regulations pertaining to the uniform glossary and have made a copy available to plans via the Internet.[13] The final regulations direct plans to make the uniform glossary available upon request within seven business days. A plan may satisfy this requirement by providing an Internet address in the summary of benefits and coverage.[14] The insurance-related terms include terms such as:

- Premium;
- Deductible;
- Co-insurance;
- Copayment;
- Out-of-pocket limit;
- Preferred provider;
- Non-preferred provider;
- Out-of-network copayments;
- Usual, customary, and reasonable (UCR) fees;
- Excluded services;
- Grievance and appeals;

and other terms that HHS determines are important to define.

The medical terms to be defined include:

- Hospitalization;
- Hospital outpatient care;
- Emergency room care;
- Physician services;
- Prescription drug coverage;

---

[10] *See* http://cciio.cms.gov/resources/factsheets/clas-data.html (list of counties provided by CMS and applicable non-English languages, which the regulations provide must be updated each year).

[11] 45 C.F.R. § 147.136(e).

[12] PHSA § 2715(a).

[13] See the uniform glossary, available at *http://cciio.cms.gov/resources/files/Files2/02102012/uniform-glossary-final.pdf.*

[14] 45 C.F.R. § 147.200.

- Durable medical equipment;

- Home health care;

- Skilled nursing care;

- Rehabilitation services;

- Hospice services;

- Emergency medical transportation;

and such other terms as HHS determines are important to define.[15]

[C] Benefits Description

The final regulations provide guidance on the content and appearance requirements of the summary. In addition, HHS and the related agencies have provided two sets of frequently asked questions intended to assist plans with specific content, format, and method of delivery guidance related to the summary.[16] A sample template and completed template of the summary were also made available by HHS and the related agencies.[17]

The summary must describe the benefits coverage, including:

1. Cost-sharing for each of the categories of the essential health benefits[18] and other benefits, as identified by HHS;

2. Any exceptions, reductions, and limitations on coverage;

3. The cost-sharing provisions, including deductible, co-insurance, and copayment obligations;

4. The renewability and continuation of coverage provisions;

5. A coverage facts label that includes examples to illustrate common benefits scenarios, including pregnancy and serious or chronic medical conditions and related cost-sharing, with such scenarios based on recognized clinical practice guidelines;

6. A statement of whether the plan or coverage provides minimum essential coverage (as defined under Section 5000A(f) of the Code), and whether it ensures that the share of the total allowed costs of benefits provided under the plan or coverage is not less than 60 percent of costs (the preamble to the final regulations provides that this information is not required until other elements of the Affordable Care Act are implemented, but that this information must be included for summaries related to coverage beginning on or after January 1, 2014, and will be addressed in future guidance);

7. A statement that the outline is a summary of the plan, policy, or certificate and that the plan or coverage document itself should be consulted to determine the governing contractual provisions; and

8. A contact number for the individual to call with additional questions and an Internet Web address where a copy of the actual plan document, individual coverage policy, or group certificate of coverage can be reviewed and obtained.[19]

---

[15] PHSA § 2715(g).

[16] See FAQs About Affordable Care Act Implementation (Part VIII) (Mar. 19, 2012) and (Part IX) (May 11, 2012).

[17] See http://cciio.cms.gov/resources/other/index.html#5bcug. The sample blank and completed templates are in **Appendix P**.

[18] Essential health benefits are defined in Section 1302(b) of the PPACA. See **Section 11.04[C][1]**.

[19] PHSA § 2715(b)(3).

If a plan makes any material modifications in any of the terms involved, the summary must be updated to provide notice of the modification to enrollees not later than 60 days prior to the date that the modification becomes effective.[20] By way of comparison, the current requirement applicable to employment-based group health plans subject to ERISA is that notice of any material reduction in coverage must be provided not later than 60 days *after* its date of adoption.[21]

Any entity that willfully fails to provide the notice shall be subject to a fine of not more than $1,000 for each such failure. A failure with respect to each enrollee shall constitute a separate offense for purposes of this fine.[22]

§ 10.02 Reporting on Claims Practices and Plan Financing

Another transparency provision requires group health plans and health insurers in the group health and individual markets (other than grandfathered health plans) to submit accurate and timely disclosures to participants of group health plans of plan terms and conditions, periodic financial disclosures, and other information required by standards to be established by HHS.[23] The information covers such items as claims payment policies and practices, cost-sharing and claims payments information, and information on enrollee and participant rights.[24] The information must be submitted to HHS and the state insurance commission, and made available to the public.[25]

§ 10.03 Quality-of-Care Reporting

For years, the federal government has attempted to drive various quality-of-care initiatives through Medicare reimbursement policies. Under the Affordable Care Act, these efforts are expanded to the group health plan and health insurance market (other than grandfathered health plans). The law requires that HHS have issued regulations by March 23, 2012, providing criteria for determining whether the reimbursement structures of a group health plan or health insurance coverage improve health outcomes, prevent hospital readmissions, improve patient safety, reduce medical errors, and promote health and wellness activities.[26] Each group health plan and health insurance issuer will be required to report annually regarding the extent to which the design of its plan or coverage satisfies the criteria.[27] No regulations have been issued as of September 2012, but, in the comments to the final rule on the establishment of state Exchanges, HHS indicates that the transparency reporting requirements under Section 2715A of the ACA will be aligned within the Exchange reporting rules.

The reports will be filed with HHS and the state Exchanges and will be made available to enrollees or potential enrollees during each open enrollment period.[28] HHS also will make the reports available to the public through the Web portal, *http://www.healthcare.gov*.[29] The regulations may include appropriate penalties for noncompliance with the reporting obligation.

HHS must develop the reporting criteria in consultation with experts in health care quality and stakeholders. The criteria must address implementation activities such as quality reporting, effective

---

[20] PHSA § 2715(d)(4) (referencing ERISA § 102 for a description of what constitutes a material modification).
[21] 29 C.F.R. § 2520.104b-3(d).
[22] PHSA § 2715(f).
[23] PPACA § 10101(c) (adding PHSA § 2715A).
[24] PHSA § 2715A (referencing PPACA § 1311(e)(3)).
[25] PHSA § 2715A.
[26] PPACA § 1001 (adding PHSA § 2717).
[27] PHSA § 2717(a)(2).
[28] PHSA § 2717(a)(2).
[29] PHSA § 2717(a)(2)(C).

case management, care coordination, chronic disease management, and medication and care compliance initiatives, including the use of the medical homes model[30] for treatments and services under the plan or coverage.[31]

In addition, the Affordable Care Act suggests that health plans should have reimbursement structures that address provider performance by implementing activities to prevent hospital readmissions through a comprehensive program for hospital discharge that includes patient-centered education and counseling, comprehensive discharge planning, and post-discharge reinforcement by an appropriate health care professional.[32] Likewise, plans will have to report on their activities addressing patient safety and medical error reduction through the appropriate use of best clinical practices, evidence-based medicine, and health information technology. For health plans, these provisions are designed to encourage the private payer market (employer plans and insured plans) to adopt programs similar to those initiated by Medicare. For example, with respect to medical error reduction, in 2008 Medicare began reducing reimbursement for claims of hospitals for readmissions attributable to certain hospital-acquired conditions and health care providers for services related to incidents that Medicare classified as serious, preventable errors, commonly referred to as "never events." The National Quality Forum has compiled a list of Serious Reportable Events (SREs) to help the health care industry assess, measure, and report performance in providing safe care.[33] The "never-event" conditions include:

- Wrong surgical or other invasive procedures performed on a patient;

- Surgical or other invasive procedures performed on the wrong body part;

- Surgical or other invasive procedures performed on the wrong patient;

- Objects left in after surgery;

- Air embolisms;

- Blood incompatibility;

- Pressure ulcers;

- Falls in the hospital;

- Catheter-associated urinary tract infections;

- Catheter-associated vascular infections;

- Mediastinitis after coronary artery bypass graft surgery (CABG);

- Inadequate glycemic control;

- Surgical site infections;

- Deep vein thrombosis and pulmonary embolism; and

- Drug-induced delirium.[34]

---

[30] A medical home is an evolving approach to managing the medical care of patients through their primary care physician. A new generation of the gatekeeper model of reimbursement, focused on quality outcomes and chronic disease management, it is a team-based model of care led by a personal physician who provides continuous and coordinated care throughout a patient's lifetime to maximize health outcomes. American Academy of Family Physicians, American Academy of Pediatrics, American College of Physicians, & American Osteopathic Ass'n, Joint principles of the patient-centered medical home (Mar. 2007), http://www.acponline.org/advocacy/where_we_stand/medical_home/approve_jp.pdf.

[31] PHSA § 2717(a)(1)(A).

[32] PHSA § 2717(a)(1).

[33] See 77 Fed. Reg. 18,417 (Mar. 27, 2012). A list of the current National Quality Forum SREs can be found at its Web site, http://www.qualityforum.org.

[34] Medicare Benefit Policy Manual, http://www.cms.gov/manuals/Downloads.

Medicare has also initiated various pay-for-performance and other reimbursement programs to provide financial incentives for improved health quality outcomes. These are the types of reimbursement structures that HHS will most likely address when it issues the quality reporting regulations. CMS's proposed clinical quality measures for 2014 are posted on its Web site.[35]

Finally, each plan or issuer will have to report on its health and wellness programs.[36] The Affordable Care Act's definition of health and wellness programs includes:

- Smoking cessation;

- Weight management;

- Stress management;

- Physical fitness;

- Nutrition;

- Heart disease prevention;

- Healthy lifestyle support; and

- Diabetes prevention.[37]

The Affordable Care Act's health and wellness provisions include an express protection of each individual health plan member's Second Amendment right to own or possess a gun.[38] The Act prohibits a health and wellness program provided under a plan or coverage from collecting any data relating to the presence or storage of a lawfully possessed firearm or ammunition in the residence or on the property of an individual or the lawful use, possession, or storage of a firearm or ammunition by an individual.[39] Accordingly, no health risk assessment program can include questions about firearms or ammunition in the home. HHS is prohibited from collecting any such information and the Act shall not be construed as authorizing the collection of any data or maintenance of any records or data banks with any such information. Further, a premium rate may not be increased on the basis of an individual's ownership or residency in a home where firearms or ammunition are possessed or stored.

The first quality outcomes reports will need to be filed by health plans shortly after the publication of the regulations, as the Affordable Care Act calls for an independent report on the impact of the reporting six months later.[40] Not later than 180 days after the publication of the regulations, the Government Accountability Office is supposed to report to committees of the U.S. Senate and House of Representatives on the impact that the activities have had on the quality and cost of health care.

§ 10.04 Containing the Cost of Health Insurance Coverage

To generate immediate change in the health insurance markets in advance of the introduction of the Exchanges in 2014, there are three measures that take effect immediately. Two address health insurance issuers only (and not employment-based group health plans that are self-funded) and relate to the use of premium revenues. The third relates to the transparency of hospital charges.

---

[35] http://www.cms.gov/Medicare/Quality-Initiatives-Patient-Assessment-Instruments/QualityMeasures/ProposedClinicalQuality Measuresfor2014.html.

[36] PHSA § 2717(b).

[37] PHSA § 2717(b).

[38] PHSA § 2717(c).

[39] PHSA § 2717(b).

[40] PHSA § 2717(e).

[A]   Rebates from Insurers for Excessive Medical Loss Ratios

[1]   Reporting Premium Revenues and Coverage Expenses

With the aim of bringing down the cost of health insurance, beginning January 1, 2011, the Affordable Care Act requires all health insurance issuers offering group or individual health insurance coverage to track and report publicly their premium revenues and the amounts expended from those revenues on major categories of costs such as clinical services to enrollees, health care quality improvement program costs, and all other non-claims costs and administrative expenses.[41]

In addition, the law establishes medical loss ratio (MLR) standards for insurers. If an insurer's MLR exceeds the established threshold for the coverage, the insurer is required to rebate to the group or individual enrollees a portion of the premium paid, starting in 2012. The first rebate payments were issued by insurers on or before August 1, 2012. The intent of the rebate provisions is to provide value to the policyholders but also to create incentives for the insurers to become more efficient in their operations. The law charged the NAIC with the responsibility of making recommendations to HHS on the appropriate definitions and MLR methodologies by December 31, 2010. The NAIC released its recommendations in November 2010, and HHS acted upon them in Interim Regulations published on December 1, 2010.[42]

The annual rebate provision applies to grandfathered health insurance coverage. Self-funded plans are not subject to the MLR reporting and rebate provisions of the Act.

For the large-group market,[43] the MLR standard is 85 percent, and for the small-group and individual markets,[44] the MLR standards are 80 percent. The law gives the Secretary of HHS the authority to adjust the MLR in the individual market in a state. As of July 1, 2012, 18 states had applied for adjustments.[45]

The disclosure and reporting obligations include annual reports to HHS, reporting the required information on a state-by-state basis, aggregated separately for the large-group, small-group, and individual markets. Experience on each policy must be included in the report. There are several basic components that are the foundation of the MLR and the rebate provisions: premium revenue, incurred claims, health care quality improvement activities, and non-claims costs.

On the revenue side, the report must include earned premium revenue (with adjustments for high-risk pool subsidies, experience rating refunds, and unearned premiums).[46]

On the expense side, expenses for clinical services ("incurred claims") to be reported include (1) direct claims paid to providers (including capitated payments), (2) claims reserves for claims incurred but not reported during the MLR reporting year, (3) any change in contract reserves, (4) reserves for contingent benefits and contested claims, and (5) experience rating refunds paid or received. There are numerous adjustments that must deducted from incurred claims for items such as prescription drug rebates, provider overpayment recoveries, and incentive and bonus payments made to providers.[47]

---

[41] PPACA § 1001, adding PHSA § 2718.

[42] 75 Fed. Reg. 74,864–934 (Dec. 1, 2010). *See* HHS Regulations on Medical Loss Ratios, 75 Fed. Reg. 74,864–82,279 (Dec. 30, 2010).

[43] Large-group market is defined as the market for large employers, i.e., employers with an average of at least 101 employees in a plan year. PHSA § 2791(e)(3). Until 2016, a state may substitute 50 employees for 100 in the definition. 45 C.F.R. § 158.103. An employee is "any individual employed by employer," including all full-time and part-time employees. PHSA § 2791(d)(5).

[44] The small-group market includes small employer group plans and individual plans. A small employer for this purpose has no more than 100 employees (50 if in a state with an adjusted large-group plan definition). PHSA § 2791(e)(5); 45 C.F.R. § 158.103.

[45] *See* http://www.cciio.hhs.gov/programs/marketreforms/mlr/index.html for the states involved and the status of their applications.

[46] 45 C.F.R. § 158.30.

[47] 45 C.F.R. § 158.140.

To qualify as a health care quality improvement activity expense, the activity must improve health quality, increase the likelihood of desired health outcomes in ways that are capable of being objectively measured and producing verifiable results and achievements or be directed toward individual enrollees, and be grounded in evidence based medicine and widely accepted best clinical practice.[48] The activity must be primarily designed to improve outcomes, prevent hospital readmissions, improve patient safety, reduce medical errors and lower infection and mortality rates, and provide wellness and health activities. Examples of such activities include direct interaction with enrollees for case management, care coordination, chronic disease management, medication and care compliance, discharge planning, patient-centered education and counseling, development of best practices to avoid medical errors, prospective prescription utilization review programs, wellness assessments, health promotion coaching programs, and health information technology to support these activities. Any function or activity not expressly described in the regulations as an activity that improves health care quality is excluded from this category of expenses.[49]

Health information technology expenses related to health improvement activities, the implementation and meaningful use of electronic health records, and monitoring and measuring clinical effectiveness through recognized accrediting agencies such as the National Committee for Quality Assurance (NCQA) and URAC (formerly known as the Utilization Review Accreditation Commission) may be included in the costs related to improving health care quality.[50]

All other premium revenue expenditures, other than taxes and regulatory fees, are considered "non-claims" costs. These include cost-containment expenses that are not related to health improvement, direct sales workforce expenses, agent and broker fees, general and administrative expenses of the issuer, and community benefit expenditures.[51] Costs for establishing and maintaining claims adjudication systems, HIPAA transaction standard implementation costs, ICD-10 coding updates, retrospective and concurrent utilization review, fraud prevention, provider credentialing, marketing, and other costs related to administering individual enrollee and employee incentives are expressly excluded from incurred claims and health improvement activity costs and are considered non-claims costs.

[2] Calculating the MLR

For all policies issued in the large-group market in a state, the issuer must provide a rebate to the enrollees if the issuer has an MLR of less than 85 percent for the plan year. For all policies issued in the small-group or the individual market in a state, the issuer must provide a rebate if the policies issued in that market have an MLR of less than 80 percent.[52] States have the option to set a higher MLR as long as the state ensures adequate competition and value for consumers.

An issuer's MLR is the ratio of the numerator (the issuer's incurred claims plus health care improvement activity expenditures) to the denominator (the issuer's premium revenues minus federal and state taxes and licensing and regulatory fees). A credibility adjustment is available for MLRs that are based on insufficient experience.[53]

---

[48] 45 C.F.R. § 158.150.
[49] 45 C.F.R. § 158.150(c)(14).
[50] 45 C.F.R. § 158.160.
[51] 45 C.F.R. § 158.160.
[52] 45 C.F.R. § 158.210.
[53] 45 C.F.R. § 158.232.

[3]   Paying the Rebates; Plan Sponsor Allocation Responsibilities

The Affordable Care Act provides that an annual rebate shall be provided to each enrollee under such coverage on a prorated basis if the issuer has not satisfied the applicable MLR standard.[54] The regulations establish a process for distributing the rebates but do not dictate to whom and how they must be paid. The regulators acknowledge that the purpose of the rebate is to ensure that value is achieved for the premium and that the rebates should be paid to those who actually paid the premium, which is not always the enrollee in the case of an employment-based group health plan.

For purposes of the issuer's distribution of the rebates, an enrollee is the individual subscriber, policyholder, or government entity *that paid the premium* for the coverage. In other words, in an employment-based group health plan, if the employer paid 100 percent of the premium, the employer is the entity entitled to receive the rebate. Because group policyholders are in a better position to fairly distribute the rebates, in the large- and small-group markets, the issuer may meet its obligation to provide a rebate by entering into an agreement with the group policyholder to distribute the rebate on behalf of the issuer.

The issuer must take steps to ensure that each enrollee receives a rebate that is proportional to the amount of the premium paid by the enrollee and that the group policyholder does not retain more of the rebate than is proportional to the amount of the premium paid. The issuer remains liable for complying with its obligations and must maintain records evidencing the amount of premium paid by each subscriber, the amount of premium paid by the policyholder, the amount of the rebate due to each subscriber, the amount of the rebate retained by the group policyholder, and the amount of any unclaimed rebate.[55] In the individual market, the issuer must provide the rebate to the enrollee. If the individual policy covers more than one person, one lump-sum rebate may be provided to the subscriber on behalf of all enrollees covered by the policy. Unclaimed rebates are subject to state escheat laws.

For each MLR reporting year, the issuer must rebate to the enrollee the net premium revenue received (i.e., the premium paid, less federal and state taxes and licensing and regulatory fees) multiplied by the difference between the required MLR and the issuer's MLR for that group). For example: If an issuer's MLR for the large-group market is 81 percent, it must rebate 4 percent of premiums (minimum required MLR of 85 percent minus actual MLR of 81 percent) paid by the enrollee. If the employer paid $20,000 in premiums and the issuer had $1,500 of taxes and regulatory fees, the employer would be entitled to a rebate of 4 percent of $18,500 ($20,000 – $1,500) or $740. If the total rebate owed to the policyholder and the subscribers is less than $5 per subscriber, an issuer is not required to provide a rebate. The unpaid rebates must be used by the issuer to increase the rebates paid to enrollees upon the same MLR standard in the same reporting year.

The issuer must provide the rebate no later than August 1 following the end of the MLR reporting year.

It is the issuer's choice whether the rebate is paid in the form of a premium credit, a lump-sum check, or reimbursement to a credit card or direct debit (if that was how the enrollee paid the premium). Any rebate paid as a premium credit must be applied in the full amount to the first premium due on or after August 1.

A plan that is subject to ERISA must determine whether the rebate received from an insurer constitutes plan assets that can only be used for plan purposes, whether the employees are entitled to a share of the rebate based on their contributions toward the premium costs, and the tax consequences of the allocation. Decisions on how to use the rebate are subject to ERISA's fiduciary standards. The allocation of the rebates should be completed within three months.[56] If the employer and the

---

[54] PHSA § 2718(b)(1)(A).

[55] 45 C.F.R. § 158.242; 75 Fed. Reg. 74,884 (Dec. 1, 2010).

[56] See **Appendix Q** for DOL Technical Release No. 2011-04 (Dec. 2, 2011), Guidance on Rebates for Group Health Plans Paid Pursuant to the Medical Loss Ratio Requirements of the Public Health Service Act.

participants each paid a percentage of the cost of the insurance coverage, a percentage of the rebate equal to the the percentage of the cost paid by participants would be attributable to participant contributions and should be allocated to the participant.[57] However, if participants pay only a fixed amount and the employer is responsible for paying any additional costs, the employer may recover all of its costs from the rebate before any portion of the rebate is allocated to participants.[58] Conversely, if the employer pays a fixed amount and participants are responsible for paying any additional costs, the rebate must be allocated to participants first to reimburse their costs before it can be used for employer purposes.[59] If distributing rebate payments to any participants is not cost-effective (e.g., payments are of *de minimis* amounts, or would give rise to tax consequences to participants in the plan), the employer or plan fiduciary may utilize the rebate for other permissible plan purposes, including applying the rebate toward future participant premium payments or toward benefit enhancements.

The issuer must also provide a notice to the enrollees at the time a rebate is provided that describes the MLR concept, the applicable standard, the issuer's MLR and the rebate percentage, and the amount owed to enrollees based on the issuer's MLR and the applicable MLR standard. This notice provides the information that the group policyholder needs for making any pro rata distributions to the individual enrollees.

[B] Hospital Rate Transparency

Another measure adopted for early implementation with the intent of bringing down the cost of coverage is a requirement that each hospital establish (and update annually) and make public a list of the hospital's standard charges for items and services, including diagnostic related groups (DRGs) charged under the Medicare program.[60] HHS is to develop guidelines for the publication of this information.

§ 10.05 Ensuring That Consumers Get Value for Their Dollars

Beginning with the 2010 plan year, the Affordable Care Act directs HHS to develop a process for an annual review of "unreasonable" health insurance coverage premium increases.[61] Insurers will be required to provide justification for the increase to HHS's Center for Medicare and Medicaid Services (CMS) and the related state agency. If the insurer implements a rate increase that is deemed unreasonable, the CMS or state finding of unreasonableness as well as the insurer's justification for the increase must be posted on the insurance company's Web site.

On May 23, 2011, HHS published final regulations addressing rate increase disclosure and review issues.[62] The regulations establish a federal review process for small-group and individual market health insurance coverage that does not preempt or supplant any existing state law process governing insurance premiums. States would continue to have the primary responsibility for the review of rate increases. HHS found that 43 of 50 states currently have some form of rate review process in either the individual or small-group markets, or both. The Affordable Care Act makes available a total of $250 million for premium review grants to states to support their efforts to enhance their review of premium increases. CMS will adopt a state's determination of whether a rate increase is reasonable if

---

[57] DOL Tech. Rel. No. 2011-04 (Dec. 2, 2011).

[58] *Id.*

[59] *Id.*

[60] PPACA § 1001 (adding PHSA § 2718(e)).

[61] PPACA § 1003.

[62] 76 Fed. Reg. 29,964–98. The proposed rule is at 75 Fed. Reg. 81,004–29. The final regulation's definitions of "individual market" and "small group market" were amended September 6, 2011. *See* 76 Fed. Reg. 54,969–77.

it concludes that the state has an Effective Rate Review Program (as defined by the regulations). CMS will post on its Web site a list of the states that meet its requirements.

If a proposed rate increase equals or exceeds a defined threshold, it would be considered "subject to review." The review process would determine if the increase is, in fact, unreasonable. For rate increases filed in a state on or after September 1, 2011, or effective on or after September 1, 2011, in a state that does not require a rate review, the threshold is (1) a rate increase of 10 percent or more, applicable to a 12-month period that begins on September 1; or (2) a rate increase that meets or exceeds a state-specific threshold applicable to a 12-month period that begins on September 1.[63] The state-specific threshold is intended to reflect local variations and factors affecting insurance rates, to the extent data for such purpose is available. HHS will publish a notice no later than June 1 of each year regarding whether the national or state-specific threshold applies to a state.[64] A rate increase will meet or exceed such applicable threshold if the average increase for all enrollees weighted by premium volume meets or exceeds the threshold.[65]

The regulations outline the premium increase review process, including the filing of preliminary and final justifications for the increase and related information and the factors for determining whether a rate increase is unreasonable, unjustified, or unfairly discriminatory.[66] Except when it will defer to the determination of a state with an Effective Rate Review Program, CMS will review and conclude whether a rate increase is unreasonable.[67]

A determination by CMS that a rate increase is "unreasonable" would not prevent or delay any health insurance issuer from implementing a rate increase permitted by state law.[68] If an issuer implements an increase that HHS or a state has determined is unreasonable, the insurance company must post on its Web site the final determination of CMS or the state and the insurer's justification for continuing with the increase, and must keep the information available on its Web site for at least three years.[69]

Rates in the large-group market are not subject to the review process. HHS concluded that large-group rates are subject to greater negotiation and leverage by the large employers and are less subject to abuse. Only 18 states have authority to review rates in the large-group market. The Affordable Care Act also authorizes funds for grants to establish medical reimbursement data centers to provide better information to plans and consumers about the actual cost of coverage.[70] The centers are to be established at academic or other nonprofit institutions to collect medical reimbursement information from health insurance issuers, to analyze and organize such information, and to make such information

---

[63] 45 C.F.R. § 154.200(a).

[64] 45 C.F.R. § 154.200(b).

[65] 45 C.F.R. § 154.200(c).

[66] 45 C.F.R. §§ 154.205(b), (c), and (d).

A rate increase is "excessive" if the increase causes the coverage premium to be unreasonably high in relation to the benefits provided, as determined by CMS based on whether the rate increase results in a projected medical loss ratio below the federal standard in the applicable market, or whether one or more of the assumptions on which the rate increase is based are not supported by substantial evidence, or whether the choice of assumptions on which the rate increase is based is unreasonable.

A rate increase is "unjustified" if the data or documentation submitted to justify the increase is incomplete, inadequate, or otherwise does not provide a basis upon which the reasonableness of the increase may be determined.

A rate increase is "unfairly discriminatory" if the increase results in premium differences between insureds within similar risk categories that are not permissible under applicable state law, or if there is no such applicable law, do not reasonably correspond to differences in expected costs.

[67] 45 C.F.R. § 154.210.

[68] The preamble to the final regulation notes that, under the statute, HHS/CMS only has the authority to require justification and disclosure of proposed rate increases, not to rescind such an increase. However, HHS/CMS can seek a court order against an insurer to enforce compliance with the requirements set forth in the final regulation.

[69] 45 C.F.R. § 154.230.

[70] PPACA § 10101(i)(2) (adding PHSA § 2794(d)). The law authorizes $250 million for these expenditures.

available to such issuers, health care providers, health researchers, health care policy makers, and the general public.[71]

§ 10.06   Empowering Consumers With Information

A major thrust of the Affordable Care Act is to empower health care consumers through access to information. Throughout the Act, HHS is charged with the responsibility of making information available to the public. This is being implemented through a Web portal developed by HHS (*http://www.healthcare.gov*). The portal enables consumers to access information gathered from group health plans and insurance issuers by HHS under the Act and will link to Web sites of state-organized offices and programs. The intent is that through the HHS-established Internet portal, any resident of any state may identify the affordable health insurance coverage options in that state.[72] The Web site or Web portal is to provide, at a minimum, information on the following coverage options:

- Health insurance coverage offered by insurers;
- Medicaid coverage;
- CHIP coverage;
- State high-risk pool coverage;
- Federal high-risk pool; and
- Coverage within the small-group market for small businesses and their employees, including reinsurance for early retirees, tax credits available under Section 45R of the Code, and other information specifically for small businesses regarding affordable care options.[73]

On May 5, 2010, HHS published an interim final rule with comment period[74] describing the information that will be collected and displayed on the Web portal. HHS released initial summary information as of July 1, 2010, which included basic information provided by insurance issuers and states on issuers and their products in the individual and small-group markets. The Web portal was updated in October 2010 to add detailed pricing and benefit information for individual and small-group coverage. It now includes an interactive program that enables an individual to find all of the private insurance coverage available within a state by zip code. The site now includes consumer pricing information, benefit summaries, provider network information, and contact information. It also provides a glimpse into the type of information that will be available on the Exchange plans.

Beginning during the transition period and continuing even after the Exchanges are accessible, a wealth of information will be collected and made available to the regulators and the public about:

- The cost and availability of coverage;
- The quality of care being paid for by that coverage;
- The quality, efficiency, and integrity of the providers; and
- The research trends in quality care and other related topics.

---

[71] PHSA § 2794(d).
[72] PPACA § 1103(a).
[73] PPACA § 1103.
[74] 75 Fed. Reg. 24,470 *et seq.* (May 5, 2010).

§ 10.07   State Health Insurance Consumer Information

The Affordable Care Act appropriates $30 million for HHS to award grants to the states to establish offices of health insurance consumer assistance or health insurance ombudsman programs.[75] Future appropriations for subsequent years are authorized in the Act. The office must be independent of, but work in coordination with, the state insurance regulators and consumer assistance offices to receive and respond to inquiries and complaints regarding federal health insurance requirements and state law.[76] Each office must provide consumer assistance and data collection for HHS. The office is directed to assist with the filing of complaints and appeals in both the initial and external appeal stages; to collect, track, and quantify problems and inquiries encountered by consumers; to provide consumer education about the rights and responsibilities of group health plans and health insurers; to provide information, referral, and enrollment assistance for consumers; and to resolve problems relating to an individual's obtaining the premium tax credit available under the Exchanges beginning in 2014.[77]

In addition, as a condition of receiving the grant, the office will be required to collect and report data requested by HHS on the types of problems consumers are encountering.[78] HHS is to use the information to identify areas where more enforcement is necessary and shall share the information with the state insurance regulators, the DOL, and Treasury.[79]

States also have obligations to post information publicly on the Internet and to link to some of the provider comparison Web sites[80] being established by HHS and CMS for state-licensed facilities such as skilled nursing facilities and nursing homes.

By far the largest new Internet obligation on states will be the Exchange site. The Exchange Internet portal will include plan rating, enrollee satisfaction information, and enrollment information.[81] See **Chapter 11** for more information about the Exchange information to be posted on the Internet for consumers.

States are also required to facilitate Medicaid enrollment through the Internet Exchange portal beginning in 2014.[82]

---

[75] PPACA § 1002 (adding PHSA § 2793).

[76] PHSA § 2793.

[77] PHSA § 2793(3). See **Section 11.04[E]** for a description of the premium tax credit available for individuals beginning January 1, 2014.

[78] PHSA § 2793(d).

[79] PHSA § 2793(d).

[80] See **Appendix D.**

[81] PPACA § 1311.

[82] PPACA § 2401.

CHAPTER 11

MANDATES AND EXCHANGES

§ 11.01 Individual Enroll-or-Pay

A cornerstone of national health care reform is that all American citizens should have access to health care coverage, regardless of their health status and income level. The group market reforms discussed earlier in Chapters 8 and 9 revealed many of the changes that will expand access to health care coverage for millions of Americans who are currently uninsured or grossly underinsured. Increased access is only effective if the uninsured segment of the population actually enrolls in coverage. Therefore, along with these changes comes a requirement for individuals to enroll in health care coverage. Beginning on January 1, 2014, "applicable individuals" will be required to enroll in "minimum essential coverage" or pay a tax penalty to the federal government.[1] We refer to this concept as "enroll or pay" or the "individual mandate."

[A] Applicable Individuals

The term *applicable individuals* encompasses all U.S. citizens except those who qualify for a religious exemption or are incarcerated.[2] Also specifically exempted from the enroll-or-pay requirement are non–U.S. citizens and U.S. nationals.[3]

[B] Minimum Essential Coverage

Currently, the definition of *minimum essential coverage* is very simplistic, but this term may change over time. An individual can satisfy the minimum essential coverage requirement by obtaining health care coverage through one of the following sources:

- Government-sponsored programs, including Medicare, Medicaid, TRICARE, and the Children's Health Insurance Program;[4]

- Eligible employer-sponsored health plans, which may include governmental plans or any other plans or coverage offered in the small- or large-group market within a state, including self-funded plans,[5] provided that the employee's share of the premiums is affordable and the coverage provides minimum value;[6]

- Continuation coverage required under COBRA or a similar state law;[7]

- Grandfathered health plans,[8] including those that are self-funded; or

- Individual health plans, including a plan purchased through an Exchange or outside an Exchange.[9]

---

[1] PPACA § 1501(b) (adding I.R.C. § 5000A(b)).

[2] I.R.C. § 5000A(d).

[3] I.R.C. § 5000A(d); see **Section 2.01** note 1 and accompanying text (regarding the subtraction of illegal aliens from the uninsured statistics).

[4] I.R.C. § 5000A(f).

[5] I.R.C. § 5000A(f)(1)(B). As drafted, the Affordable Care Act appears to exclude self-funded plans from the definition of "eligible-employer-sponsored" health plans. Proposed Treasury regulations confirm that self-funded plans are intended to be eligible employer-sponsored plans. *See* Preamble to Department of Treasury Proposed Regulations on Health Insurance Premium Tax Credit, 76 Fed. Reg. 50,935 (Aug. 17, 2011). See **Section 11.02[C][2]** for a discussion of the affordability and adequacy requirements.

[6] See **Section 11.02[C][2]** for a discussion of how to determine minimum value.

[7] Prop. Treas. Reg. § 1.36B-2(c)(3)(iv).

[8] See **Chapter 5** for a discussion of grandfathered health plans.

[9] I.R.C. § 5000A(f).

Minimum essential coverage will not include coverage for excepted benefits, which include:

- Coverage only for accident, or disability income insurance;
- Coverage issued as a supplement to liability insurance;
- Liability insurance;
- Workers' compensation or similar insurance;
- Automobile medical payment insurance;
- Credit-only insurance;
- Coverage for on-site medical clinics; and
- Other similar insurance under which benefits for medical care are secondary or incidental to other benefits.[10]

[C] Penalties

Effective January 1, 2014, any individual who is required to enroll in minimum essential coverage but chooses not to do so must pay a penalty to the federal government, subject to a few exemptions.[11] Those who are exempted include the following:

- Individuals whose required contribution for the lowest-cost plan option would be in excess of 8 percent of household income.[12]

- Individuals who do not file Form 1040 tax returns because they do not earn enough income. The filing threshold comprises two numbers—the personal exemption amount plus the standard deduction amount. For the 2012 taxable year, the sum of these amounts is $9,750 for individuals filing as "single" and $19,500 for individuals filing as "married filing jointly."[13]

- Individuals who were not covered by minimum essential coverage for a continuous period of at least three months. Once the continuous period without minimum essential coverage reaches a period of three months or more, this exemption expires and the penalty applies retroactively for the entire period.[14]

- Individuals who do not have an affordable coverage option, either through an employment-based group health plan or a qualified health plan offered through an Exchange.[15]

- Members of Indian tribes.[16]

The penalty for not having minimum essential coverage will be calculated on a monthly basis and is based on the annual amounts set forth in Table 11-1. The penalty is calculated as the greater of (1) a set dollar amount, or (2) a percentage of household income that exceeds the dollar threshold required to file a Form 1040 tax return.[17] For 2012, those thresholds were $9,500 for single filers and

---

[10] I.R.C. § 5000A(f).

[11] I.R.C. § 5000A(e).

[12] I.R.C. § 5000A(e)(1).

[13] I.R.C. § 5000A(e)(2). The 2012 threshold is $9,750 for married taxpayers filing separately and at least $12,500 for taxpayers filing as head of household.

[14] I.R.C. § 5000A(e)(4).

[15] I.R.C. § 5000A(e)(5); PPACA § 1311(d)(4)(H).

[16] I.R.C. § 5000A(e)(3).

[17] I.R.C. § 5000A(c).

$19,000 for married taxpayers filing jointly. The thresholds will be adjusted for cost-of-living increases for future years.

TABLE 11-1.
Annual Enroll-or-Pay Penalties for Individuals

Year	Individual Dollar Penalty	Individual % of Income Penalty
2014	$95	1.0%
2015	$325	2.0%
2016 (and after)	$695 (as indexed)	2.5%

The individual dollar penalty in Table 11-1 is for individuals who have attained age 18 at the beginning of a month. For individuals who have not attained age 18 at the beginning of a month, the individual dollar penalties are reduced by 50 percent. For a family, the sum of the individual dollar penalties cannot exceed 300 percent of the values in the table. For example, the annual individual dollar penalty for a family comprising two parents and six children would be no more than $285 ($95 × 300%) for 2014. However, because there is no cap on the percentage of household income penalty, the enroll-or-pay penalty could be significantly more than $285 for the 2014 calendar year.

Example. Joe and Jen Jones are married adults with three dependent children (Amber, age 14; Brad, age 16; Cindy, age 19). For the 2014 calendar year, Joe and Jen decide not to enroll in minimum essential coverage. The standard deduction and personal exemptions for their family total $29,650 (based on 2010 figures). The *annual* individual dollar penalties are calculated as follows.

Name	2014 Annual Individual Dollar Penalty
Joe	$95.00
Jen	$95.00
Amber	$47.50
Brad	$47.50
Cindy	$95.00
Total	**$380.00**

If the combined income for Joe and Jen's family in 2014 is $40,000, the monthly percent of household income penalty would be $103.50 (1 percent of the household income that exceeds the sum of the applicable standard deduction and personal exemptions). The $103.50 is calculated as follows:

$40,000 − $29,650 = $10,350
$10,350 × 1% = $103.50

Thus, the family would be subject to the $285 maximum individual dollar penalty, which is greater than the $103.50 percent of household income penalty.

However, if the combined family income is $100,000, the family would be subject to an annual penalty of $703.50 because 1 percent of household income that exceeds the sum of the applicable standard deduction and personal exemptions is greater than the maximum individual dollar penalty of $285.

[D] Payment of Penalty

Individuals subject to the enroll-or-pay penalty must remit payment to the IRS. While the penalty is assessed on a monthly basis, payment will be made annually and will be administered through the Form 1040 tax return, which will have to be redesigned to accommodate this change. Taxpayers who fail to remit an enroll-or-pay penalty will be subject to interest and the traditional IRS penalties for underpayments of tax.[18] However, such taxpayers will not be subject to criminal charges for tax underpayments[19] or to liens or levies on property.[20] These limitations on the collectability of enroll-or-pay penalties strips away some of the effectiveness of the provision.

[E] Constitutionality

The individual mandate concept was at the core of the constitutional challenges to the Affordable Care Act. Critics charged that the U.S. Constitution did not authorize Congress to penalize Americans for failing to purchase health insurance. On June 28, 2012, the U.S. Supreme Court decided, in *National Federation of Independent Business v. Sebelius*, that the individual mandate is a tax for constitutional purposes, and Congress has the authority to impose taxes.[21] See **Chapter 3** for a broader discussion of the constitutional issues.

§ 11.02   Employer Pay-or-Play (Shared Responsibility)

Complementing the requirement that individuals enroll in minimum essential coverage or pay a tax penalty is a requirement that certain employers offer minimum essential coverage or pay a tax penalty.[22] We refer to this concept as "pay-or-play."[23] Beginning January 1, 2014, certain employers will be required to offer full-time employees the chance to enroll in employment-based group health plan coverage that satisfies the definition of minimum essential coverage and that is both adequate and affordable. "Applicable employers" that fail to provide minimum essential coverage to any "full-time employee" eligible to receive a subsidy for coverage obtained through an Exchange will be subject to a nondeductible federal tax penalty. The calculation of this penalty will vary depending upon whether the employer is offering minimum essential coverage to all its full-time employees, including full-time employees covered by a collective bargaining agreement. These defined terms and penalties are discussed below.

[A] Applicable Employers

Pay-or-play is applicable only to large employers.[24] Large employers are employers that employed, on average, 50 or more full-time employees on business days during the preceding calendar year.[25] For a new business or one that was not in existence for the entire *preceding* calendar year,

---

[18] I.R.C. § 5000A(g)(1); *see* I.R.C. § 6651(a)(2) (providing penalties for tax underpayments).

[19] I.R.C. § 5000A(g)(2)(A).

[20] I.R.C. § 5000A(g)(2)(B).

[21] National Fed'n of Indep. Bus. v. Sebelius, 132 S. Ct. 1958 (2012).

[22] PPACA § 1513 (adding I.R.C. § 4980H).

[23] The IRS refers to this requirement as "shared responsibility." I.R.S. Notice 2011-36, 2011-21 I.R.B. 792 (May 23, 2011).

[24] I.R.C. § 4980H(a) and (b). It is expected that the term "employer" will refer to the employer of an employee under the common law test. *See* I.R.S. Notice 2011-36, 2011-21 I.R.B. 792 (May 23, 2011) (requesting comments on the employee-counting provisions of the pay-or-play requirement).

[25] I.R.C. § 4980H(c)(2)(A).

the large employer determination will be based on the average number of employees the business reasonably expects to employ on business days during the *current* calendar year.[26] An employer will not be subject to the pay-or-play rules if during the preceding calendar year it (1) employed 50 or more full-time employees for 120 days or less; and (2) the employees in excess of 50 for such period were seasonal workers.[27] The controlled group rules under Code Sections 414(b), (c), (m), and (o) will apply when determining the size of an employer.[28]

[B] Calculation of Employees

Because only large employers are subject to the pay-or-play rules, employers must pay careful attention to how a "full-time employee" is defined. *Full-time employees* are employees who work, on average, at least 30 hours of service per week.[29] For purposes of determining which employers are large employers, full-time equivalent employees also must be included in the employee count.[30] *Full-time equivalent employees* are determined by adding all the hours worked by non–full-time employees in a given month and dividing that number by 120.[31]

The following example illustrates how full-time employees are calculated in determining whether an employer is a "large employer" for purposes of the pay-or-play rules.

> **Example 1.** November Pain Corp. (NPC), which sells guns and roses, employs 45 employees who each work, on average, 37.5 hours per week for the entire year and an additional 100 part-time sales employees who work 12 hours per week for the entire year. Based solely on the total of 45 full-time employees, NPC would not be a large employer because it does not meet the requisite 50 full-time-employees threshold. However, full-time equivalent employees must be taken into consideration. For purposes of this example, assume that each month contains four weeks. NPC would calculate its full-time equivalent employees as follows:
>
> [(100 employees × 12 hours per week × 4 weeks) ÷ 120] = 40
>
> Therefore, once the part-time employees are factored in, NPC is a large employer for purposes of determining employer size under the pay-or-play rules, because it is deemed to employ 85 full-time employees.

The pay-or-play penalty, and the determination of whether an employer is a large employer, generally are determined on a monthly basis.[32] Recognizing that it would be difficult for employers to make these determinations every month, particularly where employee schedules are erratic, Treasury has indicated that it intends to issue guidance that would allow employers to use one or more safe

---

[26] I.R.C. § 4980H(c)(2)(C)(ii); I.R.S. Notice 2011-36, 2011-21 I.R.B. 792 (May 23, 2011).

[27] I.R.C. § 4980H(c)(2)(B)(i). Work is done on a seasonal basis where, ordinarily, the employment pertains to or is of the kind exclusively performed at certain seasons or periods of the year and that, from its nature, may not be continuous or carried on throughout the year. A worker who moves from one seasonal activity to another, while employed in agriculture or performing agricultural labor, is employed on a seasonal basis even though he may continue to be employed during a major portion of the year. 29 U.S.C. § 500.20(s)(1). Seasonal workers also include retail employees.

[28] I.R.C. § 4980H(c)(2)(C)(i). The controlled group rules require certain related companies under common control to be treated as a single employer.

[29] I.R.C. § 4980H(c)(4). The IRS has suggested that it may adopt an equivalency method of counting hours that employers could elect to use, whereby an employee could be considered a full-time employee if he or she completed at least 130 hours in a month. I.R.S. Notice 2011-36, 2011-21 I.R.B. 792 (May 23, 2011).

[30] I.R.C. § 4980H(c)(2)(E).

[31] I.R.C. § 4980H(c)(2)(E); I.R.S. Notice 2011-36, 2011-21 I.R.B. 792 (May 23, 2011).

[32] PPACA § 1513.

harbors in determining large-employer status for purpose of the pay-or-play penalty.[33] Under the contemplated safe harbor, an employer would be permitted to determine an employee's full-time status by looking back over a defined "measurement period" of between 3 and 12 months to determine whether the employee averaged at least 30 hours of service per week over the measurement period.[34] If the employee averaged at least 30 hours per week, the employer could deem the employee to be a full-time employee going forward for a "stability period" of at least 6 months (or, if greater, for at least the same length of time as the measurement period), regardless of the actual hours worked by the employee (so long as the employee remains an employee). If the employee averaged fewer than 30 hours per week, the employer must treat the employee as not a full-time employee going forward over a stability period that does not exceed the length of the measurement period. Treasury also has indicated that it intends to issue guidance regarding the determination of full-time employee status for new employees, and is considering giving employers up to 6 months to make a determination for a new employee in certain circumstances.[35]

[C] Penalties

There are two types of penalties that may be assessed under the pay-or-play rules—penalties for employers that choose not to provide minimum essential coverage (i.e., employers who are no longer in the business of providing health benefits to their employees),[36] and penalties for employers that provide minimum essential coverage (e.g., employer-sponsored health coverage) that is inadequate or unaffordable.[37] A large employer may be subject to only one of these penalties, not both, and the latter penalty cannot exceed the amount that would have been payable under the former penalty had the employer not offered minimum essential coverage. These penalties are excise taxes and are not deductible for federal tax purposes.

[1] Penalty for No Minimum Essential Coverage

An employer that chooses not to provide minimum essential coverage to its full-time employees and has at least one full-time employee who receives a premium tax credit or cost-sharing reduction related to enrollment in a qualified health plan through an Exchange will be subject to a penalty of $166.67 per month per full-time employee.[38] The monthly penalty amount will be adjusted for inflation beginning in 2015. The first 30 full-time employees are excluded from the penalty calculation.[39]

The following example illustrates how the pay-or-play penalty is calculated for employers that do not offer minimum essential coverage.

> **Example 2.** As we established in Example 1, November Pain Corp. (NPC) is subject to pay-or-play. Because of rising health care premiums and the market for guns and roses not being what it used to be, NPC eliminates its employment-based group health plan. In turn, all NPC employees enroll in a qualified health plan through a state Exchange. Many of NPC's

---

[33] I.R.S. Notice 2012-17, A-4, 2012-9 I.R.B. 430 (Feb. 9, 2012).

[34] I.R.S. Notice 2011-36, 2011-21 I.R.B. 792 (May 3, 2011).

[35] I.R.S. Notice 2012-17, A-5, 2012-9 I.R.B. 430 (Feb. 9, 2012).

[36] I.R.C. § 4980H(a).

[37] I.R.C. § 4980H(b).

[38] I.R.C. § 4980H(a). The IRS has acknowledged that calculating penalties on a monthly basis may be impractical for employers, and is contemplating one or more safe harbors that would enable employers to use a lookback/stability period approach in order to better predict exposure to the penalty. I.R.S. Notice 2011-36, 2011-21 I.R.B. 792 (May 23, 2011). The IRS also has requested comments as to how permissible eligibility waiting periods should be coordinated with the pay-or-play provisions. I.R.S. Notice 2011-36, 2011-21 I.R.B. 792 (May 23, 2011).

[39] I.R.C. § 4980H(d)(2)(D).

employees are lower paid; as a result, all of its 100 part-time employees and 10 of its 45 full-time employees receive a premium tax credit to help defray the cost of coverage under an Exchange-provided qualified health plan. Because NPC does not offer minimum essential coverage and has *at least one full-time employee* enrolled in a qualified health plan through a state Exchange who receives a premium tax credit, it must pay a monthly penalty of $166.67 for *each full-time employee* after the first 30 full-time employees. This translates into a penalty of $2,500.05 per month: [(45 full-time employees – 30 full-time employees) × $166.67]. Again, this penalty is not deductible for federal tax purposes.

Because pay-or-play penalties are assessed on a monthly basis, an employer that begins the calendar year without offering minimum essential coverage could change its mind at any point during the year and begin to offer minimum essential coverage (either through an employment-based group health plan or an Exchange plan, in certain cases). Thus, an employer that had been paying the penalties under pay-or-play from January 1, 2014, through June 30, 2014, could, effective July 1, 2014, begin offering minimum essential coverage that is adequate and affordable to eliminate future monthly pay-or-play penalties.

[2] Penalty for Inadequate or Unaffordable Coverage

An employer that offers minimum essential coverage that is either inadequate or unaffordable will be subject to a pay-or-play penalty of $250 per month per full-time employee who receives a premium tax credit or cost-sharing reduction related to enrollment in a qualified health plan through a state Exchange.[40] Minimum essential coverage is inadequate if the plan fails to provide minimum value, meaning that the plan's share of the total cost of benefits is less than 60 percent. Minimum essential coverage is unaffordable if the employee premium constitutes more than 9.5 percent of the employee's household income.[41] The monthly penalty amount will be adjusted for inflation beginning in 2015. However, unlike employers that choose not to offer minimum essential coverage, employers that offer inadequate or unaffordable minimum essential are *not* able to exclude the first 30 full-time employees from the penalty calculation.

The Treasury Department and the IRS have not yet issued regulations on how an employer will determine whether its plan provides minimum value for purposes of the employer pay-or-play penalty, as well as for purposes of determining whether an employee who is eligible for such coverage can qualify for premium subsidies through an Exchange. Measuring minimum value will be particularly difficult for employers with self-funded group health plans. The IRS has issued a notice requesting comments on the following three potential approaches for employers to determine whether their plans provide minimum value:

1. An actuarial value calculator and/or a minimum value calculator made available by HHS and Treasury online that would enable an employer to enter information about plan benefits, coverage of services, and cost-sharing items to calculate minimum value;

2. A series of plan design-based safe harbors, in the form of checklists; and

---

[40] I.R.C. § 4980H(b)(1).

[41] I.R.C. § 36B(c)(2)(C). *Household income* is determined by adding an individual's "modified adjusted gross income" plus the aggregate modified gross income of all other individuals who are taken into account in determining the taxpayer's family size that were required to file a tax return for the taxable year. *Modified adjusted gross income* means gross income *decreased* by (1) trade and business deductions; (2) losses from sale or exchange of property; (3) rents and royalties deductions; and (4) alimony; and *increased* by (1) tax-exempt interest and income earned by U.S. citizens living abroad (Code § 911 income). I.R.C. § 36B(d)(2).

    3. A required certification by a certified actuary in accordance with recognized actuarial standards.[42]

The IRS guidance acknowledges that an HHS report issued in November 2011 found that approximately 98 percent of individuals covered by employer-sponsored group health plans would be enrolled in minimum value coverage under the measurement criteria outlined in the guidance.[43] The primary drivers of minimum value in an employer-sponsored group health plan are physician and mid-level practitioner care, hospital and emergency room services, pharmacy benefits, and laboratory and imaging services.[44] Unfortunately, for employers with sophisticated, customized group health plans, the online calculator and the design-based safe harbors likely will not be helpful. Such an employer may need to hire an actuary to make a formal certification.

Employers generally do not have access to information about an employee's total household income, which might include, for example, wages from a second job or income from other family members. As drafted, the Affordable Care Act would either create great uncertainty among employers as to whether they would be subject to the pay-or-play penalty, or cause employers to make invasive requests of employees regarding their other household income. Fortunately it appears that the Treasury Department has recognized this problem and has indicated that it intends to propose a safe harbor for employers, whereby an employer could rely on the Form W-2 wages it pays to its employee as equaling the employee's household income.[45] This special safe harbor would apply only for purposes of the employer's evaluation and calculation of the pay-or-play penalty. Actual household income would still be used to determine an employee's eligibility for advance payments of premium assistance from an Exchange and the refundable premium tax credit.[46] Another consideration is whether employers will be subject to a pay-or-play penalty to the extent that new employees are not permitted to enroll in the employer's group health plan during the plan's initial waiting period, which may be as long as 90 days after an employee's date of hire.[47] The failure to provide coverage during the waiting period could be viewed as either providing no minimum essential coverage or providing inadequate coverage. Again, the Treasury Department recognized this issue and has announced that it intends to issue guidance indicating that employers will not be subject to a pay-or-play penalty solely by reason of a failure to offer group health plan coverage to an employee during an initial waiting period.[48]

The following example illustrates how the pay-or-play penalty is calculated for employers that offer minimum essential coverage that is inadequate or unaffordable.

> **Example 3.** As we established in Example 1, NPC is subject to pay-or-play. To avoid negative publicity, NPC decides that it will provide its employees with minimum essential coverage for the 2014 calendar year. However, because of rising health care costs, NPC decides that it can only contribute 30 percent of the total health insurance premium, leaving employees to pay the other 70 percent, which would cost most employees more than 9.5 percent of their household income. In turn, all NPC employees enroll in a qualified health plan through

---

[42] I.R.S. Notice 2012-31, 2012-20 I.R.B. 906 (Apr. 26, 2012).

[43] I.R.S. Notice 2012-31, 2012-20 I.R.B. 906 (Apr. 26, 2012) (citing ASPE Research Brief, U.S. Dep't of Health & Human Servs., Actuarial Value and Employer-Sponsored Insurance (Nov. 2011), http://aspe.hhs.gov/health/reports/2011/AV-ESI/rb.shtml).

[44] I.R.S. Notice 2012-31, 2012-20 I.R.B. 906 (Apr. 26, 2012).

[45] *See* I.R.S. Notice 2012-17, A-2, 2012-9 I.R.B. 430 (Feb. 9, 2012) (indicating Treasury's intent to issue proposed regulations regarding the safe harbor); I.R.S. Notice 2011-73, 2011-40 I.R.B. 474 (Sept. 13, 2011); Preamble to Proposed Treasury Regulations on Health Insurance Premium Tax Credit, 76 Fed. Reg. 50,931, 50,936 (Aug. 17, 2011).

[46] I.R.S. Notice 2011-73, 2011-40 I.R.B. 474 (Sept. 13, 2011); see **Section 11.04[E]** for a discussion of advance payments of premium assistance and refundable premium tax credits.

[47] *See* PPACA § 1201 (adding PHSA § 2708) (limiting waiting periods to no more than 90 days). See **Section 9.06** for a discussion of limits on waiting periods.

[48] I.R.S. Notice 2012-17, A-3, 2012-9 I.R.B. 430 (Feb. 9, 2012).

an Exchange. As indicated in Example 2, many of NPC's employees are lower paid, and all of its part-time employees and 10 of its full-time employees receive a premium tax credit to help defray the cost of coverage under a qualified health plan. Because NPC does not offer minimum essential coverage that is affordable and has at least one full-time employee enrolled in a qualified health plan through a state Exchange who receives a premium tax credit, it must pay a monthly penalty of $250 for *each* full-time employee receiving a subsidy. This translates into a penalty of $2,500 per month [(10 full-time employees receiving a subsidy) × $250]. Again, this penalty is not deductible for federal tax purposes.

§ 11.03 Free Choice Vouchers

While large employers are subject to the pay-or-play rules, the Affordable Care Act originally provided that all "offering employers" would be required to provide free choice vouchers to their "qualified employees" beginning on January 1, 2014.[49] Offering employers that provided qualified employees with a free choice voucher would have been able to deduct the amount of the voucher for federal income tax purposes and would not be subject to pay-or-play penalties with respect to any employee receiving a free choice voucher.[50] Employees receiving a free choice voucher would not have been subject to the enroll-or-pay penalties, so long as they used their voucher to obtain health care coverage through an Exchange.[51]

On April 15, 2011, President Obama signed the Department of Defense and Full-Year Continuing Appropriations Act, 2011, which repeals the free choice voucher provisions of the Affordable Care Act.[52] The remainder of this **Section 11.03** describes how free choice vouchers would have worked under the Affordable Care Act.

[A] Offering Employer

An *offering employer* is any employer that (1) offers minimum essential coverage through an eligible employer-sponsored plan, and (2) pays any portion of the costs of such plan.[53] There is no requirement that an offering employer have 50 or more employees, so small businesses may be classified as offering employers.

[B] Qualified Employee

A *qualified employee* is any employee (1) whose required contribution for minimum essential coverage through an eligible employer-sponsored plan is at least 8 percent but does not exceed 9.8 percent[54] of the employee's household income for the applicable taxable year (as indexed for years beginning after 2014); (2) whose household income for the applicable taxable year is not greater than 400 percent of the federal poverty level for the appropriate family size; and (3) who does not participate in the health plan offered by the offering employer.[55]

---

[49] PPACA § 10108 (this provision does not amend an existing law or add a new provision to any law).

[50] I.R.C. § 162(a).

[51] I.R.C. § 4980H(b)(3).

[52] Department of Defense and Full-Year Continuing Appropriations Act, 2011 § 1858, Pub. L. No. 112-10 (enacted Apr. 15, 2011).

[53] PPACA § 10108(b).

[54] This likely should have been changed to 9.5%, corresponding with the change made to premium tax credits. It may be corrected through a technical correction.

[55] PPACA § 10108(c).

[C]   Voucher Amounts

The amount of a free choice voucher provided by an offering employer to a qualified employee will be equal to the monthly portion of the cost of the eligible employer-sponsored plan that would have been paid by the offering employer if the qualified employee were covered under the plan.[56] The qualified employee will be able to apply the amount of the voucher toward the purchase of a qualified health plan through an Exchange.[57] The offering employer is responsible for remitting the amount of the voucher to the Exchange on behalf of the employee. If the amount of the voucher exceeds the premium of the qualified health plan, the employee is entitled to the difference.[58] The portion of a voucher that is used to reduce the premiums associated with a qualified health plan purchased through an Exchange is not taxable to the qualified employee.[59] The portion of a voucher, if any, that is not used to defray the cost of premiums associated with a qualified health plan is includable in the qualified employee's gross income and treated as taxable compensation.

The following example illustrates how free choice vouchers work.

> **Example 4.** As previously noted in Examples 1, 2, and 3, NPC has 45 full-time employees. Assume also that NPC continues to offer minimum essential coverage but requires employees to pay a share of the premium. Ten of the full-time employees who have household income between 100 percent and 400 percent of the federal poverty level (and who therefore may be eligible for subsidies under an Exchange plan) decline participation in NPC's health plan because they would rather purchase coverage through the Exchange. Assume that if these 10 employees had enrolled in NPC's plan, each of them would have to pay a share of the premium in an amount that is between 8 percent and 9.8 percent of household income. The other 35 full-time employees (whose household income exceeds 400 percent of the federal poverty level) enroll in the NPC plan.
>
> In this example, because NPC is an offering employer, it must provide the 10 qualified employees with a free choice voucher. Because these employees would receive a free choice voucher, they would not be eligible for subsidies under an Exchange plan. The 35 full-time employees who enrolled in minimum essential coverage provided through NPC's health plan are not, by definition, qualified employees and are not eligible for a voucher. Because free choice vouchers are not limited to only full-time employees, whether or not NPC is required to provide part-time employees with a free choice voucher depends on the terms of the employment-based group health plan. If part-time employees are eligible to enroll in NPC's plan, NPC would have to provide a free choice voucher to any part-time employee who is a qualified employee. If part-time employees are not eligible to enroll in the NPC plan, NPC would not have to provide a free choice voucher to part-time employees.

§ 11.04   Health Care Exchanges

Traditionally, most individuals with health care coverage in the United States receive that coverage through an employment-based group health plan.[60] Employer-sponsored plans still play a significant role in providing health care coverage, but their role has begun to diminish due to a number

---

[56] PPACA § 10108(d)(1).

[57] PPACA § 10108(d)(2).

[58] PPACA § 10108(d)(3). It is not clear whether the difference must be paid to the employee by the Exchange or by the employer, and if paid by the Exchange, whether the Exchange or the employer is responsible for tax reporting.

[59] I.R.C. § 139D.

[60] *See* http://www.bls.gov/ncs/ebs/sp/ebnr0015.pdf.

of factors.[61] First, the recession of the last few years has added millions of Americans to the ranks of the unemployed, many of whom are eligible for COBRA continuation coverage for only 18 months after termination of employment. Second, over the past decade, health care costs have grown at rates far eclipsing the rise in the consumer price index and the growth in real wages, causing many small employers to eliminate or cut back their health plans. Third, systemic changes in the American workforce have pushed more workers employed in non-agricultural pursuits than ever before to enter the ranks of the self-employed.[62] These three significant changes, among others, have left millions of Americans with only one option to obtain health care coverage—the individual insurance market. Because high quality comes with high costs in the individual insurance market, it is not uncommon to see individuals purchasing coverage through the individual insurance market take out "catastrophic" policies that do not provide for preventive care or prescription drug benefits, which ultimately can lead to higher use and more expensive treatment down the road.

To help solve this growing problem, the Affordable Care Act introduces a new concept called the American Health Benefit Exchange (more commonly known as an "Exchange"). An Exchange is a marketplace of health insurance issuers composed of traditional for-profit insurance companies and nonprofit cooperatives that will sell a type of health plan called a qualified health plan (QHP), defined more fully in **Section 11.04[C],** below. States, acting through a state governmental agency or non-profit entity established and operated by the state, will establish the Exchanges using $6 billion in federal grant funds.[63] Because each state operates its own Exchange, each state may require QHPs sold through its Exchange to offer additional benefits other than those required by HHS.[64] After January 1, 2015, each Exchange is expected to be self-sustaining and will not receive aid from the federal government.[65] Funds used to operate and maintain the Exchange will likely come from fees on health insurance issuers or individuals enrolling in an Exchange plan.

The goals of an Exchange are as follows:

1. To enhance consumer choice;

2. Create single risk pools based on community ratings that are subject to strict underwriting requirements;[66]

3. Lessen the reliance on employer-sponsored health care coverage; and

4. Allow consumers to make "apples to apples" comparisons of available health plans. To accomplish these goals and more, each Exchange will feature an Internet Web site through which comparative information may be obtained, a rating system that rates QHPs based on quality and price, and annual enrollee satisfaction surveys for each QHP that has more than 500 enrollees. Each Exchange will be responsible for preparing, maintaining, and updating this information.

---

[61] See **Section 2.02** notes 10–11 and accompanying text (providing statistics on health plan coverage).

[62] *See* http://www.bls.gov/opub/mlr/2004/07/art2full.pdf.

[63] PPACA § 1322(g).

[64] PPACA § 1311(d)(3)(B). However, the state is required to make payments either to the individual or to the QHP to defray their cost. PPACA § 1311(d)(3)(B)(ii).

[65] PPACA § 1311(d)(5).

[66] Insurers will not be able to charge tobacco users more than 1.5 times the rate of non–tobacco users and premiums may not vary by a ratio of more than 3 to 1 based on age.

[A] Eligibility

Beginning January 1, 2014, individuals and small employers will be able to purchase health insurance coverage through an Exchange.[67] Small employers are employers with at least one but not more than 100 employees on business days during the preceding calendar year and who employ at least one employee on the first day of the plan year.[68] Large employers are not eligible to purchase a QHP through an Exchange until 2017, at the earliest.[69] Large employers are employers that have employed on average at least 101 employees on business days during the preceding calendar year and who employ at least one employee on the first day of the plan year.[70] For purposes of determining the size of an employer, the controlled group rules set forth in Code Sections 414(b), (c), (m), and (o) will apply.[71] Prior to 2016, each state may opt to reduce the maximum employee limit for small employers from 100 employees to 50 employees and large employers from 101 employees to 51 employees.[72]

[B] Special Eligibility Rules

There are a couple of special eligibility rules for new employers and small employers. A new employer that was not in existence during the preceding calendar year will determine whether it is a small or large employer based on the average number of employees it reasonably expects to employ on business days during the current calendar year.[73] A small employer that makes coverage available to its employees through a QHP in the Exchange will continue to be treated as a small employer, even if it would otherwise cease to be a small employer due to an increase in the number of its employees, for the period beginning with the increase in employees and ending with the first day on which the employer does not make such QHP available to its employees.[74] Essentially, small employers whose businesses grow can keep their existing QHP.

[C] Qualified Health Plans

A *QHP* is defined as a health plan offered through an Exchange that

1. Provides for an "essential health benefits package";

2. Has a certificate of approval signifying its compliance with the certification criteria established by HHS; and

3. Is offered by an "approved" health insurance issuer.[75]

---

[67] PPACA § 1312(f).

[68] PPACA § 1304(b)(2).

[69] PPACA § 1312(f)(2)(B).

[70] PPACA § 1304(b)(1).

[71] PPACA § 1304(b)(4)(A). The controlled group rules require related companies under common control to be treated as a single employer.

[72] PPACA § 1304(b)(3).

[73] PPACA § 1304(b)(4)(B).

[74] PPACA § 1304(b)(4)(D).

[75] PPACA § 1301(a)(1).

[1] Essential Health Benefits Package

An *essential health benefits package* must satisfy the following criteria:

1. Provide a level of coverage described in Table 11-2;

2. Limit cost-sharing (deductibles, co-insurance, copayments, etc.) for essential health benefits to the annual out-of-pocket expense limit for high-deductible health plans coupled with HSAs ($5,950 and $11,900 for 2012) and cap annual deductibles on health plans offered through the small-group market to $2,000 for self-only coverage and $4,000 for family coverage, as adjusted beginning in 2015; and

3. Provide essential health benefits in at least the following general categories:[76]

   - Ambulatory patient services;

   - Emergency services;

   - Hospitalization;

   - Maternity and newborn care;

   - Mental health and substance abuse, including behavioral health treatment (it is unclear whether this would include autism coverage);

   - Prescription drugs;

   - Preventive and wellness services;

   - Chronic disease management;

   - Pediatric services, including dental and vision care;

   - Rehabilitative and habilitative services; and

   - Laboratory services.

When defining the specific services covered under each essential health benefit listed above, HHS will ensure an appropriate balance among the categories, not unduly weighting coverage toward any one category.[77] HHS will take into account the health care needs of the entire population, including women, children, and persons with disabilities and ensure that essential benefits will not be denied to individuals against their wishes on the basis of age, life expectancy, quality of life, etc. (i.e., there will be no "death panels," at least not as suggested by various opponents of the legislation).[78] HHS will not make coverage decisions, determine reimbursement rates, establish incentive programs, or design benefits in ways that discriminate based on age, disability, or life expectancy.[79] HHS will periodically review and revise the essential health benefits listed above and the services covered under each benefit.[80]

---

[76] PPACA §§ 1302(a), (b).

[77] PPACA § 1302(b)(4). HHS has released a Bulletin and related FAQs that further explain the agency's thought process for developing essential health benefit package parameters. See **Chapter 4** and **Appendix R**.

[78] PPACA § 1302(b)(4). While there are no "death panels," an argument can be made that health care could be rationed.

[79] PPACA § 1302(b)(4).

[80] PPACA § 1302(b)(4).

TABLE 11-2.
Coverage Tiers for Plan Offered Through an Exchange

Tier	Includes Essential Benefits?	Percentage of Covered Benefit Costs	Out-of-Pocket Limit for Individual/Family
Bronze	Yes	60%	$5,950 / $11,900
Silver	Yes	70%	$5,950 / $11,900
Gold	Yes	80%	$5,950 / $11,900
Platinum	Yes	90%	$5,950 / $11,900

[2] HHS Certification Criteria

At a minimum, a QHP must be certified to satisfy the following criteria[81] established by HHS:

- Meets marketing requirements and does not employ marketing practices that discourage individuals with significant health needs from enrolling in health care coverage.[82]

- Ensures a sufficient choice of providers, both in-network and out-of-network.[83]

- Includes within health plan networks those essential community providers that service predominantly low-income and medically underserved individuals.[84]

- Implements a quality improvement strategy that provides increased reimbursement or other incentives for:[85]

    — Implementation of wellness and health promotion activities;
    — Quality reporting, effective case management, care coordination, chronic disease management, and care compliance initiatives;
    — Implementation of activities to prevent hospital readmissions; and
    — Implementation of activities to improve patient safety and reduce medical errors.

- Uses a standardized enrollment form.[86]

- Uses a standard format for presenting health benefit options.[87]

- Provides information to enrollees and prospective enrollees on quality measures for each health plan offered in each Exchange.[88]

[3] Approved Health Insurance Issuer

An *approved health insurance issuer* is a health insurance issuer that:

- Is licensed and in good standing in each state where the issuer offers health insurance coverage through an Exchange;

---

[81] PPACA § 1301(a)(1)(A).
[82] PPACA § 1311(c)(1)(A).
[83] PPACA § 1311(c)(1)(B).
[84] PPACA § 1311(c)(1)(C).
[85] PPACA § 1311(c)(1)(E).
[86] PPACA § 1311(c)(1)(F).
[87] PPACA § 1311(c)(1)(G).
[88] PPACA § 1311(c)(1)(H).

- Offers at least one QHP at the "silver level" and "gold level" in each state Exchange in which the issuer participates;

- Charges the same premium rate for a QHP purchased through an Exchange as it does for the same plan purchased outside an Exchange or through a broker;

- Charges the same rate for a QHP for an entire year, submits justification for rate increases to the Exchange, and posts those justifications on the issuer's Internet Web site;[89]

- Varies premium rates by geographic rating area, age, tobacco use, and family size (individual, two adults, adult plus child or children, and family);[90]

- Must not discriminate on the basis of race, color, national origin, disability, age, sex, gender identity, or sexual orientation;[91] and

- Complies with other applicable HHS regulations and other requirements an Exchange may establish.

[D] Catastrophic Plan

In addition to QHPs, health insurance issuers may offer a catastrophic plan through an Exchange.[92] A catastrophic plan would be available only to (1) individuals who have not yet attained age 30 (determined at the beginning of the plan year), (2) individuals who are exempt from the enroll-or-pay penalties because of a hardship, and (3) individuals who would not otherwise have access to affordable coverage.

A catastrophic plan provides coverage for at least three primary care visits per year and the essential health benefits listed above.[93] However, no reimbursement will occur for essential health benefits (other than primary care visits) in a given plan year until the individual has incurred cost-sharing expenses in excess of the annual out-of-pocket expense limit for high-deductible health plans coupled with HSAs ($5,950 for single coverage and $11,900 for family coverage for 2011).

[E] Exchange Subsidies

Beginning in 2014, applicable taxpayers who enroll in a QHP offered through an Exchange may be eligible to receive premium assistance from the Exchange. If the Exchange determines that the applicable taxpayer is eligible, the Exchange will make an advance payment of the premium assistance credit to the issuer of the QHP, thereby reducing the premium due from the applicable taxpayer to the QHP.[94] The applicable taxpayer also will be allowed a refundable tax credit for the premiums he or she pays to purchase a QHP through an Exchange during a taxable year, reduced by the amount of any advance payment of premium assistance made by the Exchange.[95]

An *applicable taxpayer* is a taxpayer whose "household income" for the taxable year is between 100 percent and 400 percent of the FPL for the appropriate family size.[96] Table 11-3 shows the applicable FPL income thresholds (for 2012).

---

[89] 45 C.F.R. § 156.210(a).

[90] *See* PPACA § 1201 (limiting variations in premiums); 45 C.F.R. § 156.255.

[91] 45 C.F.R. § 156.200(e).

[92] PPACA § 1302(e).

[93] PPACA § 1302(e)(1)(B).

[94] PPACA § 1412(a).

[95] PPACA § 1401(a) (adding Section 36B to the Code); Treas. Reg. § 1.36B-4.

[96] PPACA § 1401(a) (adding Section 36B(c)(2)(C) to the Code); Treas. Reg. § 1.36B-2(b). In addition, an applicable taxpayer cannot be claimed as a dependent by another taxpayer and must file a joint return if married. For purposes of the advance payment of premium

TABLE 11-3.
2012 Federal Poverty Level (FPL)[97]

Family Size	100% of FPL	200% of FPL	300% of FPL	400% of FPL
1	$11,170	$22,340	$33,501	$44,680
2	$15,103	$30,260	$45,390	$60,520
3	$19,090	$38,180	$57,270	$76,360
4	$23,050	$46,100	$69,150	$92,200

Household income is defined as the modified adjusted gross income (MAGI) of all individuals in the taxpayer's family size who are required to file an income tax return.[98] A taxpayer's MAGI for this purpose means the taxpayer's adjusted gross income increased by amounts excluded from gross income through a foreign tax credit, tax-exempt interest, and Social Security benefits not included in gross income.[99]

An applicable taxpayer is eligible for the advance payment of premium assistance and the refundable tax credit for premiums paid so long as he or she is not eligible for minimum essential coverage from another source (e.g., an employer-sponsored group health plan) other than in the individual market.[100] The applicable taxpayer will be deemed to be eligible to enroll in minimum essential coverage under an employer-sponsored group health plan if he or she had the opportunity to enroll even if he or she did not actually enroll and enrollment has closed.[101] Also, if the applicable taxpayer actually enrolls in an employer-sponsored group health plan, he or she will be deemed to be eligible for minimum essential coverage even if the employer's plan does not meet the requirements for affordability and minimum value.[102] If the applicable taxpayer is automatically enrolled in an employer-sponsored group health plan, he or she will not be deemed to have enrolled for this purpose if participation in such coverage is terminated by the end of the second calendar month of the plan year or other period (or by the end of the opt-out period to be established by the DOL).[103] Note that if the employer-sponsored group health plan is affordable and provides minimum value, the employee who opts out will still be deemed to be eligible for minimum essential coverage, and therefore ineligible for the advance payment of premium assistance and the refundable tax credit.

In general, to be treated as minimum essential coverage for purposes of the advance payment of premium assistance and the refundable premium tax credit, the employer-sponsored group health coverage must be affordable and provide minimum value.[104] To meet the affordability test, the employee's share of the premium for self-only coverage must not exceed 9.5 percent of the employee's household income.[105] The affordability test is always based on the cost of self-only coverage, even if

---

assistance, an Exchange may treat a taxpayer with household income under 100% of FPL as an applicable taxpayer if it projects that the taxpayer's household income will be between 100% and 400% of FPL for the year. Treas. Reg. § 1.36B-2(b)(6).

[97] Annual Update of HHS Poverty Guidelines, 77 Fed. Reg. 4034–35 (Jan. 26, 2012). Additional FPL guidelines are published for larger families and individuals and families in Alaska and Hawaii.

[98] PPACA § 1401(a) (adding Section 36B(d)(2) to the Code); Treas. Reg. § 1.36B-1(e)(1). See **Section 11.02[C][2]** for a contemplated special safe harbor to enable employers to calculate household income for purposes of the pay-or-play penalty based on the employee's Form W-2 compensation.

[99] PPACA § 1401(a) (adding Section 36B(d)(2) to the Code); Treas. Reg. § 1.36B-1(e)(2).

[100] PPACA § 1401(a) (adding Section 36B(c)(2)(B) to the Code); Treas. Reg. § 1.36B-2(a)(2). See **Section 11.01[B]** for the definition of minimum essential coverage.

[101] Treas. Reg. § 1.36B-2(c)(3)(iii).

[102] PPACA § 1401(a) (adding Section 36B(c)(2)(C) to the Code); Treas. Reg. § 1.36B-2(c)(3)(vii). See **Section 11.02[C][2]** for a discussion of the affordability and minimum value requirements for employer-sponsored group health coverage to constitute minimum essential coverage.

[103] Treas. Reg. § 1.36B-2(c)(3)(vii)(B).

[104] PPACA § 1401(a) (adding Section 36B(c)(2)(C) to the Code); Treas. Reg. §§ 1.36B-2(c)(3)(v), (vi).

[105] PPACA § 1401(a) (adding Section 36B(c)(2)(C)(i) to the Code); Treas. Reg. § 1.36B-2(c)(3)(v).

the employee actually enrolls in family or some other level of coverage.[106] Treasury regulations indicate that the IRS will issue guidance on how employer-provided wellness program incentives and amounts under a health reimbursement account (HRA) are treated for purposes of the affordability test.[107] To meet the minimum value test, the employer-sponsored group health plan's share of total allowed costs of benefits provided under the plan must be at least 60 percent of those costs.[108]

The amount of premium tax credit an applicable taxpayer receives depends on the taxpayer's household income and is the lesser of (1) the total amount of premiums payable by the taxpayer for a QHP; or (2) the excess of the adjusted monthly premium based on the second-lowest-cost silver plan (with some exceptions) over an amount equal to one-twelfth of the product of the applicable percentage provided in Table 11-4 below times the taxpayer's household income.[109]

An example best illustrates how the premium tax credit is calculated.

Example 1. William and his wife Erin have no children. Both work at Paradise City Pools, a small employer that does not offer any health care coverage. Their household income is $58,840 per year. Both William and Erin are enrolled in a QHP through an Exchange that provides them with health care coverage. The adjusted monthly premium for the second-lowest-cost silver plan is $500 per month. William and Erin pay a $600 monthly premium for their QHP. Because William and Erin have household income between 100 percent and 400 percent of the FPL, they may be eligible for a premium tax credit. The calculation of their annual premium tax credit is shown below.

1. Multiply $58,840 by 9.5%, which equals $5,589.80.

2. Divide $5,589.80 by 12 months, which equals $465.82.

3. Subtract $465.82 from $500, which equals $34.18.

4. Take the lesser of $600 and $34.18.

Result: The monthly premium tax credit for William and Erin is $34.18.

TABLE 11-4.
Exchange Premium Limits for Eligible Individuals

Income Level (in terms of FPL)	Max. % of Income Paid Toward Health Care Coverage
Up to 133%	2%
133–150%	3–4%
150–200%	4–6.3%
200–250%	6.3%–8.05%
250–300%	8.05%–9.5%
300–400%	9.5%

[106] PPACA § 1401(a) (adding Section 36B(c)(2)(C)(i) to the Code); Treas. Reg. § 1.36B-2(c)(3)(v). The Treasury Department anticipates that for purposes of the individual enroll-or-pay penalty applicable to an employee's family members, the affordability test for an employer-sponsored group health plan will be based on the family level of coverage. Preamble to the Department of Treasury Proposed Regulations on Health Insurance Premium Tax Credit, 76 Fed. Reg. 50,931, 50,935.

[107] Treas. Reg. § 1.36B-2(c)(3)(v)(4). HSA contributions would not affect the affordability test.

[108] PPACA § 1401(a) (adding Section 36B(c)(2)(C)(ii) to the Code); Treas. Reg. § 1.36B-2(c)(3)(vi). See **Section 11.02[C][2]** for a discussion of minimum value.

[109] I.R.C. § 36B(b); Treas. Reg. § 1.36B-3(d).

TABLE 11-5.
Exchange Out-of-Pocket Spending Limits for Eligible Individuals

Income Level (in terms of FPL)	Out-of-Pocket Spending Limits
100–200%	$1,983 (I) / $3,967 (F)
200–300%	$2,975 (I) / $5,950 (F)
300–400%	$3,987 (I) / $7,973 (F)

TABLE 11-6.
Exchange Cost-Sharing Subsidies for Eligible Individuals

Income Level (in terms of FPL)	Cost-Sharing Limits
100–150%	6%
>150–200%	13%
>200–250%	27%
>250–400%	30%

The Affordable Care Act provides for two other subsidies—reductions in out-of-pocket spending limits and reductions in cost-sharing limits—for an "eligible insured" who is enrolled in a QHP through an Exchange and whose household income is between 100 percent and 400 percent of the FPL.[110] The issuer of the QHP will be notified by HHS if an eligible insured is eligible for a reduction in the out-of-pocket spending limits and cost-sharing limits, and such issuer must reduce the cost-sharing accordingly. See Table 11-5 for a graphical illustration of the reductions in out-of-pocket spending limits and Table 11-6 for a graphical illustration of the reductions in cost-sharing limits.

[F] Special Rules

Cost-sharing subsidies are not available to individuals who are not lawfully present in the United States. To be lawfully present, an individual must be a citizen or national of the United States or an alien lawfully present in the United States.[111]

An Native American Indian who has household income of not more than 300 percent of the FPL will be classified as an eligible insured, and the issuer of the plan will eliminate any cost-sharing under the QHP.[112]

Cost-sharing subsidies are not available to an individual who received a free choice voucher from his or her employer (the free choice voucher provisions have since been repealed).[113]

[G] State Innovation Waivers

Finally, the Affordable Care Act gives states some flexibility to pursue their own innovative strategies for providing residents with quality affordable health insurance.[114] HHS and Treasury are authorized to evaluate and grant "state innovation waivers" for up to five years from certain provisions of

---

[110] PPACA § 1402(a).

[111] PPACA § 1402(e).

[112] PPACA § 1402(d).

[113] I.R.C. § 36B(c)(2)(D). See **Section 11.03** for a discussion on free choice vouchers and their repeal.

[114] PPACA § 1332.

the Affordable Care Act.[115] The waivers allow states to implement their own policies that are different from the Affordable Care Act so long as the state policies (1) provide coverage that is at least as comprehensive as the coverage offered under the Exchanges, (2) make coverage at least as affordable as it would be under the Exchanges, (3) provide coverage to at least as many residents as the Affordable Care Act would provide, and (4) do not increase the federal deficit.[116] For example, a state innovation waiver would enable a state to allow larger employers to purchase coverage through an Exchange.

State innovation waivers are available under the Affordable Care Act beginning in 2017.[117] However, proposed legislation would accelerate the availability of such waivers by up to three years.[118]

[H] Guidance for States

In March 2012, HHS issued final (and interim final) regulations designed to coordinate and assist states in complying with the mandate to establish Exchanges.[119] The regulations and related guidance cover a broad range of topics but still leave states with many obstacles to overcome. A summary of the HHS guidance to states regarding the establishment of Exchanges is set forth below.

[1] State Flexibility

The Affordable Care Act does not require any state to establish an Exchange. Rather, it provides each state with an opportunity to design and establish its own Exchange that facilitates the purchase of health insurance by eligible individuals through a QHP, assists certain qualified employers in enrolling their employees in QHPs, and satisfies other HHS standards established under the Act.[120] However, if a state elects not to establish an Exchange, or HHS determines on or before January 1, 2013, that a state will not have an operable Exchange by January 1, 2014, then HHS may take action to establish and implement an Exchange on behalf of that state.[121]

Under the proposed regulations, states that elect to establish their own Exchanges have some flexibility as to the structure of the Exchange.[122] States may establish the Exchange as part of an existing or new state agency, or as a nonprofit organization. States also may collaborate and partner with other states or with HHS to carry out some or all of the Exchange functions. Finally, states may enter into contracts with private entities to perform certain Exchange operations.

---

[115] PPACA § 1332; *see* White House Office of the Press Secretary, FACTSHEET: The Affordable Care Act: Supporting Innovation, Empowering States (Feb. 28, 2011), *available at* http://whitehouse.gov/the-press-office/2011/02/28/fact-sheet-affordable-care-act-supporting-innovation-empowering-states.

[116] PPACA § 1332; *see* White House Office of the Press Secretary, FACTSHEET: The Affordable Care Act: Supporting Innovation, Empowering States (Feb. 28, 2011), *available at* http://whitehouse.gov/the-press-office/2011/02/28/fact-sheet-affordable-care-act-supporting-innovation-empowering-states.

[117] PPACA § 1332.

[118] *See* White House Office of the Press Secretary, Remarks by the President and the Vice President to the National Governors Association, *available at* http://www.whitehouse.gov/the-press-office/2011/02/28/remarks-president-and-vice-president (referencing the "Empowering States to Innovate Act," S. 3958, proposed by Senators Wyden (D. Or.) and Brown (R. Mass.) on November 18, 2010, and indicating President Obama's support for the bipartisan measure).

[119] 45 C.F.R. pts. 155 and 156.

[120] PPACA §§ 1311, 1321.

[121] PPACA § 1321(c)(1)(B).

[122] 45 C.F.R. § 155.100(b).

[2] HHS Approval Process

To meet the requirement that HHS determine, by January 1, 2013, whether a state Exchange will be "operational," HHS has proposed a formal application process.[123] Under the process, a state would submit a written application to HHS regarding its proposed Exchange design and an "Exchange Blueprint" to show how it will satisfy the Affordable Care Act requirements, and HHS would perform a readiness assessment. If, after assessing the submitted application and meeting with state and Exchange officials, HHS believes that the proposed Exchange will be operational by January 1, 2014, HHS will issue its conditional approval, acknowledging that further actions will need to be taken during 2013 to fully implement the Exchange by January 1, 2014. It a state does not get an Exchange approved initially, it can reapply for future years by submitting an application to HHS at least 12 months in advance of the proposed effective date.[124]

[3] Self-Sustainability

The Affordable Care Act requires that each state Exchange must be self-sustainable financially by January 1, 2015.[125] One way an Exchange can raise the revenue necessary to pay for its operations is to impose assessments or user fees on the insurance issuers that participate in the Exchange by offering QHPs to eligible individuals and employers. The HHS regulations confirm that federal funds may not be provided to sustain Exchanges after January 1, 2015.[126]

[4] Basic Exchange Functions

Under the final regulations, HHS indicates that, to be approved, an Exchange must be capable of performing the following functions:

- Evaluating and certifying QHPs;[127]

- Certifying exemptions for individuals from the individual enroll-or-pay requirements;[128]

- Determining an individual's eligibility for enrollment in a QHP, advance payments of the premium tax credit, cost-sharing reductions, Medicaid, and CHIP,[129] both initially and annually thereafter;

- Notifying individuals of determinations and coordinating with Medicaid, CHIP, and other programs to implement determinations;[130]

- Enrolling eligible individuals in a QHP;[131]

- Establishing a process for appeals of eligibility determinations;[132]

---

[123] 45 C.F.R. § 155.105.

[124] 45 C.F.R. § 155.106.

[125] PPACA § 1311(d)(5). The Affordable Care Act also specifies that any funds intended for the administrative and operational functions of the Exchange shall not be used for "staff retreats, promotional giveaways, excessive executive compensation, or promotion of Federal or State legislative and regulatory modifications." PPACA § 1311(d)(5)(B).

[126] 45 C.F.R. § 155.160(b)(2).

[127] 45 C.F.R. §§ 155.1000 *et seq.*

[128] 45 C.F.R. § 155.200(b).

[129] 45 C.F.R. §§ 155.200(a), .302.

[130] 45 C.F.R. §§ 155.340, .345.

[131] 45 C.F.R. § 155.400.

[132] 45 C.F.R. §§ 155.310(e), .335(h).

- Keeping accurate accounting records and satisfying the related oversight and financial integrity requirements;[133]

- Evaluating quality improvement strategies;[134]

- Overseeing implementation of enrollee satisfaction surveys, assessment and ratings of health care quality and outcomes, information disclosures, and data-reporting requirements;[135]

- Establishing a call center to respond to requests for assistance from consumers via a toll-free number;[136]

- Operating an Internet Web site that will serve as the primary source of information regarding QHPs offered on the Exchange, Exchange activities, and related information;[137] and

- Awarding grants to public and private entities to carry out the functions of the Affordable Care Act's "Navigator" program, which include public education activities to raise awareness of QHPs, the availability of premium tax credits, and cost-sharing reductions.[138]

[5] Enrollment in QHPs

Perhaps the most basic function of an Exchange is the enrollment of qualified individuals in a QHP, and the related administration of advance payments of the premium tax credit and cost-sharing reductions. Under the final regulations, HHS indicates that it will develop and provide a single, streamlined application that Exchanges may furnish to individuals for purposes of QHP enrollment, advance payments of the premium tax credit, cost-sharing reductions, Medicaid, and CHIP.[139] An Exchange may use an alternative application, but it must be approved in advance by HHS.[140]

The initial open enrollment period for an Exchange will run from October 1, 2013, through March 31, 2014.[141] To the extent that an Exchange receives an individual's application by December 15, 2013, the Exchange must ensure a QHP coverage date of January 1, 2014.[142] For future annual open enrollment periods, the Exchange must send an open enrollment notice to enrollees in September preceding the open enrollment period.[143] Exchanges also must offer special and other mid-year enrollment periods, similar to the rules already applicable to cafeteria plans under Section 125 of the Code.[144]

[6] Small Business Health Options Program (SHOP)

In addition to facilitating individual enrollment in QHPs, Exchanges are required to establish health insurance options for small businesses.[145] The purpose of SHOP is to give small businesses access to the types of health insurance choices and purchasing power that larger businesses have. A small employer, for this purpose, is an employer with no more than 100 employees, although a state

---

[133] 45 C.F.R. § 155.200(c); *see* PPACA § 1313 (providing oversight requirements).
[134] 45 C.F.R. § 155.200(d).
[135] 45 C.F.R. § 155.200(d) (citing PPACA §§ 1311(c)(1), (3), and (4)).
[136] 45 C.F.R. § 155.205(a).
[137] 45 C.F.R. § 155.205(b).
[138] 45 C.F.R. § 155.210; *see* PPACA § 1311(i) (describing the Navigator program).
[139] 45 C.F.R. § 155.405(a); *see* PPACA 1413(b)(1)(A) (directing HHS to develop a streamlined application).
[140] 45 C.F.R. § 155.405(b).
[141] 45 C.F.R. § 155.410(b).
[142] 45 C.F.R. § 155.410(c).
[143] 45 C.F.R. § 155.410(d).
[144] 45 C.F.R. § 155.420.
[145] PPACA § 1311(b)(1)(B).

may elect to limit SHOP enrollment to employers with no more than 50 employees prior to 2016.[146] The number of employees is based on the employer's average number of employees in the preceding year, and part-time employees would be counted on the same basis as full-time employees (although seasonal employees could be counted as fractions based on the period worked).[147] States may expand SHOP to include larger employers beginning in 2017.[148]

---

[146] PPACA §§ 1304(b)(2), (3); 45 C.F.R. § 155.710(b).
[147] PPACA § 1304(b)(2); 45 C.F.R. § 155.20.
[148] PPACA § 1312(f)(2)(B).

Chapter 12

OPERATIONAL CHANGES FOR HEALTH PLANS

§ 12.01 Medicare Part D

[A] Background

In 2003, President Bush signed the Medicare Prescription Drug, Improvement and Modernization Act of 2003 (the MMA),[1] which at the time was the most significant overhaul of the federal Medicare program since its inception nearly 40 years before. The MMA created Medicare Part D, which, effective January 1, 2006, extended the Medicare entitlement to prescription drug coverage for the first time.[2] Whereas Medicare Part A (hospitalization coverage) and Part B (outpatient and doctor visit coverage) are run almost entirely by the federal government, Part C (Medicare Advantage) and Part D are based on a system where private insurers provide coverage subject to certain federal minimum requirements and receive significant subsidies from the federal government.

A Medicare Part D plan offered by a private insurer must offer enrollees "qualified prescription drug coverage," which satisfies the standard requirements outlined below, or coverage that is actuarially equivalent to the standard prescription drug coverage.[3] The insurer must submit the proposed Medicare Part D plan to the Centers for Medicare and Medicaid Services (CMS) and receive CMS approval before the plan can be offered as a Medicare Part D plan entitling the insurer to a federal subsidy.[4] Qualified prescription drug coverage in a standard Medicare Part D plan consists of the following elements:

- An annual deductible, which for 2013 is $325. An individual who enrolls in the standard Medicare Part D plan must pay 100 percent of the first $325 in annual prescription drug costs incurred during 2013.[5]

- An initial corridor of coverage, which for 2013 runs from $325 to $2,970 in annual prescription drug costs. An individual who incurs prescription drug costs in this corridor pays only 25 percent of the costs. The Medicare Part D plan picks up the remaining 75 percent as a cost-sharing benefit.[6]

- A coverage gap (commonly known as the "donut hole") for annual prescription drug costs between $2,970 and $4,750 in 2013. The $4,750 is referred to as the "out-of-pocket expense limit." An individual who incurs prescription drug costs within the donut hole will have to pay 100 percent of such costs. No cost-sharing is available in the donut hole under the original version of the Medicare Part D program.[7]

- Catastrophic coverage for annual prescription drug costs in excess of $4,750 for 2013. An individual who incurs prescription drug costs at this level is deemed to have incurred catastrophic costs, and is only required to pay 5 percent of such costs. The Medicare Part D plan picks up the remaining 95 percent as a cost-sharing benefit.[8]

---

[1] Pub. L. No. 108-173, 117 Stat. 2066 (2003).

[2] 42 U.S.C. §§ 1395w-101 et seq.

[3] 42 U.S.C. § 1395w-101(a). Qualified prescription drug coverage must be available for covered Part D prescription drugs, and must include access to negotiated prices. 42 U.S.C. § 1395w-102.

[4] 42 U.S.C. § 1395w-101(b).

[5] 42 U.S.C. § 1395w-102(b)(1).

[6] 42 U.S.C. §§ 1395w-102(b)(2), (3).

[7] 42 U.S.C. § 1395w-102(b)(3).

[8] 42 U.S.C. § 1395w-102(b)(4). Once an eligible individual reaches the out-of-pocket expense limit for a year, the individual is only required to pay the greater of 5% of the cost, or a $5 copay for any prescription drug ($2 for generics and preferred multiple source drugs). Id.

Viewing all of the elements together graphically, the standard Medicare Part D plan coverage for 2013 would look like this:

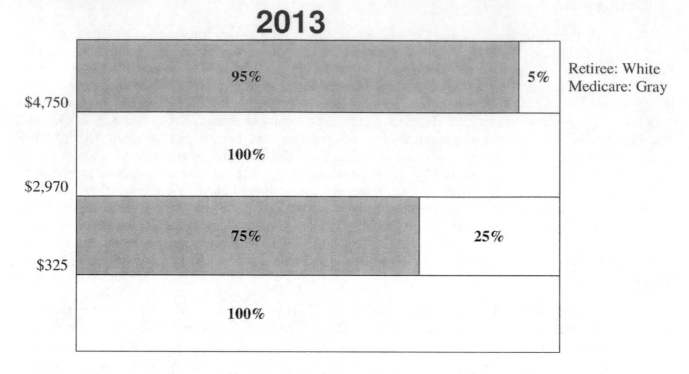

Or like this (assuming $7,500 in annual prescription drug costs):

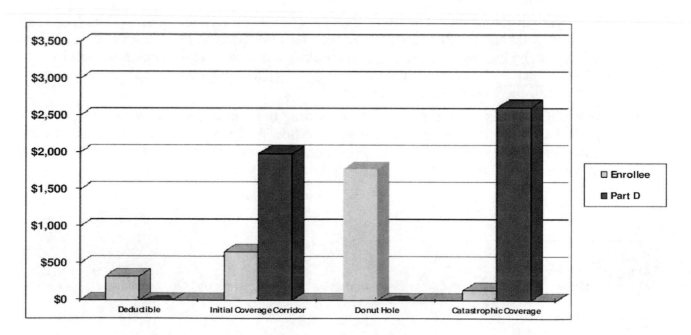

The total out-of-pocket expenses for an individual enrolled in a standard Medicare Part D plan for 2013 at various levels of annual prescription drug costs are as follows:

Prescription Drug Cost	Average Monthly Premium	Medicare Pays	Enrollee Pays (Including Premium)
$1,000	$30	$506.25	$853.75 (85%)
$5,000	$30	$2,221.25	$3,138.75 (63%)
$10,000	$30	$6,971.25	$3,388.75 (34%)

[B] Closing the Donut Hole

Notwithstanding a significant narrowing of the donut hole since 2006, when it spanned annual prescription drug costs from $2,250 to $5,100, Medicare Part D was viewed by many as incomplete coverage. Those with donut hole expenses received no cost-sharing benefits for those expenses, unless the Medicare Part D plan in which they were enrolled provided coverage in excess of the standard coverage or on some actuarially equivalent basis. Congress addressed this perceived problem in the Affordable Care Act.

[1] 2010 Rebate

The Affordable Care Act closes the donut hole by adding Part D cost-sharing at every level of cost (except the deductible) through 2020.[9] For 2010, the donut hole relief took the form of a rebate. Any individual who was enrolled in a Medicare Part D plan as of the last day of a calendar quarter in 2010, and who incurred costs for covered Part D prescription drugs in excess of the initial coverage limit of $2,830 for 2010 (which was the cap on the initial coverage corridor described above), was entitled to receive a rebate payment of $250 no later than the 15th calendar day of the third month following the end of the quarter.[10] An individual could receive only one such payment, and individuals who were already receiving income-related subsidies or reduction in premium subsidies under Medicare Part D were not eligible for the rebate.[11] Thus, if an eligible individual was covered under a Part D plan and incurred prescription drug costs in excess of $2,830 in the first calendar quarter of 2010 (ending March 31, 2010), that individual was entitled to receive a $250 rebate check from HHS by June 15, 2010.

[2] 2011 and Forward

After 2010, the Affordable Care Act creates a Medicare Coverage Gap Discount Program, which provides eligible individuals with access to manufacturers' discounts for certain brand-name drugs, the cost of which would fall into the donut hole.[12] In general, the manufacturer's discount is equal to 50 percent of the negotiated price.[13] In addition, the Act modifies the definition of qualified prescription

---

[9] HCERA § 1101.

[10] HCERA § 1101(a) (adding new subsection (c) to 42 U.S.C. § 1395w-152).

[11] HCERA § 1101(a). Section 1101(a) of the HCERA amends Section 3301(b) of the PPACA, which had added a new Section 1395w-114A, entitled "Medicare Coverage Gap Discount Program." Individuals with income up to 150% of the federal poverty level are eligible to receive income-related subsidies under Medicare Part D.

[12] PPACA § 3301.

[13] *See* Memorandum to all Part D Sponsors from Cynthia G. Tudor, Ph.D., Director, Medicare Drug Benefit and C&C Data Group, and Cheri Rice, Deputy Director, Medicare Plan Payment Group (May 21, 2010). Note that the manufacturer's discount on brand-name drug expenses incurred in the donut hole generally is applied after any other supplemental coverage, so that the discount applies to the

drug coverage in a standard Medicare Part D plan to include coverage for generic and certain other non-generic drugs in the donut hole.[14] However, individuals who are already receiving income-related subsidies or reduction in premium subsidies under Medicare Part D are not eligible for the new donut hole coverage.[15]

For generic drugs, an individual enrolled in a standard Medicare Part D plan has a "generic-gap co-insurance" requirement for annual prescription drug costs incurred in the donut hole equal to 93 percent in 2011 (as opposed to 100 percent in 2010).[16] The generic-gap co-insurance is reduced by 7 percentage points each year through 2019.[17] In 2020 and future years, the generic-gap co-insurance will be 25 percent, which is equivalent to the current co-insurance requirement in the initial coverage corridor.[18]

If we incorporate the Affordable Care Act's changes into the standard Medicare Part D coverage, the coverage will look like this for 2013 (assuming all drug costs relate to generic drugs):

2013—Generic Only

Retiree: White
Medicare: Gray

	95%	5%
$4,750	21%	79%
$2,970	75%	25%
$325	100%	

Or like this (assuming $7,500 in annual prescription drug costs):

---

individual's actual cost. However, when an employer adopts its own Part D plan for its retirees, known as an "employer group waiver plan" (EGWP), the manufacturer's discount applies before any other commercial wraparound or supplemental coverage provided by the employer. *See* Memorandum to all Part D Sponsors from Cynthia G. Tudor, Ph.D., Director, Medicare Drug Benefit and C&C Data Group, and Cheri Rice, Deputy Director, Medicare Plan Payment Group (June 2, 2010). This special rule could have the effect of creating substantial savings for employers that provide retiree prescription drug coverage through an EGWP and a supplemental wrap plan.

[14] HCERA § 1101(b) (adding new subparagraph (C) to 42 U.S.C. § 1395w-102(b)(2)).

[15] HCERA § 1101(b) (adding new subparagraph (C) to 42 U.S.C. § 1395w-102(b)(2)); *see* 42 U.S.C. 1395w-114A(g)(1), as added by Section 3301(b) of the PPACA, for a definition of an "applicable individual" who is eligible to receive the new donut hole coverage.

[16] HCERA § 1101(b) (adding new subparagraph (C) to 42 U.S.C. § 1395w-102(b)(2)); *see* 42 U.S.C. § 1395w-114A(g)(1), as added by Section 3301(b) of the PPACA, for a definition of an "applicable individual" who is eligible to receive the new donut hole coverage.

[17] HCERA § 1101(b) (adding new subparagraph (C)(ii)(II) to 42 U.S.C. § 1395w-102(b)(2)).

[18] HCERA § 1101(b) (adding new subparagraph (C)(ii)(II) to 42 U.S.C. § 1395w-102(b)(2)).

2013—Generic Only

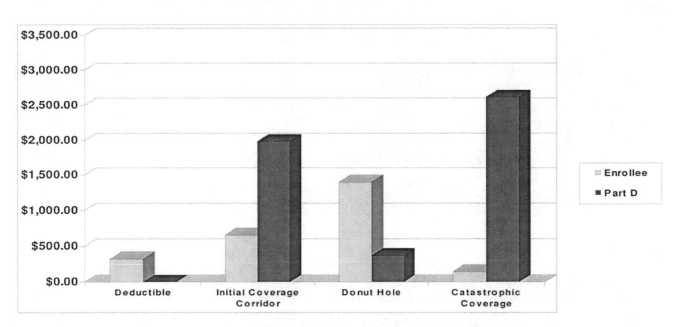

The total out-of-pocket expenses for an individual enrolled in standard Medicare Part D coverage for 2013, after incorporating the Affordable Care Act's changes, at various levels of annual prescription drug costs for generic drugs are as follows:

2013—Generic Only

Prescription Drug Cost	Average Monthly Premium	Medicare Pays	Enrollee Pays (Including Premium)
$1,000	$30	$506.25	$853.75 (85%)
$5,000	$30	$2,595.05	$2,764.95 (55%)
$10,000	$30	$7,345.05	$3,014.95 (30%)

For non-generic drugs, an individual enrolled in a standard Medicare Part D plan will have co-insurance for annual prescription drug costs (based on the negotiated price) incurred in the donut hole equal to the difference between the "applicable gap percentage" and the discount percentage.[19] The applicable gap percentage is 97.5 percent for 2013 and 2014, 95 percent for 2015 and 2016, 90 percent for 2017, 85 percent for 2018, 80 percent for 2019, and 75 percent for 2020 and each year thereafter.[20] The discount percentage is a flat 50 percent.[21] Again, if we incorporate the Affordable

---

[19] HCERA § 1101(b) (adding new subparagraph (D) to 42 U.S.C. § 1395w-102(b)(2)).

[20] HCERA § 1101(b) (adding new subparagraph (D)(ii) to 42 U.S.C. § 1395w-102(b)(2)).

[21] HCERA § 1101(b) (adding new subparagraph (D) to 42 U.S.C. § 1395w-102(b)(2)). *See* 42 U.S.C. § 1395w-114A(g)(4)(A), as added by Section 3301(b) of the PPACA (providing the discount percentage).

Care Act's changes into the standard Medicare Part D coverage, the coverage will look like this for 2013:

2013—Non-Generic Only

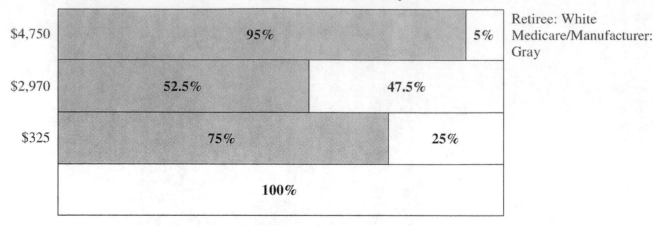

$4,750	95%	5%
$2,970	52.5%	47.5%
$325	75%	25%
	100%	

Retiree: White
Medicare/Manufacturer: Gray

Or like this (assuming $7,500 in annual prescription drug costs):

2013—Non-Generic Only

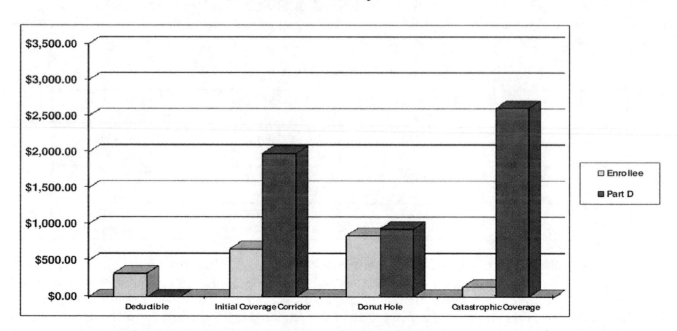

The total out-of-pocket expenses for an individual enrolled in standard Medicare Part D coverage for 2013, after incorporating the Affordable Care Act's changes, at various levels of annual prescription drug costs for non-generic drugs, are as follows:

2013—Non-Generic Only

Prescription Drug Cost	Average Monthly Premium	Medicare Pays	Enrollee Pays (Including Premium)
$1,000	$30	$506.25	$853.75 (85%)
$5,000	$30	$3,155.75	$2,204.25 (44%)
$10,000	$30	$7,905.75	$2,094.25 (21%)

[C] Nondeductibility of Retiree Drug Subsidy Payments

While Congress envisioned a Medicare Part D prescription drug coverage program based on the private insurance system, it did not want to discourage employers from providing or continuing to provide prescription drug coverage for their Medicare-eligible retirees. To incentivize employers to maintain such coverage, the MMA authorized the payment of a retiree drug subsidy (RDS) to employers that maintained retiree prescription drug plans that were at least actuarially equivalent to the standard Medicare Part D plan.[22] On an annual basis, employers can apply electronically to CMS for the RDS and provide an actuarial certification that their plans are actuarially equivalent to the standard Medicare Part D plan.[23] If approved, plan sponsors will receive RDS payments from CMS on an annual, quarterly, or monthly basis equal to 28 percent of each qualifying retiree's allowable prescription drug costs incurred within a certain corridor.[24] For 2012, the RDS applies to allowable prescription drug expenses between $320 and $6,500.[25] Allowable prescription drug costs are actual incurred expenses for any Part D drugs, net of any discounts, rebates, or other price concessions.[26] Thus, to the extent that a qualifying retiree incurs $6,500 in allowable prescription drug costs in 2012, the plan sponsor may be eligible to receive an RDS payment for that qualifying retiree of $1,730.40 (28% × ($6,500 − $320)).

One significant benefit of the RDS for companies subject to federal income tax was that, under the MMA, RDS payments were tax-exempt.[27] Thus, for-profit employers received a double tax benefit. They could deduct any expenses incurred by the employer to pay for retiree prescription drug costs,[28] and then receive an RDS payment from CMS for those same expenses without including the RDS payment in taxable income. This double tax benefit made the RDS payments more valuable for employers subject to tax than for government, church, and other tax-exempt employers.

The Affordable Care Act addresses and eliminates the double tax benefit associated with RDS payments for tax years beginning after December 31, 2012.[29] The Act amends Section 139A of the Code to provide that an employer's tax deduction for allowable prescription drug expenses is reduced to the extent the employer is reimbursed for such expenses through the receipt of RDS payments. Even

---

[22] 42 U.S.C. § 1395w-132. The changes made by the Affordable Care Act to Medicare Part D will make the standard Medicare Part D plan more valuable on an actuarial basis, which will make it more difficult for employer-sponsored retiree prescription drug plans to qualify for RDS payments. See **Section 12.01** notes 1–21 and accompanying text for a discussion of the Act's changes to the standard Medicare Part D plan.

[23] See http://www.cms.gov/EmployerRetireeDrugSubsid/Downloads/OviewoftheRDSrev1.pdf for information on how an employer can apply for RDS payments.

[24] 42 U.S.C. § 1395w-132(a)(3).

[25] See http://rds.cms.hhs.gov/reference_materials/threshold_limit.htm.

[26] 42 U.S.C. § 1395w-132(a)(3)(C).

[27] I.R.C. § 139A (as added by the MMA § 1202(a)).

[28] I.R.C. § 162 (providing a deduction for trade or business expenses).

[29] PPACA § 9012.

though the Act changes do not become effective until 2013,[30] for-profit employers receiving RDS payments were required to recognize the full accounting impact of this change in the employer's financial statements for the first quarter of 2010 (the quarter in which the Affordable Care Act was enacted). For example, Verizon Communications announced shortly after the Act was enacted that it would post a one-time accounting charge of $970 million in the first quarter of 2010 due to the 2013 change in the tax treatment of the RDS payments.[31] Ultimately, the Act puts for-profit employers back on equal footing with tax-exempt employers with respect to the value of the RDS payments.

§ 12.02   Nondiscrimination Rules Applicable to Insured Health Benefits

Sections 105 and 106 of the Code provide the basis for an employee to exclude from gross income for federal income tax purposes the value of employer-provided health coverage.[32] Section 105 allows an employee to exclude from income the amounts actually reimbursed by an employer for the medical care of an employee, his or her spouse, and dependents.[33] Section 106 allows an employee to exclude from income the cost of group health plan coverage paid by the employer.[34] Together, they house the single largest tax expenditure in the Internal Revenue Code and incentivize employers to provide health care coverage to employees.[35]

As with any tax expenditure, there are limits on the incentive. Section 105(h) of the Code provides that benefits made available in a self-funded group health plan will qualify for the Section 105 tax exclusion only if the plan does not discriminate in favor of highly compensated individuals.[36] A "highly compensated individual," for this purpose, means one of the five highest paid officers, a shareholder who owns more than 10 percent of the employer, or an individual who is among the highest-paid 25 percent of all employees.[37] Certain employees are excluded from the eligibility portion of the nondiscrimination analysis (as described below), including employees who have completed less than three years of service, employees who have not attained age 25, part-time or seasonal employees, collectively bargained employees, and employees who are nonresident aliens who receive no U.S.-source earned income.[38] This definition of "highly compensated individual" tends to be broader than the definition of "highly compensated employee" used for purposes of the nondiscrimination requirements applicable to tax-qualified retirement plans.[39]

The Section 105(h) nondiscrimination requirement applies in two ways. First, a self-funded group health plan cannot discriminate in favor of highly compensated individuals as to eligibility to participate. This requirement can be satisfied by passing a percentage test that is similar to the minimum coverage test applicable to tax-qualified retirement plans under Section 410(b) of the Code. Second, the benefits provided under a self-funded group health plan cannot discriminate in favor of highly compensated individuals. This requirement is satisfied only if all benefits provided under the plan to

---

[30] HCERA § 1407 (delaying the effective date of Section 9012 of the PPACA from tax years beginning after December 31, 2010, to tax years beginning after December 31, 2012).

[31] James A. White, *Corporate Charges Pegged to New Health Law Keep Adding Up*, Wall. St. J., Apr. 2, 2010.

[32] I.R.C. §§ 105, 106.

[33] I.R.C. § 105(b).

[34] I.R.C. § 106(a).

[35] *See* http://www.taxpolicycenter.org/briefing-book/background/expenditures/largest.cfm (comparing tax expenditures for the 2008 tax year).

[36] I.R.C. § 105(h).

[37] I.R.C. § 105(h)(5).

[38] I.R.C. § 105(h)(3)(B).

[39] *Compare* I.R.C. § 105(h)(5) *with* I.R.C. § 414(q) (providing a definition of highly compensated employee that generally is limited to 5% shareholders and employees who earn compensation in the previous year in excess of a dollar threshold ($110,000 for 2011)).

highly compensated individuals are also provided to other plan participants. To the extent that a self-funded health plan provides benefits to retirees, the nondiscrimination requirements will apply separately to the retiree population.[40]

Notwithstanding the existence of the Section 105(h) nondiscrimination limitation, employers that wish to provide additional health benefits to top executives and other highly compensated individuals have been undeterred. Employers could provide discriminatory health benefits either on an insured basis, thereby avoiding Section 105(h) (which only applies to self-funded group health plans), or by imputing the cost of the additional health benefits as income for federal income tax purposes. Employers often use these techniques to enhance incentive or retention compensation packages for executives, to provide additional coverage to certain highly compensated retirees, and to equalize benefits for highly compensated expatriates.

The Affordable Care Act closes what may be viewed as a loophole in the existing tax law by extending the nondiscrimination requirements of Section 105(h) to insured group health plans.[41] However, in December 2010, Treasury issued a notice indefinitely delaying the effective date of such nondiscrimination requirements until regulations or other guidance has been issued.[42] In order to provide insured group health plan sponsors time to implement any changes required as a result of the regulations or other guidance, Treasury has indicated that the guidance will not apply until plan years beginning a specified period after issuance.[43] Once guidance is issued, employers will be prohibited from providing discriminatory health coverage to highly compensated individuals on an insured basis. However, if the discriminatory health coverage is provided as part of a grandfathered health plan,[44] the prohibition will not apply unless and until the plan loses its grandfathered status.[45] Employers that make significant use of insured arrangements that discriminate in favor of highly compensated individuals should consider whether it is possible and desirable to take advantage of the grandfathering exemption.

Curiously, the penalties for providing discriminatory health coverage appear to be different based on whether the coverage is provided through a self-funded or an insured plan. Because the new provision does not apply to self-funded plans, the provision of discriminatory health coverage in violation of Section 105(h) of the Code continues to result in the inclusion of the value of the discriminatory benefits in the gross income of the affected highly compensated individuals.[46] Employers and highly compensated individuals may be able to reduce the tax exposure by designing the self-funded arrangement to impute the cost of the discriminatory coverage in income, as opposed to the value of the actual benefits provided.

On the other hand, the penalty for providing discriminatory health coverage through an insured arrangement is a tax of $100 per day per individual affected by the violation.[47] Because the penalty is not dependent on the taxability of the coverage, imputing the amount of discriminatory benefits or the cost of the discriminatory coverage in income for the covered highly compensated individuals would not seem to be sufficient to avoid the penalty tax. If this is the case, employers may shift back to self-funded arrangements to provide discriminatory health coverage to highly compensated individuals on an after-tax basis.

---

[40] Treas. Reg. § 1.105-11(c)(3)(iii).

[41] PPACA § 1001(5) (adding PHSA § 2716).

[42] I.R.S. Notice 2011-1, 2011-2 I.R.B. 259.

[43] I.R.S. Notice 2011-1, 2011-2 I.R.B. 259.

[44] See **Chapter 5** for a discussion of grandfathered health plans.

[45] PPACA § 1251(a). Also, if the discriminatory health coverage is provided only to retirees, the coverage may be exempt under the retiree-only plan exemption. See **Section 5.03** for a discussion of the retiree-only plan exemption.

[46] I.R.C. § 105(h).

[47] I.R.C. § 4980D. For governmental plans, other than a federal government plan, the penalty is an equivalent civil money penalty imposed under the Public Health Service Act. PHSA § 2723(b)(2).

§ 12.03   Auto-Enrollment

In the Pension Protection Act of 2006 (PPA),[48] Congress paved the way for most employers to institute automatic enrollment arrangements in their Section 401(k) and 403(b) retirement savings programs. The PPA amended ERISA to supersede any state wage payment laws that would otherwise prohibit automatic enrollment arrangements for ERISA-covered plans.[49] By encouraging employers to establish automatic enrollment arrangements in their retirement plans, Congress hoped to increase retirement savings among American workers by leveraging employee inertia.

In a retirement plan automatic enrollment arrangement, new employees (and sometimes existing employees) are deemed to have elected to participate in the plan and to make contributions at a level set by the employer (e.g., 3 percent of pay).[50] The employer must provide sufficient advance notice of the automatic enrollment arrangement to employees, and employees must have the ability to opt out of the arrangement.[51] Employees can opt out by affirmatively electing not to participate in the retirement plan, or to participate at a different contribution level (e.g., 1 percent or 5 percent of pay).

The Affordable Care Act extends the automatic enrollment concept to employment-based group health plans. The Act adds a new Section 18A to the Fair Labor Standards Act of 1938, as amended (FLSA),[52] which requires large employers that offer enrollment in one or more group health plans to automatically enroll new full-time employees in one of the plans (subject to any waiting periods authorized by law) and to continue enrollment of current employees.[53] "Large employers" are defined, for this purpose, as having more than 200 full-time employees.[54] Further guidance will be necessary to determine whether the threshold number of employees is determined as an average over some period and whether full-time equivalents are counted.

Large employers subject to the new requirement must provide adequate advance notice to employees regarding the automatic enrollment arrangement, and an opportunity to opt out of any coverage in which the employee is automatically enrolled.[55] Following in the footsteps of the PPA, the Affordable Care Act specifically supersedes any state wage payment law that would prevent an employer from implementing an automatic enrollment arrangement in a group health plan.[56]

The Affordable Care Act does not include a specific effective date for the automatic enrollment provision. The lack of a specific effective date suggested that the requirement becomes effective on the PPACA's date of enactment, March 23, 2010. However, the DOL has clarified that the provision will not be effective until after regulations have been published.[57] In 2012, the DOL announced that, due to the need to coordinate automatic enrollment rules with other Affordable Care Act guidance, it did not expect the automatic enrollment rules to become effective until after 2014.[58]

---

[48] Pub. L. No. 109-280, 120 Stat. 780.

[49] PPA § 902(f) (adding Section 514(e)(1) of ERISA). The ERISA preemption provision does not apply to non-ERISA plans, such as those sponsored by church and governmental employers.

[50] *See* I.R.C. § 401(k)(13), as added by PPA § 902(a) (providing a safe harbor from Section 401(k) plan nondiscrimination testing for certain plans with qualified automatic contribution arrangements).

[51] I.R.C. § 401(k)(13).

[52] Pub. L. No. 75-718, 52 Stat. 1060; *see* 29 U.S.C. §§ 201 *et seq.*

[53] PPACA § 1511.

[54] FLSA § 18A.

[55] FLSA § 18A.

[56] FLSA § 18A; *see also* PPA § 902(f) (adding Section 514(e)(1) of ERISA relating to preemption of state laws inhibiting automatic enrollment for retirement plans).

[57] FLSA § 18A; *see* http://www.dol.gov/ebsa/faqs/faq-aca5.html. On April 8, 2011, the DOL held an open forum to discuss issues relating to the new automatic enrollment provisions. *See* I.R.S. Notice 2011-36, 2011-21 I.R.B. 792 (May 23, 2011).

[58] *See* I.R.S. Notice 2012-17, A-1, 2012-9 I.R.B. 430 (Feb. 9, 2012).

§ 12.04 Employer Notice of Coverage Options

While employers are busy figuring out exactly how their employment-based group health plans compare to the Exchange options that will be available beginning in 2014, they need to be cognizant of a new employee notice requirement that requires disclosure of information relating to the employer's plan(s) and the Exchange. The Affordable Care Act adds a new Section 18B to the FLSA, which sets forth the details of the new notice requirement.[59] All employers subject to the FLSA must disclose, in a written notice, the following:

- Information regarding the existence of an Exchange, including a description of the services provided by the Exchange as well as information regarding how employees can contact the Exchange for assistance and further information;[60]

- If the employment-based group health plan is deemed to be "inadequate," i.e., the plan's share of total allowed costs under the plan is less than 60 percent of such costs, information regarding the employees' possible eligibility for a premium tax credit or cost-sharing reduction for coverage purchased through the Exchange;[61] and

- If an employee purchases a QHP through the Exchange, information regarding the possibility that the employee may lose the benefit of any tax-free employer contribution to the employment-based group health plan.[62]

The new notice requirement becomes effective on March 1, 2013, which is slightly less than three years following the enactment of the Affordable Care Act.[63] Employers must provide the notice to all then-current employees by March 1, 2013, and to all new hires thereafter at the time of hiring.

§ 12.05 Nursing Mothers

The Affordable Care Act also amends the FLSA to require employers to make certain accommodations for nursing mothers. The Act adds new Section 7(r) to the FLSA to require employers to provide:

- A "reasonable break time" for an employee to express breast milk for a nursing child for one year following the child's birth each time the employee has the need to express milk; and

- A place, other than a bathroom, that is shielded from view and intrusion by the public and co-workers, where the employee can express breast milk.[64]

The new provision does not require employers to compensate an employee for the breaks, notwithstanding the fact that many rest periods or breaks of short duration are treated as "working time" by employers.

An employer with fewer than 50 employees may be exempt from the requirements for nursing mothers if such requirements would impose an undue hardship on the employer.[65] The Affordable Care Act defines "undue hardship" as imposing on the employer "significant difficulty or expense when

---

[59] PPACA § 1512 (adding FLSA § 18B).

[60] FLSA § 18B(a); see **Chapter 11** (discussing Exchanges).

[61] FLSA § 18B(a); see **Section 11.04[E]** for a discussion of premium tax credits and cost-sharing reductions.

[62] FLSA § 18B(a).

[63] FLSA § 18B(b).

[64] PPACA § 4207 (adding FLSA § 7(r)).

[65] FLSA § 7(r).

considered in relation to the size, financial resources, nature or structure of the employer's business."[66] Significantly, the Act does not preempt the laws in several states that may provide equivalent or greater protections to employees who are nursing mothers.[67]

§ 12.06   Reporting Cost of Coverage on Form W-2

[A]   Background

The Affordable Care Act requires all employers that provide an employment-based group health plan to employees to report, on each employee's Form W-2, the aggregate cost of the plan for a calendar year.[68] The reporting requirement is informational only and will not affect the amount includable in income or the amount reported in any other box on Form W-2.[69] The IRS has indicated that the purpose of the reporting is to provide useful and comparable consumer information to employees on the cost of their health care coverage.[70] For 2013, certain employers will be required to report the aggregate cost of all health coverage in box 12 of Form W-2, using code DD.[71] The 2013 Forms W-2 generally are due by January 31, 2014.

[B]   Aggregate Cost of Coverage

The "aggregate cost" of coverage is determined by using one of three methods: the COBRA Applicable Premium Method, the Premium Charged Method, or the Modified COBRA Premium Method.[72]

[1]   COBRA Applicable Premium Method

Under the COBRA applicable premium method, the reportable cost for a period equals the COBRA applicable premium for that coverage for that period. If the employer applies this method, the employer must calculate the COBRA applicable premium in a manner that satisfies the requirements under Section 4980B(f)(4) of the Internal Revenue Code. Under current guidance, the COBRA applicable premium calculation would meet these requirements if the employer made such calculation in good-faith compliance with a reasonable interpretation of the statutory requirements under Code Section 4980B.[73]

[2]   Premium Charged Method

The premium charged method may be used to determine the reportable cost only for an employer's insured group health plan. If the employer applies this method, the employer must use the premium charged by the insurer for that employee's coverage (e.g., for self-only coverage or for family coverage, as applicable to the employee) for each period as the reportable cost for that period.[74]

---

[66] FLSA § 7(r).

[67] *See, e.g.*, N.J. Rev. Stat. § 26:4B-4/5 (entitling a nursing mother to breastfeed in any place of public accommodation).

[68] PPACA § 9002 (adding I.R.C. § 6051(a)(14)); I.R.S. Notice 2012-9, A-31, 2012-4 I.R.B. 315.

[69] I.R.S. Notice 2012-9, A-2, 2012-4 I.R.B. 315.

[70] I.R.S. Notice 2012-9, A-2, 2012-4 I.R.B. 315.

[71] I.R.S. Notice 2012-9, A-5, 2012-4 I.R.B. 315. Special rules apply for employees who leave or are hired during the year. I.R.S. Notice 2012-9, A-6, A-7, and A-8, 2012-4 I.R.B. 315.

[72] I.R.S. Notice 2012-9, A-24, 2012-4 I.R.B. 315.

[73] I.R.S. Notice 2012-9, A-25, 2012-4 I.R.B. 315.

[74] I.R.S. Notice 2012-9, A-26, 2012-4 I.R.B. 315.

[3]　Modified COBRA Premium Method

The modified COBRA premium method can be used by an employer with respect to a plan only where it subsidizes the cost of COBRA coverage (so that the premium charged to COBRA qualified beneficiaries is less than the COBRA applicable premium) or where the actual premium charged by the employer to COBRA qualified beneficiaries for each period in the current year is equal to the COBRA applicable premium for each period in a prior year.[75]

The aggregate cost includes the cost of coverage provided under hospital indemnity or other fixed indemnity insurance, or the cost of coverage for a specified disease or illness, if the employer makes any contribution to the cost of coverage that is excludable under Section 106 of the Internal Revenue Code or if the employee purchases the policy on a pretax basis under a cafeteria plan.[76] However, the aggregate cost to be reported on Form W-2 does not include any employee salary reduction contributions to a health flexible spending account (Health FSA), or any contributions to an HSA or an Archer MSA, a health reimbursement account (HRA), long-term care coverage, and coverage under stand-alone dental or vision benefit plans. In addition, an employer that makes contributions to a multi-employer health plan is not required to report the cost of that coverage on Form W-2.[77] This new reporting requirement was originally intended to apply to the 2011 tax year, which meant that employers would have had to report the aggregate cost of their group health plans on 2011 Forms W-2 by January 31, 2012[78] However, subsequent guidance provides that the reporting requirement is not mandatory for 2011 Forms W-2.[79] Therefore, employers will not be subject to the penalties associated with failing to report the aggregate cost of employer-sponsored coverage on 2011 Forms W-2.

[C]　Exemptions from Filing Requirement

An employer is not subject to the new Form W-2 reporting requirement if it was required to file fewer than 250 Forms W-2 for the preceding calendar year.[80] Thus, for example, if an employer is required to file, on January 31, 2013, only 225 Forms W-2 for the 2012 calendar year, the employer will not be subject to the new reporting rule for 2013. However, if the same employer is required to file, on January 31, 2013, 250 or more Forms W-2 for the 2012 calendar year, the employer will be subject to the new rule for the 2013 Forms W-2. Employers will not be required to report aggregate cost information for individuals who would not otherwise be provided a Form W-2 for the year, such as retirees and other former employees who receive no Form W-2 compensation.[81]

In addition, certain employers are exempt from the new reporting requirement, such as employers that provide health coverage through self-funded church plans (or other group health plans not subject to COBRA or other federal continuation coverage requirements), and government employers that provide health plans primarily for members of the military and their families.[82]

---

[75] I.R.S. Notice 2012-9, A-27, 2012-4 I.R.B. 315.
[76] I.R.S. Notice 2012-9, A-37, 2012-4 I.R.B. 315.
[77] I.R.C. § 6051(a)(14); I.R.S. Notice 2012-9, A-17, A-18, and A-20, 2012-4 I.R.B. 315.
[78] I.R.C. § 6051(a).
[79] I.R.S. Notice 2010-69, 2010-44 I.R.B. 576.
[80] I.R.S. Notice 2012-9, A-3, 2012-4 I.R.B. 315.
[81] I.R.S. Notice 2012-9, A-9, 2012-4 I.R.B. 315.
[82] I.R.S. Notice 2012-9, A-21 and A-22, 2012-4 I.R.B. 315.

§ 12.07   Simple Cafeteria Plans for Small Businesses

[A]   Background

Many employers that provide employment-based group health plans and charge a portion of the cost of the group health plan to employees offer employees an opportunity to pay that cost on a pretax basis through a "cafeteria plan" that satisfies the requirements of Section 125 of the Code. A cafeteria plan is a written plan document under which participating employees may choose to receive cash or one or more qualified benefits.[83] A "qualified benefit" is any benefit that is not includable in the gross income of an employee by reason of a specific provision of the Code.[84] Qualified benefits generally include employer-provided health coverage, group term life and accidental death and dismemberment (AD&D) insurance, disability benefits, Health FSAs, and dependent care flexible spending accounts.[85] Employees who elect to receive qualified benefits under a cafeteria plan generally make pretax salary reduction contributions to pay for those benefits.

Cafeteria plans are subject to certain nondiscrimination requirements under Section 125 of the Code. Generally, a cafeteria plan cannot discriminate in favor of highly compensated individuals as to eligibility to participate in the plan or with respect to contributions and benefits provided under the plan.[86] If the cafeteria plan is discriminatory, highly compensated individuals will be treated as being in constructive receipt (for tax purposes) of a cash benefit.[87] A "highly compensated individual" is defined as an officer, 5 percent shareholder, or highly compensated employee of the employer.[88] In addition, the benefits provided to key employees in a cafeteria plan cannot exceed 25 percent of the aggregate of such benefits provided to all employees under the plan.[89]

A cafeteria plan does not discriminate as to eligibility to participate if (1) the plan benefits a classification of employees that does not discriminate in favor of officers, shareholders, or highly compensated individuals; (2) no more than three years of employment are required to participate in the plan and the employment requirement is uniform for all employees; and (3) eligible employees begin participation by the first day of the first plan year after the employment requirement is satisfied.[90] Under proposed Treasury regulations, a cafeteria plan does not discriminate as to eligibility if the plan satisfies certain nondiscriminatory classification tests based on the tests that apply to tax-qualified retirement plans.[91]

A cafeteria plan that offers group health plan benefits does not discriminate with respect to contributions and benefits if (1) contributions for each participant equal 100 percent of the cost of the health benefit coverage under the plan of the majority of highly compensated participants similarly situated, or 75 percent of the cost of the most expensive health benefit coverage of the similarly situated participant having the highest-cost health benefit coverage under the plan; and (2) contributions and benefits in excess of those described in clause (1) bear a uniform relationship to compensation.[92] Many view these rules as unworkable, and it is expected that Treasury will issue new regulations to provide guidance as to how the cafeteria plan nondiscrimination rules should be applied.

---

[83] I.R.C. § 125(d).

[84] I.R.C. § 125(f).

[85] I.R.C. § 125(f).

[86] I.R.C. § 125(b)(1).

[87] I.R.C. § 125(b)(1); Prop. Treas. Reg. § 1.125-7(m)(2).

[88] I.R.C. § 125(e). Spouses and dependents of highly compensated individuals are themselves considered highly compensated individuals. I.R.C. § 125(e)(1)(D).

[89] I.R.C. § 125(b)(2). "Key employees" are defined in the same manner as under the top-heavy rules and the rules regarding nonqualified deferred compensation under Section 409A of the Code. See I.R.C. § 416(i).

[90] I.R.C. § 125(g)(3); Prop. Treas. Reg. § 1.125-7.

[91] Prop. Treas. Reg. § 1.125-7(b)(1). See generally I.R.C. § 410(b); Treas. Reg. §§ 1.410(b)-2 et seq. (discussing the minimum coverage rules applicable to tax-qualified retirement plans).

[92] I.R.C. § 125(g)(2); Prop. Treas. Reg. § 1.125-7(e).

[B] New Option for Small Businesses

Beginning in 2011, the Affordable Care Act provides small employers with a means of establishing a cafeteria plan that is automatically exempt from the Section 125 nondiscrimination requirements.[93] A "small employer" means an employer that employed, on average, 100 or fewer employees on business days during either of the two preceding years.[94] If the employer was not in existence in a preceding year (and throughout the whole preceding year), the calculation is based on the number of employees that the employer reasonably expects to employ on business days in the current year.[95] If a small employer establishes a "simple cafeteria plan" described in this section, and subsequently increases its employee base such that it can no longer satisfy the 100-employee test, the employer is deemed to remain a small employer until such time as it employs, on average, 200 or more employees in any preceding year.[96] All affiliates that are in the employer's controlled group are treated as a single employer for purposes of determining whether the employer is a small employer.[97]

The simple cafeteria plan contemplated by the Affordable Care Act must meet both an employer contribution requirement and minimum eligibility and participation requirements. To satisfy the employer contribution requirement, the employer must contribute, on behalf of each qualified employee (i.e., those who are not highly compensated individuals or key employees), an amount (1) equal to a uniform percentage (at least 2 percent) of the employee's compensation for the plan year, or (2) that is at least equal to the lesser of 6 percent of the employee's compensation or two times (2×) the amount of the employee's salary reduction contributions for the plan year.[98] If the employer seeks to satisfy the contribution requirement using matching contributions, the rate of matching contributions for any highly compensated or key employee cannot be greater than the rate of matching contributions for any other non–highly compensated or non-key employee.[99] To satisfy the minimum eligibility and participation requirements, any employee who completes at least 1,000 hours of service for the employer for the preceding plan year must be eligible to participate in the plan, and any eligible employee must be permitted to elect any benefit available under the plan, subject to any terms and conditions of the plan applicable to all participants.[100] Certain employees may be excluded for this purpose, such as employees who have not attained age 21 by the end of the plan year, have less than one year of service with the employer, are covered by a collective bargaining agreement, or are nonresident aliens with no U.S.-source income.[101]

---

[93] PPACA § 9022 (adding I.R.C. § 125(j)).

[94] I.R.C. § 125(j)(5).

[95] I.R.C. § 125(j)(5)(B). Any predecessor employer is treated as the employer for purposes of applying the 100-employee test. I.R.C. § 125(j)(5)(D)(i).

[96] I.R.C. § 125(j)(5)(C).

[97] I.R.C. § 125(j)(5)(D)(ii) (referencing the controlled group rules set forth in Section 414 of the Code).

[98] I.R.C. § 125(j)(3). The contribution rule is similar to the contribution obligation applicable to safe harbor Section 401(k) plans that are exempt from the annual nondiscrimination tests. *See* I.R.C. §§ 401(k)(12), (13).

[99] I.R.C. § 125(j)(3)(B).

[100] I.R.C. § 125(j)(4).

[101] I.R.C. § 125(j)(4)(B).

Chapter 13

NEW TAXES AND OTHER REVENUE RAISERS

§ 13.01   "Cadillac" Tax

One potential way to control the rising cost of health coverage is to incentivize employees (and their dependents) to use only the necessary and appropriate health-related products and services. Requiring employees to pay for a portion of such products and services may provide such an incentive. However, if an employee has very valuable "Cadillac" health coverage for which he or she pays little or nothing, the incentive to act as a rational consumer of health-related products and services vanishes.

The Affordable Care Act attempts to address this issue (and raise revenue to help pay for health care reform) by adding a new nondeductible tax on "Cadillac" health coverage. The Act adds Section 4980I to the Internal Revenue Code, which imposes a 40 percent excise tax on the "excess benefit" in "applicable employer-sponsored coverage."[1] The excise tax is imposed on the insurance company in an insured health plan and on the employer/plan sponsor in an employment-based group health plan that is self-funded.[2]

The excess amount, determined on a monthly basis, is equal to the aggregate monthly cost of employer-sponsored coverage over one-twelfth of the annual limitation.[3] The cost of a plan is determined in the same manner as the COBRA premium.[4] Beginning in 2018, the annual limitation is $10,200 for self-only coverage and $27,500 for family coverage.[5] Both figures are adjusted, beginning in 2018, by the "health cost adjustment percentage," which basically measures the growth in health insurance costs, adjusted by age and gender factors, by reference to the growth in the cost of the standard benefit option in the Federal Employees Health Benefit Plan after 2010.[6]

The threshold for determining excess amounts is higher for qualified retirees and those participating in a plan sponsored by an employer where the majority of the employees covered by the plan are engaged in a high-risk profession or are employed to repair or install electrical or telecommunication lines.[7] Beginning in 2018, the annual limitation for these individuals is $11,850 for self-only coverage and $30,950 for family coverage, adjusted in each case for cost-of-living increases.[8] A "qualified retiree" is an individual who is receiving retiree coverage, is over age 55, and is not Medicare eligible.[9] High-risk professions include police and fire personnel, emergency medical technicians and other first responders, longshoremen, and individuals engaged in the construction, mining, agriculture (not including food processing), forestry, and fishing industries.[10] Retirees of high-risk professions are included if they have at least 20 years of employment in the profession.[11]

The term "applicable employer-sponsored coverage" includes any employment-based group health plan provided to any employee, former employee, or surviving spouse (or any other primary

---

[1] PPACA § 9001 (adding I.R.C. § 4980I).

[2] I.R.C. § 4980I(c)(2).

[3] I.R.C. § 4980I(b)(2).

[4] I.R.C. § 4980I(d)(2) (citing the COBRA premium calculation rules located at Section 4980B(f)(4) of the Code).

[5] I.R.C. § 4980I(b)(3)(C)(i).

[6] I.R.C. §§ 4980I(b)(3)(C)(ii), (iii).

[7] I.R.C. § 4980I(b)(3)(C)(iv). This is substantially identical to the definition of "early retiree" that is applicable to the temporary early retiree reinsurance program. See **Section 7.01[A]** notes 1–27 for a discussion of the reinsurance program. Therefore, to some extent the Act creates conflicting incentives for employers. Through the end of 2013, the reinsurance program encourages employers to continue to provide early retiree health coverage by providing reimbursements of 80% of the health expenses between $15,000 and $90,000. However, beginning in 2018, employers are penalized for providing retiree health coverage with a value in excess of $11,850 (self) or $30,950 (family), as adjusted.

[8] I.R.C. § 4980I(b)(3)(C)(iv).

[9] I.R.C. § 4980I(f)(2).

[10] I.R.C. § 4980I(f)(3).

[11] I.R.C. § 4980I(f)(3).

insured individual) on a pretax basis, other than a plan providing certain "excepted" benefits, long-term care, dental, or vision benefits.[12] Applicable employer-sponsored coverage is determined without regard to whether the employee pays for all or a portion of the coverage, and includes Health FSAs and plans covering government employees.[13]

In the event that the insurer or employer/plan sponsor underpays the excise tax for any month, a penalty equal to 100 percent of any underpayment amount is imposed, plus interest calculated at the IRS tax underpayment rate.[14] However, the penalty may not apply if the employer/plan sponsor can show that it neither knew, nor by exercising reasonable diligence would have known, that an underpayment existed, if the underpayment is corrected within 30 days, and in such other circumstances as may be specified in regulations.[15]

§ 13.02   Health FSAs

[A]   Background

In the 1980s, after about a decade of administering defined benefit pension plans in accordance with the ERISA rules, employers and employees started to look for ways to supplement the standard pension benefits. Section 401(k) plans, which had first appeared in the late 1970s, started to become a popular addition to employer retirement benefits packages because they allowed employees to supplement their employer-funded pensions with their own contributions on a pretax basis.[16] As defined benefit pension plans fell out of favor in the 1990s due to their complexity and unpredictable costs, Section 401(k) plans and their progeny ultimately became the primary retirement benefits vehicle for most employers.[17] Thus, for better or for worse, there has been an evolutionary shift in the manner in which retirement benefits are provided, from the paternalistic employer-funded defined benefit pension plans to the more flexible employer and employee-funded defined contribution Section 401(k) plans.

A similar evolutionary cycle is under way for employment-based group health plans. In the years following ERISA's enactment, many employers provided health benefits to employees through traditional indemnity arrangements funded entirely or almost entirely by employers. Employees (and their spouses and dependents) could go to any health care provider to receive treatment, and the insurance company would pay most or all of the expenses. As health care costs rose in the 1980s, 1990s, and 2000s, employers started to adopt arrangements with cost-containment structures, such as PPOs, HMOs, and POS arrangements. Employers also introduced the concept of employee co-insurance and cost-sharing to shift a portion of the increasing costs to employees.

To supplement the traditional employment-based group health plans, employers began to make health flexible spending accounts (Health FSAs) available to employees. Like Section 401(k) plans on

---

[12] I.R.C. § 4980I(d)(1). Excepted benefits, for this purpose, include coverage only for accident or disability income insurance, liability insurance or coverage issued as a supplement to liability insurance, workers' compensation or similar insurance, automobile medical payment insurance, credit-only insurance, and other similar coverage. I.R.C. § 9832(c)(1). However, coverage for on-site medical clinics may be applicable employer-sponsored coverage. I.R.C. § 4980I(d)(1)(B)(i). Applicable employer-sponsored coverage also does not include coverage for a specified disease or illness, or hospital indemnity or fixed indemnity insurance if such coverage is not excludable from gross income. I.R.C. § 4980I(d)(1)(B)(iii).

[13] I.R.C. § 4980I(d)(1).

[14] I.R.C. § 4980I(e).

[15] I.R.C. § 4980I(e)(2).

[16] I.R.C. § 401(k), as added by the Revenue Act of 1978, Pub. L. No. 95-600, § 135, 92 Stat. 2763.

[17] Over the years, Section 403(b) tax-sheltered annuity plans, which are available only for public school and nonprofit employers, and Section 457(b) eligible deferred compensation plans, which are available for government and nonprofit employers, have become subject to many of the same requirements and principles as apply to Section 401(k) plans.

the retirement side, Health FSAs are accounts to which employees (and employers) can make contributions on a pretax basis to reimburse the employee for medical expenses incurred by the employee (or former employee), spouse, or dependent that are not otherwise covered by health insurance.[18] Unlike Section 401(k) plans, contributions to Health FSAs do not have to be held in trust. A Health FSA can simply be recorded as an unfunded liability in the employer's bookkeeping records.

[B] New Contribution Limit of Health FSAs

Prior to the Affordable Care Act, there was no limit on the annual amount that an employee could elect to contribute to a Health FSA on a pretax basis. However, Health FSAs are subject to a "use it or lose it" rule, whereby any amounts remaining in the Health FSA at the end of the plan year (or at the end of a grace period following the plan year) after all claims are incurred must be forfeited to the employer.[19] In addition, Health FSAs are subject to a uniform coverage rule, whereby the maximum amount of reimbursement elected by the employee must be available at all times during the plan year.[20] For example, if prior to the plan year an employee elects to contribute $5,000 on a pretax basis to a Health FSA for the plan year, the entire $5,000 must be available to the employee as reimbursement on the first day of the plan year. If the employee incurs $5,000 in reimbursable expenses on the first day of the plan year, receives the full reimbursement from the Health FSA, and then terminates employment before contributing the full $5,000 to the Health FSA, the employer is liable for the loss and cannot seek recovery from the terminated employee. Thus, as a practical matter, most employers have implemented an annual limit of $5,000 or less to avoid material exposure to employees under the use-it-or-lose-it rule, or to the employer under the uniform coverage rule.

For plan years beginning in 2013, annual salary reduction contributions to Health FSAs are limited to $2,500.[21] The limit applies only to employee salary reduction contributions to Health FSAs, and not to employer contributions (sometimes called "flex credits").[22] If the Health FSA provides for a grace period after the end of a plan year during which a participant is still permitted to use up any remaining Health FSA balance, unused salary reduction contributions that are carried over into the grace period do not count against the limit for the subsequent plan year.[23] The $2,500 annual limit is adjusted for cost-of-living increases after 2013.[24]

Inadvertent violations of the annual Health FSA limit may be corrected if:

- The violation arose from a reasonable mistake by the employer (or the employer's agent) and is not due to willful neglect;

- The Health FSA plan document has been timely amended to reflect the annual limit;

- The employer's cafeteria plan (and/or Health FSA) is not under IRS audit, and the employer has not received written notification from the IRS of such an audit; and

---

[18] I.R.C. § 105(b); Prop. Treas. Reg. § 1.125-5(a).

[19] I.R.C. § 125(d)(2); Prop. Treas. Reg. § 1.125-5(c). A Health FSA plan may provide a grace period following the plan year during which claims may be incurred and reimbursed from the Health FSA for the plan year just ended. I.R.S. Notice 2005-42, 2005-23 I.R.B. 1204; Prop. Treas. Reg. § 1.125-1(e). The grace period can extend for up to 2½ months following the end of the plan year. I.R.S. Notice 2005-42, 2005-23 I.R.B. 1204; Prop. Treas. Reg. § 1.125-1(e).

[20] I.R.C. § 125(d)(2); Prop. Treas. Reg. § 1.125-5(d)(1).

[21] PPACA § 9005 (adding I.R.C. § 125(i)); I.R.S. Notice 2012-40, 2012-25 I.R.B. 1046 (May 30, 2012). An employer cannot change the plan year of a Health FSA if the primary purpose of the change is to delay application of the limit. I.R.S. Notice 2012-40 § III, 2012-25 I.R.B. 1046 (May 30, 2012).

[22] I.R.S. Notice 2012-40 § III, 2012-25 I.R.B. 1046 (May 30, 2012).

[23] *Id.* In other words, salary reduction contributions are not double counted.

[24] I.R.C. § 125(i).

- The excess salary reduction contributions are distributed to the employee as additional wages (for income and employment tax purposes) for the year of the correction and are reported on a Form W-2.[25]

Employers will need to amend their Health FSA plan documents and summary plan descriptions to reflect this change by December 31, 2014,[26] but the amendment must be retroactively effective as of the beginning of the plan year that starts in 2013. This change, which obviously does not expand health coverage, is one of the revenue-raisers intended to provide a part of the funding for health care reform.

[C] Prohibition of Reimbursement of OTC Drug Expenses

Amounts held in Health FSAs can be used to reimburse an employee for expenses incurred for "medical care" of the employee (or former employee), spouse, and dependents.[27] In 2003, the Internal Revenue Service ruled, for the first time, that expenses incurred for medicines and drugs purchased "over the counter" (i.e., without a prescription of a physician) could constitute expenses for medical care that can be reimbursed from a Health FSA.[28] Such "OTC" expenses included purchases of allergy medicine, pain relievers, antacids, and cold medicine. However, expenses for dietary supplements and similar items that are merely beneficial to the general health of the employee, spouse, and dependents were not expenses for medical care and could not be reimbursed from a Health FSA.[29] While many employer-sponsored Health FSAs were amended to provide for reimbursements of OTC medicines and drugs, it remained a challenge for employees, employers, and third-party administrators to substantiate the differences between OTC expenses for medical care (which could be reimbursed) and OTC expenses for the general health of the employee, spouse, or dependent (which could not).

In another effort to raise revenue for health care reform, the Affordable Care Act added Section 106(f) to the Code to provide that OTC medicines and drugs would no longer be eligible for reimbursement from Health FSAs after December 31, 2010.[30] Only the costs of prescription medicines and drugs, OTC medicines and drugs purchased with a prescription, and insulin would be considered medical expenses eligible for reimbursement.[31] Other items that are not medicines or drugs, such as equipment, supplies, and diagnostic devices, are not subject to the new rule, and the cost of these items may be reimbursed out of a Health FSA if such items otherwise qualify as medical care.[32] The new rule generally applies to all OTC medicines and drugs purchased after December 31, 2010, even if the purchases are made within a grace period applicable to the 2010 plan year.[33]

Many employers and third-party administrators have implemented debit card features for their Health FSAs to simplify the reimbursement process for employees. Due to a concern that the Health FSA debit card administrators would not have enough time to update their systems to recognize whether medicines and drugs have been prescribed, the IRS offered limited relief.[34] Pursuant to this relief, the IRS will not challenge Health FSA reimbursements for expenses incurred through January

---

[25] I.R.S. Notice 2012-40 § III, 2012-25 I.R.B. 1046 (May 30, 2012).

[26] I.R.S. Notice 2012-40 § IV, 2012-25 I.R.B. 1046 (May 30, 2012).

[27] I.R.C. § 105(b).

[28] I.R.S. Rev. Rul. 2003-102, 2003-2 C.B. 559. This revenue ruling was made obsolete as of January 1, 2011. I.R.S. Rev. Rul. 2010-23, 2010-39 I.R.B. 388.

[29] I.R.S. Rev. Rul. 2003-102, 2003-2 C.B. 559.

[30] PPACA § 9003(c) (adding I.R.C. § 106(f)). A similar rule applies for HSAs and Archer MSAs. PPACA §§ 9003(a), (b); see **Section 13.03** notes 47–50 discussing the HSA's prohibition of reimbursement of OTC drug expenses.

[31] I.R.C. § 106(f); I.R.S. Notice 2010-59, 2010-39 I.R.B. 396.

[32] I.R.S. Notice 2010-59, 2010-39 I.R.B. 396 (citing crutches, bandages, and blood sugar test kits as examples).

[33] PPACA § 9003(c) (adding I.R.C. § 106(f)); I.R.S. Notice 2010-59, 2010-39 I.R.B. 396.

[34] I.R.S. Notice 2011-5, 2011-3 I.R.B. 314; I.R.S. Notice 2010-59, 2010-39 I.R.B. 396.

15, 2011, if purchased with a debit card.[35] After January 15, 2011, Health FSA debit cards may continue to be used to purchase medicines and drugs as long as the following requirements are satisfied:

- A prescription is presented to the pharmacist;

- The pharmacist dispenses the OTC medicine or drug in accordance with applicable law;

- An Rx number is assigned;

- The pharmacy (or other vendor) retains records of the Rx number, the name of the purchaser (or the name of the person to whom the prescription applies), and the date and amount of the purchase;

- All records are available to the employer or its agents upon request;

- The debit card system will not accept a charge for an OTC medicine or drug unless an Rx number has been assigned; and

- The requirements otherwise applicable to Health FSA debit cards are satisfied.[36]

Employers needed to amend their cafeteria plan documents and/or Health FSA plan documents by June 30, 2011, to reflect the new Health FSA reimbursement rules for OTC medicines and drugs. The amendment needed to be made retroactively effective to January 1, 2011 (or January 15, 2011, for OTC medicines and drugs purchased with Health FSA debit cards).[37] This change required employers and third-party administrators that offer Health FSAs, and particularly those that have implemented debit card features for their Health FSAs, to redesign the structure of their Health FSAs.

§ 13.03 HSAs

[A] Background

Another vehicle that employees may use to supplement their employer-sponsored health plan coverage is a health savings account (HSA). HSAs, which first became available in 2004, are trust or custodial accounts that may be established by eligible individuals who have coverage under a high-deductible health plan (HDHP).[38] Eligible individuals (and their employers) may contribute to the HSA on a pretax basis, and the HSA account may be used by the individual for reimbursement of certain medical expenses of the individual or his or her spouse or dependents.[39]

HSAs have certain advantages as compared to Health FSAs. HSAs are not subject to the use-it-or-lose-it rules that apply to Health FSAs, so unused account balances can be carried forward from year to year, and eligible individuals can never be reimbursed in an amount greater than the then-current HSA account balances.[40] Also, HSAs are portable, which means that an employee who switches jobs does not need to set up multiple HSAs.[41] All contributions can be made to the same HSA. Finally, whereas Health FSA balances must be used to reimburse medical expenses, an individual can withdraw funds from an HSA for any reason, provided that the individual pays federal

---

[35] I.R.S. Notice 2010-59, 2010-39 I.R.B. 396.

[36] I.R.S. Notice 2011-5, 2011-3 I.R.B. 314.

[37] I.R.S. Notice 2010-59, 2010-39 I.R.B. 396.

[38] Medicare Prescription Drug, Improvement, and Modernization Act of 2003, Pub. L. No. 108-173, § 1201(a), 117 Stat. 2066.

[39] I.R.C. §§ 223(d), (f). Investment earnings held within the HSA are not taxed until they are distributed to the individual. I.R.C. § 223(e).

[40] See **Section 13.02[B]** notes 19–20 (discussing use-it-or-lose-it and uniform coverage rules applicable to Health FSAs).

[41] I.R.C. § 223(d) (indicating that the individual is the owner of the account).

income taxes (and possibly an excise tax) if funds are withdrawn from an HSA other than as reimbursement for qualified medical expenses.[42]

HSAs have some disadvantages as well. Unlike Health FSAs (at least until 2013),[43] monthly contributions to an HSA are capped at one-twelfth of $3,250 (for those individuals with single coverage under an HDHP for 2013) and $6,450 (for those individuals with family coverage under an HDHP for 2013).[44] For individuals who will attain age 55 before the end of the year, those limits are increased by $1,000.[45] Also, an individual is eligible to contribute to an HSA only if he or she is covered under an HDHP that meets certain requirements. For 2013, an HDHP must have a deductible of at least $1,250 (for single coverage) or $2,500 (for family coverage) and an out-of-pocket expense limit of no more than $6,250 (for single coverage) or $12,500 (for family coverage).[46]

[B]   Prohibition of Reimbursement of OTC Drug Expenses

If HSA funds are used to reimburse an individual for "qualified medical expenses," the reimbursements are not subject to federal income tax for the individual.[47] Qualified medical expenses are defined in the same fashion as "expenses for medical care" in the Health FSA context.[48] Therefore, the provisions of the Affordable Care Act that exclude expenses for OTC medicines and drugs from being eligible medical expenses that can be reimbursed from Health FSAs apply equally to HSAs.[49] Accordingly, beginning in 2011, the only medicine and drug expenses that are treated as qualified medical expenses for purposes of tax-free reimbursement from an HSA are prescription medicine and drug expenses, OTC medicine and drug expenses purchased with a prescription, and insulin expenses.[50]

[C]   Tax Increase for Non-Qualified Medical Expense Reimbursements

As indicated above, HSA reimbursements for qualified medical expenses are tax-free to the individual. However, the HSA rules permit individuals to withdraw funds from their HSAs for reasons other than qualified medical expenses. In such cases, the amounts withdrawn are subject to federal income tax at the individual's normal tax rate.[51] However, if the individual is not yet Medicare eligible (which generally means that the individual has not yet reached age 65), there is an additional 10 percent tax applied to the amount withdrawn for purposes other than qualified medical expenses.[52] The additional tax does not apply if the withdrawal is made after the individual has become disabled or has died.[53]

---

[42] I.R.C. § 223(f); see **Section 13.03[C]** notes 51–54 for a discussion of the Act's change to the additional tax on HSA withdrawals used for purposes other than the reimbursement of qualified medical expenses.

[43] See **Section 13.02[B]** notes 19–26 for a discussion of the Act's limit on annual Health FSA contributions.

[44] I.R.C. § 223(b)(2); I.R.S. Rev. Proc. 2012-26, 2012-20 I.R.B. 933.

[45] I.R.C. § 223(b)(3); I.R.S. Rev. Proc. 2010-22, 2010-23 I.R.B. 747.

[46] I.R.C. § 223(c)(2); I.R.S. Rev. Proc. 2012-26, 2012-20 I.R.B. 933.

[47] I.R.C. § 223(f)(1).

[48] I.R.C. § 223(d)(2)(A) (defining qualified medical expenses as amounts paid by an HSA beneficiary for medical care (as defined in Section 213(d) of the Code) of the individual, his or her spouse, and his or her dependents, provided that such expenses have not been reimbursed by insurance or otherwise).

[49] PPACA § 9003(a) (amending I.R.C. § 223(d)(2)(A)); see **Section 13.02[C]** notes 27–37 for a discussion of the change to reimbursements of OTC medicines and drugs from Health FSAs.

[50] I.R.C. § 223(d)(2)(A); I.R.S. Notice 2011-5, 2011-3 I.R.B. 314; I.R.S. Notice 2010-59, 2010-39 I.R.B. 396.

[51] I.R.C. § 223(f)(2).

[52] I.R.C. § 223(f)(4)(C). An individual also may become eligible for Medicare by reason of certain disabilities prior to age 65.

[53] I.R.C. § 223(f)(4)(B).

Under the Affordable Care Act, beginning in 2011, the additional tax applicable to HSA distributions used for purposes other than qualified medical expenses is increased to 20 percent.[54] The existing exceptions for withdrawals after Medicare eligibility, death, or disability continue to apply.

§ 13.04 Administrative Fees for Self-Funded and Insured Plans

[A] Background

The Affordable Care Act generally provides funding for new studies and research on how the quality and efficiency of the United States health care system can be improved. One example is contained in Section 6301 of the Act, which provides for comparative clinical effectiveness research.[55] Basically, this means research to compare health outcomes and the clinical effectiveness, risks, and benefits of two or more medical treatments, services, or items.[56] The research will be conducted by a new nonprofit organization called the Patient-Centered Outcomes Research Institute (the Institute), and funding for the Institute will be generated, in part, from new fees (known as "PCORI fees") imposed upon insured and self-funded health plans.[57]

Another revenue raiser provided for by the ACA is a temporary transitional reinsurance fee that will be assessed on group health plans, including self-funded plans. The fee is to be used to help fund a transitional reinsurance program for insurers in the individual insurance market, to protect them against the prospect that an undue number of high-risk individuals will enroll for coverage under their policies when the state insurance exchanges take effect. Codification of this fee is contained in Section 1341 of the ACA and is further addressed in final regulations that were published in the *Federal Register* on March 23, 2012.

[B] PCORI Fees

For insured health plans, the Affordable Care Act imposes a PCORI fee on each health insurance policy for each policy year ending after September 30, 2012.[58] The fee, which is payable by the insurance company that issues the policy, is equal to $2.00 multiplied by the average number of lives covered under the policy.[59] Note that the PCORI fee is based on the number of covered lives, which would include spouses, surviving spouses, dependents, and others eligible for coverage. However, for calendar years ending in fiscal year 2013, the fee is reduced from $2.00 to $1.00 per covered life.[60] The PCORI fee is adjusted for policy years beginning in fiscal years ending after September 30, 2014, by the percentage increase in the projected per capita amount of National Health Expenditures, as published by the U.S. Treasury Department.[61]

For self-funded health plans, the Affordable Care Act imposes a similar PCORI fee to fund the Institute. Again, the fee is equal to $2.00 multiplied by the average number of lives covered under the plan, with a similar reduction to $1.00 for plan years ending during fiscal year 2013, and similar

---

[54] PPACA § 9004(a) (amending I.R.C. § 223(f)(4)(A)). A similar excise tax for Archer MSAs is increased from 15% to 20%. PPACA § 9004(b).

[55] PPACA § 6301, adding new Subtitle D to 42 U.S.C. §§ 1301 *et seq.*

[56] 42 U.S.C. § 1181(a)(2).

[57] 42 U.S.C. § 1181(b).

[58] PPACA § 6301 (adding I.R.C. § 4375). The fee does not apply to policies where substantially all of the coverage is for excepted benefits, as defined in Section 9832(c) of the Code. I.R.C. § 4375(b)(2).

[59] I.R.C. § 4375(a).

[60] I.R.C. § 4375(a).

[61] I.R.C. § 4375(d).

adjustments for the percentage increase in the projected per capita amount of National Health Expenditures.[62] The major difference is that the PCORI fee for self-funded health plans must be paid by the plan sponsor, which generally is the employer in the case of a single-employer plan.[63] Also, unlike the case in other areas, the Act makes clear that a self-funded health plan includes any portion of a health plan that is not insured.[64]

In both cases, the PCORI fees to fund the Institute are applied on a temporary basis. The Affordable Care Act specifies that these fees will not apply for policy years (in the case of insured health plans) and plan years (in the case of self-funded health plans) that end after September 30, 2019.[65]

[C] Plans Subject to PCORI Fees

The PCORI fees apply to group health plans, including HMOs and retiree-only health plans, with specific exceptions for:

- Certain excepted benefits, including accident and disability benefits, workers' compensation, on-site medical clinics, limited scope vision or dental benefits, long-term care benefits, and most Health FSAs;

- HSAs;

- Employee assistance, disease management, and wellness programs that do not provide significant benefits in the nature of medical care or treatment;

- Expatriate plans primarily designed to cover individuals who work and reside outside the United States (individuals who do not reside in the United States are excepted from the fee calculation, irrespective of whether coverage is provided under such an expatriate plan); and

- Stop-loss coverage.[66]

The sponsor of multiple self-funded group health plans with the same plan year needs to pay only one PCORI fee for such plans. Thus, an employer with a medical plan and a separate prescription drug plan (with the same plan year) will not need to pay multiple PCORI fees for the same individual. Similarly, if an employer sponsors a self-funded high-deductible health plan (HDHP) that is integrated with a health reimbursement account (HRA), the HDHP and HRA would be treated as a single arrangement and would be subject to a single PCORI fee. However, if the HDHP in the previous example is insured, the insurance company that issues the policy would be assessed a PCORI fee with respect to the HDHP, and the employer would be assessed the PCORI fee with respect to the HRA.[67]

[D] Determination of Covered Lives

Self-funded plan sponsors are provided the three following alternative methods for determining the average number of lives covered under the plan for the plan year.[68]

---

[62] PPACA § 6301 (adding I.R.C. § 4376).

[63] I.R.C. § 4376(b).

[64] I.R.C. § 4376(c)(1); see **Section 5.02** for a discussion of the grandfathered health plan exception for collectively bargained insured plans and the statutory ambiguity regarding what constitutes an insured plan.

[65] I.R.C. §§ 4375(e), 4376(e).

[66] Treas. Reg. §§ 46.4375-1(b)(1)(ii), 46.4376-1(b)(1)(ii).

[67] Treas. Reg. § 46.4376-1(b)(1)(iii).

[68] Treas. Reg. § 46.4376-1(c)(2)(i).

- *Actual Count Method.* The number of covered individuals would be counted each day and-divided by the total number of days in the year.

- *Snapshot Method.* This appr oach uses information from a particular date or dates in each quarter to develop the average. Under this method, a self-funded plan sponsor has two alternatives for counting the number of lives covered, the snapshot factor method or the snapshot count method.

  - *Snapshot Factor Method.* The number of lives covered on a date is equal to the number of participants with self-only coverage on that date, plus 2.35 multiplied by the number of participants with coverage other than self-only coverage on the date.
  - *Snapshot Count Method.* The actual number of lives covered on a designated date.

- *Form 5500 Method.* The average number of lives covered is based on the number of reportable participants from the Form 5500 for the corresponding plan year.

Because the first plan year subject to these rules may have already started, the rules give latitude to self-funded plans (with plan years beginning before July 11, 2012) to use any reasonable method for determining the average number of covered lives for the first plan year.[69] The proposed regulations provide another special rule for a plan sponsor whose only self-funded plan is a Health FSA or HRA. In this situation, the plan sponsor may treat each participant's Health FSA or HRA as covering a single covered life. Therefore, the plan sponsor is not required to include as covered lives any spouse, dependent, or other beneficiary of the participant in the Health FSA or HRA.[70]

Insurers may use similar methods for making the determination based on the applicable policy year, but the Form 5500 approach is replaced by a method based on the information included in the National Association of Insurance Commissioners Supplemental Health Care Exhibit or other applicable state form.[71]

A plan sponsor must use the same method of calculation throughout a plan year but may change methods from one plan year to the next.[72] Insurers also must use the same method of calculation throughout a plan year but have less flexibility to change methods from one plan year to the next.[73]

[E] Reporting and Payment of Fees

Because the PCORI fees are considered to be an excise tax under the Code, they must be reported on a Form 720 (Quarterly Federal Excise Tax Return) by July 31 of the calendar year immediately following the last day of the plan year.[74] Despite the use of the Form 720, a quarterly form, plan sponsors and insurers only have to report PCORI fees annually. Plans with plan years that end between October 1, 2012, and December 31, 2012, must report and pay their first PCORI fees by July 31, 2013. Plans with plan years that began after January 1, 2012, but prior to October 2, 2012, will not have to report and pay their first PCORI fees until July 31, 2014. Form 720 may be submitted electronically.

---

[69] Treas. Reg. § 46.4376-1(c)(2)(vii).
[70] Treas. Reg. § 46.4376-1(c)(2)(vi).
[71] Treas. Reg. § 46.4375-1(c)(2)(i).
[72] Treas. Reg. § 46.4376-1(c)(2)(ii).
[73] Treas. Reg. § 46.4375-1(c)(2)(ii).
[74] Treas. Reg. § 40.6071(a)-1(c).

[F] Transitional Reinsurance Fee

According to Section 1341 of the ACA, a transitional reinsurance fee will be assessed for three years (2014 through 2016) and is designed to raise a total of $25 billion. Of that $25 billion, $20 billion will be used to pay claims under the transitional reinsurance program while the remaining $5 billion will be paid into the U.S. Treasury, presumably to reimburse the federal government for the payments it made under the Early Retiree Reinsurance Program (which is discussed in detail in **Section 7.01**). The final regulations provide that HHS will set the transitional reinsurance fee annually on a national per capita basis and publish it in the HHS Notice of Benefit and Payment Parameters. The fee will be payable on a quarterly basis, beginning on January 15, 2014. The fee is estimated to be in the range of $60 to $105 per covered life, which includes spouses, surviving spouses, dependents, and others (e.g., domestic partners, non-dependent family members) eligible for coverage under an applicable plan. Although the transitional reinsurance program is directed toward the protection of insurers in the individual insurance market, the transitional reinsurance fee applies equally to group health plans, including those that are self-funded. Unlike the vast array of health plans that are exempt from the PCORI fee, only certain HIPAA-excepted benefits (e.g., accident and disability benefits, standalone dental and vision plans, and most health flexible spending accounts) are exempt from the transitional reinsurance fee. Furthermore, unlike the PCORI fee, the transitional reinsurance fee does not contain an offset provision that would prevent enrollees in multiple self-funded plans with the same plan year from being counted twice. Thus, an employer who sponsors separate medical and prescription plans will need to pay multiple transitional reinsurance fees for those individuals who are enrolled in both plans. The breadth of group health plans that are subject to the fee and the double-counting of participants may be remedied in future guidance if HHS (which oversees the transitional reinsurance fee) decides to administer the fee in a manner similar to how the IRS has indicated it will administer the PCORI fee. Liability for the transitional reinsurance fee falls on the issuer in an insured arrangement (which will likely be passed through to the plan sponsor in the form of higher premiums) and appears to rest with the plan sponsor in a self-funded arrangement, even though the third-party administrator will likely collect and remit the fee. Failure to properly remit this fee may result in a $100 per day penalty for each affected individual.

§ 13.05 Additional Taxes on High Earners

[A] Increase in Basic HI Tax

One of the obvious challenges in crafting the new health care reform law was to find ways to pay for the changes to the system. While much of the funding is expected to come from changes to make the Medicare system more efficient, the Affordable Care Act imposes new taxes on high-earning individuals to create additional sources of funding.

The Affordable Care Act amends the Hospital Insurance (HI) portion of the Federal Insurance Contributions Act (FICA) tax to increase the rate at which high-earning employees are taxed from 1.45 percent of wages to 2.35 percent of wages—a 62 percent increase.[75] The increase applies only to annual wages in excess of $250,000 for taxpayers who are married filing jointly for federal income tax purposes, $125,000 for taxpayers who are married filing separately, or $200,000 for taxpayers with any other filing status.[76] For purposes of wage withholding, employers may assume that the additional tax applies to the employee's wages in excess of $200,000.[77] There is no corresponding additional HI tax assessed against employers.

---

[75] PPACA § 9015 (amending I.R.C. § 3101(b)).
[76] I.R.C. § 3101(b)(2).
[77] PPACA § 9015(a)(2) (adding I.R.C. § 3102(f)).

The additional HI tax applies on the same basis to self-employed individuals who are subject to the Self-Employment Contributions Act (SECA) tax.[78] However, self-employed individuals are not permitted to deduct any portion of the additional HI tax.[79] Thus, a self-employed individual who is a high earner may continue to deduct one-half of the 2.9 percent HI tax imposed under SECA, but cannot deduct any portion of the additional 0.9 percent HI tax imposed on self-employment income in excess of $250,000, $125,000, or $200,000 as applicable.[80] The inability of self-employed individuals to deduct the additional 0.9 percent HI tax under SECA is consistent with the fact that the additional 0.9 percent HI tax under FICA applies only to employees and not employers.

The additional HI taxes will apply to taxable years beginning after December 31, 2012.[81]

[B] HI Tax on Unearned Income

In addition to the increase in the rate of the HI tax under both FICA and SECA, the Affordable Care Act imposes a significant new tax on certain taxpayers who have unearned income.[82] The new tax is equal to 3.8 percent of the *lesser* of (1) the taxpayer's net investment income for the taxable year, or (2) the excess of the taxpayer's modified adjusted gross income for the taxable year over the threshold amount.[83] Because the threshold amount is equal to $250,000 for taxpayers who are married filing jointly for federal income tax purposes and for surviving spouses, or $200,000 for other filers, the new tax on unearned income applies only to high earners who have unearned income.[84]

"Net investment income" means, for this purpose, the sum of all income derived from interest, dividends, annuities, royalties, and rents (other than such income derived from the ordinary course of a trade or business); all income derived from the disposition of property other than property held in a trade or business; and all income derived from a trade or business that is a passive activity or the trading of financial instruments or commodities; less deductions allocable to such gross income or net gain.[85] Special rules apply to income on investments in working capital, certain active interests in partnerships and Subchapter S corporations, and self-employment income.[86] Finally, net investment income does not include distributions from qualified retirement plans under Section 401(a) of the Code, qualified annuities under Section 403(a), tax-sheltered annuities under Section 403(b), traditional or Roth individual retirement arrangements under Sections 408 and 408A, respectively, and eligible deferred compensation plans under Section 457(b).[87] "Modified adjusted gross income" is defined, for this purpose, as adjusted gross income increased by the excess of the taxpayer's foreign earned income and housing costs (as defined in Section 911(a)(1) of the Code) over the amount of any deductions or exclusions disallowed under Section 911(d)(6).[88]

The new tax on unearned income is extended to certain trusts and estates in addition to high-earning individual taxpayers. The tax on trusts and estates is equal to 3.8 percent of the lesser of (1) the undistributed net investment income for the taxable year, or (2) the excess of the adjusted gross

---

[78] PPACA § 9015(b) (amending I.R.C. § 1401(b)).

[79] PPACA § 9015(b)(2) (amending I.R.C. § 164(f)).

[80] I.R.C. § 1402(a)(12).

[81] PPACA § 9015(c).

[82] HCERA § 1402(a) (adding new I.R.C. § 1411). The new tax does not apply to nonresident aliens. I.R.C. § 1411(e).

[83] I.R.C. § 1411(a)(1).

[84] I.R.C. § 1411(b).

[85] I.R.C. § 1411(c).

[86] I.R.C. §§ 1411(c)(3), (4), and (6).

[87] I.R.C. § 1411(c)(5). The existence of this exception for "qualified"-type retirement plans raises a question as to whether the new tax applies to distributions from nonqualified deferred compensation plans such as supplemental executive retirement plans and Section 401(k) excess plans.

[88] I.R.C. § 1411(d).

income for the taxable year over the dollar amount at which the highest tax bracket applicable to trusts and estates begins for such taxable year ($7,500 for 2010).[89]

The new tax on unearned income will apply to taxable years beginning after December 31, 2012.[90]

§ 13.06   Other Taxes

[A]   Tax on Charitable Hospitals

The Affordable Care Act adds a new Section 501(r) to the Code, which imposes additional requirements on tax-exempt charitable hospitals relating to community health needs assessments, financial assistance policies, limits on charges, and billing and collections.[91] Charitable hospitals that fail to meet the requirements of Section 501(r) are subject to a tax on the organization equal to $50,000.[92] New reporting and monitoring mandates also apply.

[B]   Fees on Constituencies Participating in the U.S. Health System

The Affordable Care Act imposes fees on several different constituencies that form the U.S. health system, including branded pharmaceutical manufacturers and importers,[93] medical device manufacturers and importers,[94] and health insurance providers.[95]

[C]   Increased Threshold for Itemized Medical Expense Deductions

Currently, taxpayers are permitted to deduct their unreimbursed medical expenses in excess of 7.5 percent of their adjusted gross income.[96] The Affordable Care Act increases the threshold from 7.5 percent to 10 percent, effective for taxable years beginning after December 31, 2012.[97] However, for the 2013–2016 taxable years, if the taxpayer or the taxpayer's spouse has attained age 65 or older, the threshold remains at 7.5 percent for such taxable year.[98]

[D]   Limitation on Compensation Deduction for Health Insurance Executives

Section 162(m) of the Code generally limits an employer's deduction on annual compensation paid to certain covered employees to $1 million, subject to exceptions for commissions and certain

---

[89] I.R.C. § 1411(a)(2). The new tax does not apply to a trust if all of the unexpired interests are devoted to charitable purposes. I.R.C. § 1411(e)(2) (referencing charitable interests described in Section 170(c)(2)(B) of the Code).

[90] HCERA § 1402(a)(4).

[91] PPACA § 9007 (adding I.R.C. § 501(r)); *see* Prop. Treas. Reg. §§ 1.501(r)-l *et seq.* (proposed June 22, 2012); I.R.S. Notice 2011-52, 2011-30 I.R.B. 60 (July 8, 2011); I.R.S. Notice 2010-39, 2010-24 I.R.B. 756 (May 27, 2010).

[92] PPACA § 9007 (adding I.R.C. § 4959).

[93] PPACA § 9008, *as amended by* HCERA § 1404(a); Treas. Reg. §§ 51.1T *et seq.*; *see* I.R.S. Notice 2011-92, 2011-48 I.R.B. (Nov. 3, 2011) (describing the 2012 fee-year procedure); I.R.S. Notice 2011-46, 2011-25 I.R.B. 887 (May 27, 2011) (delaying deadlines for determining applicable fee); I.R.S. Notice 2011-9, 2011-6 I.R.B. 459 (Jan. 14, 2011) (outlining the process for providing preliminary assessments and dispute resolution).

[94] HCERA § 1405(a) (adding I.R.C. § 4191); I.R.S. Notice 2010-89, 2010-52 I.R.B. 908 (requesting comments relating to exemptions from excise tax). Section 1405(d) of the HCERA repealed the original version of the annual fee on medical device manufacturers and importers, as set forth in Section 9009 of the PPACA, as amended by Section 10904(a) of the PPACA.

[95] PPACA § 9010, *as amended by* PPACA § 10905 and HCERA § 1406.

[96] I.R.C. § 213.

[97] PPACA § 9013 (amending I.R.C. § 213).

[98] I.R.C. § 213(f).

performance-based compensation.[99] Section 162(m) is limited in that it applies only to the compensation paid by a publicly held corporation to its chief executive officer and the three other highest paid executives (other than the CFO) whose compensation for the year is required to be reported to shareholders.[100]

The Affordable Care Act extends the Section 162(m) deduction limitation to *any* officer, director, or employee[101] of a "covered health insurance provider," which is defined as any insurance company that issues health insurance coverage and receives premiums for such coverage.[102] For taxable years beginning after December 31, 2012, a health insurance issuer is subject to Section 162(m) only if at least 25 percent of its gross premiums from providing health insurance coverage is from minimum essential coverage.[103] The limitation also applies to any affiliated entity that is in the same controlled group as the covered health insurance provider.[104] For purposes of applying the Section 162(m) deduction limitation to covered health insurance providers, the limitation on annual compensation is reduced to $500,000, and annual compensation is determined without regard to the exceptions for commissions and performance-based compensation.[105] Also, deferred compensation attributable to a year in which the $500,000 limit is reached will be nondeductible, even if it is paid in a later year.[106]

The extension of a modified version of Section 162(m) generally applies to covered health insurance providers for taxable years beginning after December 31, 2012.[107] However, it also applies to any remuneration attributable to services performed after December 31, 2009, that is otherwise deductible by the covered health insurance provider in a taxable year beginning after December 31, 2012 (e.g., nonqualified deferred compensation benefits).[108] The employer would have to be a covered health insurance provider during the years in which the services are performed (2010 to 2012) as well as the year in which the employer takes the deduction for Section 162(m)(6) to apply to deferred deduction remuneration earned prior to 2013.[109] Employers that receive annual premiums for taxable years after December 31, 2012, for minimum essential coverage that are less than 2 percent of the employer's gross revenues for that year are exempt from Section 162(m)(6).[110]

[E] Tax on Indoor Tanning Services

The Affordable Care Act imposes a tax equal to 10 percent of the amount paid for any indoor tanning services.[111] The tax is paid by the individual who receives the indoor tanning services, but it

---

[99] I.R.C. § 162(m).

[100] I.R.C. § 162(m); *see* IRS Notice 2007-49, 2007-25 I.R.B. 1429 (providing that the chief financial officer of a publicly traded corporation generally is not subject to the Section 162(m) limitation).

[101] PPACA § 9014 (adding I.R.C. § 162(m)(6)). Applicable individuals also include independent contractors, except those who provide substantial services to multiple unrelated customers. I.R.S. Notice 2011-2, 2011-2 I.R.B. 260.

[102] PPACA § 9014 (adding I.R.C. § 162(m)(6)). Premiums received under an indemnity reinsurance contract are not counted as premiums related to health insurance coverage. I.R.S. Notice 2011-2, 2011-2 I.R.B. 260. However, the IRS requests comments on how to treat captive reinsurers or reinsurance with very low attachment points. *Id.*

[103] I.R.C. § 162(m)(6)(C)(i)(II); see **Section 11.01[B]** notes 4–10 and accompanying text for a discussion of minimum essential coverage.

[104] I.R.C. § 162(m)(6)(C)(ii).

[105] I.R.C. §§ 162(m)(6)(A)(i) and (D).

[106] I.R.C. § 162(m)(6)(A)(ii).

[107] PPACA § 9014(b).

[108] PPACA § 9014(b).

[109] I.R.S. Notice 2011-2, 2011-2 I.R.B. 260.

[110] I.R.S. Notice 2011-2, 2011-2 I.R.B. 260. For the 2010–2012 taxable years, an employer is exempt if the annual premiums received for all health insurance coverage are less than 2% of the employer's gross revenues for that year. *Id.*

[111] PPACA § 10907(b) (adding I.R.C. § 5000B). "Indoor tanning services" means a service employing an electronic product designed to incorporate one or more ultraviolet lamps and intended to irradiate the individual with ultraviolet radiation. I.R.C. § 5000B(a)(1).

is collected at the point of sale by the party providing the services and remitted quarterly to the IRS.[112] The excise tax is reported on Form 720, "Quarterly Federal Excise Tax Return." If the tax is not paid at the point of sale and ultimately not collected from the individual who received the tanning services, the indoor tanning provider is secondarily liable for the tax.[113]

Section 10907(a) of the PPACA nullified an earlier PPACA provision, set forth in Section 9017 of the PPACA, that would have imposed an excise tax on certain elective cosmetic medical procedures.

[112] I.R.C. § 5000B(c); *see* Treas. Reg. §§ 1.1361-4T, 301.7701-2T (providing that a disregarded entity must be treated as a corporation for purposes of collecting, reporting, and transmitting the indoor tanning excise tax).

[113] I.R.C. § 5000B(c)(3).

Chapter 14

ANALYZING THE IMPACT OF HEALTH CARE REFORM

As the preceding chapters of this book describe in detail, health care reform will have a significant effect on the way employers provide health benefits and the way individuals obtain health coverage. As currently constructed, health care reform can make the delivery of health benefits very different in 2014 than in the several preceding decades. Going forward, employers of all sizes will have many difficult decisions to make. In this chapter, we will highlight some of the major differences in the Affordable Care Act for different types of employers and employees.

§ 14.01 Difference Based on Employer Size

One of the recurring themes in the Affordable Care Act is an effort to avoid imposing economic and administrative burdens on small businesses. The Act imposes far fewer restrictions on small employers, and even provides some cost-savings opportunities for small employers. The IRS suggested potential approaches that it might take with respect to employee-counting problems set forth in the pay-or-play provisions, and has indicated that it intends to publish certain safe harbor counting methods.[1]

[A] Employers With Fewer Than 25 Full-Time Equivalent Employees

Perhaps the most significant difference between large employers and small employers is the manner in which the Affordable Care Act encourages employers to provide coverage. For the smallest employers (i.e., those with fewer than 25 full-time equivalent employees and an average payroll of less than $50,000 per full-time equivalent employee), the Act creates a "reward," in the form of a tax credit, to incentivize employers to provide health insurance coverage to employees.[2] Note that the Act applies the controlled group rules in determining which entities are small employers. Thus, an employer cannot divide its workforce among separate related entities in order to fit under the 25-employee threshold to take advantage of the small employer tax credit.

For the 2010 through 2013 taxable years, the tax credit amount is 35 percent (25 percent for tax-exempt entities) of the aggregate amount of non-elective employer contributions made on behalf of employees to an insured health plan. For taxable years beginning on or after January 1, 2014, the amount of the tax credit increases to 50 percent (35 percent for tax-exempt entities) of the aggregate amount of non-elective employer contributions made on behalf of employees to a QHP. The tax credit is subject to a phase-out provision, so the full tax credit is only available for employers with ten or fewer employees and that pay average annual wages of $25,000 or less.

If a small employer chooses not to provide health insurance to its employees, it does not qualify for the tax incentive "reward," but it also is not subject to the tax penalties that otherwise apply to larger employers beginning in 2014.[3]

[B] Employers With Fewer Than 50 Full-Time Equivalent Employees

Employers that employ at least 25, but fewer than 50, employees are still considered small employers for purposes of the Affordable Care Act and are exempt from certain tax penalties, but they are not eligible for the tax credit reward described in **Section 14.01[A]**. Significantly, these small

---

[1] See **Section 11.02[B]** for a discussion of employee-counting issues.

[2] See **Section 7.03** for a full description of the small-employer tax credit.

[3] The only penalty provision that might have applied to small employers was the free choice voucher requirement. See **Section 11.03** for a discussion of the free choice voucher requirement. That requirement was repealed in subsequent legislation. Department of Defense and Full-Year Continuing Appropriations Act, 2011 § 1858, Pub. L. No. 112-10.

employers are exempt from the pay-or-play penalty, which is one of the key elements of health care reform.[4]

Small employers should consider whether it continues to make sense to offer employer-sponsored group health plans to employees. Employers offer health coverage to recruit and retain employees at every level of the organization. However, employer-sponsored group health coverage is a valuable recruiting and retention tool primarily because employees historically have not had a viable alternative to obtain individual health coverage. The individual insurance market is expensive, and individuals may be subject to preexisting-condition limitations and significant premium variations based on the individual's own experience. The Affordable Care Act attempts to bring order to the individual insurance market by creating state Exchanges, eliminating preexisting-condition limitations, and restricting an insurance company's ability to vary premiums. In doing so, the Affordable Care Act may finally create in the Exchanges a viable alternative to employer-sponsored group health coverage, particularly for employees who can qualify for subsidies through the Exchange. Small employers should consider whether the recruiting and retention benefits of employer-sponsored group health coverage outweigh the significant cost savings of dropping such coverage, sending employees to an Exchange, and possibly providing additional compensation to offset the cost of the insurance coverage.

Small employers with fewer than 50 employees also may be exempt from the Affordable Care Act's requirement to make certain accommodations for nursing mothers.[5] If a small employer can show that the requirement to provide a reasonable break time and a private location for nursing mothers to express breast milk would impose an undue hardship on the employer, the employer may be exempt from the Affordable Care Act's requirement (but not necessarily exempt from similar state law requirements).

[C] Employers With 50 or More Full-Time Equivalent Employees

Beginning January 1, 2014, a large employer will be required to offer full-time employees the chance to enroll in employment-based group health plan coverage that satisfies the definition of minimum essential coverage and is both adequate and affordable. Large employers that fail to provide such coverage on these terms are subject to an annual penalty of either $2,000 per full-time employee (where the large employer fails to offer minimum essential coverage and at least one employee receives a subsidy through an Exchange), or $3,000 per full-time employee who receives a premium tax credit or cost-sharing reduction related to enrollment in a QHP through an Exchange (where the large employer's coverage is either inadequate or unaffordable).

A "large employer," for this purpose, is one that employs, on average, 50 or more full-time equivalent employees on business days during the preceding calendar year. In determining the 50-employee threshold, full-time equivalent employees are counted, and the controlled group rules are applied to aggregate the employees of related employers. Thus, a small employer with fewer than 50 full-time equivalent employees that chooses not to provide employment-based health coverage to its employees is not subject to tax penalties.

[D] Employers With 100 or Fewer Employees

Beginning on January 1, 2014, the Affordable Care Act directs that the State Exchanges will make available health insurance for individuals and small employers.[6] Small employers, defined for this purpose as having at least one but not more than 100 employees during the preceding calendar year, will

---

[4] See **Section 11.02** for a full description of the employer pay-or-play penalty.
[5] See **Section 12.05** for a full description of the nursing mother requirements.
[6] See **Section 11.04** for a full description of Exchanges.

be able to purchase a group QHP through the Exchange for their employees. Purchasing a QHP through an Exchange allows a small employer to take advantage of a single, statewide risk pool, Exchange-approval requirements for QHPs, and a variety of options that can be compared on an apples-to-apples basis.

Large employers will face the same decision as small employers regarding whether to continue offering employer-sponsored group health coverage. Large employers that choose to drop coverage, however, are subject to the Affordable Care Act's pay-or-play penalties. Even with these penalties, a large employer could save significant amounts by dropping coverage, sending employees to an Exchange, and providing supplemental compensation.

Beginning in 2016, each state has the option to reduce the 100-employee limit for Exchange access for small employers to 50 employees. Also, Exchanges may begin to provide access to large employers beginning in 2017. The controlled-group rules are applied to these limits for purposes of aggregating related employers.

[E] Employers With Fewer Than 200 Full-Time Employees

The Affordable Care Act makes one other major distinction between large and small employers, and the distinction relates to the automatic enrollment requirements.[7] The Act requires large employers that offer enrollment in one or more group health plans to automatically enroll new full-time employees in one of the plans (subject to any waiting periods authorized by law) and to continue the enrollment of current employees. A "large employer," for this purpose, is defined as an employer having more than 200 full-time employees. Such employers also must provide advance notice of the automatic enrollment feature, as well as an opportunity for employees to opt out of coverage. A "small" employer with at least 50 but less than 200 full-time employees will be exempt from the automatic enrollment requirement, but generally will be subject to all other aspects of health care reform.

[F] Cost-Benefit Analysis

[1] Large Employers

In the long run, large employers may have the most to gain from the Affordable Care Act. For years, large employers have been expected to provide employment-based group health plans to their employees. When the Exchanges become operational on January 1, 2014, coverage will be available to all individuals, regardless of where they work, potentially freeing employers of the expectation to provide health care coverage. Large employers will need to engage in a cost-benefit analysis to determine whether they should continue to offer an employment-based group health plan to their employees or pay a penalty under pay-or-play. Because the penalty for not providing an employment-based group health plan is much less than the current cost of providing employees with such a plan, large employers will need to take a close look at the recruiting and retention advantages that a group health plan presents. See Tables 14-1 and 14-2 below for two sample cost-benefit analyses for large employers.

---

[7] See **Section 12.03** for a full description of the automatic enrollment requirements.

TABLE 14-1.
Sample Cost-Benefit Analyses for Large Employers

Thinking About Providing a Plan?	
Costs	*Benefits*
• Possibility of an annual $3,000 penalty for each full-time employee who receives a subsidy under an Exchange plan because the large employer has an employment-based group health plan that constitutes minimum essential coverage, but the plan is inadequate or unaffordable. • Increases in administrative costs due to compliance with new plan design requirements, a new administrative scheme, and a multitude of additional regulations. • Increases in administrative costs related to navigating the free choice voucher system. • Beginning in 2018, possible exposure to the "Cadillac" tax.	• Potentially effective tool for recruiting and retaining employees. • If the Exchanges prove difficult to navigate or offer inadequate coverage networks, employees may put a premium on employment-based group health plans. • Continuity of benefits. • Large employers may face pressure from employees to keep employment-based group health plans in and beyond 2014. Many employees have become accustomed to obtaining coverage through a large employer and would rather interact with internal personnel on benefits matters than external representatives employed by insurance companies or Exchanges. • Prevents benefit selection burden from being placed on employees. • Sometimes having more choices is not always beneficial. While the Exchange concept is supposed to foster a system that promotes ease of use, individuals will have to analyze many competing options when it comes to picking an appropriate plan, a stark change from the current system where the typical employer offers employees just a few options. While some employees may see an opportunity to customize their desired level of benefits by purchasing coverage through an Exchange, this option will be much less appealing to those employees who are not interested in taking a more active role in the benefit selection process.

TABLE 14-2.

Thinking About NOT Providing a Plan?	
Costs	*Benefits*
• Annual penalty of $2,000 per full-time employee (in excess of 30 employees) per year.	• If large employers choose to discontinue employment-based group health plans, they could pass along the cost savings to employees in the form of salary increases. Employers currently can spend approximately $800–$1,200 or more per month per employee on health care coverage. This would translate into large employer annual savings of approximately $10,000–$15,000 per employee. These savings could be passed along to employees in the form of increased compensation and employees could, in turn, choose the level of coverage they desire through an Exchange. • Reduction in administrative costs because there is no need to comply with the Act's new administrative scheme and a multitude of additional regulation. This could result in the reduction of HR staff needed to operate group health plans and open enrollment procedures. • Employees can choose from a wide array of coverage options through an Exchange. • Lower-paid employees may be eligible for federal government subsidies and credits. If employers increased the wages of subsidy-eligible individuals, these individuals may get the best of both worlds—additional take-home pay and adequate health care coverage.

[2] Small Employers

Unlike large employers, small employers are not subject to the Affordable Care Act's pay-or-play rules. However, small employers still have some decisions to make. Like large employers, small employers will need to engage in a cost-benefit analysis to determine whether they should provide employment-based group health plans to their employees, which could allow them to take advantage of tax credits. Small employers will need to consider a few factors. First, the household incomes of employees will determine how many may be eligible for federal subsidies and credits if they obtained health care coverage through the Exchange rather than through an employment-based group health plan. Second, competitors may be seeking to hire from the same labor market, and they may offer employment-based group health plans as an incentive. Small employers that provide an employment-based group health plan, even with a 25 percent to 50 percent tax credit from the federal government, are still likely to incur more health care–related costs than small employers who send employees directly to the Exchange for coverage. This will likely affect the amount of wages that small employers with employment-based group health plans could afford. Employees who value an employment-based group health plan may be more inclined to look for employment with small employers offering such a plan, while employees who place little value on health care coverage may elect to find an employer who offers higher compensation in exchange for not providing health care coverage. See Tables 14-3 and 14-4 below for two sample cost-benefit analyses for small employers.

TABLE 14-3.
Sample Cost-Benefit Analyses for Small Employers

Thinking About Providing a Plan?	
Costs	*Benefits*
Before January 1, 2014 • Increases in administrative costs due to compliance with new plan design requirements, a new administrative scheme, and a multitude of additional regulation. *January 1, 2014, and after* • Limited additional plan administrative costs if health care coverage is purchased through an Exchange (which is required for the tax credits).	• Tax credits. • A valuable benefit prior to 2014 when health coverage is not yet available through an Exchange. • Prevents benefit selection burden from being placed on employees. • Sometimes having more choices is not always beneficial. While the Exchange concept is supposed to foster a system that promotes ease of use, individuals will have to analyze many competing options when it comes to picking an appropriate plan, a stark change from the current system where the typical employer offers employees just a few options. While some employees may see an opportunity to customize their desired level of benefits by purchasing coverage through an Exchange, this option will be much less appealing to those employees who are not interested in taking a more active role in the benefit selection process.

TABLE 14-4.

Thinking About NOT Providing a Plan?	
Costs	*Benefits*
• None (except possibly higher wages if offered by the small employer).	• If small employers choose to discontinue employer-sponsored coverage, they could pass along the cost savings to employees in the form of salary increases. Employers currently can spend approximately $800–$1,200 or more per month per employee on health care coverage. This would translate into small-employer annual savings of approximately $10,000–$15,000 per employee. These savings could be passed along to employees in the form of increased compensation and employees could, in turn, choose the level of coverage they desire through an Exchange. • No need to comply with a new administrative scheme and a multitude of additional regulations. • Employees can choose from a wide array of coverage options through an Exchange. • Lower-paid employees may be eligible for federal government subsidies and credits. If employers increased the wages of subsidy-eligible individuals, these individuals may get the best of both worlds—additional take-home pay and adequate health care coverage.

§ 14.02   Differences Based on Full-Time vs. Part-Time Employees

Many employers provide employment-based group health plans for only their full-time employee workforce. As a result, part-time employees make up a significant percentage of the uninsured. One common question is whether the Affordable Care Act mandates that employers provide coverage for part-time employees. Simply put, no such mandate exists.[8]

Uninsured part-time employees do benefit from the Affordable Care Act in the sense that they, like all other individuals, will be able to purchase health insurance in a QHP at group rates through an Exchange beginning on January 1, 2014. Until that time, those uninsured part-time employees who have preexisting conditions may obtain health insurance coverage through the state-based temporary high-risk insurance pools.[9]

Employers that have significant part-time workforces will need to consider the part-timers in determining whether certain aspects of health care reform will apply. For example, part-time employees must be aggregated in determining the number of full-time equivalent employees for the following purposes:

- Determining eligibility for small employer tax incentives for providing employment-based group health plans to employees (must employ fewer than 25 FTEs);[10] and

- Determining whether an employer is a "large employer" subject to the pay-or-play rules (all employers with 50 or more FTEs are subject to pay-or-play).[11] Once it is established that an employer is subject to the pay-or-play rules, the penalties only apply with respect to the employer's full-time employees.

---

[8] *See, e.g.*, I.R.S. Notice 2012-17, A-5, 2012-9 I.R.B. 430 (Feb. 9, 2012).
[9] See **Section 7.02** for a full description of the temporary high-risk pools.
[10] See **Section 7.03** for a full description of the small-employer tax incentives.
[11] See **Section 11.02** for a full description of the pay-or-play rules.

§ 14.03 Differences Based on Union vs. Non-Union Workforces

Employers with unionized workforces do not have any significant advantages or disadvantages over employers with non-union workforces when it comes to health care reform, except possibly in the timing of the health care reform changes. Employers that have "health insurance coverage maintained pursuant to one or more collective bargaining agreements . . . ratified before [March 23, 2010]" may be able to take advantage of the grandfathered health plan exemption.[12] The exemption would apply until the date on which the last of the collective bargaining agreements relating to the health coverage terminates.

Employers and unions that engage in collective bargaining, particularly in 2010 or 2011 in advance of regulatory guidance, will face a daunting task when it comes to health care reform. Employers and unions will need to estimate and allocate the expected costs arising from health care reform changes at a time when the impact of such changes is not well understood. Evaluating the impact of the Exchanges in 2014 on health care costs, for example, probably cannot be done with any confidence until each state gets a better idea of the structure of the Exchange and the degree of participation from health insurers.

§ 14.04 Employers Providing Retiree Health Coverage

Due to rising costs and changes in the accounting rules that force employers to recognize the present value of promised benefits as a liability, fewer and fewer employers are providing quality health coverage for their retiree population. The Affordable Care Act acknowledges the efforts of employers that provide retiree health coverage, and provides several incentives for employers to continue retiree health coverage.

First and foremost, the Affordable Care Act exempts retiree-only plans from many of the plan design changes, such as coverage of adult children through age 26 and coverage of preventive health services without cost-sharing.[13] Second, the Affordable Care Act establishes the Early Retiree Reinsurance Program (ERRP), which allows employers to seek substantial reimbursements from the federal government for the employers' costs in maintaining health coverage for retirees who are at least age 55 but not yet eligible for Medicare.[14] Third, the Affordable Care Act closes the donut hole in the Medicare Part D by instituting co-insurance in the Medicare Part D coverage gap and providing access to a 50 percent manufacturer's discount on brand-name drugs purchased in the donut hole.[15] While the Affordable Care Act eliminates the double-tax benefit for employers receiving Medicare Part D retiree drug subsidy (RDS) payments beginning in 2013, the Medicare Part D structural changes present new and potentially more lucrative plan design opportunities for employers providing retiree prescription drug coverage.[16]

§ 14.05 Looking Ahead

There is no doubt that the Affordable Care Act will change the role employers currently play in providing access to health care coverage for employees and their families. But unless the tax laws eliminate the tax advantages of employer-provided welfare benefits, including health care, large employers and small employers with well-paid workforces probably will, at a minimum, continue to

---

[12] See **Section 5.02** for a full description of the grandfathered health plan exemption and its application to collectively bargained insured health plans.

[13] See **Section 5.03** for a discussion of the retiree-only plan exemption.

[14] See **Section 7.01** for a discussion of the ERRP provisions.

[15] See **Section 12.01[B]** for a discussion of Medicare Part D changes.

[16] See **Section 12.01[C]** for a discussion of the taxability of RDS payments.

have a role in providing access to health care coverage for their employees. While the type of coverage may change, employers can still provide financing for health coverage and/or the coverage itself on a tax-preferred basis.

As health care reform evolves, and the universality, quality, and cost-effectiveness of the Affordable Care Act's measures become better known, each employer will need to remain informed, maintain compliance with the immediate reforms, and continue to analyze what course is best for it and its workforce. Maintaining focus and pressure on the reduction of costs, particularly by insurance issuers, will be as much or more of a challenge for employers than ever. Employers will also have larger communication and education roles with respect to employees as their options for coverage change.

We are confident that further changes and refinements to the Affordable Care Act will be made prior to the rollout of the Exchanges. In the face of these seemingly overwhelming changes, we remind our readers that the trends prior to reform were unsustainable and that health care reform is a national imperative for our long-term economic stability. We are optimistic that the national dialogue will continue and that over time, these reforms will spur needed changes to the delivery of and access to health care. We hope that the cost curve also will begin to improve.

A. Affordable Care Act Provisions Applicable to Grandfathered Health Plans

- A "grandfathered health plan" is defined as a group health plan (insured or self-funded) in which individuals were enrolled for coverage as of March 23, 2010.

  —New employees and their families may be enrolled in a grandfathered plan after 3/23/2010.

  Family members of new employees and existing enrollees may be added after 3/23/2010.

  —A grandfathered plan may be renewed indefinitely.

SUBJECT	SECTION(S) OF PHSA (UNLESS NOTED)	EFFECTIVE DATE	APPLY TO GRANDFATHERED PLAN?
Extension of dependent coverage to age 26	2714	1st plan year after 9/23/2010	Yes
Pre-existing exclusions prohibited for children under age 19	2704	1st plan year after 9/23/2010	Yes
Prohibition on lifetime dollar maximum on benefits	2711	1st plan year after 9/23/2010	Yes
Prohibition on annual dollar limits on restricted benefits	2711	1st plan year after 9/23/2010	Yes
Rescissions of coverage for reasons other than fraud or non-payment	2712	1st plan year after 9/23/2010	Yes
Required preventive health services without cost-sharing	2713	1st plan year after 9/23/2010	No
Mandated appeals process with binding external review	2719	1st plan year after 9/23/2010	No
Nondiscrimination against health care providers	2706	1st plan year after 1/1/2014	No
Summary communication requirements for enrollees	2715	24 months after date of enactment	Yes
No discrimination based on salary permitted	2716	1st plan year after 9/23/2010	No
Insured plans must rebate prorated share of premiums if medical claims ratios too low	2718	1st plan year after 9/23/2010	Yes (insured plans only)
HHS reporting requirements (quality outcomes, etc.)	2717	24 months after date of enactment	No
Reinsurance for retirees	PPACA 1102	June 23, 2010	Yes
Adm. Simplification—amends HIPAA to add new transaction standards	PPACA 1104	1/1/2013–1/1/2014	Yes (electronic funds transfer standards)
All insured plans must guarantee eligibility and renewability	2702, 2703	1st plan year on or after 1/1/2014	No
All insured plans are subject to premium underwriting restrictions	2701, 1252	1st plan year on or after 1/1/2014	No
Prohibitions on health status discrimination	2704, 2705	1st plan year on or after 1/1/2014	No
Comprehensive health insurance—annual cost-sharing limits	2707	1st plan year on or after 1/1/2014	No
Nondiscrimination in health care coverage (provider)	2706	1st plan year on or after 1/1/2014	No

SUBJECT	SECTION(S) OF PHSA (UNLESS NOTED)	EFFECTIVE DATE	APPLY TO GRANDFATHERED PLAN?
No waiting period in excess of 90 days	2708	1st plan year on or after 1/1/2014	Yes
Coverage for clinical trials	2709 (Can be found in Title X)	1st plan year on or after 1/1/2014	No
Reinsurance for early retirees	PPACA 1101	6/23/2010 to 1/1/2014	Yes
Automatic enrollment for large employers	FLSA, 1511	1/1/2011	Yes, employer responsibility
Employee notice re: coverage options (FLSA amendment)	FLSA, 1512	3/1/2013	Yes, employer responsibility
Health insurance fee	PPACA 9010	Calendar year 2014	Yes, except it does not apply to self-insured or government plans

B. Tri-Agency Regulations on Grandfathered Health Plans

Thursday,
June 17, 2010

Part II

Department of the Treasury
Internal Revenue Service
26 CFR Parts 54 and 602

Department of Labor
Employee Benefits Security
Administration

29 CFR Part 2590

**Department of Health and
Human Services**

45 CFR Part 147

Group Health Plans and Health Insurance
Coverage Relating to Status as a
Grandfathered Health Plan Under the
Patient Protection and Affordable Care
Act; Interim Final Rule and Proposed
Rule

34538   Federal Register/Vol. 75, No. 116/Thursday, June 17, 2010/Rules and Regulations

DEPARTMENT OF THE TREASURY

Internal Revenue Service

26 CFR Parts 54 and 602

[TD 9489]

RIN 1545–BJ51

DEPARTMENT OF LABOR

Employee Benefits Security Administration

29 CFR Part 2590

RIN 1210–AB42

DEPARTMENT OF HEALTH AND HUMAN SERVICES

[OCIIO–9991–IFC]

45 CFR Part 147

RIN 0991–AB68

Interim Final Rules for Group Health Plans and Health Insurance Coverage Relating to Status as a Grandfathered Health Plan Under the Patient Protection and Affordable Care Act

AGENCY: Internal Revenue Service, Department of the Treasury; Employee Benefits Security Administration, Department of Labor; Office of Consumer Information and Insurance Oversight, Department of Health and Human Services.

ACTION: Interim final rules with request for comments.

SUMMARY: This document contains interim final regulations implementing the rules for group health plans and health insurance coverage in the group and individual markets under provisions of the Patient Protection and Affordable Care Act regarding status as a grandfathered health plan.

DATES: *Effective date.* These interim final regulations are effective on June 14, 2010, except that the amendments to 26 CFR 54.9815–2714T, 29 CFR 2590.715–2714, and 45 CFR 147.120 are effective July 12, 2010.

Comment date. Comments are due on or before August 16, 2010.

ADDRESSES: Written comments may be submitted to any of the addresses specified below. Any comment that is submitted to any Department will be shared with the other Departments. Please do not submit duplicates.

All comments will be made available to the public. *Warning:* Do not include any personally identifiable information (such as name, address, or other contact information) or confidential business information that you do not want

publicly disclosed. All comments are posted on the Internet exactly as received, and can be retrieved by most Internet search engines. No deletions, modifications, or redactions will be made to the comments received, as they are public records. Comments may be submitted anonymously.

Department of Labor. Comments to the Department of Labor, identified by RIN 1210–AB42, by one of the following methods:

• *Federal eRulemaking Portal: http://www.regulations.gov.* Follow the instructions for submitting comments.

• *E-mail: E-OHPSCA1251.EBSA@dol.gov.*

• *Mail or Hand Delivery:* Office of Health Plan Standards and Compliance Assistance, Employee Benefits Security Administration, Room N–5653, U.S. Department of Labor, 200 Constitution Avenue, NW., Washington, DC 20210, *Attention:* RIN 1210–AB42.

Comments received by the Department of Labor will be posted without change to *http://www.regulations.gov* and *http://www.dol.gov/ebsa,* and available for public inspection at the Public Disclosure Room, N–1513, Employee Benefits Security Administration, 200 Constitution Avenue, NW., Washington, DC 20210.

Department of Health and Human Services. In commenting, please refer to file code OCIIO–9991–IFC. Because of staff and resource limitations, the Departments cannot accept comments by facsimile (FAX) transmission.

You may submit comments in one of four ways (please choose only one of the ways listed):

1. *Electronically.* You may submit electronic comments on this regulation to *http://www.regulations.gov.* Follow the instructions under the "More Search Options" tab.

2. *By regular mail.* You may mail written comments to the following address ONLY: Office of Consumer Information and Insurance Oversight, Department of Health and Human Services, Attention: OCIIO–9991–IFC, P.O. Box 8016, Baltimore, MD 21244–1850.

Please allow sufficient time for mailed comments to be received before the close of the comment period.

3. *By express or overnight mail.* You may send written comments to the following address ONLY: Office of Consumer Information and Insurance Oversight, Department of Health and Human Services, Attention: OCIIO–9991–IFC, Mail Stop C4–26–05, 7500 Security Boulevard, Baltimore, MD 21244–1850.

4. *By hand or courier.* If you prefer, you may deliver (by hand or courier) your written comments before the close of the comment period to either of the following addresses:

a. For delivery in Washington, DC—Office of Consumer Information and Insurance Oversight, Department of Health and Human Services, Room 445–G, Hubert H. Humphrey Building, 200 Independence Avenue, SW., Washington, DC 20201.

(Because access to the interior of the Hubert H. Humphrey Building is not readily available to persons without Federal government identification, commenters are encouraged to leave their comments in the OCIIO drop slots located in the main lobby of the building. A stamp-in clock is available for persons wishing to retain a proof of filing by stamping in and retaining an extra copy of the comments being filed.)

b. For delivery in Baltimore, MD—Centers for Medicare & Medicaid Services, Department of Health and Human Services, 7500 Security Boulevard, Baltimore, MD 21244–1850.

If you intend to deliver your comments to the Baltimore address, please call (410) 786–7195 in advance to schedule your arrival with one of our staff members.

Comments mailed to the addresses indicated as appropriate for hand or courier delivery may be delayed and received after the comment period.

Submission of comments on paperwork requirements. You may submit comments on this document's paperwork requirements by following the instructions at the end of the "Collection of Information Requirements" section in this document.

Inspection of Public Comments: All comments received before the close of the comment period are available for viewing by the public, including any personally identifiable or confidential business information that is included in a comment. The Departments post all comments received before the close of the comment period on the following Web site as soon as possible after they have been received: *http://www.regulations.gov.* Follow the search instructions on that Web site to view public comments.

Comments received timely will also be available for public inspection as they are received, generally beginning approximately three weeks after publication of a document, at the headquarters of the Centers for Medicare & Medicaid Services, 7500 Security Boulevard, Baltimore, Maryland 21244, Monday through Friday of each week from 8:30 a.m. to 4 p.m. EST. To schedule an appointment to view public comments, phone 1–800–743–3951.

Internal Revenue Service. Comments to the IRS, identified by REG–118412–10, by one of the following methods:

• *Federal eRulemaking Portal: http:// www.regulations.gov.* Follow the instructions for submitting comments.

• *Mail:* CC:PA:LPD:PR (REG–118412–10), room 5205, Internal Revenue Service, P.O. Box 7604, Ben Franklin Station, Washington, DC 20044.

• *Hand or courier delivery:* Monday through Friday between the hours of 8 a.m. and 4 p.m. to: CC:PA:LPD:PR (REG–118412–10), Courier's Desk, Internal Revenue Service, 1111 Constitution Avenue, NW., Washington, DC 20224.

All submissions to the IRS will be open to public inspection and copying in room 1621, 1111 Constitution Avenue, NW., Washington, DC from 9 a.m. to 4 p.m.

FOR FURTHER INFORMATION CONTACT: Amy Turner or Beth Baum, Employee Benefits Security Administration, Department of Labor, at (202) 693–8335; Karen Levin, Internal Revenue Service, Department of the Treasury, at (202) 622–6080; Jim Mayhew, Office of Consumer Information and Insurance Oversight, Department of Health and Human Services, at (410) 786–1565.

Customer Service Information: Individuals interested in obtaining information from the Department of Labor concerning employment-based health coverage laws may call the EBSA Toll-Free Hotline at 1–866–444–EBSA (3272) or visit the Department of Labor's Web site (*http://www.dol.gov/ebsa*). In addition, information from HHS on private health insurance for consumers can be found on the Centers for Medicare & Medicaid Services (CMS) Web site (*http://www.cms.hhs.gov/ HealthInsReformforConsume/ 01_Overview.asp*) and information on health reform can be found at *http:// www.healthreform.gov.*

SUPPLEMENTARY INFORMATION:

I. Background

The Patient Protection and Affordable Care Act (the Affordable Care Act), Public Law 111–148, was enacted on March 23, 2010; the Health Care and Education Reconciliation Act (the Reconciliation Act), Public Law 111–152, was enacted on March 30, 2010. The Affordable Care Act and the Reconciliation Act reorganize, amend, and add to the provisions in part A of title XXVII of the Public Health Service Act (PHS Act) relating to group health plans and health insurance issuers in the group and individual markets. The

term "group health plan" includes both insured and self-insured group health plans.[1] The Affordable Care Act adds section 715(a)(1) to the Employee Retirement Income Security Act (ERISA) and section 9815(a)(1) to the Internal Revenue Code (the Code) to incorporate the provisions of part A of title XXVII of the PHS Act into ERISA and the Code, and make them applicable to group health plans, and health insurance issuers providing health insurance coverage in connection with group health plans. The PHS Act sections incorporated by this reference are sections 2701 through 2728. PHS Act sections 2701 through 2719A are substantially new, though they incorporate some provisions of prior law. PHS Act sections 2722 through 2728 are sections of prior law renumbered, with some, mostly minor, changes. Section 1251 of the Affordable Care Act, as modified by section 10103 of the Affordable Care Act and section 2301 of the Reconciliation Act, specifies that certain plans or coverage existing as of the date of enactment (that is, grandfathered health plans) are only subject to certain provisions.

The Affordable Care Act also adds section 715(a)(2) of ERISA, which provides that, to the extent that any provision of part 7 of ERISA conflicts with part A of title XXVII of the PHS Act with respect to group health plans or group health insurance coverage, the PHS Act provisions apply. Similarly, the Affordable Care Act adds section 9815(a)(2) of the Code, which provides that, to the extent that any provision of subchapter B of chapter 100 of the Code conflicts with part A of title XXVII of the PHS Act with respect to group health plans or group health insurance coverage, the PHS Act provisions apply. Therefore, although ERISA section 715(a)(1) and Code section 9815(a)(1) incorporate by reference new provisions, they do not affect preexisting sections of ERISA or the Code unless they cannot be read consistently with an incorporated provision of the PHS Act. For example, ERISA section 732(a) generally provides that part 7 of ERISA—and Code section 9831(a) generally provides that chapter 100 of the Code—does not apply to plans with less than two participants who are current employees (including retiree-only plans that cover less than two participants who are current employees). Prior to enactment of the

Affordable Care Act, the PHS Act had a parallel provision at section 2721(a). After the Affordable Care Act amended, reorganized, and renumbered most of title XXVII of the PHS Act, that exception no longer exists. Similarly, ERISA section 732(b) and (c) generally provides that the requirements of part 7 of ERISA—and Code section 9831(b) and (c) generally provides that the requirements of chapter 100 of the Code—do not apply to excepted benefits.[2] Prior to enactment of the Affordable Care Act, the PHS Act had a parallel section 2721(c) and (d) that indicated that the provisions of subparts 1 through 3 of part A of title XXVII of the PHS Act did not apply to excepted benefits. After the Affordable Care Act amended and renumbered PHS Act section 2721(c) and (d) as section 2722(b) and (c), that exception could be read to be narrowed so that it applies only with respect to subpart 2 of part A of title XXVII of the PHS Act, thus, in effect requiring excepted benefits to comply with subparts I and II of part A.

The absence of an express provision in part A of title XXVII of the PHS Act does not create a conflict with the relevant requirements of ERISA and the Code. Accordingly, the exceptions of ERISA section 732 and Code section 9831 for very small plans and certain retiree-only health plans, and for excepted benefits, remain in effect and, thus, ERISA section 715 and Code section 9815, as added by the Affordable Care Act, do not apply to such plans or excepted benefits.

Moreover, there is no express indication in the legislative history of an intent to treat issuers of group health insurance coverage or nonfederal governmental plans (that are subject to the PHS Act) any differently in this respect from plans subject to ERISA and the Code. The Departments of Health and Human Services, Labor, and the Treasury (the Departments) operate under a Memorandum of Understanding (MOU)[3] that implements section 104 of the Health Insurance Portability and Accountability Act of 1996 (HIPAA), enacted on August 21, 1996, and subsequent amendments, and provides that requirements over which two or more Secretaries have responsibility ("shared provisions") must be administered so as to have the same effect at all times. HIPAA section 104

---

[1] The term "group health plan" is used in title XXVII of the PHS Act, part 7 of ERISA, and chapter 100 of the Code, and is distinct from the term "health plan," as used in other provisions of title I of the Affordable Care Act. The term "health plan" does not include self-insured group health plans.

[2] Excepted benefits generally include dental-only and vision-only plans, most health flexible spending arrangements, Medigap policies, and accidental death and dismemberment coverage. For more information on excepted benefits, see 26 CFR 54.9831–1, 29 CFR 2590.732, 45 CFR 146.145, and 45 CFR 148.220.

[3] *See* 64 FR 70164 (December 15, 1999).

also requires the coordination of policies relating to enforcing the shared provisions in order to avoid duplication of enforcement efforts and to assign priorities in enforcement.

There is no express statement of intent that nonfederal governmental retiree-only plans should be treated differently from private sector plans or that excepted benefits offered by nonfederal governmental plans should be treated differently from excepted benefits offered by private sector plans. Because treating nonfederal governmental retiree-only plans and excepted benefits provided by nonfederal governmental plans differently would create confusion with respect to the obligations of issuers that do not distinguish whether a group health plan is subject to ERISA or the PHS Act, and in light of the MOU, the Department of Health and Human Services (HHS) does not intend to use its resources to enforce the requirements of HIPAA or the Affordable Care Act with respect to nonfederal governmental retiree-only plans or with respect to excepted benefits provided by nonfederal governmental plans.

PHS Act section 2723(a)(2) (formerly section 2722(a)(2)) gives the States primary authority to enforce the PHS Act group and individual market provisions over group and individual health insurance issuers. HHS enforces these provisions with respect to issuers only if it determines that the State has "failed to substantially enforce" one of the Federal provisions. Furthermore, the PHS Act preemption provisions allow States to impose requirements on issuers in the group and individual markets that are more protective than the Federal provisions. However, HHS is encouraging States not to apply the provisions of title XXVII of the PHS Act to issuers of retiree-only plans or of excepted benefits. HHS advises States that if they do not apply these provisions to the issuers of retiree-only plans or of excepted benefits, HHS will not cite a State for failing to substantially enforce the provisions of part A of title XXVII of the PHS Act in these situations.

Subtitles A and C of title I of the Affordable Care Act amend the requirements of title XXVII of the PHS Act (changes to which are incorporated into ERISA section 715). The preemption provisions of ERISA section 731 and PHS Act section 2724 [4] (implemented in 29 CFR 2590.731(a)

---

4 Code section 9815 incorporates the preemption provisions of PHS Act section 2724. Prior to the Affordable Care Act, there were no express preemption provisions in chapter 100 of the Code.

and 45 CFR 146.143(a)) apply so that the requirements of part 7 of ERISA and title XXVII of PHS Act, as amended by the Affordable Care Act, are not to be "construed to supersede any provision of State law which establishes, implements, or continues in effect any standard or requirement solely relating to health insurance issuers in connection with group or individual health insurance coverage except to the extent that such standard or requirement prevents the application of a requirement" of the Affordable Care Act. Accordingly, State laws that impose on health insurance issuers requirements that are stricter than the requirements imposed by the Affordable Care Act will not be superseded by the Affordable Care Act.

The Departments are issuing regulations implementing the revised PHS Act sections 2701 through 2719A in several phases. The first publication in this series was a Request for Information relating to the medical loss ratio provisions of PHS Act section 2718, published in the **Federal Register** on April 14, 2010 (75 FR 19297). The second publication was interim final regulations implementing PHS Act section 2714 (requiring dependent coverage of children to age 26), published in the **Federal Register** on May 13, 2010 (75 FR 27122). This document contains interim final regulations implementing section 1251 of the Affordable Care Act (relating to grandfathered health plans), as well as adding a cross-reference to these interim final regulations in the regulations implementing PHS Act section 2714. The implementation of other provisions in PHS Act sections 2701 through 2719A will be addressed in future regulations.

II. Overview of the Regulations: Section 1251 of the Affordable Care Act, Preservation of Right To Maintain Existing Coverage (26 CFR 54.9815–1251T, 29 CFR 2590.715–1251, and 45 CFR 147.140)

A. Introduction

Section 1251 of the Affordable Care Act, as modified by section 10103 of the Affordable Care Act and section 2301 of the Reconciliation Act, provides that certain group health plans and health insurance coverage existing as of March 23, 2010 (the date of enactment of the Affordable Care Act), are subject only to certain provisions of the Affordable Care Act. The statute and these interim final regulations refer to these plans and health insurance coverage as grandfathered health plans.

The Affordable Care Act balances the objective of preserving the ability of individuals to maintain their existing coverage with the goals of ensuring access to affordable essential coverage and improving the quality of coverage. Section 1251 provides that nothing in the Affordable Care Act requires an individual to terminate the coverage in which the individual was enrolled on March 23, 2010. It also generally provides that, with respect to group health plans or health insurance coverage in which an individual was enrolled on March 23, 2010, various requirements of the Act shall not apply to such plan or coverage, regardless of whether the individual renews such coverage after March 23, 2010. However, to ensure access to coverage with certain particularly significant protections, Congress required grandfathered health plans to comply with a subset of the Affordable Care Act's health reform provisions. Thus, for example, grandfathered health plans must comply with the prohibition on rescissions of coverage except in the case of fraud or intentional misrepresentation and the elimination of lifetime limits (both of which apply for plan years, or in the individual market, policy years, beginning on or after September 23, 2010). On the other hand, grandfathered health plans are not required to comply with certain other requirements of the Affordable Care Act; for example, the requirement that preventive health services be covered without any cost sharing (which otherwise becomes generally applicable for plan years, or in the individual market, policy years, beginning on or after September 23, 2010).

A number of additional reforms apply for plan years (in the individual market, policy years) beginning on or after January 1, 2014. As with the requirements effective for plan years (in the individual market, policy years) beginning on or after September 23, 2010, grandfathered health plans must then comply with some, but not all of these reforms. See Table 1 in section II.D of this preamble for a list of various requirements that apply to grandfathered health plans.

In making grandfathered health plans subject to some but not all of the health reforms contained in the Affordable Care Act, the statute balances its objective of preserving the ability to maintain existing coverage with the goals of expanding access to and improving the quality of health coverage. The statute does not, however, address at what point changes to a group health plan or health insurance coverage in which an individual was enrolled on March 23, 2010 are significant enough to cause the plan or health insurance coverage to cease to be a grandfathered health plan, leaving that question to be addressed by regulatory guidance.

These interim final regulations are designed to ease the transition of the healthcare industry into the reforms established by the Affordable Care Act by allowing for gradual implementation of reforms through a reasonable grandfathering rule. A more detailed description of the basis for these interim final regulations and other regulatory alternatives considered is included in section IV.B later in this preamble.

B. Definition of Grandfathered Health Plan Coverage in Paragraph (a) of 26 CFR 54.9815–1251T, 29 CFR 2590.715–1251, and 45 CFR 147.140 of These Interim Final Regulations

Under the statute and these interim final regulations, a group health plan or group or individual health insurance coverage is a grandfathered health plan with respect to individuals enrolled on March 23, 2010. Paragraph (a)(1) of 26 CFR 54.9815–1251T, 29 CFR 2590.715–1251, and 45 CFR 147.140 of these interim final regulations provides that a group health plan or group health insurance coverage does not cease to be grandfathered health plan coverage merely because one or more (or even all) individuals enrolled on March 23, 2010 cease to be covered, provided that the plan or group health insurance coverage has continuously covered someone since March 23, 2010 (not necessarily the same person, but at all times at least one person). The determination under the rules of these interim final regulations is made separately with respect to each benefit package made available under a group health plan or health insurance coverage.

Moreover, these interim final regulations provide that, subject to the rules of paragraph (f) of 26 CFR 54.9815–1251T, 29 CFR 2590.715–1251, and 45 CFR 147.140 for collectively bargained plans, if an employer or employee organization enters into a new policy, certificate, or contract of insurance after March 23, 2010 (because, for example, any previous policy, certificate, or contract of insurance is not being renewed), then that policy, certificate, or contract of insurance is not a grandfathered health plan with respect to the individuals in the group health plan. Any policies sold in the group and individual health insurance markets to new entities or individuals after March 23, 2010 will not be grandfathered health plans even if the health insurance products sold to

those subscribers were offered in the group or individual market before March 23, 2010.

To maintain status as a grandfathered health plan, a plan or health insurance coverage (1) must include a statement, in any plan materials provided to participants or beneficiaries (in the individual market, primary subscribers) describing the benefits provided under the plan or health insurance coverage, that the plan or health insurance coverage believes that it is a grandfathered health plan within the meaning of section 1251 of the Affordable Care Act and (2) must provide contact information for questions and complaints.

Model language is provided in these interim final regulations that can be used to satisfy this disclosure requirement. Comments are invited on possible improvements to the model language of grandfathered health plan status. Some have suggested, for example, that each grandfathered health plan be required to list and describe the various consumer protections that do not apply to the plan or health insurance coverage because it is grandfathered, together with their effective dates. The Departments intend to consider any comments regarding possible improvements to the model language in the near term; any changes to the model language that may result from such comments could be published in additional administrative guidance other than in the form of regulations.

Similarly, under these interim final regulations, to maintain status as a grandfathered health plan, a plan or issuer must also maintain records documenting the terms of the plan or health insurance coverage that were in effect on March 23, 2010, and any other documents necessary to verify, explain, or clarify its status as a grandfathered health plan. Such documents could include intervening and current plan documents, health insurance policies, certificates or contracts of insurance, summary plan descriptions, documentation of premiums or the cost of coverage, and documentation of required employee contribution rates. In addition, the plan or issuer must make such records available for examination. Accordingly, a participant, beneficiary, individual policy subscriber, or State or Federal agency official would be able to inspect such documents to verify the status of the plan or health insurance coverage as a grandfathered health plan. The plan or issuer must maintain such records and make them available for examination for as long as the plan or issuer takes the position that the plan or

health insurance coverage is a grandfathered health plan.

Under the statute and these interim final regulations, if family members of an individual who is enrolled in a grandfathered health plan as of March 23, 2010 enroll in the plan after March 23, 2010, the plan or health insurance coverage is also a grandfathered health plan with respect to the family members.

C. Adding New Employees in Paragraph (b) of 26 CFR 54.9815–1251T, 29 CFR 2590.715–1251, and 45 CFR 147.140 of These Interim Final Regulations

These interim final regulations at 26 CFR 54.9815–1251T, 29 CFR 2590.715–1251, and 45 CFR 147.140 provide that a group health plan that provided coverage on March 23, 2010 generally is also a grandfathered health plan with respect to new employees (whether newly hired or newly enrolled) and their families who enroll in the grandfathered health plan after March 23, 2010. These interim final regulations clarify that in such cases, any health insurance coverage provided under the group health plan in which an individual was enrolled on March 23, 2010 is also a grandfathered health plan. To prevent abuse, these interim final regulations provide that if the principal purpose of a merger, acquisition, or similar business restructuring is to cover new individuals under a grandfathered health plan, the plan ceases to be a grandfathered health plan. The goal of this rule is to prevent grandfather status from being bought and sold as a commodity in commercial transactions. These interim final regulations also contain a second anti-abuse rule designed to prevent a plan or issuer from circumventing the limits on changes that cause a plan or health insurance coverage to cease to be a grandfathered health plan under paragraph (g) (described more fully in section II.F of this preamble). This rule in paragraph (b)(2)(ii) addresses a situation under which employees who previously were covered by a grandfathered health plan are transferred to another grandfathered health plan. This rule is intended to prevent efforts to retain grandfather status by indirectly making changes that would result in loss of that status if those changes were made directly.

D. Applicability of Part A of Title XXVII of the PHS Act to Grandfathered Health Plans Paragraphs (c), (d), and (e) of 26 CFR 54.9815–1251T, 29 CFR 2590.715– 1251, and 45 CFR 147.140 of These Interim Final Regulations

A grandfathered health plan generally is not subject to subtitles A and C of title I of the Affordable Care Act, except as specifically provided by the statute and these interim final regulations. The statute and these interim final regulations provide that some provisions of subtitles A and C of title I of the Affordable Care Act continue to apply to all grandfathered health plans and some provisions continue to apply only to grandfathered health plans that are group health plans. These interim final regulations clarify that a grandfathered health plan must continue to comply with the requirements of the PHS Act, ERISA, and the Code that were applicable prior to the changes enacted by the Affordable Care Act, except to the extent supplanted by changes made by the Affordable Care Act. Therefore, the HIPAA portability and nondiscrimination requirements and the Genetic Information Nondiscrimination Act requirements applicable prior to the effective date of the Affordable Care Act continue to apply to grandfathered health plans. In addition, the mental health parity provisions, the Newborns' and Mothers' Health Protection Act provisions, the Women's Health and Cancer Rights Act, and Michelle's Law continue to apply to grandfathered health plans. The following table lists the new health coverage reforms in part A of title XXVII of the PHS Act (as amended by the Affordable Care Act) that apply to grandfathered health plans:

TABLE 1—LIST OF THE NEW HEALTH REFORM PROVISIONS OF PART A OF TITLE XXVII OF THE PHS ACT THAT APPLY TO GRANDFATHERED HEALTH PLANS

PHS Act statutory provisions	Application to grandfathered health plans
§ 2704 Prohibition of preexisting condition exclusion or other discrimination based on health status.	Applicable to grandfathered group health plans and group health insurance coverage. Not applicable to grandfathered individual health insurance coverage.
§ 2708 Prohibition on excessive waiting periods	Applicable.
§ 2711 No lifetime or annual limits	Lifetime limits: Applicable. Annual limits: Applicable to grandfathered group health plans and group health insurance coverage; not applicable to grandfathered individual health insurance coverage.
§ 2712 Prohibition on rescissions	Applicable.
§ 2714 Extension of dependent coverage until age 26	Applicable [5].
§ 2715 Development and utilization of uniform explanation of coverage documents and standardized definitions.	Applicable.
§ 2718 Bringing down cost of health care coverage (for insured coverage).	Applicable to insured grandfathered health plans.

[5] For a group health plan or group health insurance coverage that is a grandfathered health plan for plan years beginning before January 1, 2014, PHS Act section 2714 is applicable in the case of an adult child only if the adult child is not eligible for other employer-sponsored health plan coverage. The interim final regulations relating to PHS Act section 2714, published in 75 FR 27122 (May 13, 2010), and these interim final regulations clarify that, in the case of an adult child who is eligible for coverage under the employer-sponsored plans of both parents, neither parent's plan may exclude the adult child from coverage based on the fact that the adult child is eligible to enroll in the other parent's employer-sponsored plan.

E. Health Insurance Coverage Maintained Pursuant to a Collective Bargaining Agreement of Paragraph (f) of 26 CFR 54.9815–1251T, 29 CFR 2590.715–1251, and 45 CFR 147.140 of These Interim Final Regulations

In paragraph (f) of 26 CFR 54.9815– 1251T, 29 CFR 2590.715–1251, and 45 CFR 147.140, these interim final regulations provide that in the case of health insurance coverage maintained pursuant to one or more collective bargaining agreements ratified before March 23, 2010, the coverage is a grandfathered health plan at least until the date on which the last agreement relating to the coverage that was in effect on March 23, 2010 terminates. Thus, before the last of the applicable collective bargaining agreement terminates, any health insurance coverage provided pursuant to the collective bargaining agreements is a grandfathered health plan, even if there is a change in issuers (or any other change described in paragraph (g)(1) of 26 CFR 54.9815–1251T, 29 CFR 2590.715–1251, and 45 CFR 147.140 of these interim final regulations) during the period of the agreement. The statutory language of the provision refers solely to "health insurance coverage" and does not refer to a group health plan; therefore, these interim final regulations apply this provision only to insured plans maintained pursuant to a collective bargaining agreement and not to self-insured plans. After the date on which the last of the collective bargaining agreements terminates, the determination of whether health insurance coverage maintained pursuant to a collective bargaining agreement is grandfathered health plan coverage is made under the rules of paragraph (g). This determination is made by comparing the terms of the coverage on the date of determination with the terms of the coverage that were in effect on March 23, 2010. A change in issuers during the period of the agreement, by itself, would not cause the plan to cease to be a grandfathered health plan at the termination of the agreement. However, for a change in issuers after the termination of the agreement, the rules of paragraph (a)(1)(ii) of 26 CFR 54.9815–1251T, 29 CFR 2590.715–1251, and 45 CFR 147.140 of these interim final regulations apply.

Similar language to section 1251(d) in related bills that were not enacted would have provided a delayed effective date for collectively bargained plans with respect to the Affordable Care Act requirements. Questions have arisen as to whether section 1251(d) as enacted in the Affordable Care Act similarly operated to delay the application of the Affordable Care Act's requirements to collectively bargained plans— specifically, whether the provision of section 1251(d) that exempts collectively bargained plans from requirements for the duration of the agreement effectively provides the plans with a delayed effective date with respect to all new PHS Act requirements (in contrast to the rules for grandfathered health plans which provide that specified PHS Act provisions apply to all plans, including grandfathered health plans). However, the statutory language that applies only to collectively bargained plans, as signed into law as part of the Affordable Care Act, provides that insured collectively bargained plans in which individuals were enrolled on the date of enactment are included in the definition of a grandfathered health plan. Therefore, collectively bargained plans (both insured and self-insured) that are grandfathered health plans are subject to the same requirements as other grandfathered health plans, and are not provided with a delayed effective date for PHS Act provisions with which other grandfathered health plans must comply. Thus, the provisions that apply to grandfathered health plans apply to collectively bargained plans before and after termination of the last of the applicable collective bargaining agreement.

F. Maintenance of Grandfather Status of Paragraph (g) of 26 CFR 54.9815–1251T, 29 CFR 2590.715–1251, and 45 CFR 147.140 of These Interim Final Regulations)

Questions have arisen regarding the extent to which changes can be made to a plan or health insurance coverage and still have the plan or coverage considered the same as that in existence on March 23, 2010, so as to maintain status as a grandfathered health plan. Some have suggested that any change would cause a plan or health insurance coverage to be considered different and thus cease to be a grandfathered health plan. Others have suggested that any degree of change, no matter how large, is irrelevant provided the plan or health insurance coverage can trace some continuous legal relationship to the plan or health insurance coverage that was in existence on March 23, 2010.

In paragraph (g)(1) of 26 CFR 54.9815–1251T, 29 CFR 2590.715–1251, and 45 CFR 147.140 of these interim final regulations, coordinated rules are set forth for determining when changes to the terms of a plan or health insurance coverage cause the plan or coverage to cease to be a grandfathered health plan. The first of those rules (in paragraph (g)(1)(i) constrains the extent to which the scope of benefits can be reduced. It provides that the elimination of all or substantially all benefits to diagnose or treat a particular condition causes a plan or health insurance coverage to cease to be a grandfathered health plan. If, for example, a plan eliminates all benefits for cystic fibrosis, the plan ceases to be a grandfathered

health plan (even though this condition may affect relatively few individuals covered under the plan). Moreover, for purposes of paragraph (g)(1)(i), the elimination of benefits for any necessary element to diagnose or treat a condition is considered the elimination of all or substantially all benefits to diagnose or treat a particular condition. An example in these interim final regulations illustrates that if a plan provides benefits for a particular mental health condition, the treatment for which is a combination of counseling and prescription drugs, and subsequently eliminates benefits for counseling, the plan is treated as having eliminated all or substantially all benefits for that mental health condition.

A second set of rules (in paragraphs (g)(1)(ii) through (g)(1)(iv)) limits the extent to which plans and issuers can increase the fixed-amount and the percentage cost-sharing requirements that are imposed with respect to individuals for covered items and services. Plans and issuers can choose to make larger increases to fixed-amount or percentage cost-sharing requirements than permissible under these interim final regulations, but at that point the individual's plan or health insurance coverage would cease to be grandfathered health plan coverage. A more detailed description of the basis for the cost-sharing requirements in these interim final regulations is included in section IV.B later in this preamble.

These interim final regulations provide different standards with respect to coinsurance and fixed-amount cost sharing. Coinsurance automatically rises with medical inflation. Therefore, changes to the level of coinsurance (such as moving from a requirement that the patient pay 20 percent to a requirement that the patient pay 30 percent of inpatient surgery costs) would significantly alter the level of benefits provided. On the other hand, fixed-amount cost-sharing requirements (such as copayments and deductibles) do not take into account medical inflation. Therefore, changes to fixed-amount cost-sharing requirements (for example, moving from a $35 copayment to a $40 copayment for outpatient doctor visits) may be reasonable to keep up with the rising cost of medical items and services. Accordingly, paragraph (g)(1)(ii) provides that any increase in a percentage cost-sharing requirement (such as coinsurance) causes a plan or health insurance coverage to cease to be a grandfathered health plan.

With respect to fixed-amount cost-sharing requirements, paragraph (g)(1)(iii) provides two rules: a rule for

cost-sharing requirements other than copayments and a rule for copayments. Fixed-amount cost-sharing requirements include, for example, a $500 deductible, a $30 copayment, or a $2,500 out-of-pocket limit. With respect to fixed-amount cost-sharing requirements other than copayments, a plan or health insurance coverage ceases to be a grandfathered health plan if there is an increase, since March 23, 2010, in a fixed-amount cost-sharing requirement that is greater than the maximum percentage increase. The maximum percentage increase is defined as medical inflation (from March 23, 2010) plus 15 percentage points. For this purpose, medical inflation is defined in these interim final regulations by reference to the overall medical care component of the Consumer Price Index for All Urban Consumers, unadjusted (CPI), published by the Department of Labor. For fixed-amount copayments, a plan or health insurance coverage ceases to be a grandfathered health plan if there is an increase since March 23, 2010 in the copayment that exceeds the greater of (A) the maximum percentage increase or (B) five dollars increased by medical inflation. A more detailed description of the basis for these rules relating to cost-sharing requirements is included in section IV.B later in this preamble.

With respect to employer contributions, these interim final regulations include a standard for changes that would result in cessation of grandfather status. Specifically, paragraph (g)(1)(v) limits the ability of an employer or employee organization to decrease its contribution rate for coverage under a group health plan or group health insurance coverage. Two different situations are addressed. First, if the contribution rate is based on the cost of coverage, a group health plan or group health insurance coverage ceases to be a grandfathered health plan if the employer or employee organization decreases its contribution rate towards the cost of any tier of coverage for any class of similarly situated individuals [6] by more than 5 percentage points below the contribution rate on March 23, 2010. For this purpose, contribution rate is defined as the amount of contributions made by an employer or employee organization compared to the total cost of coverage, expressed as a percentage. These interim final regulations provide that total cost of coverage is determined in the same manner as the applicable

---

[6] Similarly situated individuals are described in the HIPAA nondiscrimination regulations at 26 CFR 54.9802–1(d), 29 CFR 2590.702(d), and 45 CFR 146.121(d).

premium is calculated under the COBRA continuation provisions of section 604 of ERISA, section 4980B(f)(4) of the Code, and section 2204 of the PHS Act. In the case of a self-insured plan, contributions by an employer or employee organization are calculated by subtracting the employee contributions towards the total cost of coverage from the total cost of coverage. Second, if the contribution rate is based on a formula, such as hours worked or tons of coal mined, a group health plan or group health insurance coverage ceases to be a grandfathered health plan if the employer or employee organization decreases its contribution rate towards the cost of any tier of coverage for any class of similarly situated individuals by more than 5 percent below the contribution rate on March 23, 2010.

Finally, paragraph (g)(1)(vi) addresses the imposition of a new or modified annual limit by a plan, or group or individual health insurance coverage.[7] Three different situations are addressed:

• A plan or health insurance coverage that, on March 23, 2010, did not impose an overall annual or lifetime limit on the dollar value of all benefits ceases to be a grandfathered health plan if the plan or health insurance coverage imposes an overall annual limit on the dollar value of benefits.

• A plan or health insurance coverage, that, on March 23, 2010, imposed an overall lifetime limit on the dollar value of all benefits but no overall annual limit on the dollar value of all benefits ceases to be a grandfathered health plan if the plan or health insurance coverage adopts an overall annual limit at a dollar value that is lower than the dollar value of the lifetime limit on March 23, 2010.

• A plan or health insurance coverage that, on March 23, 2010, imposed an overall annual limit on the dollar value of all benefits ceases to be a grandfathered health plan if the plan or health insurance coverage decreases the dollar value of the annual limit (regardless of whether the plan or health insurance coverage also imposed an overall lifetime limit on March 23, 2010 on the dollar value of all benefits).

Under these interim final regulations, changes other than the changes

---

[7] Independent of these rules regarding the impact on grandfather status of newly adopted or reduced annual limits, group health plans and group or individual health insurance coverage (other than individual health insurance policies that are grandfathered health plans) are required to comply with PHS Act section 2711, which permits restricted annual limits (as defined in regulations) until 2014. The Departments expect to publish regulations regarding restricted annual limits in the very near future.

described in 26 CFR 54.9815–1251T(g)(1), 29 CFR 2590.715–1251(g)(1), and 45 CFR 147.140(g)(1) will not cause a plan or coverage to cease to be a grandfathered health plan. Examples include changes to premiums, changes to comply with Federal or State legal requirements, changes to voluntarily comply with provisions of the Affordable Care Act, and changing third party administrators, provided these changes are made without exceeding the standards established by paragraph (g)(1).

These interim final regulations provide transitional rules for plans and issuers that made changes after the enactment of the Affordable Care Act pursuant to a legally binding contract entered into prior to enactment, made changes to the terms of health insurance coverage pursuant to a filing before March 23, 2010 with a State insurance department, or made changes pursuant to written amendments to a plan that were adopted prior to March 23, 2010. If a plan or issuer makes changes in any of these situations, the changes are effectively considered part of the plan terms on March 23, 2010 even though they are not then effective. Therefore, such changes are not taken into account in considering whether the plan or health insurance coverage remains a grandfathered health plan.

Because status as a grandfathered health plan under section 1251 of the Affordable Care Act is determined in relation to coverage on March 23, 2010, the date of enactment of the Affordable Care Act, the Departments considered whether they should provide a good-faith compliance period from Departmental enforcement until guidance regarding the standards for maintaining grandfather status was made available to the public. Group health plans and health insurance issuers often make routine changes from year to year, and some plans and issuers may have needed to implement such changes prior to the issuance of these interim final regulations.

Accordingly, for purposes of enforcement, the Departments will take into account good-faith efforts to comply with a reasonable interpretation of the statutory requirements and may disregard changes to plan and policy terms that only modestly exceed those changes described in paragraph (g)(1) of 26 CFR 54.9815–1251T, 29 CFR 2590.715–1251, and 45 CFR 147.140 and that are adopted before June 14, 2010, the date the regulations were made publicly available.

In addition, these interim final regulations provide employers and issuers with a grace period within

which to revoke or modify any changes adopted prior to June 14, 2010, where the changes might otherwise cause the plan or health insurance coverage to cease to be a grandfathered health plan. Under this rule, grandfather status is preserved if the changes are revoked, and the plan or health insurance coverage is modified, effective as of the first day of the first plan or policy year beginning on or after September 23, 2010 to bring the terms within the limits for retaining grandfather status in these interim final regulations. For this purpose, and for purposes of the reasonable good faith standard changes will be considered to have been adopted before these interim final regulations are publicly available if the changes are effective before that date, the changes are effective on or after that date pursuant to a legally binding contract entered into before that date, the changes are effective on or after that date pursuant to a filing before that date with a State insurance department, or the changes are effective on or after that date pursuant to written amendments to a plan that were adopted before that date.

While the Departments have determined that the changes identified in paragraph (g)(1) of these interim final regulations would cause a group health plan or health insurance coverage to cease to be a grandfathered health plan, the Departments invite comments from the public on whether this list of changes is appropriate and what other changes, if any, should be added to this list. Specifically, the Departments invite comments on whether the following changes should result in cessation of grandfathered health plan status for a plan or health insurance coverage: (1) Changes to plan structure (such as switching from a health reimbursement arrangement to major medical coverage or from an insured product to a self-insured product); (2) changes in a network plan's provider network, and if so, what magnitude of changes would have to be made; (3) changes to a prescription drug formulary, and if so, what magnitude of changes would have to be made; or (4) any other substantial change to the overall benefit design. In addition, the Departments invite comments on the specific standards included in these interim final regulations on benefits, cost sharing, and employer contributions. The Departments specifically invite comments on whether these standards should be drawn differently in light of the fact that changes made by the Affordable Care Act may alter plan or issuer practices in the next several years. Any new standards published in the final regulations that are more restrictive than these interim final regulations would only apply prospectively to changes to plans or health insurance coverage after the publication of the final rules.

Moreover, the Departments may issue, as appropriate, additional administrative guidance other than in the form of regulations to clarify or interpret the rules contained in these interim final regulations for maintaining grandfathered health plan status prior to the issuance of final regulations. The ability to issue prompt, clarifying guidance is especially important given the uncertainty as to how plans or issuers will alter their plans or policies in response to these rules. This guidance can address unanticipated changes by plans and issuers to ensure that individuals benefit from the Affordable Care Act's new health care protections while preserving the ability to maintain the coverage individuals had on the date of enactment.

III. Interim Final Regulations and Request for Comments

Section 9833 of the Code, section 734 of ERISA, and section 2792 of the PHS Act authorize the Secretaries of the Treasury, Labor, and HHS (collectively, the Secretaries) to promulgate any interim final rules that they determine are appropriate to carry out the provisions of chapter 100 of the Code, part 7 of subtitle B of title I of ERISA, and part A of title XXVII of the PHS Act, which include PHS Act sections 2701 through 2728 and the incorporation of those sections into ERISA section 715 and Code section 9815. The rules set forth in these interim final regulations govern the applicability of the requirements in these sections and are therefore appropriate to carry them out. Therefore, the foregoing interim final rule authority applies to these interim final regulations.

In addition, under Section 553(b) of the Administrative Procedure Act (APA) (5 U.S.C. 551 *et seq.*) a general notice of proposed rulemaking is not required when an agency, for good cause, finds that notice and public comment thereon are impracticable, unnecessary, or contrary to the public interest. The provisions of the APA that ordinarily require a notice of proposed rulemaking do not apply here because of the specific authority granted by section 9833 of the Code, section 734 of ERISA, and section 2792 of the PHS Act. However, even if the APA were applicable, the Secretaries have determined that it would be impracticable and contrary to the public

interest to delay putting the provisions in these interim final regulations in place until a full public notice and comment process was completed. As noted above, numerous provisions of the Affordable Care Act are applicable for plan years (in the individual market, policy years) beginning on or after September 23, 2010, six months after date of enactment. Grandfathered health plans are exempt from many of these provisions while group health plans and group and individual health insurance coverage that are not grandfathered health plans must comply with them. The determination of whether a plan or health insurance coverage is a grandfathered health plan therefore could substantially affect the design of the plan or health insurance coverage.

The six-month period between the enactment of the Affordable Care Act and the applicability of many of the provisions affected by grandfather status would not allow sufficient time for the Departments to draft and publish proposed regulations, receive and consider comments, and draft and publish final regulations. Moreover, regulations are needed well in advance of the effective date of the requirements of the Affordable Care Act. Many group health plans and health insurance coverage that are not grandfathered health plans must make significant changes in their provisions to comply with the requirements of the Affordable Care Act. Moreover, plans and issuers considering other modifications to their terms need to know whether those modifications will affect their status as grandfathered health plans. Accordingly, in order to allow plans and health insurance coverage to be designed and implemented on a timely basis, regulations must be published and available to the public well in advance of the effective date of the requirements of the Affordable Care Act. It is not possible to have a full notice and comment process and to publish final regulations in the brief time between enactment of the Affordable Care Act and the date regulations are needed.

The Secretaries further find that issuance of proposed regulations would not be sufficient because the provisions of the Affordable Care Act protect significant rights of plan participants and beneficiaries and individuals covered by individual health insurance policies and it is essential that participants, beneficiaries, insureds, plan sponsors, and issuers have certainty about their rights and responsibilities. Proposed regulations are not binding and cannot provide the necessary certainty. By contrast, the

interim final regulations provide the public with an opportunity for comment, but without delaying the effective date of the regulations.

For the foregoing reasons, the Departments have determined that it is impracticable and contrary to the public interest to engage in full notice and comment rulemaking before putting these regulations into effect, and that it is in the public interest to promulgate interim final regulations.

IV. Economic Impact and Paperwork Burden

A. Overview—Department of Labor and Department of Health and Human Services

As stated earlier in this preamble, these interim final regulations implement section 1251 of the Affordable Care Act, as modified by section 10103 of the Affordable Care Act and section 2301 of the Reconciliation Act. Pursuant to section 1251, certain provisions of the Affordable Care Act do not apply to a group health plan or health insurance coverage in which an individual was enrolled on March 23, 2010 (a grandfathered health plan).[8] The statute and these interim final regulations allow family members of individuals already enrolled in a grandfathered health plan to enroll in the plan after March 23, 2010; in such cases, the plan or coverage is also a grandfathered health plan with respect to the family members. New employees (whether newly hired or newly enrolled) and their families can enroll in a grandfathered group health plan after March 23, 2010 without affecting status as a grandfathered health plan.[9]

---

[8] The Affordable Care Act adds section 715(a)(1) to ERISA and section 9815(a)(1) to the Code to incorporate the provisions of part A of title XXVII of the PHS Act into ERISA and the Code, and make them applicable to group health plans, and health insurance issuers providing health insurance coverage in connection with group health plans. The PHS Act sections incorporated by this reference are sections 2701 through 2728. PHS Act sections 2701 through 2719A are substantially new, though they incorporate some provisions of prior law. PHS Act sections 2722 through 2728 are sections of prior law renumbered, with some, mostly minor, changes. Section 1251 of the Affordable Care Act, as modified by section 10103 of the Affordable Care Act and section 2301 of the Reconciliation Act, specifies that certain plans or coverage existing as of the date of enactment (that is, grandfathered health plans) are only subject to certain provisions.

[9] For individuals who have coverage through an insured group health plans subject to a collective bargaining agreement ratified before March 23, 2010, an individual's coverage is grandfathered at least until the date on which the last agreement relating to the coverage that was in effect on March 23, 2010, terminates. These collectively bargained plans may make any permissible changes to the benefit structure before the agreement terminates and remain grandfathered. After the termination

Continued

As addressed earlier in this preamble, and further discussed below, these interim final regulations include rules for determining whether changes to the terms of a grandfathered health plan made by issuers and plan sponsors allow the plan or health insurance coverage to remain a grandfathered health plan. These rules are the primary focus of this regulatory impact analysis.

The Departments have quantified the effects where possible and provided a qualitative discussion of the economic effects and some of the transfers and costs that may result from these interim final regulations.

B. Executive Order 12866—Department of Labor and Department of Health and Human Services

Under Executive Order 12866 (58 FR 51735), "significant" regulatory actions are subject to review by the Office of Management and Budget (OMB). Section 3(f) of the Executive Order defines a "significant regulatory action" as an action that is likely to result in a rule (1) having an annual effect on the economy of $100 million or more in any one year, or adversely and materially affecting a sector of the economy, productivity, competition, jobs, the environment, public health or safety, or State, local or tribal governments or communities (also referred to as "economically significant"); (2) creating a serious inconsistency or otherwise interfering with an action taken or planned by another agency; (3) materially altering the budgetary impacts of entitlement grants, user fees, or loan programs or the rights and obligations of recipients thereof; or (4) raising novel legal or policy issues arising out of legal mandates, the President's priorities, or the principles set forth in the Executive Order. OMB has determined that this regulation is economically significant within the meaning of section 3(f)(1) of the Executive Order, because it is likely to have an annual effect on the economy of $100 million in any one year. Accordingly, OMB has reviewed these rules pursuant to the Executive Order. The Departments provide an assessment of the potential costs, benefits, and transfers associated with these interim final regulations below. The Departments invite comments on this assessment and its conclusions.

---

date, grandfather status will be determined by comparing the plan, as it existed on March 23, 2010 to the changes that the plan made before termination under the rules established by these interim final regulations.

1. Need for Regulatory Action

As discussed earlier in this preamble, Section 1251 of the Affordable Care Act, as modified by section 10103 of the Affordable Care Act and section 2301 of the Reconciliation Act, provides that grandfathered health plans are subject only to certain provisions of the Affordable Care Act. The statute, however, is silent regarding changes plan sponsors and issuers can make to plans and health insurance coverage while retaining grandfather status. These interim final regulations are necessary in order to provide rules that plan sponsors and issuers can use to determine which changes they can make to the terms of the plan or health insurance coverage while retaining their grandfather status, thus exempting them from certain provisions of the Affordable Care Act and fulfilling a goal of the legislation, which is to allow those that like their healthcare to keep it. These interim final regulations are designed to allow individuals who wish to maintain their current health insurance plan to do so, to reduce short term disruptions in the market, and to ease the transition to market reforms that phase in over time.

In drafting this rule, the Departments attempted to balance a number of competing interests. For example, the Departments sought to provide adequate flexibility to plan sponsors and issuers to ease transition and mitigate potential premium increases while avoiding excessive flexibility that would conflict with the goal of permitting individuals who like their healthcare to keep it and might lead to longer term market segmentation as the least costly plans remain grandfathered the longest. In addition, the Departments recognized that many plan sponsors and issuers make changes to the terms of plans or health insurance coverage on an annual basis: Premiums fluctuate, provider networks and drug formularies change, employer and employee contributions and cost-sharing change, and covered items and services may vary. Without some ability to make some adjustments while retaining grandfather status, the ability of individuals to maintain their current coverage would be frustrated, because most plans or health insurance coverage would quickly cease to be regarded as the same group health plan or health insurance coverage in existence on March 23, 2010. At the same time, allowing unfettered changes while retaining grandfather status would also be inconsistent with Congress's intent to preserve coverage that was in effect on March 23, 2010.

Therefore, as further discussed below, these interim final regulations are designed, among other things, to take into account reasonable changes routinely made by plan sponsors or issuers without the plan or health insurance coverage relinquishing its grandfather status so that individuals can retain the ability to remain enrolled in the coverage in which they were enrolled on March 23, 2010. Thus, for example, these interim final regulations generally permit plan sponsors and issuers to make voluntary changes to increase benefits, to conform to required legal changes, and to adopt voluntarily other consumer protections in the Affordable Care Act.

2. Regulatory Alternatives

Section 6(a)(3)(C)(iii) of Executive Order 12866 requires an economically significant regulation to include an assessment of the costs and benefits of potentially effective and reasonable alternatives to the planned regulation, and an explanation of why the planned regulatory action is preferable to the potential alternatives. The alternatives considered by the Departments fall into two general categories: Permissible changes to cost sharing and benefits. The discussion below addresses the considered alternatives in each category.

The Departments considered allowing looser cost-sharing requirements, such as 25 percent plus medical inflation. However, the data analysis led the Departments to believe that the cost-sharing windows provided in these interim final regulations permit enough flexibility to enable a smooth transition in the group market over time, and further widening this window was not necessary and could conflict with the goal of allowing those who like their healthcare to keep it.

Another alternative the Departments considered was an annual allowance for cost-sharing increases above medical inflation, as opposed to the one-time allowance of 15 percent above medical inflation. An annual margin of 15 percent above medical inflation, for example, would permit plans to increase cost sharing by medical inflation plus 15 percent every year. The Departments concluded that the effect of the one-time allowance (15 percent of the original, date-of-enactment level plus medical inflation) would diminish over time insofar as it would represent a diminishing fraction of the total level of cost sharing with the cumulative effects of medical inflation over time. Accordingly, the one-time allowance would better reflect (i) the potential need of grandfathered health plans to make adjustments in the near term to reflect the requirement that they comply with the market reforms that apply to grandfathered health plans in the near term as well as (ii) the prospect that, for many plans and health insurance coverage, the need to recover the costs of compliance in other ways will diminish in the medium term, in part because of the changes that will become effective in 2014 and in part because of the additional time plan sponsors and issuers will have to make gradual adjustments that take into account the market reforms that are due to take effect in later years.

The Departments considered establishing an overall prohibition against changes that, in the aggregate, or cumulatively over time, render the plan or coverage substantially different than the plan or coverage that existed on March 23, 2010, or further delineating other examples of changes that could cause a plan to relinquish grandfather status. This kind of "substantially different" standard would have captured significant changes not anticipated in the interim final regulation. However, it would rely on a "facts and circumstances" analysis in defining "substantially different" or "significant changes," which would be less transparent and result in greater uncertainty about the status of a health plan. That, in turn, could hinder plan sponsor or issuer decisions as well as enrollee understanding of what protections apply to their coverage.

An actuarial equivalency standard was another considered option. Such a standard would allow a plan or health insurance coverage to retain status as a grandfathered health plan if the actuarial value of the coverage remains in approximately the same range as it was on March 23, 2010. However, under such a standard, a plan could make fundamental changes to the benefit design, potentially conflicting with the goal of allowing those who like their healthcare to keep it, and still retain grandfather status. Moreover, the complexity involved in defining and determining actuarial value for these purposes, the likelihood of varying methodologies for determining such value unless the Departments promulgate very detailed prescriptive rules, and the costs of administering and ensuring compliance with such rules led the Departments to reject that approach.

Another alternative was a requirement that employers continue to contribute the same dollar amount they were contributing for the period including March 23, 2010, plus an inflation component. However, the Departments were concerned that this approach would not provide enough flexibility to accommodate the year-to-year volatility in premiums that can result from changes in some plans' covered populations or other factors.

The Departments also considered whether a change in third party administrator by a self-insured plan should cause the plan to relinquish grandfather status. The Departments decided that such a change would not necessarily cause the plan to be so different from the plan in effect on March 23, 2010 that it should be required to relinquish grandfather status.

After careful consideration, the Departments opted against rules that would require a plan sponsor or issuer to relinquish its grandfather status if only relatively small changes are made to the plan. The Departments concluded that plan sponsors and issuers of grandfathered health plans should be permitted to take steps within the boundaries of the grandfather definition to control costs, including limited increases in cost-sharing and other plan changes not prohibited by these interim final regulations. As noted earlier, deciding to relinquish grandfather status is a one-way sorting process: after some period of time, more plans will relinquish their grandfather status. These interim final regulations will likely influence plan sponsors' decisions to relinquish grandfather status.

3. Discussion of Regulatory Provisions

As discussed earlier in this preamble, these interim final regulations provide that a group health plan or health insurance coverage no longer will be considered a grandfathered health plan if a plan sponsor or an issuer:

• Eliminates all or substantially all benefits to diagnose or treat a particular condition. The elimination of benefits for any necessary element to diagnose or treat a condition is considered the elimination of all or substantially all benefits to diagnose or treat a particular condition;

• Increases a percentage cost-sharing requirement (such as coinsurance) above the level at which it was on March 23, 2010;

• Increases fixed-amount cost-sharing requirements other than copayments, such as a $500 deductible or a $2,500 out-of-pocket limit, by a total percentage measured from March 23, 2010 that is more than the sum of medical inflation and 15 percentage points.[10]

• Increases copayments by an amount that exceeds the greater of: a total percentage measured from March 23, 2010 that is more than the sum of medical inflation plus 15 percentage points, or $5 increased by medical inflation measured from March 23, 2010;

• For a group health plan or group health insurance coverage, an employer or employee organization decreases its contribution rate by more than five percentage points below the contribution rate on March 23, 2010; or

• With respect to annual limits (1) a group health plan, or group or individual health insurance coverage, that, on March 23, 2010, did not impose an overall annual or lifetime limit on the dollar value of all benefits imposes an overall annual limit on the dollar value of benefits; (2) a group health plan, or group or individual health insurance coverage, that, on March 23, 2010, imposed an overall lifetime limit on the dollar value of all benefits but no overall annual limit on the dollar value of all benefits adopts an overall annual limit at a dollar value that is lower than the dollar value of the lifetime limit on March 23, 2010; or (3) a group health plan, or group or individual health insurance coverage, that, on March 23, 2010, imposed an overall annual limit on the dollar value of all benefits decreases the dollar value of the annual limit (regardless of whether the plan or health insurance coverage also imposes an overall lifetime limit on the dollar value of all benefits).

Table 1, in section II.D of this preamble, lists the relevant Affordable Care Act provisions that apply to grandfathered health plans.

In accordance with OMB Circular A–4,[11] Table 2 below depicts an accounting statement showing the Departments' assessment of the benefits, costs, and transfers associated with this regulatory action. In accordance with Executive Order 12866, the Departments believe that the benefits of this regulatory action justify the costs.

---

[10] Medical inflation is defined in these interim regulations by reference to the overall medical care component of the CPI.

[11] Available at *http://www.whitehouse.gov/omb/circulars/a004/a-4.pdf.*

34548   Federal Register / Vol. 75, No. 116 / Thursday, June 17, 2010 / Rules and Regulations

TABLE 2—ACCOUNTING TABLE

Benefits

Qualitative: These interim final regulations provide plans with guidance about the requirements for retaining grandfather status. Non-grand-fathered plans are required to offer coverage with minimum benefit standards and patient protections as required by the Affordable Care Act, while grandfathered plans are required only to comply with certain provisions. The existence of grandfathered health plans will provide individuals with the benefits of plan continuity, which may have a high value to some. In addition, grandfathering could potentially slow the rate of premium growth, depending on the extent to which their current plan does not include the benefits and protections of the new law. It could also provide incentives to employers to continue coverage, potentially reducing new Medicaid enrollment and spending and lowering the number of uninsured individuals. These interim final regulations also provide greater certainty for plans and issuers about what changes they can make without affecting their grandfather status. As compared with alternative approaches, these regulations provide significant economic and noneconomic benefits to both issuers and beneficiaries, though these benefits cannot be quantified at this time.

Costs	Low-end estimate	Mid-range estimate	High-end estimate	Year dollar	Discount rate	Period covered
Annualized	22.0	25.6	27.9	2010	7%	2011–2013
Monetized ($millions/year)	21.2	24.7	26.9	2010	3%	2011–2013

Monetized costs are due to a requirement to notify participants and beneficiaries of a plan's grandfather status and maintain plan documents to verify compliance with these interim final regulation's requirements to retain grandfather status.

Qualitative: Limitations on cost-sharing increases imposed by these interim final regulations could result in the cost of some grandfathered health plans increasing more (or decreasing less) than they otherwise would. This increased cost may encourage some sponsors and issuers to replace their grandfathered health plans with new, non-grandfathered ones. Market segmentation (adverse selection) due to the decision of higher risk plans to relinquish grandfathering could cause premiums in the exchanges to be higher than they would have been absent grandfathering.

Transfers
Qualitative: Limits on the changes to cost-sharing in grandfathered plans and the elimination of cost-sharing for some services in non-grand-fathered plans, leads to transfers of wealth from premium payers overall to individuals using covered services. Once pre-existing conditions are fully prohibited and other insurance reforms take effect, the extent to which individuals are enrolled in grandfathered plans could affect adverse selection, as higher risk plans relinquish grandfather status to gain new protections while lower risk grandfathered plans retain their grandfather status. This could result in a transfer of wealth from non-grandfathered plans to grandfathered health plans.

4. Discussion of Economic Impacts of Retaining or Relinquishing Grandfather Status

The economic effects of these interim final regulations will depend on decisions by plan sponsors and issuers, as well as by those covered under these plans and health insurance coverage. The collective decisions of plan sponsors and issuers over time can be viewed as a one-way sorting process in which these parties decide whether, and when, to relinquish status as a grandfathered health plan.

Plan sponsors and issuers can decide to:

1. Continue offering the plan or coverage in effect on March 23, 2010 with limited changes, and thereby retain grandfather status;

2. Significantly change the terms of the plan or coverage and comply with Affordable Care Act provisions from which grandfathered health plans are excepted; or

3. In the case of a plan sponsor, cease to offer any plan.

For a plan sponsor or issuer, the potential economic impact of the application of the provisions in the Affordable Care Act may be one consideration in making its decisions. To determine the value of retaining the health plan's grandfather status, each plan sponsor or issuer must determine whether the rules applicable to grandfathered health plans are more or less favorable than the rules applicable to non-grandfathered health plans. This determination will depend on such factors as the respective prices of grandfathered and non-grandfathered health plans, as well as on the preferences of grandfathered health plans' covered populations and their willingness to pay for benefits and patient protections available under non-grandfathered health plans. In making its decisions about grandfather status, a plan sponsor or issuer is also likely to consider the market segment (because different rules apply to the large and small group market segments), and the utilization pattern of its covered population.

In deciding whether to change a plan's benefits or cost sharing, a plan sponsor or issuer will examine its short-run business requirements. These requirements are regularly altered by, among other things, rising costs that result from factors such as technological changes, changes in risk status of the enrolled population, and changes in utilization and provider prices. As shown below, changes in benefits and cost sharing are typical in insurance markets. Decisions about the extent of changes will determine whether a plan retains its grandfather status. Ultimately, these decisions will involve a comparison by the plan sponsor or issuer of the long run value of grandfather status to the short-run need of that plan sponsor or issuer to adjust plan structure in order to control premium costs or achieve other business objectives.

Decisions by plan sponsors and issuers may be significantly affected by the preferences and behavior of the enrollees, especially a tendency among many towards inertia and resistance to change. There is limited research that has directly examined what drives this tendency—whether individuals remain with health plans because of simple inertia and procrastination, a lack of relevant information, or because they want to avoid risk associated with switching to new plans. One study that examined the extent to which premium changes influenced plan switching determined that younger low-risk employees were the most price-sensitive to premium changes; older, high-risk employees were the least price-sensitive. This finding suggests that, in particular, individuals with substantial health needs may be more apt to remain with a plan because of inertia as such or uncertainties associated with plan

Federal Register / Vol. 75, No. 116 / Thursday, June 17, 2010 / Rules and Regulations   34549

switching rather than quality per se—a phenomenon some behavioral economists have called "status quo bias,"[12] which can be found when people stick with the status quo even though a change would have higher expected value.

Even when an enrollee could reap an economic or other advantage from changing plans, that enrollee may not make the change because of inertia, a lack of relevant information, or because of the cost and effort involved in examining new options and uncertainty about the alternatives. Consistent with well-known findings in behavioral economics, studies of private insurance demonstrate the substantial effect of inertia in the behavior of the insured. One survey found that approximately 83 percent of privately insured individuals stuck with their plans in the year prior to the survey.[13] Among those who did change plans, well over half sought the same type of plan they had before. Those who switched plans also tended to do so for reasons other than preferring their new plans. For example, many switched because they changed jobs or their employer changed insurance offerings, compelling them to switch.

Medicare beneficiaries display similar plan loyalties. On average, only seven percent of the 17 million seniors on Medicare drug plans switch plans each year, according to the Centers for Medicare and Medicaid Services.[14] Researchers have found this comparatively low rate of switching is maintained whether or not those insured have higher quality information about plan choices, and that switching has little effect on the satisfaction of the insured with their health plans.[15]

The incentives to change are different for people insured in the individual market than they are for those covered by group health plans or group health insurance coverage. The median length of coverage for people entering the individual market is eight months.[16] In

part, this "churn" stems from the individual market's function as a stopping place for people between jobs with employer-sponsored or other types of health insurance, but in part, the churn is due to the behavior of issuers. Evidence suggests that issuers often make policy changes such as raising deductibles as a means of attracting new, healthy enrollees who have few medical costs and so are little-concerned about such deductibles. There is also evidence that issuers use such changes to sort out high-cost enrollees from low-cost ones.[17]

Decisions about the value of retaining or relinquishing status as a grandfathered health plan are complex, and the wide array of factors affecting issuers, plan sponsors, and enrollees poses difficult challenges for the Departments as they try to estimate how large the presence of grandfathered health plans will be in the future and what the economic effects of their presence will be. As one example, these interim final regulations limit the extent to which plan sponsors and issuers can increase cost sharing and still remain grandfathered. The increases that are allowed provide plans and issuers with substantial flexibility in attempting to control expenditure increases. However, there are likely to be some plans and issuers that would, in the absence of these regulations, choose to make even larger increases in cost sharing than are specified here. Such plans will need to decide whether the benefits of maintaining grandfather status outweigh those expected from increasing cost sharing above the levels permitted in the interim final regulations.

A similar analysis applies to the provision that an employer's or employee organization's share of the total premium of a group health plan cannot be reduced by more than 5 percentage points from the share it was paying on March 23, 2010 without that plan or health insurance coverage relinquishing its grandfather status. Employers and employee organizations sponsoring group health plans or health insurance coverage may be faced with economic circumstances that would lead them to reduce their premium contributions. But reductions of greater than 5 percentage points would cause them to relinquish the grandfather status of their plans. These plan sponsors must decide whether the benefit of such premium reductions

outweigh those of retaining grandfather status.

Market dynamics affecting these decisions change in 2014, when the Affordable Care Act limits variation in premium rates for individual and small group policies. Small groups for this purpose include employers with up to 100 employees (States may limit this threshold to 50 employees until 2016). The Affordable Care Act rating rules will not apply to grandfathered health plans, but such plans will remain subject to State rating rules, which vary widely and typically apply to employers with up to 50 employees. Based on the current State rating rules, it is likely that, in many States, no rating rules will apply to group health insurance policies that are grandfathered health plans covering employers with 51 to 100 employees.[18]

The interaction of the Affordable Care Act and State rating rules implies that, beginning in 2014, premiums can vary more widely for grandfathered plans than for non-grandfathered plans for employers with up to 100 employees in many States. This could encourage both plan sponsors and issuers to continue grandfathered health plans that cover lower-risk groups, because these groups will be isolated from the larger, higher-risk, non-grandfathered risk pool. On the other hand, this scenario likely will encourage plan sponsors and issuers that cover higher-risk groups to end grandfathered health plans, because the group would be folded into the larger, lower-risk non-grandfathered pool. Depending on the size of the grandfathered health plan market, such adverse selection by grandfathered health plans against non-grandfathered plans could cause premiums in the exchanges to be higher than they would have been absent grandfathering. To accommodate these changes in market dynamics in 2014, the Departments have structured a cost-sharing rule whose parameters enable greater flexibility in early years and less over time. It is likely that few plans will delay for many years before making changes that exceed medical inflation. This is because the cumulative increase in copayments from March 23, 2010 is compared to a maximum percentage increase that includes a fixed amount—15 percentage points—that does not increase annually with any type of inflator. This should help mitigate adverse selection and require plans and issuers that seek to maintain grandfather status to find ways other than increased

[12] http://www.nber.org/reporter/summer06/buchmueller.html. "Consumer Demand for Health Insurance" The National Bureau of Economic Research (Buchmueller, 2006).

[13] http://content.healthaffairs.org/cgi/reprint/19/3/158.pdf. "Health Plan Switching: Choice Or Circumstance?" (Cunningham and Kohn, 2000).

[14] http://www.kaiserhealthnews.org/Stories/2009/December/01/Medicare-Drug-Plan.aspx. "Seniors Often Reluctant To Switch Medicare Drug Plans" (2009, Kaiser Health News/Washington Post).

[15] http://www.ncbi.nlm.nih.gov/pubmed/16704882. "The effect of quality information on consumer health plan switching: evidence from the Buyers Health Care Action Group." (Abraham, Feldman, Carlin, and Christianson, 2006).

[16] Erika C. Ziller, Andrew F. Coburn, Timothy D. McBride, and Courtney Andrews. Patterns of

Individual Health Insurance Coverage, 1996–2000. Health Affairs Nov/Dec 2004: 210–221.

[17] Melinda Beeuwkes Bustin, M. Susan Marquis, and Jill M. Yegian. The Role of the Individual Health Insurance Market and Prospects for Change. Health Affairs 2004; 23(6): 79–90.

[18] Kaiser Family Foundation State Health Facts (2010). http://www.statehealthfacts.org/comparetable.jsp?ind=351&cat=7.

34550 **Federal Register**/Vol. 75, No. 116/Thursday, June 17, 2010/Rules and Regulations

copayments to limit cost growth. As discussed in the preamble, the Departments are also soliciting comments to make any adjustments needed for the final rule prior to 2014. Therefore it is premature to estimate the economic effects described above in 2014 and beyond. In the following section, the Departments provide a range of estimates of how issuers and sponsors might respond to these interim final regulations, with the caveat that there is substantial uncertainty about actual outcomes, especially considering that available data are historical and so do not account for behavioral changes in plans and the insured as a result of enactment of the Affordable Care Act.

5. Estimates of Number of Plans and Employees Affected

The Affordable Care Act applies to group health plans and health insurance issuers in the group and individual markets. The large and small group markets will be discussed first, followed by a discussion of impacts on the individual market. The Departments have defined a large group health plan as a plan at an employer with 100 or more workers and a small group plan as a plan at an employer with less than 100 workers. Using data from the 2008 Medical Expenditure Survey—Insurance Component, the Departments estimated that there are approximately 72,000 large ERISA-covered health plans and 2.8 million small group health plans with an estimated 97.0 million participants and beneficiaries [19] in large group plans and 40.9 million participants and beneficiaries in small group plans. The Departments estimate that there are 126,000 governmental plans [20] with 36.1 million participants in large plans and 2.3 million participants in small plans. The Departments estimate there are 16.7 million individuals under age 65 covered by individually purchased policies.

a. Methodology for Analyzing Plan Changes Over Time in the Group Market

For the large and small group markets, the Departments analyzed three years of Kaiser-HRET data to assess the changes that plans made between plan years 2007 to 2008 and 2008 to 2009. Specifically, the Departments examined changes made to deductibles, out-of-pocket maximums, copayments, coinsurance, and the employer's share of the premium or cost of coverage. The

Departments also estimated the number of fully-insured plans that changed issuers.[21] The distribution of changes made within the two time periods were nearly identical and ultimately the 2008–2009 changes were used as a basis for the analyses.

As discussed previously, plans will need to make decisions that balance the value they (and their enrollees) place on maintaining grandfather status with the need to meet short run objectives by changing plan features including the various cost sharing requirements that are the subject of this rule. The 2008–2009 data reflect changes in plan benefit design that were made under very different market conditions and expectations than will exist in 2011 and beyond. Therefore, there is a significant degree of uncertainty associated with using the 2008–2009 data to project the number of plans whose grandfather status may be affected in the next few years. Because the level of uncertainty becomes substantially greater when trying to use this data to predict outcomes once the full range of reforms takes effect in 2014 and the exchanges begin operating, substantially changing market dynamics the Departments restrict our estimates to the 2011–2013 period and use the existing data and a range of assumptions to estimate possible outcomes based on a range of assumptions concerning how plans' behavior regarding cost sharing changes may change relative to what is reflected in the 2008–2009 data.

Deriving projections of the number of plans that could retain grandfather status under the requirements of these interim final regulations required several steps:

• Using Kaiser/HRET data for 2008–2009, estimates were generated of the number of plans in the large and small group markets that made changes in employer premium share or any of the cost-sharing parameters that were larger than permitted for a plan to retain grandfather status under these interim final regulations;

• In order to account for a range of uncertainty with regard to changes in plan behavior toward cost sharing changes, the Departments assumed that many plans will want to maintain grandfather status and will look for ways to achieve short run cost control and still maintain that status. One plausible assumption is that plans would look to a broader range of cost sharing strategies in order to achieve

cost containment and other objectives than they had in the past. In order to examine this possibility, the Departments carefully analyzed those plans that would have relinquished grandfather status based on a change they made from 2008–2009. The Departments then estimated the proportion of these plans that could have achieved similar cost control by using one or more other cost-sharing changes in addition to the one they made in a manner that would not have exceeded the limits set by these interim final regulations for qualifying as a grandfathered health plan. For example, if a plan was estimated to relinquish grandfather status because it increased its deductible by more than the allowed 15 percentage points plus medical inflation, the Departments analyze whether the plan could have achieved the same cost control objectives with a smaller change in deductible, but larger changes (within the limits set forth in these interim final regulations) in copayments, out-of-pocket maximums, and employer contributions to the premium or cost of coverage.

• Finally, the Departments examined the impact of alternative assumptions about sponsor behavior. For example, it is possible that some sponsors who made changes from 2008–2009 in plan parameters that were so large that they would have relinquished their grandfather status would not make similar changes in 2011–2013. It is also possible that even though a sponsor could make an equivalent change that conforms to the rules established in these interim final regulations to maintain grandfather status, it would decide not to.

The estimates in this example rely on several other assumptions. Among them: (1) The annual proportion of plans relinquishing grandfather status is the same throughout the period; (2) all group health plans existing at the beginning of 2010 qualify for grandfather status; (3) all changes during 2010 occur after March 23, 2010; (4) annual medical inflation is 4 percent (based on the average annual change in the medical CPI between 2000 and 2009); and (5) firms for which the Kaiser-HRET survey has data for both 2008 and 2009 are representative of all firms.[22] The assumption used for

---

[19] All participant counts and the estimates of individual policies are from the 2009 Current Population Survey (CPS).

[20] Estimate is from the 2007 Census of Government.

[21] Under the Affordable Care Act and these interim final regulations, if a plan that is not a collectively bargained plan changes issuers after March 23, 2010, it is no longer a grandfathered health plan.

[22] The analysis is limited to firms that responded to the Kaiser/HRET survey in both 2008 and 2009. Large firms are overrepresented in the analytic sample. New firms and firms that went out of business in 2008 or 2009 are underrepresented. The Departments present results separately for large firms and small firms, and weight the results to the number of employees in each firm-size category. Results are presented for PPO plans. The Kaiser/

estimating the effects of the limits on copayment increases does not take into account the greater flexibility in the near term than in the long term; the estimated increase in firms losing their grandfather status over time reflects cumulative effects of a constant policy. To the extent that the data reflect plans that are more likely to make frequent changes in cost sharing, the assumption that a constant share of plans relinquishing grandfather status throughout the period may underestimate the number of plans that will retain grandfather status through 2013. In addition, data on substantial benefit changes were not available and thus not included in the analysis. The survey data is limited, in that it covers only one year of changes in healthcare plans. The Departments' analysis employed data only on PPO plans, the predominant type of plan. In addition, the difficulties of forecasting behavior in response to this rule create uncertainties for quantitative evaluation. However, the analysis presented here is illustrative of the rule's goal of balancing flexibility with maintaining current coverage.

b. Impacts on the Group Market Resulting From Changes From 2008 to 2009

The Departments first estimated the percentage of plans that had a percent change in the dollar value of deductibles, copayments, or out-of-pocket maximums that exceeded 19 percent (the sum of medical inflation (assumed in these analyses to be four percent) plus 15 percentage points measured from March 23, 2010. Plans making copayment changes of five dollars or less were considered to have satisfied the copayment limit, even if that change exceeded 19 percent.[23] The Departments also estimated the number of plans for whom the percentage of

total premium paid by the employer declined by more than 5 percentage points. For fully-insured plans only, estimates were made of the proportion that switched to a different issuer.[24] This estimate does not take into account collectively bargained plans, which can change issuers during the period of the collective bargaining agreement without a loss of grandfather status, because the Departments could not quantify this category of plans. Accordingly, this estimate represents an upper bound.

Using the Kaiser/HRET data, the Departments estimated that 55 percent of small employers and 36 percent of large employers made at least one change in cost-sharing parameters above the thresholds provided in these interim final regulations. Similarly, 33 percent of small employers and 21 percent of large employers decreased the employer's share of premium by more than five percentage points. In total, approximately 66 percent of small employers and 48 percent of large employers made a change in either cost sharing or premium contribution during 2009 that would require them to relinquish grandfather status if the same change were made in 2011.[25]

The changes made by employers from 2008 to 2009 were possibly made in anticipation of the recession. As discussed previously, analysis of changes from 2007 to 2008 suggests that the 2007–08 changes were not much different from the 2008–09 changes. Nevertheless, as a result of improvements in economic conditions, it makes sense to think that the pressure on employers to reduce their contributions to health insurance will be smaller in 2011 than they were in 2009, and that the Department's analysis of changes in 2009 may overestimate the changes that should be expected in 2011.[26]

As discussed previously, it is highly unlikely that plans would continue to exhibit the same behavior in 2011 to 2013 as in 2008 to 2009. In order to guide the choice of behavioral assumptions, the Departments

conducted further analyses of the 2008–2009 data. Many employers who made changes between 2008 and 2009 that would have caused them to relinquish grandfather status did so based on exceeding one of the cost-sharing limits. Assuming that the sponsor's major objective in implementing these changes was to restrain employer costs or overall premiums, the Departments examined whether the sponsor could have achieved the same net effect on employer cost or premiums by spreading cost sharing over two or more changes without exceeding the limits on any of these changes. For example, an employer that increased its deductible by 30 percent would have relinquished grandfather status. However, it is possible that the employer could have achieved the same cost control objectives by limiting the deductible increase to 19 percent, and, also increasing the out-of-pocket maximum or copayments, or decreasing the employer share of the premium.

The Departments estimate that approximately two-thirds of the employers that made changes in 2009 that would have exceeded the threshold implemented by this rule could have achieved the same cost-control objective and remained grandfathered by making changes in other cost-sharing parameters or in the employer share of the premium. Only 24 percent of small employers and 16 percent of large employers could not have reconfigured the cost-sharing parameters or employer contributions in such a manner that would have allowed them to stay grandfathered. If benefit changes that are allowed within the grandfathered health plan definition were also taken into account (not possible with available data), these percentages would be even lower.

For fully insured group health plans, another change that would require a plan to relinquish grandfather status is a change in issuer. Between 2008 and 2009, 15 percent of small employers and four percent of large employers changed insurance carriers.[27] However, it is likely that the incentive to stay grandfathered would lead some of these employers to continue with the same issuer, making the actual share of firms relinquishing grandfather status as a result of an issuer change lower than the percentage that switched in 2009. There appears to be no empirical evidence to

---

HRET survey gathers information about the PPO with the most enrollment in each year. If enrollment at a given employer shifted from one PPO to a different PPO between 2008 and 2009, then the PPO with the most enrollment in 2009 may be different than the PPO with the most enrollment in 2008. To the extent this occurred, the estimates presented here may overestimate the fraction of plans that will relinquish grandfather status. However, given the behavioral assumptions of the analysis and the need to present a range of results, the Departments believe that such overestimation will not have a noticeable effect on estimates presented here.

[23] The regulation allows plans to increase fixed-amount copayments by an amount that does not exceed $5 increased by medical inflation. In this analysis, the Departments used a threshold of $5, rather than the threshold of approximately $5.20 that would be allowed by these interim final regulations. There would have been no difference in the results if the Departments had used $5.20 rather than $5 as the threshold.

[24] In contrast, for self-insured plans, a change in third party administrator in and of itself does not cause a group health plan to cease to be a grandfathered health plan, provided changes do not exceed the limits of paragraph (g)(1) of these interim final regulations.

[25] Some employers made changes which exceeded at least one cost-sharing threshold and decreased the employer's share of contribution by more than five percent.

[26] Employers who offer plans on a calendar year basis generally make decisions about health plan offerings during the preceding summer. Thus, decisions for calendar 2009 were generally made during the summer of 2008. At that time, the depth of the coming recession was not yet clear to most observers.

[27] Among the 76 percent of small employers and 84 percent of large employers who could have accommodated the cost-sharing changes they desired to make within the parameters of these interim final regulations, 13 percent of the small employers and three percent of the large employers changed issuers.

34552   **Federal Register** / Vol. 75, No. 116 / Thursday, June 17, 2010 / Rules and Regulations

provide guidance on the proportion of employers that would choose to remain with their issuer rather than relinquish grandfather status. That being so, an assumption was made that 50 percent of employers that changed issuers in 2009 would not have made a similar change in 2011 in order to retain grandfather status. It is likely that fewer employers will elect to change carriers than in recent years given that some will prefer to retain grandfather status. But it is also likely that many employers will prefer to switch carriers given a change in the issuer's network or other factors. Because there is little empirical evidence regarding the fraction of firms that would elect to switch in response to the change in regulations, we take the midpoint of the plausible range of no switching carriers at one extreme and all switching carriers at the other extreme. We therefore assume that 50 percent of employers that changed issuers in 2009 would not make a similar change in 2011 to retain grandfather status.

Combining the estimates of the percentage of employers that would relinquish grandfather status because they chose to make cost-sharing, benefit or employer contribution changes beyond the permitted parameters with the estimates of the percentage that would relinquish grandfather status because they change issuers, the Departments estimate that approximately 31 percent of small employers and 18 percent of large employers would make changes that would require them to relinquish grandfather status in 2011. The Departments use these estimates as our mid-range scenario.

c. Sensitivity Analysis: Assuming That Employers Will Be Willing To Absorb a Premium Increase in Order To Remain Grandfathered

To the extent that a large number of plans placed a high value on remaining grandfathered, it is reasonable to assume that some would consider other measures to maintain that status. In addition to the adjustments that employers could relatively easily make by simply adjusting the full set of cost-sharing parameters rather than focusing changes on a single parameter, the Departments expect that further behavioral changes in response to the incentives created by the Affordable Care Act and these interim final regulations is possible. For instance, plans could alter other benefits or could decide to accept a slight increase in plan premium or in premium contribution. All of these options would further lower the percentage of firms that would relinquish grandfather status. There is

substantial uncertainty, however, about how many firms would utilize these other avenues.

To examine the impact of this type of behavior on the estimates on the number of plans that would not maintain grandfather status, the Departments examined the magnitude of additional premium increases plans would need to implement if they were to modify their cost-sharing changes to stay within the allowable limits. Among the 24 percent of small firms that would have relinquished grandfather status based on the changes they made in 2009, 31 percent would have needed to increase premiums by 3 percent or less in order to maintain grandfather status. The analogous statistic for the 16 percent of large firms that would have relinquished grandfather status is 41 percent. It is reasonable to think that employers that are facing only a relatively small premium increase might choose to remain grandfathered.

Using these estimates, if employers value grandfathering enough that they are willing to allow premiums to increase by three percent more than their otherwise intended level (or can make changes to benefits other than cost-sharing that achieve a similar result), then 14 percent of small employers and 11 percent of large employers would relinquish grandfather status if they made the same changes in 2011 as they had in 2009. Adding in the employers who would relinquish grandfather status because they change issuers, the Departments' lower bound estimate is that approximately 21 percent of small employers and 13 percent of large employers will relinquish grandfather status in 2011.

d. Sensitivity Analysis: Incomplete Flexibility To Substitute One Cost-Sharing Mechanism for Another

Although economic conditions may cause more plans to remain grandfathered in 2011 than might be expected from analysis of the 2009 data, there are other factors that may cause the Departments' estimates of the fraction of plans retaining grandfather status to be overestimates of the fraction that will retain grandfather status. The estimates are based on the assumption that all plans that could accommodate the 2009 change they made in a single cost-sharing parameter by spreading out those changes over multiple parameters would actually do so. However, some plans and sponsors may be concerned about the labor relations consequences of reducing the employer contribution to premium. For example, if a plan increases its out-of-pocket maximum from $3,000 to $5,000 in 2009, it could

choose to remain grandfathered by limiting the out-of-pocket maximum to $3,570, reducing the employer contribution and increasing the employee contribution to premium. It is not clear, however, that all plan sponsors would do so—some may see the costs in negative employee relations as larger than the benefits from remaining grandfathered. Moreover, because some plans may already nearly comply with all provisions of the Affordable Care Act, or because enrollees are of average to less favorable health status, some employers may place less value on retaining grandfather status.

With this in mind, the Departments replicated the analysis, but assumed that one-half of the employers who made a change in cost-sharing parameter that could not be accommodated without reducing the employer contribution will be unwilling to reduce the employer contribution as a share of premium. Under this assumption, the 24 percent and 16 percent estimates of the proportion of employers relinquishing grandfather status increases to approximately 37 percent and 28 percent among small and large employers, respectively. Adding in the number of employers that it is estimated will change issuers, the Departments' high-end estimate for the proportion that will relinquish grandfather status in 2011 is approximately 42 percent for small employers and 29 percent for large employers.

e. Estimates for 2011–2013

Estimates are provided above for the percentage of employers that will retain grandfather status in 2011. These estimates are extended through 2013 by assuming that the identical percentage of plan sponsors will relinquish grandfathering in each year. Again, to the extent that the 2008–2009 data reflect plans that are more likely to make frequent changes in cost sharing, this assumption will overestimate the number of plans relinquishing grandfather status in 2012 and 2013.

Under this assumption, the Departments' mid-range estimate is that 66 percent of small employer plans and 45 percent of large employer plans will relinquish their grandfather status by the end of 2013. The low-end estimates are for 49 percent and 34 percent of small and large employer plans, respectively, to have relinquished grandfather status, and the high-end estimates are 80 percent and 64 percent, respectively.

TABLE 3—ESTIMATES OF THE CUMULATIVE PERCENTAGE OF EMPLOYER PLANS RELINQUISHING THEIR GRANDFATHERED STATUS, 2011–2013

	2011	2012	2013
Low-end Estimate			
Small Employer Plans	20%	36%	49%
Large Employer Plans	13%	24%	34%
All Employer Plans	15%	28%	39%
Mid-range Estimate			
Small Employer Plans	30%	51%	66%
Large Employer Plans	18%	33%	45%
All Employer Plans	22%	38%	51%
High-end Estimate			
Small Employer Plans	42%	66%	80%
Large Employer Plans	29%	50%	64%
All Employer Plans	33%	55%	69%

Notes: Represents full-time employees. Small Employers=3 to 99 employees; Large Employers=100+ employees. All three scenarios assume that two percent of all large employer plans and six percent of small employer plans would relinquish grandfathered status due to a change in issuer. Estimates are based on enrollment in PPOs.
Source: Kaiser/RHET Employer Survey, 2008–2009

f. Impacts on the Individual Market

The market for individual insurance is significantly different than that for group coverage. This affects estimates of the proportion of plans that will remain grandfathered until 2014. As mentioned previously, the individual market is a residual market for those who need insurance but do not have group coverage available and do not qualify for public coverage. For many, the market is transitional, providing a bridge between other types of coverage. One study found a high percentage of individual insurance policies began and ended with employer-sponsored coverage.[28] More importantly, coverage on particular policies tends to be for short periods of time. Reliable data are scant, but a variety of studies indicate that between 40 percent and 67 percent of policies are in effect for less than one year.[29] Although data on changes in benefit packages comparable to that for the group market is not readily available, the high turnover rates described here would dominate benefit changes as the chief source of changes in grandfather status.

While a substantial fraction of individual policies are in force for less than one year, a small group of individuals maintain their policies over longer time periods. One study found that 17 percent of individuals maintained their policies for more than two years,[30] while another found that

nearly 30 percent maintained policies for more than three years.[31]

Using these turnover estimates, a reasonable range for the percentage of individual policies that would terminate, and therefore relinquish their grandfather status, is 40 percent to 67 percent. These estimates assume that the policies that terminate are replaced by new individual policies, and that these new policies are not, by definition, grandfathered. In addition, the coverage that some individuals maintain for long periods might lose its grandfather status because the cost-sharing parameters in policies change by more than the limits specified in these interim final regulations. The frequency of this outcome cannot be gauged due to lack of data, but as a result of it, the Departments estimate that the percentage of individual market policies losing grandfather status in a given year exceeds the 40 percent to 67 percent range that is estimated based on the fraction of individual policies that turn over from one year to the next.

g. Application to Extension of Dependent Coverage to Age 26

One way to assess the impact of these interim final regulations is to assess how they interact with other Affordable Care Act provisions. One such provision is the requirement that, in plan years on or after September 23, 2010, but prior to January 1, 2014, grandfathered group health plans are required to offer dependent coverage to a child under the age of 26 who is not eligible for employer-sponsored insurance. In the Regulatory Impact Assessment (RIA) for the regulation that was issued on May

13, 2010 (75 FR 27122), the Departments estimated that there were 5.3 million young adults age 19–25 who were covered by employer-sponsored coverage (ESI) and whose parents were covered by employer-sponsored insurance, and an additional 480,000 young adults who were uninsured, were offered ESI, and whose parents were covered by ESI. In that impact assessment, the Departments assumed that all parents with employer-sponsored insurance would be in grandfathered health plans, and that none of their 19–25 year old dependents with their own offer of employer-sponsored insurance would gain coverage as a result of that regulation.

As estimated here, approximately 80 percent of the parents with ESI are likely to be in grandfathered health plans in 2011, leaving approximately 20 percent of these parents in non-grandfathered health plans. Young adults under 26 with employer-sponsored insurance or with an offer of such coverage whose parents are in non-grandfathered plans potentially could enroll in their parents' coverage. The Departments assume that a large percentage of the young adults who are uninsured will enroll in their parents' coverage when given the opportunity. It is more difficult to model the choices of young adults with an offer of employer-sponsored insurance whose parents also have group coverage. One assumes these young adults will compare the amount that they must pay for their own employer's coverage with the amount that they (or their parents) would pay if they were covered under their parents' policies. Such a decision will incorporate the type of plan that the parent has, since if the parent already has a family plan whose premium does not vary by number of dependents, the

[28] Adele M. Kirk. The Individual Insurance Market: A Building Block for Health Care Reform? *Health Care Financing Organization Research Synthesis.* May 2008.

[29] Ibid.

[30] http://content.healthaffairs.org/cgi/content/full/23/6/210#R14. "Patterns of Individual Health Insurance Coverage" *Health Affairs* (Ziller et al, 2004).

[31] http://content.healthaffairs.org/cgi/content/full/hlthaff.25.w226v1/DC1. "Consumer Decision Making in the Individual Health Insurance Market" *Health Affairs* (Marquis et al., 2006).

adult child could switch at no additional cost to the parents. A very rough estimate therefore is that approximately 25 percent of young adults with ESI will switch to their parents' coverage when their parents' coverage is not grandfathered. The Departments assume that 15 percent of young adults who are offered ESI but are uninsured and whose parents have non-grandfathered health plans will switch to their parents' plan. This latter estimate roughly corresponds to the assumption made in the low-take up rate scenario in the RIA for dependent coverage for young adults who are uninsured.

These assumptions imply that an additional approximately 414,000 young adults whose parents have non-grandfathered ESI will be covered by their parents' health coverage in 2011, of whom 14,000 would have been uninsured, compared with the dependent coverage regulation impact analysis that assumed that all existing plans would have remained grandfathered and none of these adult children would have been eligible for coverage under their parents' plans. By 2013, an estimated 698,000 additional young adults with ESI or an offer of ESI will be covered by their parent's non-grandfathered health policy, of which 36,000 would have been uninsured.

6. Grandfathered Health Plan Document Retention and Disclosure Requirements

To maintain grandfathered health plan status under these interim final regulations, a plan or issuer must maintain records that document the plan or policy terms in connection with the coverage in effect on March 23, 2010, and any other documents necessary to verify, explain or clarify is status as a grandfathered health plan. The records must be made available for examination by participants, beneficiaries, individual policy subscribers, or a State or Federal agency official.

Plans or health insurance coverage that intend to be a grandfathered health plan, also must include a statement, in any plan materials provided to participants or beneficiaries (in the individual market, primary subscriber) describing the benefits provided under the plan or health insurance coverage, and that the plan or coverage is intended to be a grandfathered health plan within the meaning of section 1251 of the Affordable Care Act. In these interim final regulations, the Departments provide a model statement plans and issuers may use to satisfy the disclosure requirement. The Department's estimate that the one time

cost to plans and insurance issuers of preparing and distributing the grandfathered health plan disclosure is $39.6 million in 2011. The one time cost to plans and insurance issuers for the record retention requirement is estimated to be $32.2 million in 2011. For a discussion of the grandfathered health plan document retention and disclosure requirements, see the Paperwork Reduction Act section later in this preamble.

C. Regulatory Flexibility Act— Department of Labor and Department of Health and Human Services

The Regulatory Flexibility Act (5 U.S.C. 601 *et seq.*) (RFA) imposes certain requirements with respect to federal rules that are subject to the notice and comment requirements of section 553(b) of the APA (5 U.S.C. 551 *et seq.*) and that are likely to have a significant economic impact on a substantial number of small entities. Under Section 553(b) of the APA, a general notice of proposed rulemaking is not required when an agency, for good cause, finds that notice and public comment thereon are impracticable, unnecessary, or contrary to the public interest. These interim final regulations are exempt from the APA, because the Departments made a good cause finding that a general notice of proposed rulemaking is not necessary earlier in this preamble. Therefore, the RFA does not apply and the Departments are not required to either certify that the regulations would not have a significant economic impact on a substantial number of small entities or conduct a regulatory flexibility analysis.

Nevertheless, the Departments carefully considered the likely impact of the regulations on small entities in connection with their assessment under Executive Order 12866. Consistent with the policy of the RFA, the Departments encourage the public to submit comments that suggest alternative rules that accomplish the stated purpose of section 1251 of the Affordable Care Act and minimize the impact on small entities.

D. Special Analyses—Department of the Treasury

Notwithstanding the determinations of the Department of Labor and Department of Health and Human Services, for purposes of the Department of the Treasury, it has been determined that this Treasury decision is not a significant regulatory action for purposes of Executive Order 12866. Therefore, a regulatory assessment is not required. It has also been determined that section 553(b) of the Administrative

Procedure Act (5 U.S.C. chapter 5) does not apply to these regulations. For the applicability of the RFA, refer to the Special Analyses section in the preamble to the cross-referencing notice of proposed rulemaking published elsewhere in this issue of the **Federal Register**. Pursuant to section 7805(f) of the Code, these temporary regulations have been submitted to the Chief Counsel for Advocacy of the Small Business Administration for comment on their impact on small businesses.

E. Paperwork Reduction Act

1. Department of Labor and Department of Treasury: Affordable Care Act Grandfathered Plan Disclosure and Record Retention Requirements

As part of their continuing efforts to reduce paperwork and respondent burden, the Departments conduct a preclearance consultation program to provide the general public and federal agencies with an opportunity to comment on proposed and continuing collections of information in accordance with the Paperwork Reduction Act of 1995 (PRA) (44 U.S.C. 3506(c)(2)(A)). This helps to ensure that requested data can be provided in the desired format, reporting burden (time and financial resources) is minimized, collection requirements on respondents can be properly assessed.

As discussed earlier in this preamble, if a plan or health insurance coverage intends to be a grandfathered health plan, it must include a statement in any plan materials provided to participants or beneficiaries (in the individual market, primary subscriber) describing the benefits provided under the plan or health insurance coverage, and that the plan or coverage is intended to be grandfathered health plan within the meaning of section 1251 of the Affordable Care Act ("grandfathered health plan disclosure"). Model language has been provided in these interim final regulations, the use of which will satisfy this disclosure requirement

To maintain status as a grandfathered health plan under these interim final regulations, a plan or issuer must maintain records documenting the plan or policy terms in connection with the coverage in effect on March 23, 2010, and any other documents necessary to verify, explain, or clarify its status as a grandfathered health plan ("recordkeeping requirement"). In addition, the plan or issuer must make such records available for examination. Accordingly, a participant, beneficiary, individual policy subscriber, or State or Federal agency official would be able to inspect such documents to verify the status of the plan or health insurance coverage as a grandfathered health plan.

As discussed earlier in this preamble, grandfathered health plans are not required to comply with certain Affordable Care Act provisions. These interim regulations define for plans and issuers the scope of changes that they can make to their grandfathered health plans and policies under the Affordable Care Act while retaining their grandfathered health plan status.

The Affordable Care Act grandfathered health plan disclosure and recordkeeping requirements are information collection requests (ICR) subject to the PRA. Currently, the Departments are soliciting public comments for 60 days concerning these disclosures. The Departments have submitted a copy of these interim final regulations to OMB in accordance with 44 U.S.C. 3507(d) for review of the information collections. The Departments and OMB are particularly interested in comments that:

• Evaluate whether the collection of information is necessary for the proper performance of the functions of the agency, including whether the information will have practical utility;

• Evaluate the accuracy of the agency's estimate of the burden of the collection of information, including the validity of the methodology and assumptions used;

• Enhance the quality, utility, and clarity of the information to be collected; and

• Minimize the burden of the collection of information on those who are to respond, including through the use of appropriate automated, electronic, mechanical, or other technological collection techniques or other forms of information technology, for example, by permitting electronic submission of responses.

Comments should be sent to the Office of Information and Regulatory Affairs, Attention: Desk Officer for the Employee Benefits Security Administration either by fax to (202) 395–7285 or by e-mail to *oira_submission@omb.eop.gov*. A copy of the ICR may be obtained by contacting the PRA addressee: G. Christopher Cosby, Office of Policy and Research, U.S. Department of Labor, Employee Benefits Security Administration, 200 Constitution Avenue, NW., Room N–5718, Washington, DC 20210. Telephone: (202) 693–8410; Fax: (202) 219–2745. These are not toll-free numbers. E-mail: *ebsa.opr@dol.gov*. ICRs submitted to OMB also are available at reginfo.gov

(*http://www.reginfo.gov/public/do/ PRAMain*).

a. Grandfathered Health Plan Disclosure

In order to satisfy the interim final regulations' grandfathered health plan disclosure requirement, the Departments estimate that 2.2 million ERISA-covered plans will need to notify an estimated 56.3 million policy holders of their plans' grandfathered health plan status.[32] The following estimates, except where noted, are based on the mid-range estimates of the percent of plans retaining grandfather status. Because the interim final regulations provide model language for this purpose, the Departments estimate that five minutes of clerical time (with a labor rate of $26.14/hour) will be required to incorporate the required language into the plan document and ten minutes of an human resource professional's time (with a labor rate of $89.12/hour) will be required to review the modified language.[33] After plans first satisfy the grandfathered health plan disclosure requirement in 2011, any additional burden should be de minimis if a plan wants to maintain its grandfather status in future years. The Departments also expect the cost of removing the notice from plan documents as plans relinquish their grandfather status to be de minimis and therefore is not estimated. Therefore, the Departments estimate that plans will incur a one-time hour burden of 538,000 hours with an equivalent cost of $30.0 million to meet the disclosure requirement.

The Departments assume that only printing and material costs are associated with the disclosure requirement, because the interim final regulations provide model language that can be incorporated into existing plan documents, such as a summary plan description (SPD). The Departments estimate that the notice will require one-half of a page, five cents per page printing and material cost will be incurred, and 38 percent of the notices will be delivered electronically. This results in a cost burden of $873,000 ($0.05 per page* ½ pages per notice * 34.9 million notices*0.62).

32 The Departments' estimate of the number of ERISA-covered health plans was obtained from the 2008 Medical Expenditure Panel Survey's Insurance component. The estimate of the number of policy holders was obtained from the 2009 Current Population Survey. The methodology used to estimate the percentage of plans that will retain their grandfathered plans was discussed above.

33 EBSA estimates of labor rates include wages, other benefits, and overhead based on the National Occupational Employment Survey (May 2008, Bureau of Labor Statistics) and the Employment Cost Index June 2009, Bureau of Labor Statistics).

b. Record-Keeping Requirement

The Departments assume that most of the documents required to be retained to satisfy recordkeeping requirement of these interim final regulations already are retained by plans for tax purposes, to satisfy ERISA's record retention and statute of limitations requirements, and for other business reasons. Therefore, the Departments estimate that the recordkeeping burden imposed by this ICR will require five minutes of a legal professional's time (with a rate of $119.03/hour) to determine the relevant plan documents that must be retained and ten minutes of clerical staff time (with a labor rate of $26.14/hour) to organize and file the required documents to ensure that they are accessible to participants, beneficiaries, and Federal and State governmental agency officials.

With an estimated 2.2 million grandfathered plans in 2011, the Departments estimate an hour burden of approximately 538,000 hours with equivalent costs of $30.7 million. The Departments have estimated this as a one-time cost incurred in 2011, because after the first year, the Departments anticipate that any future costs will be de minimis.

Overall, for both the grandfathering notice and the recordkeeping requirement, the Departments expect there to be a total hour burden of 1.1 million hours and a cost burden of $291,000.

The Departments note that persons are not required to respond to, and generally are not subject to any penalty for failing to comply with, an ICR unless the ICR has a valid OMB control number.

These paperwork burden estimates are summarized as follows:

Type of Review: New Collection.

Agencies: Employee Benefits Security Administration, Department of Labor; Internal Revenue Service, U.S. Department of Treasury.

Title: Disclosure and Recordkeeping Requirements for Grandfathered Health Plans under the Affordable Care Act.

OMB Number: 1210–0140; 1545–2178.

Affected Public: Business or other for-profit; not-for-profit institutions.

Total Respondents: 2,151,000.

Total Responses: 56,347,000.

Frequency of Response: One time.

Estimated Total Annual Burden Hours: 538,000 (Employee Benefits Security Administration); 538,000 (Internal Revenue Service).

Estimated Total Annual Burden Cost: $437,000 (Employee Benefits Security Administration); $437,000 (Internal Revenue Service).

34556   Federal Register / Vol. 75, No. 116 / Thursday, June 17, 2010 / Rules and Regulations

2. Department of Health and Human Services: Affordable Care Act Grandfathered Plan Disclosure and Record Retention Requirements

As discussed above in the Department of Labor and Department of the Treasury PRA section, these interim final regulations contain a record retention and disclosure requirement for grandfathered health plans. These requirements are information collection requirements under the PRA.

a. Grandfathered Health Plan Disclosure

In order to satisfy the interim final regulations' grandfathered health plan disclosure requirement, the Department estimates that 98,000 state and local governmental plans will need to notify approximately 16.2 million policy holders of their plans' status as a grandfathered health plan. The following estimates except where noted are based on the mid-range estimates of the percent of plans retaining grandfather status. An estimated 490 insurers providing coverage in the individual market will need to notify an estimated 4.3 million policy holders of their policies' status as a grandfathered health plan.[34]

Because the interim final regulations provide model language for this purpose, the Department estimates that five minute of clerical time (with a labor rate of $26.14/hour) will be required to incorporate the required language into the plan document and ten minutes of a human resource professional's time (with a labor rate of $89.12/hour) will be required to review the modified language.[35] After plans first satisfy the grandfathered health plan disclosure requirement in 2011, any additional burden should be *de minimis* if a plan wants to maintain its grandfather status in future years. The Department also expects the cost of removing the notice from plan documents as plans relinquish their grandfather status to be de minimis and therefore is not estimated. Therefore, the Department estimates that plans and insurers will incur a one-time hour burden of 26,000 hours with an equivalent cost of $1.8

million to meet the disclosure requirement.

The Department assumes that only printing and material costs are associated with the disclosure requirement, because the interim final regulations provide model language that can be incorporated into existing plan documents, such as an SPD. The Department estimates that the notice will require one-half of a page, five cents per page printing and material cost will be incurred, and 38 percent of the notices will be delivered electronically. This results in a cost burden of $318,000 ($0.05 per page*½ pages per notice * 12.7 million notices*0.62).

b. Record-Keeping Requirement

The Department assumes that most of the documents required to be retained to satisfy the Affordable Care Act's recordkeeping requirement already are retained by plans for tax purposes, to satisfy ERISA's record retention and statute of limitations requirements, and for other business reasons. Therefore, the Department estimates that the recordkeeping burden imposed by this ICR will require five minutes of a legal professional's time (with a rate of $119.03/hour) to determine the relevant plan documents that must be retained and ten minutes of clerical staff time (with a labor rate of $26.14/hour) to organize and file the required documents to ensure that they are accessible to participants, beneficiaries, and Federal and State governmental agency officials.

With an estimated 98,000 grandfathered plans and 7,400 grandfathered individual insurance products[36] in 2011, the Department estimates an hour burden of approximately 26,000 hours with equivalent costs of $1.5 million. The Department's have estimated this as a one-time cost incurred in 2011, because after the first year, the Department assumes any future costs will be *de minimis*.

Overall, for both the grandfathering notice and the recordkeeping requirement, the Department expects there to be a total hour burden of 53,000 hours and a cost burden of $318,000.

The Department notes that persons are not required to respond to, and generally are not subject to any penalty for failing to comply with, an ICR unless

the ICR has a valid OMB control number.

These paperwork burden estimates are summarized as follows:

Type of Review: New collection.

Agency: Department of Health and Human Services.

Title: Disclosure and Recordkeeping Requirements for Grandfathered Health Plans under the Affordable Care Act.

OMB Number: 0938–1093.

Affected Public: Business; State, Local, or Tribal Governments.

Respondents: 105,000.

Responses: 20,508,000.

Frequency of Response: One-time.

Estimated Total Annual Burden Hours: 53,000 hours.

Estimated Total Annual Burden Cost: $318,000.

If you comment on this information collection and recordkeeping requirements, please do either of the following:

1. Submit your comments electronically as specified in the **ADDRESSES** section of this proposed rule; or

2. Submit your comments to the Office of Information and Regulatory Affairs, Office of Management and Budget,

Attention: OCIIO Desk Officer, OCIIO–9991–IFC.

Fax: (202) 395–6974; or

E-mail: OIRA_submission@omb.eop.gov.

F. Congressional Review Act

These interim final regulations are subject to the Congressional Review Act provisions of the Small Business Regulatory Enforcement Fairness Act of 1996 (5 U.S.C. 801 *et seq.*) and have been transmitted to Congress and the Comptroller General for review.

G. Unfunded Mandates Reform Act

The Unfunded Mandates Reform Act of 1995 (Pub. L. 104–4) requires agencies to prepare several analytic statements before proposing any rules that may result in annual expenditures of $100 million (as adjusted for inflation) by State, local and tribal governments or the private sector. These interim final regulations are not subject to the Unfunded Mandates Reform Act, because they are being issued as an interim final regulation. However, consistent with the policy embodied in the Unfunded Mandates Reform Act, these interim final regulations have been designed to be the least burdensome alternative for State, local and tribal governments, and the private sector, while achieving the objectives of the Affordable Care Act.

---

[34] The Department's estimate of the number of state and local governmental health plans was obtained from the 2007 Census of Governments. The estimate of the number of policy holders in the individual market were obtained from the 2009 Current Population Survey. The methodology used to estimate the percentage of state and local governmental plans and individual market policies that will retain their grandfathered health plan status was discussed above.

[35] EBSA estimates of labor rates include wages, other benefits, and overhead based on the National Occupational Employment Survey (May 2008, Bureau of Labor Statistics) and the Employment Cost Index June 2009, Bureau of Labor Statistics).

[36] The Department is not certain on the number of products offered in the individual market and requests comments. After reviewing the number of products offered by various insurers in the individual market the Department used an estimate of 15 which it believes is a high estimate.

H. Federalism Statement—Department of Labor and Department of Health and Human Services

Executive Order 13132 outlines fundamental principles of federalism, and requires the adherence to specific criteria by Federal agencies in the process of their formulation and implementation of policies that have "substantial direct effects" on the States, the relationship between the national government and States, or on the distribution of power and responsibilities among the various levels of government. Federal agencies promulgating regulations that have these federalism implications must consult with State and local officials, and describe the extent of their consultation and the nature of the concerns of State and local officials in the preamble to the regulation.

In the Departments' view, this regulation has federalism implications, because it has direct effects on the States, the relationship between the national government and States, or on the distribution of power and responsibilities among various levels of government. However, in the Departments' view, the federalism implications of the regulation is substantially mitigated because, with respect to health insurance issuers, the Departments expect that the majority of States will enact laws or take other appropriate action resulting in their meeting or exceeding the Federal standard.

In general, through section 514, ERISA supersedes State laws to the extent that they relate to any covered employee benefit plan, and preserves State laws that regulate insurance, banking, or securities. While ERISA prohibits States from regulating a plan as an insurance or investment company or bank, the preemption provisions of ERISA section 731 and PHS Act section 2724 (implemented in 29 CFR 2590.731(a) and 45 CFR 146.143(a)) apply so that the HIPAA requirements (including those of the Affordable Care Act) are not to be "construed to supersede any provision of State law which establishes, implements, or continues in effect any standard or requirement solely relating to health insurance issuers in connection with group health insurance coverage except to the extent that such standard or requirement prevents the application of a requirement" of a Federal standard. The conference report accompanying HIPAA indicates that this is intended to be the "narrowest" preemption of State laws. (See House Conf. Rep. No. 104–736, at 205, reprinted in 1996 U.S. Code

Cong. & Admin. News 2018.) States may continue to apply State law requirements except to the extent that such requirements prevent the application of the Affordable Care Act requirements that are the subject of this rulemaking. State insurance laws that are more stringent than the federal requirements are unlikely to "prevent the application of" the Affordable Care Act, and be preempted. Accordingly, States have significant latitude to impose requirements on health insurance issuers that are more restrictive than the Federal law.

In compliance with the requirement of Executive Order 13132 that agencies examine closely any policies that may have federalism implications or limit the policy making discretion of the States, the Departments have engaged in efforts to consult with and work cooperatively with affected State and local officials, including attending conferences of the National Association of Insurance Commissioners and consulting with State insurance officials on an individual basis. It is expected that the Departments will act in a similar fashion in enforcing the Affordable Care Act requirements. Throughout the process of developing these regulations, to the extent feasible within the specific preemption provisions of HIPAA as it applies to the Affordable Care Act, the Departments have attempted to balance the States' interests in regulating health insurance issuers, and Congress' intent to provide uniform minimum protections to consumers in every State. By doing so, it is the Departments' view that they have complied with the requirements of Executive Order 13132.

Pursuant to the requirements set forth in section 8(a) of Executive Order 13132, and by the signatures affixed to these regulations, the Departments certify that the Employee Benefits Security Administration and the Office of Consumer Information and Insurance Oversight have complied with the requirements of Executive Order 13132 for the attached regulation in a meaningful and timely manner.

V. Statutory Authority

The Department of the Treasury temporary regulations are adopted pursuant to the authority contained in sections 7805 and 9833 of the Code.

The Department of Labor interim final regulations are adopted pursuant to the authority contained in 29 U.S.C. 1027, 1059, 1135, 1161–1168, 1169, 1181–1183, 1181 note, 1185, 1185a, 1185b, 1191, 1191a, 1191b, and 1191c; section 101(g), Public Law 104–191, 110 Stat. 1936; section 401(b), Public Law 105–

200, 112 Stat. 645 (42 U.S.C. 651 note); section 512(d), Public Law 110–343, 122 Stat. 3881; section 1001, 1201, and 1562(e), Public Law 111–148, 124 Stat. 119, as amended by Public Law 111–152, 124 Stat. 1029; Secretary of Labor's Order 6–2009, 74 FR 21524 (May 7, 2009).

The Department of Health and Human Services interim final regulations are adopted pursuant to the authority contained in sections 2701 through 2763, 2791, and 2792 of the PHS Act (42 U.S.C. 300gg through 300gg–63, 300gg–91, and 300gg–92), as amended.

List of Subjects

26 CFR Part 54

Excise taxes, Health care, Health insurance, Pensions, Reporting and recordkeeping requirements.

26 CFR Part 602

Reporting and recordkeeping requirements.

29 CFR Part 2590

Continuation coverage, Disclosure, Employee benefit plans, Group health plans, Health care, Health insurance, Medical child support, Reporting and recordkeeping requirements.

45 CFR Part 147

Health care, Health insurance, Reporting and recordkeeping requirements, and State regulation of health insurance.

Steven T. Miller,
Deputy Commissioner for Services and Enforcement, Internal Revenue Service.

Approved: June 10, 2010.

Michael F. Mundaca,
Assistant Secretary of the Treasury (Tax Policy).

Signed this 4th day of June, 2010.

Phyllis C. Borzi,
Assistant Secretary, Employee Benefits Security Administration, Department of Labor.

Approved: June 8, 2010.

Jay Angoff,
Director, Office of Consumer Information and Insurance Oversight.

Approved: June 9, 2010.

Kathleen Sebelius,
Secretary.

DEPARTMENT OF THE TREASURY

Internal Revenue Service

26 CFR Chapter I

■ Accordingly, 26 CFR parts 54 and 602 are amended as follows:

34558   Federal Register / Vol. 75, No. 116 / Thursday, June 17, 2010 / Rules and Regulations

PART 54—PENSION EXCISE TAXES

■ 1. The authority citation for part 54 is amended by adding entries for §§ 54.9815–1251T and 54.9815–2714T in numerical order to read in part as follows:

Authority: 26 U.S.C. 7805. * * *

Section 54.9815–1251T also issued under 26 U.S.C. 9833.

Section 54.9815–2714T also issued under 26 U.S.C. 9833. * * *

■ 2. Section 54.9815–1251T is added to read as follows:

§ 54.9815–1251T   Preservation of right to maintain existing coverage (temporary).

(a) *Definition of grandfathered health plan coverage*—(1) *In general*—(i) *Grandfathered health plan coverage* means coverage provided by a group health plan, or a health insurance issuer, in which an individual was enrolled on March 23, 2010 (for as long as it maintains that status under the rules of this section). A group health plan or group health insurance coverage does not cease to be grandfathered health plan coverage merely because one or more (or even all) individuals enrolled on March 23, 2010 cease to be covered, provided that the plan or group health insurance coverage has continuously covered someone since March 23, 2010 (not necessarily the same person, but at all times at least one person). For purposes of this section, a plan or health insurance coverage that provides grandfathered health plan coverage is referred to as a grandfathered health plan. The rules of this section apply separately to each benefit package made available under a group health plan or health insurance coverage.

(ii) Subject to the rules of paragraph (f) of this section for collectively bargained plans, if an employer or employee organization enters into a new policy, certificate, or contract of insurance after March 23, 2010 (because, for example, any previous policy, certificate, or contract of insurance is not being renewed), then that policy, certificate, or contract of insurance is not a grandfathered health plan with respect to the individuals in the group health plan.

(2) *Disclosure of grandfather status*— (i) To maintain status as a grandfathered health plan, a plan or health insurance coverage must include a statement, in any plan materials provided to a participant or beneficiary describing the benefits provided under the plan or health insurance coverage, that the plan or coverage believes it is a grandfathered health plan within the meaning of section 1251 of the Patient Protection and Affordable Care Act and must provide contact information for questions and complaints.

(ii) The following model language can be used to satisfy this disclosure requirement:

This [group health plan or health insurance issuer] believes this [plan or coverage] is a "grandfathered health plan" under the Patient Protection and Affordable Care Act (the Affordable Care Act). As permitted by the Affordable Care Act, a grandfathered health plan can preserve certain basic health coverage that was already in effect when that law was enacted. Being a grandfathered health plan means that your [plan or policy] may not include certain consumer protections of the Affordable Care Act that apply to other plans, for example, the requirement for the provision of preventive health services without any cost sharing. However, grandfathered health plans must comply with certain other consumer protections in the Affordable Care Act, for example, the elimination of lifetime limits on benefits.

Questions regarding which protections apply and which protections do not apply to a grandfathered health plan and what might cause a plan to change from grandfathered health plan status can be directed to the plan administrator at [insert contact information]. [For ERISA plans, insert: You may also contact the Employee Benefits Security Administration, U.S. Department of Labor at 1–866–444–3272 or *www.dol.gov/ebsa/healthreform*. This website has a table summarizing which protections do and do not apply to grandfathered health plans.] [For individual market policies and nonfederal governmental plans, insert: You may also contact the U.S. Department of Health and Human Services at *www.healthreform.gov*.]

(3) *Documentation of plan or policy terms on March 23, 2010.* To maintain status as a grandfathered health plan, a group health plan, or group health insurance coverage, must, for as long as the plan or health insurance coverage takes the position that it is a grandfathered health plan—

(i) Maintain records documenting the terms of the plan or health insurance coverage in connection with the coverage in effect on March 23, 2010, and any other documents necessary to verify, explain, or clarify its status as a grandfathered health plan; and

(ii) Make such records available for examination upon request.

(4) *Family members enrolling after March 23, 2010.* With respect to an individual who is enrolled in a group health plan or health insurance coverage on March 23, 2010, grandfathered health plan coverage includes coverage of family members of the individual who enroll after March 23, 2010 in the grandfathered health plan coverage of the individual.

(5) *Examples.* The rules of this paragraph (a) are illustrated by the following examples:

Example 1. (i) *Facts.* A group health plan not maintained pursuant to a collective bargaining agreement provides coverage through a group health insurance policy from Issuer X on March 23, 2010. For the plan year beginning January 1, 2012, the plan enters into a new policy with Issuer Z.

(ii) *Conclusion.* In this *Example 1*, for the plan year beginning January 1, 2012, the group health insurance coverage issued by Z is not a grandfathered health plan under the rules of paragraph (a)(1)(ii) of this section because the policy issued by Z did not provide coverage on March 23, 2010.

Example 2. (i) *Facts.* A group health plan not maintained pursuant to a collective bargaining agreement offers three benefit packages on March 23, 2010. Option F is a self-insured option. Options G and H are insured options. Beginning July 1, 2013, the plan replaces the issuer for Option H with a new issuer.

(ii) *Conclusion.* In this *Example 2*, the coverage under Option H is not grandfathered health plan coverage as of July 1, 2013, consistent with the rule in paragraph (a)(1)(ii) of this section. Whether the coverage under Options F and G is grandfathered health plan coverage is determined under the rules of this section, including paragraph (g) of this section. If the plan enters into a new policy, certificate, or contract of insurance for Option G, Option G's status as a grandfathered health plan would cease under paragraph (a)(1)(ii) of this section.

(b) *Allowance for new employees to join current plan*—(1) *In general.* Subject to paragraph (b)(2) of this section, a group health plan (including health insurance coverage provided in connection with the group health plan) that provided coverage on March 23, 2010 and has retained its status as a grandfathered health plan (consistent with the rules of this section, including paragraph (g) of this section) is grandfathered health plan coverage for new employees (whether newly hired or newly enrolled) and their families enrolling in the plan after March 23, 2010.

(2) *Anti-abuse rules*—(i) *Mergers and acquisitions.* If the principal purpose of a merger, acquisition, or similar business restructuring is to cover new individuals under a grandfathered health plan, the plan ceases to be a grandfathered health plan.

(ii) *Change in plan eligibility.* A group health plan or health insurance coverage (including a benefit package under a group health plan) ceases to be a grandfathered health plan if—

(A) Employees are transferred into the plan or health insurance coverage (the transferee plan) from a plan or health insurance coverage under which the employees were covered on March 23, 2010 (the transferor plan);

(B) Comparing the terms of the transferee plan with those of the transferor plan (as in effect on March 23, 2010) and treating the transferee plan as if it were an amendment of the transferor plan would cause a loss of grandfather status under the provisions of paragraph (g)(1) of this section; and

(C) There was no bona fide employment-based reason to transfer the employees into the transferee plan. For this purpose, changing the terms or cost of coverage is not a bona fide employment-based reason.

(3) *Examples.* The rules of this paragraph (b) are illustrated by the following examples:

Example 1. (i) *Facts.* A group health plan offers two benefit packages on March 23, 2010, Options F and G. During a subsequent open enrollment period, some of the employees enrolled in Option F on March 23, 2010 switch to Option G.

(ii) *Conclusion.* In this *Example 1,* the group health coverage provided under Option G remains a grandfathered health plan under the rules of paragraph (b)(1) of this section because employees previously enrolled in Option F are allowed to enroll in Option G as new employees.

Example 2. (i) *Facts.* Same facts as *Example 1,* except that the plan sponsor eliminates Option F because of its high cost and transfers employees covered under Option F to Option G. If instead of transferring employees from Option F to Option G, Option F was amended to match the terms of Option G, then Option F would cease to be a grandfathered health plan.

(ii) *Conclusion.* In this *Example 2,* the plan did not have a bona fide employment-based reason to transfer employees from Option F to Option G. Therefore, Option G ceases to be a grandfathered health plan with respect to all employees. (However, any other benefit package maintained by the plan sponsor is analyzed separately under the rules of this section.)

Example 3. (i) *Facts.* A group health plan offers two benefit packages on March 23, 2010, Options H and I. On March 23, 2010, Option H provides coverage only for employees in one manufacturing plant. Subsequently, the plant is closed, and some employees in the closed plant are moved to another plant. The employer eliminates Option H and the employees that are moved are transferred to Option I. If instead of transferring employees from Option H to Option I, Option H was amended to match the terms of Option I, then Option H would cease to be a grandfathered health plan.

(ii) *Conclusion.* In this *Example 3,* the plan has a bona fide employment-based reason to transfer employees from Option H to Option I. Therefore, Option I does not cease to be a grandfathered health plan.

(c) *General grandfathering rule*—(1) Except as provided in paragraphs (d) and (e) of this section, subtitles A and C of title I of the Patient Protection and Affordable Care Act (and the amendments made by those subtitles,

and the incorporation of those amendments into section 9815 and ERISA section 715) do not apply to grandfathered health plan coverage. Accordingly, the provisions of PHS Act sections 2701, 2702, 2703, 2705, 2706, 2707, 2709 (relating to coverage for individuals participating in approved clinical trials, as added by section 10103 of the Patient Protection and Affordable Care Act), 2713, 2715A, 2716, 2717, 2719, and 2719A, as added or amended by the Patient Protection and Affordable Care Act, do not apply to grandfathered health plans. (In addition, *see* 45 CFR 147.140(c), which provides that the provisions of PHS Act section 2704, and PHS Act section 2711 insofar as it relates to annual limits, do not apply to grandfathered health plans that are individual health insurance coverage.)

(2) To the extent not inconsistent with the rules applicable to a grandfathered health plan, a grandfathered health plan must comply with the requirements of the Code, the PHS Act, and ERISA applicable prior to the changes enacted by the Patient Protection and Affordable Care Act.

(d) *Provisions applicable to all grandfathered health plans.* The provisions of PHS Act section 2711 insofar as it relates to lifetime limits, and the provisions of PHS Act sections 2712, 2714, 2715, and 2718, apply to grandfathered health plans for plan years beginning on or after September 23, 2010. The provisions of PHS Act section 2708 apply to grandfathered health plans for plan years beginning on or after January 1, 2014.

(e) *Applicability of PHS Act sections 2704, 2711, and 2714 to grandfathered group health plans and group health insurance coverage*—(1) The provisions of PHS Act section 2704 as it applies with respect to enrollees who are under 19 years of age, and the provisions of PHS Act section 2711 insofar as it relates to annual limits, apply to grandfathered health plans that are group health plans (including group health insurance coverage) for plan years beginning on or after September 23, 2010. The provisions of PHS Act section 2704 apply generally to grandfathered health plans that are group health plans (including group health insurance coverage) for plan years beginning on or after January 1, 2014.

(2) For plan years beginning before January 1, 2014, the provisions of PHS Act section 2714 apply in the case of an adult child with respect to a grandfathered health plan that is a group health plan only if the adult child is not eligible to enroll in an eligible employer-sponsored health plan (as

defined in section 5000A(f)(2)) other than a grandfathered health plan of a parent. For plan years beginning on or after January 1, 2014, the provisions of PHS Act section 2714 apply with respect to a grandfathered health plan that is a group health plan without regard to whether an adult child is eligible to enroll in any other coverage.

(f) *Effect on collectively bargained plans*—(1) *In general.* In the case of health insurance coverage maintained pursuant to one or more collective bargaining agreements between employee representatives and one or more employers that was ratified before March 23, 2010, the coverage is grandfathered health plan coverage at least until the date on which the last of the collective bargaining agreements relating to the coverage that was in effect on March 23, 2010 terminates. Any coverage amendment made pursuant to a collective bargaining agreement relating to the coverage that amends the coverage solely to conform to any requirement added by subtitles A and C of title I of the Patient Protection and Affordable Care Act (and the amendments made by those subtitles, and the incorporation of those amendments into section 9815 and ERISA section 715) is not treated as a termination of the collective bargaining agreement. After the date on which the last of the collective bargaining agreements relating to the coverage that was in effect on March 23, 2010 terminates, the determination of whether health insurance coverage maintained pursuant to a collective bargaining agreement is grandfathered health plan coverage is made under the rules of this section other than this paragraph (f) (comparing the terms of the health insurance coverage after the date the last collective bargaining agreement terminates with the terms of the health insurance coverage that were in effect on March 23, 2010) and, for any changes in insurance coverage after the termination of the collective bargaining agreement, under the rules of paragraph (a)(1)(ii) of this section.

(2) *Examples.* The rules of this paragraph (f) are illustrated by the following examples:

Example 1. (i) *Facts.* A group health plan maintained pursuant to a collective bargaining agreement provides coverage through a group health insurance policy from Issuer W on March 23, 2010. The collective bargaining agreement has not been amended and will not expire before December 31, 2011. The group health plan enters into a new group health insurance policy with Issuer Y for the plan year starting on January 1, 2011.

(ii) *Conclusion.* In this *Example 1,* the group health plan, and the group health insurance policy provided by Y, remains a grandfathered health plan with respect to existing employees and new employees and their families because the coverage is maintained pursuant to a collective bargaining agreement ratified prior to March 23, 2010 that has not terminated.

Example 2. (i) *Facts.* Same facts as *Example 1,* except the coverage with Y is renewed under a new collective bargaining agreement effective January 1, 2012, with the only changes since March 23, 2010 being changes that do not cause the plan to cease to be a grandfathered health plan under the rules of this section, including paragraph (g) of this section.

(ii) *Conclusion.* In this *Example 2,* the group health plan remains a grandfathered health plan pursuant to the rules of this section. Moreover, the group health insurance policy provided by Y remains a grandfathered health plan under the rules of this section, including paragraph (g) of this section.

(g) *Maintenance of grandfather status*—(1) *Changes causing cessation of grandfather status.* Subject to paragraph (g)(2) of this section, the rules of this paragraph (g)(1) describe situations in which a group health plan or health insurance coverage ceases to be a grandfathered health plan.

(i) *Elimination of benefits.* The elimination of all or substantially all benefits to diagnose or treat a particular condition causes a group health plan or health insurance coverage to cease to be a grandfathered health plan. For this purpose, the elimination of benefits for any necessary element to diagnose or treat a condition is considered the elimination of all or substantially all benefits to diagnose or treat a particular condition.

(ii) *Increase in percentage cost-sharing requirement.* Any increase, measured from March 23, 2010, in a percentage cost-sharing requirement (such as an individual's coinsurance requirement) causes a group health plan or health insurance coverage to cease to be a grandfathered health plan.

(iii) *Increase in a fixed-amount cost-sharing requirement other than a copayment.* Any increase in a fixed-amount cost-sharing requirement other than a copayment (for example, deductible or out-of-pocket limit), determined as of the effective date of the increase, causes a group health plan or health insurance coverage to cease to be a grandfathered health plan, if the total percentage increase in the cost-sharing requirement measured from March 23, 2010 exceeds the maximum percentage increase (as defined in paragraph (g)(3)(ii) of this section).

(iv) *Increase in a fixed-amount copayment.* Any increase in a fixed-amount copayment, determined as of the effective date of the increase, causes

a group health plan or health insurance coverage to cease to be a grandfathered health plan, if the total increase in the copayment measured from March 23, 2010 exceeds the greater of:

(A) An amount equal to $5 increased by medical inflation, as defined in paragraph (g)(3)(i) of this section (that is, $5 times medical inflation, plus $5), or

(B) The maximum percentage increase (as defined in paragraph (g)(3)(ii) of this section), determined by expressing the total increase in the copayment as a percentage.

(v) *Decrease in contribution rate by employers and employee organizations*—(A) *Contribution rate based on cost of coverage.* A group health plan or group health insurance coverage ceases to be a grandfathered health plan if the employer or employee organization decreases its contribution rate based on cost of coverage (as defined in paragraph (g)(3)(iii)(A) of this section) towards the cost of any tier of coverage for any class of similarly situated individuals (as described in § 54.9802–1(d)) by more than 5 percentage points below the contribution rate for the coverage period that includes March 23, 2010.

(B) *Contribution rate based on a formula.* A group health plan or group health insurance coverage ceases to be a grandfathered health plan if the employer or employee organization decreases its contribution rate based on a formula (as defined in paragraph (g)(3)(iii)(B) of this section) towards the cost of any tier of coverage for any class of similarly situated individuals (as described in § 54.9802–1(d)) by more than 5 percent below the contribution rate for the coverage period that includes March 23, 2010.

(vi) *Changes in annual limits*—(A) *Addition of an annual limit.* A group health plan, or group health insurance coverage, that, on March 23, 2010, did not impose an overall annual or lifetime limit on the dollar value of all benefits ceases to be a grandfathered health plan if the plan or health insurance coverage imposes an overall annual limit on the dollar value of benefits.

(B) *Decrease in limit for a plan or coverage with only a lifetime limit.* A group health plan, or group health insurance coverage, that, on March 23, 2010, imposed an overall lifetime limit on the dollar value of all benefits but no overall annual limit on the dollar value of all benefits ceases to be a grandfathered health plan if the plan or health insurance coverage adopts an overall annual limit at a dollar value that is lower than the dollar value of the lifetime limit on March 23, 2010.

(C) *Decrease in limit for a plan or coverage with an annual limit.* A group health plan, or group health insurance coverage, that, on March 23, 2010, imposed an overall annual limit on the dollar value of all benefits ceases to be a grandfathered health plan if the plan or health insurance coverage decreases the dollar value of the annual limit (regardless of whether the plan or health insurance coverage also imposed an overall lifetime limit on March 23, 2010 on the dollar value of all benefits).

(2) *Transitional rules*—(i) *Changes made prior to March 23, 2010.* If a group health plan or health insurance issuer makes the following changes to the terms of the plan or health insurance coverage, the changes are considered part of the terms of the plan or health insurance coverage on March 23, 2010 even though they were not effective at that time and such changes do not cause a plan or health insurance coverage to cease to be a grandfathered health plan:

(A) Changes effective after March 23, 2010 pursuant to a legally binding contract entered into on or before March 23, 2010;

(B) Changes effective after March 23, 2010 pursuant to a filing on or before March 23, 2010 with a State insurance department; or

(C) Changes effective after March 23, 2010 pursuant to written amendments to a plan that were adopted on or before March 23, 2010.

(ii) *Changes made after March 23, 2010 and adopted prior to issuance of regulations.* If, after March 23, 2010, a group health plan or health insurance issuer makes changes to the terms of the plan or health insurance coverage and the changes are adopted prior to June 14, 2010, the changes will not cause the plan or health insurance coverage to cease to be a grandfathered health plan if the changes are revoked or modified effective as of the first day of the first plan year (in the individual market, policy year) beginning on or after September 23, 2010, and the terms of the plan or health insurance coverage on that date, as modified, would not cause the plan or coverage to cease to be a grandfathered health plan under the rules of this section, including paragraph (g)(1) of this section. For this purpose, changes will be considered to have been adopted prior to June 14, 2010 if:

(A) The changes are effective before that date;

(B) The changes are effective on or after that date pursuant to a legally binding contract entered into before that date;

(C) The changes are effective on or after that date pursuant to a filing before that date with a State insurance department; or

(D) The changes are effective on or after that date pursuant to written amendments to a plan that were adopted before that date.

(3) *Definitions*—(i) *Medical inflation defined.* For purposes of this paragraph (g), the term *medical inflation* means the increase since March 2010 in the overall medical care component of the Consumer Price Index for All Urban Consumers (CPI–U) (unadjusted) published by the Department of Labor using the 1982–1984 base of 100. For this purpose, the increase in the overall medical care component is computed by subtracting 387.142 (the overall medical care component of the CPI–U (unadjusted) published by the Department of Labor for March 2010, using the 1982–1984 base of 100) from the index amount for any month in the 12 months before the new change is to take effect and then dividing that amount by 387.142.

(ii) *Maximum percentage increase defined.* For purposes of this paragraph (g), the term *maximum percentage increase* means medical inflation (as defined in paragraph (g)(3)(i) of this section), expressed as a percentage, plus 15 percentage points.

(iii) *Contribution rate defined.* For purposes of paragraph (g)(1)(v) of this section:

(A) *Contribution rate based on cost of coverage.* The term *contribution rate based on cost of coverage* means the amount of contributions made by an employer or employee organization compared to the total cost of coverage, expressed as a percentage. The total cost of coverage is determined in the same manner as the applicable premium is calculated under the COBRA continuation provisions of section 4980B(f)(4), section 604 of ERISA, and section 2204 of the PHS Act. In the case of a self-insured plan, contributions by an employer or employee organization are equal to the total cost of coverage minus the employee contributions towards the total cost of coverage.

(B) *Contribution rate based on a formula.* The term *contribution rate based on a formula* means, for plans that, on March 23, 2010, made contributions based on a formula (such as hours worked or tons of coal mined), the formula.

(4) *Examples.* The rules of this paragraph (g) are illustrated by the following examples:

Example 1. (i) *Facts.* On March 23, 2010, a grandfathered health plan has a coinsurance requirement of 20% for inpatient surgery. The plan is subsequently amended to increase the coinsurance requirement to 25%.

(ii) *Conclusion.* In this *Example 1*, the increase in the coinsurance requirement from 20% to 25% causes the plan to cease to be a grandfathered health plan.

Example 2. (i) *Facts.* Before March 23, 2010, the terms of a group health plan provide benefits for a particular mental health condition, the treatment for which is a combination of counseling and prescription drugs. Subsequently, the plan eliminates benefits for counseling.

(ii) *Conclusion.* In this *Example 2*, the plan ceases to be a grandfathered health plan because counseling is an element that is necessary to treat the condition. Thus the plan is considered to have eliminated substantially all benefits for the treatment of the condition.

Example 3. (i) *Facts.* On March 23, 2010, a grandfathered health plan has a copayment requirement of $30 per office visit for specialists. The plan is subsequently amended to increase the copayment requirement to $40. Within the 12-month period before the $40 copayment takes effect, the greatest value of the overall medical care component of the CPI–U (unadjusted) is 475.

(ii) *Conclusion.* In this *Example 3*, the increase in the copayment from $30 to $40, expressed as a percentage, is 33.33% (40 − 30 = 10; 10 ÷ 30 = 0.3333; 0.3333 = 33.33%). Medical inflation (as defined in paragraph (g)(3)(i) of this section) from March 2010 is 0.2269 (475 − 387.142 = 87.858; 87.858 ÷ 387.142 = 0.2269). The maximum percentage increase permitted is 37.69% (0.2269 − 22.69%; 22.69% + 15% = 37.69%). Because 33.33% does not exceed 37.69%, the change in the copayment requirement at that time does not cause the plan to cease to be a grandfathered health plan.

Example 4. (i) *Facts.* Same facts as *Example 3*, except the grandfathered health plan subsequently increases the $40 copayment requirement to $45 for a later plan year. Within the 12-month period before the $45 copayment takes effect, the greatest value of the overall medical care component of the CPI–U (unadjusted) is 485.

(ii) *Conclusion.* In this *Example 4*, the increase in the copayment from $30 (the copayment that was in effect on March 23, 2010) to $45, expressed as a percentage, is 50% (45 − 30 = 15; 15 ÷ 30 = 0.5; 0.5 = 50%). Medical inflation (as defined in paragraph (g)(3)(i) of this section) from March 2010 is 0.2527 (485 − 387.142 = 97.858; 97.858 ÷ 387.142 = 0.2527). The increase that would cause a plan to cease to be a grandfathered health plan under paragraph (g)(1)(iv) of this section is the greater of the maximum percentage increase of 40.27% (0.2527 = 25.27%; 25.27% + 15% = 40.27%), or $6.26 ($5 × 0.2527 = $1.26; $1.26 + $5 = $6.26). Because 50% exceeds 40.27% and $15 exceeds $6.26, the change in the copayment requirement at that time causes the plan to cease to be a grandfathered health plan.

Example 5. (i) *Facts.* On March 23, 2010, a grandfathered health plan has a copayment of $10 per office visit for primary care providers. The plan is subsequently amended to increase the copayment requirement to $15. Within the 12-month period before the

$15 copayment takes effect, the greatest value of the overall medical care component of the CPI–U (unadjusted) is 415.

(ii) *Conclusion.* In this *Example 5*, the increase in the copayment, expressed as a percentage, is 50% (15 − 10 = 5; 5 ÷ 10 = 0.5; 0.5 = 50%). Medical inflation (as defined in paragraph (g)(3) of this section) from March 2010 is 0.0720 (415.0 − 387.142 = 27.858; 27.858 ÷ 387.142 = 0.0720). The increase that would cause a plan to cease to be a grandfathered health plan under paragraph (g)(1)(iv) of this section is the greater of the maximum percentage increase of 22.20% (0.0720 = 7.20%; 7.20% + 15% = 22.20), or $5.36 ($5 × 0.0720 = $0.36; $0.36 + $5 = $5.36). The $5 increase in copayment in this *Example 5* would not cause the plan to cease to be a grandfathered health plan pursuant to paragraph (g)(1)(iv) of this section, which would permit an increase in the copayment of up to $5.36.

Example 6. (i) *Facts.* The same facts as *Example 5*, except on March 23, 2010, the grandfathered health plan has no copayment ($0) for office visits for primary care providers. The plan is subsequently amended to increase the copayment requirement to $5.

(ii) *Conclusion.* In this *Example 6*, medical inflation (as defined in paragraph (g)(3)(i) of this section) from March 2010 is 0.0720 (415.0 − 387.142 = 27.858; 27.858 ÷ 387.142 = 0.0720). The increase that would cause a plan to cease to be a grandfathered health plan under paragraph (g)(1)(iv)(A) of this section is $5.36 ($5 × 0.0720 = $0.36; $0.36 + $5 = $5.36). The $5 increase in copayment in this *Example 6* is less than the amount calculated pursuant to paragraph (g)(1)(iv)(A) of this section of $5.36. Thus, the $5 increase in copayment does not cause the plan to cease to be a grandfathered health plan.

Example 7. (i) *Facts.* On March 23, 2010, a self-insured group health plan provides two tiers of coverage—self-only and family. The employer contributes 80% of the total cost of coverage for self-only and 60% of the total cost of coverage for family. Subsequently, the employer reduces the contribution to 50% for family coverage, but keeps the same contribution rate for self-only coverage.

(ii) *Conclusion.* In this *Example 7*, the decrease of 10 percentage points for family coverage in the contribution rate based on cost of coverage causes the plan to cease to be a grandfathered health plan. The fact that the contribution rate for self-only coverage remains the same does not change the result.

Example 8. (i) *Facts.* On March 23, 2010, a self-insured grandfathered health plan has a COBRA premium for the 2010 plan year of $5000 for self-only coverage and $12,000 for family coverage. The required employee contribution for the coverage is $1000 for self-only coverage and $4000 for family coverage. Thus, the contribution rate based on cost of coverage for 2010 is 80% ((5000 − 1000)/5000) for self-only coverage and 67% ((12,000 − 4000)/12,000) for family coverage. For a subsequent plan year, the COBRA premium is $6000 for self-only coverage and $15,000 for family coverage. The employee contributions for that plan year are $1200 for self-only coverage and $5000 for family coverage. Thus, the contribution rate based on cost of coverage is

80% ((6000 − 1200)/6000) for self-only coverage and 67% ((15,000 − 5000)/15,000) for family coverage.

(ii) *Conclusion.* In this *Example 8,* because there is no change in the contribution rate based on cost of coverage, the plan retains its status as a grandfathered health plan. The result would be the same if all or part of the employee contribution was made pre-tax through a cafeteria plan under section 125 of the Internal Revenue Code.

Example 9. (i) *Facts.* Before March 23, 2010, Employer W and Individual B enter into a legally binding employment contract that promises B lifetime health coverage upon termination. Prior to termination, B is covered by W's self-insured grandfathered group health plan. B is terminated after March 23, 2010 and W purchases a new health insurance policy providing coverage to B, consistent with the terms of the employment contract.

(ii) *Conclusion.* In this *Example 9,* because no individual is enrolled in the health insurance policy on March 23, 2010, it is not a grandfathered health plan.

(h) *Expiration date.* This section expires on or before June 14, 2013.

■ 3. Section 54.9815–2714T is amended by revising paragraphs (h) and (i) to read as follows:

*   *   *   *   *

(h) *Applicability date.* The provisions of this section apply for plan years beginning on or after September 23, 2010. *See* § 54.9815–1251T for determining the application of this section to grandfathered health plans.

(i) *Expiration date.* This section expires on or before May 10, 2013.

PART 602—OMB CONTROL NUMBERS UNDER THE PAPERWORK REDUCTION ACT

■ 4. The authority citation for part 602 continues to read in part as follows:

Authority: 26 U.S.C. 7805. * * *

■ 5. Section 602.101(b) is amended by adding the following entry in numerical order to the table to read as follows:

§ 602.101   OMB Control numbers.

(b) * * *

CFR part or section where identified and described	Current OMB control No.
*　　*　　*　　*　　*	
54.9815–1251T	1545–2178
*　　*　　*　　*　　*	

DEPARTMENT OF LABOR

Employee Benefits Security Administration

29 CFR Chapter XXV

■ 29 CFR part 2590 is amended as follows:

PART 2590—RULES AND REGULATIONS FOR GROUP HEALTH PLANS

■ 1. The authority citation for part 2590 continues to read as follows:

Authority: 29 U.S.C. 1027, 1059, 1135, 1161–1168, 1169, 1181–1183, 1181 note, 1185, 1185a, 1185b, 1191, 1191a, 1191b, and 1191c; sec. 101(g), Pub. L. 104–191, 110 Stat. 1936; sec. 401(b), Pub. L. 105–200, 112 Stat. 645 (42 U.S.C. 651 note); sec. 512(d), Pub. L. 110–343, 122 Stat. 3881; sec. 1001, 1201, and 1562(e), Pub. L. 111–148, 124 Stat. 119, as amended by Pub. L. 111–152, 124 Stat. 1029; Secretary of Labor's Order 6–2009, 74 FR 21524 (May 7, 2009).

■ 2. Section 2590.715–1251 is added to subpart C to read as follows:

§ 2590.715–1251   Preservation of right to maintain existing coverage.

(a) *Definition of grandfathered health plan coverage*—(1) *In general*—(i) *Grandfathered health plan coverage* means coverage provided by a group health plan, or a health insurance issuer, in which an individual was enrolled on March 23, 2010 (for as long as it maintains that status under the rules of this section). A group health plan or group health insurance coverage does not cease to be grandfathered health plan coverage merely because one or more (or even all) individuals enrolled on March 23, 2010 cease to be covered, provided that the plan or group health insurance coverage has continuously covered someone since March 23, 2010 (not necessarily the same person, but at all times at least one person). For purposes of this section, a plan or health insurance coverage that provides grandfathered health plan coverage is referred to as a grandfathered health plan. The rules of this section apply separately to each benefit package made available under a group health plan or health insurance coverage.

(ii) Subject to the rules of paragraph (f) of this section for collectively bargained plans, if an employer or employee organization enters into a new policy, certificate, or contract of insurance after March 23, 2010 (because, for example, any previous policy, certificate, or contract of insurance is not being renewed), then that policy, certificate, or contract of insurance is not a grandfathered health plan with respect to the individuals in the group health plan.

(2) *Disclosure of grandfather status*—(i) To maintain status as a grandfathered health plan, a plan or health insurance coverage must include a statement, in any plan materials provided to a participant or beneficiary describing the benefits provided under the plan or health insurance coverage, that the plan or coverage believes it is a grandfathered health plan within the meaning of section 1251 of the Patient Protection and Affordable Care Act and must provide contact information for questions and complaints.

(ii) The following model language can be used to satisfy this disclosure requirement:

This [group health plan or health insurance issuer] believes this [plan or coverage] is a "grandfathered health plan" under the Patient Protection and Affordable Care Act (the Affordable Care Act). As permitted by the Affordable Care Act, a grandfathered health plan can preserve certain basic health coverage that was already in effect when that law was enacted. Being a grandfathered health plan means that your [plan or policy] may not include certain consumer protections of the Affordable Care Act that apply to other plans, for example, the requirement for the provision of preventive health services without any cost sharing. However, grandfathered health plans must comply with certain other consumer protections in the Affordable Care Act, for example, the elimination of lifetime limits on benefits.

Questions regarding which protections apply and which protections do not apply to a grandfathered health plan and what might cause a plan to change from grandfathered health plan status can be directed to the plan administrator at [insert contact information]. [For ERISA plans, insert: You may also contact the Employee Benefits Security Administration, U.S. Department of Labor at 1–866–444–3272 or *www.dol.gov/ebsa/ healthreform.* This Web site has a table summarizing which protections do and do not apply to grandfathered health plans.] [For individual market policies and nonfederal governmental plans, insert: You may also contact the U.S. Department of Health and Human Services at *www.healthreform.gov.*]

(3) *Documentation of plan or policy terms on March 23, 2010.* To maintain status as a grandfathered health plan, a group health plan, or group health insurance coverage, must, for as long as the plan or health insurance coverage takes the position that it is a grandfathered health plan—

(i) Maintain records documenting the terms of the plan or health insurance coverage in connection with the coverage in effect on March 23, 2010, and any other documents necessary to verify, explain, or clarify its status as a grandfathered health plan; and

(ii) Make such records available for examination upon request.

(4) *Family members enrolling after March 23, 2010.* With respect to an individual who is enrolled in a group health plan or health insurance coverage on March 23, 2010, grandfathered health plan coverage includes coverage of family members of the individual who

enroll after March 23, 2010 in the grandfathered health plan coverage of the individual.

(5) *Examples.* The rules of this paragraph (a) are illustrated by the following examples:

Example 1. (i) *Facts.* A group health plan not maintained pursuant to a collective bargaining agreement provides coverage through a group health insurance policy from Issuer *X* on March 23, 2010. For the plan year beginning January 1, 2012, the plan enters into a new policy with Issuer *Z*.

(ii) *Conclusion.* In this *Example 1.* for the plan year beginning January 1, 2012, the group health insurance coverage issued by *Z* is not a grandfathered health plan under the rules of paragraph (a)(1)(ii) of this section because the policy issued by *Z* did not provide coverage on March 23, 2010.

Example 2. (i) *Facts.* A group health plan not maintained pursuant to a collective bargaining agreement offers three benefit packages on March 23, 2010. Option *F* is a self-insured option. Options *G* and *H* are insured options. Beginning July 1, 2013, the plan replaces the issuer for Option *H* with a new issuer.

(ii) *Conclusion.* In this *Example 2,* the coverage under Option *H* is not grandfathered health plan coverage as of July 1, 2013, consistent with the rule in paragraph (a)(1)(ii) of this section. Whether the coverage under Options *F* and *G* is grandfathered health plan coverage is determined under the rules of this section, including paragraph (g) of this section. If the plan enters into a new policy, certificate, or contract of insurance for Option *G*, Option *G*'s status as a grandfathered health plan would cease under paragraph (a)(1)(ii) of this section.

(b) *Allowance for new employees to join current plan*—(1) *In general.* Subject to paragraph (b)(2) of this section, a group health plan (including health insurance coverage provided in connection with the group health plan) that provided coverage on March 23, 2010 and has retained its status as a grandfathered health plan (consistent with the rules of this section, including paragraph (g) of this section) is grandfathered health plan coverage for new employees (whether newly hired or newly enrolled) and their families enrolling in the plan after March 23, 2010.

(2) *Anti-abuse rules*—(i) *Mergers and acquisitions.* If the principal purpose of a merger, acquisition, or similar business restructuring is to cover new individuals under a grandfathered health plan, the plan ceases to be a grandfathered health plan.

(ii) *Change in plan eligibility.* A group health plan or health insurance coverage (including a benefit package under a group health plan) ceases to be a grandfathered health plan if—

(A) Employees are transferred into the plan or health insurance coverage (the transferee plan) from a plan or health insurance coverage under which the employees were covered on March 23, 2010 (the transferor plan);

(B) Comparing the terms of the transferee plan with those of the transferor plan (as in effect on March 23, 2010) and treating the transferee plan as if it were an amendment of the transferor plan would cause a loss of grandfather status under the provisions of paragraph (g)(1) of this section; and

(C) There was no bona fide employment-based reason to transfer the employees into the transferee plan. For this purpose, changing the terms or cost of coverage is not a bona fide employment-based reason.

(3) *Examples.* The rules of this paragraph (b) are illustrated by the following examples:

Example 1. (i) *Facts.* A group health plan offers two benefit packages on March 23, 2010, Options *F* and *G.* During a subsequent open enrollment period, some of the employees enrolled in Option *F* on March 23, 2010 switch to Option *G.*

(ii) *Conclusion.* In this *Example 1,* the group health coverage provided under Option *G* remains a grandfathered health plan under the rules of paragraph (b)(1) of this section because employees previously enrolled in Option *F* are allowed to enroll in Option *G* as new employees.

Example 2. (i) *Facts.* Same facts as *Example 1.* except that the plan sponsor eliminates Option *F* because of its high cost and transfers employees covered under Option *F* to Option *G.* If instead of transferring employees from Option *F* to Option *G,* Option *F* was amended to match the terms of Option *G,* then Option *F* would cease to be a grandfathered health plan.

(ii) *Conclusion.* In this *Example 2,* the plan did not have a bona fide employment-based reason to transfer employees from Option *F* to Option *G.* Therefore, Option *G* ceases to be a grandfathered health plan with respect to all employees. (However, any other benefit package maintained by the plan sponsor is analyzed separately under the rules of this section.)

Example 3. (i) *Facts.* A group health plan offers two benefit packages on March 23, 2010, Options *H* and *I.* On March 23, 2010, Option *H* provides coverage only for employees in one manufacturing plant. Subsequently, the plant is closed, and some employees in the closed plant are moved to another plant. The employer eliminates Option *H* and the employees that are moved are transferred to Option *I.* If instead of transferring employees from Option *H* to Option *I,* Option *H* was amended to match the terms of Option *I,* then Option *H* would cease to be a grandfathered health plan.

(ii) *Conclusion.* In this *Example 3,* the plan has a bona fide employment-based reason to transfer employees from Option *H* to Option *I.* Therefore, Option *I* does not cease to be a grandfathered health plan.

(c) *General grandfathering rule*—(1) Except as provided in paragraphs (d)

and (e) of this section, subtitles A and C of title I of the Patient Protection and Affordable Care Act (and the amendments made by those subtitles, and the incorporation of those amendments into ERISA section 715 and Internal Revenue Code section 9815) do not apply to grandfathered health plan coverage. Accordingly, the provisions of PHS Act sections 2701, 2702, 2703, 2705, 2706, 2707, 2709 (relating to coverage for individuals participating in approved clinical trials, as added by section 10103 of the Patient Protection and Affordable Care Act), 2713, 2715A, 2716, 2717, 2719, and 2719A, as added or amended by the Patient Protection and Affordable Care Act, do not apply to grandfathered health plans. (In addition, *see* 45 CFR 147.140(c), which provides that the provisions of PHS Act section 2704, and PHS Act section 2711 insofar as it relates to annual limits, do not apply to grandfathered health plans that are individual health insurance coverage.)

(2) To the extent not inconsistent with the rules applicable to a grandfathered health plan, a grandfathered health plan must comply with the requirements of the PHS Act, ERISA, and the Internal Revenue Code applicable prior to the changes enacted by the Patient Protection and Affordable Care Act.

(d) *Provisions applicable to all grandfathered health plans.* The provisions of PHS Act section 2711 insofar as it relates to lifetime limits, and the provisions of PHS Act sections 2712, 2714, 2715, and 2718, apply to grandfathered health plans for plan years beginning on or after September 23, 2010. The provisions of PHS Act section 2708 apply to grandfathered health plans for plan years beginning on or after January 1, 2014.

(e) *Applicability of PHS Act sections 2704, 2711, and 2714 to grandfathered group health plans and group health insurance coverage*—(1) The provisions of PHS Act section 2704 as it applies with respect to enrollees who are under 19 years of age, and the provisions of PHS Act section 2711 insofar as it relates to annual limits, apply to grandfathered health plans that are group health plans (including group health insurance coverage) for plan years beginning on or after September 23, 2010. The provisions of PHS Act section 2704 apply generally to grandfathered health plans that are group health plans (including group health insurance coverage) for plan years beginning on or after January 1, 2014.

(2) For plan years beginning before January 1, 2014, the provisions of PHS Act section 2714 apply in the case of an

adult child with respect to a grandfathered health plan that is a group health plan only if the adult child is not eligible to enroll in an eligible employer-sponsored health plan (as defined in section 5000A(f)(2) of the Internal Revenue Code) other than a grandfathered health plan of a parent. For plan years beginning on or after January 1, 2014, the provisions of PHS Act section 2714 apply with respect to a grandfathered health plan that is a group health plan without regard to whether an adult child is eligible to enroll in any other coverage.

(f) *Effect on collectively bargained plans*—(1) *In general.* In the case of health insurance coverage maintained pursuant to one or more collective bargaining agreements between employee representatives and one or more employers that was ratified before March 23, 2010, the coverage is grandfathered health plan coverage at least until the date on which the last of the collective bargaining agreements relating to the coverage that was in effect on March 23, 2010 terminates. Any coverage amendment made pursuant to a collective bargaining agreement relating to the coverage that amends the coverage solely to conform to any requirement added by subtitles A and C of title I of the Patient Protection and Affordable Care Act (and the amendments made by those subtitles, and the incorporation of those amendments into ERISA section 715 and Internal Revenue Code section 9815) is not treated as a termination of the collective bargaining agreement. After the date on which the last of the collective bargaining agreements relating to the coverage that was in effect on March 23, 2010 terminates, the determination of whether health insurance coverage maintained pursuant to a collective bargaining agreement is grandfathered health plan coverage is made under the rules of this section other than this paragraph (f) (comparing the terms of the health insurance coverage after the date the last collective bargaining agreement terminates with the terms of the health insurance coverage that were in effect on March 23, 2010) and, for any changes in insurance coverage after the termination of the collective bargaining agreement, under the rules of paragraph (a)(1)(ii) of this section.

(2) *Examples.* The rules of this paragraph (f) are illustrated by the following examples:

Example 1. (i) *Facts.* A group health plan maintained pursuant to a collective bargaining agreement provides coverage through a group health insurance policy from Issuer *W* on March 23, 2010. The collective bargaining agreement has not been amended and will not expire before December 31, 2011. The group health plan enters into a new group health insurance policy with Issuer *Y* for the plan year starting on January 1, 2011.

(ii) *Conclusion.* In this *Example 1*, the group health plan, and the group health insurance policy provided by *Y*, remains a grandfathered health plan with respect to existing employees and new employees and their families because the coverage is maintained pursuant to a collective bargaining agreement ratified prior to March 23, 2010 that has not terminated.

Example 2. (i) *Facts.* Same facts as *Example 1.* except the coverage with *Y* is renewed under a new collective bargaining agreement effective January 1, 2012, with the only changes since March 23, 2010 being changes that do not cause the plan to cease to be a grandfathered health plan under the rules of this section, including paragraph (g) of this section.

(ii) *Conclusion.* In this *Example 2*, the group health plan remains a grandfathered health plan pursuant to the rules of this section. Moreover, the group health insurance policy provided by *Y* remains a grandfathered health plan under the rules of this section, including paragraph (g) of this section.

(g) *Maintenance of grandfather status*—(1) *Changes causing cessation of grandfather status.* Subject to paragraph (g)(2) of this section, the rules of this paragraph (g)(1) describe situations in which a group health plan or health insurance coverage ceases to be a grandfathered health plan.

(i) *Elimination of benefits.* The elimination of all or substantially all benefits to diagnose or treat a particular condition causes a group health plan or health insurance coverage to cease to be a grandfathered health plan. For this purpose, the elimination of benefits for any necessary element to diagnose or treat a condition is considered the elimination of all or substantially all benefits to diagnose or treat a particular condition.

(ii) *Increase in percentage cost-sharing requirement.* Any increase, measured from March 23, 2010, in a percentage cost-sharing requirement (such as an individual's coinsurance requirement) causes a group health plan or health insurance coverage to cease to be a grandfathered health plan.

(iii) *Increase in a fixed-amount cost-sharing requirement other than a copayment.* Any increase in a fixed-amount cost-sharing requirement other than a copayment (for example, deductible or out-of-pocket limit), determined as of the effective date of the increase, causes a group health plan or health insurance coverage to cease to be a grandfathered health plan, if the total percentage increase in the cost-sharing requirement measured from March 23, 2010 exceeds the maximum percentage increase (as defined in paragraph (g)(3)(ii) of this section).

(iv) *Increase in a fixed-amount copayment.* Any increase in a fixed-amount copayment, determined as of the effective date of the increase, causes a group health plan or health insurance coverage to cease to be a grandfathered health plan, if the total increase in the copayment measured from March 23, 2010 exceeds the greater of:

(A) An amount equal to $5 increased by medical inflation, as defined in paragraph (g)(3)(i) of this section (that is, $5 times medical inflation, plus $5), or

(B) The maximum percentage increase (as defined in paragraph (g)(3)(ii) of this section), determined by expressing the total increase in the copayment as a percentage.

(v) *Decrease in contribution rate by employers and employee organizations*—(A) *Contribution rate based on cost of coverage.* A group health plan or group health insurance coverage ceases to be a grandfathered health plan if the employer or employee organization decreases its contribution rate based on cost of coverage (as defined in paragraph (g)(3)(iii)(A) of this section) towards the cost of any tier of coverage for any class of similarly situated individuals (as described in § 2590.702(d) of this part) by more than 5 percentage points below the contribution rate for the coverage period that includes March 23, 2010.

(B) *Contribution rate based on a formula.* A group health plan or group health insurance coverage ceases to be a grandfathered health plan if the employer or employee organization decreases its contribution rate based on a formula (as defined in paragraph (g)(3)(iii)(B) of this section) towards the cost of any tier of coverage for any class of similarly situated individuals (as described in section 2590.702(d) of this part) by more than 5 percent below the contribution rate for the coverage period that includes March 23, 2010.

(vi) *Changes in annual limits*—(A) *Addition of an annual limit.* A group health plan, or group health insurance coverage, that, on March 23, 2010, did not impose an overall annual or lifetime limit on the dollar value of all benefits ceases to be a grandfathered health plan if the plan or health insurance coverage imposes an overall annual limit on the dollar value of benefits.

(B) *Decrease in limit for a plan or coverage with only a lifetime limit.* A group health plan, or group health insurance coverage, that, on March 23, 2010, imposed an overall lifetime limit

Federal Register/Vol. 75, No. 116/Thursday, June 17, 2010/Rules and Regulations 34565

on the dollar value of all benefits but no overall annual limit on the dollar value of all benefits ceases to be a grandfathered health plan if the plan or health insurance coverage adopts an overall annual limit at a dollar value that is lower than the dollar value of the lifetime limit on March 23, 2010.

(C) *Decrease in limit for a plan or coverage with an annual limit.* A group health plan, or group health insurance coverage, that, on March 23, 2010, imposed an overall annual limit on the dollar value of all benefits ceases to be a grandfathered health plan if the plan or health insurance coverage decreases the dollar value of the annual limit (regardless of whether the plan or health insurance coverage also imposed an overall lifetime limit on March 23, 2010 on the dollar value of all benefits).

(2) *Transitional rules—(i) Changes made prior to March 23, 2010.* If a group health plan or health insurance issuer makes the following changes to the terms of the plan or health insurance coverage, the changes are considered part of the terms of the plan or health insurance coverage on March 23, 2010 even though they were not effective at that time and such changes do not cause a plan or health insurance coverage to cease to be a grandfathered health plan:

(A) Changes effective after March 23, 2010 pursuant to a legally binding contract entered into on or before March 23, 2010;

(B) Changes effective after March 23, 2010 pursuant to a filing on or before March 23, 2010 with a State insurance department; or

(C) Changes effective after March 23, 2010 pursuant to written amendments to a plan that were adopted on or before March 23, 2010.

(ii) *Changes made after March 23, 2010 and adopted prior to issuance of regulations.* If, after March 23, 2010, a group health plan or health insurance issuer makes changes to the terms of the plan or health insurance coverage and the changes are adopted prior to June 14, 2010, the changes will not cause the plan or health insurance coverage to cease to be a grandfathered health plan if the changes are revoked or modified effective as of the first day of the first plan year (in the individual market, policy year) beginning on or after September 23, 2010, and the terms of the plan or health insurance coverage on that date, as modified, would not cause the plan or coverage to cease to be a grandfathered health plan under the rules of this section, including paragraph (g)(1) of this section. For this purpose, changes will be considered to have been adopted prior to June 14, 2010 if:

(A) The changes are effective before that date;

(B) The changes are effective on or after that date pursuant to a legally binding contract entered into before that date;

(C) The changes are effective on or after that date pursuant to a filing before that date with a State insurance department; or

(D) The changes are effective on or after that date pursuant to written amendments to a plan that were adopted before that date.

(3) *Definitions—(i) Medical inflation defined.* For purposes of this paragraph (g), the term *medical inflation* means the increase since March 2010 in the overall medical care component of the Consumer Price Index for All Urban Consumers (CPI–U) (unadjusted) published by the Department of Labor using the 1982–1984 base of 100. For this purpose, the increase in the overall medical care component is computed by subtracting 387.142 (the overall medical care component of the CPI–U (unadjusted) published by the Department of Labor for March 2010, using the 1982–1984 base of 100) from the index amount for any month in the 12 months before the new change is to take effect and then dividing that amount by 387.142.

(ii) *Maximum percentage increase defined.* For purposes of this paragraph (g), the term *maximum percentage increase* means medical inflation (as defined in paragraph (g)(3)(i) of this section), expressed as a percentage, plus 15 percentage points.

(iii) *Contribution rate defined.* For purposes of paragraph (g)(1)(v) of this section:

(A) *Contribution rate based on cost of coverage.* The term *contribution rate based on cost of coverage* means the amount of contributions made by an employer or employee organization compared to the total cost of coverage, expressed as a percentage. The total cost of coverage is determined in the same manner as the applicable premium is calculated under the COBRA continuation provisions of section 604 of ERISA, section 4980B(f)(4) of the Internal Revenue Code, and section 2204 of the PHS Act. In the case of a self-insured plan, contributions by an employer or employee organization are equal to the total cost of coverage minus the employee contributions towards the total cost of coverage.

(B) *Contribution rate based on a formula.* The term *contribution rate based on a formula* means, for plans that, on March 23, 2010, made contributions based on a formula (such as hours worked or tons of coal mined), the formula.

(4) *Examples.* The rules of this paragraph (g) are illustrated by the following examples:

Example 1. (i) *Facts.* On March 23, 2010, a grandfathered health plan has a coinsurance requirement of 20% for inpatient surgery. The plan is subsequently amended to increase the coinsurance requirement to 25%.

(ii) *Conclusion.* In this *Example 1*, the increase in the coinsurance requirement from 20% to 25% causes the plan to cease to be a grandfathered health plan.

Example 2. (i) *Facts.* Before March 23, 2010, the terms of a group health plan provide benefits for a particular mental health condition, the treatment for which is a combination of counseling and prescription drugs. Subsequently, the plan eliminates benefits for counseling.

(ii) *Conclusion.* In this *Example 2*, the plan ceases to be a grandfathered health plan because counseling is an element that is necessary to treat the condition. Thus the plan is considered to have eliminated substantially all benefits for the treatment of the condition.

Example 3. (i) *Facts.* On March 23, 2010, a grandfathered health plan has a copayment requirement of $30 per office visit for specialists. The plan is subsequently amended to increase the copayment requirement to $40. Within the 12-month period before the $40 copayment takes effect, the greatest value of the overall medical care component of the CPI–U (unadjusted) is 475.

(ii) *Conclusion.* In this *Example 3*, the increase in the copayment from $30 to $40, expressed as a percentage, is 33.33% ($40 − 30 = 10; 10 ÷ 30 = 0.3333; 0.3333 = 33.33%). Medical inflation (as defined in paragraph (g)(3)(i) of this section) from March 2010 is 0.2269 (475 − 387.142 = 87.858; 87.858 ÷ 387.142 = 0.2269). The maximum percentage increase permitted is 37.69% (0.2269 = 22.69%; 22.69% + 15% = 37.69%). Because 33.33% does not exceed 37.69%, the change in the copayment requirement at that time does not cause the plan to cease to be a grandfathered health plan.

Example 4. (i) *Facts.* Same facts as *Example 3*, except the grandfathered health plan subsequently increases the $40 copayment requirement to $45 for a later plan year. Within the 12-month period before the $45 copayment takes effect, the greatest value of the overall medical care component of the CPI–U (unadjusted) is 485.

(ii) *Conclusion.* In this *Example 4*, the increase in the copayment from $30 (the copayment that was in effect on March 23, 2010) to $45, expressed as a percentage, is 50% (45 − 30 = 15; 15 ÷ 30 = 0.5; 0.5 = 50%). Medical inflation (as defined in paragraph (g)(3)(i) of this section) from March 2010 is 0.2527 (485 − 387.142 = 97.858; 97.858 ÷ 387.142 = 0.2527). The increase that would cause a plan to cease to be a grandfathered health plan under paragraph (g)(1)(iv) of this section is the greater of the maximum percentage increase of 40.27% (0.2527 = 25.27%; 25.27% + 15% = 40.27%), or $6.26 ($5 x 0.2527 = $1.26; $1.26 + $5 = $6.26).

34566 **Federal Register** / Vol. 75, No. 116 / Thursday, June 17, 2010 / Rules and Regulations

Because 50% exceeds 40.27% and $15 exceeds $6.26, the change in the copayment requirement at that time causes the plan to cease to be a grandfathered health plan.

Example 5. (i) *Facts.* On March 23, 2010, a grandfathered health plan has a copayment of $10 per office visit for primary care providers. The plan is subsequently amended to increase the copayment requirement to $15. Within the 12-month period before the $15 copayment takes effect, the greatest value of the overall medical care component of the CPI–U (unadjusted) is 415.

(ii) *Conclusion.* In this *Example 5,* the increase in the copayment, expressed as a percentage, is 50% $(15 - 10 = 5; 5 \div 10 = 0.5; 0.5 = 50\%)$. Medical inflation (as defined in paragraph (g)(3) of this section) from March 2010 is 0.0720 $(415.0 - 387.142 = 27.858; 27.858 \div 387.142 = 0.0720)$. The increase that would cause a plan to cease to be a grandfathered health plan under paragraph (g)(1)(iv) of this section is the greater of the maximum percentage increase of 22.20% $(0.0720 = 7.20\%; 7.20\% + 15\% = 22.20)$, or $5.36 ($5 x 0.0720 = $0.36; $0.36 + $5 = $5.36)$. The $5 increase in copayment in this *Example 5* would not cause the plan to cease to be a grandfathered health plan pursuant to paragraph (g)(1)(iv) of this section, which would permit an increase in the copayment of up to $5.36.

Example 6. (i) *Facts.* The same facts as *Example 5,* except on March 23, 2010, the grandfathered health plan has no copayment ($0) for office visits for primary care providers. The plan is subsequently amended to increase the copayment requirement to $5.

(ii) *Conclusion.* In this *Example 6,* medical inflation (as defined in paragraph (g)(3)(i) of this section) from March 2010 is 0.0720 $(415.0 - 387.142 = 27.858; 27.858 \div 387.142 = 0.0720)$. The increase that would cause a plan to cease to be a grandfathered health plan under paragraph (g)(1)(iv)(A) of this section is $5.36 ($5 x 0.0720 = $0.36; $0.36 + $5 = $5.36)$. The $5 increase in copayment in this *Example 6* is less than the amount calculated pursuant to paragraph (g)(1)(iv)(A) of this section of $5.36. Thus, the $5 increase in copayment does not cause the plan to cease to be a grandfathered health plan.

Example 7. (i) *Facts.* On March 23, 2010, a self-insured group health plan provides two tiers of coverage—self-only and family. The employer contributes 80% of the total cost of coverage for self-only and 60% of the total cost of coverage for family. Subsequently, the employer reduces the contribution to 50% for family coverage, but keeps the same contribution rate for self-only coverage.

(ii) *Conclusion.* In this *Example 7,* the decrease of 10 percentage points for family coverage in the contribution rate based on cost of coverage causes the plan to cease to be a grandfathered health plan. The fact that the contribution rate for self-only coverage remains the same does not change the result.

Example 8. (i) *Facts.* On March 23, 2010, a self-insured grandfathered health plan has a COBRA premium for the 2010 plan year of $5000 for self-only coverage and $12,000 for family coverage. The required employee contribution for the coverage is $1000 for self-only coverage and $4000 for family coverage. Thus, the contribution rate based

on cost of coverage for 2010 is 80% ((5000–1000)/5000) for self-only coverage and 67% ((12,000–4000)/12,000) for family coverage. For a subsequent plan year, the COBRA premium is $6000 for self-only coverage and $15,000 for family coverage. The employee contributions for that plan year are $1200 for self-only coverage and $5000 for family coverage. Thus, the contribution rate based on cost of coverage is 80% ((6000–1200)/6000) for self-only coverage and 67% ((15,000–5000)/15,000) for family coverage.

(ii) *Conclusion.* In this *Example 8,* because there is no change in the contribution rate based on cost of coverage, the plan retains its status as a grandfathered health plan. The result would be the same if all or part of the employee contribution was made pre-tax through a cafeteria plan under section 125 of the Internal Revenue Code.

Example 9. (i) *Facts.* Before March 23, 2010, Employer *W* and Individual *B* enter into a legally binding employment contract that promises *B* lifetime health coverage upon termination. Prior to termination, *B* is covered by *W*'s self-insured grandfathered group health plan. *B* is terminated after March 23, 2010 and *W* purchases a new health insurance policy providing coverage to *B,* consistent with the terms of the employment contract.

(ii) *Conclusion.* In this *Example 9,* because no individual is enrolled in the health insurance policy on March 23, 2010, it is not a grandfathered health plan.

■ 3. Section 2590.715–2714 is amended by revising paragraph (h) to read as follows:

§ 2590.715–2714   Eligibility of children until at least age 26.

*   *   *   *   *

(h) *Applicability date.* The provisions of this section apply for plan years beginning on or after September 23, 2010. *See* § 2590.715–1251 of this Part for determining the application of this section to grandfathered health plans.

DEPARTMENT OF HEALTH AND HUMAN SERVICES

45 CFR Chapter I

■ For the reasons stated in the preamble, the Department of Health and Human Services amends 45 CFR part 147 as follows:

PART 147—HEALTH INSURANCE REFORM REQUIREMENTS FOR THE GROUP AND INDIVIDUAL HEALTH INSURANCE MARKETS

■ 1. The authority citation for part 147 continues to read as follows:

Authority: Secs. 2701 through 2763, 2791, and 2792 of the Public Health Service Act (42 USC 300gg through 300gg–63, 300gg–91, and 300gg–92), as amended.

■ 2. Section 147.120 is amended by revising paragraph (h) to read as follows:

(h) *Applicability date.* The provisions of this section apply for plan years (in the individual market, policy years) beginning on or after September 23, 2010. *See* § 147.140 of this part for determining the application of this section to grandfathered health plans.

■ 3. Section 147.140 is added to read as follows:

§ 147.140   Preservation of right to maintain existing coverage.

(a) *Definition of grandfathered health plan coverage*—(1) *In general*—(i) *Grandfathered health plan coverage* means coverage provided by a group health plan, or a group or individual health insurance issuer, in which an individual was enrolled on March 23, 2010 (for as long as it maintains that status under the rules of this section). A group health plan or group health insurance coverage does not cease to be grandfathered health plan coverage merely because one or more (or even all) individuals enrolled on March 23, 2010 cease to be covered, provided that the plan or group health insurance coverage has continuously covered someone since March 23, 2010 (not necessarily the same person, but at all times at least one person). For purposes of this section, a plan or health insurance coverage that provides grandfathered health plan coverage is referred to as a grandfathered health plan. The rules of this section apply separately to each benefit package made available under a group health plan or health insurance coverage.

(ii) Subject to the rules of paragraph (f) of this section for collectively bargained plans, if an employer or employee organization enters into a new policy, certificate, or contract of insurance after March 23, 2010 (because, for example, any previous policy, certificate, or contract of insurance is not being renewed), then that policy, certificate, or contract of insurance is not a grandfathered health plan with respect to the individuals in the group health plan.

(2) *Disclosure of grandfather status*—(i) To maintain status as a grandfathered health plan, a plan or health insurance coverage must include a statement, in any plan materials provided to a participant or beneficiary (in the individual market, primary subscriber) describing the benefits provided under the plan or health insurance coverage, that the plan or coverage believes it is a grandfathered health plan within the meaning of section 1251 of the Patient Protection and Affordable Care Act and must provide contact information for questions and complaints.

(ii) The following model language can be used to satisfy this disclosure requirement:

This [group health plan or health insurance issuer] believes this [plan or coverage] is a "grandfathered health plan" under the Patient Protection and Affordable Care Act (the Affordable Care Act). As permitted by the Affordable Care Act, a grandfathered health plan can preserve certain basic health coverage that was already in effect when that law was enacted. Being a grandfathered health plan means that your [plan or policy] may not include certain consumer protections of the Affordable Care Act that apply to other plans, for example, the requirement for the provision of preventive health services without any cost sharing. However, grandfathered health plans must comply with certain other consumer protections in the Affordable Care Act, for example, the elimination of lifetime limits on benefits.

Questions regarding which protections apply and which protections do not apply to a grandfathered health plan and what might cause a plan to change from grandfathered health plan status can be directed to the plan administrator at [insert contact information]. [For ERISA plans, insert: You may also contact the Employee Benefits Security Administration, U.S. Department of Labor at 1–866–444–3272 or www.dol.gov/ebsa/healthreform. This Web site has a table summarizing which protections do and do not apply to grandfathered health plans.] [For individual market policies and nonfederal governmental plans, insert: You may also contact the U.S. Department of Health and Human Services at www.healthreform.gov.]

(3) *Documentation of plan or policy terms on March 23, 2010.* To maintain status as a grandfathered health plan, a group health plan, or group or individual health insurance coverage, must, for as long as the plan or health insurance coverage takes the position that it is a grandfathered health plan—

(i) Maintain records documenting the terms of the plan or health insurance coverage in connection with the coverage in effect on March 23, 2010, and any other documents necessary to verify, explain, or clarify its status as a grandfathered health plan; and

(ii) Make such records available for examination upon request.

(4) *Family members enrolling after March 23, 2010.* With respect to an individual who is enrolled in a group health plan or health insurance coverage on March 23, 2010, grandfathered health plan coverage includes coverage of family members of the individual who enroll after March 23, 2010 in the grandfathered health plan coverage of the individual.

(5) *Examples.* The rules of this paragraph (a) are illustrated by the following examples:

Example 1. (i) *Facts.* A group health plan not maintained pursuant to a collective bargaining agreement provides coverage through a group health insurance policy from Issuer *X* on March 23, 2010. For the plan year beginning January 1, 2012, the plan enters into a new policy with Issuer *Z.*

(ii) *Conclusion.* In this *Example 1,* for the plan year beginning January 1, 2012, the group health insurance coverage issued by *Z* is not a grandfathered health plan under the rules of paragraph (a)(1)(ii) of this section because the policy issued by *Z* did not provide coverage on March 23, 2010.

Example 2. (i) *Facts.* A group health plan not maintained pursuant to a collective bargaining agreement offers three benefit packages on March 23, 2010. Option *F* is a self-insured option. Options *G* and *H* are insured options. Beginning July 1, 2013, the plan replaces the issuer for Option *H* with a new issuer.

(ii) *Conclusion.* In this *Example 2,* the coverage under Option *H* is not grandfathered health plan coverage as of July 1, 2013, consistent with the rule in paragraph (a)(1)(ii) of this section. Whether the coverage under Options *F* and *G* is grandfathered health plan coverage is determined under the rules of this section, including paragraph (g) of this section. If the plan enters into a new policy, certificate, or contract of insurance for Option *G,* Option *G's* status as a grandfathered health plan would cease under paragraph (a)(1)(ii) of this section.

(b) *Allowance for new employees to join current plan*—(1) *In general.* Subject to paragraph (b)(2) of this section, a group health plan (including health insurance coverage provided in connection with the group health plan) that provided coverage on March 23, 2010 and has retained its status as a grandfathered health plan (consistent with the rules of this section, including paragraph (g) of this section) is grandfathered health plan coverage for new employees (whether newly hired or newly enrolled) and their families enrolling in the plan after March 23, 2010.

(2) *Anti-abuse rules*—(i) *Mergers and acquisitions.* If the principal purpose of a merger, acquisition, or similar business restructuring is to cover new individuals under a grandfathered health plan, the plan ceases to be a grandfathered health plan.

(ii) *Change in plan eligibility.* A group health plan or health insurance coverage (including a benefit package under a group health plan) ceases to be a grandfathered health plan if—

(A) Employees are transferred into the plan or health insurance coverage (the transferee plan) from a plan or health insurance coverage under which the employees were covered on March 23, 2010 (the transferor plan);

(B) Comparing the terms of the transferee plan with those of the transferor plan (as in effect on March 23, 2010) and treating the transferee plan as if it were an amendment of the transferor plan would cause a loss of grandfather status under the provisions of paragraph (g)(1) of this section; and

(C) There was no bona fide employment-based reason to transfer the employees into the transferee plan. For this purpose, changing the terms or cost of coverage is not a bona fide employment-based reason.

(3) *Examples.* The rules of this paragraph (b) are illustrated by the following examples:

Example 1. (i) *Facts.* A group health plan offers two benefit packages on March 23, 2010, Options *F* and *G.* During a subsequent open enrollment period, some of the employees enrolled in Option *F* on March 23, 2010 switch to Option *G.*

(ii) *Conclusion.* In this *Example 1,* the group health coverage provided under Option *G* remains a grandfathered health plan under the rules of paragraph (b)(1) of this section because employees previously enrolled in Option *F* are allowed to enroll in Option *G* as new employees.

Example 2. (i) *Facts.* Same facts as *Example 1,* except that the plan sponsor eliminates Option *F* because of its high cost and transfers employees covered under Option *F* to Option *G.* If instead of transferring employees from Option *F* to Option *G,* Option *F* was amended to match the terms of Option *G,* then Option *F* would cease to be a grandfathered health plan.

(ii) *Conclusion.* In this *Example 2,* the plan did not have a bona fide employment-based reason to transfer employees from Option *F* to Option *G.* Therefore, Option *G* ceases to be a grandfathered health plan with respect to all employees. (However, any other benefit package maintained by the plan sponsor is analyzed separately under the rules of this section.)

Example 3. (i) *Facts.* A group health plan offers two benefit packages on March 23, 2010, Options *H* and *I.* On March 23, 2010, Option *H* provides coverage only for employees in one manufacturing plant. Subsequently, the plant is closed, and some employees in the closed plant are moved to another plant. The employer eliminates Option *H* and the employees that are moved are transferred to Option *I.* If instead of transferring employees from Option *H* to Option *I,* Option *H* was amended to match the terms of Option *I,* then Option *H* would cease to be a grandfathered health plan.

(ii) *Conclusion.* In this *Example 3,* the plan has a bona fide employment-based reason to transfer employees from Option *H* to Option *I.* Therefore, Option *I* does not cease to be a grandfathered health plan.

(c) *General grandfathering rule*—(1) Except as provided in paragraphs (d) and (e) of this section, subtitles A and C of title I of the Patient Protection and Affordable Care Act (and the amendments made by those subtitles, and the incorporation of those amendments into ERISA section 715 and Internal Revenue Code section 9815) do not apply to grandfathered health plan coverage. Accordingly, the

34568 Federal Register / Vol. 75, No. 116 / Thursday, June 17, 2010 / Rules and Regulations

provisions of PHS Act sections 2701, 2702, 2703, 2705, 2706, 2707, 2709 (relating to coverage for individuals participating in approved clinical trials, as added by section 10103 of the Patient Protection and Affordable Care Act), 2713, 2715A, 2716, 2717, 2719, and 2719A, as added or amended by the Patient Protection and Affordable Care Act, do not apply to grandfathered health plans. In addition, the provisions of PHS Act section 2704, and PHS Act section 2711 insofar as it relates to annual limits, do not apply to grandfathered health plans that are individual health insurance coverage.

(2) To the extent not inconsistent with the rules applicable to a grandfathered health plan, a grandfathered health plan must comply with the requirements of the PHS Act, ERISA, and the Internal Revenue Code applicable prior to the changes enacted by the Patient Protection and Affordable Care Act.

(d) *Provisions applicable to all grandfathered health plans.* The provisions of PHS Act section 2711 insofar as it relates to lifetime limits, and the provisions of PHS Act sections 2712, 2714, 2715, and 2718, apply to grandfathered health plans for plan years (in the individual market, policy years) beginning on or after September 23, 2010. The provisions of PHS Act section 2708 apply to grandfathered health plans for plan years (in the individual market, policy years) beginning on or after January 1, 2014.

(e) *Applicability of PHS Act sections 2704, 2711, and 2714 to grandfathered group health plans and group health insurance coverage*—(1) The provisions of PHS Act section 2704 as it applies with respect to enrollees who are under 19 years of age, and the provisions of PHS Act section 2711 insofar as it relates to annual limits, apply to grandfathered health plans that are group health plans (including group health insurance coverage) for plan years beginning on or after September 23, 2010. The provisions of PHS Act section 2704 apply generally to grandfathered health plans that are group health plans (including group health insurance coverage) for plan years beginning on or after January 1, 2014.

(2) For plan years beginning before January 1, 2014, the provisions of PHS Act section 2714 apply in the case of an adult child with respect to a grandfathered health plan that is a group health plan only if the adult child is not eligible to enroll in an eligible employer-sponsored health plan (as defined in section 5000A(f)(2) of the Internal Revenue Code) other than a grandfathered health plan of a parent.

For plan years beginning on or after January 1, 2014, the provisions of PHS Act section 2714 apply with respect to a grandfathered health plan that is a group health plan without regard to whether an adult child is eligible to enroll in any other coverage.

(f) *Effect on collectively bargained plans*—(1) *In general.* In the case of health insurance coverage maintained pursuant to one or more collective bargaining agreements between employee representatives and one or more employers that was ratified before March 23, 2010, the coverage is grandfathered health plan coverage at least until the date on which the last of the collective bargaining agreements relating to the coverage that was in effect on March 23, 2010 terminates. Any coverage amendment made pursuant to a collective bargaining agreement relating to the coverage that amends the coverage solely to conform to any requirement added by subtitles A and C of title I of the Patient Protection and Affordable Care Act (and the amendments made by those subtitles, and the incorporation of those amendments into ERISA section 715 and Internal Revenue Code section 9815) is not treated as a termination of the collective bargaining agreement. After the date on which the last of the collective bargaining agreements relating to the coverage that was in effect on March 23, 2010 terminates, the determination of whether health insurance coverage maintained pursuant to a collective bargaining agreement is grandfathered health plan coverage is made under the rules of this section other than this paragraph (f) (comparing the terms of the health insurance coverage after the date the last collective bargaining agreement terminates with the terms of the health insurance coverage that were in effect on March 23, 2010) and, for any changes in insurance coverage after the termination of the collective bargaining agreement, under the rules of paragraph (a)(1)(ii) of this section.

(2) *Examples.* The rules of this paragraph (f) are illustrated by the following examples:

Example 1. (i) *Facts.* A group health plan maintained pursuant to a collective bargaining agreement provides coverage through a group health insurance policy from Issuer *W* on March 23, 2010. The collective bargaining agreement has not been amended and will not expire before December 31, 2011. The group health plan enters into a new group health insurance policy with Issuer *Y* for the plan year starting on January 1, 2011.

(ii) *Conclusion.* In this *Example 1*, the group health plan, and the group health insurance policy provided by *Y*, remains a

grandfathered health plan with respect to existing employees and new employees and their families because the coverage is maintained pursuant to a collective bargaining agreement ratified prior to March 23, 2010 that has not terminated.

Example 2. (i) *Facts.* Same facts as *Example 1*, except the coverage with *Y* is renewed under a new collective bargaining agreement effective January 1, 2012, with the only changes since March 23, 2010 being changes that do not cause the plan to cease to be a grandfathered health plan under the rules of this section, including paragraph (g) of this section.

(ii) *Conclusion.* In this *Example 2*, the group health plan remains a grandfathered health plan pursuant to the rules of this section. Moreover, the group health insurance policy provided by *Y* remains a grandfathered health plan under the rules of this section, including paragraph (g) of this section.

(g) *Maintenance of grandfather status*—(1) *Changes causing cessation of grandfather status.* Subject to paragraph (g)(2) of this section, the rules of this paragraph (g)(1) describe situations in which a group health plan or health insurance coverage ceases to be a grandfathered health plan.

(i) *Elimination of benefits.* The elimination of all or substantially all benefits to diagnose or treat a particular condition causes a group health plan or health insurance coverage to cease to be a grandfathered health plan. For this purpose, the elimination of benefits for any necessary element to diagnose or treat a condition is considered the elimination of all or substantially all benefits to diagnose or treat a particular condition.

(ii) *Increase in percentage cost-sharing requirement.* Any increase, measured from March 23, 2010, in a percentage cost-sharing requirement (such as an individual's coinsurance requirement) causes a group health plan or health insurance coverage to cease to be a grandfathered health plan.

(iii) *Increase in a fixed-amount cost-sharing requirement other than a copayment.* Any increase in a fixed-amount cost-sharing requirement other than a copayment (for example, deductible or out-of-pocket limit), determined as of the effective date of the increase, causes a group health plan or health insurance coverage to cease to be a grandfathered health plan, if the total percentage increase in the cost-sharing requirement measured from March 23, 2010 exceeds the maximum percentage increase (as defined in paragraph (g)(3)(ii) of this section).

(iv) *Increase in a fixed-amount copayment.* Any increase in a fixed-amount copayment, determined as of the effective date of the increase, causes a group health plan or health insurance coverage to cease to be a grandfathered health plan, if the total increase in the copayment measured from March 23, 2010 exceeds the greater of:

(A) An amount equal to $5 increased by medical inflation, as defined in paragraph (g)(3)(i) of this section (that is, $5 times medical inflation, plus $5), or

(B) The maximum percentage increase (as defined in paragraph (g)(3)(ii) of this section), determined by expressing the total increase in the copayment as a percentage.

(v) *Decrease in contribution rate by employers and employee organizations*—(A) *Contribution rate based on cost of coverage.* A group health plan or group health insurance coverage ceases to be a grandfathered health plan if the employer or employee organization decreases its contribution rate based on cost of coverage (as defined in paragraph (g)(3)(iii)(A) of this section) towards the cost of any tier of coverage for any class of similarly situated individuals (as described in section 146.121(d) of this subchapter) by more than 5 percentage points below the contribution rate for the coverage period that includes March 23, 2010.

(B) *Contribution rate based on a formula.* A group health plan or group health insurance coverage ceases to be a grandfathered health plan if the employer or employee organization decreases its contribution rate based on a formula (as defined in paragraph (g)(3)(iii)(B) of this section) towards the cost of any tier of coverage for any class of similarly situated individuals (as described in section 146.121(d) of this subchapter) by more than 5 percent below the contribution rate for the coverage period that includes March 23, 2010.

(vi) *Changes in annual limits*—(A) *Addition of an annual limit.* A group health plan, or group or individual health insurance coverage, that, on March 23, 2010, did not impose an overall annual or lifetime limit on the dollar value of all benefits ceases to be a grandfathered health plan if the plan or health insurance coverage imposes an overall annual limit on the dollar value of benefits.

(B) *Decrease in limit for a plan or coverage with only a lifetime limit.* A group health plan, or group or individual health insurance coverage, that, on March 23, 2010, imposed an overall lifetime limit on the dollar value of all benefits but no overall annual limit on the dollar value of all benefits ceases to be a grandfathered health plan if the plan or health insurance coverage adopts an overall annual limit at a dollar value that is lower than the dollar

value of the lifetime limit on March 23, 2010.

(C) *Decrease in limit for a plan or coverage with an annual limit.* A group health plan, or group or individual health insurance coverage, that, on March 23, 2010, imposed an overall annual limit on the dollar value of all benefits ceases to be a grandfathered health plan if the plan or health insurance coverage decreases the dollar value of the annual limit (regardless of whether the plan or health insurance coverage also imposed an overall lifetime limit on March 23, 2010 on the dollar value of all benefits).

(2) *Transitional rules*—(i) *Changes made prior to March 23, 2010.* If a group health plan or health insurance issuer makes the following changes to the terms of the plan or health insurance coverage, the changes are considered part of the terms of the plan or health insurance coverage on March 23, 2010 even though they were not effective at that time and such changes do not cause a plan or health insurance coverage to cease to be a grandfathered health plan:

(A) Changes effective after March 23, 2010 pursuant to a legally binding contract entered into on or before March 23, 2010;

(B) Changes effective after March 23, 2010 pursuant to a filing on or before March 23, 2010 with a State insurance department; or

(C) Changes effective after March 23, 2010 pursuant to written amendments to a plan that were adopted on or before March 23, 2010.

(ii) *Changes made after March 23, 2010 and adopted prior to issuance of regulations.* If, after March 23, 2010, a group health plan or health insurance issuer makes changes to the terms of the plan or health insurance coverage and the changes are adopted prior to June 14, 2010, the changes will not cause the plan or health insurance coverage to cease to be a grandfathered health plan if the changes are revoked or modified effective as of the first day of the first plan year (in the individual market, policy year) beginning on or after September 23, 2010, and the terms of the plan or health insurance coverage on that date, as modified, would not cause the plan or coverage to cease to be a grandfathered health plan under the rules of this section, including paragraph (g)(1) of this section. For this purpose, changes will be considered to have been adopted prior to June 14, 2010 if:

(A) The changes are effective before that date;

(B) The changes are effective on or after that date pursuant to a legally

binding contract entered into before that date;

(C) The changes are effective on or after that date pursuant to a filing before that date with a State insurance department; or

(D) The changes are effective on or after that date pursuant to written amendments to a plan that were adopted before that date.

(3) *Definitions*—(i) *Medical inflation defined.* For purposes of this paragraph (g), the term *medical inflation* means the increase since March 2010 in the overall medical care component of the Consumer Price Index for All Urban Consumers (CPI–U) (unadjusted) published by the Department of Labor using the 1982–1984 base of 100. For this purpose, the increase in the overall medical care component is computed by subtracting 387.142 (the overall medical care component of the CPI–U (unadjusted) published by the Department of Labor for March 2010, using the 1982–1984 base of 100) from the index amount for any month in the 12 months before the new change is to take effect and then dividing that amount by 387.142.

(ii) *Maximum percentage increase defined.* For purposes of this paragraph (g), the term *maximum percentage increase* means medical inflation (as defined in paragraph (g)(3)(i) of this section), expressed as a percentage, plus 15 percentage points.

(iii) *Contribution rate defined.* For purposes of paragraph (g)(1)(v) of this section:

(A) *Contribution rate based on cost of coverage.* The term *contribution rate based on cost of coverage* means the amount of contributions made by an employer or employee organization compared to the total cost of coverage, expressed as a percentage. The total cost of coverage is determined in the same manner as the applicable premium is calculated under the COBRA continuation provisions of section 604 of ERISA, section 4980B(f)(4) of the Internal Revenue Code, and section 2204 of the PHS Act. In the case of a self-insured plan, contributions by an employer or employee organization are equal to the total cost of coverage minus the employee contributions towards the total cost of coverage.

(B) *Contribution rate based on a formula.* The term *contribution rate based on a formula* means, for plans that, on March 23, 2010, made contributions based on a formula (such as hours worked or tons of coal mined), the formula.

(4) *Examples.* The rules of this paragraph (g) are illustrated by the following examples:

34570 **Federal Register** / Vol. 75, No. 116 / Thursday, June 17, 2010 / Rules and Regulations

Example 1. (i) *Facts.* On March 23, 2010, a grandfathered health plan has a coinsurance requirement of 20% for inpatient surgery. The plan is subsequently amended to increase the coinsurance requirement to 25%.

(ii) *Conclusion.* In this *Example 1,* the increase in the coinsurance requirement from 20% to 25% causes the plan to cease to be a grandfathered health plan.

Example 2. (i) *Facts.* Before March 23, 2010, the terms of a group health plan provide benefits for a particular mental health condition, the treatment for which is a combination of counseling and prescription drugs. Subsequently, the plan eliminates benefits for counseling.

(ii) *Conclusion.* In this *Example 2,* the plan ceases to be a grandfathered health plan because counseling is an element that is necessary to treat the condition. Thus the plan is considered to have eliminated substantially all benefits for the treatment of the condition.

Example 3. (i) *Facts.* On March 23, 2010, a grandfathered health plan has a copayment requirement of $30 per office visit for specialists. The plan is subsequently amended to increase the copayment requirement to $40. Within the 12-month period before the $40 copayment takes effect, the greatest value of the overall medical care component of the CPI–U (unadjusted) is 475.

(ii) *Conclusion.* In this *Example 3,* the increase in the copayment from $30 to $40, expressed as a percentage, is 33.33% (40 − 30 = 10; 10 ÷ 30 = 0.3333; 0.3333 = 33.33%). Medical inflation (as defined in paragraph (g)(3)(i) of this section) from March 2010 is 0.2269 (475 − 387.142 = 87.858; 87.858 ÷ 387.142 = 0.2269). The maximum percentage increase permitted is 37.69% (0.2269 = 22.69%; 22.69% + 15% = 37.69%). Because 33.33% does not exceed 37.69%, the change in the copayment requirement at that time does not cause the plan to cease to be a grandfathered health plan.

Example 4. (i) *Facts.* Same facts as *Example 3,* except the grandfathered health plan subsequently increases the $40 copayment requirement to $45 for a later plan year. Within the 12-month period before the $45 copayment takes effect, the greatest value of the overall medical care component of the CPI–U (unadjusted) is 485.

(ii) *Conclusion.* In this *Example 4,* the increase in the copayment from $30 (the copayment that was in effect on March 23, 2010) to $45, expressed as a percentage, is 50% (45 − 30 = 15; 15 ÷ 30 = 0.5; 0.5 = 50%). Medical inflation (as defined in paragraph (g)(3)(i) of this section) from March 2010 is 0.2527 (485 − 387.142 = 97.858; 97.858 ÷ 387.142 = 0.2527). The increase that would cause a plan to cease to be a grandfathered health plan under paragraph (g)(1)(iv) of this section is the greater of the maximum percentage increase of 40.27% (0.2527 = 25.27%; 25.27% + 15% = 40.27%), or $6.26 ($5 × 0.2527 = $1.26; $1.26 + $5 = $6.26). Because 50% exceeds 40.27% and $15 exceeds $6.26, the change in the copayment requirement at that time causes the plan to cease to be a grandfathered health plan.

Example 5. (i) *Facts.* On March 23, 2010, a grandfathered health plan has a copayment of $10 per office visit for primary care providers. The plan is subsequently amended to increase the copayment requirement to $15. Within the 12-month period before the $15 copayment takes effect, the greatest value of the overall medical care component of the CPI–U (unadjusted) is 415.

(ii) *Conclusion.* In this *Example 5,* the increase in the copayment, expressed as a percentage, is 50% (15 − 10 = 5; 5 ÷ 10 = 0.5; 0.5 = 50%). Medical inflation (as defined in paragraph (g)(3) of this section) from March 2010 is 0.0720 (415.0 − 387.142 = 27.858; 27.858 ÷ 387.142 = 0.0720). The increase that would cause a plan to cease to be a grandfathered health plan under paragraph (g)(1)(iv) of this section is the greater of the maximum percentage increase of 22.20% (0.0720 = 7.20%; 7.20% + 15% = 22.20), or $5.36 ($5 × 0.0720 = $0.36; $0.36 + $5 = $5.36). The $5 increase in copayment in this *Example 5* would not cause the plan to cease to be a grandfathered health plan pursuant to paragraph (g)(1)(iv) this section, which would permit an increase in the copayment of up to $5.36.

Example 6. (i) *Facts.* The same facts as *Example 5,* except on March 23, 2010, the grandfathered health plan has no copayment ($0) for office visits for primary care providers. The plan is subsequently amended to increase the copayment requirement to $5.

(ii) *Conclusion.* In this *Example 6,* medical inflation (as defined in paragraph (g)(3)(i) of this section) from March 2010 is 0.0720 (415.0 − 387.142 = 27.858; 27.858 ÷ 387.142 = 0.0720). The increase that would cause a plan to cease to be a grandfathered health plan under paragraph (g)(1)(iv)(A) of this section is $5.36 ($5 × 0.0720 = $0.36; $0.36 + $5 = $5.36). The $5 increase in copayment in this *Example 6* is less than the amount calculated pursuant to paragraph (g)(1)(iv)(A) of this section of $5.36. Thus, the $5 increase in copayment does not cause the plan to cease to be a grandfathered health plan.

Example 7. (i) *Facts.* On March 23, 2010, a self-insured group health plan provides two tiers of coverage—self-only and family. The employer contributes 80% of the total cost of coverage for self-only and 60% of the total cost of coverage for family. Subsequently, the employer reduces the contribution to 50% for family coverage, but keeps the same contribution rate for self-only coverage.

(ii) *Conclusion.* In this *Example 7,* the decrease of 10 percentage points for family coverage in the contribution rate based on cost of coverage causes the plan to cease to be a grandfathered health plan. The fact that the contribution rate for self-only coverage remains the same does not change the result.

Example 8. (i) *Facts.* On March 23, 2010, a self-insured grandfathered health plan has a COBRA premium for the 2010 plan year of $5000 for self-only coverage and $12,000 for family coverage. The required employee contribution for the coverage is $1000 for self-only coverage and $4000 for family coverage. Thus, the contribution rate based on cost of coverage for 2010 is 80% ((5000 − 1000)/5000) for self-only coverage and 67% ((12,000 − 4000)/12,000) for family coverage. For a subsequent plan year, the COBRA premium is $6000 for self-only coverage and $15,000 for family coverage. The employee contributions for that plan year are $1200 for self-only coverage and $5000 for family coverage. Thus, the contribution rate based on cost of coverage is 80% ((6000 − 1200)/6000) for self-only coverage and 67% ((15,000 − 5000)/15,000) for family coverage.

(ii) *Conclusion.* In this *Example 8,* because there is no change in the contribution rate based on cost of coverage, the plan retains its status as a grandfathered health plan. The result would be the same if all or part of the employee contribution was made pre-tax through a cafeteria plan under section 125 of the Internal Revenue Code.

Example 9. (i) *Facts.* Before March 23, 2010, Employer *W* and Individual *B* enter into a legally binding employment contract that promises *B* lifetime health coverage upon termination. Prior to termination, *B* is covered by *W*'s self-insured grandfathered group health plan. *B* is terminated after March 23, 2010 and *W* purchases a new health insurance policy providing coverage to *B,* consistent with the terms of the employment contract.

(ii) *Conclusion.* In this *Example 9,* because no individual is enrolled in the health insurance policy on March 23, 2010, it is not a grandfathered health plan.

[FR Doc. 2010–14488 Filed 6–14–10; 11:15 am]

BILLING CODE 4830–01–P, 4510–29–P, 4120–01–P

C. Amendment to Grandfathered Health Plan Regulations

70114 Federal Register / Vol. 75, No. 221 / Wednesday, November 17, 2010 / Rules and Regulations

VI. What references are on display?

The following reference has been placed on display in the Division of Dockets Management (HFA–305), Food and Drug Administration, 5630 Fishers Lane, Rm. 1061, Rockville, MD 20852, and may be seen by interested persons between 9 a.m. and 4 p.m., Monday through Friday.

1. Petition from Spiracur, Inc., November 3, 2008.

List of Subjects in 21 CFR Part 878

Medical devices.

■ Therefore, under the Federal Food, Drug, and Cosmetic Act and under authority delegated to the Commissioner of Food and Drugs, 21 CFR part 878 is amended as follows:

PART 878—GENERAL AND PLASTIC SURGERY DEVICES

■ 1. The authority citation for 21 CFR part 878 continues to read as follows:

Authority: 21 U.S.C. 351, 360, 360c, 360e, 360j, 360l, 371.

■ 2. Section 878.4683 is added to subpart E to read as follows:

§ 878.4683 Non-Powered suction apparatus device intended for negative pressure wound therapy.

(a) *Identification.* A non-powered suction apparatus device intended for negative pressure wound therapy is a device that is indicated for wound management via application of negative pressure to the wound for removal of fluids, including wound exudate, irrigation fluids, and infectious materials. It is further indicated for management of wounds, burns, flaps, and grafts.

(b) *Classification.* Class II (special controls). The special control for this device is FDA's "Class II Special Controls Guidance Document: Non-powered Suction Apparatus Device Intended for Negative Pressure Wound Therapy (NPWT)." See § 878.1(e) for the availability of this guidance document.

Dated: November 10, 2010.

Nancy K. Stade,

Deputy Director for Policy, Center for Devices and Radiological Health.

[FR Doc. 2010–28873 Filed 11–16–10; 8:45 am]

BILLING CODE 4160–01–P

DEPARTMENT OF THE TREASURY

Internal Revenue Service

26 CFR Part 54

[TD 9506]

RIN 1545–BJ91

DEPARTMENT OF LABOR

Employee Benefits Security Administration

29 CFR Part 2590

RIN 1210–AB42

DEPARTMENT OF HEALTH AND HUMAN SERVICES

Office of Consumer Information and Insurance Oversight

45 CFR Part 147

RIN 0950–AA17

[OCIIO–9991–IFC2]

Amendment to the Interim Final Rules for Group Health Plans and Health Insurance Coverage Relating to Status as a Grandfathered Health Plan Under the Patient Protection and Affordable Care Act

AGENCY: Internal Revenue Service, Department of the Treasury; Employee Benefits Security Administration, Department of Labor; Office of Consumer Information and Insurance Oversight, Department of Health and Human Services.

ACTION: Amendment to interim final rules with request for comments.

SUMMARY: This document contains an amendment to interim final regulations implementing the rules for group health plans and health insurance coverage in the group and individual markets under provisions of the Patient Protection and Affordable Care Act regarding status as a grandfathered health plan; the amendment permits certain changes in policies, certificates, or contracts of insurance without loss of grandfathered status.

DATES: *Effective Date.* This amendment to the interim final regulations is effective on November 15, 2010.

Comment Date. Comments are due on or before December 17, 2010.

ADDRESSES: Written comments may be submitted to any of the addresses specified below. Any comment that is submitted to any Department will be shared with the other Departments. Please do not submit duplicates.

All comments will be made available to the public. Warning: Do not include any personally identifiable information (such as name, address, or other contact information) or confidential business information that you do not want publicly disclosed. All comments may be posted on the Internet and can be retrieved by most Internet search engines. Comments may be submitted anonymously.

Department of Labor. Comments to the Department of Labor, identified by RIN 1210–AB42, by one of the following methods:

• *Federal eRulemaking Portal: http:// www.regulations.gov.* Follow the instructions for submitting comments.

• *E-mail: E-OHPSCA1251amend.EBSA@dol.gov.*

• *Mail or Hand Delivery:* Office of Health Plan Standards and Compliance Assistance, Employee Benefits Security Administration, Room N–5653, U.S. Department of Labor, 200 Constitution Avenue NW., Washington, DC 20210, *Attention:* RIN 1210–AB42.

Comments received by the Department of Labor will be posted without change to *http:// www.regulations.gov* and *http:// www.dol.gov/ebsa,* and available for public inspection at the Public Disclosure Room, N–1513, Employee Benefits Security Administration, 200 Constitution Avenue, NW., Washington, DC 20210.

Department of Health and Human Services. In commenting, please refer to file code OCIIO–9991–IFC2. Because of staff and resource limitations, we cannot accept comments by facsimile (FAX) transmission.

You may submit comments in one of four ways (please choose only one of the ways listed):

• *Electronically.* You may submit electronic comments on this regulation to *http://www.regulations.gov.* Follow the instructions under the "More Search Options" tab.

• *By regular mail.* You may mail written comments to the following address ONLY: Office of Consumer Information and Insurance Oversight, Department of Health and Human Services, Attention: OCIIO–9991–IFC2, Room 445–G, Hubert H. Humphrey Building, 200 Independence Avenue, SW., Washington, DC 20201.

Please allow sufficient time for mailed comments to be received before the close of the comment period.

• *By express or overnight mail.* You may send written comments to the following address only: Office of Consumer Information and Insurance Oversight, Department of Health and Human Services, Attention: OCIIO–

Federal Register / Vol. 75, No. 221 / Wednesday, November 17, 2010 / Rules and Regulations **70115**

9991–IFC2, Room 445–G, Hubert H. Humphrey Building, 200 Independence Avenue, SW., Washington, DC 20201.

• *By hand or courier.* If you prefer, you may deliver (by hand or courier) your written comments before the close of the comment period to the following address: Office of Consumer Information and Insurance Oversight, Department of Health and Human Services, Attention: OCIIO–9991–IFC2, Room 445–G, Hubert H. Humphrey Building, 200 Independence Avenue, SW., Washington, DC 20201.

(Because access to the interior of the Hubert H. Humphrey Building is not readily available to persons without Federal government identification, commenters are encouraged to leave their comments in the OCIIO drop slots located in the main lobby of the building. A stamp-in clock is available for persons wishing to retain a proof of filing by stamping in and retaining an extra copy of the comments being filed.)

Comments mailed to the address indicated as appropriate for hand or courier delivery may be delayed and received after the comment period.

Comments received timely will also be available for public inspection as they are received, generally beginning approximately three weeks after publication of a document, at the headquarters of the Centers for Medicare & Medicaid Services, 7500 Security Boulevard, Baltimore, Maryland 21244, Monday through Friday of each week from 8:30 a.m. to 4 p.m. EST. To schedule an appointment to view public comments, phone 1–800–743–3951.

Internal Revenue Service. Comments to the IRS, identified by REG–118412–10, by one of the following methods:

• *Federal eRulemaking Portal: http://www.regulations.gov.* Follow the instructions for submitting comments.

• *Mail:* CC:PA:LPD:PR (REG–118412–10), room 5205, Internal Revenue Service, P.O. Box 7604, Ben Franklin Station, Washington, DC 20044.

• *Hand or courier delivery:* Monday through Friday between the hours of 8 a.m. and 4 p.m. to: CC:PA:LPD:PR (REG–118412–10), Courier's Desk, Internal Revenue Service, 1111 Constitution Avenue, NW., Washington, DC 20224.

All submissions to the IRS will be open to public inspection and copying in room 1621, 1111 Constitution Avenue, NW., Washington, DC from 9 a.m. to 4 p.m.

FOR FURTHER INFORMATION CONTACT: Amy Turner or Beth Baum, Employee Benefits Security Administration, Department of Labor, at (202) 693–8335; Karen Levin, Internal Revenue Service,

Department of the Treasury, at (202) 622–6080; Lisa Campbell, Office of Consumer Information and Insurance Oversight, Department of Health and Human Services, at (301) 492–4100.

Customer Service Information: Individuals interested in obtaining information from the Department of Labor concerning employment-based health coverage laws may call the EBSA Toll-Free Hotline at 1–866–444–EBSA (3272) or visit the Department of Labor's Web site (*http://www.dol.gov/ebsa*). In addition, information from HHS on private health insurance for consumers can be found on the Centers for Medicare & Medicaid Services (CMS) Web site (*http://www.cms.hhs.gov/ HealthInsReformforConsume/ 01_Overview.asp*) and the Office of Consumer Information & Insurance Oversight (OCIIO) Web site (*http:// www.hhs.gov/OCIIO*).

SUPPLEMENTARY INFORMATION:

I. Background

The Patient Protection and Affordable Care Act (the Affordable Care Act), Public Law 111–148, was enacted on March 23, 2010; the Health Care and Education Reconciliation Act (the Reconciliation Act), Public Law 111–152, was enacted on March 30, 2010. The Affordable Care Act and the Reconciliation Act reorganize, amend, and add to the provisions in part A of title XXVII of the Public Health Service Act (PHS Act) relating to group health plans and health insurance issuers in the group and individual markets. The term "group health plan" includes both insured and self-insured group health plans.[1] The Affordable Care Act adds section 715(a)(1) to the Employee Retirement Income Security Act (ERISA) and section 9815(a)(1) to the Internal Revenue Code (the Code) to incorporate the provisions of part A of title XXVII of the PHS Act into ERISA and the Code, and make them applicable to group health plans, and health insurance issuers providing health insurance coverage in connection with group health plans. The PHS Act sections incorporated by this reference are sections 2701 through 2728. PHS Act sections 2701 through 2719A are substantially new, though they incorporate some provisions of prior law. PHS Act sections 2722 through 2728 are sections of prior law renumbered, with some, mostly minor,

changes. Section 1251 of the Affordable Care Act, as modified by section 10103 of the Affordable Care Act and section 2301 of the Reconciliation Act, specifies that certain plans or coverage existing as of the date of enactment (that is, grandfathered health plans) are subject to only certain provisions.

The Departments of Health and Human Services, Labor, and the Treasury (the Departments) previously issued interim final regulations implementing section 1251 of the Affordable Care Act; these interim final regulations were published in the **Federal Register** on June 17, 2010 (75 FR 34538). Additionally, on September 20, 2010,[2] October 8, 2010,[3] October 12, 2010,[4] and October 28, 2010,[5] the Departments issued subregulatory guidance on a number of issues pertaining to the implementation of the Affordable Care Act, including several clarifications relating to the interim final regulations on grandfathered health plans.

Section 1251 of the Affordable Care Act, as modified by section 10103 of the Affordable Care Act and section 2301 of the Reconciliation Act, provides that certain plans or coverage existing as of March 23, 2010 (the date of enactment of the Affordable Care Act) are subject to only certain provisions of the Affordable Care Act. The statute and the interim final regulations refer to these plans or health insurance coverage as grandfathered health plans. The statute and the interim final regulations provide that a group health plan or group or individual health insurance coverage is a grandfathered health plan with respect to individuals enrolled on March 23, 2010 regardless of whether an individual later renews the coverage. The interim final regulations specify certain changes to a plan or coverage that would cause it to no longer be a grandfathered health plan.

In addition, the statute and the interim final regulations provide that a group health plan that provided coverage on March 23, 2010 generally is also a grandfathered health plan with

---

[1] The term "group health plan" is used in title XXVII of the PHS Act, part 7 of ERISA, and chapter 100 of the Code, and is distinct from the term "health plan," as used in other provisions of title I of the Affordable Care Act. The term "health plan," as used in those provisions, does not include self-insured group health plans.

[2] The subregulatory guidance took the form of "frequently asked questions" (FAQs). The September 20, 2010 FAQs are available at *http:// www.dol.gov/ebsa/faqs/faq-aca.html* and *http:// www.hhs.gov/ociio/regulations/questions.html.*

[3] The October 8, 2010 FAQs are available at *http://www.dol.gov/ebsa/faqs/faq-aca2.html* and *http://www.hhs.gov/ociio/regulations/ implementation_faq.html.*

[4] The October 12, 2010 FAQs are available at *http://www.dol.gov/ebsa/faqs/faq-aca3.html* and *http://www.hhs.gov/ociio/regulations/ implementation_faq.html.*

[5] The October 28, 2010 FAQs are available at *http://www.dol.gov/ebsa/faqs/faq-aca4.html* and *http://www.hhs.gov/ociio/regulations/ implementation_faq.html.*

respect to new employees (whether newly hired or newly enrolled) and their families that enroll in the grandfathered health plan after March 23, 2010. The interim final regulations clarify that, in such cases, any health insurance coverage provided under the group health plan in which an individual was enrolled on March 23, 2010 is also a grandfathered health plan.

Paragraph (g)(1) of the interim final regulations includes rules for determining when changes to the terms of a plan or health insurance coverage cause the plan or coverage to cease to be a grandfathered health plan. In addition to the changes described in paragraph (g)(1) of the interim final regulations that cause a plan to cease to be a grandfathered health plan, paragraph (a)(1)(ii) of the interim final regulations provides that if an employer or employee organization enters into a new policy, certificate, or contract of insurance after March 23, 2010, the policy, certificate, or contract of insurance is not a grandfathered health plan with respect to individuals in the group health plan. For example, under the interim final regulations, if a group health plan changes issuers after March 23, 2010, the group health plan ceases to be a grandfathered health plan, even if the plan otherwise would be a grandfathered health plan under the standards set forth in paragraph (g)(1).[6] In contrast, under the interim final regulations, a change in third party administrator (TPA) by a self-insured group health plan does not cause the plan to relinquish grandfather status, provided that the change of TPA does not result in any other change that would cause loss of grandfather status under paragraph (g)(1).

II. Overview of Amendment to the Interim Final Regulations

The Departments have received comments on paragraph (a)(1)(ii) of the interim final regulations, which provides that a group health plan will relinquish grandfather status if it changes issuers or policies. The comments expressed four principal concerns about this provision of the regulations. First, commenters raised

the concern that this provision treats insured group health plans, which cannot change issuers or policies without ceasing to be a grandfathered health plan, differently from self-insured group health plans, which can change TPAs without relinquishing grandfather status, as long as any other plan change (such as cost sharing or employer contributions) does not exceed the standards of paragraph (g)(1) of the interim final regulations. Second, commenters raised questions about circumstances in which a group health plan changes its issuer involuntarily (for example, the issuer withdraws from the market) yet the plan sponsor wants to maintain its grandfather status with a new issuer. Third, commenters noted that the provision would unnecessarily restrict the ability of issuers to reissue policies to current plan sponsors for administrative reasons unrelated to any change in the underlying terms of the health insurance coverage (for example, to transition the policy to a subsidiary of the original issuer or to consolidate a policy with its various riders or amendments) without loss of grandfather status. Finally, commenters expressed concern that the provision terminating grandfather status upon any change in issuer gives issuers undue and unfair leverage in negotiating the price of coverage renewals with the sponsors of grandfathered health plans, and that this interferes with the health care cost containment that tends to result from price competition.

The interim final regulations issued on June 17, 2010 were based on an interpretation of the language in section 1251 of the Affordable Care Act providing that grandfather status is based on "coverage under a group health plan or health insurance coverage in which such individual was enrolled on the date of the enactment of the Act." In adopting the interim final regulations, the Departments did not consider a new insurance policy issued after March 23, 2010 to be a grandfathered health plan (except for the special rule for a group health plan maintained pursuant to a collective bargaining agreement) because "coverage" under the new policy was not in place on that date.

Following review of the comments submitted on this issue and further review and consideration of the provisions of section 1251 of the Affordable Care Act, the Departments have determined it is appropriate to amend the interim final regulations to allow a group health plan to change health insurance coverage (that is, to allow a group health plan to enter into a new policy, certificate, or contract of insurance) without ceasing to be a

grandfathered health plan, provided that the plan continues to comply fully with the standards set forth in paragraph (g)(1). For purposes of section 1251 of the Affordable Care Act, the Departments now conclude that it is reasonable to construe the statutory term "group health plan" to apply the grandfather provisions uniformly to both self-insured and insured group health plans (and, consequently, to health insurance coverage offered in connection with a group health plan). Where insured coverage is provided not through a group health plan but instead in the individual market, a change in issuer would still be a change in the health insurance coverage in which the individual was enrolled on March 23, 2010, and thus the new individual policy, certificate, or contract of insurance would not be a grandfathered health plan.

This amendment modifies paragraph (a)(1) of the interim final regulations, which previously caused a group health plan to cease to be a grandfathered health plan if the plan entered into a new policy, certificate, or contract of insurance. The modification provides that a group health plan does not cease to be grandfathered health plan coverage merely because the plan (or its sponsor) enters into a new policy, certificate, or contract of insurance after March 23, 2010[7] (for example, a plan enters into a contract with a new issuer or a new policy is issued with an existing issuer). The amendment applies to such changes to group health insurance coverage that are effective on or after November 15, 2010, the date the amendment to the interim final regulations was made available for public inspection; the amendment does not apply retroactively to such changes to group health insurance coverage that were effective before this date.[8] For this purpose, the date the new coverage becomes effective is the operative date, not the date a contract for a new policy, certificate or contract of insurance is entered into. Therefore, for example, if a plan enters into an agreement with an issuer on September 28, 2010 for a new policy to be effective on January 1, 2011, then January 1, 2011 is the date the new policy is effective and, therefore, the relevant date for purposes of determining the application of the

---

[6] In accordance with statutory provisions relating to collectively bargained group health plans, the interim final regulations include an exception for a group health plan governed by a collective bargaining agreement that was in effect on March 23, 2010. In such a case, the grandfathered group health plan is permitted to change issuers, or change from a self-insured plan to an insured plan. or make a change described under paragraph (g)(1) of the interim final regulations (which would otherwise end grandfather status) and remain a grandfathered health plan for the remainder of the duration of the collective bargaining agreement.

[7] Of course, with respect to changes to group health insurance coverage on or after March 23, 2010 but before June 14, 2010, the Departments' enforcement safe harbor remains in effect for good faith efforts to comply with a reasonable interpretation of the statute.

[8] As noted below, the Departments are inviting comments on this amendment to the interim final regulations.

amendment to the interim final regulations. If, however, the plan entered into an agreement with an issuer on July 1, 2010 for a new policy to be effective on September 1, 2010, then the amendment would not apply and the plan would cease to be a grandfathered health plan.

Notwithstanding the ability to change health insurance coverage pursuant to the modification made by the amendment, if the new policy, certificate, or contract of insurance includes changes described in paragraph (g)(1) of the interim final regulations, the plan ceases to be a grandfathered health plan. In applying this amendment, as with other provisions of the interim final regulations, the rules apply separately to each benefit package made available under a group health plan.

The amendment also provides that, to maintain status as a grandfathered health plan, a group health plan that enters into a new policy, certificate, or contract of insurance must provide to the new health insurance issuer (and the new health insurance issuer must require) documentation of plan terms (including benefits, cost sharing, employer contributions, and annual limits) under the prior health coverage sufficient to determine whether any change described in paragraph (g)(1) is being made. This documentation may include a copy of the policy or summary plan description. The amendment also makes minor conforming changes to other provisions of the interim final regulations.

Thus, a plan can retain its grandfather status if it changes its carrier, so long as it has not made any other changes that would revoke its status. This amendment is being issued on an interim final basis to notify plans as soon as possible of the change and is effective prospectively to minimize disruption to participants and beneficiaries. The Departments are continuing to review and evaluate the comments received in response to the June 17, 2010 interim final regulations. In addition, the Departments invite comments on this amendment to the interim final regulations, including the prospective effective date of the rule and how that affects plans with different plan years. Final regulations on grandfathered health plans will be published in the near future.

III. Interim Final Rules and Waiver of Delay of Effective Date

Section 9833 of the Code, section 734 of ERISA, and section 2792 of the PHS Act authorize the Secretaries of the Treasury, Labor, and HHS (collectively,

the Secretaries) to promulgate any interim final rules that they determine are appropriate to carry out the provisions of chapter 100 of the Code, part 7 of subtitle B of title I of ERISA, and part A of title XXVII of the PHS Act, which include PHS Act sections 2701 through 2728 and the incorporation of those sections into ERISA section 715 and Code section 9815. The rule set forth in this amendment governs the applicability of the requirements in these sections and is therefore appropriate to carry them out. Therefore, the foregoing interim final rule authority applies to this amendment.

In addition, under Section 553(b) of the Administrative Procedure Act (APA) (5 U.S.C. 551 *et seq.*) a general notice of proposed rulemaking is not required when an agency, for good cause, finds that notice and public comment thereon are impracticable, unnecessary, or contrary to the public interest. Although the provisions of the APA that ordinarily require a notice of proposed rulemaking do not apply here because of the specific authority granted by section 9833 of the Code, section 734 of ERISA, and section 2792 of the PHS Act, even if the APA were applicable, the Secretaries have determined that it would be impracticable and contrary to the public interest to delay putting the provisions of this amendment to the June 17, 2010 interim final regulations in place until an additional public notice and comment process was completed.

As noted in the preamble to the June 17, 2010 interim final regulations, numerous provisions of the Affordable Care Act are applicable for plan years (in the individual market, policy years) beginning on or after September 23, 2010, six months after date of enactment. Because grandfathered health plans are exempt from many of these provisions while group health plans and group and individual health insurance coverage that are not grandfathered health plans must comply with them, it was critical for plans and issuers to receive clear guidance as to whether they were so exempt as soon as possible; accordingly, the June 17, 2010 interim final regulations were published without prior notice and comment. While the Affordable Care Act provisions have become effective with respect to certain plans and coverage, the majority of plans and coverage have not yet become subject to the Act. It is critical to provide those plans with the guidance in these interim final rules immediately. In addition, the provisions of this amendment essentially are the product of prior notice and comment, as

they are a logical outgrowth of the June 17, 2010 interim final regulations which provided an opportunity for public comment, and are being issued in response to public comments received.

For the foregoing reasons, the Departments have determined that it is impracticable and contrary to the public interest to engage in full notice and comment rulemaking before putting these regulations into effect, and that it is in the public interest to promulgate interim final regulations.

In addition, under Section 553(d) of the APA, regulations are to be published at least 30 days before they take effect. Again, under section 553(d)(3), this requirement may be waived "for good cause found and published with the rule." For the reasons set forth above, the Departments have determined that there is good cause for waiver of the 30 day delay of effective date requirement in section 553(d).

IV. Economic Impact and Paperwork Burden

A. Overview and Need for Regulatory Action—Department of Labor and Department of Health and Human Services

As stated earlier in this preamble, the Departments of Health and Human Services, Labor, and the Treasury (the Departments) previously issued interim final regulations implementing section 1251 of the Affordable Care Act that were published in the **Federal Register** on June 17, 2010 (75 FR 34538). Paragraph (a)(1)(ii) of the interim final regulations provides that if a group health plan changes the issuer providing the insured health coverage after March 23, 2010, the group health plan ceases to be a grandfathered health plan. Paragraph (g)(1) of the interim final regulations includes rules for determining when changes to the terms of a plan or health insurance coverage cause a plan or coverage to cease to be a grandfathered health plan.

As described earlier in this preamble, comments expressed a number of concerns regarding the change in issuer rule. Among other concerns, comments stated that the change in issuer rule provides issuers with undue leverage in negotiating the price of coverage renewals with grandfathered health plans, because a change in carrier would result in plans relinquishing their grandfathered status. Therefore, in effect, the provision could impede employers' efforts to obtain group health insurance coverage for their employees at the lowest cost. Commenters also expressed concern that the rule creates an unlevel playing field for self-insured and fully-insured group health plans, because the former could change plan administrators without relinquishing their grandfathered health plan status, while the latter could not change issuers without relinquishing such status.

After reviewing the comments concerning this issue and further analyzing the statutory provision, the Departments have determined that it is appropriate to amend the interim final regulations to allow group health plans to change a health insurance policy or issuer providing health insurance coverage without ceasing to be a grandfathered health plan, provided that the standards set forth under paragraph (g)(1) of the interim final regulations are met. The Departments expect that this amendment will result in a small increase in the number of plans retaining their grandfathered status relative to the estimates made in the interim final regulations. The Departments did not produce a range of estimates for the number of affected entities given considerable uncertainty about the behavioral response to this amendment. For a further discussion, see Section II. Overview of Amendment to the Interim Final Regulations, above.

B. Executive Order 12866—Department of Labor and Department of Health and Human Services

Under Executive Order 12866 (58 FR 51735), "significant" regulatory actions are subject to review by the Office of Management and Budget (OMB). Section 3(f) of the Executive Order defines a "significant regulatory action" as an action that is likely to result in a rule (1) having an annual effect on the economy of $100 million or more in any one year, or adversely and materially affecting a sector of the economy, productivity, competition, jobs, the environment, public health or safety, or State, local or tribal governments or communities (also referred to as "economically significant"); (2) creating a serious inconsistency or otherwise interfering with an action taken or planned by another agency; (3) materially altering the budgetary impacts of entitlement grants, user fees, or loan programs or the rights and obligations of recipients thereof; or (4) raising novel legal or policy issues arising out of legal mandates, the President's priorities, or the principles set forth in the Executive Order. OMB has determined that this amendment to the interim final regulations is significant within the meaning of section 3(f)(4) of the Executive Order. Accordingly, OMB has reviewed the amendment pursuant to the Executive Order.

C. Regulatory Flexibility Act— Department of Labor and Department of Health and Human Services

The Regulatory Flexibility Act (5 U.S.C. 601 et seq.) (RFA) imposes certain requirements with respect to Federal rules that are subject to the notice and comment requirements of section 553(b) of the APA (5 U.S.C. 551 et seq.) and that are likely to have a significant economic impact on a substantial number of small entities. Under Section 553(b) of the APA, a general notice of proposed rulemaking is not required when an agency, for good cause, finds that notice and public comment thereon are impracticable, unnecessary, or contrary to the public interest. The interim final regulations were exempt from the APA, because the Departments made a good cause finding that a general notice of proposed rulemaking is not necessary earlier in this preamble. Therefore, the RFA did not apply and the Departments were not required to either certify that the regulations or this amendment would not have a significant economic impact on a substantial number of small entities or conduct a regulatory flexibility analysis.

Nevertheless, the Departments carefully considered the likely impact of the amendment on small entities and believe that the amendment will have a positive impact on small plans, because such plans are more likely to be fully-insured. The Departments estimated in the regulatory impact analysis for the interim final regulations that small plans were more likely to relinquish grandfathered health plan status due to changes in issuers or policies than large plans. Therefore, this amendment to the interim final regulations will benefit small plans that want to retain their grandfathered health plan status while still changing health insurance issuers. This change should give employers greater flexibility to keep premiums affordable for the same plan.

D. Special Analyses—Department of the Treasury

Notwithstanding the determinations of the Department of Labor and Department of Health and Human Services, for purposes of the Department of the Treasury, it has been determined that this Treasury decision is not a significant regulatory action for purposes of Executive Order 12866. Therefore, a regulatory assessment is not required. It has also been determined that section 553(b) of the Administrative Procedure Act (5 U.S.C. chapter 5) does not apply to these regulations. For the applicability of the RFA, refer to the Special Analyses section in the preamble to the cross-referencing notice of proposed rulemaking published elsewhere in this issue of the **Federal Register**. Pursuant to section 7805(f) of the Code, these temporary regulations have been submitted to the Chief Counsel for Advocacy of the Small Business Administration for comment on their impact on small businesses.

E. Paperwork Reduction Act

As part of their continuing efforts to reduce paperwork and respondent burden, the Departments conduct a preclearance consultation program to provide the general public and Federal agencies with an opportunity to comment on proposed and continuing collections of information in accordance with the Paperwork Reduction Act of 1995 (PRA) (44 U.S.C. 3506(c)(2)(A)). This helps to ensure that requested data can be provided in the desired format, reporting burden (time and financial resources) is minimized, and collection requirements on respondents can be properly assessed.

As discussed earlier in this preamble, the amendment to the interim final regulation adds a new disclosure requirement that requires the group health plan that is changing health insurance coverage to provide to the succeeding health insurance issuer (and the succeeding health insurance issuer must require) documentation of plan terms (including benefits, cost sharing, employer contributions, and annual limits) under the prior health insurance coverage sufficient to make a determination whether the standards of paragraph (g)(1) are exceeded. The Departments expect that this amendment will result in a small increase in the number of plans retaining their grandfathered status relative to the estimates made in the interim final regulations. Although the Departments did not produce a range of estimates for the number of affected entities due to the considerable uncertainty regarding the behavioral response to this amendment, the Departments estimate that the new disclosure requirement associated with the amendment will result in a total hour burden of 3,845 hours and a total cost burden of $260,000.[9] The Departments welcome comments on this estimate.

The Office of Management and Budget has approved revisions to the ICRs contained under OMB Control Numbers

---

[9] The Departments applied the same methodology that was used in estimating the hour and cost burden associated with the information collection requests (ICRs) contained in the interim final regulations to make this estimate.

1210–0140 (Department of Labor), 1545–2178 (Department of the Treasury; Internal Revenue Service), and 0938–1093 (Department of Health and Human Services) reflecting this estimate. A copy of the ICR may be obtained by contacting the PRA addressee: G. Christopher Cosby, Office of Policy and Research, U.S. Department of Labor, Employee Benefits Security Administration, 200 Constitution Avenue, NW., Room N–5718, Washington, DC 20210. Telephone: (202) 693–8410; Fax: (202) 219–2745. These are not toll-free numbers. E-mail: *ebsa.opr@dol.gov*. ICRs submitted to OMB also are available at reginfo.gov (*http://www.reginfo.gov/public/do/PRAMain*).

F. Congressional Review Act

This amendment to the interim final regulations is subject to the Congressional Review Act provisions of the Small Business Regulatory Enforcement Fairness Act of 1996 (5 U.S.C. 801 *et seq.*) and has been transmitted to Congress and the Comptroller General for review. The interim final rule is not a "major rule" as that term is defined in 5 U.S.C. 804, because it does not result in (1) an annual effect on the economy of $100 million or more; (2) a major increase in costs or prices for consumers, individual industries, or Federal, State, or local government agencies, or geographic regions; or (3) significant adverse effects on competition, employment, investment, productivity, innovation, or on the ability of United States-based enterprises to compete with foreign-based enterprises in domestic and export markets.

G. Unfunded Mandates Reform Act

The Unfunded Mandates Reform Act of 1995 (Pub. L. 104–4) requires agencies to prepare several analytic statements before proposing any rules that may result in annual expenditures of $100 million (as adjusted for inflation) by State, local and tribal governments or the private sector. This amendment to the interim final regulations is not subject to the Unfunded Mandates Reform Act, because they are being issued as an interim final regulation. However, consistent with the policy embodied in the Unfunded Mandates Reform Act, this amendment to the interim final regulations has been designed to be the least burdensome alternative for State, local and tribal governments, and the private sector, while achieving the objectives of the Affordable Care Act.

H. Federalism Statement—Department of Labor and Department of Health and Human Services

Executive Order 13132 outlines fundamental principles of federalism, and requires the adherence to specific criteria by Federal agencies in the process of their formulation and implementation of policies that have "substantial direct effects" on the States, the relationship between the national government and States, or on the distribution of power and responsibilities among the various levels of government. Federal agencies promulgating regulations that have these federalism implications must consult with State and local officials, and describe the extent of their consultation and the nature of the concerns of State and local officials in the preamble to the regulation.

In the Departments' view, this amendment to the regulation has federalism implications, because it has direct effects on the States, the relationship between the national government and States, or on the distribution of power and responsibilities among various levels of government. However, in the Departments' view, the federalism implications of the regulation is substantially mitigated because, with respect to health insurance issuers, the Departments expect that the majority of States will enact laws or take other appropriate action resulting in their meeting or exceeding the Federal standard.

In general, through section 514, ERISA supersedes State laws to the extent that they relate to any covered employee benefit plan, and preserves State laws that regulate insurance, banking, or securities. While ERISA prohibits States from regulating a plan as an insurance or investment company or bank, the preemption provisions of ERISA section 731 and PHS Act section 2724 (implemented in 29 CFR 2590.731(a) and 45 CFR 146.143(a)) apply so that the HIPAA requirements (including those of the Affordable Care Act) are not to be "construed to supersede any provision of State law which establishes, implements, or continues in effect any standard or requirement solely relating to health insurance issuers in connection with group health insurance coverage except to the extent that such standard or requirement prevents the application of a requirement" of a Federal standard. The conference report accompanying HIPAA indicates that this is intended to be the "narrowest" preemption of State laws. (See House Conf. Rep. No. 104–

736, at 205, reprinted in 1996 U.S. Code Cong. & Admin. News 2018.) States may continue to apply State law requirements except to the extent that such requirements prevent the application of the Affordable Care Act requirements that are the subject of this rulemaking. State insurance laws that are more stringent than the Federal requirements are unlikely to "prevent the application of" the Affordable Care Act, and be preempted. Accordingly, States have significant latitude to impose requirements on health insurance issuers that are more restrictive than the Federal law.

In compliance with the requirement of Executive Order 13132 that agencies examine closely any policies that may have federalism implications or limit the policy making discretion of the States, the Departments have engaged in efforts to consult with and work cooperatively with affected State and local officials, including attending conferences of the National Association of Insurance Commissioners and consulting with State insurance officials on an individual basis. It is expected that the Departments will act in a similar fashion in enforcing the Affordable Care Act requirements. Throughout the process of developing this amendment, to the extent feasible within the specific preemption provisions of HIPAA as it applies to the Affordable Care Act, the Departments have attempted to balance the States' interests in regulating health insurance issuers, and Congress' intent to provide uniform minimum protections to consumers in every State. By doing so, it is the Departments' view that they have complied with the requirements of Executive Order 13132.

Pursuant to the requirements set forth in section 8(a) of Executive Order 13132, and by the signatures affixed to these regulations, the Departments certify that the Employee Benefits Security Administration and the Office of Consumer Information and Insurance Oversight have complied with the requirements of Executive Order 13132 for the attached amendment to the interim final regulations in a meaningful and timely manner.

V. Statutory Authority

The Department of the Treasury temporary regulations are adopted pursuant to the authority contained in sections 7805 and 9833 of the Code.

The Department of Labor interim final regulations are adopted pursuant to the authority contained in 29 U.S.C. 1027, 1059, 1135, 1161–1168, 1169, 1181–1183, 1181 note, 1185, 1185a, 1185b, 1191, 1191a, 1191b, and 1191c; sec.

101(g), Pub. L. 104–191, 110 Stat. 1936; sec. 401(b), Pub. L. 105–200, 112 Stat. 645 (42 U.S.C. 651 note); sec. 512(d), Pub. L. 110–343, 122 Stat. 3881; sec. 1001, 1201, and 1562(e), Pub. L. 111–148, 124 Stat. 119, as amended by Public Law 111–152, 124 Stat. 1029; Secretary of Labor's Order 6–2009, 74 FR 21524 (May 7, 2009).

The Department of Health and Human Services interim final regulations are adopted pursuant to the authority contained in sections 2701 through 2763, 2791, and 2792 of the PHS Act (42 U.S.C. 300gg through 300gg–63, 300gg–91, and 300gg–92), as amended.

List of Subjects

26 CFR Part 54

Excise taxes, Health care, Health insurance, Pensions, Reporting and recordkeeping requirements.

29 CFR Part 2590

Continuation coverage, Disclosure, Employee benefit plans, Group health plans, Health care, Health insurance, Medical child support, Reporting and recordkeeping requirements.

45 CFR Part 147

Health care, Health insurance, Reporting and recordkeeping requirements, and State regulation of health insurance.

Approved: November 8, 2010.

Steven T. Miller,

Deputy Commissioner for Services and Enforcement, Internal Revenue Service.

Michael F. Mundaca,

Assistant Secretary of the Treasury (Tax Policy).

Signed this 5th day of November 2010.

Phyllis C. Borzi,

Assistant Secretary, Employee Benefits Security Administration, Department of Labor.

Approved: November 9, 2010.

Jay Angoff,

Director, Office of Consumer Information and Insurance Oversight.

Approved: November 9, 2010.

Kathleen Sebelius,

Secretary, Department of Health and Human Services.

Department of the Treasury

Internal Revenue Service

26 CFR Chapter I

■ Accordingly, 26 CFR part 54 is amended as follows:

PART 54—PENSION EXCISE TAXES

■ **Paragraph 1.** The authority citation for part 54 continues to read in part as follows:

Authority: 26 U.S.C. 7805. * * *

■ **Par. 2.** Section 54.9815–1251T is amended by:

■ 1. Revising paragraph (a)(1).
■ 2. Redesignating paragraphs (a)(3) introductory text, (a)(3)(i), and (a)(3)(ii) as paragraphs (a)(3)(i), (a)(3)(i)(A) and (a)(3)(i)(B), respectively.
■ 3. Adding new paragraph (a)(3)(ii).
■ 4. Removing paragraphs (a)(5) and (f)(2).
■ 5. Redesignating paragraph (f)(1) as paragraph (f).
■ 6. Revising the last sentence in newly-designated paragraph (f).
■ 7. Revising paragraph (g)(4) *Example 9.*

The revisions and addition reads as follows:

§ 54.9815–1251T Preservation of right to maintain existing coverage (temporary).

(a) *Definition of grandfathered health plan coverage*—(1) *In general*—(i) *Grandfathered health plan coverage.* Grandfathered health plan coverage means coverage provided by a group health plan, or a health insurance issuer, in which an individual was enrolled on March 23, 2010 (for as long as it maintains that status under the rules of this section). A group health plan or group health insurance coverage does not cease to be grandfathered health plan coverage merely because one or more (or even all) individuals enrolled on March 23, 2010 cease to be covered, provided that the plan has continuously covered someone since March 23, 2010 (not necessarily the same person, but at all times at least one person). In addition, subject to the limitation set forth in paragraph (a)(1)(ii) of this section, a group health plan (and any health insurance coverage offered in connection with the group health plan) does not cease to be a grandfathered health plan merely because the plan (or its sponsor) enters into a new policy, certificate, or contract of insurance after March 23, 2010 (for example, a plan enters into a contract with a new issuer or a new policy is issued with an existing issuer). For purposes of this section, a plan or health insurance coverage that provides grandfathered health plan coverage is referred to as a grandfathered health plan. The rules of this section apply separately to each benefit package made available under a group health plan or health insurance coverage.

(ii) *Changes in group health insurance coverage.* Subject to paragraphs (f) and

(g)(2) of this section, if a group health plan (including a group health plan that was self-insured on March 23, 2010) or its sponsor enters into a new policy, certificate, or contract of insurance after March 23, 2010 that is effective before November 15, 2010, then the plan ceases to be a grandfathered health plan.

*   *   *   *   *

(3)(i) * * *

(ii) *Change in group health insurance coverage.* To maintain status as a grandfathered health plan, a group health plan that enters into a new policy, certificate, or contract of insurance must provide to the new health insurance issuer (and the new health insurance issuer must require) documentation of plan terms (including benefits, cost sharing, employer contributions, and annual limits) under the prior health coverage sufficient to determine whether a change causing a cessation of grandfathered health plan status under paragraph (g)(1) of this section has occurred.

*   *   *   *   *

(f) * * * After the date on which the last of the collective bargaining agreements relating to the coverage that was in effect on March 23, 2010 terminates, the determination of whether health insurance coverage maintained pursuant to a collective bargaining agreement is grandfathered health plan coverage is made under the rules of this section other than this paragraph (f) (comparing the terms of the health insurance coverage after the date the last collective bargaining agreement terminates with the terms of the health insurance coverage that were in effect on March 23, 2010).

(g) * * *
(4) * * *

Example 9. (i) *Facts.* A group health plan not maintained pursuant to a collective bargaining agreement offers three benefit packages on March 23, 2010. Option F is a self-insured option. Options G and H are insured options. Beginning July 1, 2013, the plan increases coinsurance under Option H from 10% to 15%.

(ii) *Conclusion.* In this *Example 9,* the coverage under Option H is not grandfathered health plan coverage as of July 1, 2013, consistent with the rule in paragraph (g)(1)(ii) of this section. Whether the coverage under Options F and G is grandfathered health plan coverage is determined separately under the rules of this paragraph (g).

Department of Labor

Employee Benefits Security Administration

29 CFR Chapter XXV

■ 29 CFR part 2590 is amended as follows:

PART 2590—RULES AND REGULATIONS FOR GROUP HEALTH PLANS

■ 1. The authority citation for part 2590 continues to read as follows:

Authority: 29 U.S.C. 1027, 1059, 1135, 1161–1168, 1169, 1181–1183, 1181 note, 1185, 1185a, 1185b, 1191, 1191a, 1191b, and 1191c; sec. 101(g), Pub. L.104–191, 110 Stat. 1936; sec. 401(b), Pub. L. 105–200, 112 Stat. 645 (42 U.S.C. 651 note); sec. 512(d), Pub. L. 110–343, 122 Stat. 3881; sec. 1001, 1201, and 1562(e), Pub. L. 111–148, 124 Stat. 119, as amended by Pub. L. 111–152, 124 Stat. 1029; Secretary of Labor's Order 6–2009, 74 FR 21524 (May 7, 2009).

■ 2. Section 2590.715–1251 is amended by:
■ 1. Revising paragraph (a)(1).
■ 2. Redesignating paragraphs (a)(3), (a)(3)(i) and (a)(3)(ii) as paragraphs (a)(3)(i), (a)(3)(i)(A) and (a)(3)(i)(B), respectively.
■ 3. Adding new paragraph (a)(3)(ii).
■ 4. Removing paragraphs (a)(5) and (f)(2).
■ 5. Redesignating paragraph (f)(1) as paragraph (f).
■ 6. Revising the last sentence in newly-designated paragraph (f).
■ 7. Revising paragraph (g)(4) *Example 9*.

The revisions and addition reads as follows:

§ 2590.715–1251   Preservation of right to maintain existing coverage.

(a) *Definition of grandfathered health plan coverage*—(1) *In general*—(i) *Grandfathered health plan coverage. Grandfathered health plan coverage* means coverage provided by a group health plan, or a health insurance issuer, in which an individual was enrolled on March 23, 2010 (for as long as it maintains that status under the rules of this section). A group health plan or group health insurance coverage does not cease to be grandfathered health plan coverage merely because one or more (or even all) individuals enrolled on March 23, 2010 cease to be covered, provided that the plan has continuously covered someone since March 23, 2010 (not necessarily the same person, but at all times at least one person). In addition, subject to the limitation set forth in paragraph (a)(1)(ii) of this section, a group health plan (and any health insurance coverage offered in connection with the group health plan) does not cease to be a grandfathered health plan merely because the plan (or its sponsor) enters into a new policy, certificate, or contract of insurance after March 23, 2010 (for example, a plan enters into a contract with a new issuer or a new policy is issued with an existing issuer). For

purposes of this section, a plan or health insurance coverage that provides grandfathered health plan coverage is referred to as a grandfathered health plan. The rules of this section apply separately to each benefit package made available under a group health plan or health insurance coverage.

(ii) *Changes in group health insurance coverage.* Subject to paragraphs (f) and (g)(2) of this section, if a group health plan (including a group health plan that was self-insured on March 23, 2010) or its sponsor enters into a new policy, certificate, or contract of insurance after March 23, 2010 that is effective before November 15, 2010, then the plan ceases to be a grandfathered health plan.

*   *   *   *   *

(3)(i) * * *

(ii) *Change in group health insurance coverage.* To maintain status as a grandfathered health plan, a group health plan that enters into a new policy, certificate, or contract of insurance must provide to the new health insurance issuer (and the new health insurance issuer must require) documentation of plan terms (including benefits, cost sharing, employer contributions, and annual limits) under the prior health coverage sufficient to determine whether a change causing a cessation of grandfathered health plan status under paragraph (g)(1) of this section has occurred.

*   *   *   *   *

(f) * * * After the date on which the last of the collective bargaining agreements relating to the coverage that was in effect on March 23, 2010 terminates, the determination of whether health insurance coverage maintained pursuant to a collective bargaining agreement is grandfathered health plan coverage is made under the rules of this section other than this paragraph (f) (comparing the terms of the health insurance coverage after the date the last collective bargaining agreement terminates with the terms of the health insurance coverage that were in effect on March 23, 2010).

(g) * * *
(4) * * *
Example 9. (i) *Facts.* A group health plan not maintained pursuant to a collective bargaining agreement offers three benefit packages on March 23, 2010. Option *F* is a self-insured option. Options *G* and *H* are insured options. Beginning July 1, 2013, the plan increases coinsurance under Option *H* from 10% to 15%.

(ii) *Conclusion.* In this *Example 9*, the coverage under Option *H* is not grandfathered health plan coverage as of July 1, 2013, consistent with the rule in paragraph (g)(1)(ii) of this section. Whether the coverage under Options *F* and *G* is grandfathered health plan coverage is determined

separately under the rules of this paragraph (g).

Department of Health and Human Services

45 CFR Chapter I

■ Accordingly, 45 CFR part 147 is amended as follows:

PART 147—HEALTH INSURANCE REFORM REQUIREMENTS FOR THE GROUP AND INDIVIDUAL HEALTH INSURANCE MARKETS

■ 1. The authority citation for part 147 continues to read as follows:

Authority: Secs. 2701 through 2763, 2791, and 2792 of the Public Health Service Act (42 U.S.C. 300gg through 300gg–63, 300gg–91, and 300gg–92), as amended.

■ 2. Section 147.140 is amended by:
■ 1. Revising paragraph (a)(1).
■ 2. Redesignating paragraphs (a)(3), (a)(3)(i) and (a)(3)(ii) as paragraphs (a)(3)(i), (a)(3)(i)(A) and (a)(3)(i)(B), respectively.
■ 3. Adding new paragraph (a)(3)(ii).
■ 4. Removing paragraphs (a)(5) and (f)(2).
■ 5. Redesignating paragraph (f)(1) as paragraph (f).
■ 6. Revising the last sentence in newly-designated paragraph (f).
■ 7. Revising paragraph (g)(4) *Example 9*.

The revisions and addition reads as follows:

§ 147.140   Preservation of right to maintain existing coverage.

(a) *Definition of grandfathered health plan coverage*—(1) *In general*—(i) *Grandfathered health plan coverage. Grandfathered health plan coverage* means coverage provided by a group health plan, or a group or individual health insurance issuer, in which an individual was enrolled on March 23, 2010 (for as long as it maintains that status under the rules of this section). A group health plan or group health insurance coverage does not cease to be grandfathered health plan coverage merely because one or more (or even all) individuals enrolled on March 23, 2010 cease to be covered, provided that the plan has continuously covered someone since March 23, 2010 (not necessarily the same person, but at all times at least one person). In addition, subject to the limitation set forth in paragraph (a)(1)(ii) of this section, a group health plan (and any health insurance coverage offered in connection with the group health plan) does not cease to be a grandfathered health plan merely because the plan (or its sponsor) enters into a new policy, certificate, or contract of insurance after March 23, 2010 (for example, a plan enters into a contract with a new issuer or a new policy is issued with an existing issuer). For purposes of this section, a plan or health insurance coverage that provides grandfathered health plan coverage is referred to as a grandfathered health plan. The rules of this section apply separately to each benefit package made available under a group health plan or health insurance coverage.

(ii) *Changes in group health insurance coverage.* Subject to paragraphs (f) and (g)(2) of this section, if a group health plan (including a group health plan that was self-insured on March 23, 2010) or its sponsor enters into a new policy, certificate, or contract of insurance after March 23, 2010 that is effective before November 15, 2010, then the plan ceases to be a grandfathered health plan.

* * * * *

(3)(i) * * *

(ii) *Change in group health insurance coverage.* To maintain status as a grandfathered health plan, a group health plan that enters into a new policy, certificate, or contract of insurance must provide to the new health insurance issuer (and the new health insurance issuer must require) documentation of plan terms (including benefits, cost sharing, employer contributions, and annual limits) under the prior health coverage sufficient to determine whether a change causing a cessation of grandfathered health plan status under paragraph (g)(1) of this section has occurred.

* * * * *

(f) * * * After the date on which the last of the collective bargaining agreements relating to the coverage that was in effect on March 23, 2010 terminates, the determination of whether health insurance coverage maintained pursuant to a collective bargaining agreement is grandfathered health plan coverage is made under the rules of this section other than this paragraph (f) (comparing the terms of the health insurance coverage after the date the last collective bargaining agreement terminates with the terms of the health insurance coverage that were in effect on March 23, 2010).

(g) * * *

(4) * * *

Example 9. (i) *Facts.* A group health plan not maintained pursuant to a collective bargaining agreement offers three benefit packages on March 23, 2010. Option *F* is a self-insured option. Options *G* and *H* are insured options. Beginning July 1, 2013, the plan increases coinsurance under Option *H* from 10% to 15%.

(ii) *Conclusion.* In this *Example 9*, the coverage under Option *H* is not grandfathered health plan coverage as of July

1, 2013, consistent with the rule in paragraph (g)(1)(ii) of this section. Whether the coverage under Options *F* and *G* is grandfathered health plan coverage is determined separately under the rules of this paragraph (g).

[FR Doc. 2010–28861 Filed 11–15–10; 4:15 pm]

BILLING CODE 4830–01–4510–29–4120–01–P

D. HHS Regulations on Web Portal Requirements

24470   Federal Register / Vol. 75, No. 86 / Wednesday, May 5, 2010 / Rules and Regulations

of the decision. The Secretary sends a written decision to the sponsor or the applicable Secretary's designee upon request.

Subpart G—Disclosure of Data Inaccuracies

§ 149.600 Sponsor's duty to report data inaccuracies.

A sponsor is required to disclose any data inaccuracies upon which a reimbursement determination is made, including inaccurate claims data and negotiated price concessions, in a manner and at a time specified by the Secretary in guidance.

§ 149.610 Secretary's authority to reopen and revise a reimbursement determination.

(a) The Secretary may reopen and revise a reimbursement determination upon the Secretary's own motion or upon the request of a sponsor:

(1) Within 1 year of the reimbursement determination for any reason.

(2) Within 4 years of a reimbursement determination for good cause.

(3) At any time, in instances of fraud or similar fault.

(b) For purposes of this section, the Secretary does not find good cause if the only reason for the revision is a change of legal interpretation or administrative ruling upon which the determination to reimburse was made.

(c) A decision by the Secretary not to revise a reimbursement determination is final and binding (unless fraud or similar fault is found) and cannot be appealed.

Subpart H—Change of Ownership Requirements

§ 149.700 Change of ownership requirements.

(a) *Change of ownership consists of:*
(1) *Partnership.* The removal, addition, or substitution of a partner, unless the partners expressly agree otherwise as permitted by applicable state law.

(2) *Asset sale.* Transfer of all or substantially all of the assets of the sponsor to another party.

(3) *Corporation.* The merger of the sponsor's corporation into another corporation or the consolidation of the sponsor's organization with one or more other corporations, resulting in a new corporate body.

(b) *Change of ownership; exception.* Transfer of corporate stock or the merger of another corporation into the sponsor's corporation, with the sponsor surviving, does not ordinarily constitute change of ownership.

(c) *Advance notice requirement.* A sponsor that has a sponsor agreement in effect under this part and is considering or negotiating a change in ownership must notify the Secretary at least 60 days before the anticipated effective date of the change.

(d) *Assignment of agreement.* When there is a change of ownership as specified in paragraph (a) of this section, and this results in a transfer of the liability for health benefits, the existing sponsor agreement is automatically assigned to the new owner.

(e) *Conditions that apply to assigned agreements.* The new owner to whom a sponsor agreement is assigned is subject to all applicable statutes and regulations and to the terms and conditions of the sponsor agreement.

(f) Failure to notify the Secretary at least 60 days before the anticipated effective date of the change may result in the Secretary recovering funds paid under this program.

Dated: April 29, 2010.

Jay Angoff,

Director, Office of Consumer Information and Insurance Oversight.

Dated: April 29, 2010

Kathleen Sebelius,

Secretary.

[FR Doc. 2010–10658 Filed 5–4–10; 8:45 am]

BILLING CODE 4150–03–P

DEPARTMENT OF HEALTH AND HUMAN SERVICES

Office of the Secretary

45 CFR Part 159

RIN 0991–AB63

Health Care Reform Insurance Web Portal Requirements

AGENCY: Office of the Secretary, HHS.

ACTION: Interim final rule with comment period.

SUMMARY: The Patient Protection and Affordable Care Act (the Affordable Care Act) was enacted on March 23, 2010. It requires the establishment of an internet Web site (hereinafter referred to as a Web portal) through which individuals and small businesses can obtain information about the insurance coverage options that may be available to them in their State. The Department of Health and Human Services (HHS) is issuing this interim final rule in order to implement this mandate. This interim final rule adopts the categories of information that will be collected and displayed as Web portal content, and the data we will require from issuers and request from States, associations, and high risk pools in order to create this content.

DATES: *Effective Date:* These regulations are effective on May 10, 2010.

Comment Date: To be assured consideration, comments must be received at the address provided below, no later than 5 p.m. on June 4, 2010.

ADDRESSES: In commenting, please refer to file code DHHS–9997–IFC. Because of staff and resource limitations, we cannot accept comments by facsimile (FAX) transmission.

You may submit comments in one of four ways (please choose only one of the ways listed):

• *Electronically.* You may submit electronic comments on this regulation to *http://www.regulations.gov.* Follow the instructions on the home page.

• *By regular mail.* You may mail written comments to the following address ONLY: Centers for Medicare & Medicaid Services, Department of Health and Human Services, Attention: DHHS–9997–IFC, P.O. Box 8014, Baltimore, MD 21244–8014.

Please allow sufficient time for mailed comments to be received before the close of the comment period.

• *By express or overnight mail.* You may send written comments to the following address ONLY: Centers for Medicare & Medicaid Services, Department of Health and Human Services, Attention: DHHS–9997–IFC, Mail Stop C4–26–05, 7500 Security Boulevard, Baltimore, MD 21244–1850.

• *By hand or courier.* If you prefer, you may deliver (by hand or courier) your written comments before the close of the comment period to either of the following addresses:

a. For delivery in Washington, DC— Centers for Medicare & Medicaid Services, Department of Health and Human Services, Room 445–G, Hubert H. Humphrey Building, 200 Independence Avenue, SW., Washington, DC 20201

(Because access to the interior of the Hubert H. Humphrey Building is not readily available to persons without Federal government identification, commenters are encouraged to leave their comments in the CMS drop slots located in the main lobby of the building. A stamp-in clock is available for persons wishing to retain a proof of filing by stamping in and retaining an extra copy of the comments being filed.)

b. For delivery in Baltimore, MD— Centers for Medicare & Medicaid Services, Department of Health and Human Services, 7500 Security Boulevard, Baltimore, MD 21244–1850.

If you intend to deliver your comments to the Baltimore address,

Federal Register / Vol. 75, No. 86 / Wednesday, May 5, 2010 / Rules and Regulations **24471**

please call telephone number (410) 786–9994 in advance to schedule your arrival with one of our staff members.

Comments mailed to the addresses indicated as appropriate for hand or courier delivery may be delayed and received after the comment period.

Submission of comments on paperwork requirements. You may submit comments on this document's paperwork requirements by following the instructions at the end of the "Collection of Information Requirements" section in this document.

For information on viewing public comments, see the beginning of the **SUPPLEMENTARY INFORMATION** section.

FOR FURTHER INFORMATION CONTACT: Danielle Harris, (410) 786–1819.

SUPPLEMENTARY INFORMATION: *Inspection of Public Comments:* All comments received before the close of the comment period are available for viewing by the public, including any personally identifiable or confidential business information that is included in a comment. We post all comments received before the close of the comment period on the following Web site as soon as possible after they have been received: *http://regulations.gov.* Follow the search instructions on that Web site to view public comments.

Comments received timely will be also available for public inspection as they are received, generally beginning approximately 3 weeks after publication of a document, at the headquarters of the Centers for Medicare & Medicaid Services, 7500 Security Boulevard, Baltimore, Maryland 21244, Monday through Friday of each week from 8:30 a.m. to 4 p.m. To schedule an appointment to view public comments, phone 1–800–743–3951.

I. Background

The Patient Protection and Affordable Care Act (Pub. L. 111–148), hereinafter referred to as the Affordable Care Act, was enacted on March 23, 2010. Section 1103(a), as amended by section 10102(b) of the same act, directs the Secretary to immediately establish a mechanism, including an internet Web site, through which a resident of, or small business in, any State may identify affordable health insurance coverage options in that State.

In implementing these requirements, we seek to develop a Web site (hereinafter called the Web portal) that would empower consumers by increasing informed choice and promoting market competition. To achieve these ends, we intend to provide a Web portal that provides information to consumers in a clear,

salient, and easily navigated manner. We plan to minimize the use of technical language, jargon, or excessive complexity in order to promote the ability of consumers to understand the information and act in accordance with what they have learned. We will engage in careful consumer testing to identify the best methods to achieve these goals.

In obtaining information to populate the Web portal, we will be seeking all the statutorily required information from issuers, and we anticipate adopting electronic submission capabilities. As we develop the Web portal, and engage with consumers, this information will be used to create an effective consumer-friendly presentation of affordable health coverage option plans. In addition, we plan to provide information, consistent with applicable laws, in a format that is accessible for use by members of the public, allowing them to download and repackage the information, promoting innovation and the goal of consumer choice.

As we develop the Web portal, we are also seeking to balance the need to obtain information that will promote informed choice with the principles of the Paperwork Reduction Act and Executive Order 12866, which call for minimizing burdens and maximizing net benefits. To that end, we are seeking comments on how best to achieve that balance, and in particular how to reduce unnecessary burdens on the private sector.

This is an interim final rule that becomes effective May 10, 2010. We invite public comments on all relevant issues to make improvements.

A. Statutory Basis

As discussed above, Section 1103(a) of the Affordable Care Act, as amended by section 10102(b) of the same act, directs the Secretary to immediately establish a mechanism, including an internet Web site, through which a resident of, or small business in, any State may identify affordable health insurance coverage options in that State. To the extent practicable, the Web site (hereinafter called the Web portal) is to provide, at minimum, information on the following coverage options:

1. Health insurance coverage offered by health insurance issuers,

2. Medicaid coverage,

3. Children's Health Insurance Program (CHIP) coverage,

4. State health benefits high risk pool coverage,

5. Coverage under the high risk pool created by section 1101 of the Affordable Care Act, and

6. Coverage within the small group market for small businesses and their employees.

In order to provide this information in a standardized format, section 1103(b) requires the Secretary to develop a standardized format to present the coverage information described above. This format is to provide for, at a minimum, the inclusion of information on the percentage of total premium revenue expended on nonclinical costs (as reported under section 2718(a) of the Public Health Service Act), eligibility, availability, premium rates, and cost sharing with respect to such coverage options. The format must be consistent with the standards that are adopted for the uniform explanation of coverage under section 2715 of the Public Health Service Act. Defining the minimum content of the format required under section 1103(b) in effect defines what we will publish as the minimum content of the Web portal. This regulation, therefore, specifies the data that will be collected and disseminated through the Web portal in accordance with 1103(a) as amended by section 10102(b).

B. General Overview

Section 1103(a) of the Affordable Care Act, as amended by section 10102(b) of the same act, requires the establishment of a Web portal through which individuals can obtain information about the health insurance options that may be available to them in their "State." Section 1304(d) of the Affordable Care Act defines "State" to include the fifty states and the District of Columbia. The territories are not included in this definition. We therefore will interpret "State" in the Web portal context to mean the 50 States and the District of Columbia.

By statute, the Web portal must be available for public use no later than July 1, 2010. We will use the data collections and processes described in this rule to make the initial release of the Web portal available to the public on July 1, 2010, through a government sponsored Web site. We intend for the future development and updating of the Web portal to be an evolutionary process that involves all stakeholders, and we anticipate future updates, including annual and periodic revisions, to be released as the result of a continued refinement of the Web portal content.

In the July 1, 2010 release we will provide summary information about health insurance products that are available in the individual and small business markets including issuers of the products, types of products, location, summaries of services offered, links to provider networks, and contact information (including Web site links and customer service telephone contact) to enable interaction with specific issuers. In addition, the Web portal will provide information on eligibility, coverage limitations and premium information for existing high risk pools operating in the States, to the extent that it is provided to us by the responding parties. It will also provide introductory information on eligibility and services for Medicaid and CHIP. We will include contact information and Web site links for the Medicaid and CHIP programs for individuals who believe that they or family members may meet eligibility criteria. In addition, we will provide information on coverage options for small businesses, including reinsurance for early retirees under section 1102 of the Affordable Care Act (which is being administered by HHS), and tax credits available under section 45R of the Internal Revenue Code, as added by section 1421 of the Affordable Care Act. We also will include Web site links to these programs so that small businesses can obtain further information.

We note that Section 1103(b)(1) requires the Secretary to present the Web portal information in a format that is consistent with the standards that are adopted for the uniform explanation of coverage under section 2715 of the Public Health Service Act (PHSA) as added by section 1001(a) of the Affordable Care Act. Section 2715 of the PHSA provides for the establishment of these standards within 12 months of the Affordable Care Act's enactment date. As a result, these standards will not be in place for the July 1, 2010 release of the Web portal. We will modify the format used to present the initial release of the Web portal to ensure Web portal consistency with these standards in accordance with the implementation schedule that is established for these standards.

In an effort to make the Web portal as comprehensive as possible, we will enhance the content over time to include more than the statutory minimum requirements that are discussed above. We will include any information that we have that we believe would be useful to consumers, such as medical loss ratios, quality and performance information, links to appropriate Web sites such as the Web site of the association that represents existing State health benefits high risk pools, and more State-specific information on Medicaid and CHIP eligibility and service coverage. Because of the complexity of pricing information and the need to incorporate pricing

engines into the Web site, detailed pricing and benefit information will be provided in the second release of the Web portal on October 1, 2010.

As we discuss in more detail in section III "Waiver of Proposed Rulemaking and the 30-Day Delay in the Effective Date," the statutory requirement for a July 1, 2010 Web portal release does not allow time for full notice and comment rulemaking. While this timeframe necessitates going directly to final, in order to maximize public input we are using an interim final rule with comment to establish the categories of information that we will collect for inclusion in the Web portal, including the data production requirements that we impose on health insurance issuers, and the data collection requests for States, associations, and high risk pools.

II. Provisions of the Interim Final Rule

A. Definitions

For any terms defined by the Affordable Care Act, including the definitions in section 1304, as well as any definitions in the Public Health Service Act that are incorporated by reference under sections 1301(b) or 1551 of the Affordable Care Act, we adopt those definitions. We discuss these definitions below. The regulatory text provides cross references to these provisions. We also explain here how we are defining the terms that are not defined in the Affordable Care Act or the PHSA. These terms are "State health benefits high risk pool," "section 1101 high risk pool," "health insurance product" and "portal plan."

Section 2791(b)(1) of the PHSA, as incorporated by reference into the Affordable Care Act, defines "health insurance coverage" as "benefits consisting of medical care (provided directly, through insurance or reimbursement, or otherwise and including items and services paid for as medical care) under any hospital or medical service policy or certificate, hospital or medical service plan contract, or health maintenance organization contract offered by a health insurance issuer." Section 2791(b)(2) in turn defines an insurance issuer (also referred to here as an "issuer") to be an entity "licensed to engage in the business of insurance in a State and which is subject to State law which regulates insurance" and specifies that it does not include a group health plan.

For purposes of the Affordable Care Act and the PHSA, a distinction is made between health insurance coverage sold to group health plans, and other health insurance coverage. The term "group

health plan," as defined in section 2791(a)(1) of the PHSA, exclusively refers to health coverage sold to group health plans. Section 1304(a)(2) of the Affordable Care Act, which adopts the identical definition as section 2791(e)(1)(A) of the PHSA, defines "individual market" as the "market for health insurance coverage offered to individuals other than in connection with a group health plan."

Section 2791(b)(5) of the PHSA in turn defines "individual health insurance coverage" as health insurance coverage "offered to individuals in the individual market, but does not include short-term limited duration insurance."

The Affordable Care Act and the PHSA further divide the group health insurance market into coverage sold to large employers (the "large group market," and coverage sold to small employers (the "small group market"). See section 1304(a)(3) of Affordable Care Act. Section 1304(b)(2) of the Affordable Care Act defines a "small employer" as, in connection with a group health plan with respect to a calendar year and a plan year, an employer who employed an average at least 1, but not more than 100 employees on business days during the preceding calendar year, and who employs at least 1 employee on the first day of the plan year. Section 1304(b)(3) of the Affordable Care Act allows for a State to elect the option to define "small employer" as an employer who employed on average at least 1, but not more than 50 employees on business days during the preceding calendar year in the case of plan years beginning before January 1, 2016. As such, for any State that elects this option, we would apply this alternate definition of "small employer" for their State for plan years beginning before January 1, 2016.

For purposes of this regulation, we will refer to health insurance coverage offered to employees of small employers in the small group market as "small group coverage."

Sections 1103(a)(2)(D) of the Affordable Care Act provides for Web portal reporting of "State health benefits high risk pools." For the purpose of this rule, we define "State health benefits high risk pools" as nonprofit organizations created by State law to offer comprehensive health coverage to individuals who otherwise would be unable to secure such coverage because of their health status. This language was adopted, with modification, from the National Association of Comprehensive Health Insurance Plans (NASCHIP) annual report. Our understanding is that this definition is generally understood to identify existing high risk pools.

Federal Register / Vol. 75, No. 86 / Wednesday, May 5, 2010 / Rules and Regulations   24473

Section 1103(a)(2)(E) provides for Web portal reporting of pools established pursuant to section 1101 of the Affordable Care Act. For purposes of this regulation, we define "section 1101 high risk pools" as any entity described in regulations implementing section 1101 of the Affordable Care Act.

The Affordable Care Act and the PHSA do not include the term "health insurance product." We are creating this term as a short hand reference to the information that we will publish in the first release of the Web portal. This term is needed in order to differentiate the information that will be collected for the July 1, 2010 release and the post-July 1, 2010 releases. We define "health insurance product" ("product") as a package of benefits that an issuer offers that is reported to State regulators in an insurance filing.

The Affordable Care Act and the PHSA also do not define the term "portal plan." We are creating this term to describe certain data that we will collect and disseminate in post-July 1, 2010 releases of the Web portal. We understand that consumers apply for coverage under individual health insurance products that issuers develop and market to offer a package of benefits. In applying for a package of benefits, we further understand that consumers are offered a range of cost-sharing arrangements, including deductibles and copayments but not including premium rates or premium rate quotes. As a result, each package of benefits can be paired with a multitude of cost sharing options. We will use the word "portal plan" to refer to the discrete pairing of a package of benefits with a particular cost-sharing option (not including premium rates or premium rate quotes). We will collect portal plan information for publication in post-July 1, 2010 releases of the Web portal. We believe that portal plan information is precise enough to provide a potential consumer with enough information to discern the relative costs and benefits of selecting a particular coverage option.

We welcome comments on the adequacy of these definitions, and, if applicable, suggestions to improve them.

B. Individual and Small Group Market Data Collection and Dissemination

In order to meet the mandate, we must collect information on individual and small group coverage from health insurance issuers and prepare the information to be presented publicly in a clear and concise fashion. We will have a two part rollout of the Web portal for 2010, and then annual and periodic updates to allow for the inclusion of updated data as well as consumer education content.

1. Data Submission Mandate

The Secretary currently regulates health insurance industry practices for private insurance plans offered through public programs such as Medicare, Medicaid, and CHIP. While she either has or has access to data on Federal government sponsored plans, we must issue regulations to mandate the production of the necessary information from issuers in order to fulfill the statutory mandate as it applies to private plans not offered through Federal government programs. To facilitate the development of a robust Web portal with comprehensive pricing and benefit information on individual and small group coverage, our current plan is to contract with a vendor that has a health insurance pricing engine and a related Web site with portal plan identification and comparison functionality through a full and open competition. The work on this contract will not be completed in time for the July 1, 2010 release of the Web portal. Accordingly, we will collect an initial set of data (health insurance product information) from issuers in order to present basic information on all issuers and health insurance products in the July 1, 2010 release of the Web portal. This release of the Web portal will only contain the basic information on issuers and their products in the individual and small group markets that was practicable to obtain in the constrained timeframe for meeting the statutory requirement that the Web portal be available for public use by July 1, 2010. We will provide a second release of the Web portal on October 1, 2010 with comprehensive pricing and benefit information for individual and small group coverage.

We will communicate to consumers through the Web portal and other public communication processes, such as presentations and reports to stakeholders, the names of those issuers who fail to timely meet the reporting requirements or who provide incomplete or inaccurate information.

a. July 1, 2010

To meet the July 1, 2010 deadline, we will require issuers to provide data that we will use to develop introductory information for consumers on the universe of issuers and health insurance products in their geographic area. By May 21, 2010 we will require issuers to submit corporate and contact information, such as corporate addresses and Web sites; administrative information, such as enrollment codes; enrollment data by product; product names and types, such as Preferred Provider Organization (PPO) or Health Maintenance Organization (HMO); whether enrollment is currently open for each product; geographic availability information, such as product availability by zip code or county; customer service phone numbers; Web site links to the issuer Web site, brochure documents such as benefit summaries, and provider networks; and financial ratings, such as those offered by financial rating firms including AM Best, Standard and Poor, and Moody's, if available.

We invite comment on whether enrollment information is considered by issuers to be confidential business information.

We are aware that some issuers are rated on their financial status and other performance measures. We considered excluding issuers with no or low financial ratings from firms such as AM Best, Standard and Poor, and Moody. However, it is our understanding that not all issuers seek financial ratings, and that the private firms that conduct them do not use standardized approaches. Therefore, we will instead require each issuer to submit information on whether they obtained a financial rating, from which firm, and what the rating is. We will use this information to help analyze whether such ratings are or could be useful in conveying meaningful differences to consumers. For the same purpose we will allow, but not require issuers to report other types of ratings they have received, such as ratings from The National Committee for Quality Assurance (NCQA) Accreditation.

Certain administrative information that we are collecting, such as an issuer's technical contact information (that is, the person who will work directly with us and our contractors to submit and validate data), tax identification number, and enrollment count in an issuer's products, will be used to support the structure of the database in which this information will be warehoused so that the data can be easily retrieved to support uploading information to the Web portal test site, and so that issuers and their portal plans can be reliably recognized by HHS and issuers and counted to support analyses for improving the Web portal. This information will also be used to support analysis necessary to improve the meaningfulness and usefulness of the Web portal in future releases. In addition, certain contact information will allow the Federal government and its contractors to provide useful updates and reminders to issuers and to provide technical support.

Data submitted under the requirements contained in this regulation must be submitted by issuers in accordance with instructions issued by the Secretary.

b. October 1, 2010

We will release a more comprehensive version of the Web portal on October 1, 2010. This version will include benefit and pricing information. Benefit and pricing information includes data such as premiums, cost-sharing options, types of services covered, coverage limitations, and exclusions.

We note that for States in which premiums are not community rated, the premium data that we intend to collect will include manual rates that represent only standard risks. As a result of medical underwriting, issuers may charge individuals rates that are above the manual rate based on the applicant's health status. We recognize that there is not a feasible method for collecting or displaying information on the rate that an individual who is underwritten might actually be charged, and in the absence of that are proposing to provide information on the manual rates with the understanding that they do not represent actual premium rates that an individual may be charged.

While the initial release of the Web portal will list all issuers and all health insurance products, we believe that it would confuse users if we were to display portal plans that are not open for enrollment. Furthermore, we believe that it is inappropriate to impose a pricing and benefits information reporting burden on issuers for products and portal plans that are not open for enrollment. Therefore, we will exempt issuers of products and portal plans that are not open to new enrollments from additional pricing and benefits reporting requirements. Such issuers will be required to provide the data defined under the May 21 collection to assure we have the universe of issuers and their health insurance products.

In the event that an issuer establishes new products or new portal plans under a product, or opens enrollment in products or portal plans under a product that was previously closed to enrollment, we will require the submission of the pricing and benefits information within 30 days of offering new, or newly re-opened to enrollment, products or portal plans.

We considered excluding issuers with minimal market share from the benefits and cost sharing data collection. However, we believe that some of the portal plans offered by these issuers serve niche markets that would be particularly appealing to some consumers. At this time, we will include portal plans with minimal market share, but we will collect enrollment data for use in analyzing the effect, if any, of market share and our ability to meet consumer needs.

The intent of the Web portal is to present consumers with the full range of meaningful insurance options available to them. We believe this will be best accomplished through providing all plans that have a non-de minimus portion of the issuer's enrollment in an area and allowing for additional plans to be submitted based on the issuers perception of need. Our initial overview of the market indicates that most areas have coverage which is concentrated in a limited number of portal plans. One percent of an issuers' enrollment in the service area was seen as a reasonable cut off balancing the consumer's right to know with the burden imposed on issuers. Therefore, for each zip code, issuers will be required to submit information on at least all portal plans that are open for enrollment and that represent 1 percent or more of the issuer's total enrollment for the respective individual or small group market within that zip code.

We invite comments from the public on what information should be required from issuers to ensure consumer access to meaningful information about coverage options is included in the Web portal, and on the ways that information should be presented to allow for sorting and comparing portal plans. We are particularly interested in comments from consumers, to make certain that the Web portal meets the needs of those individuals who will use it as part of their health coverage decision making.

The data submissions for the October 1, 2010 Web portal release will be due by September 3, 2010. Data must be submitted by issuers in accordance with instructions issued by the Secretary.

c. Future Updates

After the initial data collection efforts described in the prior two subsections, we will require issuers to perform an annual verification and update of the data they submitted. In addition, we recognize that many issuers update pricing and benefit information for their portal plans more frequently than annually, and we therefore will require issuers to submit updated data whenever they change premiums, cost-sharing, types of services covered, coverage limitations, or exclusions for one or more of their individual or small group portal plans. Furthermore, we will require issuers that develop new health insurance products between annual verifications to submit pricing and benefit information for the new product within 30 days of opening enrollment.

Finally, while not included in the statutory list of minimum requirements for the Web portal, we will collect from issuers and report on the Web portal in 2011 the following performance ratings: percent of individual market and small group market policies that are rescinded; the percent of individual market policies sold at the manual rate; the percent of claims that are denied under individual market and small group market policies; and the number and disposition of appeals on denials to insure, pay claims and provide required preauthorizations.

Updated data, including the required data updates previously discussed and annual verifications, must be submitted by issuers in accordance with instructions issued by the Secretary in a future Paperwork Reduction Act Package.

d. Data Validation

All data that is collected for the July 1, 2010, October 1, 2010, and future releases of the Web portal will be validated by the issuers to assure the information they provided is correct. We will require the issuer's CEO or CFO to electronically certify to the completeness and accuracy of the initial data collection for the October 1, 2010 release of the Web portal and for any future updates to these requirements. Following the submission of the data, we will provide issuers with access to preview the data that we will publish on the Web portal. They will also be provided with access to edit their data submissions to update or correct information.

2. Voluntary Data Submission by States

We are requesting that States submit data on issuer corporate and contact information for licensed issuers in their State, such as corporate addresses and Web sites; underwriting status, such as whether or not premium rates in the individual market are determined based on medical underwriting or community rating; and information on any public Web sites administered by the State that provide consumer guidance on individual and small group health insurance coverage in their State.

It is our understanding that States possess the issuer corporate and contact information we are requesting them to submit as a result of their filing requirements for regulated issuers. We are requesting that States voluntarily

Federal Register / Vol. 75, No. 86 / Wednesday, May 5, 2010 / Rules and Regulations **24475**

submit issuer corporate and contact information because we believe that it is incumbent upon us to ensure that we provide information on the entire universe of issuers and health insurance products. Gathering these data from both States and issuers will help us in determining the universe and ensure that we are not inadvertently excluding an issuer or product as a result of incomplete data collection.

The underwriting information and Web site links we are requesting from States will be included on the Web portal in an effort to develop consumer education content and incorporate (by way of linking) any State-developed information on insurance coverage options in a given State. We recognize that some States may have already developed Web portals that provide comprehensive information about health insurance coverage in their State, and we will link to that information if it is available.

In asking States to provide the data identified above, we note that the information would improve the accuracy and scope of the information we can provide to consumers in each of the States. We expect that States will want to ensure full access to information about issuers, health insurance products and portal plans to their residents. We believe that doing so would support consumer choice and a more robust marketplace for insurance. We therefore anticipate that States will be responsive to this request because the information requested will enhance the ability of the citizens of each State to identify affordable options for insurance.

3. Data Dissemination

We will disseminate the information collected as a result of our data submission mandates as described above, as well as other information about health insurance coverage in the individual and small group market that may be useful to the public.

a. July 1, 2010

On July 1, 2010 the Web portal will include information on the data collected as a result of the May 21, 2010 data submission mandate outlined above, including information for consumers on the issuers that sell individual and small group products in their area and links to benefit information for those products. In addition, we will provide some consumer education information on the individual market, including describing how it operates and why its offerings might be appropriate for a consumer, as well as information that will facilitate

health insurance coverage decision-making and increased understanding of how the Web portal operates in the context of the Affordable Care Act. We also will include information for small businesses on the small group market, including information on the reinsurance and tax credit programs discussed previously.

b. October 1, 2010

On October 1, 2010 the Web portal will include expanded content that will incorporate the data collected as a result of the September 3, 2010 data submission mandate outlined above with the data collected for the May 21, 2010 mandate previously discussed. Using the pricing and benefit information gathered as a result of the September 3rd collection, we will display portal plans as packages of benefits and cost sharing, with associated premiums, based on geographic availability.

The display of portal plans will be driven by interactive functionality that accounts for geographic and personal demographic information such as State and zip code of residence, sex, family composition, smoking status and other health indicators. We intend for the order and layering of search results to be based on consumer choice parameters such as range of premium, high and low deductibles, ranges of out-of-pocket maximums, provider network, and indicators of market interest in the product including enrollment. We intend that consumers will also have the ability to select on all available issuers and portal plans and view them alphabetically.

We invite comments on the sort and selection functionality of the Web portal, and on the order and layering of portal plans that we will display.

Certain administrative data collected for the October 1 Web portal release will not be displayed directly on the Web portal but these data are important to the functionality of a pricing engine, such as input data that defines the geographic and demographic variables that affect premium price and cost sharing that will be displayed on the Web portal.

We also will retain and enhance the consumer education content established for the July 1, 2010 Web portal release.

c. Future Updates

We will update the portal plan pricing and benefit information as frequently as monthly to reflect updates that issuers submit as a result of changes to their portal plans. As discussed previously, because issuers may update pricing and benefit information more frequently

than annually, we are requiring updated data submissions whenever an issuer changes the premiums, cost-sharing, types of services covered, coverage limitations, or exclusions for one or more of their individual or small group portal plans. Our monthly updates will also reflect these updates. Consumer education content will be updated periodically in the event that new and pertinent information about either of these markets becomes available that would be beneficial for a consumer to know.

In addition, we are required by section 1103(b)(1) to provide information on the percentage of total premium revenue expended on nonclinical costs, as reported under section 2718(a) of the Public Health Service Act (PHSA). We will report medical loss ratios to meet this requirement, which will provide more than the minimally required information and is believed to be more useful to the public. Section 2718 of the PHSA requires issuers to report this information to HHS beginning with plan years starting on or after September 23, 2010, and the Secretary is promulgating rules on these reporting requirements. After the regulations for this provision are implemented, we anticipate including medical loss ratio information on the Web portal.

As discussed previously, we anticipate including portal plan performance rating information, such as percent of individual market and small group market policies that are rescinded, the percent of individual market policies sold at the manual rate, the percent of claims that are denied under individual market and small group market policies, and the number and disposition of appeals, on the Web portal in the future.

We also anticipate posting information derived from standards and reporting obligations that will apply to insurance sold under the exchanges. For example, we might post information on issuers' financial stability, trends in enrollment and disenrollment, appeals and grievances, and other indicators of fiscal viability, customer service and policy-holder satisfaction.

The Affordable Care Act directs the Secretary to develop quality measures and standards to inform the public about quality of care and to drive improvements in the service delivery system. When such measures and standards become available they will be incorporated into the Web portal.

We invite comments on the content of futures updates to the Web portal, including the frequency of updates, the inclusion of performance rating

24476 Federal Register / Vol. 75, No. 86 / Wednesday, May 5, 2010 / Rules and Regulations

information, and the incorporation of quality measures and standards.

C. Information to be Collected and Disseminated on High Risk Pool Coverage

Sections 1103(a)(2)(D) and (E) of the Affordable Care Act requires HHS to include information about State health benefits high risk pools and high risk pools established under section 1101 of the Affordable Care Act. In order to fulfill this mandate, HHS must establish a mechanism for collecting and preparing this information for public dissemination in a clear and concise fashion.

1. Data Submission Request

Pursuant to the requirement that the Web portal include information on coverage through these high risk pools, this rule requests that certain information on State health benefits high risk pools and high risk pools that will operate under authority established in section 1101 of the Affordable Care Act be reported.

a. July 1, 2010

We will ask the National Association of State Comprehensive Health Insurance Plans (NASCHIP) for information about State health benefit high risk pools. This information will include administrative and contact information, such as a customer service phone number and a Web site for pool information; pool eligibility information, such as state residency and health condition requirements; pool coverage limitations, such as restrictive riders; and pool premium information, such as rules and restrictions for premium subsidy programs. We understand that this information is currently collected and maintained by NASCHIP, and that all of the existing State health benefits high risk pools are members of NASCHIP. As such, we believe that NASCHIP is strategically equipped to work with the State health benefits high risk pools to gather and transmit data to HHS on behalf of State health benefits high risk pools. Therefore, we will ask NASCHIP to provide the data as discussed above by May 21, 2010.

b. Future Updates

We understand that coverage that is offered by State health benefits high risk pools is updated on an annual calendar-year basis. We will therefore ask NASCHIP to provide annual updates of the information that we will request for the May 21, 2010 data collection. If NASCHIP is unable to provide this information in the future, we will ask

State health benefits high risk pools to provide this information.

Because the initial release of the Web portal is July 1, 2010, which is in the middle of a calendar-year, we will initiate the annual update data submission requests in the fall of 2010.

In addition, we request that any State health benefits high risk pool that is established after May 21, 2010, including any high risk pool established pursuant to section 1101 of the Affordable Care Act, report the requested information within 30 days of when the pool begins accepting enrollment, and then annually thereafter.

2. Data Dissemination

a. July 1, 2010

The July 1, 2010 release of the Web portal will include eligibility, coverage limitations and premium information as collected under the request as described above, as well as consumer education content that would aid consumer understanding about high risk pools generally, and whether such pools might offer a potential source of coverage for them.

b. Future Updates

Future updates to the high risk pool content of the Web portal will include updates to the eligibility, coverage, and premium information requested above. These updates may include data for new high risk pools that are established subsequent to the July 1, 2010 release of the Web portal, including those established pursuant to section 1101 of the Affordable Care Act. We understand NASCHIP intends to build a Web site to contain detailed information that today is only available in NASCHIP's hard copy annual report. We will therefore also provide a link to a NASCHIP Web site in a future release in order to provide even more comprehensive information on those State health benefits high risk pools that are represented by NASCHIP.

D. Information to be Disseminated on Medicaid and CHIP

Sections 1103(a)(2)(B) and (C) of the Affordable Care Act require that Medicaid and CHIP information be included on the Web portal. Title XIX of the Social Security Act, the law governing the Medicaid program, has allowed States broad discretion over Medicaid eligibility policy and therefore, Medicaid eligibility varies widely across States. In general, Medicaid eligibility is dependent on categorical and income requirements. Title XXI of the Social Security Act outlines the eligibility rules in CHIP,

and such eligibility requirements are generally based on certain income requirements for children under age 19. There are instances where pregnant women and parents can be eligible for CHIP. The Affordable Care Act simplifies Medicaid and CHIP income eligibility rules for most populations beginning January 2014. In the meantime, individuals will need to directly contact their State programs for definitive determinations of their eligibility or for their family members. However, the Web portal can serve as a resource to educate potential beneficiaries that they or their family members may be eligible for Medicaid and CHIP and provide information about how they can contact their State programs to determine eligibility and services available to them. The portal will serve as a resource for understanding what their State Medicaid and CHIP programs generally cover and how to apply for benefits.

To implement sections 1103(a)(2)(B) and (C) we will provide information guiding consumers on general eligibility criteria for the individual State programs in an effort to assist them in assessing the need to pursue the application processes for these programs. There are no new reporting requirements to support implementation of this section. The data will come from existing Federal sources. The Web portal will also be designed to offer links to the various State Medicaid and CHIP agencies in order to facilitate consumers' submission of program applications.

For each eligibility category, the Web portal will present information regarding the services that are available to eligible applicants. General cost sharing requirements will also be presented on the Web portal, to the extent that they are permitted for the eligibility category in these programs.

In order to provide this information, data are being compiled within CMS across all Medicaid and CHIP eligibility categories regarding the services available under each program. This includes both mandatory and optional Medicaid services for which States receive Federal funding as defined in each State Medicaid plan and any waiver of such plan, as well as the services available under each State's CHIP plan and any waiver of such plan. Mandatory services are specific services States are required to cover for certain groups of Medicaid beneficiaries, both adults and children under the age of 21. Each required service is defined in Federal regulations 42 CFR part 440. Optional Medicaid services are defined as those services not required by Federal

Federal Register / Vol. 75, No. 86 / Wednesday, May 5, 2010 / Rules and Regulations   24477

law that States may elect to provide Medicaid beneficiaries. Optional services are also defined in Federal regulation at 42 CFR part 440. CHIP regulations define mandatory and optional services at 42 CFR part 457.

The portal will include data elements for mandatory services for each mandatory and optional categorical group defined in each Medicaid State plan, such as: Inpatient hospital care (excluding inpatient services in institutions for mental disease for working age adults); outpatient hospital care; physician's services; nurse midwife services; pediatric and family nurse practitioner services; laboratories and x-ray services; rural health clinic services including Federally qualified health centers ("FQHC") and if permitted by State law, rural health clinic and other ambulatory services provided by a rural health clinic which are otherwise included under a State Medicaid plan; prenatal care and family planning services, skilled nursing facility services for persons over age 21, home health care services for persons over 21 who are eligible for skilled nursing services (includes medical supplies and equipment), early and periodic screening, diagnosis, and treatment for persons under age 21 ("EPSDT"), necessary transportation services, and vaccines for children.

If States include optional services in their Medicaid State plan, they must be provided in a manner that is consistent with all Federal requirements. The Web portal will include data elements to reflect the availability of optional services such as home health therapy services, rehabilitative services, case management services, medical or remedial care services or other licensed practitioners (chiropractors, podiatrists, optometrist, psychologists and nurse anesthetists), smoking cessation services and palliative care for children in each State Medicaid plan. Additional program specific service information will be provided with regard to Demonstration programs designed by States under the authority of section 1115 of the Social Security Act as well as services provided through the Children's Health Insurance Program.

Appropriate information on a specific State's Demonstration programs, including variations in eligibility, coverage and service delivery systems used under the Demonstrations, will also be provided on the portal. Demonstrations that are Statewide or high impact, meaning that they have a significant penetration in the market and serve more than a narrow coverage group, will also be included in the initial release of the Web portal. Other

Demonstration programs in Medicaid and CHIP will be added in future releases.

Additionally, the Web portal will provide information to consumers on the Home and Community-Based Waiver program (Section 1915(c) of the Act), including a broad range of State defined services that enable independence in a consumer's own home.

All of the above data will be derived from sources internal to CMS and include Medicaid State Plan Amendments, CHIP State Plans, CHIP annual reports, home and community based waivers applications and renewals, 1115 Demonstration documents, and the contacts database used for *http://www.cms.gov* which includes consumer contacts to state Medicaid and CHIP program offices. We are not collecting any new data elements for the Medicaid and CHIP portions of the Web portal under the authorities that were granted to us under section 1103 of the Affordable Care Act. All information will come from data that CMS already collects for program management and administration purposes.

Certain State-based variations in Medicaid and CHIP programs, such as specific income and resource disregards, and variations in services, such as limits on the number of visits, cannot be presented with a high degree of detail in early releases of the Web portal. We expect to list the services and note that there are limitations, giving consumers enough information to ask questions of the State program if they pursue an application to enroll.

Finally, while a significant amount of data is being compiled to populate the Web portal, some of the data for the Medicaid and CHIP portion will be presented in an aggregated format to enhance public understanding. For example, eligibility categories may be collapsed together for purposes of maximizing public understanding. By way of example, there are several working disabled eligibility categories in Medicaid that inter-relate. We would expect, given the complexity of these definitions, that consumers may have difficulty fully understanding these categories. Therefore, we are presenting the public with summary-level information, such as collapsing information about the working disabled into one category.

III. Waiver of Proposed Rulemaking and the 30-Day Delay in the Effective Date

We ordinarily publish a notice of proposed rulemaking in the **Federal**

Register and invite public comment on the proposed rule in accordance with 5 U.S.C. 553(b) of the Administrative Procedure Act (APA). The notice of proposed rulemaking includes a reference to the legal authority under which the rule is proposed, and the terms and substances of the proposed rule or a description of the subjects and issues involved. This procedure can be waived, however, if an agency finds good cause for concluding that a notice-and-comment procedure is impracticable, unnecessary, or contrary to the public interest and incorporates a statement of the finding and its reasons in the rule issued. Section 1103(a), as amended by section 10102(b), and section 1103(b) of the Affordable Care Act provide for the establishment by July 1, 2010 of a Web portal through which a resident or small business of any State may identify affordable health insurance coverage options in that State. In order to meet this mandate, we have to collect and prepare for dissemination a broad array of data on issuers, health insurance products, and plans, including administrative and product information for the individual and small group markets; information on eligibility and coverage limits for high risk pools; and information on eligibility and services for Medicaid and CHIP. This cannot be accomplished unless issuers are made aware of the data submission requirements in short order and States, associations and high risk pools are made aware of opportunities to aide in this information dissemination effort within the established narrow timeframes. In order to allow sufficient time for data submission and validation prior to public presentation, we must be in possession of the data that is to be included on the Web portal in the July 1, 2010 release no later than May 21, 2010.

As a result of this data collection timeline, it is impracticable to issue a notice of proposed rulemaking prior to publishing a final rule that would implement these data production requirements. Therefore, we find good cause to waive notice and comment rulemaking, and we are proceeding with issuing this final rule on an interim basis. We are providing a 30-day public comment period.

In addition, we ordinarily provide a 30-day delay in the effective date of the provisions of an interim final rule. While the Administrative Procedures Act (5 U.S.C. 551 *et seq.*) generally requires the publication of a substantive rule not less than thirty days prior to its effective date, agencies may establish a shorter time frame based on good cause.

5 U.S.C. 553(d)(3). In accordance with the good cause basis explained below, these regulations are effective on May 10, 2010.

Section 1103(a) of the Affordable Care Act requires the public release of the Web portal on July 1, 2010. As shown below, a sequenced order of activities must be completed in order to meet this statutory deadline.

Data will be uploaded into the database supporting the Web portal to populate the Web portal test site, and based on observations adjustments to the actual Web site may be made. Any problems with the actual data would be adjusted as well. This is a four week iterative process that continues until the test site is functioning and presenting data output as expected, which begins with the first data upload on June 3 and ends with the release of the Web portal on July 1.

Prior to this, the data that is submitted must be formatted in preparation for upload to the database that supports the Web portal test site. First upload to the test site takes approximately two days, from June 1 to June 3. There can be subsequent uploads through June 14, as noted below.

Prior to this, beginning May 21, we must have time to view the submitted data to assure it is complete and clean. At this same time we believe that the regulated parties should be offered an opportunity to validate the data they submit and resubmit any erroneous data. We believe that the minimum time required to accomplish such work is three weeks, which brings us to June 14, 2010. There is a 10 day overlap between this process and the two processes described above.

Prior to this, we must afford those submitting the data with adequate time to gather and submit the data. We believe that the minimum time that should be provided for this work is 7 business days from May 12 through to May 21, 2010.

In order to submit that data, these parties will need to establish accounts that will allow secure data entry into the data collection tool. This will entail approximately 3 business days from May 10 to May 12.

Furthermore, we anticipate that these parties will need training and guidance on gathering data, obtaining an account and entering data. This will include a webinar on or about May 7 and other technical support through a help desk. This collection of activities would take at least 4 business days which brings us to May 12, 2010.

Thus, in order to meet the statutory deadline of July 1, 2010, the processes

described above must commence no later than May 10, 2010.

Furthermore, certain activities had to occur within the agency prior to our being able to publish a rule to implement the Web portal requirements, or enter the contracts necessary to support work under this rule. The Affordable Care Act was enacted on March 23, 2010. We immediately established a workgroup to analyze policy options and the contractual and regulatory needs of the Web portal program. This work was completed on April 22. We then commenced task-specific workgroups to draft the necessary documents, including this regulation, and to procure the initial contractors. While these activities would usually take at least 6 months we have accomplished them in just under six weeks. It was impossible to have accomplished this work any faster, and the brief timeframe between the publication of this document and the effective date of its provisions could not have been avoided through more diligent use of time by the individuals working to implement this mandate.

To afford a full thirty days between publication and the effective date we would have to hold the parties submitting the data and ourselves to inadequate timeframes in which to accomplish the necessary tasks. The timeframes and dates described above therefore establish good cause for an effective date that is fewer than thirty days after publication.

We will accept comments on the content of this regulation until June 4, 2010. This schedule will allow for a ten day comment period prior to the initial reporting requirement under these regulations.

IV. Collection of Information Requirements

In accordance with section 3507(j) of the Paperwork Reduction Act of 1995 (44 U.S.C. 3501 et seq.), the information collection included in this interim rule have been submitted for emergency approval to the Office of Management and Budget (OMB). OMB has assigned control number 0938–1086 to the information collection requirements.

Under the Paperwork Reduction Act of 1995, we are required to provide 60-day notice in the **Federal Register** and solicit public comment before a collection of information requirement is submitted to the Office of Management and Budget (OMB) for review and approval. In order to fairly evaluate whether an information collection should be approved by OMB, section 3506(c)(2)(A) of the Paperwork

Reduction Act of 1995 requires that we solicit comment on the following issues:
• The need for the information collection and its usefulness in carrying out the proper functions of our agency.
• The accuracy of our estimate of the information collection burden.
• The quality, utility, and clarity of the information to be collected.
• Recommendations to minimize the information collection burden on the affected public, including automated collection techniques.

We are soliciting public comment on each of these issues for the following sections of this document that contain information collection requirements (ICRs):

ICRs Regarding Data Submission for the Individual and Small Group Markets (§ 159.120)

Section 159.120(a) requires health insurance issuers (issuers), in accordance with guidance issued by the Secretary, to submit corporate and contact information; administrative information; enrollment data by health insurance product; health insurance product name and type; whether enrollment is currently open for each health insurance product; geographic availability information; customer service phone numbers; and Web site links to the issuer Web site, brochure documents, and provider networks; and financial ratings on or before May 21, 2010, and annually thereafter. The information must be submitted via a template furnished by the Secretary. The burden associated with these reporting requirements is both the time and effort necessary to review the regulations, analyze data, and train issuer staff and the time and effort necessary for an issuer to compile the necessary information, to download and complete the template, and to submit the required information. We estimate that this requirement affects 650 issuers. We believe it will take each issuer 30 hours to review the regulations, analyze data, and train its staff on how to comply with the requirements. The total one-time burden associated with this requirement is 19,500 hours. The estimated cost associated with complying with this part of the requirement is $1,950,000.

Based on our experience with Medicare Part C, we also estimate that each issuer will submit information on 9 of its portal plans and that it will take each issuer a total of 19 minutes to download the information submission template, complete the template, and submit the template. The estimated annual burden associated with the requirements in § 159.120 is 206 hours.

The estimate cost associated with complying with these requirements is $13,390.

Section 159.120(b) requires issuers, in accordance with the guidance issued by the Secretary, to submit pricing and benefit data for their portal plans on or before September 3, 2010, and annually thereafter. The information must be submitted via a template furnished by the Secretary. The burden associated with this requirement is the time and effort necessary for issuers to compile and submit pricing and benefit information. We estimate that it will take each of the 650 issuers 533 minutes to comply with these requirements. The total annual burden associated with these requirements is 51,968 hours. The estimated cost associated with complying with these requirements is $3,377,920.

Section 159.120(c) requires issuers to submit updated pricing and benefit data for their portal plans whenever they change premiums, cost-sharing, types of services covered, coverage limitations, or exclusions for one or more of their individual or small group portal plans. Section 159.120(d) requires issuers to submit pricing and benefit data for portal plans associated with products that are newly open or reopened for enrollment within 30 days of opening for enrollment. Each submission would include a certification on the completeness and accuracy of the submission. The burden associated with these requirements is the time and effort necessary for an issuer to submit the aforementioned data. While these requirements are subject to the PRA, we do not have sufficient data to estimate the associated burden. We do not know the frequency with which issuers will make the aforementioned updates. For that reason, we are estimating a total burden of 1 hour for these requirements.

The estimate of one hour acknowledges that there is a burden associated with this requirement. The total estimated annual burden to industry associated with these updates is 13,000 hours, or 20 hours per issuer. This estimate is based on a three times a year, 19 minute per batch response update. The total cost associated with this requirement is $845,000.

Section 159.120(e) requires issuers to annually verify the data submitted under § 159.120(a) through (d). Section 159.120(f) requires issuers to submit administrative data on product and performance rating information for future releases of the Web portal in accordance with guidance issued by the Secretary. While these requirements are subject to the PRA, we will seek OMB approval at a later date under notice and comment periods separate from this interim final rule with comment.

TABLE 1—RECORDKEEPING AND REPORTING BURDEN

Regulation section(s)	OMB control No.	Respond-ents	Responses	Burden per response (hours)	Total annual burden (hours)	Hourly labor cost of reporting ($)	Total labor cost of reporting ($)	Total cap-ital/mainte-nance costs ($)	Total cost ($)
§ 159.120(a)	0938–1086	650	650	30	19,500	100	1,950,000	0	1,950,000
		650	650	.317	206	65	13,390	0	13,390
§ 159.120(b)	0938–1086	650	650	4	52,000	65	3,380,000		3,380,000
§ 159.120(c) and (d)	0938–1086	650	13,000	1	13,000	65	845,000	0	845,000
Total		650	14,950		84,706				6,188,390

This interim final rule imposes information collection requirements as outlined in the regulation text and specified above. However, this interim final rule also makes reference to several associated information collections that are not discussed in the regulation text contained in this document. The following is a discussion of these information collections.

State Data Submissions

As previously stated in Section II.B.2 of the preamble of this interim final rule, we are requesting that States, in accordance with guidance issued by the Secretary, submit issuer corporate and contact information, underwriting status, and information on any State-administered Web sites that provide consumer information on health insurance coverage in their State by May 21, 2010. The information must be submitted via a template furnished by the Secretary.

The burden associated with these voluntary reporting requests is both the time and effort necessary to review the regulations, analyze data, and train issuer staff and the time and effort necessary for an issuer to compile the

necessary information, to download and complete the template, and to submit the required information. We estimate that this request affects all 50 States and the District of Columbia. We believe it will take each State 10 hours to review the preamble discussion, analyze data, and train its staff on how to comply with the request. The total one-time burden associated with this request is 500 hours. The total estimated cost associated with complying with this part of the requirement is $50,000.

We further estimate that it will take each State a total of 10 minutes to download the information submission template, complete the template, and submit the template. The estimated annual burden associated with this request is 8 hours. The estimated cost associated with complying with this request is $520.

Data Submissions for High Risk Pools

As discussed in section II.C.1 of the preamble of this interim final rule, we are asking the National Association of State Comprehensive Health Insurance Plans (NASCHIP) to provide data pertaining to the information listed in section II.C.1., in accordance with

guidance issued by the Secretary, no later than May 21, 2010. In the event that NSACHIP is unable to provide this information, State health benefits high risk pools have been asked to submit it to HHS. While this request is subject to the PRA, we anticipate that this information will be collected from NASCHIP. Therefore, we are not assigning any burden to these entities within the first year of this collection.

In section II.C.1, we also request that NASCHIP or State health benefits high risk pools submit annual updates on the aforementioned information. While these requests are subject to the PRA, we will seek OMB approval at a later date under notice and comment periods separate from this interim final rule with comment.

Similarly, in the case of a high risk pool established under section 1101 of the Affordable Care Act, we are requesting that the pool submit to HHS the aforementioned information within thirty days of accepting enrollment and then annually thereafter. While these requests are subject to the PRA, we will seek OMB approval at a later date under notice and comment periods separate from this interim final rule with comment.

All of the information collection requirements contained in this interim final rule were submitted to the Office of Management and Budget (OMB) for emergency review and approval as part of a single information collection request (ICR). As part of the emergency review and approval process, OMB waived the notification requirements. The ICR was approved under OMB control number 0938–1086 with an expiration date of October 31, 2010. However, we are still seeking public comments on the information collection requirements discussed in this interim final rule with comment. All comments will be considered as we continue to develop the ICR as we must resubmit the ICR to obtain a standard 3-year approval.

If you comment on these information collection and recordkeeping requirements, please do either of the following:

1. Submit your comments electronically as specified in the **ADDRESSES** section of this rule; or

2. Submit your comments to the Office of Information and Regulatory Affairs, Office of Management and Budget,

Attention: CMS Desk Officer, DHHS–9997–IFC.

Fax: (202) 395–6974; or *E-mail:* OIRA_submission@omb.eop.gov.

V. Response to Comments

Because of the large number of public comments we normally receive on **Federal Register** documents, we are not able to acknowledge or respond to them individually. We will consider all comments we receive by the date and time specified in the **DATES** section of this preamble, and, when we proceed with a subsequent document, we will respond to the comments in the preamble to that document.

VI. Regulatory Impact Statement

We have examined the impacts of this rule as required by Executive Order 12866 (September 1993, Regulatory Planning and Review), the Regulatory Flexibility Act (RFA) (September 19, 1980, Pub. L. 96–354), section 1102(b) of the Social Security Act, the Unfunded Mandates Reform Act of 1995 (Pub. L. 104–4), Executive Order 13132 on Federalism, and the Congressional Review Act (5 U.S.C. 804(2)).

Executive Order 12866 directs agencies to assess all costs and benefits of available regulatory alternatives and, if regulation is necessary, to select regulatory approaches that maximize net benefits (including potential

economic, environmental, public health and safety effects, distributive impacts, and equity). A regulatory impact analysis (RIA) must be prepared for major rules with economically significant effects ($100 million or more in any 1 year). As discussed below, we have concluded that this rule does not have economic impacts of $100 million or more or otherwise meet the definitions of "significant rule" under EO 12866.

Based primarily on data that we have obtained from the National Association of Insurance Commissioners (NAIC), we believe that there are about 650 insurance firms that sell insurance in the individual and small group markets and are hence subject to this interim final rule. This estimate is consistent with other data on the size of the health insurance industry estimated by HHS in previous rulemakings. In addition, about 50 States and other governmental entities will be encouraged to provide voluntarily administrative data on Medicaid and CHIP and (as applicable) data on high risk pool programs. We estimate that on average these approximately 700 respondents will spend 40 hours of time reading this rule, determining what information sources will be used to respond, determining how to provide that information in the newly required formats, and completing a certification on the completeness and accuracy of the information. Assuming that high level staff (for example, managers, attorneys, actuaries, and senior IT professionals) are involved in these efforts, at an average compensation cost of $100 an hour, total one-time costs will be approximately $3 million dollars. Actual provision of data we estimate to cost approximately $3 million a year both in the first year and annually thereafter. Federal government planning, oversight, preparation, and maintenance of the portal web site we estimate to cost $11 million in one-time costs in 2010, and $12 million to oversee and operate in 2011 and annually thereafter. In total, we estimate costs in calendar 2010 to be approximately $17 million, and annual costs thereafter to be approximately $15 million. Additional detail on these estimates can be found in the Paperwork Reduction Act section of this preamble and we welcome comment on them.

All or virtually all of the information needed for the Web portal is standard information that is already made available to individuals, insurance agents, or existing IT contractors with pricing engines and other entities that sell or otherwise provide health insurance to individuals and small groups. For example, information on

deductibles, coverage, cost-sharing, and catastrophic protection limits is routinely available on all or virtually all insurance available to individuals or small groups. Nothing in this rule requires preparation of entirely new information. In essence, we simply require that relatively comprehensive information be provided in standardized formats so that plan comparisons can be automated in ways that present comparable information in comparable levels of detail to facilitate consumer understanding of available choices. We believe that carriers that offer large numbers of plans will find that once they have determined how best to provide the data for a few of those plans, adding additional plans will involve very little if any additional cost. We have also limited the number of plans on which carriers will be required to provide data. Because we appreciate that the time schedule provided in the statute is extremely short, and because the Federal government itself needs time to prepare and populate its Web portal, we have provided for two data submissions in 2010, the first in May and a second more detailed collection in September. This will provide the Federal government with the time needed to competitively bid for a contractor that has a sophisticated pricing engine, as well as for issuers and States time to plan for and compile some of the more detailed information that we are deferring until later in the year.

Nothing in this interim final rule prevents other parties from aggregating and presenting similar information. For example, the State of Massachusetts already presents essentially the entire set of information we will obtain, and more, on its Connector Web site. Several online firms aggregate and present information for some of the policies sold in all or most States. Many insurance brokers and agents, and some consumer organizations, present information on subsets of plans available to their client target groups in their geographic areas. In fact, the Web portal we will provide may facilitate such efforts and improve the scope and accuracy of information provided by alternative sources.

As specified in the statute, our Web portal will include the range of insurance coverage options available to individuals or small businesses, including both public (for example, Medicaid, CHIP, and high risk pool) and private plans, and all types of plans including health maintenance organization, preferred provider organization and indemnity plans. To the best of our knowledge no web sites include such a broad range of health care coverage and specific plan information on a national scale, with the intent of serving such a broad range of consumers needing health insurance coverage. (There are, however, similarly broad portals for some specific population groups, such as Medicare beneficiaries and Federal employees).

It is difficult if not impossible to quantify the benefits of such a broad expansion of consumer information. Moreover, the benefits of this information will change over time, most importantly as State-specific insurance exchanges expand their presence. We do believe, however, that the benefits of improved information will facilitate informed consumer choices as well as benefit the insurance market more broadly. We expect that our Web portal will inform State decisions on the design of exchanges both by positive example and, doubtless, through ideas on ways to improve on the information and formats and tools we provide. Among the likely effects of this effort will be increased use of State high risk insurance pools, increased sale of private policies to uninsured individuals, increased enrollment in Medicaid and CHIP, and commensurate reductions in spending on care for the uninsured. We believe, however, that the most important effect of the Web portal will be to improve health insurance coverage choices. For example, private plans that offer better benefit packages at lower premium costs are likely to benefit from improved consumer information.

We have considered a range of alternatives to the Web portal approach we describe in this final rule with comment, including both more and less ambitious efforts. For example, we could provide less complete information on health insurance coverage choices, and rely on States and private efforts to provide more complete comparisons. In our view, however, costs would not be significantly less were we to require less plan-specific information. Moreover, the full range of information we specify is likely to facilitate other efforts. For example, we do not believe that any other service has been able to assemble in one source information on all insurance issuers and programs serving the individual and small group markets across a broad range of States. One specific alternative on which we request comment is on our proposal to limit the number of plan variations on which we present information for an issuer in a particular area to those that represent at least one percent of their total enrollment in that area (that is, never more than 100 variations, and usually far fewer). Without such a limitation, if

a particular issuer offers twenty or more possible products and twenty alternative cost sharing arrangements applied to the products in a particular geographic area, the combinations and permutations of offerings would be 400 for this one issuer alone. Our use of zip codes for plan service areas is an essential simplifying approach to reducing the number of alternative plans presented, by eliminating irrelevant plans, but does not solve this problem.

We welcome comments on the likely costs and benefits of this rule as presented, on alternatives that would improve the consumer and small business purchaser information to be provided, and on our quantitative estimates of burden. Comments are welcome to address both regulatory changes and changes that might be made through administrative decisions in planning and implementing the Web portal. Comments on ways to design our Internet portal to best meet consumer information needs are especially welcome.

The RFA requires agencies to analyze options for regulatory relief of small businesses, if a rule has a significant impact on a substantial number of small entities. For purposes of the RFA, small entities include small businesses, nonprofit organizations, and small government jurisdictions. Small businesses are those with sizes below thresholds established by the Small Business Administration (SBA). We examined the health insurance industry in depth in the Regulatory Impact Analysis we prepared for the proposed rule on establishment of the Medicare Advantage program (69 FR 46866, August 3, 2004). In that analysis we determined that there were few if any insurance firms underwriting comprehensive health insurance policies (in contrast, for example, to travel insurance policies or dental discount policies) that fell below the size thresholds for "small" business established by the SBA. In fact, then and even more so now, the market for health insurance is dominated by a relative handful of firms with substantial market shares. For example, nationally the approximately 40 Blue Cross and Blue Shield companies account for approximately half of all private insurance sold in the United States. A recent GAO study focused on the small business market and found that the five largest issuers in the small group market, when combined, represented three-quarters or more of the market in 34 of 39 States for which this information was available (GAO, February 27, 2009, *Private Health*

Insurance: 2008 Survey Results on Number and Market Share of Issuers in the Small Group Health Insurance Market). These firms included Blue Cross companies, and also other major insurers such as United HealthCare, Aetna, and Kaiser. Small government jurisdictions do not sell insurance in the individual or small business markets. There are, however, a number of health maintenance organizations (HMOs) that are small entities by virtue of their non-profit status, including Kaiser, even though few if any of them are small by SBA size standards. There are approximately one hundred such HMOs. These HMOs and those Blue Cross and Blue Shield plans that are non-profit organizations, like the other firms affected by this interim final rule, will be required to provide information on their insurance policies to the Department. Accordingly, this interim final rule will affect a "substantial number" of small entities.

We estimate, however, that the one-time costs of this interim final rule are approximately $5 thousand per covered entity (regardless of size or non-profit status) and about $5 thousand annually both in the first year and thereafter. Numbers of this magnitude do not remotely approach the amounts necessary to be a "significant economic impact" on firms with revenues of tens of millions of dollars (usually hundreds of millions or billions of dollars annually). Moreover, the Regulatory Flexibility Act only requires an analysis for those final rules for which a Notice of Proposed Rule Making was required. Accordingly, we have determined, and certify, that this rule will not have a significant economic impact on a substantial number of small entities and that a regulatory flexibility analysis is not required.

In addition, section 1102(b) of the Social Security Act requires us to prepare a regulatory impact analysis if a rule may have a significant economic impact on the operations of a substantial number of small rural hospitals. This analysis must conform to the provisions of section 604 of the RFA. This interim final rule would not affect small rural hospitals. Therefore, the Secretary has determined that this rule would not have a significant impact on the operations of a substantial number of small rural hospitals.

Section 202 of the Unfunded Mandates Reform Act of 1195 requires that agencies assess anticipated costs and benefits before issuing any rule that includes a Federal mandate that could result in expenditure in any one year by State, local or tribal governments, in the aggregate, or by the private sector, of

24482   Federal Register / Vol. 75, No. 86 / Wednesday, May 5, 2010 / Rules and Regulations

$100 million in 1995 dollars, updated annually for inflation. That threshold level is currently about $135 million. This interim final rule contains reporting mandates for private sector firms, but these will not cost more than the approximately $6 million that we have estimated. It includes no mandates on State, local, or tribal governments.

Executive Order 13132 establishes certain requirements that an agency must meet when it promulgates a proposed rule and subsequent final rule that imposes substantial direct requirement costs on State and local governments, preempts State law, or otherwise has Federalism implications. This interim final rule does not impose substantial direct requirement costs on State and local governments, preempt State law, or otherwise have Federalism implications.

In accordance with the provisions of Executive Order 12866, this interim final rule was reviewed by the Office of Management and Budget.

List of Subjects in 45 CFR Part 159

Administrative practice and procedure, Computer technology, Health care, Health facilities, Health insurance, Health records, Hospitals, Medicaid, Medicare, Penalties, Reporting and recordkeeping requirements.

■ For the reasons set forth in the preamble, the Department of Health and Human Services amends 45 CFR subtitle A, subchapter B, by adding a new part 159 to read as follows:

PART 159—HEALTH CARE REFORM INSURANCE WEB PORTAL

Sec.
159.100 Basis and Scope.
159.110 Definitions.
159.120 Data Submission for the individual and small group markets.

Authority: Section 1103 of the Patient Protection and Affordable Care Act (Pub. L. 111–148).

§ 159.100 Basis and scope.

This part establishes provisions governing a Web portal that will provide information on health insurance coverage options in each of the 50 States and the District of Columbia. It sets forth data submission requirements for health insurance issuers. It covers the individual market and the small group market.

§ 159.110 Definitions.

For purposes of part 159, the following definitions apply unless otherwise provided:

Health Insurance Coverage: We adopt the Public Health Service Act (PHSA)

definition of "health insurance coverage" found at section 2791(b)(1) of the Public Health Service Act (PHSA).

Health Insurance Issuer: We adopt the PHSA definition of "health insurance issuer" found at section 2791(b)(2) of the PHSA.

Health Insurance Product: Means a package of benefits that an issuer offers that is reported to State regulators in an insurance filing.

Individual Health Insurance Coverage: We adopt the PHSA definition of "individual health insurance coverage" found at section 2791(b)(5) of the PHSA.

Individual Market: We adopt the Affordable Care Act definition of "individual market" found at section 1304(a)(2) of the Affordable Care Act and 2791(e)(1)(A) of the PHSA.

Portal Plan: Means the discrete pairing of a package of benefits and a particular cost sharing option (not including premium rates or premium quotes).

Section 1101 High Risk Pools: We define section 1101 high risk pools as any entity described in regulations implementing section 1101 of the Affordable Care Act.

Small Employer: We adopt the Affordable Care Act definition of "small employer" found at section 1304(b)(2) and (3).

Small Group Coverage: Means health insurance coverage offered to employees of small employers in the small group market.

Small Group Market: We adopt the Affordable Care Act definition of "small group market" found at section 1304(a)(3).

State Health Benefits High Risk Pools: Means nonprofit organizations created by State law to offer comprehensive health insurance to individuals who otherwise would be unable to secure such coverage because of their health status.

§ 159.120 Data submission for the individual and small group markets.

(a) Health insurance issuers (hereinafter referred to as issuers) must, in accordance with guidance issued by the Secretary, submit corporate and contact information; administrative information; enrollment data by health insurance product; product names and types; whether enrollment is currently open for each health insurance product; geographic availability information; customer service phone numbers; and Web site links to the issuer Web site, brochure documents, and provider networks; and financial ratings on or before May 21, 2010, and annually thereafter.

(b) Issuers must, as determined by the Secretary, submit pricing and benefit information for their portal plans on or before September 3, 2010, and annually thereafter.

(c) Issuers must submit updated pricing and benefit data for their portal plans whenever they change premiums, cost-sharing, types of services covered, coverage limitations, or exclusions for one or more of their individual or small group portal plans.

(d) Issuers must submit pricing and benefit data for portal plans associated with products that are newly open or newly reopened for enrollment within 30 days of opening for enrollment.

(e) Issuers must annually verify the data submitted under paragraphs (a) through (d) of this section, and make corrections to any errors that are found.

(f) Issuers must submit administrative data on products and portal plans, and these performance ratings, percent of individual market and small group market policies that are rescinded; the percent of individual market policies sold at the manual rate; the percent of claims that are denied under individual market and small group market policies; and the number and disposition of appeals on denials to insure, pay claims and provide required preauthorizations, for future releases of the Web portal in accordance with guidance issued by the Secretary.

(g) The issuer's CEO or CFO must electronically certify to the completeness and accuracy of all data submitted for the October 1, 2010, release of the Web portal and for any future updates to these requirements.

Dated: April 29, 2010.
Jay Angoff,
Director, Office of Consumer Information and Insurance Oversight.
Dated: April 29, 2010.
Kathleen Sebelius,
Secretary.
[FR Doc. 2010–10504 Filed 4–30–10; 4:15 pm]
BILLING CODE 4150–03–P

DEPARTMENT OF COMMERCE

National Oceanic and Atmospheric Administration

50 CFR Part 660

[Docket No. 100218107–0199–01]

RIN 0648–AY60

Fisheries Off West Coast States; West Coast Salmon Fisheries; 2010 Management Measures

AGENCY: National Marine Fisheries Service (NMFS), National Oceanic and

D-15

E. IRS Form 8941 and Instructions (Small Employer Tax Credit)

Form 8941

Credit for Small Employer Health Insurance Premiums

Department of the Treasury
Internal Revenue Service

▶ Information about Form 8941 and its instructions is available at *www.irs.gov/form8941*.
▶ Attach to your tax return.

OMB No. 1545-2198

2011

Attachment
Sequence No. 63

Name(s) shown on return | Identifying number

1	Enter the number of individuals you employed during the tax year who are considered employees for purposes of this credit (see instructions)	1	
2	Enter the number of full-time equivalent employees you had for the tax year (see instructions). If you entered 25 or more, skip lines 3 through 11 and enter -0- on line 12	2	
3	Average annual wages you paid for the tax year (see instructions). If you entered $50,000 or more, skip lines 4 through 11 and enter -0- on line 12	3	
4	Premiums you paid during the tax year for employees included on line 1 for health insurance coverage under a qualifying arrangement (see instructions)	4	
5	Premiums you would have entered on line 4 if the total premium for each employee equaled the average premium for the small group market in which you offered health insurance coverage (see instructions)	5	
6	Enter the **smaller** of line 4 or line 5	6	
7	Multiply line 6 by the applicable percentage: • Tax-exempt small employers, multiply line 6 by 25% (.25) • All other small employers, multiply line 6 by 35% (.35)	7	
8	If line 2 is 10 or less, enter the amount from line 7. Otherwise, see instructions	8	
9	If line 3 is $25,000 or less, enter the amount from line 8. Otherwise, see instructions	9	
10	Enter the total amount of any state premium subsidies paid and any state tax credits available to you for premiums included on line 4 (see instructions)	10	
11	Subtract line 10 from line 4. If zero or less, enter -0-	11	
12	Enter the **smaller** of line 9 or line 11	12	
13	If line 12 is zero, skip lines 13 and 14 and go to line 15. Otherwise, enter the number of employees included on line 1 for whom you paid premiums during the tax year for health insurance coverage under a qualifying arrangement (see instructions)	13	
14	Enter the number of full-time equivalent employees you would have entered on line 2 if you only included employees included on line 13	14	
15	Credit for small employer health insurance premiums from partnerships, S corporations, cooperatives, estates, and trusts (see instructions)	15	
16	Add lines 12 and 15. Cooperatives, estates, and trusts, go to line 17. Tax-exempt small employers, skip lines 17 and 18 and go to line 19. Partnerships and S corporations, stop here and report this amount on Schedule K. All others, stop here and report this amount on Form 3800, line 4h	16	
17	Amount allocated to patrons of the cooperative or beneficiaries of the estate or trust (see instructions)	17	
18	Cooperatives, estates, and trusts, subtract line 17 from line 16. Stop here and report this amount on Form 3800, line 4h	18	
19	Enter the amount you paid in 2011 for taxes considered payroll taxes for purposes of this credit (see instructions)	19	
20	Tax-exempt small employers, enter the **smaller** of line 16 or line 19 here and on Form 990-T, line 44f	20	

For Paperwork Reduction Act Notice, see separate instructions.   Cat. No. 37757S   Form **8941** (2011)

2011

Department of the Treasury
Internal Revenue Service

Instructions for Form 8941

Credit for Small Employer Health Insurance Premiums

Section references are to the Internal Revenue Code unless otherwise noted.

What's New

Carryforwards, carrybacks, and passive activity limitations. The carryforwards, carrybacks, and passive activity limitations for this credit are no longer reported on this form. Instead, they must be reported on Form 3800, *General Business Credit.*

Future developments. The IRS has created a page on IRS.gov for information about Form 8941 and its instructions, at *www.irs.gov/form8941.* Information about any future developments affecting Form 8941 (such as legislation enacted after we release it) will be posted on that page.

General Instructions

Purpose of Form

Eligible small employers (defined below) use Form 8941 to figure the credit for small employer health insurance premiums for tax years beginning after 2009. The maximum credit is a percentage of premiums the employer paid during the tax year for certain health insurance coverage the employer provided to certain employees. But the credit may be reduced by limitations based on the employer's full-time equivalent employees, average annual wages, state average premiums, and state premium subsidies and tax credits.

For **tax-exempt small employers**, the credit is generally 25% of premiums paid, is also limited to the amount of certain payroll taxes paid, and is claimed as a refundable credit on Form 990-T, Exempt Organization Business Income Tax Return. A tax-exempt small employer is an eligible small employer described in section 501(c) that is exempt from taxation under section 501(a). A tax-exempt employer not described in section 501(c) is generally not eligible to claim this credit. However, a tax-exempt farmers' cooperative subject to tax under section 1381 may be able to claim the credit as a general business credit as discussed next.

For **all other small employers**, the credit is generally 35% of premiums paid, can be taken against both regular and alternative minimum tax, and is claimed as part of the general business credit on Form 3800.

 Taxpayers other than partnerships, S corporations, cooperatives, estates, and trusts, whose only source of this credit is from those pass-through entities, are not required to complete or file this form. Instead, they can report this credit directly on Form 3800.

Eligible Small Employers

You are an eligible small employer for the tax year if you meet the following three requirements.

1. You paid premiums for employee health insurance coverage under a qualifying arrangement. A qualifying arrangement is generally an arrangement that requires you to pay a uniform percentage (not less than 50%) of the premium cost for each enrolled employee's health insurance coverage (defined later). However, an arrangement that requires you to pay a uniform premium for each enrolled employee (composite billing) and offers different tiers of coverage (for example, self-only, self plus one, and family coverage) can be a qualifying arrangement even if it requires you to pay a uniform percentage that is less than 50% of the premium cost for employees not enrolled in self-only coverage.

In addition, an arrangement that requires you to pay a separate premium for each employee based on age or other factors (list billing) can be a qualifying arrangement even if it requires you to pay a uniform percentage that is less than 50% of the premium cost for some employees.

For details, see *Employer Premiums Paid, Health Insurance Coverage,* and *Qualifying Arrangement,* later.

2. You had fewer than 25 full-time equivalent employees (FTEs) for the tax year. You may be able to meet this requirement even if you had 25 or more employees. For details, see *Individuals Considered Employees* and *Full-Time Equivalent Employee (FTE) Limitation,* later.

3. You paid average annual wages for the tax year of less than $50,000 per FTE. For details, see *Individuals Considered Employees* and *Average Annual Wage Limitation,* later.

> *If you had more than 10 FTEs **and** average annual wages of more than $25,000, the FTE and average annual wage limitations (discussed later) will separately reduce your credit. This may reduce your credit to zero even if you had fewer than 25 FTEs and average annual wages of less than $50,000.*

Employers treated as a single employer. Treat the following employers as a single employer to figure the credit.
- Employers who are corporations in a controlled group of corporations.
- Employers who are members of an affiliated service group.
- Employers who are partnerships, proprietorships, etc., under common control. See Regulations sections 1.414(c)-2, 1.414(c)-3, and 1.414(c)-4 for details.
- Tax-exempt employers under common control. See Regulations section 1.414(c)-5.

For details, see section 45R(e)(5)(A).

 No more than one Form 8941 can be filed with a tax return, unless the exception described in Example 2 below applies.

Example 1. You are a sole proprietor with two separate businesses and you file a separate Schedule C (Form 1040) for each business. You must treat both businesses as a single employer to figure the credit. You will file one Form 8941 for both businesses.

Example 2. You and your spouse are both sole proprietors and file a separate Schedule C (Form 1040) for each of your separate businesses. Neither spouse was an employee of the other spouse or participated in the management of the other spouse's business at any time during the tax year. No more than 50% of the gross income of either business was derived from royalties, rents, dividends, interest, and annuities and you otherwise meet the requirements listed in Regulations section 1.414(c)-4(b)(5)(ii). Do not treat both businesses as a single employer to figure the credit. If you and your spouse are both eligible small employers, you can file two Forms 8941 with a jointly filed Form 1040.

Individuals Considered Employees

In general, all employees who perform services for you during the tax year are taken into account in determining your FTEs, average annual wages, and premiums paid. Rules that apply to certain types of employees are discussed below.

Excluded employees. The following individuals are not considered employees when you figure this credit. Hours and wages of these employees and premiums paid for them are not counted when you figure your credit.
• The owner of a sole proprietorship.
• A partner in a partnership.
• A shareholder who owns (after applying the section 318 constructive ownership rules) more than 2% of an S corporation.
• A shareholder who owns (after applying the section 318 constructive ownership rules) more than 5% of the outstanding stock or stock possessing more than 5% of the total combined voting power of all stock of a corporation that is not an S corporation.
• A person who owns more than 5% of the capital or profits interest in any other business that is not a corporation.
• Family members or a member of the household who is not a family member but qualifies as a dependent on the individual income tax return of a person listed above. Family members include a child (or descendant of a child), a sibling or step sibling, a parent (or ancestor of a parent), a step-parent, a niece or nephew, an aunt or uncle, or a son-in-law, daughter-in-law, father-in-law, mother-in-law, brother-in-law, or sister-in-law. A spouse is also considered a family member for this purpose.

Leased employees. Do not use premiums paid by the leasing organization to figure your credit. Also, a leased employee who is not a common law employee is considered an employee for credit purposes if he or she does all the following.
• Provides services to you under an agreement between you and a leasing organization.
• Has performed services for you (or for you and a related person) substantially full time for at least 1 year.
• Performs services under your primary direction or control.

But do not use hours, wages, or premiums paid with respect to the initial year of service on which leased employee status is based.

Seasonal employees. Seasonal employees who work for you 120 or fewer days during the tax year are not considered employees in determining FTEs and average annual wages. But premiums paid on their behalf are counted in determining the amount of the credit. Seasonal workers include retail workers employed exclusively during holiday seasons.

Household and other nonbusiness employees. Household employees and other employees who are not performing services in your trade or business are considered employees if they otherwise qualify as discussed above. A sole proprietor must include both business and nonbusiness employees to determine FTEs, average annual wages, and premiums paid.

Ministers. A minister performing services in the exercise of his or her ministry is treated as self-employed for social security and Medicare purposes. However, for credit purposes, whether a minister is an employee or self-employed is determined under the common law test for determining worker status. Self-employed ministers are not considered employees.

Full-Time Equivalent Employee (FTE) Limitation

Your credit is reduced if you had more than 10 FTEs for the tax year. If you had 25 or more FTEs for the tax year, your credit is reduced to zero. However, you can still receive a credit from a partnership, S corporation, cooperative, estate, or trust (see the instructions for line 15, later).

How to figure FTEs. To figure the number of FTEs you had for the tax year, you must do the following.
   1. Figure the total hours of service (discussed below) for the tax year of all individuals considered employees.
   2. Divide the total hours of service by 2,080.
   3. If the result is not a whole number (0, 1, 2, etc.), generally round the result down to the next lowest whole number. For example, 10.99 is rounded down to 10. However, if the result is less than one, round up to 1.

Employee hours of service. An employee's hours of service for a year include the following.
• Each hour for which the employee is paid, or entitled to payment, for the performance of duties for the employer during the employer's tax year.
• Each hour for which an employee is paid, or entitled to payment, by the employer on account of a period of time during the employer's tax year during which no duties are performed due to vacation, holiday, illness, incapacity (including disability), layoff, jury duty, military duty, or leave of absence (except that no more than 160 hours of service are required to be counted for an employee on account of any single continuous period during which the employee performs no duties).

Do not include hours of service of any seasonal employee who worked 120 or fewer days during the tax year. Also, do not include more than 2,080 hours of service from any employee.

To figure the total number of hours of service you must take into account for an employee for the year, you can use any of the following methods.

Actual hours worked method. Determine actual hours of service from records of hours worked and hours for which payment is made or due (payment is made or due for vacation, holiday, illness, incapacity, etc., as described above).

Days-worked equivalency method. Use a days-worked equivalency whereby the employee is credited with 8 hours of service for each day for which the employee would be required to be credited with at least one hour of service under the rules described above.

Weeks-worked equivalency method. Use a weeks-worked equivalency whereby the employee is credited with 40 hours of service for each week for which the employee would be required to be credited with at

-2-

least one hour of service under the rules described above.

Average Annual Wage Limitation

Your credit is reduced if you paid average annual wages of more than $25,000 for the tax year. If you paid average annual wages of $50,000 or more for the tax year, your credit is reduced to zero. However, you can still receive a credit from a partnership, S corporation, cooperative, estate, or trust (see the instructions for line 15, later).

How to figure average annual wages. To figure the average annual wages you paid for the tax year, you must do the following.

    1. Figure the total wages paid (discussed below) for the tax year to all individuals considered employees.

    2. Divide the total wages paid by the number of FTEs you had for the tax year (discussed earlier).

    3. If the result is not a multiple of $1,000 ($1,000, $2,000, $3,000, etc.), round the result down to the next lowest multiple of $1,000. For example, $25,999 is rounded down to $25,000.

Employee wages paid. Wages, for this purpose, mean wages subject to social security and Medicare tax withholding determined without considering any wage base limit. But do not include wages paid to any seasonal employees who worked 120 or fewer days during the tax year.

Employer Premiums Paid

Only premiums you paid for health insurance coverage under a qualifying arrangement (discussed later) for individuals considered employees are counted when figuring your credit. For this purpose, if you are entitled to a state tax credit or a state premium subsidy paid directly to you for premiums you paid, do not reduce the amount you paid by the credit or subsidy amount. Also, if a state pays a premium subsidy directly to your insurance provider, treat the subsidy amount as an amount you paid for employee health insurance coverage.

If you pay only a portion of the premiums and your employees pay the rest, only the portion you pay is taken into account. For this purpose, any premium paid through a salary reduction arrangement under a section 125 cafeteria plan is not treated as an employer paid premium. For more information on cafeteria plans, see section 1 of Publication 15-B, Employer's Tax Guide to Fringe Benefits.

Example 3. You offer health insurance coverage to employees under a qualifying arrangement that requires you to pay 60% of the premium cost for single (employee-only) coverage for each employee enrolled in any health insurance coverage you provide to employees. The total premium for each employee enrolled in single (employee-only) coverage is $5,200 per year or $100 ($5,200 ÷ 52) for each weekly payday. The total premium for each employee enrolled in family coverage is $12,376 per year or $238 ($12,376 ÷ 52) for each weekly payday.

Each payday you contribute $60 (60% of $100) toward the premium cost of each employee enrolled in single (employee-only) coverage and withhold the remaining $40 from the employee's paycheck to obtain the $100 total weekly premium. Each payday you contribute $60 (the same amount you pay toward the premiums of employees enrolled in single coverage) toward the premium cost of each employee enrolled in family

coverage and withhold the remaining $178 from the employee's paycheck to obtain the $238 total weekly premium.

To determine the premiums you paid during the tax year, multiply the number of pay periods during which the employee was enrolled in the health insurance coverage by $60. For example, you would have paid $3,120 ($60 × 52) for an employee who was enrolled for the entire tax year. You would have paid $600 ($60 × 10) for an employee who was only enrolled for 10 pay periods. You will need an additional set of calculations if the premium amounts changed during the tax year.

Health Insurance Coverage

For credit purposes, health insurance coverage means benefits consisting of medical care (provided directly, through insurance or reimbursement, or otherwise) under any hospital or medical service policy or certificate, hospital or medical service plan contract, or health maintenance organization contract offered by a health insurance provider.

A health insurance provider is either an insurance company or another entity licensed under state law to provide health insurance coverage.

Health insurance coverage also includes coverage under the following plans.
- Limited scope dental or vision plans.
- Long-term care plans.
- Nursing home care plans.
- Home health care plans.
- Community-based care plans.
- Any combination of the above.

In addition, health insurance coverage includes the following.
- Coverage only for a specified disease or illness.
- Hospital indemnity or other fixed indemnity insurance.
- Medicare supplemental health insurance.
- Certain other supplemental coverage.
- Similar supplemental coverage provided to coverage under a group health plan.

 Employer premiums paid for health insurance coverage can be counted in figuring the credit only if the premiums are paid under a qualifying arrangement.

Health insurance coverage **does not** include the following benefits.
- Coverage only for accident, or disability income insurance, or any combination thereof.
- Coverage issued as a supplement to liability insurance.
- Liability insurance, including general liability insurance and automobile liability insurance.
- Workers' compensation or similar insurance.
- Automobile medical payment insurance.
- Credit-only insurance.
- Coverage for on-site medical clinics.
- Other similar insurance coverage, specified in regulations, under which benefits for medical care are secondary or incidental to other insurance benefits.

Also, because the coverage must be offered by a health insurance provider as discussed above, health insurance coverage does not include benefits provided by the following.
- Health reimbursement arrangements (HRAs).
- Flexible spending arrangements (health FSAs).
- Coverage under other self-insured plans.
- Health savings accounts (HSAs).

However, health insurance coverage may include coverage under the following plans.
- Church welfare benefit plans.
- Multiemployer health and welfare plans that provide coverage through a health insurance provider.

For details, see Notice 2010-82 as discussed under *More Information,* later.

Qualifying Arrangement

A qualifying arrangement is generally an arrangement that requires you to pay a uniform percentage (not less than 50%) of the premium cost for each enrolled employee's health insurance coverage (defined earlier). An arrangement that offers different tiers of coverage (for example, self-only, self-plus one, and family coverage) is generally a qualifying arrangement if it requires you to pay a uniform percentage (not less than 50%) separately for each tier of coverage you offer. However, an arrangement can be a qualifying arrangement even if it requires you to pay a uniform percentage that is less than 50% of the premium cost for some employees. For more details about the following exceptions, see Notice 2010-82 as discussed under *More Information,* later.

Arrangements with composite billing. An arrangement that requires you to pay a uniform premium for each enrolled employee (composite billing) and offers different tiers of coverage can be a qualifying arrangement even if it requires you to pay a uniform percentage that is less than 50% of the premium cost for employees not enrolled in self-only coverage. It is a qualifying arrangement (assuming self-only coverage is the least expensive tier of coverage) if it requires you to pay the following amounts.
- A uniform percentage (not less than 50%) of the premium cost for each employee (if any) enrolled in self-only coverage,
- A uniform amount that is no less than the amount you would have paid toward self-only coverage for each employee (if any) enrolled in self plus one coverage.
- A uniform amount that is no less than the amount you would have paid toward self-only coverage for each employee (if any) enrolled in family coverage.
- A uniform amount that is no less than the amount you would have paid toward self-only coverage for each employee (if any) enrolled in any other tier of coverage (figured separately for each tier).

Arrangements with list billing and only self-only coverage. An arrangement that requires you to pay a separate premium for each employee based on age or other factors (list billing) that only provides self-only coverage can be a qualifying arrangement even if it requires you to pay a uniform percentage that is less than 50% of the premium cost for some employees. It is a qualifying arrangement if it requires you to pay either of the following amounts.
- A uniform percentage (not less than 50%) of the premium charged for each employee enrolled in the self-only coverage, or
- A uniform percentage (not less than 50%) of your employer-computed composite rate (defined later) for your self-only coverage for each employee enrolled in the self-only coverage.

Arrangements with list billing and other tiers of coverage. An arrangement that requires you to pay a separate premium for each employee based on age or other factors (list billing) that provides other tiers of coverage can be a qualifying arrangement even if it requires you to pay a uniform percentage that is less than

50% of the premium cost for some employees. It is a qualifying arrangement (assuming self-only coverage is the least expensive tier of coverage) if it requires you to pay the following amounts.
- A uniform percentage (not less than 50%) for each employee enrolled in self-only coverage as discussed under *Arrangements with list billing and only self-only coverage* above.
- A uniform amount that is either equal to the amount you would have paid toward self-only coverage (as discussed above), a uniform percentage (not less than 50%) of the premium charged, or a uniform percentage (not less than 50%) of your employer-computed composite rate (defined below) for your self plus one coverage, for each employee (if any) enrolled in self plus one coverage.
- A uniform amount that is either equal to the amount you would have paid toward self-only coverage (as discussed above), a uniform percentage (not less than 50%) of the premium charged, or a uniform percentage (not less than 50%) of your employer-computed composite rate (defined below) for your family coverage, for each employee (if any) enrolled in family coverage.
- A uniform amount that is either equal to the amount you would have paid toward self-only coverage (as discussed above), a uniform percentage (not less than 50%) of the premium charged, or a uniform percentage (not less than 50%) of your employer-computed composite rate (defined below) for any other tier of coverage, for each employee (if any) enrolled in any other tier of coverage (figured separately for each tier).

Employer-computed composite rate. The employer-computed composite rate for a tier of coverage is the average rate determined by adding the premiums for that tier of coverage for all employees eligible to participate in the health insurance plan (whether or not they actually receive coverage under the plan or under that tier of coverage) and dividing by the total number of such eligible employees.

More than one plan. Different types of health insurance plans are generally not aggregated for purposes of meeting the qualifying arrangement requirement. For example, if you offer a major medical insurance plan and a stand-alone vision plan, you generally must separately satisfy the requirements for a qualifying arrangement with respect to each type of coverage. For exceptions, see Notice 2010-82 as discussed under *More Information,* later.

State subsidies and credits. For this purpose, if you are entitled to a state tax credit or a state premium subsidy paid directly to you for premiums you paid, do not reduce the amount you paid by the credit or subsidy amount. Also, if a state pays a premium subsidy directly to your insurance provider, treat the subsidy amount as an amount you paid for employee health insurance coverage.

Multiemployer health and welfare plans. For a special rule that applies to multiemployer health and welfare plans, see Notice 2010-82 as discussed under *More Information,* later.

State Average Premium Limitation

Your credit is reduced if the employer premiums paid are more than the employer premiums that would have been paid if individuals considered employees enrolled in a plan with a premium equal to the average premium for the small group market in the state in which the employee works.

-4-

The following table lists the average premium for the small group market in each state for tax years beginning in 2011. Family coverage includes any coverage other than single (employee-only) coverage.

Table A. 2011 State Average Premiums for Small Group Markets

State	Single (Employee-Only) Coverage	Family Coverage
Alabama	$4,778	$12,084
Alaska	6,729	14,701
Arizona	4,614	11,063
Arkansas	4,378	9,849
California	4,790	11,493
Colorado	5,007	12,258
Connecticut	5,640	14,096
Delaware	5,902	13,411
District of Columbia	5,721	14,024
Florida	5,218	12,550
Georgia	5,085	11,440
Hawaii	4,622	11,529
Idaho	4,379	10,066
Illinois	5,565	13,176
Indiana	5,262	12,097
Iowa	4,694	11,051
Kansas	4,693	11,909
Kentucky	4,456	10,560
Louisiana	5,143	11,911
Maine	5,261	12,255
Maryland	5,073	12,530
Massachusetts	5,900	15,262
Michigan	5,195	12,539
Minnesota	5,048	12,790
Mississippi	4,787	10,860
Missouri	4,843	11,379
Montana	4,923	10,789
Nebraska	5,130	12,057
Nevada	4,781	10,836
New Hampshire	5,858	14,523
New Jersey	5,868	14,093
New Mexico	5,146	12,328
New York	5,589	13,631
North Carolina	5,136	11,949
North Dakota	4,545	11,328
Ohio	4,706	11,627
Oklahoma	4,922	11,200
Oregon	4,881	11,536

State	Single (Employee-Only) Coverage	Family Coverage
Pennsylvania	5,186	12,671
Rhode Island	5,956	14,553
South Carolina	5,036	11,780
South Dakota	4,733	11,589
Tennessee	4,744	11,035
Texas	5,172	12,432
Utah	4,532	11,346
Vermont	5,426	12,505
Virginia	5,060	12,213
Washington	4,776	11,151
West Virginia	5,356	12,724
Wisconsin	5,284	13,911
Wyoming	5,430	12,867

Example 4. Assume the same facts that were used in *Example 3.* The $60 you contribute each payday toward employee health insurance coverage is 60% ($60 ÷ $100) of the weekly premium for each employee enrolled in single (employee-only) coverage and 25.21% ($60 ÷ $238) of the weekly premium for each employee enrolled in family coverage.

In this situation, the total average premium limitation amounts that apply are 60% of the applicable amounts shown in the single coverage column of Table A for each employee enrolled in single coverage and 25.21% of the applicable amounts shown in the family coverage column of Table A for each employee enrolled in family coverage.

You have an employee enrolled in single (employee-only) coverage who works for you in Maryland. The single coverage amount shown in Table A for Maryland is $5,073 or $98 ($5,073 ÷ 52) for each weekly payday. The amount you are considered to have paid toward this employee's health insurance coverage based on the average premiums in Table A is $58.80 (60% of $98) each payday.

To determine the premiums you would have paid for this employee during the tax year if the employee had enrolled in a state-average-premium plan, multiply the number of pay periods during which your employee was enrolled in the health insurance coverage by $58.80. For example, you would have paid $3,057.60 ($58.80 × 52) if the employee was enrolled for the entire tax year. You would have paid $588 ($58.80 × 10) if the employee was only enrolled for 10 pay periods. You will need an additional set of calculations if the premium amounts changed during the tax year.

State Premium Subsidy and Tax Credit Limitation

Your credit may be reduced if you are entitled to a state tax credit or a state premium subsidy for the cost of health insurance coverage you provide under a qualifying arrangement to individuals considered employees. The state tax credit may be refundable or nonrefundable and the state premium subsidy may be paid to you or directly to your insurance provider.

Although a state tax credit or premium subsidy paid directly to you does not reduce the amount of your employer premiums paid, and although a state premium subsidy paid directly to an insurance provider is treated as an employer premium you paid, the amount of your credit cannot be more than your net premium payments.

Net premium payments are employer premiums paid (discussed earlier) minus the amount of any state tax credits you received or will receive and any state premium subsides paid either to you or directly to your insurance provider for premiums for health insurance coverage you provide under a qualifying arrangement to individuals considered employees.

Payroll Tax Limitation for Tax-Exempt Small Employers

The credit for tax-exempt small employers cannot exceed the amount of certain payroll taxes. For tax years beginning in 2011, payroll taxes, for this purpose, mean only the following taxes.
• Federal income taxes the tax-exempt employer was required to withhold from employees' wages in calendar year 2011.
• Medicare taxes the tax-exempt employer was required to withhold from employees' wages in calendar year 2011.
• Medicare taxes the tax-exempt employer was required to pay for calendar year 2011.

Premium Deduction Reduced

Your deduction for the cost of providing health insurance coverage to your employees is reduced by the amount of any credit for small employer health insurance premiums allowed with respect to the coverage.

More Information

For more information about this credit, see the following.
• Section 45R.
• Notice 2010-44, 2010-22 I.R.B. 717, available at *www.irs.gov/irb/2010-22_IRB/ar12.html*.
• Notice 2010-82, 2010-51 I.R.B. 857, available at *www.irs.gov/irb/2010-51_IRB/ar09.html*.
• IRS.gov.

Specific Instructions

Worksheets 1 through 7 can help you figure the amounts to report on various lines of Form 8941.
• Use Worksheets 1, 2, and 3 to figure the amounts to report on lines 1 through 3 of Form 8941.
• Use Worksheet 4 to figure the amounts to report on lines 4 and 5 of Form 8941.
• Use Worksheets 5, 6, and 7 if you need to figure amounts to report on lines 8, 9, and 14 of Form 8941.

Line 1

Enter the total number of individuals considered employees shown in column (a) of Worksheet 1. For details, see *Individuals Considered Employees,* earlier.

Instructions for Worksheet 1

Column (a). Enter the name or other identifying information for all individuals considered employees for purposes of this credit. For details, see *Individuals Considered Employees,* earlier.

Column (b). Enter the total hours of service for the tax year for each employee listed in column (a). Do not enter more than 2,080 hours for any employee. But enter -0-

for seasonal employees who worked 120 or fewer days during the tax year. The information in this column is used to figure your number of full-time equivalent employees on Worksheet 2. For details, see *Full-Time Equivalent Employee (FTE) Limitation,* earlier.

 *Complete Worksheet 2 before you complete column (c) of Worksheet 1. **Do not** complete column (c) if Worksheet 2, line 3, is 25 or more.*

Column (c). Enter the total wages paid for the tax year for each employee listed in column (a). But enter -0- for seasonal employees who worked 120 or fewer days during the tax year. The information in this column is used to figure your average annual wages on Worksheet 3. For details, see *Average Annual Wage Limitation,* earlier.

Worksheet 1. Information Needed To Complete Line 1 and Worksheets 2 and 3

If you need more rows, use a separate sheet and include the additional amounts in the totals below.

	(a) Individuals Considered Employees	(b) Employee Hours of Service	(c) Employee Wages Paid
1.			
2.			
3.			
4.			
5.			
6.			
7.			
8.			
9.			
10.			
11.			
12.			
13.			
14.			
15.			
16.			
17.			
18.			
19.			
20.			
21.			
22.			
23.			
24.			
25.			
Totals:			

Line 2

Enter the number of full-time equivalent employees shown on line 3 of Worksheet 2. For details, see *Full-Time Equivalent Employee (FTE) Limitation,* earlier.

Worksheet 2. Full-Time Equivalent Employees (FTEs)

1. Enter the total employee hours of service from Worksheet 1, column (b) . . . . 1.	
2. Hours of service per FTE . . . . 2.	2,080
3. **Full-time equivalent employees.** Divide line 1 by line 2. If the result is not a whole number (0, 1, 2, etc.), generally round the result down to the next lowest whole number. However, if the result is less than one, enter 1. Report this amount on Form 8941, line 2 . . . . 3.	

Line 3

Enter the average annual wages shown on line 3 of Worksheet 3. For details, see *Average Annual Wage Limitation,* earlier.

Worksheet 3. Average Annual Wages

1. Enter the total employee wages paid from Worksheet 1, column (c) . . . . 1.	
2. Enter FTEs from Worksheet 2, line 3 . . . 2.	
3. **Average annual wages.** Divide line 1 by line 2. If the result is not a multiple of $1,000 ($1,000, $2,000, $3,000, etc.), round the result down to the next lowest multiple of $1,000. Report this amount on Form 8941, line 3 . . . . 3.	

Line 4

Enter the total employer premiums paid shown in column (b) of Worksheet 4. For details, see *Instructions for Worksheet 4* below.

Line 5

Enter the total employer-state-average premiums shown in column (c) of Worksheet 4. For details, see *Instructions for Worksheet 4* below.

Instructions for Worksheet 4

Column (a). Enter the name or other identifying information for each individual listed in column (a) of Worksheet 1 who was enrolled in health insurance coverage you provided to employees during the tax year under a qualifying arrangement. For details, see *Health Insurance Coverage* and *Qualifying Arrangement,* earlier.

Column (b). Enter the total employer premiums paid for the tax year for each employee listed in column (a). For details, see *Employer Premiums Paid,* earlier.

Column (c). Enter, for each employee listed in column (a), the premiums you would have paid if the employee had enrolled in a plan or plans with a total premium equal to the average premium for the small group market in the state in which the employee works. For details, see *State Average Premium Limitation,* earlier.

 Do not *complete column (d) if Form 8941, line 12, is zero.*

Column (d). Enter the amount from column (b) of Worksheet 1 for each employee listed in column (a) of Worksheet 4.

Worksheet 4. Information Needed To Complete Lines 4 and 5 and Worksheet 7

If you need more rows, use a separate sheet and include the additional amounts in the totals below.

(a) Enrolled Individuals Considered Employees	(b) Employer Premiums Paid	(c) Employer State Average Premiums	(d) Enrolled Employee Hours of Service
1.			
2.			
3.			
4.			
5.			
6.			
7.			
8.			
9.			
10.			
11.			
12.			
13.			
14.			
15.			
16.			
17.			
18.			
19.			
20.			
21.			
22.			
23.			
24.			
25.			
Totals:			

Line 8

If the number of FTEs reported on line 2 is 10 or less, your credit is not reduced by the FTE limitation. Enter on line 8 the amount from line 7. If line 2 is more than 10, enter on line 8 the reduced credit amount shown on Worksheet 5, line 6.

Worksheet 5. FTE Limitation

```
1. Enter the amount from Form 8941, line 7 .. 1. _____
2. Enter the amount from Form
   8941, line 2 .............. 2. _____
3. Subtract 10 from line 2 ...... 3. _____
4. Divide line 3 by 15. Enter the
   result as a decimal (rounded to
   at least 3 places) ........... 4. _____
5. Multiply line 1 by line 4 .............. 5. _____
6. Subtract line 5 from line 1. Report this
   amount on Form 8941, line 8 ........... 6. _____
```

Line 9

If the average annual wages reported on line 3 are $25,000 or less, your credit is not reduced by the average annual wage limitation. Enter on line 9 the amount from line 8. If line 3 is more than $25,000, enter on line 9 the reduced credit amount shown on Worksheet 6, line 7.

Worksheet 6. Average Annual Wage Limitation

```
1. Enter the amount from Form 8941, line 8 ... 1. _____
2. Enter the amount from Form
   8941, line 7 ................ 2. _____
3. Enter the amount from Form
   8941, line 3 ................ 3. _____
4. Subtract $25,000 from line 3 .... 4. _____
5. Divide line 4 by $25,000. Enter
   the result as a decimal (rounded
   to at least 3 places) .......... 5. _____
6. Multiply line 2 by line 5 ............... 6. _____
7. Subtract line 6 from line 1. Report this
   amount on Form 8941, line 9 ........... 7. _____
```

Line 10

Enter the total amount of any state premium subsidies paid and any state tax credits available to you for premiums included on line 4. For details, see *State Premium Subsidy and Tax Credit Limitation,* earlier.

Line 13

Enter the total number of individuals shown in column (a) of Worksheet 4. These are individuals considered employees for whom you paid premiums during the tax year for health insurance coverage under a qualifying arrangement.

Line 14

Enter the number of full-time equivalent employees (FTEs) shown on line 3 of Worksheet 7. These are FTEs for whom you paid premiums for health insurance coverage under a qualifying arrangement during the tax year.

Worksheet 7. FTEs Enrolled in Coverage

```
1. Enter the total enrolled employee hours of
   service from Worksheet 4, column (d) .. 1. _____
2. Hours of service per FTE .......... 2.   2,080
3. Divide line 1 by line 2. If the result is not a
   whole number (0, 1, 2, etc.), generally
   round the result down to the next lowest
   whole number. However, if the result is
   less than one, enter 1. Report this amount
   on Form 8941, line 14 .............. 3. _____
```

Line 15

Enter any credit for small employer health insurance premiums from:
- Schedule K-1 (Form 1065), box 15 (code P),
- Schedule K-1 (Form 1120S), box 13 (code P),
- Schedule K-1 (Form 1041), box 13 (code G), and
- Any notice of credit allocation you receive from a cooperative.

Line 17

Cooperatives. A cooperative described in section 1381(a) must allocate to its patrons the credit in excess of its tax liability. Therefore, to figure the unused amount of the credit allocated to patrons, the cooperative must first figure its tax liability. While any excess is allocated to patrons, any credit recapture applies as if the cooperative had claimed the entire credit.

If the cooperative is subject to the passive activity rules, include on line 15 any credit for small employer health insurance premiums from passive activities disallowed for prior years and carried forward to this year. Complete Form 8810, Corporate Passive Activity Loss and Credit Limitations, to determine the allowed credit that must be allocated to patrons. For details, see the Instructions for Form 8810.

Estates and Trusts. Allocate the credit on line 16 between the estate or trust and the beneficiaries in the same proportion as income was allocated and enter the beneficiaries' share on line 17.

If the estate or trust is subject to the passive activity rules, include on line 15 any credit for small employer health insurance premiums from passive activities disallowed for prior years and carried forward to this year. Complete Form 8582-CR, Passive Activity Credit Limitations, to determine the allowed credit that must be allocated between the estate or trust and the beneficiaries. For details, see the Instructions for Form 8582-CR.

Line 19

Enter the total amount of certain payroll taxes. Payroll taxes, for this purpose, means only the following taxes.
- Federal income taxes the tax-exempt employer was required to withhold from employees' wages in calendar year 2011.
- Medicare taxes the tax-exempt employer was required to withhold from employees' wages in calendar year 2011.
- Medicare taxes the tax-exempt employer was required to pay for calendar year 2011.

-8-

Paperwork Reduction Act Notice. We ask for the information on this form to carry out the Internal Revenue laws of the United States. You are required to give us the information. We need it to ensure that you are complying with these laws and to allow us to figure and collect the right amount of tax.

You are not required to provide the information requested on a form that is subject to the Paperwork Reduction Act unless the form displays a valid OMB control number. Books or records relating to a form or its instructions must be retained as long as their contents may become material in the administration of any Internal Revenue law. Generally, tax returns and return information are confidential, as required by section 6103.

The time needed to complete and file this form will vary depending on individual circumstances. The estimated burden for individual taxpayers filing this form is approved under OMB control number 1545-0074 and is included in the estimates shown in the instructions for their individual income tax return. The estimated burden for all other taxpayers who file this form is shown below.

Recordkeeping . . . . 12 hr., 46 min.
Learning about the law or the form . . . . 1 hr., 23 min.
Preparing and sending the form to the IRS . . . . 2 hr., 48 min.

If you have comments concerning the accuracy of these time estimates or suggestions for making this form simpler, we would be happy to hear from you. See the instructions for the tax return with which this form is filed.

F. Tri-Agency Regulations on Preventive Care

(b) The additive is used or intended for use as a feed acidifying agent, to lower the pH, in complete swine feeds at levels not to exceed 1.2 percent of the complete feed.

(c) To assure safe use of the additive, in addition to the other information required by the Federal Food, Drug, and Cosmetic Act (the act), the label and labeling shall contain:

(1) The name of the additive.

(2) Adequate directions for use including a statement that ammonium formate must be uniformly applied and thoroughly mixed into complete swine feeds and that the complete swine feeds so treated shall be labeled as containing ammonium formate.

(d) To assure safe use of the additive, in addition to the other information required by the act and paragraph (c) of this section, the label and labeling shall contain:

(1) Appropriate warnings and safety precautions concerning ammonium formate (37 percent ammonium salt of formic acid and 62 percent formic acid).

(2) Statements identifying ammonium formate in formic acid (37 percent ammonium salt of formic acid and 62 percent formic acid) as a corrosive and possible severe irritant.

(3) Information about emergency aid in case of accidental exposure as follows:

(i) Statements reflecting requirements of applicable sections of the Superfund Amendments and Reauthorization Act (SARA), and the Occupational Safety and Health Administration's (OSHA) human safety guidance regulations.

(ii) Contact address and telephone number for reporting adverse reactions or to request a copy of the Material Safety Data Sheet (MSDS).

Dated: July 14, 2010.

Tracey H. Forfa,

Acting Director, Center for Veterinary Medicine.

[FR Doc. 2010–17565 Filed 7–16–10; 8:45 am]

BILLING CODE 4160–01–S

DEPARTMENT OF THE TREASURY

Internal Revenue Service

26 CFR Part 54

[TD 9493]

RIN 1545–BJ60

DEPARTMENT OF LABOR

Employee Benefits Security Administration

29 CFR Part 2590

RIN 1210–AB44

DEPARTMENT OF HEALTH AND HUMAN SERVICES

[OCIIO–9992–IFC]

45 CFR Part 147

RIN 0938–AQ07

Interim Final Rules for Group Health Plans and Health Insurance Issuers Relating to Coverage of Preventive Services Under the Patient Protection and Affordable Care Act

AGENCIES: Internal Revenue Service, Department of the Treasury; Employee Benefits Security Administration, Department of Labor; Office of Consumer Information and Insurance Oversight, Department of Health and Human Services.

ACTION: Interim final rules with request for comments.

SUMMARY: This document contains interim final regulations implementing the rules for group health plans and health insurance coverage in the group and individual markets under provisions of the Patient Protection and Affordable Care Act regarding preventive health services.

DATES: *Effective date.* These interim final regulations are effective on September 17, 2010.

Comment date. Comments are due on or before September 17, 2010.

Applicability dates. These interim final regulations generally apply to group health plans and group health insurance issuers for plan years beginning on or after September 23, 2010. These interim final regulations generally apply to individual health insurance issuers for policy years beginning on or after September 23, 2010.

ADDRESSES: Written comments may be submitted to any of the addresses specified below. Any comment that is submitted to any Department will be shared with the other Departments. Please do not submit duplicates.

All comments will be made available to the public. *WARNING:* Do not include any personally identifiable information (such as name, address, or other contact information) or confidential business information that you do not want publicly disclosed. All comments are posted on the Internet exactly as received, and can be retrieved by most Internet search engines. No deletions, modifications, or redactions will be made to the comments received, as they are public records. Comments may be submitted anonymously.

Department of Labor. Comments to the Department of Labor, identified by RIN 1210–AB44, by one of the following methods:

• *Federal eRulemaking Portal: http:// www.regulations.gov.* Follow the instructions for submitting comments.

• *E-mail:* E-OHPSCA2713.EBSA@dol.gov.

• *Mail or Hand Delivery:* Office of Health Plan Standards and Compliance Assistance, Employee Benefits Security Administration, Room N–5653, U.S. Department of Labor, 200 Constitution Avenue, NW., Washington, DC 20210, *Attention:* RIN 1210–AB44.

Comments received by the Department of Labor will be posted without change to *http:// www.regulations.gov* and *http:// www.dol.gov/ebsa,* and available for public inspection at the Public Disclosure Room, N–1513, Employee Benefits Security Administration, 200 Constitution Avenue, NW., Washington, DC 20210.

Department of Health and Human Services. In commenting, please refer to file code OCIIO–9992–IFC. Because of staff and resource limitations, we cannot accept comments by facsimile (FAX) transmission.

You may submit comments in one of four ways (please choose only one of the ways listed):

1. *Electronically.* You may submit electronic comments on this regulation to *http://www.regulations.gov.* Follow the instructions under the "More Search Options" tab.

2. *By regular mail.* You may mail written comments to the following address ONLY: Office of Consumer Information and Insurance Oversight, Department of Health and Human Services, Attention: OCIIO–9992–IFC. P.O. Box 8016, Baltimore, MD 21244–1850.

Please allow sufficient time for mailed comments to be received before the close of the comment period.

3. *By express or overnight mail.* You may send written comments to the

Federal Register / Vol. 75, No. 137 / Monday, July 19, 2010 / Rules and Regulations   **41727**

following address ONLY: Office of Consumer Information and Insurance Oversight, Department of Health and Human Services, Attention: OCIIO–9992–IFC, Mail Stop C4–26–05, 7500 Security Boulevard, Baltimore, MD 21244–1850.

4. *By hand or courier.* If you prefer, you may deliver (by hand or courier) your written comments before the close of the comment period to either of the following addresses:

a. For delivery in Washington, DC—Office of Consumer Information and Insurance Oversight, Department of Health and Human Services, Room 445–G, Hubert H. Humphrey Building, 200 Independence Avenue, SW., Washington, DC 20201.

(Because access to the interior of the Hubert H. Humphrey Building is not readily available to persons without Federal government identification, commenters are encouraged to leave their comments in the OCIIO drop slots located in the main lobby of the building. A stamp-in clock is available for persons wishing to retain a proof of filing by stamping in and retaining an extra copy of the comments being filed.)

b. For delivery in Baltimore, MD—Centers for Medicare & Medicaid Services, Department of Health and Human Services, 7500 Security Boulevard, Baltimore, MD 21244–1850.

If you intend to deliver your comments to the Baltimore address, please call (410) 786–7195 in advance to schedule your arrival with one of our staff members.

Comments mailed to the addresses indicated as appropriate for hand or courier delivery may be delayed and received after the comment period.

Submission of comments on paperwork requirements. You may submit comments on this document's paperwork requirements by following the instructions at the end of the "Collection of Information Requirements" section in this document.

Inspection of Public Comments. All comments received before the close of the comment period are available for viewing by the public, including any personally identifiable or confidential business information that is included in a comment. We post all comments received before the close of the comment period on the following Web site as soon as possible after they have been received: *http:// www.regulations.gov.* Follow the search instructions on that Web site to view public comments.

Comments received timely will also be available for public inspection as they are received, generally beginning approximately three weeks after publication of a document, at the headquarters of the Centers for Medicare & Medicaid Services, 7500 Security Boulevard, Baltimore, Maryland 21244, Monday through Friday of each week from 8:30 a.m. to 4 p.m. EST. To schedule an appointment to view public comments, phone 1–800–743–3951.

Internal Revenue Service. Comments to the IRS, identified by REG–120391–10, by one of the following methods:

• *Federal eRulemaking Portal: http:// www.regulations.gov.* Follow the instructions for submitting comments.

• *Mail:* CC:PA:LPD:PR (REG–120391–10), room 5205, Internal Revenue Service, P.O. Box 7604, Ben Franklin Station, Washington, DC 20044.

• *Hand or courier delivery:* Monday through Friday between the hours of 8 a.m. and 4 p.m. to: CC:PA:LPD:PR (REG–120391–10), Courier's Desk, Internal Revenue Service, 1111 Constitution Avenue, NW., Washington DC 20224.

All submissions to the IRS will be open to public inspection and copying in room 1621, 1111 Constitution Avenue, NW., Washington, DC from 9 a.m. to 4 p.m.

FOR FURTHER INFORMATION CONTACT: Amy Turner or Beth Baum, Employee Benefits Security Administration, Department of Labor, at (202) 693–8335; Karen Levin, Internal Revenue Service, Department of the Treasury, at (202) 622–6080; Jim Mayhew, Office of Consumer Information and Insurance Oversight, Department of Health and Human Services, at (410) 786–1565.

Customer Service Information: Individuals interested in obtaining information from the Department of Labor concerning employment-based health coverage laws may call the EBSA Toll-Free Hotline at 1–866–444–EBSA (3272) or visit the Department of Labor's Web site (*http://www.dol.gov/ebsa*). In addition, information from HHS on private health insurance for consumers can be found on the Centers for Medicare & Medicaid Services (CMS) Web site (*http://www.cms.hhs.gov/ HealthInsReformforConsume/01_ Overview.as*) and information on health reform can be found at *http:// www.healthreform.gov.*

SUPPLEMENTARY INFORMATION:

I. Background

The Patient Protection and Affordable Care Act (the Affordable Care Act). Public Law 111–148, was enacted on March 23, 2010; the Health Care and Education Reconciliation Act (the Reconciliation Act), Public Law 111–152, was enacted on March 30, 2010. The Affordable Care Act and the Reconciliation Act reorganize, amend, and add to the provisions of part A of title XXVII of the Public Health Service Act (PHS Act) relating to group health plans and health insurance issuers in the group and individual markets. The term "group health plan" includes both insured and self-insured group health plans.[1] The Affordable Care Act adds section 715(a)(1) to the Employee Retirement Income Security Act (ERISA) and section 9815(a)(1) to the Internal Revenue Code (the Code) to incorporate the provisions of part A of title XXVII of the PHS Act into ERISA and the Code, and make them applicable to group health plans, and health insurance issuers providing health insurance coverage in connection with group health plans. The PHS Act sections incorporated by this reference are sections 2701 through 2728. PHS Act sections 2701 through 2719A are substantially new, though they incorporate some provisions of prior law. PHS Act sections 2722 through 2728 are sections of prior law renumbered, with some, mostly minor, changes.

Subtitles A and C of title I of the Affordable Care Act amend the requirements of title XXVII of the PHS Act (changes to which are incorporated into ERISA section 715). The preemption provisions of ERISA section 731 and PHS Act section 2724[2] (implemented in 29 CFR 2590.731(a) and 45 CFR 146.143(a)) apply so that the requirements of part 7 of ERISA and title XXVII of the PHS Act, as amended by the Affordable Care Act, are not to be "construed to supersede any provision of State law which establishes, implements, or continues in effect any standard or requirement solely relating to health insurance issuers in connection with group or individual health insurance coverage except to the extent that such standard or requirement prevents the application of a requirement" of the Affordable Care Act. Accordingly, State laws that impose on health insurance issuers requirements that are stricter than those imposed by the Affordable Care Act will not be superseded by the Affordable Care Act.

---

[1] The term "group health plan" is used in title XXVII of the PHS Act, part 7 of ERISA, and chapter 100 of the Code, and is distinct from the term "health plan," as used in other provisions of title I of the Affordable Care Act. The term "health plan" does not include self-insured group health plans.

[2] Code section 9815 incorporates the preemption provisions of PHS Act section 2724. Prior to the Affordable Care Act, there were no express preemption provisions in chapter 100 of the Code.

The Departments of Health and Human Services, Labor, and the Treasury (the Departments) are issuing regulations in several phases implementing the revised PHS Act sections 2701 through 2719A and related provisions of the Affordable Care Act. The first phase in this series was the publication of a Request for Information relating to the medical loss ratio provisions of PHS Act section 2718, published in the **Federal Register** on April 14, 2010 (75 FR 19297). The second phase was interim final regulations implementing PHS Act section 2714 (requiring dependent coverage of children to age 26), published in the **Federal Register** on May 13, 2010 (75 FR 27122). The third phase was interim final regulations implementing section 1251 of the Affordable Care Act (relating to status as a grandfathered health plan), published in the **Federal Register** on June 17, 2010 (75 FR 34538). The fourth phase was interim final regulations implementing PHS Act sections 2704 (prohibiting preexisting condition exclusions), 2711 (regarding lifetime and annual dollar limits on benefits), 2712 (regarding restrictions on rescissions), and 2719A (regarding patient protections), published in the **Federal Register** on June 28, 2010 (75 FR 37188). These interim final regulations are being published to implement PHS Act section 2713 (relating to coverage for preventive services). PHS Act section 2713 is generally effective for plan years (in the individual market, policy years) beginning on or after September 23, 2010, which is six months after the March 23, 2010 date of enactment of the Affordable Care Act. The implementation of other provisions of PHS Act sections 2701 through 2719A will be addressed in future regulations.

II. Overview of the Regulations: PHS Act Section 2713, Coverage of Preventive Health Services (26 CFR 54.9815–2713T, 29 CFR 2590.715–2713, 45 CFR 147.130)

Section 2713 of the PHS Act, as added by the Affordable Care Act, and these interim final regulations require that a group health plan and a health insurance issuer offering group or individual health insurance coverage provide benefits for and prohibit the imposition of cost-sharing requirements with respect to:

• Evidence-based items or services that have in effect a rating of A or B in the current recommendations of the United States Preventive Services Task

Force (Task Force) with respect to the individual involved.[3]

• Immunizations for routine use in children, adolescents, and adults that have in effect a recommendation from the Advisory Committee on Immunization Practices of the Centers for Disease Control and Prevention (Advisory Committee) with respect to the individual involved. A recommendation of the Advisory Committee is considered to be "in effect" after it has been adopted by the Director of the Centers for Disease Control and Prevention. A recommendation is considered to be for routine use if it appears on the Immunization Schedules of the Centers for Disease Control and Prevention.

• With respect to infants, children, and adolescents, evidence-informed preventive care and screenings provided for in the comprehensive guidelines supported by the Health Resources and Services Administration (HRSA).

• With respect to women, evidence-informed preventive care and screening provided for in comprehensive guidelines supported by HRSA (not otherwise addressed by the recommendations of the Task Force). The Department of HHS is developing these guidelines and expects to issue them no later than August 1, 2011.

The complete list of recommendations and guidelines that are required to be covered under these interim final regulations can be found at *http://www.HealthCare.gov/center/regulations/prevention.html*. Together, the items and services described in these recommendations and guidelines are referred to in this preamble as "recommended preventive services."

These interim final regulations clarify the cost-sharing requirements when a recommended preventive service is provided during an office visit. First, if a recommended preventive service is billed separately (or is tracked as individual encounter data separately) from an office visit, then a plan or issuer may impose cost-sharing requirements with respect to the office visit. Second, if a recommended preventive service is

not billed separately (or is not tracked as individual encounter data separately) from an office visit and the primary purpose of the office visit is the delivery of such an item or service, then a plan or issuer may not impose cost-sharing requirements with respect to the office visit. Finally, if a recommended preventive service is not billed separately (or is not tracked as individual encounter data separately) from an office visit and the primary purpose of the office visit is not the delivery of such an item or service, then a plan or issuer may impose cost-sharing requirements with respect to the office visit. The reference to tracking individual encounter data was included to provide guidance with respect to plans and issuers that use capitation or similar payment arrangements that do not bill individually for items and services.

Examples in these interim final regulations illustrate these provisions. In one example, an individual receives a cholesterol screening test, a recommended preventive service, during a routine office visit. The plan or issuer may impose cost-sharing requirements for the office visit because the recommended preventive service is billed as a separate charge. A second example illustrates that treatment resulting from a preventive screening can be subject to cost-sharing requirements if the treatment is not itself a recommended preventive service. In another example, an individual receives a recommended preventive service that is not billed as a separate charge. In this example, the primary purpose for the office visit is recurring abdominal pain and not the delivery of a recommended preventive service; therefore the plan or issuer may impose cost-sharing requirements for the office visit. In the final example, an individual receives a recommended preventive service that is not billed as a separate charge, and the delivery of that service is the primary purpose of the office visit. Therefore, the plan or issuer may not impose cost-sharing requirements for the office visit.

With respect to a plan or health insurance coverage that has a network of providers, these interim final regulations make clear that a plan or issuer is not required to provide coverage for recommended preventive services delivered by an out-of-network provider. Such a plan or issuer may also impose cost-sharing requirements for recommended preventive services delivered by an out-of-network provider.

These interim final regulations provide that if a recommendation or

---

[3] Under PHS Act section 2713(a)(5), the Task Force recommendations regarding breast cancer screening, mammography, and prevention issued in or around November of 2009 are not to be considered current recommendations on this subject for purposes of any law. Thus, the recommendations regarding breast cancer screening, mammography, and prevention issued by the Task Force prior to those issued in or around November of 2009 (*i.e.,* those issued in 2002) will be considered current until new recommendations in this area are issued by the Task Force or appear in comprehensive guidelines supported by the Health Resources and Services Administration concerning preventive care and screenings for women.

guideline for a recommended preventive service does not specify the frequency, method, treatment, or setting for the provision of that service, the plan or issuer can use reasonable medical management techniques to determine any coverage limitations. The use of reasonable medical management techniques allows plans and issuers to adapt these recommendations and guidelines to coverage of specific items and services where cost sharing must be waived. Thus, under these interim final regulations, a plan or issuer may rely on established techniques and the relevant evidence base to determine the frequency, method, treatment, or setting for which a recommended preventive service will be available without cost-sharing requirements to the extent not specified in a recommendation or guideline.

The statute and these interim final regulations clarify that a plan or issuer continues to have the option to cover preventive services in addition to those required to be covered by PHS Act section 2713. For such additional preventive services, a plan or issuer may impose cost-sharing requirements at its discretion. Moreover, a plan or issuer may impose cost-sharing requirements for a treatment that is not a recommended preventive service, even if the treatment results from a recommended preventive service.

The statute requires the Departments to establish an interval of not less than one year between when recommendations or guidelines under PHS Act section 2713(a)[4] are issued, and the plan year (in the individual market, policy year) for which coverage of the services addressed in such recommendations or guidelines must be in effect. These interim final regulations provide that such coverage must be provided for plan years (in the

individual market, policy years) beginning on or after the later of September 23, 2010, or one year after the date the recommendation or guideline is issued. Thus, recommendations and guidelines issued prior to September 23, 2009 must be provided for plan years (in the individual market, policy years) beginning on or after September 23, 2010. For the purpose of these interim final regulations, a recommendation or guideline of the Task Force is considered to be issued on the last day of the month on which the Task Force publishes or otherwise releases the recommendation; a recommendation or guideline of the Advisory Committee is considered to be issued on the date on which it is adopted by the Director of the Centers for Disease Control and Prevention; and a recommendation or guideline in the comprehensive guidelines supported by HRSA is considered to be issued on the date on which it is accepted by the Administrator of HRSA or, if applicable, adopted by the Secretary of HHS. For recommendations and guidelines adopted after September 23, 2009, information at *http:// www.HealthCare.gov/center/ regulations/prevention.html* will be updated on an ongoing basis and will include the date on which the recommendation or guideline was accepted or adopted.

Finally, these interim final regulations make clear that a plan or issuer is not required to provide coverage or waive cost-sharing requirements for any item or service that has ceased to be a recommended preventive service.[5] Other requirements of Federal or State law may apply in connection with ceasing to provide coverage or changing cost-sharing requirements for any such item or service. For example, PHS Act section 2715(d)(4) requires a plan or issuer to give 60 days advance notice to an enrollee before any material modification will become effective.

Recommendations or guidelines in effect as of July 13, 2010 are described in section V later in this preamble. Any change to a recommendation or guideline that has—at any point since September 23, 2009—been included in the recommended preventive services will be noted at *http:// www.HealthCare.gov/center/ regulations/prevention.html.* As described above, new recommendations and guidelines will also be noted at this

site and plans and issuers need not make changes to coverage and cost-sharing requirements based on a new recommendation or guideline until the first plan year (in the individual market, policy year) beginning on or after the date that is one year after the new recommendation or guideline went into effect. Therefore, by visiting this site once per year, plans or issuers will have straightforward access to all the information necessary to determine any additional items or services that must be covered without cost-sharing requirements, or to determine any items or services that are no longer required to be covered.

The Affordable Care Act gives authority to the Departments to develop guidelines for group health plans and health insurance issuers offering group or individual health insurance coverage to utilize value-based insurance designs as part of their offering of preventive health services. Value-based insurance designs include the provision of information and incentives for consumers that promote access to and use of higher value providers, treatments, and services. The Departments recognize the important role that value-based insurance design can play in promoting the use of appropriate preventive services. These interim final regulations, for example, permit plans and issuers to implement designs that seek to foster better quality and efficiency by allowing cost-sharing for recommended preventive services delivered on an out-of-network basis while eliminating cost-sharing for recommended preventive health services delivered on an in-network basis. The Departments are developing additional guidelines regarding the utilization of value-based insurance designs by group health plans and health insurance issuers with respect to preventive benefits. The Departments are seeking comments related to the development of such guidelines for value-based insurance designs that promote consumer choice of providers or services that offer the best value and quality, while ensuring access to critical, evidence-based preventive services.

The requirements to cover recommended preventive services without any cost-sharing requirements do not apply to grandfathered health plans. *See* 26 CFR 54.9815–1251T, 29 CFR 2590.715–1251, and 45 CFR 147.140 (75 FR 34538, June 17, 2010).

III. Interim Final Regulations and Request for Comments

Section 9833 of the Code, section 734 of ERISA, and section 2792 of the PHS

---

[4] Section 2713(b)(1) refers to an interval between "the date on which a recommendation described in subsection (a)(1) or (a)(2) or a guideline under subsection (a)(3) is issued and the plan year with respect to which the requirement described in subsection (a) is effective with respect to the service described in such recommendation or guideline." While the first part of this statement does not mention guidelines under subsection (a)(4), it would make no sense to treat the services covered under (a)(4) any differently than those in (a)(1), (a)(2), and (a)(3). First, the same sentence refers to "the requirement described in subsection (a)," which would include a requirement under (a)(4). Secondly, the guidelines under (a)(4) are from the same source as those under (a)(3), except with respect to women rather than infants, children and adolescents; and other preventive services involving women are addressed in (a)(1), so there is no plausible policy rationale for treating them differently. Third, without this clarification, it would be unclear when such services would have to be covered. These interim final regulations accordingly apply the intervals established therein to services under section 2713(a)(4).

[5] For example, if a recommendation of the United States Preventive Services Task Force is downgraded from a rating of A or B to a rating of C or D, or if a recommendation or guideline no longer includes a particular item or service.

Act authorize the Secretaries of the Treasury, Labor, and HHS (collectively, the Secretaries) to promulgate any interim final rules that they determine are appropriate to carry out the provisions of chapter 100 of the Code, part 7 of subtitle B of title I of ERISA, and part A of title XXVII of the PHS Act, which include PHS Act sections 2701 through 2728 and the incorporation of those sections into ERISA section 715 and Code section 9815.

In addition, under Section 553(b) of the Administrative Procedure Act (APA) (5 U.S.C. 551 *et seq.*) a general notice of proposed rulemaking is not required when an agency, for good cause, finds that notice and public comment thereon are impracticable, unnecessary, or contrary to the public interest. The provisions of the APA that ordinarily require a notice of proposed rulemaking do not apply here because of the specific authority granted by section 9833 of the Code, section 734 of ERISA, and section 2792 of the PHS Act. However, even if the APA were applicable, the Secretaries have determined that it would be impracticable and contrary to the public interest to delay putting the provisions in these interim final regulations in place until a full public notice and comment process was completed. As noted above, the preventive health service provisions of the Affordable Care Act are applicable for plan years (in the individual market, policy years) beginning on or after September 23, 2010, six months after date of enactment. Had the Departments published a notice of proposed rulemaking, provided for a 60-day comment period, and only then prepared final regulations, which would be subject to a 60-day delay in effective date, it is unlikely that it would have been possible to have final regulations in effect before late September, when these requirements could be in effect for some plans or policies. Moreover, the requirements in these interim final

regulations require significant lead time in order to implement. These interim final regulations require plans and issuers to provide coverage for preventive services listed in certain recommendations and guidelines without imposing any cost-sharing requirements. Preparations presumably would have to be made to identify these preventive services. With respect to the changes that would be required to be made under these interim final regulations, group health plans and health insurance issuers subject to these provisions have to be able to take these changes into account in establishing their premiums, and in making other changes to the designs of plan or policy benefits, and these premiums and plan or policy changes would have to receive necessary approvals in advance of the plan or policy year in question.

Accordingly, in order to allow plans and health insurance coverage to be designed and implemented on a timely basis, regulations must be published and available to the public well in advance of the effective date of the requirements of the Affordable Care Act. It is not possible to have a full notice and comment process and to publish final regulations in the brief time between enactment of the Affordable Care Act and the date regulations are needed.

The Secretaries further find that issuance of proposed regulations would not be sufficient because the provisions of the Affordable Care Act protect significant rights of plan participants and beneficiaries and individuals covered by individual health insurance policies and it is essential that participants, beneficiaries, insureds, plan sponsors, and issuers have certainty about their rights and responsibilities. Proposed regulations are not binding and cannot provide the necessary certainty. By contrast, the interim final regulations provide the public with an opportunity for

comment, but without delaying the effective date of the regulations.

For the foregoing reasons, the Departments have determined that it is impracticable and contrary to the public interest to engage in full notice and comment rulemaking before putting these interim final regulations into effect, and that it is in the public interest to promulgate interim final regulations.

IV. Economic Impact

Under Executive Order 12866 (58 FR 51735), a "significant" regulatory action is subject to review by the Office of Management and Budget (OMB). Section 3(f) of the Executive Order defines a "significant regulatory action" as an action that is likely to result in a rule (1) having an annual effect on the economy of $100 million or more in any one year, or adversely and materially affecting a sector of the economy, productivity, competition, jobs, the environment, public health or safety, or State, local or tribal governments or communities (also referred to as "economically significant"); (2) creating a serious inconsistency or otherwise interfering with an action taken or planned by another agency; (3) materially altering the budgetary impacts of entitlement grants, user fees, or loan programs or the rights and obligations of recipients thereof; or (4) raising novel legal or policy issues arising out of legal mandates, the President's priorities, or the principles set forth in the Executive Order. OMB has determined that this regulation is economically significant within the meaning of section 3(f)(1) of the Executive Order, because it is likely to have an annual effect on the economy of $100 million in any one year. Accordingly, OMB has reviewed these rules pursuant to the Executive Order. The Departments provide an assessment of the potential costs, benefits, and transfers associated with these interim final regulations, summarized in the following table.

TABLE 1—ACCOUNTING TABLE (2011–2013)

Benefits:

Qualitative: By expanding coverage and eliminating cost sharing for the recommended preventive services, the Departments expect access and utilization of these services to increase. To the extent that individuals increase their use of these services the Departments anticipate several benefits: (1) prevention and reduction in transmission of illnesses as a result of immunization and screening of transmissible diseases; (2) delayed onset, earlier treatment, and reduction in morbidity and mortality as a result of early detection, screening, and counseling; (3) increased productivity and fewer sick days; and (4) savings from lower health care costs. Another benefit of these interim final regulations will be to distribute the cost of preventive services more equitably across the broad insured population.

Costs:

Qualitative: New costs to the health care system result when beneficiaries increase their use of preventive services in response to the changes in coverage and cost-sharing requirements of preventive services. The magnitude of this effect on utilization depends on the price elasticity of demand and the percentage change in prices facing those with reduced cost sharing or newly gaining coverage.

Transfers:

TABLE 1—ACCOUNTING TABLE (2011–2013)—Continued

Qualitative: Transfers will occur to the extent that costs that were previously paid out-of-pocket for certain preventive services will now be covered by group health plans and issuers under these interim final regulations. Risk pooling in the group market will result in sharing expected cost increases across an entire plan or employee group as higher average premiums for all enrollees. However, not all of those covered will utilize preventive services to an equivalent extent. As a result, these interim final regulations create a small transfer from those paying premiums in the group market utilizing less than the average volume of preventive services in their risk pool to those whose utilization is greater than average. To the extent there is risk pooling in the individual market, a similar transfer will occur.

A. The Need for Federal Regulatory Action

As discussed later in this preamble, there is current underutilization of preventive services, which stems from three main factors. First, due to turnover in the health insurance market, health insurance issuers do not currently have incentives to cover preventive services, whose benefits may only be realized in the future when an individual may no longer be enrolled. Second, many preventive services generate benefits that do not accrue immediately to the individual that receives the services, making the individual less likely to take-up, especially in the face of direct, immediate costs. Third, some of the benefits of preventive services accrue to society as a whole, and thus do not get factored into an individual's decision-making over whether to obtain such services.

These interim final regulations address these market failures through two avenues. First, they require coverage of recommended preventive services by non-grandfathered group health plans and health insurance issuers in the group and individual markets, thereby overcoming plans' lack of incentive to invest in these services. Second, they eliminate cost-sharing requirements, thereby removing a barrier that could otherwise lead an individual to not obtain such services, given the long-term and partially external nature of benefits.

These interim final regulations are necessary in order to provide rules that plan sponsors and issuers can use to determine how to provide coverage for certain preventive health care services without the imposition of cost sharing in connection with these services.

B. PHS Act Section 2713, Coverage of Preventive Health Services (26 CFR 54.9815–2713T, 29 CFR 2590.715–2713, 45 CFR 147.130)

1. Summary

As discussed earlier in this preamble, PHS Act section 2713, as added by the Affordable Care Act, and these interim final regulations require a group health plan and a health insurance issuer offering group or individual health insurance coverage to provide benefits for and prohibit the imposition of cost-sharing requirements with respect to the following preventive health services:

• Evidence-based items or services that have in effect a rating of A or B in the current recommendations of the United States Preventive Services Task Force (Task Force). While these guidelines will change over time, for the purposes of this impact analysis, the Departments utilized currently available guidelines, which include blood pressure and cholesterol screening, diabetes screening for hypertensive patients, various cancer and sexually transmitted infection screenings, and counseling related to aspirin use, tobacco cessation, obesity, and other topics.

• Immunizations for routine use in children, adolescents, and adults that have in effect a recommendation from the Advisory Committee on Immunization Practices of the Centers for Disease Control and Prevention (Advisory Committee) with respect to the individual involved.

• With respect to infants, children, and adolescents, evidence-informed preventive care and screenings provided for in the comprehensive guidelines supported by the Health Resources and Services Administration (HRSA).

• With respect to women, evidence-informed preventive care and screening provided for in comprehensive guidelines supported by HRSA (not otherwise addressed by the recommendations of the Task Force). The Department of HHS is developing these guidelines and expects to issue them no later than August 1, 2011.

2. Preventive Services

For the purposes of this analysis, the Departments used the relevant recommendations of the Task Force and Advisory Committee and current HRSA guidelines as described in section V later in this preamble. In addition to covering immunizations, these lists include such services as blood pressure and cholesterol screening, diabetes screening for hypertensive patients, various cancer and sexually transmitted infection screenings, genetic testing for the BRCA gene, adolescent depression screening, lead testing, autism testing, and oral health screening and counseling related to aspirin use, tobacco cessation, and obesity.

3. Estimated Number of Affected Entities

For purposes of the new requirements in the Affordable Care Act that apply to group health plans and health insurance issuers in the group and individual markets, the Departments have defined a large group health plan as an employer plan with 100 or more workers and a small group plan as an employer plan with less than 100 workers. The Departments estimated that there are approximately 72,000 large and 2.8 million small ERISA-covered group health plans with an estimated 97.0 million participants in large group plans and 40.9 million participants in small group plans.[6] The Departments estimate that there are 126,000 governmental plans with 36.1 million participants in large plans and 2.3 million participants in small plans.[7] The Departments estimate there are 16.7 million individuals under age 65 covered by individual health insurance policies.[8]

As described in the Departments' interim final regulations relating to status as a grandfathered health plan,[9] the Affordable Care Act preserves the ability of individuals to retain coverage under a group health plan or health insurance coverage in which the individual was enrolled on March 23, 2010 (a grandfathered health plan). Group health plans, and group and individual health insurance coverage, that are grandfathered health plans do not have to meet the requirements of these interim final regulations. Therefore, only plans and issuers offering group and individual health insurance coverage that are not grandfathered health plans will be affected by these interim final regulations.

---

[6] All participant counts and the estimates of individual policies are from the U.S. Department of Labor. EBSA calculations using the March 2008 Current Population Survey Annual Social and Economic Supplement and the 2008 Medical Expenditure Panel Survey.

[7] Estimate is from the 2007 Census of Government.

[8] US Census Bureau, Current Population Survey, March 2009.

[9] 75 FR 34538 (June 17, 2010).

41732 Federal Register / Vol. 75, No. 137 / Monday, July 19, 2010 / Rules and Regulations

Plans can choose to relinquish their grandfather status in order to make certain otherwise permissible changes to their plans.[10] The Affordable Care Act provides plans with the ability to maintain grandfathered status in order to promote stability for consumers while allowing plans and sponsors to make reasonable adjustments to lower costs and encourage the efficient use of services. Based on an analysis of the changes plans have made over the past few years, the Departments expect that more plans will choose to make these changes over time and therefore the number of grandfathered health plans is expected to decrease. Correspondingly, the number of plans and policies affected by these interim final regulations is likely to increase over time. In addition, the number of individuals receiving the benefits of the Affordable Care Act is likely to increase over time. The Departments' mid-range estimate is that 18 percent of large employer plans and 30 percent of small employer plans would relinquish grandfather status in 2011, increasing over time to 45 percent and 66 percent respectively by 2013, although there is substantial uncertainty surrounding these estimates.[11]

Using the mid-range assumptions, the Departments estimate that in 2011, roughly 31 million people will be enrolled in group health plans subject to the prevention provisions in these interim final regulations, growing to approximately 78 million in 2013.[12] The mid-range estimates suggest that approximately 98 million individuals will be enrolled in grandfathered group health plans in 2013, many of which already cover preventive services (see discussion of the extent of preventive services coverage in employer-sponsored plans later in this preamble).

In the individual market, one study estimated that 40 percent to 67 percent of individual policies terminate each year. Because all newly purchased individual policies are not grandfathered, the Departments expect that a large proportion of individual policies will not be grandfathered, covering up to and perhaps exceeding 10 million individuals.[13]

However, not all of the individuals potentially affected by these interim final regulations will directly benefit given the prevalence and variation in insurance coverage today. State laws will affect the number of entities affected by all or some provision of these interim final regulations, since plans, policies, and enrollees in States that already have certain requirements will be affected to different degrees.[14] For instance, 29 States require that health insurance issuers cover most or all recommended immunizations for children.[15] Of these 29 States, 18 States require first-dollar coverage of immunizations so that the insurers pay for immunizations without a deductible and 12 States exempt immunizations from copayments (e.g., $5, $10, or $20 per vaccine) or coinsurance (e.g., 10 percent or 20 percent of charges). State laws also require coverage of certain other preventive health services. Every State except Utah mandates coverage for some type of breast cancer screening for women. Twenty-eight States mandate coverage for some cervical cancer screening and 13 States mandate coverage for osteoporosis screening.[16]

Estimation of the number of entities immediately affected by some or all provisions of these interim final regulations is further complicated by the fact that, although not all States require insurance coverage for certain preventive services, many health plans have already chosen to cover these services. For example, most health plans cover most childhood and some adult immunizations contained in the recommendations from the Advisory Committee. A survey of small, medium and large employers showed that 78 percent to 80 percent of their point of service, preferred provider organization (PPO), and health maintenance organization (HMO) health plans covered childhood immunizations and 57 percent to 66 percent covered influenza vaccines in 2001.[17] All 61 health plans (HMOs and PPOs) responding to a 2005 America's Health Insurance Plans (AHIP) survey covered childhood immunizations [18] in their best-selling products and almost all health plans (60 out of 61) covered diphtheria-tetanus-pertussis vaccines and influenza vaccines for adults.[19] A survey of private and public employer health plans found that 84 percent covered influenza vaccines in 2002–2003.[20]

Similarly, many health plans already cover preventive services today, but there are differences in the coverage of these services in the group and individual markets. According to a 2009 survey of employer health benefits, over 85 percent of employer-sponsored health insurance plans covered preventive services without having to meet a deductible.[21] Coverage of preventive services does vary slightly by employer size, with large employers being more likely to cover such services than small employers.[22] In contrast, coverage of preventive services is less prevalent and varies more significantly in the individual market.[23] For PPOs,

---

[10] See 75 FR 34538 (June 17, 2010).

[11] See 75 FR 34538 (June 17, 2010) for a detailed description of the derivation of the estimates for the percentages of grandfathered health plans. In brief, the Departments used data from the 2008 and 2009 Kaiser Family Foundations/Health Research and Educational Trust survey of employers to estimate the proportion of plans that made changes in cost-sharing requirements that would have caused them to relinquish grandfather status if those same changes were made in 2011, and then applied a set of assumptions about how employer behavior might change in response to the incentives created by the grandfather regulations to estimate the proportion of plans likely to relinquish grandfather status. The estimates of changes in 2012 and 2013 were calculated by using the 2011 calculations and assuming that an identical percentage of plan sponsors will relinquish grandfather status in each year.

[12] To estimate the number of individuals covered in grandfathered health plans, the Departments extended the analysis described in 75 FR 34538, and estimated a weighted average of the number of employees in grandfathered health plans in the large employer and small employer markets separately, weighting by the number of employees in each employer's plan. Estimates for the large employer and small employer markets were then combined, using the estimates supplied above that there are 133.1 million covered lives in the large group market, and 43.2 million in the small group market.

[13] Adele M. Kirk. The Individual Insurance Market: A Building Block for Health Care Reform? *Health Care Financing Organization Research Synthesis.* May 2008.

[14] Of note, State insurance requirements do not apply to self-insured group health plans, whose participants and beneficiaries make up 57 percent of covered employees (in firms with 3 or more employees) in 2009 according to a major annual survey of employers due to ERISA preemption of State insurance laws. See e.g., Kaiser Family Foundation and Health Research and Education Trust, *Employer Health Benefits 2009 Annual Survey* (2009).

[15] See e.g., American Academy of Pediatrics, *State Legislative Report* (2009).

[16] See Kaiser Family Foundation, www.statehealthfacts.org.

[17] See e.g., Mary Ann Bondi et. al., "Employer Coverage of Clinical Preventive Services in the United States," *American Journal of Health Promotion,* 20(3), pp. 214–222 (2006).

[18] The specific immunizations include: DTaP (diphtheria and tetanus toxoids and acellular Pertussis), Hib (*Haemophilus influenza* type b), Hepatitis B, inactivated polio, influenza, MMR (measles, mumps, and rubella), pneumococcal, and varicella vaccine.

[19] McPhillips-Tangum C., Rehm B., Hilton O. "Immunization practices and policies: A survey of health insurance plans." *AHIP Coverage.* 47(1), 32–7 (2006).

[20] See e.g., Matthew M. Davis et. al., "Benefits Coverage for Adult Vaccines in Employer-Sponsored Health Plans," University of Michigan for the CDC National Immunizations Program (2003).

[21] See e.g., Kaiser Family Foundation and Health Research and Education Trust, *Employer Health Benefits 2009 Annual Survey* (2009) available at http://ehbs.kff.org/pdf/2009/7936.pdf.

[22] See e.g., Mary Ann Bondi et. al., "Employer Coverage of Clinical Preventive Services in the United States," American Journal of Health Promotion, 20(3), pp. 214–222 (2006).

[23] See e.g., Matthew M. Davis et. al., "Benefits Coverage for Adult Vaccines in Employer-Sponsored Health Plans," University of Michigan

only 66.2 percent of single policies purchased covered adult physicals, while 94.1 percent covered cancer screenings.[24]

In summary, the number of affected entities depends on several factors, such as whether a health plan retains its grandfather status, the number of new health plans, whether State benefit requirements for preventive services apply, and whether plans or issuers voluntarily offer coverage and/or no cost sharing for recommended preventive services. In addition, participants, beneficiaries, and enrollees in such plans or health insurance coverage will be affected in different ways: Some will newly gain coverage for recommended preventive services, while others will have the cost sharing that they now pay for such services eliminated. As such, there is considerable uncertainty surrounding estimation of the number of entities affected by these interim final regulations.

4. Benefits

The Departments anticipate that four types of benefits will result from these interim final regulations. First, individuals will experience improved health as a result of reduced transmission, prevention or delayed onset, and earlier treatment of disease. Second, healthier workers and children will be more productive with fewer missed days of work or school. Third, some of the recommended preventive services will result in savings due to lower health care costs. Fourth, the cost of preventive services will be distributed more equitably.

By expanding coverage and eliminating cost sharing for recommended preventive services, these interim final regulations could be expected to increase access to and utilization of these services, which are not used at optimal levels today. Nationwide, almost 38 percent of adult residents over 50 have never had a colorectal cancer screening (such as a sigmoidoscopy or a colonoscopy)[25] and almost 18 percent of women over age 18 have not been screened for cervical cancer in the past three years.[26] Vaccination rates for childhood vaccines are generally high due to State laws requiring certain vaccinations for children to enter school, but recommended childhood vaccines that are not subject to State laws and adult vaccines have lower vaccination rates (e.g., the meningococcal vaccination rate among teenagers is 42 percent).[27] Studies have shown that improved coverage of preventive services leads to expanded utilization of these services,[28] which would lead to substantial benefits as discussed further below.

In addition, these interim final regulations limit preventive service coverage under this provision to services recommended by the Task Force, Advisory Committee, and HRSA. The preventive services given a grade of A or B by the Task Force have been determined by the Task Force to have at least fair or good [29] evidence that the preventive service improves important health outcomes and that benefits outweigh harms in the judgment of an independent panel of private sector experts in primary care and prevention.[30] Similarly, the mission of the Advisory Committee is to provide advice that will lead to a reduction in the incidence of vaccine preventable diseases in the United States, and an increase in the safe use of vaccines and related biological products. The comprehensive guidelines for infants, children, and adolescents supported by HRSA are developed by multidisciplinary professionals in the relevant fields to provide a framework for improving children's health and reducing morbidity and mortality based on a review of the relevant evidence. The statute and interim final regulations limit the preventive services covered to those recommended by the Task Force, Advisory Committee, and HRSA because the benefits of these preventive services will be higher than others that may be popular but unproven.

Research suggests significant health benefits from a number of the preventive services that would be newly covered with no cost sharing by plans and issuers under the statute and these interim final regulations. A recent article in *JAMA* stated, "By one account, increasing delivery of just five clinical preventive services would avert 100,000 deaths per year." [31] These five services are all items and services recommended by the Task Force, Advisory Committee, and/or the comprehensive guidelines supported by HRSA. The National Council on Prevention Priorities (NCPP) estimated that almost 150,000 lives could potentially be saved by increasing the 2005 rate of utilization to 90 percent for eight of the preventive services recommended by the Task Force or Advisory Committee.[32] Table 2 shows eight of the services and the number of lives potentially saved if utilization of preventive services were to increase to 90 percent.

---

for the CDC National Immunizations Program (2003).

[24] See Individual Health Insurance 2006–2007: A Comprehensive Survey of Premiums, Availability, and Benefits. Available at *http://www.ahipresearch.org/pdfs/Individual_Market_Survey_December_2007.pdf*.

[25] This differs from the Task Force recommendation that individuals aged 50–75 receive fecal occult blood testing, sigmoidoscopy, or colonoscopy screening for colorectal cancer.

[26] For Behavioral Risk Factor Surveillance System Numbers *see e.g.* Centers for Disease Control and Prevention (CDC). *Behavioral Risk Factor Surveillance System Survey Data.* Atlanta, Georgia: U.S. Department of Health and Human Services, Centers for Disease Control and Prevention, (2008) at *http://apps.nccd.cdc.gov/BRFSS/page.asp?cat=CC&yr=2008&state=UB#CC*.

[27] See *http://www.cdc.gov/vaccines/stats-surv/imz-coverage.htm#nis* for vaccination rates.

[28] *See e.g.*, Jonathan Gruber, *The Role of Consumer Copayments for Health Care: Lessons from the RAND Health Insurance Experiment and Beyond,* Kaiser Family Foundation (Oct. 2006). This paper examines an experiment in which copays randomly vary across several thousand individuals.

The author finds that individuals are sensitive to prices for health services—i.e. as copays decline, more services are demanded. *See e.g.*, Sharon Long, "On the Road to Universal Coverage: Impacts of Reform in Massachusetts At One Year," *Health Affairs*, Volume 27, Number 4 (June 2008). The author investigated the case of Massachusetts, where coverage of preventive services became a requirement in 2007, and found that for individuals under 300 percent of the poverty line, doctor visits for preventive care increased by 6.1 percentage points in the year after adoption, even after controlling for observable characteristics. Additionally, the incidence of individuals citing cost as the reason for not receiving preventive screenings declined by 2.8 percentage points from 2006 to 2007. In the Massachusetts case, these preventive care services were not necessarily free; therefore, economists would expect a higher differential under these interim final rules because of the price sensitivity of health care usage.

[29] The Task Force defines good and fair evidence as follows. Good: Evidence includes consistent results from well-designed, well-conducted studies in representative populations that directly assess effects on health outcomes.

Fair: Evidence is sufficient to determine effects on health outcomes, but the strength of the evidence is limited by the number, quality or consistency of the individual studies, generalizability to routine practice or indirect nature of the evidence on health outcomes. See *http://www.ahrq.gov/clinic/uspstf/gradespre.htm#drec*.

[30] See *http://www.ahrq.gov/clinic/uspstf/gradespre.htm#drec* for details of the Task Force grading.

[31] Woolf, Steven. A Closer Look at the Economic Argument for Disease Prevention. *JAMA* 2009;301(5):536–538.

[32] See National Commission on Prevention Priorities. *Preventive Care: A National Profile on Use, Disparities, and Health Benefits.* Partnership for Prevention. August 2007 at *http://www.prevent.org/content/view/129/72/#citations* accessed on 6/22/2010. Lives saved were estimated using models previously developed to rank clinical preventive services. See Maciosek MV, Edwards NM, Coffield AB, Flottemesch TJ, Nelson WW, Goodman MJ, Rickey DA, Butani AB, Solberg LI. Priorities among effective clinical preventive services: methods. *Am J Prev Med* 2006; 31(1):90–96.

TABLE 2.—LIVES SAVED FROM INCREASING UTILIZATION OF SELECTED PREVENTIVE SERVICES TO 90 PERCENT

Preventive service	Population group	Percent utilizing preventive service in 2005	Lives saved annually if percent utilizing preventive service increased to 90 percent
Regular aspirin use	Men 40+ and women 50+	40	45,000
Smoking cessation advice and help to quit	All adult smokers	28	42,000
Colorectal cancer screening	Adults 50+	48	14,000
Influenza vaccination	Adults 50+	37	12,000
Cervical cancer screening in the past 3 years	Women 18–64	83	620
Cholesterol screening	Men 35+ and women 45+	79	2,450
Breast cancer screening in the past 2 years	Women 40+	67	3,700
Chlamydia screening	Women 16–25	40	30,000

Source: National Commission on Prevention Priorities, 2007.

Since financial barriers are not the only reason for sub-optimal utilization rates, population-wide utilization of preventive services is unlikely to increase to the 90 percent level assumed in Table 2 as a result of these interim final regulations. Current utilization of preventive services among insured populations varies widely, but the Departments expect that utilization will increase among those individuals in plans affected by the regulation because the provisions eliminate cost sharing and require coverage for these services.

These interim final regulations are expected to increase the take-up rate of preventive services and are likely, over time, to lead physicians to increase their use of these services knowing that they will be covered, and covered with zero copayment. In the absence of data on the elasticity of demand for these specific services, it is difficult to know precisely how many more patients will use these services. Evidence from studies comparing the utilization of preventive services such as blood pressure and cholesterol screening between insured and uninsured individuals with relatively high incomes suggests that coverage increases usage rates in a wide range between three and 30 percentage points, even among those likely to be able to afford basic preventive services out-of-pocket.[33] A reasonable assumption is that the average increase in utilization of these services will be modest, perhaps on the order of 5 to 10 percentage points for some of them. For services that are generally covered without cost sharing in the current market, the Departments would expect minimal change in utilization.

Preventive services' benefits have also been evaluated individually. Effective cancer screening, early treatment, and sustained risk reduction could reduce the death rate due to cancer by 29 percent.[34] Improved blood sugar control could reduce the risk for eye disease, kidney disease and nerve disease by 40 percent in people with Type 1 or Type 2 diabetes.[35]

Some recommended preventive services have both individual and public health value. Vaccines have reduced or eliminated serious diseases that, prior to vaccination, routinely caused serious illnesses or deaths. Maintaining high levels of immunization in the general population protects the un-immunized from exposure to the vaccine-preventable disease, so that individuals who cannot receive the vaccine or who do not have a sufficient immune response to the vaccine to protect against the disease are indirectly protected.[36]

A second type of benefit from these interim final regulations is improved workplace productivity and decreased absenteeism for school children. Numerous studies confirm that ill health compromises worker output and that health prevention efforts can improve worker productivity. For example, one study found that 69 million workers reported missing days due to illness and 55 million workers reported a time when they were unable to concentrate at work because of their own illness or a family member's

illness.[37] Together, labor time lost due to health reasons represents lost economic output totaling $260 billion per year.[38] Prevention efforts can help prevent these types of losses. Studies have also shown that reduced cost-sharing for medical services results in fewer restricted-activity days at work,[39] and increased access to health insurance coverage improves labor market outcomes by improving worker health.[40] Thus, the expansion of benefits and the elimination of cost sharing for preventive services as provided in these

---

[33] The Commonwealth Fund. "Insurance Coverage and the Receipt of Preventive Care." 2005. http:// www.commonwealthfund.org/Content/ Performance-Snapshots/Financial-and-Structural-Access-to-Care/Insurance-Coverage-and-Receipt-of-Preventive-Care.aspx.

[34] Curry, Susan J., Byers, Tim, and Hewitt, Maria, eds. 2003. Fulfilling the Potential of Cancer Prevention and Early Detection. Washington. DC: National Academies Press.

[35] Centers for Disease Control and Prevention. 2010. Diabetes at a Glance. See http://www.cdc.gov/ chronicdisease/resources/publications/aag/pdf/ 2010/diabetes_aag.pdf.

[36] See Modern Infectious Disease Epidemiology by Johan Giesecke 1994, Chapter 18, The Epidemiology of Vaccination.

[37] Health and Productivity Among U.S. Workers, Karen Davis, Ph.D., Sara R. Collins, Ph.D., Michelle M. Doty, Ph.D., Alice Ho, and Alyssa L. Holmgren. The Commonwealth Fund, August 2005 http:// www.commonwealthfund.org/Content/ Publications/Issue-Briefs/2005/Aug/Health-and-Productivity-Among-U-S-Workers.aspx.

[38] Ibid.

[39] See e.g., RAND, The Health Insurance Experiment: A Classic RAND Study Speaks to the Current Health Care Reform Debate, Rand Research Brief, Number 9174 (2006), at http://www.rand.org/pubs/research_briefs/2006/ RAND_RB9174.pdf and Janet Currie et al., "Has Public Health Insurance for Older Children Reduced Disparities in Access to Care and Health Outcomes?", Journal of Health Economics, Volume 27, Issue 6, pages 1567–1581 (Dec. 2008). With early childhood interventions, there appear to be improved health outcomes in later childhood. Analogously, health interventions in early adulthood could have benefits for future productivity.

[40] In a RAND policy brief, the authors cite results from the RAND Health Insurance Experiment in which cost-sharing is found to correspond with workers having fewer restricted-activity days— evidence that free care for certain services may be productivity enhancing. See e.g., RAND, The Health Insurance Experiment: A Classic RAND Study Speaks to the Current Health Care Reform Debate, Rand Research Brief, Number 9174 (2006), at http://www.rand.org/pubs/research_briefs/2006/ RAND_RB9174.pdf. See e.g. Janet Currie et. al., "Has Public Health Insurance for Older Children Reduced Disparities in Access to Care and Health Outcomes?" Journal of Health Economics, Volume 27, Issue 6, pages 1567–1581 (Dec. 2008). With early childhood interventions, there appears to be improved health outcomes in later childhood. Analogously, health interventions in early adulthood could have benefits for future productivity. Council of Economic Advisers. "The Economic Case for Health Reform." (2009).

interim final regulations can be expected to have substantial productivity benefits in the labor market.

Illnesses also contribute to increased absenteeism among school children, which could be avoided with recommended preventive services. In 2006, 56 percent of students missed between one and five days of school due to illness, 10 percent missed between six and ten days and five percent missed 11 or more days.[41] Obesity in particular contributes to missed school days: One study from the University of Pennsylvania found that overweight children were absent on average 20 percent more than their normal-weight peers.[42] Studies also show that influenza contributes to school absenteeism, and vaccination can reduce missed school days and indirectly improve community health.[43] These interim final regulations will ensure that children have access to preventive services, thus decreasing the number of days missed due to illness.[44] Similarly, regular pediatric care, including care by physicians specializing in pediatrics, can improve child health outcomes and avert preventable health care costs. For example, one study of Medicaid enrolled children found that when children were up to date for their age on their schedule of well-child visits, they were less likely to have an avoidable hospitalization at a later time.[45]

A third type of benefit from some preventive services is cost savings. Increasing the provision of preventive services is expected to reduce the incidence or severity of illness, and, as a result, reduce expenditures on treatment of illness. For example, childhood vaccinations have generally been found to reduce such expenditures by more than the cost of the vaccinations themselves and generate considerable benefits to society. Researchers at the Centers for Disease

Control and Prevention (CDC) studying the economic impact of DTaP (diphtheria and tetanus toxoids and acellular Pertussis), Td (tetanus and diphtheria toxoids), Hib (*Haemophilus influenza* type b), IPV (inactivated poliovirus), MMR (measles, mumps and rubella), Hepatitis B and varicella routine childhood vaccines found that every dollar spent on immunizations in 2001 was estimated to save $5.30 on direct health care costs and $16.50 on total societal costs of the diseases as they are prevented or reduced (direct health care associated with the diseases averted were $12.1 billion and total societal costs averted were $33.9 billion).[46]

A review of preventive services by the National Committee on Prevention Priorities found that, in addition to childhood immunizations, two of the recommended preventive services—discussing aspirin use with high-risk adults and tobacco use screening and brief intervention—are cost-saving on net.[47] By itself, tobacco use screening with a brief intervention was found to save more than $500 per smoker.[48]

Another area where prevention could achieve savings is obesity prevention and reduction. Obesity is widely recognized as an important driver of higher health care expenditures.[49] The Task Force recommends children over age six and adults be screened for obesity and be offered or referred to counseling to improve weight status or promote weight loss. Increasing obesity screening and referrals to counseling should decrease obesity and its related costs. If providers are able to proactively identify and monitor obesity in child patients, they may reduce the incidence of adult health conditions that can be expensive to treat, such as diabetes,

hypertension, and adult obesity.[50] One recent study estimated that a one-percentage-point reduction in obesity among twelve-year-olds would save $260.4 million in total medical expenditures.[51]

A full quantification of the cost savings from the extension of coverage of preventive services in these interim final regulations is not possible, but to illustrate the potential savings, an assessment of savings from obesity reduction was conducted. According to the CDC, in 2008, 34.2 percent of U.S. adults and 16.9 percent of children were obese (defined as having a body mass index (BMI) of 30.0 or greater).[52] Obesity is associated with increased risk for coronary heart disease, hypertension, stroke, type 2 diabetes, several types of cancer, diminished mobility, and social stigmatization.[53] As a result, obesity is widely recognized as an important driver of higher health care expenditures on an individual [54] and national level.[55]

As described below, the Departments' analysis assumes that the utilization of preventive services will increase when they are covered with zero copayment, and these interim final regulations are expected to increase utilization of dietary counseling services both among people who currently have the service covered with a copayment and among people for whom the service is not currently covered at all.

Data from the 2009 Kaiser Family Foundation Employer Health Benefits Survey shows that 73 percent of employees with employer-sponsored insurance from a small (< 200 employees) employer do not currently have coverage for weight loss programs,

[41] Bloom B, Cohen RA. Summary health statistics for U.S. children: National Health Interview Survey, 2006. Vital Health Stat 2007;10(234). Available at *http://www.cdc.gov/nchs/nhis.htm*.

[42] University of Pennsylvania 2007: *http://www.upenn.edu/pennnews/news/childhood-obesity-indicates-greater-risk-school-absenteeism-university-pennsylvania-study-revea*.

[43] Davis, Mollie M., James C. King, Ginny Cummings, and Laurence S. Madger. "Countywide School-Based Influenza Immunization: Direct and Indirect Impact on Student Absenteeism." *Pediatrics* 122.1 (2008).

[44] Moonie, Sheniz, David A. Sterling, Larry Figgs, and Mario Castro. "Asthma Status and Severity Affects Missed School Days." *Journal of School Health* 76.1 (2006): 18–24.

[45] Bye, "Effectiveness of Compliance with Pediatric Preventative Care Guidelines Among Medicaid Beneficiaries."

[46] Fangjun Zhou, Jeanne Santoli, Mark L. Messonnier, Hussain R. Yusuf, Abigail Shefer, Susan Y. Chu, Lance Rodewald, Rafael Harpaz. Economic Evaluation of the 7-Vaccine Routine Childhood Immunization Schedule in the United States. *Archives of Pediatric and Adolescent Medicine 2005;* 159(12): 1136–1144. The estimates of the cost savings are based on current immunization levels. The incremental impact of increasing immunization rates is likely to be smaller, but still significant and positive.

[47] Maciosek MV, Coffield AB, Edwards NM, Coffield AB, Flottemesch TJ, Goodman MJ, Solberg LI. Priorities among effective clinical preventive services: Results of a Systematic Review and Analysis. *Am J Prev Med 2006;* 31(1):52–61.

[48] Solberg LI, Maciosek, MV, Edwards NM, Khanchandani HS, and Goodman MJ. Repeated tobacco-use screening and intevention in clinical practice: Health impact and cost effectiveness. American Journal of Preventive Medicine. 2006;31(1).

[49] Congressional Budget Office. "Technological Change and the Growth of Health Care Spending." January 2008. Box 1, pdf p. 18. *http://www.cbo.gov/ftpdocs/89xx/doc8947/01-31-TechHealth.pdf*.

[50] "Working Group Report on Future Research Directions in Childhood Obesity Prevention and Treatment." National Heart, Lung and Blood Institute, National Institutes of Health, U.S. Department of Health and Human Services (2007), available at *http://www.nhlbi.nih.gov/meetings/workshops/child-obesity/index.htm*.

[51] *Ibid.*

[52] Centers for Disease Control and Prevention. "Obesity and Overweight." 2010. *http://www.cdc.gov/nchs/fastats/overwt.htm*.

[53] Agency for Healthcare Research and Quality (AHRQ). "Screening for Obesity in Adults." December 2003. *http://www.ahrq.gov/clinic/3rduspstf/obesity/obesrr.pdf*.

[54] Thorpe, Kenneth E. "The Future Costs of Obesity: National and State Estimates of the Impact of Obesity on Direct Health Care Expenses." November 2009; McKinsey Global Institute. "Sample data suggest that obese adults can incur nearly twice the annual health care costs of normal-weight adults." 2007.

[55] Congressional Budget Office. "Technological Change and the Growth of Health Care Spending." January 2008. Box 1, pdf p. 18. *http://www.cbo.gov/ftpdocs/89xx/doc8947/01-31-TechHealth.pdf*.

compared to 38 percent at large firms.[56] In the illustrative analysis below, the share of individuals without weight loss coverage in the individual market is assumed to be equal to the share in the small group market.

The size of the increase in the number of individuals receiving dietary counseling or other weight loss services will be limited by current physician practice patterns, in which relatively few individuals who are obese receive physician recommendations for dietary counseling. In one study of patients at an internal medicine clinic in the Bronx, NY, approximately 15 percent of obese patients received a recommendation for dietary counseling.[57] Similarly, among overweight and obese patients enrolled in the Cholesterol Education and Research Trial, approximately 15 to 20 percent were referred to nutrition counseling.[58]

These interim final regulations are expected to increase the take-up rate of counseling among patients who are referred to it, and may, over time, lead physicians to increase their referral to such counseling, knowing that it will be covered, and covered without cost sharing. The effect of these interim final regulations is expected to be magnified because of the many other public and private sector initiatives dedicated to combating the obesity epidemic.

In the absence of data on take-up of counseling among patients who are referred by their physicians, it is difficult to know what fraction of the estimated 15 percent to 20 percent of patients who are currently referred to counseling follow through on that referral, or how that fraction will change after coverage of these services is expanded. A reasonable assumption is that utilization of dietary counseling among patients who are obese might increase by five to 10 percentage points as a result of these interim final regulations. If physicians change their behavior and increase the rate at which they refer to counseling, the effect might be substantially larger.

The share of obese individuals without weight loss coverage is estimated to be 29 percent.[59] It is assumed that obese individuals have health care costs 39 percent above average, based on a McKinsey Global Institute analysis.[60] The Task Force noted that counseling interventions led to sustained weight loss ranging from four percent to eight percent of body weight, although there is substantial heterogeneity in results across interventions, with many interventions having little long-term effect.[61] Assuming midpoint reduction of six percent of body weight, the BMI for an individual taking up such an intervention would fall by six percent as well, as height would remain constant. Based on the aforementioned McKinsey Global Institute analysis, a six percent reduction in BMI for an obese individual (from 32 to around 30, for example) would result in a reduction in health care costs of approximately five percent. This parameter for cost reduction is subject to considerable uncertainty, given the wide range of potential weight loss strategies with varying degrees of impact on BMI, and their interconnectedness with changes in individual health care costs.

Multiplying the percentage reduction in health care costs by the total premiums of obese individuals newly gaining obesity prevention coverage allows for an illustrative calculation of the total dollar reduction in premiums, and dividing by total premiums for the affected population allows for an estimate of the reduction in average premiums across the entire affected population. Doing so results in a potential private premium reduction of 0.05 percent to 0.1 percent from lower health care costs due to a reduction in obesity for enrollees in non-grandfathered plans. This does not account for potential savings in Medicaid, Medicare, or other health programs.

A fourth benefit of these interim final regulations will be to distribute the cost of preventive services more equitably across the broad insured population. Some Americans in plans affected by these regulations currently have no coverage of certain recommended preventive services, and pay for them entirely out-of-pocket. For some individuals who currently have no coverage of certain recommended preventive services, these interim final regulations will result in a large savings in out-of-pocket payments, and only a small increase in premiums. Many other Americans have limited coverage of certain recommended preventive services, with large coinsurance or deductibles, and also make substantial out-of-pocket payments to obtain preventive services. Some with limited coverage of preventive services will also experience large savings as a result of these interim final regulations. Reductions in out-of-pocket costs are expected to be largest among people in age groups in which relatively expensive preventive services are most likely to be recommended.

5. Costs and Transfers

The changes in how plans and issuers cover the recommended preventive services resulting from these interim final regulations will result in changes in covered benefits and premiums for individuals in plans and health insurance coverage subject to these interim final regulations. New costs to the health system result when beneficiaries increase their use of preventive services in response to the changes in coverage of preventive services. Cost sharing, including coinsurance, deductibles, and copayments, divides the costs of health services between the insurer and the beneficiaries. The removal of cost sharing increases the quantity of services demanded by lowering the direct cost of the service to consumers. Therefore, the Departments expect that the statute and these interim final regulations will increase utilization of the covered preventive services. The magnitude of this effect on utilization depends on the price elasticity of demand.

Several studies have found that individuals are sensitive to prices for health services.[62] Evidence that consumers change their utilization of preventive services is available from CDC researchers who studied out-of-pocket costs of immunizations for

[56] Kaiser Family Foundation. 2009 Employer Health Benefits Annual Survey. Public Use File provided to CEA; documentation of statistical analysis available upon request. See http://ehbs.kff.org.

[57] Davis NJ, Emerenini A, Wylie-Rosett J. "Obesity management: physician practice patterns and patient preference," Diabetes Education. 2006 Jul–Aug; 32(4):557–61.

[58] Molly E. Waring, PhD, Mary B. Roberts, MS, Donna R. Parker, ScD and Charles B. Eaton, MD, MS. "Documentation and Management of Overweight and Obesity in Primary Care," The Journal of the American Board of Family Medicine 22 (5): 544–552 (2009).

[59] This estimate is constructed using a weighted average obesity rate taking into account the share of the population aged 0 to 19 and 20 to 74 and their respective obesity rates, derived from Census Bureau and Centers for Disease Control and Prevention data. U.S. Census Bureau. "Current Population Survey (CPS) Table Creator." 2010. http://www.census.gov/hhes/www/cpstc/cps_table_creator.html. Centers for Disease Control and Prevention. "Obesity and Overweight." 2010. http://www.cdc.gov/nchs/fastats/overwt.htm.

[60] McKinsey Global Institute Analysis provided to CEA.

[61] Agency for Healthcare Research and Quality (AHRQ). "Screening for Obesity in Adults." December 2003. p. 4. http://www.ahrq.gov/clinic/3rduspstf/obesity/obesrr.pdf.

[62] See e.g., Jonathan Gruber, The Role of Consumer Copayments for Health Care: Lessons from the RAND Health Insurance Experiment and Beyond, Kaiser Family Foundation (Oct. 2006). This paper examines an experiment in which copays randomly vary across several thousand individuals. The author finds that individuals are sensitive to prices for health services—i.e., as copays decline, more services are demanded.

privately insured children up to age 5 in families in Georgia in 2003, to find that a one percent increase in out-of-pocket costs for routine immunizations (DTaP, IPV, MMR, Hib, and Hep B) was associated with a 0.07 percent decrease in utilization.[63]

Along with new costs of induced utilization, there are transfers associated with these interim final regulations. A transfer is a change in who pays for the services, where there is not an actual change in the level of resources used. For example, costs that were previously paid out-of-pocket for certain preventive services will now be covered by plans and issuers under these interim final regulations. Such a transfer of costs could be expected to lead to an increase in premiums.

a. Estimate of Average Changes in Health Insurance Premiums

The Departments assessed the impact of eliminating cost sharing, increases in services covered, and induced utilization on the average insurance premium using a model to evaluate private health insurance plans against a nationally representative population. The model is based on the Medical Expenditure Panel Survey data from 2004, 2005, and 2006 on household spending on health care, which are scaled to levels consistent with the CMS projections of the National Health Expenditure Accounts.[64] This data is combined with data from the Employer Health Benefits Surveys conducted by the Kaiser Family Foundation and Health Research and Education Trust to model a "typical PPO coverage" plan. The model then allows the user to assess changes in covered expenses, benefits, premiums, and induced utilization of services resulting from changes in the characteristics of the plan. The analysis of changes in coverage is based on the average per-person covered expenses and insurance benefits. The average covered expense is the total charge for covered services; insurance benefits are the part of the covered expenses covered by the insurer. The effect on the average premium is then estimated based on the percentage changes in the insurance benefits and the distribution of the individuals across individual and group markets in non-grandfathered plans.

The Departments assume that the percent increase for insurance benefits and premiums will be the same. This is based on two assumptions: (1) That administrative costs included in the premium will increase proportionally with the increase in insurance benefits; and (2) that the increases in insurance benefits will be directly passed on to the consumer in the form of higher premiums. These assumptions bias the estimates of premium changes upward. Using this model, the Departments assessed: (1) Changes in cost-sharing for currently covered and utilized services, (2) changes in services covered, and (3) induced utilization of preventive services. There are several additional sources of uncertainty concerning these estimates. First, there is no accurate, granular data on exactly what baseline coverage is for the particular preventive services addressed in these interim final regulations. Second, there is uncertainty over behavioral assumptions related to additional utilization that results from reduced cost-sharing. Therefore, after providing initial estimates, the Departments provide a sensitivity analysis to capture the potential range of impacts of these interim final regulations.

From the Departments' analysis of the Medical Expenditure Panel Survey (MEPS) data, controlled to be consistent with projections of the National Health Expenditure Accounts, the average person with employer-sponsored insurance (ESI) has $264 in covered expenses for preventive services, of which $240 is paid by insurance, and $24 is paid out-of-pocket.[65] When preventive services are covered with zero copayment, the Departments expect the average preventive benefit (holding utilization constant) will increase by $24. This is a 0.6 percent increase in insurance benefits and premiums for plans that have relinquished their grandfather status. A similar, but larger effect is expected in the individual market because existing evidence suggests that individual health insurance policies generally have less generous benefits for preventive services than group health plans. However, the evidence base for current coverage and cost sharing for preventive services in individual health insurance policies is weaker than for group health plans, making estimation of the increase in average benefits and premiums in the individual market highly uncertain.

For analyses of changes in covered services, the Departments used the Blue Cross/Blue Shield Standard (BC/BS) plan offered through the Federal Employees Health Benefits Program as an average plan.[66] Other analyses have used the BC/BS standard option as an average plan as it was designed to reflect standard practice within employer-sponsored health insurance plans.[67] BC/BS covers most of the preventive services listed in the Task Force and Advisory Committee recommendations, and most of the preventive services listed in the comprehensive guidelines for infants, children, and adolescents supported by HRSA. Not covered by the BC/BS Standard plan are the recommendations for genetic testing for the BRCA gene, adolescent depression screening,[68] lead testing, autism testing, and oral health screening.[69]

The Departments estimated the increase in benefits from newly covered services by estimating the number of new services that would be provided times the cost of providing the services, and then spread these new costs across the total insured population. The Departments estimated that adding coverage for genetic screening and depression screening would increase insurance benefits an estimated 0.10 percent. Adding lead testing, autism testing, and oral health screening would increase insurance benefits by an estimated 0.02 percent. This results in a total average increase in insurance benefits on these services of 0.12 percent, or just over $4 per insured person. This increase represents a mixture of new costs and transfers, dependent on whether beneficiaries previously would have purchased these services on their own. It is also important to remember that actual plan

---

[63] See e.g., Noelle-Angelique Molinari et al., "Out-of-Pocket Costs of Childhood Immunizations: A Comparison by Type of Insurance Plan," Pediatrics, 120(5) pp. 148–156 (2006).

[64] The National Health Expenditure Accounts (NHEA) are the official estimates of total health care spending in the United States. See http://www.cms.gov/NationalHealthExpendData/02_NationalHealthAccountsHistorical.asp.

[65] The model does not distinguish between recommended and non-recommended preventive services, and so this likely represents an overestimate of the insurance benefits for preventive services.

[66] The Blue Cross Blue Shield standard option plan documentation is available online at http://fepblue.org/benefitplans/standard-option/index.html.

[67] Frey A, Mika S, Nuzum R, and Schoen C. "Setting a National Minimum Standard for Health Benefits: How do State Benefit Mandates Compare with Benefits in Large-Group Plans?" Issue Brief. Commonwealth Fund June 2009 available at http://www.commonwealthfund.org/Content/Publications/Issue-Briefs/2009/Jun/Setting-a-National-Minimum-Standard-for-Health-Benefits.aspx.

[68] The Task Force recommends that women whose family history is associated with an increased risk for deleterious mutations in BRCA1 or BRCA2 genes be referred for genetic counseling and evaluation for BRCA testing and screening of adolescents (12–18 years of age) for major depressive disorder (MDD) when systems are in place to ensure accurate diagnosis, psychotherapy (cognitive-behavioral or interpersonal), and follow-up.

[69] Lead, autism, and oral health screening are from the HRSA comprehensive guidelines.

impacts will vary depending on baseline benefit levels, and that grandfathered health plans will not experience any impact from these interim final regulations. The Departments expect the increase to be larger in the individual market because coverage of preventive services in the individual market is less complete than coverage in the group market, but as noted previously, the evidence base for the individual market is weaker than that of the group market, making detailed estimates of the size of this effect difficult and highly uncertain.

Actuaries use an "induction formula" to estimate the behavioral change in response to changes in the relative levels of coverage for health services. For this analysis, the Departments used the model to estimate the induced demand (the increased use of preventive services). The model uses a standard actuarial formula for induction $1/(1+alpha*P)$, where alpha is the "induction parameter" and P is the average fraction of the cost of services paid by the consumer. The induction parameter for physician services is 0.7, derived by the standard actuarial formula that is generally consistent with the estimates of price elasticity of demand from the RAND Health Insurance Experiment and other economic studies.[70] Removing cost sharing for preventive services lowers the direct cost to consumers of using preventive services, which induces additional utilization, estimated with the model above to increase covered expenses and benefits by approximately $17, or 0.44 percent in insurance benefits in group health plans. The Departments expect a similar but larger effect in the individual market, although these estimates are highly uncertain.

The Departments calculated an estimate of the average impact using the information from the analyses described above, using estimates of the number of individuals in non-grandfathered health plans in the group and individual markets in 2011. The Departments estimate that premiums will increase by approximately 1.5 percent on average for enrollees in non-grandfathered plans. This estimate assumes that any changes in insurance benefits will be directly passed on to the consumer in the form of changes in premiums. As mentioned earlier, this assumption biases the estimates of premium change upward.

[70] Standard formula best described in "Quantity-Price Relationships in Health Insurance", Charles L. Trowbridge, Chief Actuary, Social Security Administration (DHEW Publication No. (SSA)73–11507, November 1972).

b. Sensitivity analysis

As discussed previously, there is substantial uncertainty associated with the estimates presented above. To address the uncertainty in the group market, the Departments first varied the estimated change to underlying benefits, to address the particular uncertainty behind the estimate of baseline coverage of preventive services in the group market. The estimate for the per person annual increase in insurance benefits from adding coverage for new services is approximately $4. The Departments considered the impact of a smaller and larger addition in benefits of approximately $2 and $6 per person. To consider the impact of uncertainty around the size of the behavioral change (that is, the utilization of more services when cost sharing is eliminated), the Departments analyzed the impact on insurance benefits if the behavioral change were 15 percent smaller and 15 percent larger.

In the individual market, to accommodate the greater uncertainty relative to the group market, the Departments considered the impact of varying the increase in benefits resulting from cost shifting due to the elimination of cost sharing, in addition to varying the cost of newly covered services and behavioral change.

Combining results in the group and individual markets for enrollees in non-grandfathered plans, the Departments' low-end is a few tenths of a percent lower than the mid-range estimate of approximately 1.5 percent, and the high-end estimate is a few tenths of a percent higher. Grandfathered health plans are not subject to these interim final regulations and therefore would not experience this premium change.

6. Alternatives Considered

Several provisions in these interim final regulations involved policy choices. One was whether to allow a plan or issuer to impose cost sharing for an office visit when a recommended preventive service is provided in that visit. Sometimes a recommended preventive service is billed separately from the office visit; sometimes it is not. The Departments decided that the cost sharing prohibition of these interim final regulations applies to the specific preventive service as recommended by the guidelines. Therefore, if the preventive service is billed separately from the office visit, it is the preventive service that has cost sharing waived, not the entire office visit.

A second policy choice was if the preventive service is not billed separately from the office visit, whether

these interim final regulations should prohibit cost sharing for any office visit in which any recommended preventive service was administered, or whether cost sharing should be prohibited only when the preventive service is the primary purpose of the office visit. Prohibiting cost sharing for office visits when any recommended preventive service is provided, regardless of the primary purpose of the visit, could lead to an overly broad application of these interim final regulations; for example, a person who sees a specialist for a particular condition could end up with a zero copayment simply because his or her blood pressure was taken as part of the office visit. This could create financial incentives for consumers to request preventive services at office visits that are intended for other purposes in order to avoid copayments and deductibles. The increased prevalence of the application of zero cost sharing would lead to increased premiums compared with the chosen option, without a meaningful additional gain in access to preventive services.

A third issue involves health plans that have differential cost sharing for services provided by providers who are in and out of their networks. These interim final regulations provide that a plan or issuer is not required to provide coverage for recommended preventive services delivered by an out-of-network provider. The plan or issuer may also impose cost sharing for recommended preventive services delivered by an out-of-network provider. The Departments considered that requiring coverage by out-of-network providers at no cost sharing would result in higher premiums for these interim final regulations. Plans and issuers negotiate allowed charges with in-network providers as a way to promote effective, efficient health care, and allowing differences in cost sharing in- and out-of-network enables plans to encourage use of in-network providers. Allowing zero cost sharing for out of network providers could reduce providers' incentives to participate in insurer networks. The Departments decided that permitting cost sharing for recommended preventive services provided by out-of-network providers is the appropriate option to preserve choice of providers for individuals, while avoiding potentially larger increases in costs and transfers as well as potentially lower quality care.

C. Regulatory Flexibility Act—Department of Labor and Department of Health and Human Services

The Regulatory Flexibility Act (5 U.S.C. 601 et seq.) (RFA) imposes

Federal Register / Vol. 75, No. 137 / Monday, July 19, 2010 / Rules and Regulations   **41739**

certain requirements with respect to Federal rules that are subject to the notice and comment requirements of section 553(b) of the APA (5 U.S.C. 551 *et seq.*) and that are likely to have a significant economic impact on a substantial number of small entities. Section 9833 of the Code, section 734 of ERISA, and section 2792 of the PHS Act authorize the Secretaries to promulgate any interim final rules that they determine are appropriate to carry out the provisions of chapter 100 of the Code, part 7 of subtitle B or title I of ERISA, and part A of title XXVII of the PHS Act, which include PHS Act sections 2701 through 2728 and the incorporation of those sections into ERISA section 715 and Code section 9815.

Moreover, under Section 553(b) of the APA, a general notice of proposed rulemaking is not required when an agency, for good cause, finds that notice and public comment thereon are impracticable, unnecessary, or contrary to the public interest. These interim final regulations are exempt from APA, because the Departments made a good cause finding that a general notice of proposed rulemaking is not necessary earlier in this preamble. Therefore, the RFA does not apply and the Departments are not required to either certify that the rule would not have a significant economic impact on a substantial number of small entities or conduct a regulatory flexibility analysis.

Nevertheless, the Departments carefully considered the likely impact of the rule on small entities in connection with their assessment under Executive Order 12866. Consistent with the policy of the RFA, the Departments encourage the public to submit comments that suggest alternative rules that accomplish the stated purpose of the Affordable Care Act and minimize the impact on small entities.

D. Special Analyses—Department of the Treasury

Notwithstanding the determinations of the Department of Labor and Department of Health and Human Services, for purposes of the Department of the Treasury, it has been determined that this Treasury decision is not a significant regulatory action for purposes of Executive Order 12866. Therefore, a regulatory assessment is not required. It has also been determined that section 553(b) of the APA (5 U.S.C. chapter 5) does not apply to these interim final regulations. For the applicability of the RFA, refer to the Special Analyses section in the preamble to the cross-referencing notice of proposed rulemaking published

elsewhere in this issue of the **Federal Register**. Pursuant to section 7805(f) of the Code, these temporary regulations have been submitted to the Chief Counsel for Advocacy of the Small Business Administration for comment on their impact on small businesses.

E. Paperwork Reduction Act: Department of Labor, Department of the Treasury, and Department of Health and Human Services

These interim final regulations are not subject to the requirements of the Paperwork Reduction Act of 1980 (44 U.S.C. 3501 *et seq.*) because it does not contain a "collection of information" as defined in 44 U.S.C. 3502 (11).

F. Congressional Review Act

These interim final regulations are subject to the Congressional Review Act provisions of the Small Business Regulatory Enforcement Fairness Act of 1996 (5 U.S.C. 801 *et seq.*) and have been transmitted to Congress and the Comptroller General for review.

G. Unfunded Mandates Reform Act

The Unfunded Mandates Reform Act of 1995 (Pub. L. 104–4) requires agencies to prepare several analytic statements before proposing any rules that may result in annual expenditures of $100 million (as adjusted for inflation) by State, local and tribal governments or the private sector. These interim final regulations are not subject to the Unfunded Mandates Reform Act because they are being issued as interim final regulations. However, consistent with the policy embodied in the Unfunded Mandates Reform Act, these interim final regulations have been designed to be the least burdensome alternative for State, local and tribal governments, and the private sector, while achieving the objectives of the Affordable Care Act.

H. Federalism Statement—Department of Labor and Department of Health and Human Services

Executive Order 13132 outlines fundamental principles of federalism, and requires the adherence to specific criteria by Federal agencies in the process of their formulation and implementation of policies that have "substantial direct effects" on the States, the relationship between the national government and States, or on the distribution of power and responsibilities among the various levels of government. Federal agencies promulgating regulations that have these federalism implications must consult with State and local officials, and describe the extent of their

consultation and the nature of the concerns of State and local officials in the preamble to the regulation.

In the Departments' view, these interim final regulations have federalism implications, because they have direct effects on the States, the relationship between the national government and States, or on the distribution of power and responsibilities among various levels of government. However, in the Departments' view, the federalism implications of these interim final regulations are substantially mitigated because, with respect to health insurance issuers, the Departments expect that the majority of States will enact laws or take other appropriate action resulting in their meeting or exceeding the Federal standards.

In general, through section 514, ERISA supersedes State laws to the extent that they relate to any covered employee benefit plan, and preserves State laws that regulate insurance, banking, or securities. While ERISA prohibits States from regulating a plan as an insurance or investment company or bank, the preemption provisions of section 731 of ERISA and section 2724 of the PHS Act (implemented in 29 CFR 2590.731(a) and 45 CFR 146.143(a)) apply so that the HIPAA requirements (including those of the Affordable Care Act) are not to be "construed to supersede any provision of State law which establishes, implements, or continues in effect any standard or requirement solely relating to health insurance issuers in connection with group health insurance coverage except to the extent that such standard or requirement prevents the application of a requirement" of a Federal standard. The conference report accompanying HIPAA indicates that this is intended to be the "narrowest" preemption of State laws. (*See* House Conf. Rep. No. 104–736, at 205, reprinted in 1996 U.S. Code Cong. & Admin. News 2018.) States may continue to apply State law requirements except to the extent that such requirements prevent the application of the Affordable Care Act requirements that are the subject of this rulemaking. State insurance laws that are more stringent than the Federal requirements are unlikely to "prevent the application of" the Affordable Care Act, and be preempted. Accordingly, States have significant latitude to impose requirements on health insurance issuers that are more restrictive than the Federal law.

In compliance with the requirement of Executive Order 13132 that agencies examine closely any policies that may have federalism implications or limit the policy making discretion of the States, the Departments have engaged in efforts to consult with and work cooperatively with affected State and local officials, including attending conferences of the National Association of Insurance Commissioners and consulting with State insurance officials on an individual basis. It is expected that the Departments will act in a similar fashion in enforcing the Affordable Care Act requirements. Throughout the process of developing these interim final regulations, to the extent feasible within the specific preemption provisions of HIPAA as it applies to the Affordable Care Act, the Departments have attempted to balance the States' interests in regulating health insurance issuers, and Congress' intent to provide uniform minimum protections to consumers in every State. By doing so, it is the Departments' view that they have complied with the requirements of Executive Order 13132.

Pursuant to the requirements set forth in section 8(a) of Executive Order 13132, and by the signatures affixed to these interim final regulations, the Departments certify that the Employee Benefits Security Administration and the Centers for Medicare & Medicaid Services have complied with the requirements of Executive Order 13132 for the attached regulations in a meaningful and timely manner.

V. Recommended Preventive Services as of July 14, 2010

The materials that follow list recommended preventive services, current as of July 14, 2010, that will have to be covered without cost-sharing when delivered by an in-network provider. In many cases, the recommendations or guidelines went into effect before September 23, 2009; therefore the recommended services must be covered under these interim final regulations in plan years (in the individual market, policy years) that begin on or after September 23, 2010. However, there are some services that appear in the figure that are based on recommendations or guidelines that went into effect at some point later than September 23, 2009. Those services do not have to be covered under these interim final regulations until plan years (in the individual market, policy years) that begin at some point later than September 23, 2010. In addition, there are a few recommendations and guidelines that went into effect after September 23, 2009 and are not included in the figure. In both cases, information at *http:// www.HealthCare.gov/center/ regulations/prevention.html* specifically identifies those services and the relevant dates. The materials at *http:// www.HealthCare.gov/center/ regulations/prevention.html* will be updated on an ongoing basis, and will contain the most current recommended preventive services.

A. Recommendations of the United States Preventive Services Task Force (Task Force)

Recommendations of the Task Force appear in a chart that follows. This chart includes a description of the topic, the text of the Task Force recommendation, the grade the recommendation received (A or B), and the date that the recommendation went into effect.

B. Recommendations of the Advisory Committee On Immunization Practices (Advisory Committee) That Have Been Adopted by the Director of the Centers for Disease Control and Prevention

Recommendations of the Advisory Committee appear in four immunization schedules that follow: A schedule for children age 0 to 6 years, a schedule for children age 7 to 18 years, a "catch-up" schedule for children, and a schedule for adults. Immunization schedules are issued every year, and the schedules that appear here are the 2010 schedules. The schedules contain graphics that provide information about the recommended age for vaccination, number of doses needed, interval between the doses, and (for adults) recommendations associated with particular health conditions. In addition to the graphics, the schedules contain detailed footnotes that provide further information on each immunization in the schedule.

C. Comprehensive Guidelines Supported by the Health Resources and Services Administration (HRSA) for Infants, Children, and Adolescents

Comprehensive guidelines for infants, children, and adolescents supported by HRSA appear in two charts that follow: The Periodicity Schedule of the Bright Futures Recommendations for Pediatric Preventive Health Care, and the Uniform Panel of the Secretary's Advisory Committee on Heritable Disorders in Newborns and Children.
BILLING CODE 4830–01–P; 4510–29–P; 4210–01–P

Grade A and B Recommendations of the United States Preventive Services Task Force - July 13, 2010

Topic	Text	Grade	Date in Effect
Screening for abdominal aortic aneurysm	The USPSTF recommends one-time screening for abdominal aortic aneurysm (AAA) by ultrasonography in men aged 65 to 75 who have ever smoked.	B	February 28, 2005
Counseling for alcohol misuse	The U.S. Preventive Services Task Force (USPSTF) recommends screening and behavioral counseling interventions to reduce alcohol misuse (go to Clinical Considerations) by adults, including pregnant women, in primary care settings.	B	April 30, 2004
Screening for anemia	The USPSTF recommends routine screening for iron deficiency anemia in asymptomatic pregnant women.	B	May 31, 2006
Aspirin to prevent CVD: men	The USPSTF recommends the use of aspirin for men age 45 to 79 years when the potential benefit due to a reduction in myocardial infarctions outweighs the potential harm due to an increase in gastrointestinal hemorrhage.	A	March 30, 2009
Aspirin to prevent CVD: women	The USPSTF recommends the use of aspirin for women age 55 to 79 years when the potential benefit of a reduction in ischemic strokes outweighs the potential harm of an increase in gastrointestinal hemorrhage.	A	March 30, 2009
Screening for bacteriuria	The USPSTF recommends screening for asymptomatic bacteriuria with urine culture for pregnant women at 12 to 16 weeks' gestation or at the first prenatal visit, if later.	A	July 31, 2008
Screening for blood pressure	The U.S. Preventive Services Task Force (USPSTF) recommends screening for high blood pressure in adults aged 18 and older.	A	December 31, 2007
Counseling for BRCA screening	The USPSTF recommends that women whose family history is associated with an increased risk for deleterious mutations in BRCA1 or BRCA2 genes be referred for genetic counseling and evaluation for BRCA testing.	B	September 30, 2005
Screening for breast cancer (mammography)	The USPSTF recommends screening mammography for women with or without clinical breast examination (CBE), every 1-2 years for women aged 40 and older.	B	September 30, 2002
Chemoprevention of breast cancer	The USPSTF recommends that clinicians discuss chemoprevention with women at high risk for breast cancer and at low risk for adverse effects of chemoprevention. Clinicians should inform patients of the potential benefits and harms of chemoprevention.	B	July 31, 2002
Counseling for breast feeding	The USPSTF recommends interventions during pregnancy and after birth to promote and support breastfeeding.	B	October 31, 2008
Screening for cervical cancer	The USPSTF strongly recommends screening for cervical cancer in women who have been sexually active and have a cervix.	B	January 31, 2003
Screening for chlamydial infection: non-pregnant women	The U.S. Preventive Services Task Force (USPSTF) recommends screening for chlamydial infection for all sexually active non-pregnant young women aged 24 and younger and for older non-pregnant women who are at increased risk.	A	June 30, 2007
Screening for chlamydial infection: pregnant women	The USPSTF recommends screening for chlamydial infection for all pregnant women aged 24 and younger and for older pregnant women who are at increased risk.	B	June 30, 2007

Screening for cholesterol abnormalities: men 35 and older	The U.S. Preventive Services Task Force (USPSTF) strongly recommends screening men aged 35 and older for lipid disorders.	A	June 30, 2008
Screening for cholesterol abnormalities: men younger than 35	The USPSTF recommends screening men aged 20 to 35 for lipid disorders if they are at increased risk for coronary heart disease.	B	June 30, 2008
Screening for cholesterol abnormalities: women 45 and older	The USPSTF strongly recommends screening women aged 45 and older for lipid disorders if they are at increased risk for coronary heart disease.	A	June 30, 2008
Screening for cholesterol abnormalities: women younger than 45	The USPSTF recommends screening women aged 20 to 45 for lipid disorders if they are at increased risk for coronary heart disease.	B	June 30, 2008
Screening for colorectal cancer	The USPSTF recommends screening for colorectal cancer (CRC) using fecal occult blood testing, sigmoidoscopy, or colonoscopy, in adults, beginning at age 50 years and continuing until age 75 years. The risks and benefits of these screening methods vary.	A	October 31, 2008
Chemoprevention of dental caries	The USPSTF recommends that primary care clinicians prescribe oral fluoride supplementation at currently recommended doses to preschool children older than 6 months of age whose primary water source is deficient in fluoride.	B	April 30, 2004
Screening for depression: adults	The USPSTF recommends screening adults for depression when staff-assisted depression care supports are in place to assure accurate diagnosis, effective treatment, and follow-up.	B	December 31, 2009, identical to a 2002 recommendation
Screening for depression: adolescents	The USPSTF recommends screening of adolescents (12-18 years of age) for major depressive disorder (MDD) when systems are in place to ensure accurate diagnosis, psychotherapy (cognitive-behavioral or interpersonal), and follow-up.	B	March 30, 2009
Screening for diabetes	The USPSTF recommends screening for type 2 diabetes in asymptomatic adults with sustained blood pressure (either treated or untreated) greater than 135/80 mm Hg.	B	June 30, 2008
Counseling for diet	The USPSTF recommends intensive behavioral dietary counseling for adult patients with hyperlipidemia and other known risk factors for cardiovascular and diet-related chronic disease. Intensive counseling can be delivered by primary care clinicians or by referral to other specialists, such as nutritionists or dietitians.	B	January 30, 2003
Supplementation with folic acid	The USPSTF recommends that all women planning or capable of pregnancy take a daily supplement containing 0.4 to 0.8 mg (400 to 800 µg) of folic acid.	A	May 31, 2009
Screening for gonorrhea: women	The U.S. Preventive Services Task Force (USPSTF) recommends that clinicians screen all sexually active women, including those who are pregnant, for gonorrhea infection if they are at increased risk for infection (that is, if they are young or have other individual or population risk factors [go to Clinical Considerations for further discussion of risk factors]).	B	May 31, 2005
Prophylactic medication for gonorrhea: newborns	The USPSTF strongly recommends prophylactic ocular topical medication for all newborns against gonococcal ophthalmia neonatorum.	A	May 31, 2005

Screening for hearing loss	The USPSTF recommends screening for hearing loss in all newborn infants.	B	July 31, 2008
Screening for hemoglobinopathies	The U.S. Preventive Services Task Force (USPSTF) recommends screening for sickle cell disease in newborns.	A	September 30, 2007
Screening for hepatitis B	The U.S. Preventive Services Task Force (USPSTF) strongly recommends screening for hepatitis B virus (HBV) infection in pregnant women at their first prenatal visit.	A	June 30, 2009
Screening for HIV	The U.S. Preventive Services Task Force (USPSTF) strongly recommends that clinicians screen for human immunodeficiency virus (HIV) all adolescents and adults at increased risk for HIV infection (go to Clinical Considerations for discussion of risk factors).	A	July 31, 2005
Screening for congenital hypothyroidism	The USPSTF recommends screening for congenital hypothyroidism (CH) in newborns.	A	March 31, 2008
Iron supplementation in children	The U.S. Preventive Services Task Force (USPSTF) recommends routine iron supplementation for asymptomatic children aged 6 to 12 months who are at increased risk for iron deficiency anemia (go to Clinical Considerations for a discussion of increased risk)	B	May 30, 2006
Screening and counseling for obesity: adults	The USPSTF recommends that clinicians screen all adult patients for obesity and offer intensive counseling and behavioral interventions to promote sustained weight loss for obese adults.	B	December 31, 2003
Screening and counseling for obesity: children	The USPSTF recommends that clinicians screen children aged 6 years and older for obesity and offer them or refer them to comprehensive, intensive behavioral interventions to promote improvement in weight status.	B	January 31, 2010
Screening for osteoporosis	The U.S. Preventive Services Task Force (USPSTF) recommends that women aged 65 and older be screened routinely for osteoporosis. The USPSTF recommends that routine screening begin at age 60 for women at increased risk for osteoporotic fractures. (Go to Clinical Considerations for discussion of women at increased risk.)	B	September 30, 2002
Screening for PKU	The U.S. Preventive Services Task Force (USPSTF) strongly recommends screening for phenylketonuria (PKU) in newborns.	A	March 31, 2008
Screening for Rh incompatibility: first pregnancy visit	The U.S. Preventive Services Task Force (USPSTF) strongly recommends Rh (D) blood typing and antibody testing for all pregnant women during their first visit for pregnancy-related care.	A	February 29, 2004
Screening for Rh incompatibility: 24-28 weeks' gestation	The USPSTF recommends repeated Rh (D) antibody testing for all unsensitized Rh (D)-negative women at 24-28 weeks' gestation, unless the biological father is known to be Rh (D)-negative.	B	February 29, 2004
Counseling for STIs	The USPSTF recommends high-intensity behavioral counseling to prevent sexually transmitted infections (STIs) for all sexually active adolescents and for adults at increased risk for STIs.	B	October 31 2008
Counseling for tobacco use: adults	The USPSTF recommends that clinicians ask all adults about tobacco use and provide tobacco cessation interventions for those who use tobacco products.	A	April 30, 2009
Counseling for tobacco use: pregnant women	The USPSTF recommends that clinicians ask all pregnant women about tobacco use and provide augmented, pregnancy-tailored counseling for those who smoke.	A	April 30, 2009

Screening for syphilis: non-pregnant persons	The U.S. Preventive Services Task Force (USPSTF) strongly recommends that clinicians screen persons at increased risk for syphilis infection.	A	July 31, 2004
Screening for syphilis: pregnant women	The USPSTF recommends that clinicians screen all pregnant women for syphilis infection.	A	July 31, 2004
Screening for visual acuity in children	The USPSTF recommends screening to detect amblyopia, strabismus, and defects in visual acuity in children younger than age 5 years.	B	May 31, 2004

G. Recommended Immunization Schedules

2012 Recommended Immunizations for Children from Birth Through 6 Years Old

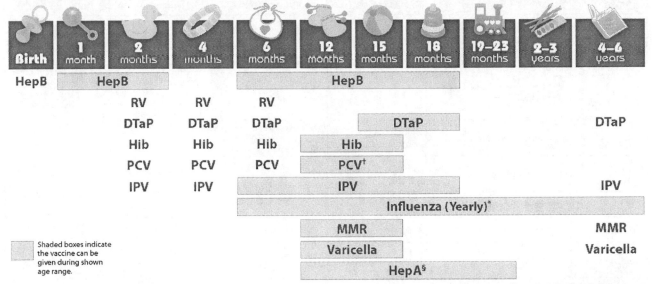

Birth	1 month	2 months	4 months	6 months	12 months	15 months	18 months	19–23 months	2–3 years	4–6 years
HepB	HepB			HepB						
		RV	RV	RV						
		DTaP	DTaP	DTaP		DTaP				DTaP
		Hib	Hib	Hib	Hib					
		PCV	PCV	PCV	PCV†					
		IPV	IPV	IPV						IPV
				Influenza (Yearly)*						
					MMR					MMR
					Varicella					Varicella
					HepA§					

Shaded boxes indicate the vaccine can be given during shown age range.

FOOTNOTES

† Children 2 years old and older with certain medical conditions may need a dose of pneumococcal vaccine (PPSV) and meningococcal vaccine (MCV4). See vaccine-specific recommendations at http://www.cdc.gov/vaccines/pubs/ACIP-list.htm.

* Two doses given at least four weeks apart are recommended for children aged 6 months through 8 years of age who are getting a flu vaccine for the first time.

§ Two doses of HepA vaccine are needed for lasting protection. The first dose of HepA vaccine should be given between 12 months and 23 months of age. The second dose should be given 6 to 18 months later. HepA vaccination may be given to any child 12 months and older to protect against HepA. Children and adolescents who did not receive the HepA vaccine and are at high-risk, should be vaccinated against HepA.

SEE BACK PAGE FOR MORE INFORMATION ON VACCINE-PREVENTABLE DISEASES AND THE VACCINES THAT PREVENT THEM.

For more information, call toll free 1-800-CDC-INFO (1-800-232-4636) or visit http://www.cdc.gov/vaccines

U.S. Department of Health and Human Services
Centers for Disease Control and Prevention

AMERICAN ACADEMY OF
FAMILY PHYSICIANS
STRONG MEDICINE FOR AMERICA

American Academy
of Pediatrics
DEDICATED TO THE HEALTH OF ALL CHILDREN™

Vaccine-Preventable Diseases and the Vaccines that Prevent Them

Disease	Vaccine	Disease spread by	Disease symptoms	Disease complications
Chickenpox	Varicella vaccine protects against chickenpox.	Air, direct contact	Rash, tiredness, headache, fever	Infected blisters, bleeding disorders, encephalitis (brain swelling), pneumonia (infection in the lungs)
Diphtheria	DTaP* vaccine protects against diphtheria.	Air, direct contact	Sore throat, mild fever, weakness, swollen glands in neck	Swelling of the heart muscle, heart failure, coma, paralysis, death
Hib	Hib vaccine protects against *Haemophilus influenzae* type b.	Air, direct contact	May be no symptoms unless bacteria enter the blood	Meningitis (infection of the covering around the brain and spinal cord), mental retardation, epiglottis (life-threatening infection that can block the windpipe and lead to serious breathing problems) and pneumonia (infection in the lungs), death
HepA	HepA vaccine protects against hepatitis A.	Personal contact, contaminated food or water	May be no symptoms, fever, stomach pain, loss of appetite, fatigue, vomiting, jaundice (yellowing of skin and eyes), dark urine	Liver failure
HepB	HepB vaccine protects against hepatitis B.	Contact with blood or body fluids	May be no symptoms, fever, headache, weakness, vomiting, jaundice (yellowing of skin and eyes), joint pain	Chronic liver infection, liver failure, liver cancer
Flu	Flu vaccine protects against influenza.	Air, direct contact	Fever, muscle pain, sore throat, cough, extreme fatigue	Pneumonia (infection in the lungs)
Measles	MMR** vaccine protects against measles.	Air, direct contact	Rash, fever, cough, runny nose, pinkeye	Encephalitis (brain swelling), pneumonia (infection in the lungs), death
Mumps	MMR** vaccine protects against mumps.	Air, direct contact	Swollen salivary glands (under the jaw), fever, headache, tiredness, muscle pain	Meningitis (infection of the covering around the brain and spinal cord), encephalitis (brain swelling), inflammation of testicles or ovaries, deafness
Pertussis	DTaP* vaccine protects against pertussis (whooping cough).	Air, direct contact	Severe cough, runny nose, apnea (a pause in breathing in infants)	Pneumonia (infection in the lungs), death
Polio	IPV vaccine protects against polio.	Through the mouth	May be no symptoms, sore throat, fever, nausea, headache	Paralysis, death
Pneumococcal	PCV vaccine protects against pneumococcus.	Air, direct contact	May be no symptoms, pneumonia (infection in the lungs)	Bacteremia (blood infection), meningitis (infection of the covering around the brain and spinal cord), death
Rotavirus	RV vaccine protects against rotavirus.	Through the mouth	Diarrhea, fever, vomiting	Severe diarrhea, dehydration
Rubella	MMR** vaccine protects against rubella.	Air, direct contact	Children infected with rubella virus sometimes have a rash, fever, and swollen lymph nodes.	Very serious in pregnant women—can lead to miscarriage, stillbirth, premature delivery, and birth defects
Tetanus	DTaP* vaccine protects against tetanus.	Exposure through cuts in skin	Stiffness in neck and abdominal muscles, difficulty swallowing, muscle spasms, fever	Broken bones, breathing difficulty, death

* DTaP is a combination vaccine that protects against diphtheria, tetanus, and pertussis.
** MMR is a combination vaccine that protects against measles, mumps, and rubella.

Last updated on 02/01/2012 · CS229312-B

H. Tri-Agency Regulations on Coverage of Contraceptive Services by Religious Employers

however, no market value threshold need be satisfied in connection with non-convertible securities eligible for registration on Form F–9 (§ 239.39 of this chapter)".

■ 34. Effective December 31, 2012, amend Form 40–F (referenced in 17 CFR 249.240f) by:

■ a. In General Instruction A.(i), removing "F–9";

■ b. Removing from paragraph (2)(iv) of General Instruction A. the phrase "; provided, however, that no market value threshold need be satisfied in connection with non-convertible securities eligible for registration on Form F–9" and adding in its place the phrase "or the Registrant filed a Form F–9 with the Commission on or before December 30, 2012"; and

■ c. Revising paragraph (2) of General Instruction C. to read as follows:

(2) Any financial statements, other than interim financial statements, included in this Form by registrants registering securities pursuant to Section 12 of the Exchange Act or reporting pursuant to the provisions of Section 13(a) or 15(d) of the Exchange Act must be reconciled to U.S. GAAP as required by Item 17 of Form 20–F under the Exchange Act, unless this Form is filed with respect to a reporting obligation under Section 15(d) that arose solely as a result of a filing made on Form F–7, F–8, F–9 or F–80, in which case no such reconciliation is required.

Note: The text of Form 40–F does not, and this amendment will not, appear in the Code of Federal Regulations.

Dated: July 27, 2011.

By the Commission.

Elizabeth M. Murphy,

Secretary.

[FR Doc. 2011–19421 Filed 8–2–11; 8:45 am]

BILLING CODE 8011–01–P

DEPARTMENT OF THE TREASURY

Internal Revenue Service

26 CFR Part 54

[TD 9541]

RIN 1545–BJ60

DEPARTMENT OF LABOR

Employee Benefits Security Administration

29 CFR Part 2590

RIN 1210–AB44

DEPARTMENT OF HEALTH AND HUMAN SERVICES

[CMS–9992–IFC2]

45 CFR Part 147

RIN 0938–AQ07

Group Health Plans and Health Insurance Issuers Relating to Coverage of Preventive Services Under the Patient Protection and Affordable Care Act

AGENCIES: Internal Revenue Service, Department of the Treasury; Employee Benefits Security Administration, Department of Labor; Centers for Medicare & Medicaid Services, Department of Health and Human Services.

ACTION: Interim final rules with request for comments.

SUMMARY: This document contains amendments to the interim final regulations implementing the rules for group health plans and health insurance coverage in the group and individual markets under provisions of the Patient Protection and Affordable Care Act regarding preventive health services.

DATES: *Effective date.* These interim final regulations are effective on August 1, 2011.

Comment date. Comments are due on or before September 30, 2011.

Applicability dates. These interim final regulations generally apply to group health plans and group health insurance issuers on August 1, 2011.

ADDRESSES: Written comments may be submitted to any of the addresses specified below. Any comment that is submitted to any Department will be shared with the other Departments. Please do not submit duplicates.

All comments will be made available to the public. *WARNING:* Do not include any personally identifiable information (such as name, address, or other contact information) or confidential business information that you do not want publicly disclosed. All comments are posted on the Internet exactly as received, and can be retrieved by most Internet search engines. No deletions, modifications, or redactions will be made to the comments received, as they are public records. Comments may be submitted anonymously.

Department of Labor. Comments to the Department of Labor, identified by RIN 1210–AB44, by one of the following methods:

• *Federal eRulemaking Portal: http://www.regulations.gov.* Follow the instructions for submitting comments.

• *E-mail:* E-OHPSCA2713.EBSA@dol.gov.

• *Mail or Hand Delivery:* Office of Health Plan Standards and Compliance Assistance, Employee Benefits Security Administration, Room N–5653, U.S. Department of Labor, 200 Constitution Avenue, NW., Washington, DC 20210, *Attention:* RIN 1210–AB44.

Comments received by the Department of Labor will be posted without change to *http://www.regulations.gov* and *http://www.dol.gov/ebsa,* and available for public inspection at the Public Disclosure Room, N–1513, Employee Benefits Security Administration, 200 Constitution Avenue, NW., Washington, DC 20210.

Department of Health and Human Services. In commenting, please refer to file code CMS–9992–IFC2. Because of staff and resource limitations, we cannot accept comments by facsimile (FAX) transmission.

You may submit comments in one of four ways (please choose only one of the ways listed):

1. *Electronically.* You may submit electronic comments on this regulation to *http://www.regulations.gov.* Follow the "Submit a comment" instructions.

2. *By regular mail.* You may mail written comments to the following address ONLY: Centers for Medicare & Medicaid Services, Department of Health and Human Services, *Attention:* CMS–9992–IFC2, P.O. Box 8010, Baltimore, MD 21244–8010.

Please allow sufficient time for mailed comments to be received before the close of the comment period.

3. *By express or overnight mail.* You may send written comments to the following address ONLY: Centers for Medicare & Medicaid Services, Department of Health and Human Services, *Attention:* CMS–9992–IFC2, Mail Stop C4–26–05, 7500 Security Boulevard, Baltimore, MD 21244–1850.

4. *By hand or courier.* Alternatively, you may deliver (by hand or courier) your written comments ONLY to the

following addresses prior to the close of the comment period: Centers for Medicare & Medicaid Services, Department of Health and Human Services, Room 445–G, Hubert H. Humphrey Building, 200 Independence Avenue, SW., Washington, DC 20201

(Because access to the interior of the Hubert H. Humphrey Building is not readily available to persons without Federal government identification, commenters are encouraged to leave their comments in the CMS drop slots located in the main lobby of the building. A stamp-in clock is available for persons wishing to retain a proof of filing by stamping in and retaining an extra copy of the comments being filed.)

b. For delivery in Baltimore, MD— Centers for Medicare & Medicaid Services, Department of Health and Human Services, 7500 Security Boulevard, Baltimore, MD 21244–1850.

If you intend to deliver your comments to the Baltimore address, call telephone number (410) 786–4492 in advance to schedule your arrival with one of our staff members.

Comments mailed to the addresses indicated as appropriate for hand or courier delivery may be delayed and received after the comment period.

Inspection of Public Comments: All comments received before the close of the comment period are available for viewing by the public, including any personally identifiable or confidential business information that is included in a comment. We post all comments received before the close of the comment period on the following Web site as soon as possible after they have been received: *http:// www.regulations.gov.* Follow the search instructions on that Web site to view public comments.

Comments received timely will also be available for public inspection as they are received, generally beginning approximately three weeks after publication of a document, at the headquarters of the Centers for Medicare & Medicaid Services, 7500 Security Boulevard, Baltimore, Maryland 21244, Monday through Friday of each week from 8:30 a.m. to 4 p.m. EST. To schedule an appointment to view public comments, phone 1–800–743–3951.

Internal Revenue Service. Comments to the IRS, identified by REG–120391– 10, by one of the following methods:

• *Federal eRulemaking Portal: http:// www.regulations.gov.* Follow the instructions for submitting comments.

• *Mail:* CC:PA:LPD:PR (REG–120391– 10), room 5205, Internal Revenue Service, P.O. Box 7604, Ben Franklin Station, Washington, DC 20044.

• *Hand or courier delivery:* Monday through Friday between the hours of 8 a.m. and 4 p.m. to: CC:PA:LPD:PR (REG–120391–10), Courier's Desk, Internal Revenue Service, 1111 Constitution Avenue, NW., Washington DC 20224.

All submissions to the IRS will be open to public inspection and copying in room 1621, 1111 Constitution Avenue, NW., Washington, DC from 9 a.m. to 4 p.m.

FOR FURTHER INFORMATION CONTACT: Amy Turner or Beth Baum, Employee Benefits Security Administration, Department of Labor, at (202) 693–8335; Karen Levin, Internal Revenue Service, Department of the Treasury, at (202) 622–6080; Robert Imes, Centers for Medicare & Medicaid Services (CMS), Department of Health and Human Services, at (410) 786–1565.

Customer Service Information: Individuals interested in obtaining information from the Department of Labor concerning employment-based health coverage laws may call the EBSA Toll-Free Hotline at 1–866–444–EBSA (3272) or visit the Department of Labor's Web site (*http://www.dol.gov/ebsa*). In addition, information from HHS on private health insurance for consumers can be found on the Centers for Medicare & Medicaid Services (CMS) Web site (*http://cciio.cms.gov*) and information on health reform can be found at *http://www.HealthCare.gov.*

SUPPLEMENTARY INFORMATION:

I. Background

The Patient Protection and Affordable Care Act, Public Law 111–148, was enacted on March 23, 2010; the Health Care and Education Reconciliation Act (the Reconciliation Act), Public Law 111–152, was enacted on March 30, 2010 (collectively known as the "Affordable Care Act"). The Affordable Care Act reorganizes, amends, and adds to the provisions of part A of title XXVII of the Public Health Service Act (PHS Act) relating to group health plans and health insurance issuers in the group and individual markets. The term "group health plan" includes both insured and self-insured group health plans.[1] The Affordable Care Act adds section 715(a)(1) to the Employee Retirement Income Security Act (ERISA) and section 9815(a)(1) to the Internal Revenue Code (the Code) to incorporate the provisions of part A of title XXVII

of the PHS Act into ERISA and the Code, and make them applicable to group health plans, and health insurance issuers providing health insurance coverage in connection with group health plans. The PHS Act sections incorporated by this reference are sections 2701 through 2728. PHS Act sections 2701 through 2719A are substantially new, though they incorporate some provisions of prior law. PHS Act sections 2722 through 2728 are sections of prior law renumbered, with some, mostly minor, changes.

Subtitles A and C of title I of the Affordable Care Act amend the requirements of title XXVII of the PHS Act (changes to which are incorporated into ERISA section 715). The preemption provisions of ERISA section 731 and PHS Act section 2724[2] (implemented in 29 CFR 2590.731(a) and 45 CFR 146.143(a)) apply so that the requirements of part 7 of ERISA and title XXVII of the PHS Act, as amended by the Affordable Care Act, are not to be "construed to supersede any provision of State law which establishes, implements, or continues in effect any standard or requirement solely relating to health insurance issuers in connection with group or individual health insurance coverage except to the extent that such standard or requirement prevents the application of a requirement" of the Affordable Care Act. Accordingly, State laws that impose requirements on health insurance issuers that are stricter than the requirements imposed by the Affordable Care Act are not superseded by the Affordable Care Act.

Section 2713 of the PHS Act, as added by the Affordable Care Act and incorporated under section 715(a)(1) of ERISA and section 9815(a)(1) of the Code, specifies that a group health plan and a health insurance issuer offering group or individual health insurance coverage provide benefits for and prohibit the imposition of cost-sharing with respect to:

• Evidence-based items or services that have in effect a rating of A or B in the current recommendations of the United States Preventive Services Task Force (Task Force) with respect to the individual involved.[3]

---

[1] The term "group health plan" is used in title XXVII of the PHS Act, part 7 of ERISA, and chapter 100 of the Code, and is distinct from the term "health plan," as used in other provisions of title I of the Affordable Care Act. The term "health plan" does not include self-insured group health plans.

[2] Code section 9815 incorporates the preemption provisions of PHS Act section 2724. Prior to the Affordable Care Act, there were no express preemption provisions in chapter 100 of the Code.

[3] Under PHS Act section 2713(a)(5), the Task Force recommendations regarding breast cancer screening, mammography, and prevention issued in or around November of 2009 are not to be considered current recommendations on this subject for purposes of PHS Act section 2713(a)(1).

- Immunizations for routine use in children, adolescents, and adults that have in effect a recommendation from the Advisory Committee on Immunization Practices of the Centers for Disease Control and Prevention (Advisory Committee) with respect to the individual involved. A recommendation of the Advisory Committee is considered to be "in effect" after it has been adopted by the Director of the Centers for Disease Control and Prevention. A recommendation is considered to be for routine use if it appears on the Immunization Schedules of the Centers for Disease Control and Prevention.

- With respect to infants, children, and adolescents, evidence-informed preventive care and screenings provided for in the comprehensive guidelines supported by the Health Resources and Services Administration (HRSA).

- With respect to women, preventive care and screening provided for in comprehensive guidelines supported by HRSA (not otherwise addressed by the recommendations of the Task Force), which will be commonly known as HRSA's Women's Preventive Services: Required Health Plan Coverage Guidelines.

The requirements to cover recommended preventive services without any cost-sharing do not apply to grandfathered health plans.[4] The Departments previously issued interim final regulations implementing PHS Act section 2713; these interim final rules were published in the **Federal Register** on July 19, 2010 (75 FR 41726). For the reasons explained below, the Departments are now issuing an amendment to these interim final rules.

II. Overview of the Amendment to the Interim Final Regulations

The interim final regulations provided that a group health plan or health insurance issuer must cover certain items and services, without cost-sharing, as recommended by the U.S. Preventive Services Task Force, the Advisory Committee on Immunization Practices of the Centers for Disease Control and Prevention, and the Health

Resources and Services Administration. Notably, to the extent not described in the U.S. Preventive Services Task Force recommendations, HRSA was charged with developing comprehensive guidelines for preventive care and screenings with respect to women (*i.e.*, the Women's Preventive Services: Required Health Plan Coverage Guidelines or "HRSA Guidelines"). The interim final regulations also require that changes in the required items and services be implemented no later than plan years (in the individual market, policy years) beginning on or after the date that is one year from when the new recommendation or guideline is issued.

In response to the request for comments on the interim final regulations, the Departments received considerable feedback regarding which preventive services for women should be considered for coverage under PHS Act section 2713(a)(4). Most commenters, including some religious organizations, recommended that HRSA Guidelines include contraceptive services for all women and that this requirement be binding on all group health plans and health insurance issuers with no religious exemption. However, several commenters asserted that requiring group health plans sponsored by religious employers to cover contraceptive services that their faith deems contrary to its religious tenets would impinge upon their religious freedom. One commenter noted that some religious employers do not currently cover such benefits under their group health plan due to their religious beliefs.

The Departments note that PHS Act section 2713(a)(4) gives HRSA the authority to develop comprehensive guidelines for additional preventive care and screenings for women "for purposes of this paragraph." In other words, the statute contemplated HRSA Guidelines that would be developed with the knowledge that certain group health plans and health insurance issuers would be required to cover the services recommended without cost-sharing, unlike the other guidelines referenced in section 2713(a), which pre-dated the Affordable Care Act and were originally issued for purposes of identifying the non-binding recommended care that providers should provide to patients. These HRSA Guidelines exist solely to bind non-grandfathered group health plans and health insurance issuers with respect to the extent of their coverage of certain preventive services for women. In the Departments' view, it is appropriate that HRSA, in issuing these Guidelines, takes into account the effect on the religious beliefs of certain

religious employers if coverage of contraceptive services were required in the group health plans in which employees in certain religious positions participate. Specifically, the Departments seek to provide for a religious accommodation that respects the unique relationship between a house of worship and its employees in ministerial positions. Such an accommodation would be consistent with the policies of States that require contraceptive services coverage, the majority of which simultaneously provide for a religious accommodation.

In light of the above, the Departments are amending the interim final rules to provide HRSA additional discretion to exempt certain religious employers from the Guidelines where contraceptive services are concerned. The amendment to the interim final rules provides HRSA with the discretion to establish this exemption. Consistent with most States that have such exemptions, as described below, the amended regulations specify that, for purposes of this policy, a religious employer is one that: (1) Has the inculcation of religious values as its purpose; (2) primarily employs persons who share its religious tenets; (3) primarily serves persons who share its religious tenets; and (4) is a non-profit organization under section 6033(a)(1) and section 6033(a)(3)(A)(i) or (iii) of the Code. Section 6033(a)(3)(A)(i) and (iii) refer to churches, their integrated auxiliaries, and conventions or associations of churches, as well as to the exclusively religious activities of any religious order. The definition of religious employer, as set forth in the amended regulations, is based on existing definitions used by most States that exempt certain religious employers from having to comply with State law requirements to cover contraceptive services. We will be accepting comments on this definition as well as alternative definitions, such as those that have been developed under Title 26 of the United States Code. The definition set forth here is intended to reasonably balance the extension of any coverage of contraceptive services under the HRSA Guidelines to as many women as possible, while respecting the unique relationship between certain religious employers and their employees in certain religious positions. The change in policy effected by this amendment to these interim final rules is intended solely for purposes of PHS Act section 2713 and the companion provisions of ERISA and the Internal Revenue Code.

Because HRSA's discretion to establish an exemption applies only to group health plans sponsored by certain

---

Thus, the recommendations regarding breast cancer screening, mammography, and prevention issued by the Task Force prior to those issued in or around November of 2009 (that is, those issued in 2002) will be considered current until new recommendations in this area are issued by the Task Force or appear in comprehensive guidelines supported by HRSA concerning preventive care and screenings for women, which will be commonly known as HRSA's Women's Preventive Services: Required Health Plan Coverage Guidelines.

[4] See 26 CFR 54.9815–1251T. 29 CFR 2590.715–1251 and 45 CFR 147.140 (75 FR 34538, June 17, 2010).

46624 **Federal Register** / Vol. 76, No. 149 / Wednesday, August 3, 2011 / Rules and Regulations

religious employers and group health insurance offered in connection with such plans, health insurance issuers in the individual health insurance market would not be covered under any such exemption.

III. Interim Final Regulations and Waiver of Delay of Effective Date

Section 9833 of the Code, section 734 of ERISA, and section 2792 of the PHS Act authorize the Secretaries of the Treasury, Labor, and HHS (collectively, the Secretaries) to promulgate any interim final rules that they determine are appropriate to carry out the provisions of chapter 100 of the Code, part 7 of subtitle B of title I of ERISA, and part A of title XXVII of the PHS Act, which include PHS Act sections 2701 through 2728 and the incorporation of those sections into ERISA section 715 and Code section 9815. The amendments promulgated in this rulemaking carry out the provisions of these statutes. Therefore, the foregoing interim final rule authority applies to these amendments.

Under the Administrative Procedure Act (APA) (5 U.S.C. 551, *et seq.*), while a general notice of proposed rulemaking and an opportunity for public comment is generally required before promulgation of regulations, an exception is made when an agency, for good cause, finds that notice and public comment thereon are impracticable, unnecessary, or contrary to the public interest. The provisions of the APA that ordinarily require a notice of proposed rulemaking do not apply here because of the specific authority to issue interim final rules granted by section 9833 of the Code, section 734 of ERISA, and section 2792 of the PHS Act.

Even if the APA requirements for notice and comment were applicable to these regulations, they have been satisfied. This is because the Secretaries find that providing for an additional opportunity for public comment is unnecessary, as the July 19, 2010 interim final rules implementing section 2713 of the PHS Act provided the public with an opportunity to comment on the implementation of the preventive services requirements in this provision, and the amendments made in these interim final rules in fact are based on such public comments. Specifically, commenters expressed concerns that HRSA-supported guidelines issued under section 2713(a)(4) that included coverage of contraceptive services could impinge upon the religious freedom of certain religious employers. The flexibility that is afforded under these amendments is being provided to HRSA in order to allow HRSA the discretion

to accommodate, in a balanced way, as discussed above, these commenter concerns.

In addition, the Departments have determined that an additional opportunity for public comment would be impractical and contrary to the public interest. The requirement in section 2713(a)(4) that preventive services supported by HRSA be provided without cost-sharing took effect at the beginning of the first plan or policy year beginning on or after September 23, 2010. At that time, however, HRSA had not issued any such guidelines. Under the July 19, 2010 interim final rules, group health plans and insurance issuers do not have to begin covering preventive services supported in HRSA guidelines until the first plan or policy year that begins one year after the guidelines are issued. Thus, while the law requiring coverage of recommended women's preventive health services was enacted on March 23, 2010, and has been in effect since September 23, 2010, no such guidelines have yet been issued, and it will be at least a full year after they are issued before group health plans and issuers will be required to start covering preventive services recommended in the guidelines without cost sharing.

The July 19, 2010 interim final rules indicated that HRSA expected to issue guidelines by August 1, 2011. After considering public comments raising the issue addressed in these amendments, however, the Departments determined that HRSA should be granted the discretion to address the commenter concerns at issue prior to issuing guidelines under section 2713(a)(4). Many college student policy years begin in August and an estimated 1.5 million young adults are estimated to be covered by such policies.[5] Providing an opportunity for public comment as described above would mean that the guidelines could not be issued until after August of 2011. This delay would mean that many students could not benefit from the new prevention coverage without cost-sharing following from the issuance of the guidelines until the 2013–14 school year, as opposed to the 2012–13 school year. Similarly, 2008 data from the Department of Labor indicate that over 4 million Americans have ERISA group health plan coverage that starts in August or September; they too would experience over a year's delay in the receipt of the new benefit if the public

comment period delayed the issuance of the guidance for over a month. The Departments have determined that such a delay in implementation of the statutory requirement that women receive vital preventive services without cost-sharing would be contrary to the public interest because it could result in adverse health consequences that may not otherwise have occurred.

While the Departments have determined that, even if the APA were applicable, issuing these regulations in proposed form, so they would not become effective until after public comment, would be contrary to the public interest in the case of these amendments, the Departments are issuing these amendments as interim final rules so as to provide the public with an opportunity for public comment on these amendments.

The APA also generally requires that a final rule be effective no sooner than 30 days after the date of publication in the **Federal Register**. This 30-day delay in effective date can be waived, however, if an agency finds good cause why the effective date should not be delayed, and the agency incorporates a statement of the findings and its reasons in the rule issued.

As indicated above, many college student policy years begin in August. Delaying the effective date of this amendment by 30 days would mean that the HRSA guidelines could not be issued until after August of 2011. This delay would mean many students could not benefit from the new prevention coverage without cost-sharing following from the issuance of the guidelines until the 2013–14 school year, as opposed to the 2012–13 school year. As discussed above, all other participants, beneficiaries and enrollees in plans or policies with a plan or a policy year beginning in the months between August 1 and whenever a final rule would be published should the Departments provide a pre-promulgation opportunity for public comment would face a similar one-year delay in receiving these important health benefits. The Departments have determined that such a delay in implementation of the statutory requirement that women receive vital preventive services without cost-sharing would be impracticable and contrary to the public interest because it could result in adverse health consequences that may not otherwise have occurred. Therefore, the Departments are waiving the 30-day delay in effective date of these amendments.

[5] Department of Health and Human Services, Notice of Proposed Rulemaking on Student Health Insurance Coverage (76 FR 7767, February 22, 2011).

IV. Economic Impact and Paperwork Burden

A. Executive Orders 13563 and 12866—Department of Labor and Department of Health and Human Services

Executive Orders 13563 and 12866 direct agencies to assess all costs and benefits of available regulatory alternatives and, if regulation is necessary, to select regulatory approaches that maximize net benefits (including potential economic, environmental, public health and safety effects, distributive impacts, and equity). Executive Order 13563 emphasizes the importance of quantifying both costs and benefits, of reducing costs, of harmonizing rules, and of promoting flexibility. This rule has been designated a "significant regulatory action," although not economically significant, under section 3(f) of Executive Order 12866. Accordingly, the rule has been reviewed by the Office of Management and Budget.

1. Need for Regulatory Action

As stated earlier in this preamble, the Departments previously issued interim final regulations implementing PHS Act section 2713 that were published in the **Federal Register** on July 19, 2010 (75 FR 41726). Comments received in response to the interim final regulations raised the issue of imposing on certain religious employers through binding guidelines the requirement to cover contraceptive services that would be in conflict with the religious tenets of the employer. The Departments have determined that it is appropriate to amend the interim final rules to provide HRSA the discretion to exempt from its guidelines group health plans maintained by certain religious employers where contraceptive services are concerned.

2. Anticipated Effects

The Departments expect that this amendment will not result in any additional significant burden or costs to the affected entities.

B. Special Analyses—Department of the Treasury

Notwithstanding the determinations of the Department of Labor and Department of Health and Human Services, for purposes of the Department of the Treasury, it has been determined that this Treasury decision is not a significant regulatory action for purposes of Executive Order 12866. Therefore, a regulatory assessment is not required. It has also been determined that section 553(b) of the APA (5 U.S.C.

chapter 5) does not apply to these interim final regulations. For the applicability of the RFA, refer to the Special Analyses section in the preamble to the cross-referencing notice of proposed rulemaking published elsewhere in this issue of the **Federal Register**. Pursuant to section 7805(f) of the Code, these temporary regulations have been submitted to the Chief Counsel for Advocacy of the Small Business Administration for comment on their impact on small businesses.

C. Paperwork Reduction Act

As stated in the previously issued interim final regulations, this rule is not subject to the requirements of the Paperwork Reduction Act of 1980 (44 U.S.C. 3501 *et seq.*) because it does not contain a "collection of information" as defined in 44 U.S.C. 3502 (11).

V. Statutory Authority

The Department of the Treasury temporary regulations are adopted pursuant to the authority contained in sections 7805 and 9833 of the Code.

The Department of Labor interim final regulations are adopted pursuant to the authority contained in 29 U.S.C. 1027, 1059, 1135, 1161–1168, 1169, 1181–1183, 1181 note, 1185, 1185a, 1185b, 1185c, 1185d, 1191, 1191a, 1191b, and 1191c; sec. 101(g), Pub. L. 104–191, 110 Stat. 1936; sec. 401(b), Pub. L. 105–200, 112 Stat. 645 (42 U.S.C. 651 note); sec. 512(d), Pub. L. 110–343, 122 Stat. 3881; sec. 1001, 1201, and 1562(e), Pub. L. 111–148, 124 Stat. 119, as amended by Pub. L. 111–152, 124 Stat. 1029; Secretary of Labor's Order 3–2010, 75 FR 55354 (September 10, 2010).

The Department of Health and Human Services interim final regulations are adopted pursuant to the authority contained in sections 2701 through 2763, 2791, and 2792 of the PHS Act (42 U.S.C. 300gg through 300gg–63, 300gg–91, and 300gg–92), as amended.

List of Subjects

26 CFR Part 54

Excise taxes, Health care, Health insurance, Pensions, Reporting and recordkeeping requirements.

29 CFR Part 2590

Continuation coverage, Disclosure, Employee benefit plans, Group health plans, Health care, Health insurance, Medical child support, Reporting and recordkeeping requirements.

45 CFR Part 147

Health care, Health insurance, Reporting and recordkeeping requirements, and State regulation of health insurance.

Department of the Treasury

Internal Revenue Service

26 CFR Chapter 1

Accordingly, 26 CFR part 54 is amended as follows:

PART 54—PENSION EXCISE TAXES

■ **Paragraph 1.** The authority citation for part 54 continues to read as follows:

Authority: 26 U.S.C. 7805. * * *

■ **Par. 2.** Section 54.9815–2713T is amended by revising paragraph (a)(1)(iv) to read as follows:

§ 54.9815–2713T Coverage of preventive health services (temporary).

(a) * * *

(1) * * *

(iv) With respect to women, to the extent not described in paragraph (a)(1)(i) of this section, preventive care and screenings provided for in binding comprehensive health plan coverage guidelines supported by the Health Resources and Services Administration and developed in accordance with 45 CFR 147.130(a)(1)(iv).

*   *   *   *   *

Department of Labor

Employee Benefits Security Administration

29 CFR Chapter XXV

29 CFR part 2590 is amended as follows:

PART 2590—RULES AND REGULATIONS FOR GROUP HEALTH PLANS

■ 1. The authority citation for part 2590 continues to read as follows:

Authority: 29 U.S.C. 1027, 1059, 1135, 1161–1168, 1169, 1181–1183, 1181 note, 1185, 1185a, 1185b, 1185c, 1185d, 1191, 1191a, 1191b, and 1191c; sec. 101(g), Pub. L. 104–191, 110 Stat. 1936; sec. 401(b), Pub. L. 105–200, 112 Stat. 645 (42 U.S.C. 651 note); sec. 512(d), Pub. L. 110–343, 122 Stat. 3881; sec. 1001, 1201, and 1562(e), Pub. L. 111–148, 124 Stat. 119, as amended by Pub. L. 111–152, 124 Stat. 1029; Secretary of Labor's Order 3–2010, 75 FR 55354 (September 10, 2010).

Subpart C—Other Requirements

■ 2. Section 2590.715–2713 is amended by revising paragraph (a)(1)(iv) to read as follows:

§ 2590.715–2713 Coverage of preventive health services.

(a) * * *

(1) * * *

(iv) With respect to women, to the extent not described in paragraph (a)(1)(i) of this section, preventive care and screenings provided for in binding comprehensive health plan coverage guidelines supported by the Health Resources and Services Administration and developed in accordance with 45 CFR 147.130(a)(1)(iv).

*   *   *   *   *

Department of Health and Human Services

For the reasons stated in the preamble, the Department of Health and Human Services amends 45 CFR part 147 as follows:

PART 147—HEALTH INSURANCE REFORM REQUIREMENTS FOR THE GROUP AND INDIVIDUAL HEALTH INSURANCE MARKETS

■ 1. The authority citation for part 147 continues to read as follows:

Authority: 2701 through 2763, 2791, and 2792 of the Public Health Service Act (42 U.S.C. 300gg through 300gg–63, 300gg–91, and 300gg–92), as amended.

■ 2. Section 147.130 is amended by revising paragraph (a)(1)(iv) to read as follows:

§ 147.130 Coverage of preventive health services.

(a) * * *

(1) * * *

(iv) With respect to women, to the extent not described in paragraph (a)(1)(i) of this section, preventive care and screenings provided for in binding comprehensive health plan coverage guidelines supported by the Health Resources and Services Administration.

(A) In developing the binding health plan coverage guidelines specified in this paragraph (a)(1)(iv), the Health Resources and Services Administration shall be informed by evidence and may establish exemptions from such guidelines with respect to group health plans established or maintained by religious employers and health insurance coverage provided in connection with group health plans established or maintained by religious employers with respect to any requirement to cover contraceptive services under such guidelines.

(B) For purposes of this subsection, a "religious employer" is an organization that meets all of the following criteria:

(1) The inculcation of religious values is the purpose of the organization.

(2) The organization primarily employs persons who share the religious tenets of the organization.

(3) The organization serves primarily persons who share the religious tenets of the organization.

(4) The organization is a nonprofit organization as described in section 6033(a)(1) and section 6033(a)(3)(A)(i) or (iii) of the Internal Revenue Code of 1986, as amended.

*   *   *   *   *

Steven T. Miller,
Deputy Commissioner for Services and Enforcement, Internal Revenue Service.

Approved: July 28, 2011.

Emily S. McMahon,
Acting Assistant Secretary of the Treasury (Tax Policy).

Signed this 29th day of July 2011.

Phyllis C. Borzi,
Assistant Secretary, Employee Benefits Security Administration, Department of Labor.

OCIIO–9992–IFC2

(Catalog of Federal Domestic Assistance Program No. 93.773, Medicare—Hospital Insurance; and Program No. 93.774, Medicare—Supplementary Medical Insurance Program)

Dated: July 28, 2011.

Donald M. Berwick,
Administrator, Centers for Medicare & Medicaid Services.

Approved: July 28, 2011.

Kathleen Sebelius,
Secretary, Department of Health and Human Services.

[FR Doc. 2011–19684 Filed 8–1–11; 8:45 am]

BILLING CODE 4120–01–P

DEPARTMENT OF HOMELAND SECURITY

Coast Guard

33 CFR Part 165

[Docket No. USCG–2011–0717]

RIN 1625–AA00

Safety Zone; Discovery World Private Wedding Firework Displays, Milwaukee, WI

AGENCY: Coast Guard, DHS.

ACTION: Temporary final rule.

SUMMARY: The Coast Guard is establishing a temporary safety zone on the waters of Milwaukee Harbor in Milwaukee, Wisconsin. This zone is intended to restrict vessels from a portion of Milwaukee Harbor during two separate firework displays on July 31, 2011 and August 26, 2011. This temporary safety zone is necessary to protect spectators and vessels from the hazards associated with these firework displays.

DATES: This rule is in the CFR on August 3, 2011 through 10:30 p.m. on August 26, 2011. This rule is effective with actual notice for purposes of enforcement at 9:30 p.m. on July 31, 2011.

ADDRESSES: Documents indicated in this preamble as being available in the docket are part of docket USCG–2011–0717 and are available online by going to *http://www.regulations.gov*, inserting USCG–2011–0717 in the Docket ID box, and then clicking "search." They are also available for inspection or copying at the Docket Management Facility (M–30), U.S. Department of Transportation, West Building Ground Floor, Room W12–140, 1200 New Jersey Avenue, SE., Washington, DC 20590, between 9 a.m. and 5 p.m., Monday through Friday, except Federal holidays.

FOR FURTHER INFORMATION CONTACT: If you have questions on this temporary rule, contact or e-mail BM1 Adam Kraft, U.S. Coast Guard Sector Lake Michigan, at 414–747–7148 or *Adam.D.Kraft@uscg.mil*. If you have questions on viewing the docket, call Renee V. Wright, Program Manager, Docket Operations, telephone 202–366–9826.

SUPPLEMENTARY INFORMATION:

Regulatory Information

The Coast Guard is issuing this temporary final rule without prior notice and opportunity to comment pursuant to authority under section 4(a) of the Administrative Procedure Act (APA) (5 U.S.C. 553(b)). This provision authorizes an agency to issue a rule without prior notice and opportunity to comment when the agency for good cause finds that those procedures are "impracticable, unnecessary, or contrary to the public interest." Under 5 U.S.C. 553(b)(B), the Coast Guard finds that good cause exists for not publishing a notice of proposed rulemaking (NPRM) with respect to this rule because waiting for a notice and comment period to run would be impracticable and contrary to the public interest. Notice of this fireworks display was not received in sufficient time for the Coast Guard to solicit public comments before the start of the event. Thus, waiting for a notice and comment period to run would be impracticable and contrary to the public interest because it would inhibit the Coast Guard's ability to protect the public from the hazards associated with these maritime fireworks displays.

Under 5 U.S.C. 553(d)(3), the Coast Guard finds that good cause exists for making this rule effective less than 30-days after publication in the **Federal Register**. For the same reasons discussed in the preceding paragraph, waiting for a 30 day notice period to run

I. CMS Temporary Enforcement Safe Harbor for Coverage of Contraceptive Services by Religious Employers

DEPARTMENT OF HEALTH & HUMAN SERVICES   Washington, DC 20201

Date: February 10, 2012

From: Center for Consumer Information and Insurance Oversight (CCIIO), Centers for Medicare & Medicaid Services (CMS)

Title: Guidance on the Temporary Enforcement Safe Harbor for Certain Employers, Group Health Plans and Group Health Insurance Issuers with Respect to the Requirement to Cover Contraceptive Services Without Cost Sharing Under Section 2713 of the Public Health Service Act, Section 715(a)(1) of the Employee Retirement Income Security Act, and Section 9815(a)(1) of the Internal Revenue Code

I.   Purpose

Section 2713(a)(4) of the Public Health Service Act (PHS Act), as added by the Patient Protection and Affordable Care Act (Affordable Care Act), requires non-grandfathered group health plans and health insurance issuers to provide coverage for recommended women's preventive health services without cost sharing. The Affordable Care Act also added section 715(a)(1) to the Employee Retirement Income Security Act (ERISA) and section 9815(a)(1) to the Internal Revenue Code (Code) to incorporate the provisions of part A of title XXVII of the PHS Act (including section 2713) into ERISA and the Code to make them applicable to group health plans.

Interim final regulations were issued by the Department of Health and Human Services (HHS), the Department of Labor, and the Department of the Treasury (collectively, the Departments) on July 19, 2010 (codified at 26 CFR §54.9815-2713T; 29 CFR §2590.715-2713; and 45 CFR §147.130), which provide that a non-grandfathered group health plan or health insurance issuer must cover certain items and services, without cost sharing, as recommended by the U.S. Preventive Services Task Force (USPSTF), the Advisory Committee on Immunization Practices of the Centers for Disease Control and Prevention, and the Health Resources and Services Administration (HRSA). Among other things, the interim final regulations provide that, if a new recommendation or guideline is issued, a plan or issuer must provide coverage consistent with the new recommendation or guideline (with no cost sharing) for plan years (or, in the individual market, policy years) that begin on or after the date that is one year after the date on which the new recommendation or guideline is issued.

HRSA was charged by statute with developing comprehensive guidelines for preventive care and screenings with respect to women, to the extent not already recommended by USPSTF. On August 1, 2011, HRSA adopted and released guidelines for women's preventive services based on recommendations developed by the Institute of Medicine at the request of HHS (Women's Preventive Services: Required Health Plan Coverage Guidelines, or HRSA Guidelines). One of HRSA's recommendations is that all Food and Drug Administration-approved contraceptives for women, as prescribed by a provider, be covered by non-grandfathered group health plans and health insurance issuers without cost sharing.

That same day, the Departments issued an amendment to the interim final regulations that provided HRSA discretion to exempt group health plans established or maintained by certain religious employers (and any group health insurance provided in connection with such plans) from any requirement to cover contraceptive services. The Departments' amended interim final regulations specified that, for purposes of this exemption, a religious employer is one that: (1) has the inculcation of religious values as its purpose; (2) primarily employs persons who share its religious tenets; (3) primarily serves persons who share its religious tenets; and (4) is a non-profit organization described in section 6033(a)(1) and section 6033(a)(3)(A)(i) or (iii) of the Code. Section 6033(a)(3)(A)(i) and (iii) of the Code refers to churches, their integrated auxiliaries, and conventions or associations of churches, as well as to the exclusively religious activities of any religious order. The definition of religious employer, as set forth in the amended interim final regulations, was based on existing definitions used by some States that exempt group health insurance coverage of certain religious employers from having to comply with State insurance law requirements to cover contraceptive services. This discretion to exempt the group health plans established or maintained by these religious employers (and any group health insurance coverage provided in connection with such plans) from any requirement to cover contraceptive services was exercised by HRSA in the HRSA Guidelines, consistent with the Departments' amended interim final regulations. Therefore, this exemption now applies to any group health plan established or maintained by a qualifying religious employer (and any group health insurance coverage provided in connection with such a plan).

For all non-exempted, non-grandfathered plans and policies, the regulations require coverage of the recommended women's preventive services, including the recommended contraceptive services, without cost sharing, for plan years (or, in the individual market, policy years) beginning on or after August 1, 2012.

On January 20, 2012, Secretary Sebelius reaffirmed the exemption authorized in the amended interim final regulations. In doing so, the Secretary indicated that a temporary enforcement safe harbor would be provided to non-exempted, non-grandfathered group health plans established and maintained by non-profit organizations with religious objections to contraceptive coverage (and any health insurance coverage offered in connection with such plans). This bulletin describes the temporary enforcement safe harbor. It is available to non-exempted, non-grandfathered group health plans established or maintained by non-profit organizations whose plans have not covered contraceptive services for religious reasons at any point from the issuance date of this bulletin (i.e., February 10, 2012) onward, consistent with any applicable State law (and any group health insurance coverage provided in connection with such plans), as described herein. This temporary enforcement safe harbor provides an additional year for these group health plans and group health insurance issuers (i.e., until the first plan year beginning on or after August 1, 2013).

The Department of Labor and the Department of the Treasury agree with the need for such transitional relief and will not take any enforcement action against an employer or group health plan that complies with the conditions of the temporary enforcement safe harbor described herein.

-3-

II.   Temporary Enforcement Safe Harbor

The temporary enforcement safe harbor will be in effect until the first plan year that begins on or after August 1, 2013. Neither employers, nor group health plans, nor group health insurance issuers will be subject to any enforcement action by the Departments for failing to cover recommended contraceptive services without cost sharing in non-exempted, non-grandfathered group health plans established or maintained by an organization, including a group or association of employers within the meaning of section 3(5) of ERISA, (and any group health insurance coverage provided in connection with such plans) meeting all of the following criteria:

1. The organization is organized and operates as a non-profit entity.

2. From February 10, 2012 onward, contraceptive coverage has not been provided at any point by the group health plan established or maintained by the organization, consistent with any applicable State law, because of the religious beliefs of the organization.

3. As detailed below, the group health plan established or maintained by the organization (or another entity on behalf of the plan, such as a health insurance issuer or third-party administrator) must provide to participants the attached notice, as described below, which states that contraceptive coverage will not be provided under the plan for the first plan year beginning on or after August 1, 2012.[1]

4. The organization self-certifies that it satisfies criteria 1-3 above, and documents its self-certification in accordance with the procedures detailed herein.

III.   Notice

The attached notice must be in any application materials distributed in connection with enrollment (or re-enrollment) in coverage that is effective beginning on the first day of the first plan year that is on or after August 1, 2012.[2] (For example, for a calendar year plan with an open enrollment period beginning November 1, the notice must be in any application materials provided to participants on or after November 1, 2012.).

This notice is required to be provided by the group health plan (although the plan may ask another entity, such as a health insurance issuer or third-party administrator, to accept responsibility for providing the notice on its behalf). With respect to insured coverage, unless it accepts in writing the responsibility for providing the notice, a group health insurance issuer does not lose its protection under the temporary enforcement safe harbor solely because the notice is not distributed by the plan as described herein, or because the issuer relies in good faith on a representation by the plan that turns out to be incorrect.

---

[1] Nothing in this bulletin precludes employers or others from expressing their opposition, if any, to the final regulations or to the use of contraceptives.

[2] CMS has determined that the notice is not a collection of information under the Paperwork Reduction Act because it is "[t]he public disclosure of information originally supplied by the Federal government to the recipient for the purpose of disclosure to the public." 5 CFR §1320.3(c)(2).

IV.   Certification

A certification must be made by the organization described in section II.[3] The certification must be signed by an organizational representative who is authorized to make the certification on behalf of the organization. The specifications for the certification are attached.

The certification must be completed and made available for examination by the first day of the plan year to which the temporary enforcement safe harbor applies.

Where to get more information:

If you have any questions regarding this bulletin, contact CCIIO at CMS at 410-786-1565 or at phig@cms.hhs.gov.

---

[3] CMS has determined that the certification is not a collection of information under the Paperwork Reduction Act because, although it is a third-party disclosure, it is a certification that does not entail burden other than that necessary to identify the respondent, the date, the respondent's address, and the nature of the instrument. 5 CFR §1320.3(h)(1).

NOTICE TO PLAN PARTICIPANTS

The organization that sponsors your group health plan has certified that it qualifies for a temporary enforcement safe harbor with respect to the Federal requirement to cover contraceptive services without cost sharing. During this one-year period, coverage under your group health plan will not include coverage of contraceptive services.

CERTIFICATION

This form is to be used to certify that the group health plan established or maintained by the organization listed below qualifies for the temporary enforcement safe harbor, as described in HHS bulletin entitled "Guidance on the Temporary Enforcement Safe Harbor for Certain Employers, Group Health Plans and Group Health Insurance Issuers with Respect to the Requirement to Cover Contraceptive Services Without Cost Sharing Under Section 2713 of the Public Health Service Act, Section 715(a)(1) of the Employee Retirement Income Security Act, and Section 9815(a)(1) of the Internal Revenue Code," pertaining to coverage of FDA-approved contraceptive services for women without cost sharing.

Please fill out this form completely.

	Name of the organization sponsoring the plan
	Name of the individual who is authorized to make, and makes, this certification on behalf of the organization
	Mailing and email addresses and phone number for the individual listed above

I certify that the organization is organized and operated as a non-profit entity; and that, at any point from February 10, 2012 onward, contraceptive coverage has not been provided by the plan, consistent with any applicable State law, because of the religious beliefs of the organization.

I declare that I have made this certification, and that, to the best of my knowledge and belief, it is true and correct. I also declare that this certification is complete.

_____

Signature of the individual listed above

_____

Date

Failure to provide the requisite notice to plan participants renders a group health plan ineligible for the temporary enforcement safe harbor.

J. Advance Notice of Tri-Agency Proposed Rulemaking on Coverage of Contraceptive Services by Religious Employers

DEPARTMENT OF THE TREASURY

Internal Revenue Service

26 CFR Part 54

RIN 1545-BJ60

DEPARTMENT OF LABOR

Employee Benefits Security Administration

29 CFR Part 2590

RIN 1210-AB44

DEPARTMENT OF HEALTH AND HUMAN SERVICES

45 CFR Part 147

[CMS-9968-ANPRM]

RIN 0938-AR42

Certain Preventive Services Under the Affordable Care Act

AGENCIES: Internal Revenue Service, Department of the Treasury; Employee Benefits Security Administration, Department of Labor; Centers for Medicare & Medicaid Services, Department of Health and Human Services.

ACTION: Advance notice of proposed rulemaking (ANPRM).

SUMMARY: This advance notice of proposed rulemaking announces the intention of the Departments of Health and Human Services, Labor, and the Treasury to propose amendments to regulations regarding certain preventive health services under provisions of the Patient Protection and Affordable Care Act (Affordable Care Act). The proposed amendments would establish alternative ways to fulfill the requirements of section 2713 of the Public Health Service Act and companion provisions under the Employee Retirement Income Security Act and the Internal Revenue Code when health coverage is sponsored or arranged by a religious organization that objects to the coverage of contraceptive services for religious reasons and that is not exempt under the final regulations published February 15, 2012. This document serves as a request for comments in advance of proposed rulemaking on the potential means of accommodating such organizations while ensuring contraceptive coverage for plan participants and beneficiaries covered under their plans (or, in the case of student health insurance plans, student enrollees and their dependents) without cost sharing.

DATES: Comments are due on or before June 19, 2012.

ADDRESSES: Written comments may be submitted as specified below. Any comment that is submitted will be shared with the other Departments. Please do not submit duplicate comments.

All comments will be made available to the public. **Please Note:** Do not include any personally identifiable information (such as name, address, or other contact information) or confidential business information that you do not want publicly disclosed. All comments are posted on the Internet exactly as received, and can be retrieved by most Internet search engines. No deletions, modifications, or redactions will be made to the comments received, as they are public records. Comments may be submitted anonymously.

In commenting, please refer to file code CMS-9968-ANPRM. Because of staff and resource limitations, the Departments cannot accept comments by facsimile (FAX) transmission.

You may submit comments in one of four ways (please choose only one of the ways listed):

1. *Electronically.* You may submit electronic comments on this ANPRM to *http://www.regulations.gov.* Follow the instructions under the "More Search Options" tab.

2. *By regular mail.* You may mail written comments to the following address only: Centers for Medicare & Medicaid Services, Department of Health and Human Services, Attention: CMS-9968-ANPRM, P.O. Box 8016, Baltimore, MD 21244-1850.

Please allow sufficient time for mailed comments to be received before the close of the comment period.

3. *By express or overnight mail.* You may send written comments to the following address only: Centers for Medicare & Medicaid Services, Department of Health and Human Services, Attention: CMS-9968-ANPRM, Mail Stop C4-26-05, 7500 Security Boulevard, Baltimore, MD 21244-1850.

4. *By hand or courier.* If you prefer, you may deliver (by hand or courier) your written comments before the close of the comment period to either of the following addresses:

a. For delivery in Washington, DC— Centers for Medicare & Medicaid Services, Department of Health and Human Services, Room 445–G, Hubert H. Humphrey Building, 200 Independence Avenue SW., Washington, DC 20201.

(Because access to the interior of the Hubert H. Humphrey Building is not readily available to persons without Federal government identification, commenters are encouraged to leave their comments in the CMS drop slots located in the main lobby of the building. A stamp-in clock is available for persons wishing to retain a proof of filing by stamping and retaining an extra copy of the comments being filed.)

b. For delivery in Baltimore, MD— Centers for Medicare & Medicaid Services, Department of Health and Human Services, 7500 Security Boulevard, Baltimore, MD 21244-1850.

If you intend to deliver your comments to the Baltimore address, call (410) 786-9994 in advance to schedule your arrival with one of our staff members.

Inspection of Public Comments: All comments received before the close of the comment period are available for viewing by the public, including any personally identifiable or confidential business information that is included in a comment. The Departments post all comments received before the close of the comment period on the following Web site as soon as possible after they have been received: *http:// www.regulations.gov.* Follow the search instructions on that Web site to view public comments.

Comments received timely will also be available for public inspection as they are received, generally beginning approximately three weeks after publication of a document, at the headquarters of the Centers for Medicare & Medicaid Services, 7500 Security Boulevard, Baltimore, Maryland 21244, Monday through Friday of each week from 8:30 a.m. to 4 p.m. EST. To schedule an appointment to view public comments, call 1-800-743-3951.

FOR FURTHER INFORMATION CONTACT: Amy Turner or Beth Baum, Employee Benefits Security Administration (EBSA), Department of Labor, at (202) 693-8335; Karen Levin, Internal Revenue Service, Department of the Treasury, at (202) 927-9639; Jacob Ackerman, Centers for Medicare & Medicaid Services (CMS), Department of Health and Human Services (HHS), at (410) 786-1565.

Customer Service Information: Individuals interested in obtaining information from the Department of Labor concerning employment-based health coverage laws may call the EBSA Toll-Free Hotline at 1-866-444-EBSA (3272) or visit the Department of Labor's Web site (*http://www.dol.gov/ebsa*). In

16502   Federal Register / Vol. 77, No. 55 / Wednesday, March 21, 2012 / Proposed Rules

addition, information from HHS on private health insurance for consumers can be found on the CMS Web site (*www.cciio.cms.gov*), and information on health reform can be found at *http://www.HealthCare.gov.*

SUPPLEMENTARY INFORMATION:

I. Background

The Patient Protection and Affordable Care Act, Public Law 111–148, was enacted on March 23, 2010; the Health Care and Education Reconciliation Act of 2010, Public Law 111–152, was enacted on March 30, 2010 (collectively, the Affordable Care Act). The Affordable Care Act reorganizes, amends, and adds to the provisions of part A of title XXVII of the Public Health Service Act (PHS Act) relating to group health plans and health insurance issuers in the group and individual markets. The Affordable Care Act adds section 715(a)(1) to the Employee Retirement Income Security Act (ERISA) and section 9815(a)(1) to the Internal Revenue Code (Code) to incorporate the provisions of part A of title XXVII of the PHS Act into ERISA and the Code, and make them applicable to group health plans.

Section 2713 of the PHS Act, as added by the Affordable Care Act and incorporated into ERISA and the Code, requires that non-grandfathered group health plans and health insurance issuers offering non-grandfathered group or individual health insurance coverage provide benefits for certain preventive health services without the imposition of cost sharing. These preventive health services include, with respect to women, preventive care and screening provided for in the comprehensive guidelines supported by the Health Resources and Services Administration (HRSA) that were issued on August 1, 2011 (HRSA Guidelines).[1] As relevant here, the HRSA Guidelines require coverage, without cost sharing, for "[a]ll Food and Drug Administration [(FDA)] approved contraceptive methods, sterilization procedures, and patient education and counseling for all women with reproductive capacity," as prescribed by a provider.[2] Except as discussed below, non-grandfathered group health plans and health insurance issuers offering non-grandfathered group or individual health insurance coverage are required to provide coverage consistent with the HRSA Guidelines, without cost sharing, in plan years (or, in the individual market, policy years) beginning on or after

August 1, 2012.[3] These guidelines were based on recommendations of the independent Institute of Medicine, which undertook a review of the scientific and medical evidence on women's preventive services.

The Departments of Health and Human Services (HHS), Labor, and the Treasury (the Departments) published interim final regulations implementing section 2713 of the PHS Act on July 19, 2010 (75 FR 41726). In response to comments, the Departments amended the interim final regulations on August 1, 2011.[4] The amendment provided HRSA with discretion to establish an exemption for group health plans established or maintained by certain religious employers (and any group health insurance coverage provided in connection with such plans) with respect to any contraceptive services that they would otherwise be required to cover consistent with the HRSA Guidelines. The amended interim final regulations further specified that, for purposes of this exemption only, a religious employer is one that—(1) has the inculcation of religious values as its purpose; (2) primarily employs persons who share its religious tenets; (3) primarily serves persons who share its religious tenets; and (4) is a non-profit organization described in section 6033(a)(1) and section 6033(a)(3)(A)(i) or (iii) of the Code. Section 6033(a)(3)(A)(i) and (iii) of the Code refers to churches, their integrated auxiliaries, and conventions or associations of churches, as well as to the exclusively religious activities of any religious order. This religious exemption is consistent with the policies in some States that currently both require contraceptive coverage and provide for some type of religious exemption from their contraceptive coverage requirement.

In the HRSA Guidelines, HRSA exercised its discretion under the amended interim final regulations such that group health plans established or maintained by these religious employers (and any group health insurance coverage provided in connection with such plans) are not required to cover any contraceptive services. In the final regulations published on February 15, 2012 (77 FR 8725), the Departments

adopted the definition of religious employer in the amended interim final regulations.

The Departments emphasize that this religious exemption is intended *solely* for purposes of the contraceptive coverage requirement pursuant to section 2713 of the PHS Act and the companion provisions of ERISA and the Code. Whether an employer is designated as "religious" for these purposes is not intended as a judgment about the mission, sincerity, or commitment of the employer, and the use of such designation is limited to defining the class that qualifies for this specific exemption. The designation will not be applied with respect to any other provision of the PHS Act, ERISA, or the Code, nor is it intended to set a precedent for any other purpose.

In addition, we note that this exemption is available to religious employers in a variety of arrangements. For example, a Catholic elementary school may be a distinct common-law employer from the Catholic diocese with which it is affiliated. If the school's employees receive health coverage through a plan established or maintained by the school, and the school meets the definition of a religious employer in the final regulations, then the religious employer exemption applies. If, instead, the same school provides health coverage for its employees through the same plan under which the diocese provides coverage for its employees, and the diocese is exempt from the requirement to cover contraceptive services, then neither the diocese nor the school is required to offer contraceptive coverage to its employees.

On February 10, 2012, when the final regulations concerning the exemption were posted, HHS issued a bulletin entitled "Guidance on the Temporary Enforcement Safe Harbor for Certain Employers, Group Health Plans and Group Health Insurance Issuers with Respect to the Requirement to Cover Contraceptive Services Without Cost Sharing Under Section 2713 of the Public Health Service Act, Section 715(a)(1) of the Employee Retirement Income Security Act, and Section 9815(a)(1) of the Internal Revenue Code."[5] The bulletin established a temporary enforcement safe harbor for group health plans sponsored by non-profit organizations that, on and after February 10, 2012, do not provide some or all of the contraceptive coverage otherwise required, consistent with any

---

[1] The HRSA Guidelines are available at: *http://www.hrsa.gov/womensguidelines.*

[2] **Note:** This excludes items and services such as vasectomies and condoms.

[3] The interim final regulations published by the Departments on July 19, 2010, generally provide that plans and issuers must cover a newly recommended preventive service starting with the first plan year (or, in the individual market, policy year) that begins on or after the date that is one year after the date on which the new recommendation or guideline is issued. 26 CFR 54.9815–2713T(b)(1); 29 CFR 2590.715–2713(b)(1); 45 CFR 147.130(b)(1).

[4] The amendment to the interim final rules was published on August 3, 2011, at 76 FR 46621.

[5] The bulletin can be found at: *http://cciio.cms.gov/resources/files/Files2/02102012/20120210-Preventive-Services-Bulletin.pdf.*

applicable State law, because of the religious beliefs of the organization (and any group health insurance coverage provided in connection with such plans). The temporary enforcement safe harbor is in effect until the first plan year that begins on or after August 1, 2013. The bulletin confirmed that all three Departments will not take any enforcement action against an employer, group health plan, or health insurance issuer that complies with the conditions of the temporary enforcement safe harbor described in the bulletin.

At the same time, the Departments announced plans to expeditiously develop and propose changes to the final regulations implementing section 2713 of the PHS Act that would meet two goals—accommodating non-exempt, non-profit religious organizations' religious objections to covering contraceptive services and assuring that participants and beneficiaries covered under such organizations' plans receive contraceptive coverage without cost sharing. The Departments intend to finalize these amendments to the final regulations such that they are effective by the end of the temporary enforcement safe harbor; that is, the amended final regulations would apply to plan years starting on or after August 1, 2013. This advance notice of proposed rulemaking (ANPRM) is the first step toward promulgating these amended final regulations. Following the receipt of public comment, a notice of proposed rulemaking (NPRM) will be published, which will permit additional public comment, followed by amended final regulations.

II. Overview of Intended Regulations

On February 10, 2012, the Departments committed to working with stakeholders to develop alternative ways of providing contraceptive coverage without cost sharing in order to accommodate non-exempt, non-profit religious organizations with religious objections to such coverage. Specifically, the Departments indicated their plans for a rulemaking to require issuers to offer group health insurance coverage without contraceptive coverage to such an organization (or its plan sponsor) and simultaneously to provide contraceptive coverage directly to the participants and beneficiaries covered under the organization's plan with no cost sharing. Under this approach, the Departments would require that, in this circumstance, there be no premium charge for the separate contraceptive coverage. Actuaries and experts have found that coverage of contraceptives is at least cost neutral, and may save money, when taking into account all

costs and benefits for the issuer.[6] If the cost of coverage is reduced, savings may accrue to employers, plan participants and beneficiaries, and the health care system. The Departments indicated their intent to develop policies to achieve the same goals with respect to self-insured group health plans sponsored by non-exempt, non-profit religious organizations with religious objections to contraceptive coverage.

In the time since this announcement, the Departments have met with representatives of religious organizations, insurers, women's groups, insurance experts, and other interested stakeholders. These initial meetings were used to help identify issues relating to the accommodation to be developed with respect to non-exempt, non-profit religious organizations with religious objections to contraceptive coverage. These consultations also began to provide more detailed information on how health coverage arrangements are currently structured, how religious accommodations work in States with contraceptive coverage requirements, and the landscape with respect to religious organizations that offer health benefits today. These discussions have informed this ANPRM.

As the consultations with interested parties continue, this ANPRM presents questions and ideas to help shape these discussions as well as an early opportunity for any interested stakeholder to provide advice and input into the policy development relating to the accommodation to be made with respect to non-exempted, non-profit religious organizations with religious objections to contraceptive coverage. The Departments welcome all points of view on how to provide women access to the important preventive services at issue without cost sharing while accommodating religious liberty interests.

The starting point for this policy development includes two goals and several ideas about how to achieve them. First, the Departments aim to maintain the provision of contraceptive coverage without cost sharing to individuals who receive coverage through non-exempt, non-profit

[6] Bertko, John, F.S.A., M.A.A.A., Director of Special Initiatives and Pricing, Center for Consumer Information and Insurance Oversight, Centers for Medicare & Medicaid Services, Glied, Sherry, Ph.D., Assistant Secretary for Planning and Evaluation, Department of Health and Human Services (ASPE/HHS), Miller, Erin, MPH, ASPE/HHS, Wilson, Lee, ASPE/HHS, Simmons, Adelle, ASPE/HHS, "The Cost of Covering Contraceptives Through Health Insurance," (February 9, 2012), available at: http://aspe.hhs.gov/health/reports/2012/contraceptives/ib.shtml.

religious organizations with religious objections to contraceptive coverage in the simplest way possible. Second, the Departments aim to protect such religious organizations from having to contract, arrange, or pay for contraceptive coverage. As described below, the Departments intend to propose a requirement that health insurance issuers providing coverage for insured group health plans sponsored by such religious organizations assume the responsibility for the provision of contraceptive coverage without cost sharing to participants and beneficiaries covered under the plan, independent of the religious organization, as a means of meeting these goals. HHS also intends to propose a comparable requirement with respect to student health insurance plans arranged by such religious organizations. For such religious organizations that sponsor self-insured plans, the Departments intend to propose that a third-party administrator of the group health plan or some other independent entity assume this responsibility. The Departments suggest multiple options for how contraceptive coverage in this circumstance could be arranged and financed in recognition of the variation in how such self-insured plans are structured and different religious organizations' perspectives on what constitutes objectionable cooperation with the provision of contraceptive coverage. The Departments seek input on these options, particularly how to enable religious organizations to avoid such objectionable cooperation when it comes to the funding of contraceptive coverage, as well as new ideas to inform the next stage of the rulemaking process.

The following sections set forth questions the Departments believe will help inform the development of proposed regulations, including the policy options the Departments are considering and potential language related to such options. Throughout this ANPRM, the term "accommodation" is used to refer to an arrangement under which contraceptive coverage is provided without cost sharing to participants and beneficiaries covered under a plan independent of the objecting religious organization that sponsors the plan, which would effectively exempt the religious organization from the requirement to cover contraceptive services. The term "religious organization" is used to describe the class of organizations that qualifies for the accommodation. An "independent entity" is an issuer, third-party administrator, or other provider of contraceptive coverage that is not a religious organization. And "contraceptive coverage" means the contraceptive coverage required under the HRSA Guidelines.

The Departments note that a number of questions have been raised about the scope and application of the contraceptive coverage requirement more generally (that is, questions apart from the religious accommodation). The Departments' interim final regulations implementing section 2713 of the PHS Act provide that "[n]othing prevents a plan or issuer from using reasonable medical management techniques to determine the frequency, method, treatment, or setting for an item or service * * * to the extent not specified in the recommendation or guideline."[7] The preamble to the interim final regulations further provides:

"The use of reasonable medical management techniques allows plans and issuers to adapt these recommendations and guidelines to coverage of specific items and services where cost sharing must be waived. Thus, under these interim final regulations, a plan or issuer may rely on established techniques and the relevant evidence base to determine the frequency, method, treatment, or setting for which a recommended preventive service will be available without cost sharing requirements to the extent not specified in a recommendation or guideline." (75 FR 41728–29).[8]

This policy applies to contraceptive coverage. The Departments plan to issue further guidance on section 2713 of the PHS Act more generally.

A. Who qualifies for the accommodation?

As previously described, group health plans sponsored by certain religious employers (and any group health insurance coverage provided in connection with such plans) are exempt from the requirement to offer coverage of contraceptive services that would otherwise be required under the HRSA Guidelines for plan years beginning on or after August 1, 2012. A second set of organizations qualifies for a temporary enforcement safe harbor: group health plans sponsored by non-exempt, non-profit organizations, that, consistent with any applicable State law, do not, on or after February 10, 2012 (the date of the posting of the final regulations), cover some or all forms of contraceptives due to the organization's religious objections to them (and any group health insurance coverage

provided in connection with such plans). The temporary enforcement safe harbor also applies to student health insurance plans arranged by non-profit institutions of higher education that meet comparable criteria. The temporary enforcement safe harbor applies for plan years beginning on or after August 1, 2012, and before August 1, 2013.

On February 10, 2012, the Departments also announced their intention to provide an accommodation with respect to non-exempt, non-profit religious organizations with religious objections to contraceptive coverage. The final regulation concerning student health insurance plans, published elsewhere in this issue of the **Federal Register**, states that this intention extends to student health insurance plans arranged by non-profit religious institutions of higher education with such objections. This accommodation would apply to some or all organizations that qualify for the temporary enforcement safe harbor, and possibly to additional organizations. Thus, a question for purposes of the intended regulations is: What entities should be eligible for the new accommodation (that is, what is a "religious organization")?[9]

One approach would be to adopt the definition of religious organization used in another statute or regulation. For example, the definition used in one or more State laws to afford a religious exemption from a contraceptive coverage requirement could be adopted. Alternatively, the intended regulations could base their definition on another Federal law, such as section 414(e) the Code and section 3(33) of ERISA, which set forth definitions for purposes of "church plans." A definition based on these provisions may include organizations such as hospitals, universities, and charities that are exempt from taxation under section 501 of the Code and that are controlled by or associated with a church or a convention or association of churches. In developing a definition of religious organization, we are cognizant of the important role of ministries of churches and, as such, seek to accommodate their religious objections to contraceptive coverage. The Departments seek comment on which religious organizations should be eligible for the accommodation and whether, as some religious stakeholders have suggested,

for-profit religious employers with such objections should be considered as well.

The Departments underscore, as we did with respect to the definition of religious employer in the final regulations, that whatever definition of religious organization is adopted will not be applied with respect to any other provision of the PHS Act, ERISA, or the Code, nor is it intended to set a precedent for any other purpose. And, while the participants and beneficiaries covered under the health plans offered by a "religious employer" compared to those covered under the health plans offered by a "religious organization" will have differential access to contraceptive coverage, nothing in the final regulations or the forthcoming regulations is intended to differentiate among the religious merits, commitment, mission, or public or private standing of the organizations themselves.

Regardless of the definition of religious organization that is proposed, the Departments are considering proposing the same or a similar process for self-certification that will be used for the temporary enforcement safe harbor referenced in the final regulations. Under that process, an individual authorized by the organization certifies that the organization satisfies the eligibility criteria, and the self-certification is made available for examination. The Departments expect that, for purposes of the proposed accommodation, religious organizations would make a similar self-certification, and similarly make the self-certification available for examination. The self-certification would be used to put the independent entity responsible for providing contraceptive coverage on notice that the religious organization has invoked the accommodation. The future rulemaking would require that the independent entity be responsible for providing the contraceptive coverage in this case.

Under the temporary enforcement safe harbor, an organization that self-certifies must also provide (or arrange to provide) notice to plan participants and beneficiaries that its plan qualifies for the one-year enforcement safe harbor. As the Departments noted in the bulletin establishing the temporary enforcement safe harbor, nothing precludes any organization or individual from expressing opposition, if any, to the regulations or to the use of contraceptives. The Departments do not anticipate that religious organizations would be required to provide such notice to plan participants and beneficiaries beyond the one-year transition period because the

---

[7] 26 CFR 54.9815–2713T(a)(4), 29 CFR 2590.715–2713(a)(4), and 45 CFR 147.130(a)(4).

[8] See also the Departments' guidance in FAQ–8 at *http://www.dol.gov/ebsa/pdf/faq-aca2.pdf* and FAQ–1 at *http://www.dol.gov/ebsa/pdf/faq-aca5.pdf*.

[9] Note that, even if the definition of religious organization for purposes of the accommodation were to include religious employers eligible for the exemption, nothing in the proposed regulations would limit eligibility of religious employers for the exemption.

responsibility to provide notice to plan participants and beneficiaries about the contraceptive coverage would be assumed by the independent entity. The Departments seek comment on how this notice should be provided.

The Departments also intend to propose an accommodation for religious organizations that are non-profit institutions of higher education with religious objections to contraceptive coverage with respect to the student health insurance plans that they arrange. In the final regulation published elsewhere in this issue of the **Federal Register**, "student health insurance coverage" is defined as a type of individual market health insurance coverage offered to students and their dependents under a written agreement between an institution of higher education and an issuer. Some non-profit religious colleges and universities object to signing a written agreement providing for student health insurance coverage that includes contraceptive coverage. Some non-profit religious colleges and universities include funding for their student health insurance plans in their student aid packages and would object if contraceptive coverage were included in the student health insurance plan. The preamble to the final regulation on student health insurance plans provides that the temporary enforcement safe harbor announced on February 10, 2012, with respect to certain non-exempt, non-profit organizations with religious objections to contraceptive coverage extends on comparable terms to student health insurance plans if offered through non-profit institutions of higher education with such objections. After the one-year transition period, the Departments would propose to treat student health insurance plans arranged by non-profit religious institutions of higher education that object to contraceptive coverage on religious grounds in a manner comparable to that in which insured group health plans sponsored by religious organizations eligible for the accommodation are treated. This means that the issuer of the student health insurance plan would, independent of the agreement with the institution of higher education, provide student enrollees and their dependents with contraceptive coverage without cost sharing and without charge.

The Departments seek comment on whether the definition of religious organization should include religious organizations that provide coverage for some, but not all, FDA-approved contraceptives consistent with their religious beliefs. That is, under the forthcoming proposed regulations, the

Departments could allow religious organizations to continue to provide coverage for some forms of contraceptives without cost sharing, and allow them to qualify for the accommodation with respect to other forms of contraceptives consistent with their religious beliefs.

B. Who administers the accommodation?

The accommodation aims to simultaneously fulfill the requirement that plan participants and beneficiaries be offered contraceptive coverage without cost sharing and without charge, and protect a non-profit religious organization that objects on religious grounds from having to provide contraceptive coverage. To achieve these goals, an independent entity is needed to assume certain functions. This entity would, separate from the religious organization and as directed by regulations and guidance, notify plan participants and beneficiaries of the availability of separate contraceptive coverage, provide this coverage automatically to participants and beneficiaries covered under the organization's plan (for example, without an application or enrollment process), and protect the privacy of participants and beneficiaries covered under the plan who use contraceptive services.

Today, in most instances, an independent entity either provides or administers health coverage for group health plans. Such group coverage falls into two categories: Insured coverage and self-insured coverage. A group that buys insured coverage pays a premium to a State-licensed and State-regulated health insurance issuer which bears the risk of claims for that coverage. A group that self-insures its coverage does not pay premiums to a health insurance issuer; instead, employer and/or employee contributions fund the health claims of participants and beneficiaries covered under the plan. Typically, self-insured plans contract with a third-party administrator, under a fee arrangement, for administrative services, such as network contracting, managed care services, and payment of claims. Insured group health plans and self-insured group health plans that are not church plans or governmental plans are generally subject to Title I of ERISA. Because there is no insurance provided by a health insurance issuer, self-insured plans are not subject to State insurance laws.

The Departments intend to propose that, when offering insured coverage to a religious organization that self-certifies as qualifying for the

accommodation, a health insurance issuer may not include contraceptive coverage in that organization's insured coverage. This means that contraceptive coverage would not be included in the plan document, contract, or premium charged to the religious organization. Instead, the issuer would be required to provide participants and beneficiaries covered under the plan separate coverage for contraceptive services, potentially as excepted benefits, without cost sharing, and notify plan participants and beneficiaries of its availability. The issuer could not charge a premium to the religious organization or plan participants or beneficiaries for the contraceptive coverage. To incorporate this proposal into regulations with respect to insured group health plans (comparable regulatory language would be developed with respect to student health insurance plans), the Departments are considering proposing new language in the existing preventive services regulations at 45 CFR 147.130, 29 CFR 2590.715–2713 and 26 CFR 54.9815–2713 providing: "In the case of an insured group health plan established or maintained by a religious organization—

• The group health plan established or maintained by the religious organization (and the group health insurance coverage provided in connection with the plan) need not comply with any requirement under this section to provide coverage for contraceptive services with respect to the insured group coverage if all of the following conditions are satisfied:

○ The organization provides the issuer with written notice that the organization is a religious organization, and will not act as the designated plan administrator or claims administrator with respect to claims for contraceptive benefits.

○ The issuer has access to information necessary to communicate with the plan's participants and beneficiaries and to act as a claims administrator and plan administrator with respect to contraceptive benefits.

• An issuer that receives the notice described above must offer to the religious organization group health insurance coverage that does not include coverage for contraceptive services otherwise required to be covered under this section. The issuer must additionally provide to the participants and beneficiaries covered under the plan separate health insurance coverage consisting solely of coverage for contraceptive services required to be covered under this section. The issuer must make such health insurance coverage for contraceptive services available without any charge to the organization, group health plan, or plan participants or beneficiaries. The issuer must notify plan participants and beneficiaries of the availability of such coverage for contraceptive services in accordance with guidance issued by the Secretary. The issuer must not impose any cost sharing requirements (such as a copayment, coinsurance, or a deductible) on such coverage for contraceptive services and must comply with all other requirements of this section with respect to coverage for contraceptive services."

Additionally, to ensure that contraceptive coverage offered by a health insurance issuer under these circumstances does not confront obstacles due to other Federal requirements (such as the guaranteed issue requirement under section 2702 of the PHS Act, the single risk pool requirement under section 1312(c) of the Affordable Care Act, and the essential health benefits requirement under section 2707 of the PHS Act), the Departments are considering adding by regulation contraceptive coverage to the types of excepted benefits in the individual market at 45 CFR 148.220(b). In so doing, the Departments would consider preserving certain PHS Act protections such as appeals and grievances rights while ensuring relief from others such as the requirement to provide essential health benefits. The Departments seek comment on whether and how to structure such a change to the excepted benefits regulations, and what PHS Act protections should (or should not) continue to apply. In addition, the Departments seek comment on ways to structure the contraceptive-only benefit as a benefit separate from the insured group coverage other than as an excepted benefit.

Issuers would pay for contraceptive coverage from the estimated savings from the elimination of the need to pay for services that would otherwise be used if contraceptives were not covered. Typically, issuers build into their premiums projected costs and savings from a set of services. Premiums from multiple organizations are pooled in a "book of business" from which the issuer pays for services. To the extent that contraceptive coverage lowers the draw-down for other health care services from the pool, funds would be available to pay for contraceptive services without an additional premium charged to the religious organization or plan participants or beneficiaries. Actuaries, insurers, and economists

estimate that covering contraceptive services is at least cost neutral.

For a religious organization that sponsors a self-insured group health plan, the Departments aim to similarly shield it from contracting, arranging, paying, or referring for contraceptive coverage. The Departments intend to propose, and invite comments on, having the third-party administrator of an objecting religious organization fulfill such responsibility. For ERISA plans,[10] the Departments are considering proposing that the self-certification of the religious organization, described above, would serve as a notice to the third-party administrator that the requirement to provide contraceptive coverage will not be fulfilled by the religious organization. The proposed regulations, in this circumstance, would set forth the circumstances and criteria under which the third-party administrator would be designated as the plan administrator for ERISA plans solely for the purpose of fulfilling the requirement to provide contraceptive coverage. As prescribed by the proposed regulations, the third-party administrator would provide or arrange for such coverage in such circumstances. The third-party administrator would notify plan participants and beneficiaries of this coverage. The religious organization would take no action other than self-certification.

To incorporate this proposal into regulations with respect to self-insured group health plans, the Departments are considering proposing new language in the existing preventive services regulations at 29 CFR 2590.715–2713 and 26 CFR 54.9815–2713 providing that: "A religious organization maintaining a self-insured group health plan is not responsible for compliance with any requirement under this section to provide coverage for contraceptive services if all of the following conditions are satisfied:

• The plan contracts with one or more third parties for processing of benefit claims,

• Before entering into each such contract, the employer provides each third party administrator (TPA) with written notice that the employer: (1) Is a religious organization, (2) will not act as the designated plan administrator or claims administrator with respect to claims for contraceptive services, (3) will not contribute to the funding of

[10] A church plan as defined under section 3(33) of ERISA is exempt from ERISA's requirements under section 4(b) of ERISA, and, therefore, any proposed ERISA regulations would not apply to church plans. Comments are sought on potential options for church plans.

contraceptive services, and (4) will not participate in claims processing with respect to claims for contraceptive services.

• With respect to contraceptive benefits, the TPAs have authority and control over the funds available to pay the benefit, authority to act as a claims administrator and plan administrator, and access to information necessary to communicate with the plan's participants and beneficiaries."

In addition, with respect to ERISA plans, the Department of Labor is considering proposing a new regulation at 29 CFR 2510.3–16 providing: "In the case of a group health plan established or maintained by a religious organization that is not responsible for compliance with any requirement under § 2590.715–2713 of this part to provide coverage for contraceptive services, the required notice from the religious organization provided to a third party administrator (TPA) of the religious organization's refusal to provide and fund such benefits shall be an instrument under which the plan is operated and shall have the effect of designating such TPA as the plan administrator under section 3(16) of ERISA for those contraceptive benefits for which that TPA processes claims in its normal course of business. A TPA that becomes a plan administrator pursuant to this section shall be responsible for—

• The plan's compliance with section 2713 of the Public Health Service Act (as incorporated into section 715 of ERISA and § 2590.715–2713 of this part) as to those categories of contraceptive benefits for which the TPA processes claims in its normal course of business (*for example,* surgical procedures, non-surgical procedures, patient education and counseling, prescription benefits and non-prescription benefits).

• Establishing and operating a procedure for determining such claims for contraceptive benefits in accordance with § 2560.503–1 of this title.

• Complying with disclosure requirements and other requirements under Title I of ERISA for such benefits to participants and beneficiaries."

We note that there is no obligation for a TPA to enter into such a contract if it objects to these terms.

Providing for an independent entity to assume responsibility for plan-related functions when other plan sponsors or officials fail or refuse to do so would not be unique to the instant context. For example, where certain retirement savings plans have been abandoned by their sponsors, Department of Labor regulations authorize asset custodians to distribute plan benefits and wind up the plan's affairs. 29 CFR 2578.1.

The Departments seek comment on the following possible approaches that a third-party administrator could use to fund the contraceptive coverage without using funds provided by the religious organization. The third-party administrator could use revenue that is not already obligated to plan sponsors such as drug rebates, service fees, disease management program fees, or other sources. These funds may inure to the third-party administrator rather than the plan or its sponsor and drug rebates, for example, could be larger if contraceptive coverage were provided. Additionally, nothing precludes a third-party administrator from receiving funds from a private, non-profit organization to pay for contraceptive services for the participants and beneficiaries covered under the plan of a religious organization. Comments should address the ways in which third-party administrators generally receive funding to pay benefits, other flows of funds, the extent to which funding from other sources may be available for payment of claims, and the monitoring responsibilities and oversight that would be associated with such arrangements.

Another option under consideration would be to have the third-party administrator receive a credit or rebate on the amount that it pays under the reinsurance program under Affordable Care Act section 1341 in order to fund contraceptive coverage for participants and beneficiaries covered under the plan of a religious organization that sponsors a self-insured plan. Section 1341 of the Affordable Care Act creates a reinsurance program to balance out risk selection from 2014 through 2016. Payments from health insurance issuers and third-party administrators on behalf of group health plans will be made to a reinsurance entity. Payments are used, among other things, to offset the cost of reinsurance for health insurance issuers. While the reinsurance program does not provide payments to group health plans, it collects payments from third-party administrators to support the program. Under this proposal, a third-party administrator that funds contraceptive coverage separate from a religious organization could offset the amount of this cost with a credit or rebate against its assessments under the reinsurance program. Such a policy could help advance the goals of the reinsurance program, which is one of many in the Act designed to make health insurance affordable, accessible, meaningful, and stable. The Departments seek comments on such an interpretation of Affordable

Care Act section 1341 and on ideas of alternative sources of funding once this temporary program ends.

An additional option would have the third-party administrator separately arrange for contraceptive coverage. In this case, an additional independent entity other than a third-party administrator would be needed. The Departments are considering having the Office of Personnel Management (OPM) identify a private insurer to provide this coverage. Under section 1334 of the Affordable Care Act, OPM is responsible for contracting with at least two insurers to offer multi-State plans in each Exchange in each State to promote choice, competition, and access to health services. The OPM Director, in consultation with the HHS Secretary, has the authority to impose appropriate requirements on the insurers that offer multi-State plans. Accordingly, OPM could incentivize or require one or more of the insurers offering a multi-State plan also to provide, at no additional charge, contraceptive coverage to participants and beneficiaries covered under religious organizations' self-insured plans. The third-party administrator would send a copy of the religious organization's self-certification to OPM along with information on plan participants and beneficiaries. One option for covering the cost of the contraceptive coverage would be a credit against any user fees such an insurer would be required to pay in order to offer coverage on the Exchanges. The Departments seek comment on the impact of this proposal on the multi-State plan program, ways to administer it, and additional funding ideas.

If adopted, the reinsurance program and multi-State plan options may require amendments to the regulations and guidance governing those programs. In addition, these programs start on January 1, 2014. There may be some religious organizations with plan years that begin on or after August 1, 2013, but before those programs begin, so, should the Departments propose these options, we would also propose a means of resolving this gap in relief. The Departments seek input on such means as well as how many religious organizations have plan years that start between August 1 and December 31.

The Departments welcome ideas on other options for the source of funds for contraceptive coverage. Some religious stakeholders have suggested, for example, the use of tax-preferred accounts that employees may in their discretion use for a range of medical services that neither precludes nor obligates funds to be used for

contraceptive services. A number of religious stakeholders have also suggested that public funding to support coverage of contraceptive services is not objectionable. The Departments seek comment on these and other proposals. Comments are also requested on additional considerations that should be taken into account with respect to these and other proposals and on suggestions for structuring the implementation of the proposals in light of these considerations.

The Departments expect that the third-party administrator could use these sources of funds individually or in combination. The Departments also note that nothing precludes a religious organization from switching from a self-insured plan to an insured plan such that a health insurance issuer rather than a third-party administrator is responsible for providing the contraceptive coverage.

The Departments also seek information on coordination when there are multiple third-party administrators and on the prevalence of multi-year contracts as well as options for addressing the application of these proposals in such instances. The Departments invite comment on the extent to which there are self-insured health plans without a third-party administrator as well as options for how the accommodation would work in these rare circumstances. One option would be to have a religious organization send its self-certification to OPM, which would be directed to independently arrange for contraceptive coverage through a private insurer. The Departments seek comment on the prevalence and number of participants and beneficiaries of health plans sponsored by religious organizations without a third-party administrator.

C. Additional Questions

To inform the notice of proposed rulemaking, the Departments seek information on several additional questions. One question that has arisen from religious stakeholders is whether an exemption or accommodation should be made for certain religious health insurance issuers or third-party administrators with respect to contraceptive coverage. The Departments have little information about the number and location of such issuers and administrators and whether and how such issuers operate in the 28 States with contraceptive coverage requirements.

The Departments also recognize that various denominations may offer coverage to institutions affiliated with those denominations. For example, their

16508 Federal Register / Vol. 77, No. 55 / Wednesday, March 21, 2012 / Proposed Rules

plans may be offered as "church plans" (described above) to individual churches as a means of pooling their risk. The Departments seek comment on whether different accommodations are needed for such plans.

In addition, the Departments are aware that 28 States have adopted laws requiring that certain health insurance issuers provide contraceptive coverage. Some of these laws contain exemptions related to religious organizations, but the scope of the exemptions varies among the States. Generally, Federal health insurance coverage regulation creates a floor to which States may add consumer protections, but may not subtract. This means that, in States with broader religious exemptions than that in the final regulations, the exemptions will be narrowed to align with that in the final regulations because this will help more consumers. Organizations that qualify for an exemption under State law but do not qualify for the exemption under the final regulations may be eligible for the temporary enforcement safe harbor. During this transition period, State laws that require contraceptive coverage with narrower or no religious exemptions will continue. The Departments seek comment on the interaction between these State laws and the intended regulations on which we are seeking comment in this notice and on the extent to which there is a need for consistency between any Federal regulations and these State laws. Similarly, the Departments solicit comment on what other Federal or State laws or accounting rules governing funding and accounting could affect the proposed options described herein.

In addition, the Departments solicit information on the number of potentially affected issuers and religious organizations as well as their plan participants and beneficiaries; the administrative cost of providing separate contraceptive coverage, including details regarding the nature of the costs (for example, one-time systems changes or ongoing administrative costs); and the average costs and savings to health plans, plan participants and beneficiaries, and the public of providing contraceptive coverage.

D. Additional Input

The 90-day comment period is designed to encourage maximum input into the development of an accommodation for religious organizations with religious objections to providing contraceptive coverage while ensuring the availability of contraceptive coverage without cost sharing for plan participants and beneficiaries. The Departments seek

comments on the ideas and questions outlined in this ANPRM as well as new suggestions to achieve its goals. The Departments also intend to hold listening sessions to ensure all voices are heard. This will not be the only opportunity for comment. The subsequent notice of proposed rulemaking will also include a public comment period. The Departments aim to ensure that the final accommodation is fully vetted and published in advance of the expiration of the temporary enforcement safe harbor.

Steven T. Miller,

Deputy Commissioner for Services and Enforcement, Internal Revenue Service.

Signed this day of March 14, 2012.

Phyllis C. Borzi.

Assistant Secretary, Employee Benefits Security Administration, Department of Labor.

Dated: March 15, 2012.

Marilyn Tavenner,

Acting Administrator, Centers for Medicare & Medicaid Services.

Approved: March 15, 2012.

Kathleen Sebelius,

Secretary, Department of Health and Human Services.

[FR Doc. 2012–6689 Filed 3–16–12; 4:15 pm]

BILLING CODE 4120–01–P

ENVIRONMENTAL PROTECTION AGENCY

40 CFR Part 63

[EPA–HQ–OAR–2011–0435; FRL–9650–3]

RIN 2060–AR02

National Emission Standards for Hazardous Air Pollutant Emissions: Group IV Polymers and Resins; Pesticide Active Ingredient Production; and Polyether Polyols Production

AGENCY: Environmental Protection Agency (EPA).

ACTION: Reopening of public comment period.

SUMMARY: On January 9, 2012, the EPA proposed amendments to three national emission standards for hazardous air pollutants: National Emission Standards for Hazardous Air Pollutant Emissions: Group IV Polymers and Resins; National Emission Standards for Hazardous Air Pollutants for Pesticide Active Ingredient Production; and National Emission Standards for Hazardous Air Pollutants for Polyether Polyols Production. The EPA is reopening the comment period until March 30, 2012. The EPA received a request for this reopening from the Sierra Club. The

Sierra Club requested the reopening in order to analyze data and review the proposed amendments. EPA finds this request to be reasonable due to the multiple source categories involved in this action.

DATES: Comments must be received on or before March 30, 2012.

ADDRESSES: Submit your comments, identified by Docket ID No. EPA–HQ–OAR–2011–0435, by one of the following methods:

• *www.regulations.gov:* Follow the on-line instructions for submitting comments.

• *Email:* a-and-r-docket@epa.gov. Attention Docket ID No. EPA–HQ–OAR–2011–0435.

• *Fax:* (202) 566–9744. Attention Docket ID No. EPA–HQ–OAR–2011–0435.

• *Mail:* U.S. Postal Service, send comments to: EPA Docket Center, EPA West (Air Docket), Attention Docket ID No. EPA–HQ–OAR–2011–0435, U.S. Environmental Protection Agency, Mailcode: 2822T, 1200 Pennsylvania Ave. NW., Washington, DC 20460. Please include a total of two copies. In addition, please mail a copy of your comments on the information collection provisions to the Office of Information and Regulatory Affairs, Office of Management and Budget (OMB), Attn: Desk Officer for EPA, 725 17th Street NW., Washington, DC 20503.

• *Hand Delivery:* U.S. Environmental Protection Agency, EPA West (Air Docket), Room 3334, 1301 Constitution Ave. NW., Washington, DC 20004. Attention Docket ID No. EPA–HQ–OAR–2011–0435. Such deliveries are only accepted during the Docket's normal hours of operation, and special arrangements should be made for deliveries of boxed information.

Instructions. Direct your comments to Docket ID No. EPA–HQ–OAR–2011–0435. The EPA's policy is that all comments received will be included in the public docket without change and may be made available online at *www.regulations.gov,* including any personal information provided, unless the comment includes information claimed to be confidential business information (CBI) or other information whose disclosure is restricted by statute. Do not submit information that you consider to be CBI or otherwise protected through *www.regulations.gov* or email. The *www.regulations.gov* Web site is an "anonymous access" system, which means the EPA will not know your identity or contact information unless you provide it in the body of your comment. If you send an email comment directly to the EPA without

K. Tri-Agency Regulations on Extended Coverage for Adult Children

Thursday,
May 13, 2010

Part II

Department of the Treasury
Internal Revenue Service
26 CFR Parts 54 and 602

Department of Labor
Employee Benefits Security
Administration

29 CFR Part 2590

Department of Health and Human Services

45 CFR Parts 144, 146, and 147

Group Health Plans and Health Insurance Issuers Relating to Dependent Coverage of Children to Age 26 Under the Patient Protection and Affordable Care Act; Interim Final Rule and Proposed Rule

27122 Federal Register / Vol. 75, No. 92 / Thursday, May 13, 2010 / Rules and Regulations

DEPARTMENT OF THE TREASURY

Internal Revenue Service

26 CFR Parts 54 and 602

[TD 9482]

RIN 1545–BJ46

DEPARTMENT OF LABOR

Employee Benefits Security Administration

29 CFR Part 2590

RIN 1210–AB41

DEPARTMENT OF HEALTH AND HUMAN SERVICES

Office of the Secretary

[OCIIO–4150–IFC]

45 CFR Parts 144, 146, and 147

RIN 0991–AB66

Interim Final Rules for Group Health Plans and Health Insurance Issuers Relating to Dependent Coverage of Children to Age 26 Under the Patient Protection and Affordable Care Act

AGENCY: Internal Revenue Service, Department of the Treasury; Employee Benefits Security Administration, Department of Labor; Department of Health and Human Services.

ACTION: Interim final rules with request for comments.

SUMMARY: This document contains interim final regulations implementing the requirements for group health plans and health insurance issuers in the group and individual markets under provisions of the Patient Protection and Affordable Care Act regarding dependent coverage of children who have not attained age 26.

DATES: *Effective date.* These interim final regulations are effective on July 12, 2010.

Comment date. Comments are due on or before August 11, 2010.

Applicability date. These interim final regulations generally apply to group health plans and group health insurance issuers for plan years beginning on or after September 23, 2010. These interim final regulations generally apply to individual health insurance issuers for policy years beginning on or after September 23, 2010.

ADDRESSES: Written comments may be submitted to any of the addresses specified below. Any comment that is submitted to any Department will be shared with the other Departments. Please do not submit duplicates.

All comments will be made available to the public. *Warning:* Do not include any personally identifiable information (such as name, address, or other contact information) or confidential business information that you do not want publicly disclosed. All comments are posted on the Internet exactly as received, and can be retrieved by most Internet search engines. No deletions, modifications, or redactions will be made to the comments received, as they are public records. Comments may be submitted anonymously.

Department of Labor. Comments to the Department of Labor, identified by RIN 1210–AB41, by one of the following methods:

• *Federal eRulemaking Portal: http://www.regulations.gov.* Follow the instructions for submitting comments.

• *E-mail: E-OHPSCA.EBSA@dol.gov.*

• *Mail or Hand Delivery:* Office of Health Plan Standards and Compliance Assistance, Employee Benefits Security Administration, Room N–5653, U.S. Department of Labor, 200 Constitution Avenue NW., Washington, DC 20210, *Attention:* RIN 1210–AB41.

Comments received by the Department of Labor will be posted without change to *http://www.regulations.gov* and *http://www.dol.gov/ebsa,* and available for public inspection at the Public Disclosure Room, N–1513, Employee Benefits Security Administration, 200 Constitution Avenue, NW., Washington, DC 20210.

Department of Health and Human Services. In commenting, please refer to file code OCIIO–4150–IFC. Because of staff and resource limitations, we cannot accept comments by facsimile (FAX) transmission.

You may submit comments in one of four ways (please choose only one of the ways listed):

1. *Electronically.* You may submit electronic comments on this regulation to *http://www.regulations.gov.* Follow the instructions under the "More Search Options" tab.

2. *By regular mail.* You may mail written comments to the following address only: Office of Consumer Information and Insurance Oversight, Department of Health and Human Services, Attention: OCIIO–4150–IFC, P.O. Box 8016, Baltimore, MD 21244–1850.

Please allow sufficient time for mailed comments to be received before the close of the comment period.

3. *By express or overnight mail.* You may send written comments to the following address only: Office of Consumer Information and Insurance Oversight, Department of Health and

Human Services, Attention: OCIIO–4150–IFC, Mail Stop C4–26–05, 7500 Security Boulevard, Baltimore, MD 21244–1850.

4. *By hand or courier.* If you prefer, you may deliver (by hand or courier) your written comments before the close of the comment period to either of the following addresses:

a. For delivery in Washington, DC— Office of Consumer Information and Insurance Oversight, Department of Health and Human Services, Room 445– G, Hubert H. Humphrey Building, 200 Independence Avenue, SW., Washington, DC 20201 (Because access to the interior of the Hubert H. Humphrey Building is not readily available to persons without Federal government identification, commenters are encouraged to leave their comments in the OCIIO drop slots located in the main lobby of the building. A stamp-in clock is available for persons wishing to retain a proof of filing by stamping in and retaining an extra copy of the comments being filed.).

b. For delivery in Baltimore, MD— Centers for Medicare & Medicaid Services, Department of Health and Human Services, 7500 Security Boulevard, Baltimore, MD 21244–1850.

If you intend to deliver your comments to the Baltimore address, please call (410) 786–7195 in advance to schedule your arrival with one of our staff members.

Comments mailed to the addresses indicated as appropriate for hand or courier delivery may be delayed and received after the comment period.

Submission of comments on paperwork requirements. You may submit comments on this document's paperwork requirements by following the instructions at the end of the "Collection of Information Requirements" section in this document.

Inspection of Public Comments: All comments received before the close of the comment period are available for viewing by the public, including any personally identifiable or confidential business information that is included in a comment. We post all comments received before the close of the comment period on the following Web site as soon as possible after they have been received: *http://www.regulations.gov.* Follow the search instructions on that Web site to view public comments.

Comments received timely will also be available for public inspection as they are received, generally beginning approximately three weeks after publication of a document, at the headquarters of the Centers for Medicare & Medicaid Services, 7500 Security

Boulevard, Baltimore, Maryland 21244, Monday through Friday of each week from 8:30 a.m. to 4 p.m. EST. To schedule an appointment to view public comments, phone 1–800–743–3951.

Internal Revenue Service. Comments to the IRS, identified by REG–114494–10, by one of the following methods:

• *Federal eRulemaking Portal: http:// www.regulations.gov.* Follow the instructions for submitting comments.

• *Mail:* CC:PA:LPD:PR (REG–114494–10), room 5205, Internal Revenue Service, P.O. Box 7604, Ben Franklin Station, Washington, DC 20044.

• *Hand or courier delivery:* Monday through Friday between the hours of 8 a.m. and 4 p.m. to: CC:PA:LPD:PR (REG–114494–10), Courier's Desk, Internal Revenue Service, 1111 Constitution Avenue, NW., Washington DC 20224.

All submissions to the IRS will be open to public inspection and copying in room 1621, 1111 Constitution Avenue, NW., Washington, DC from 9 a.m. to 4 p.m.

FOR FURTHER INFORMATION CONTACT: Amy Turner or Beth Baum, Employee Benefits Security Administration, Department of Labor, at (202) 693–8335; Karen Levin, Internal Revenue Service, Department of the Treasury, at (202) 622–6080; Jim Mayhew, Office of Consumer Information and Insurance Oversight, Department of Health and Human Services, at (410) 786–1565.

Customer Service Information: Individuals interested in obtaining information from the Department of Labor concerning employment-based health coverage laws may call the EBSA Toll-Free Hotline at 1–866–444–EBSA (3272) or visit the Department of Labor's Web site (*http://www.dol.gov/ebsa*). In addition, information from HHS on private health insurance for consumers can be found on the Centers for Medicare & Medicaid Services (CMS) Web site (*http://www.cms.hhs.gov/ HealthInsReformforConsume/ 01_Overview.asp*).

SUPPLEMENTARY INFORMATION:

I. Background

The Patient Protection and Affordable Care Act (the Affordable Care Act), Public Law 111–148, was enacted on March 23, 2010; the Health Care and Education Reconciliation Act (the Reconciliation Act), Public Law 111–152, was enacted on March 30, 2010. The Affordable Care Act and the Reconciliation Act reorganize, amend, and add to the provisions of part A of title XXVII of the Public Health Service Act (PHS Act) relating to group health plans and health insurance issuers in

the group and individual markets. The term "group health plan" includes both insured and self-insured group health plans.[1] The Affordable Care Act adds section 715 to the Employee Retirement Income Security Act (ERISA) and section 9815 to the Internal Revenue Code (the Code) to make the provisions of part A of title XXVII of the PHS Act applicable under ERISA and the Code to group health plans, and health insurance issuers providing health insurance coverage in connection with group health plans, as if those provisions of the PHS Act were included in ERISA and the Code. The PHS Act sections incorporated by this reference are sections 2701 through 2728. PHS Act sections 2701 through 2719A are substantially new, though they incorporate some provisions of prior law. PHS Act sections 2722 through 2728 are sections of prior law renumbered with some, mostly minor, changes. Section 1251 of the Affordable Care Act, as modified by section 10103 of the Affordable Care Act and section 2301 of the Reconciliation Act, specifies that certain plans or coverage existing as of the date of enactment (*i.e.,* grandfathered health plans) are subject to only certain provisions.

Subtitles A and C of title I of the Affordable Care Act amend the requirements of title XXVII of the PHS Act (changes to which are incorporated into ERISA section 715). The preemption provisions of ERISA section 731 and PHS Act section 2724[2] (implemented in 29 CFR 2590.731(a) and 45 CFR 146.143(a)) apply so that the requirements of the Affordable Care Act are not to be "construed to supersede any provision of State law which establishes, implements, or continues in effect any standard or requirement solely relating to health insurance issuers in connection with group or individual health insurance coverage except to the extent that such standard or requirement prevents the application of a requirement" of the Affordable Care Act. Accordingly, State laws that impose on health insurance issuers stricter requirements than those imposed by the Affordable Care Act will not be superseded by the Affordable Care Act.

---
[1] The term "group health plan" is used in title XXVII of the PHS Act, part 7 of ERISA, and chapter 100 of the Code, and is distinct from the term "health plan", as used in other provisions of title I of the Affordable Care Act. The term "health plan" does not include self-insured group health plans.

[2] Code section 9815 incorporates the preemption provisions of PHS Act section 2724. Prior to the Affordable Care Act, there were no express preemption provisions in chapter 100 of the Code.

The Departments of Health and Human Services, Labor, and the Treasury (the Departments) expect to issue regulations implementing the revised PHS Act sections 2701 through 2719A in several phases. The first publication in this series was a Request for Information relating to the medical loss ratio provisions of PHS Act section 2718, published in the **Federal Register** on April 14, 2010 (75 FR 19297). These interim final regulations are being published to implement PHS Act section 2714 (requiring dependent coverage of children to age 26). PHS Act section 2714 generally is effective for plan years (in the individual market, policy years) beginning on or after September 23, 2010, which is six months after the March 23, 2010 date of enactment of the Affordable Care Act.[3] The implementation of other provisions of PHS Act sections 2701 through 2719A and section 1251 of the Affordable Care Act will be addressed in future regulations.

Because subtitles A and C of title I of the Affordable Care Act contain requirements that are applicable to both the group and individual health insurance markets, it would be duplicative to insert the requirements into both the existing 45 CFR part 146 (Requirements for the Group Health Insurance Market) and 45 CFR part 148 (Requirements for the Individual Health Insurance Market). Accordingly, these interim final regulations create a new part 147 in subchapter B of 45 CFR to implement the provisions of the Affordable Care Act. The provisions of the Affordable Care Act, to the extent that they apply to group health plans and group health insurance coverage, are also implemented under new regulations added to 29 CFR part 2590 and 26 CFR part 54.

II. Overview of the Regulations

A. PHS Act Section 2714, Continued Eligibility of Children Until Age 26 (26 CFR 54.9815–2714, 29 CFR 2590.715–2714, 45 CFR 147.120)

Section 2714 of the PHS Act, as added by the Affordable Care Act (and amended by the Reconciliation Act), and these interim final regulations provide that a plan or issuer that makes available dependent coverage[4] of children must make such coverage available for children until attainment

---
[3] *See* section 1004 of the Affordable Care Act.

[4] For purposes of these interim final regulations, dependent coverage means coverage of any individual under the terms of a group health plan, or group or individual health insurance coverage, because of the relationship to a participant (in the individual market, primary subscriber).

of 26 years of age. The statute also requires the issuance of regulations to "define the dependents to which coverage shall be made available" under this rule.

Many group health plans that provide dependent coverage limit the coverage to health coverage excludible from employees' gross income for income tax purposes. Thus, dependent coverage is limited to employees' spouses and employees' children that qualify as dependents for income tax purposes. Consequently, these plans often condition dependent coverage, in addition to the age of the child, on student status, residency, and financial support or other factors indicating dependent status. However, with the expansion of dependent coverage required by the Affordable Care Act to children until age 26, conditioning coverage on whether a child is a tax dependent or a student, or resides with or receives financial support from the parent, is no longer appropriate in light of the correlation between age and these factors. Therefore, these interim final regulations do not allow plans or coverage to use these requirements to deny dependent coverage to children. Because the statute does not distinguish between coverage for minor children and coverage for adult children under age 26, these factors also may not be used to determine eligibility for dependent coverage for minor children.

Accordingly, these interim final regulations clarify that, with respect to children who have not attained age 26, a plan or issuer may not define dependent for purposes of eligibility for dependent coverage of children other than in terms of the relationship between the child and the participant (in the individual market, the primary subscriber). Examples of factors that cannot be used for defining dependent for purposes of eligibility (or continued eligibility) include financial dependency on the participant or primary subscriber (or any other person), residency with the participant or primary subscriber (or any other person), student status, employment, eligibility for other coverage, or any combination of these. These interim final regulations also provide that the terms of the plan or policy for dependent coverage cannot vary based on the age of a child, except for children age 26 or older. Examples illustrate that surcharges for coverage of children under age 26 are not allowed except where the surcharges apply regardless of the age of the child (up to age 26) and that, for children under age 26, the plan cannot vary benefits based on the age of the child. The Affordable Care Act, as

originally enacted, required plans and issuers to make dependent coverage available only to a child "who is not married." This language was struck by section 2301(b) of the Reconciliation Act. Accordingly, under these interim final regulations, plans and issuers may not limit dependent coverage based on whether a child is married. (However, a plan or issuer is not required under these interim final regulations to cover the spouse of an eligible child).

The statute and these interim final regulations provide that nothing in PHS Act section 2714 requires a plan or issuer to make available coverage for a child of a child receiving dependent coverage.

Under section 1004(d) of the Reconciliation Act and IRS Notice 2010–38 (released to the public on April 27, 2010 and scheduled to be published in 2010–20 Internal Revenue Bulletin, May 17, 2010), employers may exclude from the employee's income the value of any employer-provided health coverage for an employee's child for the entire taxable year the child turns 26 if the coverage continues until the end of that taxable year. This means that if a child turns 26 in March, but stays on the plan past December 31st (the end of most people's taxable year), the health benefits up to December 31st can be excluded for tax purposes.

Application to grandfathered health plans. Under the statute and these interim final regulations, the requirement to make available dependent coverage for children who have not attained age 26 generally applies to all group health plans and health insurance issuers offering group or individual health insurance coverage whether or not the plan or health insurance coverage qualifies as a grandfathered health plan [5] under section 1251 of the Affordable Care Act, for plan years (in the individual market, policy years) beginning on or after September 23, 2010. However, in accordance with section 2301(a) of the Reconciliation Act, for plan years beginning before January 1, 2014, these interim final regulations provide that a grandfathered health plan that is a group health plan that makes available dependent coverage of children may exclude an adult child who has not attained age 26 from coverage only if the child is eligible to enroll in an employer-sponsored health plan (as

defined in section 5000A(f)(2) of the Code) other than a group health plan of a parent. In the case of an adult child who is eligible for coverage under the plans of the employers of both parents, neither plan may exclude the adult child from coverage based on the fact that the adult child is eligible to enroll in the plan of the other parent's employer.

Regulations relating to grandfathered health plans under section 1251 of the Affordable Care Act are expected to be published in the very near future. The Departments anticipate that the regulations will make clear that changes to plan or policy terms to comply with PHS Act section 2714 and these interim final regulations, including voluntary compliance before plan years (in the individual market, policy years) beginning on or after September 23, 2010, will not cause a plan or health insurance coverage to lose grandfathered health plan status for any purpose under the Affordable Care Act, as amended.

Transitional Rule. Prior to the applicability date of PHS Act section 2714, a child who was covered under a group health plan or health insurance coverage as a dependent may have lost eligibility under the plan (or coverage) due to age prior to age 26. Moreover, if, when a parent first became eligible for coverage, a child was under age 26 but older than the age at which the plan (or coverage) stopped covering children, the child would not have become eligible for the plan (or coverage). When the provisions of section 2714 become applicable, a plan or issuer can no longer exclude coverage for the child prior to age 26 irrespective of whether or when that child was enrolled in the plan (or coverage). Also, a child of a primary subscriber with family coverage in the individual market may be entitled to an opportunity to enroll if the child previously lost coverage due to age while other family members retained the coverage.[6]

Accordingly, these interim final regulations provide transitional relief for a child whose coverage ended, or who was denied coverage (or was not

---

[5] Section 1251 of the Affordable Care Act, as modified by section 10103 of the Affordable Care Act and section 2301 of the Reconciliation Act, specifies that certain plans or coverage existing as of the March 23, 2010 date of enactment (*i.e.,* grandfathered health plans) are subject to only certain provisions.

[6] In the group market, section 9802(a) of the Code, section 702(a) of ERISA, and section 2705 of the PHS Act provide that a plan or issuer cannot impose any rule for eligibility for benefits (including any rule excluding coverage) based on a health factor, including a preexisting condition. These rules were added by HIPAA and generally became applicable for group health plans for plan years beginning on or after July 1, 1997. Similar guidance regarding re-enrollment rights for individuals previously denied coverage due to a health factor was issued by the Departments of the Treasury, Labor, and HHS on December 29, 1997, at 62 FR 67689 and on January 8, 2001 at 66 FR 1378, 1403, 1410, 1418.

eligible for coverage) under a group health plan or health insurance coverage because, under the terms of the plan or coverage, the availability of dependent coverage of children ended before the attainment of age 26.

These interim final regulations require a plan or issuer to give such a child an opportunity to enroll that continues for at least 30 days (including written notice of the opportunity to enroll), regardless of whether the plan or coverage offers an open enrollment period and regardless of when any open enrollment period might otherwise occur. This enrollment opportunity (including the written notice) must be provided not later than the first day of the first plan year (in the individual market, policy year) beginning on or after September 23, 2010. Thus, many plans can use their existing annual enrollment periods (which commonly begin and end before the start of the plan year) to satisfy the enrollment opportunity requirement. If the child is enrolled, coverage must begin not later than the first day of the first plan year (in the individual market, policy year) beginning on or after September 23, 2010, even if the request for enrollment is made after the first day of the plan year. In subsequent years, dependent coverage may be elected for an eligible child in connection with normal enrollment opportunities under the plan or coverage.

Under these interim final regulations, the notice may be provided to an employee on behalf of the employee's child (in the individual market, to a primary subscriber on behalf of the primary subscriber's child). In addition, for a group health plan or group health insurance coverage, the notice may be included with other enrollment materials that a plan distributes to employees, provided the statement is prominent. For a group health plan or group health insurance coverage, if a notice satisfying these requirements is provided to an employee whose child is entitled to an enrollment opportunity, the obligation to provide the notice of enrollment opportunity with respect to that child is satisfied for both the plan and the issuer.

Any child enrolling in group health plan coverage pursuant to this enrollment right must be treated as a special enrollee, as provided under the regulations interpreting the HIPAA portability provisions.[7] Accordingly, the child must be offered all the benefit

packages available to similarly situated individuals who did not lose coverage by reason of cessation of dependent status. The child also cannot be required to pay more for coverage than similarly situated individuals who did not lose coverage by reason of cessation of dependent status.

The Departments have been informed that many health insurance issuers have announced that they will allow continued coverage of adult children before such coverage is required by the Affordable Care Act. A plan or issuer that allows continued coverage of adult children before being required to do so by the Affordable Care Act is not required to provide the enrollment opportunity with respect to children who do not lose coverage.

Examples in these interim final regulations illustrate the application of these transitional rules. One example illustrates that, if a child qualifies for an enrollment opportunity under this section and the parent is not enrolled but is otherwise eligible for enrollment, the plan must provide an opportunity to enroll the parent, in addition to the child. Similarly, another example illustrates that, if a plan has more than one benefit package option, a child qualifies for enrollment under this section, and the parent is enrolled in one benefit package option, the plan must provide an opportunity to enroll the child in any benefit package option for which the child is otherwise eligible (thus allowing the parent to switch benefit package options). Another example illustrates that a child who qualifies for an enrollment opportunity under this section and who is covered under a COBRA continuation provision must be given the opportunity to enroll as a dependent of an active employee (i.e., other than as a COBRA-qualified beneficiary). In this situation, if the child loses eligibility for coverage due to a qualifying event (including aging out of coverage at age 26), the child has another opportunity to elect COBRA continuation coverage. (If the qualifying event is aging out, the COBRA continuation coverage could last 36 months from the loss of eligibility that relates to turning age 26.) The final example in this section illustrates that an employee who joined a plan prior to the applicability date of PHS Act section 2714, and has a child who never enrolled because the child was too old under the terms of the plan but has not yet turned 26, must be provided an opportunity to enroll the child under this section even though the child was not previously covered under the plan. If the parent is no longer eligible for coverage under the plan (for example, if

the parent has ceased employment with the plan sponsor) as of the first date on which the enrollment opportunity would be required to be given, the plan would not be required to enroll the child.

B. Conforming Changes Under the PHS Act

1. References to the Public Health Service Act

Conforming changes to references to sections of title XXVII of the PHS Act are made throughout parts 144 and 146 of title 45 of the Code of Federal Regulations to reflect the renumbering of certain sections by the Affordable Care Act.

2. Definitions (45 CFR 144.103)

These interim final regulations define "policy year" as the 12-month period that is designated in the policy documents of individual health insurance coverage. If the policy document does not designate a policy year (or no such document is available), then the policy year is the deductible or limit year used under the coverage. If deductibles or other limits are not imposed on a yearly basis, the policy year is the calendar year. The Affordable Care Act uses the term "plan year" in referring to the period of coverage in both the individual and group health insurance markets. The term "plan year", however, is generally used in the group health insurance market. Accordingly, these interim final regulations substitute the term "policy year" for "plan year" in defining the period of coverage in the individual health insurance market.

III. Interim Final Regulations and Request for Comments

Section 9833 of the Code, section 734 of ERISA, and section 2792 of the PHS Act authorize the Secretaries of the Treasury, Labor, and HHS (collectively, the Secretaries) to promulgate any interim final rules that they determine are appropriate to carry out the provisions of chapter 100 of the Code, part 7 of subtitle B of title I of ERISA, and part A of title XXVII of the PHS Act, which include PHS Act sections 2701 through 2728 and the incorporation of those sections into ERISA section 715 and Code section 9815.

In addition, under Section 553(b) of the Administrative Procedure Act (APA) (5 U.S.C. 551 et seq.) a general notice of proposed rulemaking is not required when an agency, for good cause, finds that notice and public comment thereon are impracticable, unnecessary, or contrary to the public interest. The

---

[7] HIPAA is the Health Insurance Portability and Accountability Act of 1996 (Public Law 104–191). Regulations regarding the treatment of HIPAA special enrollees are included at 26 CFR 54.9801–6(d), 29 CFR 2590.701–6(d), and 45 CFR 146.117(d).

provisions of the APA that ordinarily require a notice of proposed rulemaking do not apply here because of the specific authority granted by section 9833 of the Code, section 734 of ERISA, and section 2792 of the PHS Act. However, even if the APA was applicable, the Secretaries have determined that it would be impracticable and contrary to the public interest to delay putting the provisions in these interim final regulations in place until a full public notice and comment process is completed. The statutory requirement implemented in these interim final regulations was enacted on March 23, 2010, and applies for plan years (in the individual market, policy years) beginning on or after September 23, 2010. Having a binding rule in effect is critical to ensuring that individuals entitled to the new protections being implemented have these protections uniformly applied.

Moreover, the provisions in these interim final regulations require lead time for implementation. These interim final regulations require that an enrollment period be provided no later than the first day the obligation to allow dependent children to enroll until attainment of age 26 takes effect. Preparations presumably would have to be made to put such an enrollment process in place. Group health plans and health insurance issuers also would have to take the cost associated with this new obligation into account in establishing their premiums, and in making other changes to the designs of plan or policy benefits, and any such premiums and changes would have to receive necessary approvals in advance of the plan or policy year in question.

For the foregoing reasons, the Departments have determined that it is essential to provide certainty about what will be required of group health plans and health insurance issuers under the statutory requirements implemented in binding regulations as far in advance of September 23, 2010 as possible. This makes it impracticable to engage in full notice and comment rulemaking before putting regulations into effect, and in the public interest to do so through interim final regulations under which the public will have an opportunity for comment, but that opportunity will not delay putting rules in effect (a delay that could possibly last past September 23, 2010).

Issuance of proposed regulations would not be sufficient because the proposed regulations would not be binding, and different group health plans or health insurance issuers could interpret the statutory language in different ways. Had the Departments

published a notice of proposed rulemaking, provided for a 60-day comment period, and only then prepared final regulations, which would be subject to a 60-day delay in effective date, it is unlikely that it would have been possible to have final regulations in effect before late September, when these requirements could be in effect for some plans or policies. It therefore is in the public interest that these interim final regulations be in effect and apply when the statutory protections being implemented apply.

IV. Economic Impact and Paperwork Burden

A. Summary—Department of Labor and Department of Health and Human Services

As stated earlier in this preamble, these interim final regulations implement PHS Act section 2714, which requires plans or issuers that make dependent coverage available for children to continue to make such coverage available for an adult child until the attainment of age 26. The regulation also provides an enrollment opportunity to individuals who lost or were not eligible for dependent coverage before age 26.[8] This provision generally is effective for plan years (in the individual market, policy years) beginning on or after September 23, 2010, which is six months after the March 23, 2010 date of enactment of the Affordable Care Act.

The Departments have crafted these interim final regulations to secure the protections intended by Congress in the most economically efficient manner possible. The Departments have quantified costs where possible and provided a qualitative discussion of the economic benefits and some of the transfers and costs that may stem from these interim final regulations.

B. Executive Order 12866—Department of Labor and Department of Health and Human Services

Under Executive Order 12866 (58 FR 51735), this regulatory action has been determined "significant" and therefore subject to review by the Office of

---

[8] The Affordable Care Act adds section 715 and Code section to make the provisions of part A of title XXVII of the PHS Act applicable to group health plans, and health insurance issuers providing health insurance coverage in connection with group health plans, under ERISA and the Code as if those provisions of the PHS Act were included in ERISA and the Code. The PHS Act sections incorporated by this reference are sections 2701 through 2728. Section 1251 of the Affordable Care Act provides rules for grandfathered health plans, and these rules are further clarified in section 10103 of the Affordable Care Act and section 2301 of the Reconciliation Act.

Management and Budget (OMB). Section 3(f) of the Executive Order defines a "significant regulatory action" as an action that is likely to result in a rule (1) having an annual effect on the economy of $100 million or more in any one year, or adversely and materially affecting a sector of the economy, productivity, competition, jobs, the environment, public health or safety, or State, local or tribal governments or communities (also referred to as "economically significant"); (2) creating a serious inconsistency or otherwise interfering with an action taken or planned by another agency; (3) materially altering the budgetary impacts of entitlement grants, user fees, or loan programs or the rights and obligations of recipients thereof; or (4) raising novel legal or policy issues arising out of legal mandates, the President's priorities, or the principles set forth in the Executive Order. OMB has determined that this regulation is economically significant within the meaning of section 3(f)(1) of the Executive Order, because it is likely to have an annual effect on the economy of $100 million in any one year. Accordingly, OMB has reviewed these rules pursuant to the Executive Order. The Departments provide an assessment of the potential costs, benefits, and transfers associated with the regulatory provision below. The Departments invite comments on this assessment and its conclusions.

1. Need for Regulatory Action

PHS Act section 2714, as added by the Affordable Care Act and amended by the Reconciliation Act requires group health plans and health insurance issuers offering group or individual health insurance coverage that make dependent coverage available for children to continue to make coverage available to such children until the attainment of age 26. With respect to a child receiving dependent coverage, coverage does not have to be extended to a child or children of the child or a spouse of the child. In addition, as provided by the Reconciliation Act, grandfathered group health plans are not required to offer dependent coverage to a child under 26 who is otherwise eligible for employer-sponsored insurance other than a group health plan of a parent for plan years beginning before January 1, 2014. PHS Act section 2714 generally is effective for plan years (in the individual market, policy years) beginning on or after September 23, 2010. Thus, these interim final regulations are necessary to amend the Departments' existing regulations to implement these statutorily mandated changes.

2. Summary of Impacts

In this section, the Departments estimate the number of individuals affected by these interim final regulations, and the impact of the regulations on health insurance premiums in the group and individual markets. Beginning with the population of individuals age 19–25, the number of individuals potentially affected is estimated by applying several criteria including whether their parents have existing employer-sponsored insurance (ESI) or an individual market policy; and whether the individuals are themselves uninsured, have ESI, individual market policies or other forms of coverage. A range of assumptions concerning the percentage of the potentially affected individuals that will accept the offer of new dependent coverage—"take-up" rates— is then applied to estimate the number of newly covered individuals. The premium impact is calculated by using an estimated incremental insurance cost per newly-covered individual as a percent of average family premiums.

In accordance, with OMB Circular A–4,[9] Table 1 below depicts an accounting statement showing the Departments' assessment of the benefits, costs, and transfers associated with this regulatory action.

TABLE 1—ACCOUNTING TABLE

Benefits:

Annualized Quantified: low estimate	0.19 million previously uninsured individuals gain coverage in 2011.
mid-range estimate	0.65 million previously uninsured individuals gain coverage in 2011.
high estimate	1.64 million previously uninsured individuals gain coverage in 2011.

Qualitative: Expanding coverage options of the 19–25 population should decrease the number uninsured, which in turn should decrease the cost-shifting of uncompensated care onto those with insurance, increase the receipt of preventive health care and provide more timely access to high quality care, resulting in a healthier population. Allowing extended dependent coverage will also permit greater job mobility for this population as their insurance coverage will no longer be tied to their own jobs or student status. Dependents aged 19–25 that have chronic or other serious health conditions would still be able to continue their current coverage through a parent's plan. To the extent there is an increase in beneficial utilization of healthcare, health could improve.

Costs[10]	Low estimate	Mid-range estimate	High estimate	Year dollar	Discount rate percent	Period covered [11]
Annualized Monetized ($millions/year)	11.2	11.2	11.2	2010	7	2011–2013
	10.4	10.4	10.4	2010	3	2011–2013

A one-time notice of right to enroll must be sent to those affected.

Qualitative: To the extent additional coverage increases utilization of health care services, there will be additional costs incurred to achieve the health benefits.

Transfer: [12]

	Low estimate	Mid-range estimate	High estimate	Year dollar	Discount rate percent	Period covered
Annualized Monetized ($millions/year)	3,459.3	5,250.2	6,893.9	2010	7	2011–2013
	3,482.5	5,274.5	6,895.4	2010	3	2011–2013

Qualitative. If the rule causes family health insurance premiums to increase, there will be a transfer from individuals with family health insurance coverage who do not have dependents aged 19–25 to those individuals with family health insurance coverage that have dependents aged 19–25. To the extent that these higher premiums result in lower profits or higher prices for the employer's product, then the higher premiums will result in a transfer either from stockholders or consumers.

[10] The cost estimates are annualize across the years 2011–2013, and reflects a single point estimate of the cost to send out a notice in the first year only.

[11] The Departments limited the period covered by the RIA to 2011–2013, because it only has reliable data to make projections over this period due to the fact that in 2014, things will change drastically when the subsidies and tax credits to offset premium increases and the exchanges are in effect.

[12] The estimates in this table reflect the annualized discounted value in 2010 of the additional premium costs for family policies calculated as the product of the newly covered dependents in each year from 2011–2013 (see below) and an incremental cost per newly-covered person in those years (see below).

3. Estimated Number of Affected Individuals

The Departments' estimates in this section are based on the 2004–2006 Medical Expenditure Panel Survey Household Component (MEPS–HC) which was projected and calibrated to 2010 to be consistent with the National Health Accounts projections. The Departments estimate that in 2010, there are approximately 29.5 million individuals aged 19–25 (young adults) in the United States. Of those individuals, 9.3 million young adults (of whom 3.1 million are uninsured) do not have a parent who has either ESI or non-group insurance, and thus they have no access to dependent coverage. As shown in Table 2, among the remaining 20.2 million young adults whose parents are covered either by ESI or by non-group insurance:

- 3.44 million are currently uninsured,
- 2.42 million are covered by their own non-group insurance,
- 5.55 million are covered by their own ESI,
- 5.73 million are already on their parent's or spouse's ESI, and
- 3.01 million have some other form of coverage such as Medicaid or TRICARE.

[9] Available at *http://www.whitehouse.gov/omb/circulars/a004/a-4.pdf.*

27128 Federal Register/Vol. 75, No. 92/Thursday, May 13, 2010/Rules and Regulations

TABLE 2—YOUNG ADULTS AGED 19–25 BY INSURANCE STATUS

	Uninsured*	Non-group	Own ESI	ESI as a dependent	Other	Total
Total U.S. Population Aged 19–25	**6.59**	**2.69**	6.98	5.75	7.5	29.5
All Young Adults in U.S. with a Parent with a Policy by Young Adult Insurance Status						
Parents have ESI	**3.28**	**2.03**	5.32	5.73	2.91	19.27
Parents have non-group	**0.16**	**0.40**	0.23	....	0.10	0.88
Subtotal A	**3.44**	**2.42**	5.55	5.73	3.01	20.15

*The **bolded** numbers are potentially affected by the regulation.

Source: MEPS 2004–2006 HC Surveys, controlled to 2010 consistent with the National Health Accounts. Note: Total number of young adults, age 19–25 is 29.5 million; the 20.15 million in this Table are the subset whose parents have either ESI or non-group coverage.

Initially, the subset of this group of young adults that will be affected by these interim final regulations are those who are either uninsured (3.44 million) or covered by individual coverage (2.42 million). The statute does not require grandfathered group health plans to offer coverage to young adults who currently have their own ESI or an offer of an ESI. For the purposes of this analysis, it is assumed that all plans begin 2011 with grandfathered status. These impacts could change if plans lose their Grandfathered status.

Of these 5.86 million young adults, as shown in Table 3, 3.49 million are also unlikely to switch to their parents' coverage because:
• They are already allowed to enroll in extended dependent coverage for young adults through their State's existing laws, but have chosen not to

(2.61 million). Thirty-seven states already have requirements concerning dependent coverage in the group market, although most of these are substantially more restrictive than those contained in this regulation.[13] Using information about State laws obtained from the Kaiser Family Foundation,[14] a State by State profile of State required coverage based on a person's State of residence, age, student status, and living situation was developed. This profile was then overlaid on MEPS data to obtain an estimate of the number of individuals that would newly become eligible for coverage due to these interim final regulations.
• They have an offer of ESI and have parents who are covered by ESI (0.48 million). For the purposes of this regulatory impact statement, the Departments assume that the parents of

these young adults will be in grandfathered group health plans, and thus that these young adults will not be affected by the provisions of these interim final regulations. To the extent that some of the coverage in which these parents are enrolled is not grandfathered, the effect of these interim final regulations will be larger than the estimates provided here.

• Finally, there are 0.40 million young adults who have non-group coverage and whose parents have non-group coverage. Because the parents' non-group coverage is underwritten, there is not likely to be any financial benefit to the family in moving the young adult onto the parents' coverage, and the Departments assume that these young adults will not be affected by the regulation.

TABLE 3—"UNINSURED" AND "NON-GROUP" YOUNG ADULTS UNLIKELY TO BE AFFECTED BY EXTENDING DEPENDENT COVERAGE TO AGE 26

	Uninsured	Non-Group coverage	Total
(1) Young adults potentially covered by parent ESI due to state law	1.30	1.31	2.61
(2) Young adults with an offer of ESI whose parents have ESI	0.31	0.17	0.48
(3) Young adults with non-group coverage whose parents have non-group coverage	....	0.40	0.40
Subtotal B	1.61	1.88	3.49

As shown in Table 4, this leaves approximately 2.37 million young adults who might be affected by this provision, or approximately eight percent of the 29.5 million young adults

in the age group. Among the approximately 2.37 million young adults who are estimated to be potentially affected by this provision, approximately 1.83 million are

currently uninsured, and 0.55 million are currently covered by their own non-group coverage.

TABLE 4—YOUNG ADULTS POTENTIALLY AFFECTED BY EXTENDING DEPENDENT COVERAGE TO AGE 26

	Uninsured	Non-group coverage	Total
Parents have ESI	1.67	0.55	2.21
Parents have non-group	0.16	....	0.16

---

[13] Restrictions include requirements for financial dependency, student status, and age limits.

[14] As described in Kaiser Family Foundation, *Definition of Dependency by Age, 2010*, KFF State Health Facts, at *http://www.statehealthfacts.org/comparetable.jsp?ind=601&cat=7.*

Federal Register / Vol. 75, No. 92 / Thursday, May 13, 2010 / Rules and Regulations

27129

TABLE 4—Young Adults Potentially Affected by Extending Dependent Coverage to Age 26—Continued

	Uninsured	Non-group coverage	Total
Total (Subtotal A–Subtotal B)*	1.83	0.55	2.37

Source: MEPS 2004–2006 HC Surveys, controlled to 2010 consistent with projections of the National Health Accounts.
*Subtotal A is in Table 2 and Subtotal B is in Table 3.

It is difficult to estimate precisely what fraction of the 2.37 million young adults who might potentially be affected by the provision will actually enroll on their parents' coverage. A study by Monheit and Cantor of the early experience in States that have extended coverage to dependents suggests that few uninsured children in these States shift to their parents' policy.[15] However, data and methodological difficulties inevitably lead to substantial uncertainty about the finding.

The Departments considered two other points of reference to estimate take-up rates. One is the work that has analyzed take-up rates among people made newly eligible for public coverage by Medicaid expansions. These studies suggest take-up rates in the range of 10–34 percent.[16] However, the populations eligible for these expansions have different socio-demographic compositions than those eligible for the dependent coverage provisions covered under these interim final regulations, and the decision to take-up Medicaid is clearly different than the decision to cover a child on a parent's private insurance policy. A second point of reference are estimates from the Kaiser/HRET Employer Health benefits Survey[17] which suggest that, depending on the size of the worker contribution, between 77 percent and 90 percent of employees accept offers of family

policies. Again, these estimates would be based on a group that differs in characteristics from those eligible for new dependent coverage. These concerns notwithstanding, the analyses of Medicaid expansions and employee take-up of employer sponsored coverage provide useful points of reference.

Recognizing the uncertainty in the area, the Departments produced a range of assumptions concerning take-up rates. In developing the range of take-up rates, the Departments assume that these rates will vary by the following factors: (1) The young adult's current health coverage status (uninsured young adults are less likely to take advantage of the dependent coverage option than young adults already covered by non-group insurance, because young adults who have purchased non-group insurance have shown a strong preference for coverage, and can almost always save money and get better coverage by switching to their parents' policy); (2) the young adult's health status (young adults in fair or poor health are more likely to take advantage of the option than those in excellent, very good or good health), and (3) the young adult's living situation (those living with their parents are more likely to take up the option than those not living with their parents).

The almost fully covered or "high" take-up rate scenario assumes that

regardless of health or insurance status, 95 percent of young adults living at home and 85 percent of those not living at home would move to dependent coverage. For the mid-range scenario, the Departments assume that relative to the high take-up rate scenario, 90 percent of the uninsured whose health status was fair or poor health and 50 percent of those in good to excellent health would move to dependent coverage. In the low take-up rate scenario, the Departments adjusted the percentages to 80 percent and 10 percent of the high take-up rate scenario. In all three scenarios, the same assumptions apply to individuals with non-group policies whose parents have ESI—95 percent of those living at home and 85 percent of those living elsewhere would move to dependent coverage.

In the low take-up rate scenario, the assumptions lead to the result that approximately 30 percent of eligibles will enroll in dependent coverage. In the mid-range scenario, they result in an approximate 50 percent take-up rate, and in the high take-up scenario, they result in an approximate 90 percent take-up rate. The Departments are uncertain regarding which of these scenarios is most likely but are confident that they bracket the expected outcome.

TABLE 5—Number of Individuals with New Dependent Coverage and Impact on Group Insurance Premiums, 2011–2013

	Low estimate			Mid-range estimate			High estimate		
	2011	2012	2013	2011	2012	2013	2011	2012	2013
Individuals with New Dependent Coverage (millions)	0.68	0.97	1.08	1.24	1.60	1.65	2.12	2.07	1.98
From Uninsured (millions)	0.19	0.29	0.33	0.65	0.94	0.91	1.64	1.42	1.21
Incremental Premium Cost Per Individual Coverage	$3,670	$3,800	$4,000	$3,380	$3,500	$3,690	$3,220	$3,340	$3,510
Impact on Group Insurance Premiums (%)	0.5	0.7	0.7	0.7	1.0	1.0	1.2	1.2	1.1

[15] Monheit, A., J. Cantor, et al, "State Policies Expanding Dependent Coverage to Young Adults in Private Health Insurance Plans," presented at the Academy Health State Health Research and Policy Interest Group Meeting, Chicago IL, June 27, 2009.

[16] Bansak, Cynthia and Steven Raphael. "The Effects of State Policy Design Features on Take-Up and Crowd-out Rates fro the State Children's Health Insurance Program." Journal of Policy Analysis and Management, Vol. 26, No. 1, 149–175. 2006. Find that for the time period 1998–2002 take-up rates for SCHIP were about 10 percent.

Currie, Janet and Jonathan Gruber. "Saving babies: The Efficacy and Cost of Recent Changes in Medicaid Eligibility of Pregnant Women." The Journal of Political Economy, Vol. 104, No. 6, Dec. 1996, pp. 1263–1296. Find for Medicaid expansions during the 1979–1992 period the take-up rate for eligible pregnant women was 34 percent.

Cutler, David and Jonathan Gruber. "Does Public Insurance Crowd Out Private Insurance?" The Quarterly Journal of Economics, Vol. 111, No. 2, May 1996, pp. 391–430. Find that for the Medicaid expansions from 1987–1992 the take-up rate for the

uninsured is close to 30 percent, while for pregnant women it was seven percent.

Gruber, Jonathan and Kosali Simon. "Crowd-Out Ten years Later: Have Recent Public Insurance Expansions Crowded Out Private Health Insurance?" NBER Working Paper 12858. January 2007. Find that for the Medicaid expansions during 1996–2002 the take-up rate was 7 percent across all children, but nearly one-third for uninsured children.

[17] Found at http://www.kff.org/insurance/snapshot/chcm020707oth.cfm.

These take-up rate assumptions are then applied to the number of potentially affected individuals displayed in Table 3. The resulting number of individuals with new dependent coverage is summarized in Table 5. Under the mid-range take-up rate assumption, the Departments estimate that in 2011, 1.24 million young adults will newly be covered by their parents' ESI or non-group market policies, of whom 0.65 million were previously uninsured, and 0.6 million were previously covered by non-group coverage. The number of individuals newly covered by their parents' plans would be 0.7 and 2.12 million under the high and low take-up rate assumptions respectively, with 0.2 and 1.64 million of these individuals being previously uninsured. Relative to the individuals covered under the high take-up rate assumption, higher proportions of the low- and mid-range assumption groups are accounted for by people who previously had non-group coverage (72 percent and 48 percent respectively in contrast to 23 percent for the high take-up rate group). This difference is a result of the Departments' assumption for the low- and mid-range take-up rates that people with non-group coverage will be more likely than healthy people who were uninsured to take advantage of the dependent coverage option.

Under the mid-range take-up rate assumptions, the estimated number of young adults covered by their parents' plans in 2012 increases somewhat over the 2011 estimate to 1.6 million in total, of whom approximately 0.9 million would have been uninsured. The increase in the estimate for 2012 results from the assumption that as children reach the age that would have caused them to be excluded from their parents' policy before the implementation of these interim final regulations, a large fraction of them now will remain on their parents' policy. Similarly, the estimated number of young adults enrolling in their parents' non-group policy increases from just under 75,000 in 2011 to approximately 100,000 in 2012, and 120,000 in 2013.

4. Benefits

The benefits of these interim final regulations are expected to outweigh the costs to the regulated community. In the mid-range take-up rate assumption, the Departments estimate that in 2011, 0.65 million previously uninsured individuals will now be covered on their parent's policies due to these interim final regulations and 1.24 million individuals total will now be covered on their parent's coverage. Expanding coverage options for the

19–25 population should decrease the number uninsured, which in turn should decrease the cost-shifting of uncompensated care onto those with coverage, increase the receipt of preventive health care and provide more timely access to high quality care, resulting in a healthier population. In particular, children with chronic conditions or other serious health issues will be able to continue coverage through a parent's plan until age 26. Allowing extended dependent coverage also will permit greater job mobility for this population as their health coverage will no longer be tied to their own jobs or student status.

5. Costs and Transfers Associated With the Rule

Estimates for the incremental annual premium costs for the newly covered individuals are developed based on expenditure data from MEPS and vary based on the take-up rate assumptions. These incremental costs are lowest for the high take-up rate assumption since the newly covered group would contain a relatively high percentage of individuals whose health status was good to excellent. Conversely, the low take-up rate assumption results in the highest incremental costs because a higher percentage of the newly covered individuals would be those whose health status was fair to poor. For those enrolling in their parents' ESI, the expected annual premium cost under the mid-range take-up rate assumption would be $3,380 in 2011, $3,500 in 2012 and $3,690 in 2013. If these costs were distributed among all family ESI plans, family premiums would be expected to rise by 0.7 percent in 2011, 1.0 percent in 2012, and 1.0 percent in 2013 due to these interim final regulations.[18] The comparable incremental costs and premium effects for the low and high take-up rate assumptions are summarized in Table 5. To the extent that these increases are passed on to workers in the form of higher premiums for all workers purchasing family policies or in the form of lower wages for all workers, there will be a transfer from workers who do not have newly covered dependents to those who do. To the extent that these higher premiums result in lower profits or higher prices for the employer's product, the higher premiums will result in a transfer either from stockholders or consumers.

In addition, to the extent that these interim final regulations result in a decrease in the number of uninsured,

the Departments expect a reduction in uncompensated care, and a reduction in liability for those who fund uncompensated care, including public programs (primarily Medicaid and State and local general revenue support for public hospitals), as well as the portion of uncompensated care that is paid for by the cost shift from private premium payers. Such effects would lead to lower premiums for the insured population, both with or without newly covered children.

For the small number of children (75,000 in 2011) enrolling in their parents' non-group insurance policy under the mid-range take-up assumption, the Departments expect estimated annual premium cost to be $2,360 in 2011, $2,400 in 2012 and $2,480 in 2013. To a large extent, premiums in the non-group market are individually underwritten, and the Departments expect that most of the premium cost will be borne by the parents who are purchasing the policy to which their child is added. If, instead, these costs were distributed over the entire individual market (as would be the case in a pure community-rated market), then individual premiums would be expected to rise 0.7 percent in 2011, 1.0 percent in 2012, and 1.2 percent in 2013 due to these interim final regulations. However, the Departments expect the actual increase across the entire individual market, if any, will be much smaller than these estimates, because they expect that the costs largely will be borne by the subscribers who are directly affected rather than distributed across the entire individual market.

6. Enrollment Opportunity

These interim final regulations provide an enrollment opportunity for children excluded from coverage because of age before the effective date of the rule. The Departments estimate that this information collection request will result in approximately 105,000,000 notices being distributed with an hour burden of approximately 1,100,000 hours and cost burden of approximately $2,010,500. For a discussion of this enrollment opportunity, see the Paperwork Reduction Act section later in this preamble.

7. Regulatory Alternatives

Section 6(a)(3)(C)(iii) of Executive Order 12866 requires an economically significant regulation to include an assessment of the costs and benefits of potentially effective and reasonable alternatives to the planned regulation, and an explanation of why the planned

---

[18] For purposes of this regulatory impact analysis, the Departments assume that there would be no effect on premiums for employee-only policies.

regulatory action is preferable to the potential alternatives. The Departments carefully considered limiting the flexibility of plans and policies to define who is a child. However, the Departments concluded, as they have in other regulatory contexts, that plan sponsors and issuers should be free to determine whether to cover children or which children should be covered by their plans and policies (although they must comply with other applicable Federal or State law mandating coverage, such as ERISA section 609). Therefore, these interim final regulations have not limited a plan's or policy's flexibility to define who is a child for purposes of the determination of children to whom coverage must be made available.

C. Regulatory Flexibility Act— Department of Labor and Department of Health and Human Services

The Regulatory Flexibility Act (5 U.S.C. 601 *et seq.*) (RFA) imposes certain requirements with respect to Federal rules that are subject to the notice and comment requirements of section 553(b) of the APA (5 U.S.C. 551 *et seq.*) and that are likely to have a significant economic impact on a substantial number of small entities. Under Section 553(b) of the APA, a general notice of proposed rulemaking is not required when an agency, for good cause, finds that notice and public comment thereon are impracticable, unnecessary, or contrary to the public interest. These interim final regulations are exempt from APA, because the Departments made a good cause finding that a general notice of proposed rulemaking is not necessary earlier in this preamble. Therefore, the RFA does not apply and the Departments are not required to either certify that the regulations would not have a significant economic impact on a substantial number of small entities or conduct a regulatory flexibility analysis.

Nevertheless, the Departments carefully considered the likely impact of the regulations on small entities in connection with their assessment under Executive Order 12866. Consistent with the policy of the RFA, the Departments encourage the public to submit comments that suggest alternative rules that accomplish the stated purpose of PHS Act section 2714 and minimize the impact on small entities.

D. Special Analyses—Department of the Treasury

Notwithstanding the determinations of the Department of Labor and Department of Health and Human Services, for purposes of the Department of the Treasury, it has been determined that this Treasury decision is not a significant regulatory action for purposes of Executive Order 12866. Therefore, a regulatory assessment is not required. It has also been determined that section 553(b) of the APA (5 U.S.C. chapter 5) does not apply to these interim final regulations. For the applicability of the RFA, refer to the Special Analyses section in the preamble to the cross-referencing notice of proposed rulemaking published elsewhere in this issue of the **Federal Register**. Pursuant to section 7805(f) of the Code, these temporary regulations have been submitted to the Chief Counsel for Advocacy of the Small Business Administration for comment on their impact on small businesses.

E. Paperwork Reduction Act

1. Department of Labor and Department of the Treasury: Affordable Care Act Enrollment Opportunity Notice Relating to Extended Dependent Coverage

As part of their continuing efforts to reduce paperwork and respondent burden, the Departments conduct a preclearance consultation program to provide the general public and federal agencies with an opportunity to comment on proposed and continuing collections of information in accordance with the Paperwork Reduction Act of 1995 (PRA) (44 U.S.C. 3506(c)(2)(A)). This helps to ensure that requested data can be provided in the desired format, reporting burden (time and financial resources) is minimized, collection instruments are clearly understood, and the impact of collection requirements on respondents can be properly assessed.

As discussed earlier in this preamble, prior to the applicability date of PHS Act section 2714, a child who was covered under a group health plan (or group health insurance coverage) may have lost eligibility for coverage under the plan due to age before age 26. Moreover, if a child was under age 26 when a parent first became eligible for coverage, but older than the age at which the plan stopped covering children, the child would not have become eligible for coverage. When the provisions of PHS Act section 2714 become applicable to the plan (or coverage), the plan or coverage can no longer exclude coverage for the individual until age 26.

Accordingly, these interim final regulations require plans to provide a notice of an enrollment opportunity to individuals whose coverage ended, or who were denied coverage (or were not eligible for coverage) under a group health plan or health insurance coverage because, under the terms of the plan or coverage, the availability of dependent coverage of children ended before the attainment of age 26. The enrollment opportunity must continue for at least 30 days, regardless of whether the plan or coverage offers an open enrollment period and regardless of when any open enrollment period might otherwise occur. This enrollment opportunity must be presented not later than the first day of the first plan year (in the individual market, policy year) beginning on or after September 23, 2010 (which is the applicability date of PHS Act section 2714). Coverage must begin not later than the first day of the first plan year (in the individual market, policy year) beginning on or after September 23, 2010.[19]

The Affordable Care Act dependent coverage enrollment opportunity notice is an information collection request (ICR) subject to the PRA. Currently, the Departments are soliciting public comments for 60 days concerning these disclosures. The Departments have submitted a copy of these interim final regulations to OMB in accordance with 44 U.S.C. 3507(d) for review of the information collections. The Departments and OMB are particularly interested in comments that:

• Evaluate whether the collection of information is necessary for the proper performance of the functions of the agency, including whether the information will have practical utility;

• Evaluate the accuracy of the agency's estimate of the burden of the collection of information, including the validity of the methodology and assumptions used;

• Enhance the quality, utility, and clarity of the information to be collected; and

• Minimize the burden of the collection of information on those who are to respond, including through the use of appropriate automated, electronic, mechanical, or other technological collection techniques or other forms of information technology, for example, by permitting electronic submission of responses.

Comments should be sent to the Office of Information and Regulatory Affairs, Attention: Desk Officer for the Employee Benefits Security

---

[19] Any individual enrolling in coverage pursuant to this enrollment right must be treated as a special enrollee, as provided under HIPAA portability rules. Accordingly, the individual must be offered all the benefit packages available to similarly situated individuals who did not lose coverage by reason of cessation of dependent status. The individual also cannot be required to pay more for coverage than similarly situated individuals who did not lose coverage by reason of cessation of dependent status.

27132 **Federal Register** / Vol. 75, No. 92 / Thursday, May 13, 2010 / Rules and Regulations

Administration either by fax to (202) 395–7285 or by e-mail to *oira_submission@omb.eop.gov.* A copy of the ICR may be obtained by contacting the PRA addressee: G. Christopher Cosby, Office of Policy and Research, U.S. Department of Labor, Employee Benefits Security Administration, 200 Constitution Avenue, NW., Room N–5718, Washington, DC 20210. Telephone: (202) 693–8410; Fax: (202) 219–4745. These are not toll-free numbers. E-mail: *ebsa.opr@dol.gov.* ICRs submitted to OMB also are available at reginfo.gov (*http://www.reginfo.gov/public/do/ PRAMain*).

The Departments assume that 2,800,000 ERISA covered plans will send the enrollment opportunity notice to all 79,573,000 employees eligible for group health insurance coverage. The Departments estimate that preparing the enrollment notice will require 30 minutes of legal professional time at a labor rate of $119 per hour [20] and one minute of clerical time at $26 per hour per paper notice to distribute the notices.[21] This results in an hour burden of nearly 822,000 hours and an associated equivalent cost of nearly $21,513,000.

The Departments estimate that the cost burden associated with distributing the approximately 79,573,000 notices will be approximately $2,467,000 based on one minute of clerical time, and $.05 per page for material and printing costs. The Departments assumed that 38 percent of the notices would be sent electronically.[22] In addition, plans can send these notices with other plan

documents, such as open enrollment materials. Therefore, the Departments have not included postage costs in this estimate. The Departments note that persons are not required to respond to, and generally are not subject to any penalty for failing to comply with, an ICR unless the ICR has a valid OMB control number.[23]

These paperwork burden estimates are summarized as follows:

Type of Review: New collection.
Agencies: Employee Benefits Security Administration, Department of Labor; Internal Revenue Service, U.S. Department of the Treasury.
Title: Affordable Care Act Enrollment Opportunity Notice Relating to Extended Dependent Coverage.
OMB Number: 1210–0139; 1545–2172.
Affected Public: Business or other for-profit; not-for-profit institutions.
Total Respondents: 2,800,000.
Total Responses: 79,573,000.
Frequency of Response: One-time.
Estimated Total Annual Burden Hours: 411,000 hours (Employee Benefits Security Administration); 411,000 hours (Internal Revenue Service).
Estimated Total Annual Burden Cost: $1,233,500 (Employee Benefits Security Administration); $1,233,500 (Internal Revenue Service).

2. Department of Health and Human Services: Affordable Care Act Enrollment Opportunity Notice Relating to Extended Dependent Coverage

We are soliciting public comment on the following sections of this document that contain information collection requirements (ICR) regarding the Affordable Care Act—ICR Relating to Enrollment Opportunity Notice—Dependent Coverage. As discussed earlier in this preamble, the Affordable Care Act and these interim final regulations require issuers in the individual market and group health plans sponsored by State and local governments to notify participants regarding an enrollment opportunity related to the extension of dependent coverage. Prior to the applicability date of PHS Act section 2714, a child who was covered under a group health plan (or group health insurance coverage) as a dependent may have lost eligibility for coverage under the plan due to age before age 26. Moreover, if, when a parent first became eligible for coverage, a child was under age 26 but older than the age at which the plan stopped covering children, the child would not have become eligible for coverage.

When the provisions of PHS Act section 2714 become applicable to the plan (or coverage), the plan or coverage can no longer exclude coverage for the individual until age 26.

Accordingly, these interim final regulations require issuers in the individual insurance market and group health plans sponsored by State and local governments to provide a notice of an enrollment opportunity to individuals whose coverage ended, or who was denied coverage (or was not eligible for coverage) under a group health plan or group health insurance coverage because, under the terms of the plan or coverage, the availability of dependent coverage of children ended before the attainment of age 26. The enrollment opportunity must continue for at least 30 days, regardless of whether the plan or coverage offers an open enrollment period and regardless of when any open enrollment period might otherwise occur. This enrollment opportunity must be presented not later than the first day of the first plan year (in the individual market, policy year) beginning on or after September 23, 2010 (which is the applicability date of PHS Act section 2714). Coverage must begin not later than the first day of the first plan year (in the individual market, policy year) beginning on or after September 23, 2010.[24]

The Department estimates that 126,000 State and local governmental plans would have to send 19,627,000 notices to eligible employees and 490 insurers in the individual market would have to send approximately 5,444,000 notices to individuals with policies covering dependents.[25] For purposes of this estimate, the Department assumes that it will take a legal professional, on average, 30 minutes to prepare the notice at a labor rate of $119 per hour,[26] and one minute, on average, of a clerical professional's time at $26 per hour to copy and mail the notice.[27] While plans could prepare their own notice, the

---

[20] Hourly wage estimates are based on data from the Bureau of Labor Statistics Occupational Employment Survey (May 2008) and the Bureau of Labor Statistics Employment Cost Index (June 2009). All hourly wage rates include wages and benefits. Clerical wage and benefits estimates are based on metropolitan wage rates for executive secretaries and administrative assistants. Legal professional wage and benefits estimates are based on metropolitan wage rates for lawyers.

[21] While plans could prepare their own notice, the Departments assume that the notices will be prepared by service providers. The Departments have previously estimated that there are 630 health insurers (460 providing coverage in the group market, and 490 providing coverage in the individual market.). These estimates are from NAIC 2007 financial statements data and the California Department of Managed Healthcare (2009), *at http://wpso.dmhc.ca.gov/hpsearch/viewall.aspx.* Because the hour and cost burden is shared between the Departments of Labor/Treasury and the Department of Health and Human Services, the burden to prepare the notices is calculated using half the number of insurers (315).

[22] For purposes of this burden estimate, the Departments assume that 38 percent of the disclosures will be provided through electronic means in accordance with the Department of Labor's standards for electronic communication of required information provided under 29 CFR 2520.104b–1(c).

[23] 5 CFR 1320.1 through 1320.18.

[24] Any individual enrolling in coverage pursuant to this enrollment right must be treated as a special enrollee, as provided under HIPAA portability rules. Accordingly, the individual must be offered all the benefit packages available to similarly situated individuals who did not lose coverage by reason of cessation of dependent status. The individual also cannot be required to pay more for coverage than similarly situated individuals who did not lose coverage by reason of cessation of dependent status.

[25] The number of individual insurance notices was based on the number of individual policy holders with dependents on that policy according to the 2009 March Current Population Survey (CPS).

[26] Estimates of labor rates include wages, other benefits, and overhead based on the National Occupational Employment Survey (May 2008, Bureau of Labor Statistics) and the Employment Cost Index June 2009, Bureau of Labor Statistics).

Department assumes that the notices will be prepared by service providers. The Department has previously estimated that there are 630 health insurers [28] (460 providing coverage in the group market, and 490 providing coverage in the individual market). Because the hour and cost burden is shared among the Departments of Labor/ Treasury and the Department of Health and Human Services, the burden to prepare the notices is calculated using half the number of insurers (315). The Department assumes that 38 percent of the notices would be sent electronically.[29] Notices that are sent electronically do not require any of the clerical worker's time to mail the notice. This results in an hour burden of approximately 259,000 hours and an associated equivalent cost of about $6,791,000 to prepare and distribute 25,071,000 notices. The Department estimates that the cost burden associated with distributing the notices will be approximately $777,000.[30] The Department assumes that 38 percent of the notices would be sent electronically.[31] In addition, plans and issuers can send these notices with other plan documents (for example, during open enrollment for the government plans, or other communication at reenrollment in the individual market). Therefore, the Department did not include postage costs in this estimate. The Department notes that persons are not required to respond to, and generally are not subject to any penalty for failing to comply with, an ICR unless the ICR has a valid OMB control number.[32]

These paperwork burden estimates are summarized as follows:

Type of Review: New collection.
Agency: Department of Health and Human Services.
Title: Notice of Special Enrollment Opportunity under the Affordable Care Act Relating to Dependent Coverage.
OMB Number: 0938–1089.
Affected Public: Business; State, Local, or Tribal Governments.
Respondents: 126,000.

---

[28] These estimates are from NAIC 2007 financial statements data and the California Department of Managed Healthcare (2009), *at http:// wpso.dmhc.ca.gov/hpsearch/viewall.aspx.*

[29] For purposes of this burden estimate, the Department assumes that 38 percent of the disclosures will be provided through electronic means.

[30] This estimate is based on an average document size of one page and $.05 cents per page for material and printing costs.

[31] For purposes of this burden estimate, the Department assumes that 38 percent of the disclosures will be provided through electronic means.

[32] 5 CFR 1320.1 through 1320.18.

Responses: 25,071,000.
Frequency of Response: One-time.
Estimated Total Annual Burden Hours: 259,000 hours.
Estimated Total Annual Burden Cost: $777,000.

If you comment on this information collection and recordkeeping requirements, please do either of the following:

1. Submit your comments electronically as specified in the **ADDRESSES** section of this proposed rule; or

2. Submit your comments to the Office of Information and Regulatory Affairs, Office of Management and Budget,
Attention: CMS Desk Officer, 4140–IFC
Fax: (202) 395–6974; or
E-mail: OIRA_submission@omb.eop.gov

F. Congressional Review Act

These interim final regulations are subject to the Congressional Review Act provisions of the Small Business Regulatory Enforcement Fairness Act of 1996 (5 U.S.C. 801 *et seq.*) and have been transmitted to Congress and the Comptroller General for review.

G. Unfunded Mandates Reform Act

The Unfunded Mandates Reform Act of 1995 (Pub. L. 104–4) requires agencies to prepare several analytic statements before proposing any rules that may result in annual expenditures of $100 million (as adjusted for inflation) by State, local and tribal governments or the private sector. These interim final regulations are not subject to the Unfunded Mandates Reform Act, because they are being issued as an interim final regulation. However, consistent with the policy embodied in the Unfunded Mandates Reform Act, these interim final regulations have been designed to be the least burdensome alternative for State, local and tribal governments, and the private sector, while achieving the objectives of the Affordable Care Act.

H. Federalism Statement—Department of Labor and Department of Health and Human Services

Executive Order 13132 outlines fundamental principles of federalism, and requires the adherence to specific criteria by Federal agencies in the process of their formulation and implementation of policies that have "substantial direct effects" on the States, the relationship between the national government and States, or on the distribution of power and responsibilities among the various

levels of government. Federal agencies promulgating regulations that have these federalism implications must consult with State and local officials, and describe the extent of their consultation and the nature of the concerns of State and local officials in the preamble to the regulation.

In the Departments' view, these interim final regulations have federalism implications, because they have direct effects on the States, the relationship between the national government and States, or on the distribution of power and responsibilities among various levels of government. However, in the Departments' view, the federalism implications of these interim final regulations are substantially mitigated because, with respect to health insurance issuers, the Departments expect that the majority of States will enact laws or take other appropriate action resulting in their meeting or exceeding the Federal standard.

In general, through section 514, ERISA supersedes State laws to the extent that they relate to any covered employee benefit plan, and preserves State laws that regulate insurance, banking, or securities. While ERISA prohibits States from regulating a plan as an insurance or investment company or bank, the preemption provisions of ERISA section 731 and PHS Act section 2724 (implemented in 29 CFR 2590.731(a) and 45 CFR 146.143(a)) apply so that the HIPAA requirements (including those of the Affordable Care Act) are not to be "construed to supersede any provision of State law which establishes, implements, or continues in effect any standard or requirement solely relating to health insurance issuers in connection with group health insurance coverage except to the extent that such standard or requirement prevents the application of a requirement" of a federal standard. The conference report accompanying HIPAA indicates that this is intended to be the "narrowest" preemption of State laws. (See House Conf. Rep. No. 104–736, at 205, reprinted in 1996 U.S. Code Cong. & Admin. News 2018.) States may continue to apply State law requirements except to the extent that such requirements prevent the application of the Affordable Care Act requirements that are the subject of this rulemaking. State insurance laws that are more stringent than the Federal requirements are unlikely to "prevent the application of" the Affordable Care Act, and be preempted. Accordingly, States have significant latitude to impose requirements on health insurance issuers that are more restrictive than the Federal law.

In compliance with the requirement of Executive Order 13132 that agencies examine closely any policies that may have federalism implications or limit the policy making discretion of the States, the Departments have engaged in efforts to consult with and work cooperatively with affected State and local officials, including attending conferences of the National Association of Insurance Commissioners and consulting with State insurance officials on an individual basis. It is expected that the Departments will act in a similar fashion in enforcing the Affordable Care Act requirements. Throughout the process of developing these interim final regulations, to the extent feasible within the specific preemption provisions of HIPAA as it applies to the Affordable Care Act, the Departments have attempted to balance the States' interests in regulating health insurance issuers, and Congress' intent to provide uniform minimum protections to consumers in every State. By doing so, it is the Departments' view that they have complied with the requirements of Executive Order 13132.

Pursuant to the requirements set forth in section 8(a) of Executive Order 13132, and by the signatures affixed to these regulations, the Departments certify that the Employee Benefits Security Administration and the Office of Consumer Information and Insurance Oversight have complied with the requirements of Executive Order 13132 for the attached regulation in a meaningful and timely manner.

V. Statutory Authority

The Department of the Treasury temporary regulations are adopted pursuant to the authority contained in sections 7805 and 9833 of the Code.

The Department of Labor interim final regulations are adopted pursuant to the authority contained in 29 U.S.C. 1027, 1059, 1135, 1161–1168, 1169, 1181–1183, 1181 note, 1185, 1185a, 1185b, 1191, 1191a, 1191b, and 1191c; sec. 101(g), Pub. L. 104–191, 110 Stat. 1936; sec. 401(b), Pub. L. 105–200, 112 Stat. 645 (42 U.S.C. 651 note); sec. 512(d), Pub. L. 110–343, 122 Stat. 3881; sec. 1001, 1201, and 1562(e), Pub. L. 111–148, 124 Stat. 119, as amended by Pub. L. 111–152, 124 Stat. 1029; Secretary of Labor's Order 6–2009, 74 FR 21524 (May 7, 2009).

The Department of Health and Human Services interim final regulations are adopted pursuant to the authority contained in sections 2701 through 2763, 2791, and 2792 of the PHS Act (42

USC 300gg through 300gg–63, 300gg–91, and 300gg–92), as amended.

List of Subjects

26 CFR Part 54

Excise taxes, Health care, Health insurance, Pensions, Reporting and recordkeeping requirements.

26 CFR Part 602

Reporting and recordkeeping requirements.

29 CFR Part 2590

Continuation coverage, Disclosure, Employee benefit plans, Group health plans, Health care, Health insurance, Medical child support, Reporting and recordkeeping requirements.

45 CFR Parts 144, 146, and 147

Health care, Health insurance, Reporting and recordkeeping requirements, and State regulation of health insurance.

Steven T. Miller,

Deputy Commissioner for Services and Enforcement, Internal Revenue Service.

Approved: May 7, 2010.

Michael F. Mundaca,

Assistant Secretary of the Treasury (Tax Policy).

Signed this 6th day of May 2010.

Phyllis C. Borzi,

Assistant Secretary, Employee Benefits Security Administration, Department of Labor.

Approved: May 4, 2010.

Jay Angoff,

Director, Office of Consumer Information and Insurance Oversight.

Approved: May 7, 2010.

Kathleen Sebelius,

Secretary, Department of Health and Human Services.

Internal Revenue Service

26 CFR Chapter 1

■ Accordingly, 26 CFR Parts 54 and 602 are amended as follows:

PART 54—PENSION EXCISE TAXES

■ **Paragraph 1.** The authority citation for part 54 continues to read in part as follows:

Authority: 26 U.S.C. 7805. * * *

■ **Par. 2.** Section 54.9815–2714T is added to read as follows:

§ 54.9815–2714T Eligibility of children until at least age 26 (temporary).

(a) *In general*—(1) A group health plan, or a health insurance issuer offering group health insurance coverage, that makes available dependent coverage of children must

make such coverage available for children until attainment of 26 years of age.

(2) The rule of this paragraph (a) is illustrated by the following example:

Example. (i) *Facts.* For the plan year beginning January 1, 2011, a group health plan provides health coverage for employees, employees' spouses, and employees' children until the child turns 26. On the birthday of a child of an employee, July 17, 2011, the child turns 26. The last day the plan covers the child is July 16, 2011.

(ii) *Conclusion.* In this *Example,* the plan satisfies the requirement of this paragraph (a) with respect to the child.

(b) *Restrictions on plan definition of dependent.* With respect to a child who has not attained age 26, a plan or issuer may not define dependent for purposes of eligibility for dependent coverage of children other than in terms of a relationship between a child and the participant. Thus, for example, a plan or issuer may not deny or restrict coverage for a child who has not attained age 26 based on the presence or absence of the child's financial dependency (upon the participant or any other person), residency with the participant or with any other person, student status, employment, or any combination of those factors. In addition, a plan or issuer may not deny or restrict coverage of a child based on eligibility for other coverage, except that paragraph (g) of this section provides a special rule for plan years beginning before January 1, 2014 for grandfathered health plans that are group health plans. (Other requirements of Federal or State law, including section 609 of ERISA or section 1908 of the Social Security Act, may mandate coverage of certain children.)

(c) *Coverage of grandchildren not required.* Nothing in this section requires a plan or issuer to make coverage available for the child of a child receiving dependent coverage.

(d) *Uniformity irrespective of age.* The terms of the plan or health insurance coverage providing dependent coverage of children cannot vary based on age (except for children who are age 26 or older).

(e) *Examples.* The rules of paragraph (d) of this section are illustrated by the following examples:

Example 1. (i) *Facts.* A group health plan offers a choice of self-only or family health coverage. Dependent coverage is provided under family health coverage for children of participants who have not attained age 26. The plan imposes an additional premium surcharge for children who are older than age 18.

(ii) *Conclusion.* In this *Example 1,* the plan violates the requirement of paragraph (d) of this section because the plan varies the terms for dependent coverage of children based on age.

Example 2. (i) *Facts.* A group health plan offers a choice among the following tiers of health coverage: self-only, self plus one, self-plus two, and self-plus-three-or-more. The cost of coverage increases based on the number of covered individuals. The plan provides dependent coverage of children who have not attained age 26.

(ii) *Conclusion.* In this *Example 2,* the plan does not violate the requirement of paragraph (d) of this section that the terms of dependent coverage for children not vary based on age. Although the cost of coverage increases for tiers with more covered individuals, the increase applies without regard to the age of any child.

Example 3. (i) *Facts.* A group health plan offers two benefit packages—an HMO option and an indemnity option. Dependent coverage is provided for children of participants who have not attained age 26. The plan limits children who are older than age 18 to the HMO option.

(ii) *Conclusion.* In this *Example 3,* the plan violates the requirement of paragraph (d) of this section because the plan, by limiting children who are older than age 18 to the HMO option, varies the terms for dependent coverage of children based on age.

(f) *Transitional rules for individuals whose coverage ended by reason of reaching a dependent eligibility threshold*—(1) *In general.* The relief provided in the transitional rules of this paragraph (f) applies with respect to any child—

(i) Whose coverage ended, or who was denied coverage (or was not eligible for coverage) under a group health plan or group health insurance coverage because, under the terms of the plan or coverage, the availability of dependent coverage of children ended before the attainment of age 26 (which, under this section, is no longer permissible); and

(ii) Who becomes eligible (or is required to become eligible) for coverage under a group health plan or group health insurance coverage on the first day of the first plan year beginning on or after September 23, 2010 by reason of the application of this section.

(2) *Opportunity to enroll required.* (i) If a group health plan, or group health insurance coverage, in which a child described in paragraph (f)(1) of this section is eligible to enroll (or is required to become eligible to enroll) is the plan or coverage in which the child's coverage ended (or did not begin) for the reasons described in paragraph (f)(1)(i) of this section, and if the plan, or the issuer of such coverage, is subject to the requirements of this section, the plan and the issuer are required to give the child an opportunity to enroll that continues for at least 30 days (including written notice of the opportunity to enroll). This

opportunity (including the written notice) must be provided beginning not later than the first day of the first plan year beginning on or after September 23, 2010.

(ii) The written notice must include a statement that children whose coverage ended, or who were denied coverage (or were not eligible for coverage), because the availability of dependent coverage of children ended before attainment of age 26 are eligible to enroll in the plan or coverage. The notice may be provided to an employee on behalf of the employee's child. In addition, the notice may be included with other enrollment materials that a plan distributes to employees, provided the statement is prominent. If a notice satisfying the requirements of this paragraph (f)(2) is provided to an employee whose child is entitled to an enrollment opportunity under this paragraph (f), the obligation to provide the notice of enrollment opportunity under this paragraph (f)(2) with respect to that child is satisfied for both the plan and the issuer.

(3) *Effective date of coverage.* In the case of an individual who enrolls under paragraph (f)(2) of this section, coverage must take effect not later than the first day of the first plan year beginning on or after September 23, 2010.

(4) *Treatment of enrollees in a group health plan.* Any child enrolling in a group health plan pursuant to paragraph (f)(2) of this section must be treated as if the child were a special enrollee, as provided under the rules of § 54.9801-6(d). Accordingly, the child (and, if the child would not be a participant once enrolled in the plan, the participant through whom the child is otherwise eligible for coverage under the plan) must be offered all the benefit packages available to similarly situated individuals who did not lose coverage by reason of cessation of dependent status. For this purpose, any difference in benefits or cost-sharing requirements constitutes a different benefit package. The child also cannot be required to pay more for coverage than similarly situated individuals who did not lose coverage by reason of cessation of dependent status.

(5) *Examples.* The rules of this paragraph (f) are illustrated by the following examples:

Example 1. (i) *Facts.* Employer Y maintains a group health plan with a calendar year plan year. The plan has a single benefit package. For the 2010 plan year, the plan allows children of employees to be covered under the plan until age 19, or until age 23 for children who are full-time students. Individual B, an employee of Y, and Individual C, B's child and a full-time student, were enrolled in Y's group health

plan at the beginning of the 2010 plan year. On June 10, 2010, C turns 23 years old and loses dependent coverage under Y's plan. On or before January 1, 2011, Y's group health plan gives B written notice that individuals who lost coverage by reason of ceasing to be a dependent before attainment of age 26 are eligible to enroll in the plan, and that individuals may request enrollment for such children through February 14, 2011 with enrollment effective retroactively to January 1, 2011.

(ii) *Conclusion.* In this *Example 1,* the plan has complied with the requirements of this paragraph (f) by providing an enrollment opportunity to C that lasts at least 30 days.

Example 2. (i) *Facts.* Employer Z maintains a group health plan with a plan year beginning October 1 and ending September 30. Prior to October 1, 2010, the group health plan allows children of employees to be covered under the plan until age 22. Individual D, an employee of Z, and Individual E, D's child, are enrolled in family coverage under Z's group health plan for the plan year beginning on October 1, 2008. On May 1, 2009, E turns 22 years old and ceases to be eligible as a dependent under Z's plan and loses coverage. D drops coverage but remains an employee of Z.

(ii) *Conclusion.* In this *Example 2,* not later than October 1, 2010, the plan must provide D and E an opportunity to enroll (including written notice of an opportunity to enroll) that continues for at least 30 days, with enrollment effective not later than October 1, 2010.

Example 3. (i) *Facts.* Same facts as *Example 2,* except that D did not drop coverage. Instead, D switched to a lower-cost benefit package option.

(ii) *Conclusion.* In this *Example 3,* not later than October 1, 2010, the plan must provide D and E an opportunity to enroll in any benefit package available to similarly situated individuals who enroll when first eligible.

Example 4. (i) *Facts.* Same facts as *Example 2,* except that E elected COBRA continuation coverage.

(ii) *Conclusion.* In this *Example 4,* not later than October 1, 2010, the plan must provide D and E an opportunity to enroll other than as a COBRA qualified beneficiary (and must provide, by that date, written notice of the opportunity to enroll) that continues for at least 30 days, with enrollment effective not later than October 1, 2010.

Example 5. (i) *Facts.* Employer X maintains a group health plan with a calendar year plan year. Prior to 2011, the plan allows children of employees to be covered under the plan until the child attains age 22. During the 2009 plan year, an individual with a 22-year old child joins the plan; the child is denied coverage because the child is 22.

(ii) *Conclusion.* In this *Example 5,* notwithstanding that the child was not previously covered under the plan, the plan must provide the child, not later than January 1, 2011, an opportunity to enroll (including written notice to the employee of an opportunity to enroll the child) that continues for at least 30 days, with enrollment effective not later than January 1, 2011.

(g) *Special rule for grandfathered group health plans*—(1) For plan years beginning before January 1, 2014, a group health plan that qualifies as a grandfathered health plan under section 1251 of the Patient Protection and Affordable Care Act and that makes available dependent coverage of children may exclude an adult child who has not attained age 26 from coverage only if the adult child is eligible to enroll in an eligible employer-sponsored health plan (as defined in section 5000A(f)(2)) other than a group health plan of a parent.

(2) For plan years beginning on or after January 1, 2014, a group health plan that qualifies as a grandfathered health plan under section 1251 of the Patient Protection and Affordable Care Act must comply with the requirements of paragraphs (a) through (f) of this section.

(h) *Applicability date.* The provisions of this section apply for plan years beginning on or after September 23, 2010.

(i) *Expiration date.* This section expires on or before May 13, 2013.

PART 602—OMB CONTROL NUMBERS UNDER THE PAPERWORK REDUCTION ACT

■ **Par. 5.** The authority citation for part 602 continues to read as follows:

Authority: 26 U.S.C. 7805.

■ **Par. 6.** In § 602.101, paragraph (b) is amended by adding the following entry in numerical order to the table:

§ 602.101   OMB Control numbers.

*   *   *   *   *

(b) * * *

CFR part or section where identified and described	Current OMB control No.
* * * * *	
54.9815–2714T	1545–2172
* * * * *	

Employee Benefits Security Administration

29 CFR Chapter XXV

■ 29 CFR Part 2590 is amended as follows:

PART 2590—RULES AND REGULATIONS FOR GROUP HEALTH PLANS

■ 1. The authority citation for Part 2590 is revised to read as follows:

Authority: 29 U.S.C. 1027, 1059, 1135, 1161–1168, 1169, 1181–1183, 1181 note, 1185, 1185a, 1185b, 1191, 1191a, 1191b, and 1191c; sec. 101(g), Pub. L.104–191, 110 Stat. 1936; sec. 401(b), Pub. L. 105–200, 112 Stat.

645 (42 U.S.C. 651 note); sec. 512(d), Pub. L. 110–343, 122 Stat. 3881; sec. 1001, 1201, and 1562(e), Pub. L. 111–148, 124 Stat. 119, as amended by Pub. L. 111–152, 124 Stat. 1029; Secretary of Labor's Order 6–2009, 74 FR 21524 (May 7, 2009).

■ 2. Section 2590.715–2714 is added to Subpart C to read as follows:

§ 2590.715–2714   Eligibility of children until at least age 26.

(a) *In general*—(1) A group health plan, or a health insurance issuer offering group health insurance coverage, that makes available dependent coverage of children must make such coverage available for children until attainment of 26 years of age.

(2) The rule of this paragraph (a) is illustrated by the following example:

Example. (i) *Facts.* For the plan year beginning January 1, 2011, a group health plan provides health coverage for employees, employees' spouses, and employees' children until the child turns 26. On the birthday of a child of an employee, July 17, 2011, the child turns 26. The last day the plan covers the child is July 16, 2011.

(ii) *Conclusion.* In this *Example,* the plan satisfies the requirement of this paragraph (a) with respect to the child.

(b) *Restrictions on plan definition of dependent.* With respect to a child who has not attained age 26, a plan or issuer may not define dependent for purposes of eligibility for dependent coverage of children other than in terms of a relationship between a child and the participant. Thus, for example, a plan or issuer may not deny or restrict coverage for a child who has not attained age 26 based on the presence or absence of the child's financial dependency (upon the participant or any other person), residency with the participant or with any other person, student status, employment, or any combination of those factors. In addition, a plan or issuer may not deny or restrict coverage of a child based on eligibility for other coverage, except that paragraph (g) of this section provides a special rule for plan years beginning before January 1, 2014 for grandfathered health plans that are group health plans. (Other requirements of Federal or State law, including section 609 of ERISA or section 1908 of the Social Security Act, may mandate coverage of certain children.)

(c) *Coverage of grandchildren not required.* Nothing in this section requires a plan or issuer to make coverage available for the child of a child receiving dependent coverage.

(d) *Uniformity irrespective of age.* The terms of the plan or health insurance coverage providing dependent coverage of children cannot vary based on age

(except for children who are age 26 or older).

(e) *Examples.* The rules of paragraph (d) of this section are illustrated by the following examples:

Example 1. (i) *Facts.* A group health plan offers a choice of self-only or family health coverage. Dependent coverage is provided under family health coverage for children of participants who have not attained age 26. The plan imposes an additional premium surcharge for children who are older than age 18.

(ii) *Conclusion.* In this *Example 1,* the plan violates the requirement of paragraph (d) of this section because the plan varies the terms for dependent coverage of children based on age.

Example 2. (i) *Facts.* A group health plan offers a choice among the following tiers of health coverage: self-only, self-plus-one, self-plus-two, and self-plus-three-or-more. The cost of coverage increases based on the number of covered individuals. The plan provides dependent coverage of children who have not attained age 26.

(ii) *Conclusion.* In this *Example 2,* the plan does not violate the requirement of paragraph (d) of this section that the terms of dependent coverage for children not vary based on age. Although the cost of coverage increases for tiers with more covered individuals, the increase applies without regard to the age of any child.

Example 3. (i) *Facts.* A group health plan offers two benefit packages—an HMO option and an indemnity option. Dependent coverage is provided for children of participants who have not attained age 26. The plan limits children who are older than age 18 to the HMO option.

(ii) *Conclusion.* In this *Example 3,* the plan violates the requirement of paragraph (d) of this section because the plan, by limiting children who are older than age 18 to the HMO option, varies the terms for dependent coverage of children based on age.

(f) *Transitional rules for individuals whose coverage ended by reason of reaching a dependent eligibility threshold*—(1) *In general.* The relief provided in the transitional rules of this paragraph (f) applies with respect to any child—

(i) Whose coverage ended, or who was denied coverage (or was not eligible for coverage) under a group health plan or group health insurance coverage because, under the terms of the plan or coverage, the availability of dependent coverage of children ended before the attainment of age 26 (which, under this section, is no longer permissible); and

(ii) Who becomes eligible (or is required to become eligible) for coverage under a group health plan or group health insurance coverage on the first day of the first plan year beginning on or after September 23, 2010 by reason of the application of this section.

(2) *Opportunity to enroll required*—(i) If a group health plan, or group health

insurance coverage, in which a child described in paragraph (f)(1) of this section is eligible to enroll (or is required to become eligible to enroll) is the plan or coverage in which the child's coverage ended (or did not begin) for the reasons described in paragraph (f)(1)(i) of this section, and if the plan, or the issuer of such coverage, is subject to the requirements of this section, the plan and the issuer are required to give the child an opportunity to enroll that continues for at least 30 days (including written notice of the opportunity to enroll). This opportunity (including the written notice) must be provided beginning not later than the first day of the first plan year beginning on or after September 23, 2010.

(ii) The written notice must include a statement that children whose coverage ended, or who were denied coverage (or were not eligible for coverage), because the availability of dependent coverage of children ended before attainment of age 26 are eligible to enroll in the plan or coverage. The notice may be provided to an employee on behalf of the employee's child. In addition, the notice may be included with other enrollment materials that a plan distributes to employees, provided the statement is prominent. If a notice satisfying the requirements of this paragraph (f)(2) is provided to an employee whose child is entitled to an enrollment opportunity under this paragraph (f), the obligation to provide the notice of enrollment opportunity under this paragraph (f)(2) with respect to that child is satisfied for both the plan and the issuer.

(3) *Effective date of coverage.* In the case of an individual who enrolls under paragraph (f)(2) of this section, coverage must take effect not later than the first day of the first plan year beginning on or after September 23, 2010.

(4) *Treatment of enrollees in a group health plan.* Any child enrolling in a group health plan pursuant to paragraph (f)(2) of this section must be treated as if the child were a special enrollee, as provided under the rules of § 2590.701–6(d) of this Part. Accordingly, the child (and, if the child would not be a participant once enrolled in the plan, the participant through whom the child is otherwise eligible for coverage under the plan) must be offered all the benefit packages available to similarly situated individuals who did not lose coverage by reason of cessation of dependent status. For this purpose, any difference in benefits or cost-sharing requirements constitutes a different benefit package. The child also cannot be required to pay more for coverage than similarly situated individuals who did not lose

coverage by reason of cessation of dependent status.

(5) *Examples.* The rules of this paragraph (f) are illustrated by the following examples:

Example 1. (i) *Facts.* Employer Y maintains a group health plan with a calendar year plan year. The plan has a single benefit package. For the 2010 plan year, the plan allows children of employees to be covered under the plan until age 19, or until age 23 for children who are full-time students. Individual B, an employee of Y, and Individual C, B's child and a full-time student, were enrolled in Y's group health plan at the beginning of the 2010 plan year. On June 10, 2010, C turns 23 years old and loses dependent coverage under Y's plan. On or before January 1, 2011, Y's group health plan gives B written notice that individuals who lost coverage by reason of ceasing to be a dependent before attainment of age 26 are eligible to enroll in the plan, and that individuals may request enrollment for such children through February 14, 2011 with enrollment effective retroactively to January 1, 2011.

(ii) *Conclusion.* In this *Example 1,* the plan has complied with the requirements of this paragraph (f) by providing an enrollment opportunity to C that lasts at least 30 days.

Example 2. (i) *Facts.* Employer Z maintains a group health plan with a plan year beginning October 1 and ending September 30. Prior to October 1, 2010, the group health plan allows children of employees to be covered under the plan until age 22. Individual D, an employee of Z, and Individual E, D's child, are enrolled in family coverage under Z's group health plan for the plan year beginning on October 1, 2008. On May 1, 2009, E turns 22 years old and ceases to be eligible as a dependent under Z's plan and loses coverage. D drops coverage but remains an employee of Z.

(ii) *Conclusion.* In this *Example 2,* not later than October 1, 2010, the plan must provide D and E an opportunity to enroll (including written notice of an opportunity to enroll) that continues for at least 30 days, with enrollment effective not later than October 1, 2010.

Example 3. (i) *Facts.* Same facts as *Example 2,* except that D did not drop coverage. Instead, D switched to a lower-cost benefit package option.

(ii) *Conclusion.* In this *Example 3,* not later than October 1, 2010, the plan must provide D and E an opportunity to enroll in any benefit package available to similarly situated individuals who enroll when first eligible.

Example 4. (i) *Facts.* Same facts as *Example 2,* except that E elected COBRA continuation coverage.

(ii) *Conclusion.* In this *Example 4,* not later than October 1, 2010, the plan must provide D and E an opportunity to enroll other than as a COBRA qualified beneficiary (and must provide, by that date, written notice of the opportunity to enroll) that continues for at least 30 days, with enrollment effective not later than October 1, 2010.

Example 5. (i) *Facts.* Employer X maintains a group health plan with a calendar year plan year. Prior to 2011, the plan allows children

of employees to be covered under the plan until the child attains age 22. During the 2009 plan year, an individual with a 22-year old child joins the plan; the child is denied coverage because the child is 22.

(ii) *Conclusion.* In this *Example 5,* notwithstanding that the child was not previously covered under the plan, the plan must provide the child, not later than January 1, 2011, an opportunity to enroll (including written notice to the employee of an opportunity to enroll the child) that continues for at least 30 days, with enrollment effective not later than January 1, 2011.

(g) *Special rule for grandfathered group health plans*—(1) For plan years beginning before January 1, 2014, a group health plan that qualifies as a grandfathered health plan under section 1251 of the Patient Protection and Affordable Care Act and that makes available dependent coverage of children may exclude an adult child who has not attained age 26 from coverage only if the adult child is eligible to enroll in an eligible employer-sponsored health plan (as defined in section 5000A(f)(2) of the Internal Revenue Code) other than a group health plan of a parent.

(2) For plan years beginning on or after January 1, 2014, a group health plan that qualifies as a grandfathered health plan under section 1251 of the Patient Protection and Affordable Care Act must comply with the requirements of paragraphs (a) through (f) of this section.

(h) *Applicability date.* The provisions of this section apply for plan years beginning on or after September 23, 2010.

Department of Health and Human Services

45 CFR Subtitle A

■ For reasons set forth in the preamble, the Department of Health and Human Services is amending 45 CFR Subtitle A, Subchapter B as follows:

PART 144—REQUIREMENTS RELATING TO HEALTH INSURANCE COVERAGE

Subpart A—General Provisions

■ 1. Section 144.101 is amended by-
■ A. Revising paragraph (a).
■ B. Redesignating paragraphs (b), (c) and (d) as paragraphs (c), (d) and (e), respectively.
■ C. Adding a new paragraph (b).
■ D. Revising the first sentence of newly redesignated paragraph (c).
■ E. Amending newly redesignated paragraph (d) by removing "2722" and adding in its place "2723".

The revisions and additions read as follows:

27138   Federal Register / Vol. 75, No. 92 / Thursday, May 13, 2010 / Rules and Regulations

§ 144.101   Basis and purpose.

(a) Part 146 of this subchapter implements requirements of Title XXVII of the Public Health Service Act (PHS Act, 42 U.S.C. 300gg, *et seq.*) that apply to group health plans and group health insurance issuers.

(b) Part 147 of this subchapter implements the provisions of the Patient Protection and Affordable Care Act that apply to both group health plans and health insurance issuers in the Group and Individual Markets.

(c) Part 148 of this subchapter implements Individual Health Insurance Market requirements of the PHS Act.

* * *

*   *   *   *   *

■ 2. Section 144.103 is amended by adding the definition of "Policy Year" to read as follows:

§ 144.103   Defintions.

*   *   *   *   *

Policy Year means in the individual health insurance market the 12-month period that is designated as the policy year in the policy documents of the individual health insurance coverage. If there is no designation of a policy year in the policy document (or no such policy document is available), then the policy year is the deductible or limit year used under the coverage. If deductibles or other limits are not imposed on a yearly basis, the policy year is the calendar year.

*   *   *   *   *

PART 146—REQUIREMENTS FOR THE GROUP HEALTH INSURANCE MARKET

■ 3. Section 146.101 is amended by—
■ A. Revising the first sentence of paragraph (a).
■ B. Revising paragraph (b)(4).
The revisions read as follows:

§ 146.101   Basis and Scope.

(a) Statutory basis. This part implements the Group Market requirements of the PHS Act.* * *
(b) * * *
(4) *Subpart E.* Subpart E of this part implements requirements relating to group health plans and issuers in the Group Health Insurance Market.

*   *   *   *   *

§ 146.115   [Amended]

■ 4. Section 146.115 is amended by removing "2721(b)" wherever it appears in paragraph (a)(6) and adding in its place "2722(a)".

§ 146.130   [Amended]

■ 5. Section 146.130 is amended by—
■ A. Removing "2704" wherever it appears in paragraphs (e) and (f),

including the examples in paragraph (e)(4), and adding in its place "2725".
■ B. Removing "2723" wherever it appears in paragraph (e)(3), including the paragraph heading, and adding in its place "2724".
■ 6. A new Part 147 is added to read as follows:

PART 147—HEALTH INSURANCE REFORM REQUIREMENTS FOR THE GROUP AND INDIVIDUAL HEALTH INSURANCE MARKETS

Authority: Secs 2701 through 2763, 2791, and 2792 of the Public Health Service Act (42 USC 300gg through 300gg–63, 300gg–91, and 300gg–92), as amended.

§ 147.100   Basis and scope.

Part 147 of this subchapter implements the requirements of the Patient Protection and Affordable Care Act that apply to group health plans and health insurance issuers in the Group and Individual markets.

§ 147.120   Eligibility of children until at least age 26.

(a) *In general*—(1) A group health plan, or a health insurance issuer offering group or individual health insurance coverage, that makes available dependent coverage of children must make such coverage available for children until attainment of 26 years of age.

(2) The rule of this paragraph (a) is illustrated by the following example:

Example. (i) *Facts.* For the plan year beginning January 1, 2011, a group health plan provides health coverage for employees, employees' spouses, and employees' children until the child turns 26. On the birthday of a child of an employee, July 17, 2011, the child turns 26. The last day the plan covers the child is July 16, 2011.

(ii) *Conclusion.* In this *Example,* the plan satisfies the requirement of this paragraph (a) with respect to the child.

(b) *Restrictions on plan definition of dependent.* With respect to a child who has not attained age 26, a plan or issuer may not define dependent for purposes of eligibility for dependent coverage of children other than in terms of a relationship between a child and the participant (in the individual market, the primary subscriber). Thus, for example, a plan or issuer may not deny or restrict coverage for a child who has not attained age 26 based on the presence or absence of the child's financial dependency (upon the participant or primary subscriber, or any other person), residency with the participant (in the individual market, the primary subscriber) or with any other person, student status, employment, or any combination of

those factors. In addition, a plan or issuer may not deny or restrict coverage of a child based on eligibility for other coverage, except that paragraph (g) of this section provides a special rule for plan years beginning before January 1, 2014 for grandfathered health plans that are group health plans. (Other requirements of Federal or State law, including section 609 of ERISA or section 1908 of the Social Security Act, may mandate coverage of certain children.)

(c) *Coverage of grandchildren not required.* Nothing in this section requires a plan or issuer to make coverage available for the child of a child receiving dependent coverage.

(d) *Uniformity irrespective of age.* The terms of the plan or health insurance coverage providing dependent coverage of children cannot vary based on age (except for children who are age 26 or older).

(e) *Examples.* The rules of paragraph (d) of this section are illustrated by the following examples:

Example 1. (i) *Facts.* A group health plan offers a choice of self-only or family health coverage. Dependent coverage is provided under family health coverage for children of participants who have not attained age 26. The plan imposes an additional premium surcharge for children who are older than age 18.

(ii) *Conclusion.* In this *Example 1,* the plan violates the requirement of paragraph (d) of this section because the plan varies the terms for dependent coverage of children based on age.

Example 2. (i) *Facts.* A group health plan offers a choice among the following tiers of health coverage: Self-only, self-plus-one, self-plus-two, and self-plus-three-or-more. The cost of coverage increases based on the number of covered individuals. The plan provides dependent coverage of children who have not attained age 26.

(ii) *Conclusion.* In this *Example 2,* the plan does not violate the requirement of paragraph (d) of this section that the terms of dependent coverage for children not vary based on age. Although the cost of coverage increases for tiers with more covered individuals, the increase applies without regard to the age of any child.

Example 3. (i) *Facts.* A group health plan offers two benefit packages—an HMO option and an indemnity option. Dependent coverage is provided for children of participants who have not attained age 26. The plan limits children who are older than age 18 to the HMO option.

(ii) *Conclusion.* In this *Example 3,* the plan violates the requirement of paragraph (d) of this section because the plan, by limiting children who are older than age 18 to the HMO option, varies the terms for dependent coverage of children based on age.

(f) *Transitional rules for individuals whose coverage ended by reason of reaching a dependent eligibility threshold*—(1) *In general.* The relief provided in the transitional rules of this paragraph (f) applies with respect to any child—

(1) Whose coverage ended, or who was denied coverage (or was not eligible for coverage) under a group health plan or group or individual health insurance coverage because, under the terms of the plan or coverage, the availability of dependent coverage of children ended before the attainment of age 26 (which, under this section, is no longer permissible); and

(ii) Who becomes eligible (or is required to become eligible) for coverage under a group health plan or group or individual health insurance coverage on the first day of the first plan year (in the individual market, the first day of the first policy year) beginning on or after September 23, 2010 by reason of the application of this section.

(2) *Opportunity to enroll required*—(i) If a group health plan, or group or individual health insurance coverage, in which a child described in paragraph (f)(1) of this section is eligible to enroll (or is required to become eligible to enroll) is the plan or coverage in which the child's coverage ended (or did not begin) for the reasons described in paragraph (f)(1)(i) of this section, and if the plan, or the issuer of such coverage, is subject to the requirements of this section, the plan and the issuer are required to give the child an opportunity to enroll that continues for at least 30 days (including written notice of the opportunity to enroll). This opportunity (including the written notice) must be provided beginning not later than the first day of the first plan year (in the individual market, the first day of the first policy year) beginning on or after September 23, 2010.

(ii) The written notice must include a statement that children whose coverage ended, or who were denied coverage (or were not eligible for coverage), because the availability of dependent coverage of children ended before attainment of age 26 are eligible to enroll in the plan or coverage. The notice may be provided to an employee on behalf of the employee's child (in the individual market, to the primary subscriber on behalf of the primary subscriber's child). In addition, for a group health plan or group health insurance coverage, the notice may be included with other enrollment materials that a plan distributes to employees, provided the statement is prominent. For a group health plan or group health insurance coverage, if a notice satisfying the requirements of this paragraph (f)(2) is provided to an employee whose child is entitled to an enrollment opportunity

under this paragraph (f), the obligation to provide the notice of enrollment opportunity under this paragraph (f)(2) with respect to that child is satisfied for both the plan and the issuer.

(3) *Effective date of coverage.* In the case of an individual who enrolls under paragraph (f)(2) of this section, coverage must take effect not later than the first day of the first plan year (in the individual market, the first day of the first policy year) beginning on or after September 23, 2010.

(4) *Treatment of enrollees in a group health plan.* For purposes of this Part, any child enrolling in a group health plan pursuant to paragraph (f)(2) of this section must be treated as if the child were a special enrollee, as provided under the rules of 45 CFR 146.117(d). Accordingly, the child (and, if the child would not be a participant once enrolled in the plan, the participant through whom the child is otherwise eligible for coverage under the plan) must be offered all the benefit packages available to similarly situated individuals who did not lose coverage by reason of cessation of dependent status. For this purpose, any difference in benefits or cost-sharing requirements constitutes a different benefit package. The child also cannot be required to pay more for coverage than similarly situated individuals who did not lose coverage by reason of cessation of dependent status.

(5) *Examples.* The rules of this paragraph (f) are illustrated by the following examples:

Example 1. (i) *Facts.* Employer *Y* maintains a group health plan with a calendar year plan year. The plan has a single benefit package. For the 2010 plan year, the plan allows children of employees to be covered under the plan until age 19, or until age 23 for children who are full-time students. Individual *B*, an employee of *Y*, and Individual *C*, *B*'s child and a full-time student, were enrolled in *Y*'s group health plan at the beginning of the 2010 plan year. On June 10, 2010, *C* turns 23 years old and loses dependent coverage under *Y*'s plan. On or before January 1, 2011, *Y*'s group health plan gives *B* written notice that individuals who lost coverage by reason of ceasing to be a dependent before attainment of age 26 are eligible to enroll in the plan, and that individuals may request enrollment for such children through February 14, 2011 with enrollment effective retroactively to January 1, 2011.

(ii) *Conclusion.* In this *Example 1*, the plan has complied with the requirements of this paragraph (f) by providing an enrollment opportunity to *C* that lasts at least 30 days.

Example 2. (i) *Facts.* Employer *Z* maintains a group health plan with a plan year beginning October 1 and ending September 30. Prior to October 1, 2010, the group health plan allows children of employees to be

covered under the plan until age 22. Individual *D*, an employee of *Z*, and Individual *E*, *D*'s child, are enrolled in family coverage under *Z*'s group health plan for the plan year beginning on October 1, 2008. On May 1, 2009, *E* turns 22 years old and ceases to be eligible as a dependent under *Z*'s plan and loses coverage. *D* drops coverage but remains an employee of *Z*.

(ii) *Conclusion.* In this *Example 2*, not later than October 1, 2010, the plan must provide *D* and *E* an opportunity to enroll (including written notice of an opportunity to enroll) that continues for at least 30 days, with enrollment effective not later than October 1, 2010.

Example 3. (i) *Facts.* Same facts as *Example 2*, except that *D* did not drop coverage. Instead, *D* switched to a lower-cost benefit package option.

(ii) *Conclusion.* In this *Example 3*, not later than October 1, 2010, the plan must provide *D* and *E* an opportunity to enroll in any benefit package available to similarly situated individuals who enroll when first eligible.

Example 4. (i) *Facts.* Same facts as *Example 2*, except that *E* elected COBRA continuation coverage.

(ii) *Conclusion.* In this *Example 4*, not later than October 1, 2010, the plan must provide *D* and *E* an opportunity to enroll other than as a COBRA qualified beneficiary (and must provide, by that date, written notice of the opportunity to enroll) that continues for at least 30 days, with enrollment effective not later than October 1, 2010.

Example 5. (i) *Facts.* Employer *X* maintains a group health plan with a calendar year plan year. Prior to 2011, the plan allows children of employees to be covered under the plan until the child attains age 22. During the 2009 plan year, an individual with a 22-year old child joins the plan; the child is denied coverage because the child is 22.

(ii) *Conclusion.* In this *Example 5*, notwithstanding that the child was not previously covered under the plan, the plan must provide the child, not later than January 1, 2011, an opportunity to enroll (including written notice to the employee of an opportunity to enroll the child) that continues for at least 30 days, with enrollment effective not later than January 1, 2011.

(g) *Special rule for grandfathered group health plans*—(1) For plan years beginning before January 1, 2014, a group health plan that qualifies as a grandfathered health plan under section 1251 of the Patient Protection and Affordable Care Act and that makes available dependent coverage of children may exclude an adult child who has not attained age 26 from coverage only if the adult child is eligible to enroll in an eligible employer-sponsored health plan (as defined in section 5000A(f)(2) of the Internal Revenue Code) other than a group health plan of a parent.

(2) For plan years beginning on or after January 1, 2014, a group health plan that qualifies as a grandfathered

27140   Federal Register / Vol. 75, No. 92 / Thursday, May 13, 2010 / Rules and Regulations

health plan under section 1251 of the Patient Protection and Affordable Care Act must comply with the requirements of paragraphs (a) through (f) of this section.

(h) *Applicability date.* The provisions of this section apply for plan years (in the individual market, policy years) beginning on or after September 23, 2010.

[FR Doc. 2010–11391 Filed 5–10–10; 4:15 pm]
BILLING CODE 4830–01–P; 4510–29–P; 4120–01–P

L. IRS Notice 2010-38 (Exclusions from Income for Adult Children Coverage)

Internal Revenue Bulletin: 2010-20

May 17, 2010

Notice 2010-38

Tax Treatment of Health Care Benefits Provided With Respect to Children Under Age 27

Table of Contents

I. PURPOSE

This notice provides guidance on the tax treatment of health coverage for children up to age 27 under the Affordable Care Act. (In this notice, the "Affordable Care Act" refers to the Patient Protection and Affordable Care Act, Public Law No. 111-148 (PPACA), and the Health Care and Education Reconciliation Act of 2010, Public Law No. 111-152 (HCERA), signed into law by the President on March 23 and 30, 2010, respectively.)

The Affordable Care Act requires group health plans and health insurance issuers that provide dependent coverage of children to continue to make such coverage available for an adult child until age 26. The Affordable Care Act also amends the Internal Revenue Code (Code) to give certain favorable tax treatment to coverage for adult children. This notice addresses a number of questions regarding the tax treatment of such coverage.

Specifically, this notice provides guidance on the Affordable Care Act's amendment of § 105(b) of the Code, effective March 30, 2010, to extend the general exclusion from gross income for reimbursements for medical care under an employer-provided accident or health plan to any employee's child who has not attained age 27 as of the end of the taxable year. (See § 1004(d) of HCERA.) The Affordable Care Act also makes parallel amendments, effective March 30, 2010, to § 401(h) for retiree health accounts in pension plans, to § 501(c)(9) for voluntary employees' beneficiary associations (VEBAs), and to § 162(l) for deductions by self-employed individuals for medical care insurance. (See § 1004(d) of HCERA.)

The Affordable Care Act amended the Public Health Service Act (PHS Act) to add § 2714, which requires group health plans and health insurance issuers that provide dependent coverage of children to continue to make such coverage available for an adult child until age 26. (See § 1001 of PPACA.)

Section 2714 of the PHS Act is incorporated into § 9815 of the Code by § 1562(f) of PPACA. In certain respects, the rules of § 2714 of the PHS Act extending coverage to an adult child do not parallel the gross income exclusion rules provided by the Affordable Care Act's amendments of §§ 105(b), 401(h), 501(c)(9), and 162(l) of the Code. For example, § 2714 of the PHS Act applies to children under age 26 and is effective for the first plan year beginning on or after September 23, 2010, while, as noted above, the amendments to the Code addressed in this notice apply to children who have not attained age 27 as of the end of the taxable year and are effective March 30, 2010.

II. EXCLUSION OF EMPLOYER-PROVIDED MEDICAL CARE REIMBURSEMENTS FOR EMPLOYEE'S CHILD UNDER AGE 27

Section 105(b) generally excludes from an employee's gross income employer-provided reimbursements made directly or indirectly to the employee for the medical care of the employee, employee's spouse or employee's dependents (as defined in § 152 (determined without regard to § 152(b)(1), (b)(2) or (d)(1)(B)). As amended by the Affordable Care Act, the exclusion from gross income under § 105(b) is extended to employer-provided reimbursements for expenses incurred by the employee for the medical care of the employee's child (within the meaning of § 152(f)(1)) who has not attained age 27 as of the end of the taxable year. (The Affordable Care Act does not alter the existing definitions of spouse or dependent for purposes of § 105(b).) Under § 152(f)(1), a child is an individual who is the son, daughter, stepson, or stepdaughter of the employee, and a child includes both a legally adopted individual of the employee and an individual who is lawfully placed with the employee for legal adoption by the employee. Under § 152(f)(1), a child also includes an "eligible foster child," defined as an individual who is placed with the employee by an authorized placement agency or by judgment, decree, or other order of any court of competent jurisdiction.

As amended by the Affordable Care Act, the exclusion from gross income under § 105(b) applies with respect to an employee's child who has not attained age 27 as of the end of the taxable year, including a child of the employee who is not the employee's dependent within the meaning of § 152(a). Thus, the age limit, residency, support, and other tests described in § 152(c) do not apply with respect to such a child for purposes of § 105(b).

The exclusion applies only for reimbursements for medical care of individuals who are not age 27 or older at any time during the taxable year. For purposes of §§ 105(b) and 106, the taxable year is the employee's taxable year; employers may assume that an employee's taxable year is the calendar year; a child attains age 27 on the 27th anniversary of the date the child was born (for example, a child born on April 10, 1983 attained age 27 on April 10, 2010); and employers may rely on the employee's representation as to the child's date of birth.

III. EXCLUSION OF EMPLOYER-PROVIDED ACCIDENT OR HEALTH COVERAGE FOR EMPLOYEE'S CHILD UNDER AGE 27

Section 106 excludes from an employee's gross income coverage under an employer-provided accident or health plan. The regulations under § 106 provide that the exclusion applies to employer-provided coverage for an employee and the employee's spouse or dependents (as defined in § 152, determined without regard to § 152(b)(1), (b)(2) or (d)(1)(B)). See Prop. Treas. Reg. § 1.106-1. Prior to the Affordable Care Act, the exclusion for employer-provided accident or health plan coverage under § 106 paralleled the exclusion for reimbursements under § 105(b). There is no indication that Congress intended to provide a broader exclusion in § 105(b) than in § 106. Accordingly, IRS and Treasury intend to amend the regulations under § 106, retroactively to March 30, 2010, to provide that coverage for an employee's child under age 27 is excluded from gross income. Thus, on and after

March 30, 2010, both coverage under an employer-provided accident or health plan and amounts paid or reimbursed under such a plan for medical care expenses of an employee, an employee's spouse, an employee's dependents (as defined in § 152, determined without regard to § 152(b)(1), (b)(2) or (d)(1)(B)), or an employee's child (as defined in § 152(f)(1)) who has not attained age 27 as of the end of the employee's taxable year are excluded from the employee's gross income.

The following examples illustrate this rule. In these examples, any reference to a "dependent" means a dependent as defined in § 152, determined without regard to § 152(b)(1), (b)(2) or (d)(1)(B). Also, in these examples, it is assumed that none of the individuals are disabled.

Example (1). (i) Employer X provides health care coverage for its employees and their spouses and dependents and for any employee's child (as defined in § 152(f)(1)) who has not attained age 26. For the 2010 taxable year, Employer X provides coverage to Employee A and to A's son, C. C will attain age 26 on November 15, 2010. During the 2010 taxable year, C is not a full-time student. C has never worked for Employer X. C is not a dependent of A because prior to the close of the 2010 taxable year C had attained age 19 (and was also not a student who had not attained age 24).

(ii) C is a child of A within the meaning of § 152(f)(1). Accordingly, and because C will not attain age 27 during the 2010 taxable year, the health care coverage and reimbursements provided to him under the terms of Employer X's plan are excludible from A's gross income under §§ 106 and 105(b) for the period on and after March 30, 2010 through November 15, 2010 (when C attains age 26 and loses coverage under the terms of the plan).

Example (2). (i) Employer Y provides health care coverage for its employees and their spouses and dependents and for any employee's child (as defined in § 152(f)(1)) who has not attained age 27 as of the end of the taxable year. For the 2010 taxable year, Employer Y provides health care coverage to Employee E and to E's son, G. G will not attain age 27 until after the end of the 2010 taxable year. During the 2010 taxable year, G earns $50,000 per year, and does not live with E. G has never worked for Employer Y. G is not eligible for health care coverage from his own employer. G is not a dependent of E because G does not live with E and E does not provide more than one half of his support.

(ii) G is a child of E within the meaning of § 152(f)(1). Accordingly, and because G will not attain age 27 during the 2010 taxable year, the health care coverage and reimbursements for G under Employer Y's plan are excludible from E's gross income under §§ 106 and 105(b) for the period on and after March 30, 2010 through the end of the 2010 taxable year.

Example (3). (i) Same facts as *Example (2)*, except that G's employer offers health care coverage, but G has decided not to participate in his employer's plan.

(ii) G is a child of E within the meaning of § 152(f)(1). Accordingly, and because G will not attain age 27 during the 2010 taxable year, the health care coverage and reimbursements for G under Employer Y's plan are excludible from E's gross income under §§ 106 and 105(b) for the period on and after March 30, 2010 through the end of the 2010 taxable year.

Example (4). (i) Same facts as *Example (3)*, except that G is married to H, and neither G nor H is a dependent of E. G and H have decided not to participate in the health care coverage offered by G's employer, and Employer Y provides health care coverage to G and H.

(ii) G is a child of E within the meaning of § 152(f)(1). Accordingly, and because G will not attain age 27 during the 2010 taxable year, the health care coverage and reimbursements for G under Employer Y's plan are excludible from E's gross income under §§ 106 and 105(b) for the period on and after

March 30, 2010 through the end of the 2010 taxable year. The fair market value of the coverage for H is includible in E's gross income for the 2010 taxable year.

Example (5). (i) Employer Z provides health care coverage for its employees and their spouses and dependents. Effective May 1, 2010, Employer Z amends the health plan to provide coverage for any employee's child (as defined in § 152(f)(1)) who has not attained age 26. Employer Z provides coverage to Employee F and to F's son, K, for the 2010 taxable year. K will attain age 22 in 2010. During the 2010 taxable year, F provides more than one half of K's support. K lives with F and graduates from college on May 15, 2010 and thereafter is not a student. K has never worked for Employer Z. Prior to K's graduation from college, K is a dependent of F. Following graduation from college, K is no longer a dependent of F.

(ii) For the 2010 taxable year, the health care coverage and reimbursements provided to K under the terms of Employer Z's plan are excludible from F's gross income under §§ 106 and 105(b). For the period through May 15, 2010, the reimbursements and coverage are excludible because K was a dependent of F. For the period on and after March 30, 2010, the coverage is excludible because K is a child of F within the meaning of § 152(f)(1) and because K will not attain age 27 during the 2010 taxable year. (Thus, for the period from March 30 through May 15, 2010, there are two bases for the exclusion.)

IV. CAFETERIA PLANS, FLEXIBLE SPENDING ARRANGEMENTS, AND HEALTH REIMBURSEMENT ARRANGEMENTS

Section 125 allows employees to elect between cash and certain qualified benefits, including accident or health plans (described in § 106) and health flexible spending arrangements (health FSAs) (described in § 105(b)). Section 125(f) defines "qualified benefit" as any benefit which, with the application of § 125(a), is not includible in the gross income of the employee by reason of an express provision of chapter 1 of the Code (other than §§ 106(b) (which applies to Archer MSAs), 117, 127, or 132). Accordingly, the exclusion of coverage and reimbursements from an employee's gross income under §§ 106 and 105(b) for an employee's child who has not attained age 27 as of the end of the employee's taxable year carries forward automatically to the definition of qualified benefits for § 125 cafeteria plans, including health FSAs. Thus, a benefit will not fail to be a qualified benefit under a cafeteria plan (including a health FSA) merely because it provides coverage or reimbursements that are excludible under §§ 106 and 105(b) for a child who has not attained age 27 as of the end of the employee's taxable year.

A cafeteria plan may permit an employee to revoke an election during a period of coverage and to make a new election only in limited circumstances, such as a change in status event. See Treas. Reg. § 1.125-4(c). A change in status event includes changes in the number of an employee's dependents. The regulations under § 1.125-4(c) currently do not permit election changes for children under age 27 who are not the employee's dependents. IRS and Treasury intend to amend the regulations under § 1.125-4, effective retroactively to March 30, 2010, to include change in status events affecting non-dependent children under age 27, including becoming newly eligible for coverage or eligible for coverage beyond the date on which the child otherwise would have lost coverage.

In general, a health reimbursement arrangement (HRA) is an arrangement that is paid for solely by an employer (and not through a § 125 cafeteria plan) which reimburses an employee for medical care expenses up to a maximum dollar amount for a coverage period. Notice 2002-45, 2002-2 C.B. 93. The same rules that apply to an employee's child under age 27 for purposes of §§ 106 and 105(b) apply to an HRA.

V. FICA, FUTA, RRTA, AND INCOME TAX WITHHOLDING TREATMENT

Coverage and reimbursements under an employer-provided accident and health plan for employees generally and their dependents (or a class or classes of employees and their dependents) are excluded from wages for Federal Insurance Contributions Act (FICA) and Federal Unemployment Tax Act (FUTA) tax purposes under §§ 3121(a)(2) and 3306(b)(2), respectively. For these purposes, a child of the employee is a dependent. Treas. Reg. §§ 31.3121(a)(2)-1(c) and 31.3306(b)(2)-1(c). No age limit, residency, support, or other test applies for these purposes. Thus, coverage and reimbursements under a plan for employees and their dependents that are provided for an employee's child under age 27 are not wages for FICA or FUTA purposes. For this purpose, child has the same meaning as in § 152(f)(1), as discussed in the first paragraph in Section II of this notice. A similar exclusion applies for Railroad Retirement Tax Act (RRTA) tax purposes under § 3231(e)(1)(i) and Treas. Reg. § 31.3231(e)-1(a)(1).

Such coverage and reimbursements are also exempt from income tax withholding. See Rev. Rul. 56-632, 1956-2 C.B. 101.

VI. VEBAS, SECTION 401(h) ACCOUNTS, AND SECTION 162(l) DEDUCTIONS

A VEBA is a tax-exempt entity described in § 501(c)(9) providing for the payment of life, sick, accident, or other benefits to members of the VEBA or their dependents or designated beneficiaries. The regulations provide that, for purposes of § 501(c)(9), "dependent" means the member's spouse; any child of the member or the member's spouse who is a minor or a student (within the meaning of § 151(e)(4) (now § 152(f)(2)); any other minor child residing with the member; and any other individual who an association, relying on information furnished to it by a member, in good faith believes is a person described in § 152(a). Treas. Reg. § 1.501(c)(9)-3. As amended by the Affordable Care Act, § 501(c)(9) provides that, for purposes of providing for the payment of sick and accident benefits to members of the VEBA and their dependents, the term dependent includes any individual who is a member's child (as defined in § 152(f)(1)) and who has not attained age 27 as of the end of the calendar year.

Section 401(h) provides that a pension or annuity plan can establish and maintain a separate account to provide for the payment of benefits for sickness, accident, hospitalization, and medical expenses of retired employees, their spouses and their dependents if certain enumerated conditions are met ("401(h) Account"). The regulations provide that, for purposes of § 401(h) and § 1.401-14, the term "dependent" shall have the same meaning as that assigned to it by § 152. Treas. Reg. § 1.401-14(b)(4)(i). As amended by the Affordable Care Act, § 401(h) provides that the term dependent includes any individual who is a retired employee's child (within the meaning of § 152(f)(1)) and who has not attained age 27 as of the end of the calendar year.

Section 162(l) generally allows a self-employed individual to deduct, in computing adjusted gross income, amounts paid during the taxable year for insurance that constitutes medical care for the taxpayer, his or her spouse, and dependents, if certain requirements are satisfied. As amended by the Affordable Care Act, § 162(l) covers medical insurance for any child (within the meaning of § 152(f)(1)) who has not attained age 27 as of the end of the taxable year.

VII. TRANSITION RULE FOR CAFETERIA PLAN AMENDMENTS

Cafeteria plans may need to be amended to include employees' children who have not attained age 27 as of the end of the taxable year. Pursuant to § 1.125-1(c) of the proposed regulations, cafeteria plan amendments may be effective only prospectively. Notwithstanding this general rule, as of March 30,

2010, employers may permit employees to immediately make pre-tax salary reduction contributions for accident or health benefits under a cafeteria plan (including a health FSA) for children under age 27, even if the cafeteria plan has not yet been amended to cover these individuals. However, a retroactive amendment to a cafeteria plan to cover children under age 27 must be made no later than December 31, 2010, and must be effective retroactively to the first date in 2010 when employees are permitted to make pre-tax salary reduction contributions to cover children under age 27 (but in no event before March 30, 2010).

VIII. EFFECT ON OTHER DOCUMENTS

IRS and Treasury intend to amend the regulations at §§ 1.105-1, 1.105-2, 1.106-1, 1.125-1, 1.125-4, 1.125-5, and 1.401-14 to include children (as defined in § 152(f)(1)) who are under age 27. Additionally, IRS and Treasury intend to amend the regulations at § 1.501(c)(9)-3 to include children (as defined in § 152(f)(1)) who are under age 27, with respect to sick and accident benefits. Taxpayers may rely on this notice pending the issuance of the amended regulations.

IX. EFFECTIVE DATES

The changes relating to §§ 105(b), 106, 501(c)(9), 401(h) and 162(l) are effective on March 30, 2010.

DRAFTING INFORMATION

The principal author of this notice is Karen Levin of the Office of Division Counsel/Associate Chief Counsel (Tax Exempt and Government Entities). For further information regarding this notice, contact Ms. Levin at (202) 622-6080 (not a toll-free call).

M. Tri-Agency Regulations on Claims and Appeals Process

Friday,
July 23, 2010

Part IV

Department of the Treasury
Internal Revenue Service
26 CFR Parts 54 and 602

Department of Labor
Employee Benefits Security
Administration

29 CFR Part 2590

Department of Health and Human Services
45 CFR Part 147

Interim Final Rules for Group Health
Plans and Health Insurance Issuers
Relating to Internal Claims and Appeals
and External Review Processes Under the
Patient Protection and Affordable Care
Act; Interim Final Rule

DEPARTMENT OF THE TREASURY

Internal Revenue Service

26 CFR Parts 54 and 602

[TD 9494]

RIN 1545–BJ63

DEPARTMENT OF LABOR

Employee Benefits Security Administration

29 CFR Part 2590

RIN 1210–AB45

DEPARTMENT OF HEALTH AND HUMAN SERVICES

[OCIIO–9993–IFC]

45 CFR Part 147

RIN 0991–AB70

Interim Final Rules for Group Health Plans and Health Insurance Issuers Relating to Internal Claims and Appeals and External Review Processes Under the Patient Protection and Affordable Care Act

AGENCY: Internal Revenue Service, Department of the Treasury; Employee Benefits Security Administration, Department of Labor; Office of Consumer Information and Insurance Oversight, Department of Health and Human Services.

ACTION: Interim final rules with request for comments.

SUMMARY: This document contains interim final regulations implementing the requirements regarding internal claims and appeals and external review processes for group health plans and health insurance coverage in the group and individual markets under the Patient Protection and Affordable Care Act. The regulations will generally affect health insurance issuers; group health plans; and participants, beneficiaries, and enrollees in health insurance coverage and in group health plans. The regulations provide plans and issuers with guidance necessary to comply with the law.

DATES: *Effective date.* These interim final regulations are effective on September 21, 2010.

Comment date. Comments are due on or before September 21, 2010.

Applicability dates. These interim final regulations generally apply to group health plans and group health insurance issuers for plan years beginning on or after September 23, 2010. These interim final regulations

generally apply to individual health insurance issuers for policy years beginning on or after September 23, 2010.

ADDRESSES: Written comments may be submitted to any of the addresses specified below. Any comment that is submitted to any Department will be shared with the other Departments. Please do not submit duplicates.

All comments will be made available to the public. *Warning:* Do not include any personally identifiable information (such as name, address, or other contact information) or confidential business information that you do not want publicly disclosed. All comments are posted on the Internet exactly as received, and can be retrieved by most Internet search engines. No deletions, modifications, or redactions will be made to the comments received, as they are public records. Comments may be submitted anonymously.

Department of Labor. Comments to the Department of Labor, identified by RIN 1210–AB45, by one of the following methods:

• *Federal eRulemaking Portal: http://www.regulations.gov.* Follow the instructions for submitting comments.

• *E-mail: E-OHPSCA2719.EBSA@dol.gov.*

• *Mail or Hand Delivery:* Office of Health Plan Standards and Compliance Assistance, Employee Benefits Security Administration, Room N–5653, U.S. Department of Labor, 200 Constitution Avenue, NW., Washington, DC 20210, *Attention:* RIN 1210—AB45.

Comments received by the Department of Labor will be posted without change to *http://www.regulations.gov* and *http://www.dol.gov/ebsa,* and available for public inspection at the Public Disclosure Room, N–1513, Employee Benefits Security Administration, 200 Constitution Avenue, NW., Washington, DC 20210.

Department of Health and Human Services. In commenting, please refer to file code OCIIO–9993–IFC. Because of staff and resource limitations, we cannot accept comments by facsimile (FAX) transmission.

You may submit comments in one of four ways (please choose only one of the ways listed):

1. *Electronically.* You may submit electronic comments on this regulation to *http://www.regulations.gov.* Follow the instructions under the "More Search Options" tab.

2. *By regular mail.* You may mail written comments to the following address only: Office of Consumer Information and Insurance Oversight,

Department of Health and Human Services, Attention: OCIIO–9993–IFC, P.O. Box 8016, Baltimore, MD 21244–1850.

Please allow sufficient time for mailed comments to be received before the close of the comment period.

3. *By express or overnight mail.* You may send written comments to the following address only: Office of Consumer Information and Insurance Oversight, Department of Health and Human Services, Attention: OCIIO–9993–IFC, Mail Stop C4–26–05, 7500 Security Boulevard, Baltimore, MD 21244–1850.

4. *By hand or courier.* If you prefer, you may deliver (by hand or courier) your written comments before the close of the comment period to either of the following addresses:

a. For delivery in Washington, DC—

Office of Consumer Information and Insurance Oversight, Department of Health and Human Services, Room 445–G, Hubert H. Humphrey Building, 200 Independence Avenue, SW., Washington, DC 20201.

(Because access to the interior of the Hubert H. Humphrey Building is not readily available to persons without Federal government identification, commenters are encouraged to leave their comments in the OCIIO drop slots located in the main lobby of the building. A stamp-in clock is available for persons wishing to retain a proof of filing by stamping in and retaining an extra copy of the comments being filed.)

b. For delivery in Baltimore, MD—

Centers for Medicare & Medicaid Services, Department of Health and Human Services, 7500 Security Boulevard, Baltimore, MD 21244–1850.

If you intend to deliver your comments to the Baltimore address, please call (410) 786–7195 in advance to schedule your arrival with one of our staff members.

Comments mailed to the addresses indicated as appropriate for hand or courier delivery may be delayed and received after the comment period.

Submission of comments on paperwork requirements. You may submit comments on this document's paperwork requirements by following the instructions at the end of the "Collection of Information Requirements" section in this document.

Inspection of Public Comments: All comments received before the close of the comment period are available for viewing by the public, including any personally identifiable or confidential business information that is included in a comment. We post all comments received before the close of the comment period on the following website as soon as possible after they have been received: *http://www.regulations.gov.* Follow the search instructions on that Web site to view public comments.

Comments received timely will also be available for public inspection as they are received, generally beginning approximately three weeks after publication of a document, at the headquarters of the Centers for Medicare & Medicaid Services, 7500 Security Boulevard, Baltimore, Maryland 21244, Monday through Friday of each week from 8:30 a.m. to 4 p.m. EST. To schedule an appointment to view public comments, phone 1–800–743–3951.

Internal Revenue Service. Comments to the IRS, identified by REG–125592–10, by one of the following methods:

• *Federal eRulemaking Portal: http://www.regulations.gov.* Follow the instructions for submitting comments.

• *Mail:* CC:PA:LPD:PR (REG–125592–10), Room 5205, Internal Revenue Service, P.O. Box 7604, Ben Franklin Station, Washington, DC 20044.

• *Hand or courier delivery:* Monday through Friday between the hours of 8 a.m. and 4 p.m. to: CC:PA:LPD:PR (REG–125592–10), Courier's Desk, Internal Revenue Service, 1111 Constitution Avenue, NW., Washington DC 20224.

All submissions to the IRS will be open to public inspection and copying in Room 1621, 1111 Constitution Avenue, NW., Washington, DC from 9 a.m. to 4 p.m.

FOR FURTHER INFORMATION CONTACT: Amy Turner or Beth Baum, Employee Benefits Security Administration, Department of Labor, at (202) 693–8335; Karen Levin, Internal Revenue Service, Department of the Treasury, at (202) 622–6080; Ellen Kuhn, Office of Consumer Information and Insurance Oversight, Department of Health and Human Services, at (301) 492–4100.

Customer Service Information: Individuals interested in obtaining information from the Department of Labor concerning employment-based health coverage laws may call the EBSA Toll-Free Hotline at 1–866–444–EBSA (3272) or visit the Department of Labor's Web site (*http://www.dol.gov/ebsa*). In addition, information from HHS on private health insurance for consumers can be found on the Centers for Medicare & Medicaid Services (CMS) Web site (*http://www.cms.hhs.gov/HealthInsReformforConsume/01_Overview.asp*) and information on health reform can be found at *http://www.healthreform.gov.*

SUPPLEMENTARY INFORMATION:

I. Background

The Patient Protection and Affordable Care Act (the Affordable Care Act), Public Law 111–148, was enacted on March 23, 2010; the Health Care and Education Reconciliation Act (the Reconciliation Act), Public Law 111–152, was enacted on March 30, 2010. The Affordable Care Act and the Reconciliation Act reorganize, amend, and add to the provisions of part A of title XXVII of the Public Health Service Act (PHS Act) relating to group health plans and health insurance issuers in the group and individual markets. The term "group health plan" includes both insured and self-insured group health plans.[1] The Affordable Care Act adds section 715(a)(1) to the Employee Retirement Income Security Act (ERISA) and section 9815(a)(1) to the Internal Revenue Code (the Code) to incorporate the provisions of part A of title XXVII of the PHS Act into ERISA and the Code, and make them applicable to group health plans, and health insurance issuers providing health insurance coverage in connection with group health plans. The PHS Act sections incorporated by this reference are sections 2701 through 2728. PHS Act sections 2701 through 2719A are substantially new, though they incorporate some provisions of prior law. PHS Act sections 2722 through 2728 are sections of prior law renumbered, with some, mostly minor, changes.

Subtitles A and C of title I of the Affordable Care Act amend the requirements of title XXVII of the PHS Act (changes to which are incorporated into ERISA section 715). The preemption provisions of ERISA section 731 and PHS Act section 2724[2] (implemented in 29 CFR 2590.731(a) and 45 CFR 146.143(a)) apply so that the requirements of part 7 of ERISA and title XXVII of the PHS Act, as amended by the Affordable Care Act, are not to be "construed to supersede any provision of State law which establishes, implements, or continues in effect any standard or requirement solely relating to health insurance issuers in connection with group or individual health insurance coverage except to the extent that such standard or

[1] The term "group health plan" is used in title XXVII of the PHS Act, part 7 of ERISA, and chapter 100 of the Code, and is distinct from the term "health plan," as used in other provisions of title I of the Affordable Care Act. The term "health plan" does not include self-insured group health plans.

[2] Code section 9815 incorporates the preemption provisions of PHS Act section 2724. Prior to the Affordable Care Act, there were no express preemption provisions in chapter 100 of the Code.

requirement prevents the application of a requirement" of the Affordable Care Act. Accordingly, State laws that impose on health insurance issuers requirements that are stricter than those imposed by the Affordable Care Act will not be superseded by the Affordable Care Act.

The Departments of Health and Human Services, Labor, and the Treasury (the Departments) are issuing regulations in several phases implementing the revised PHS Act sections 2701 through 2719A and related provisions of the Affordable Care Act. The first phase in this series was the publication of a Request for Information relating to the medical loss ratio provisions of PHS Act section 2718, published in the **Federal Register** on April 14, 2010 (75 FR 19297). The second phase was interim final regulations implementing PHS Act section 2714 (requiring dependent coverage of children to age 26), published in the **Federal Register** on May 13, 2010 (75 FR 27122). The third phase was interim final regulations implementing section 1251 of the Affordable Care Act (relating to status as a grandfathered health plan), published in the **Federal Register** on June 17, 2010 (75 FR 34538). The fourth phase was interim final regulations implementing PHS Act sections 2704 (prohibiting preexisting condition exclusions), 2711 (regarding lifetime and annual dollar limits on benefits), 2712 (regarding restrictions on rescissions), and 2719A (regarding patient protections), published in the **Federal Register** on June 28, 2010 (75 FR 37188). The fifth phase was interim final regulations implementing PHS Act section 2713 (regarding preventive health services), published in the **Federal Register** on July 19, 2010 (75 FR 41726). These interim final regulations are being published to implement PHS Act section 2719, relating to internal claims and appeals and external review processes. PHS Act section 2719 is generally effective for plan years (in the individual market, policy years) beginning on or after September 23, 2010, which is six months after the March 23, 2010 date of enactment of the Affordable Care Act. The implementation of other provisions of PHS Act sections 2701 through 2719A will be addressed in future regulations.

II. Overview of the Regulations: PHS Act Section 2719, Internal Claims and Appeals and External Review Processes (26 CFR 54.9815–2719T, 29 CFR 2590.715–27109, 45 CFR 147.136)

a. Scope and Definitions

These interim final regulations set forth rules implementing PHS Act section 2719 for internal claims and appeals and external review processes for group health plans and health insurance coverage; these requirements do not apply to grandfathered health plans under section 1251 of the Affordable Care Act. With respect to internal claims and appeals processes for group health coverage, PHS Act section 2719 provides that plans and issuers must initially incorporate the internal claims and appeals processes set forth in 29 CFR 2560.503–1 and update such processes in accordance with standards established by the Secretary of Labor. Similarly, with respect to internal claims and appeals processes for individual health insurance coverage, issuers must initially incorporate the internal claims and appeals processes set forth in applicable State law and update such processes in accordance with standards established by the Secretary of Health and Human Services. These interim final regulations provide such updated standards for compliance. The Department of Labor is also considering further updates to 29 CFR 2560.503–1 and expects to issue future regulations that will propose additional, more comprehensive updates to the standards for plan internal claims and appeals processes.

With respect to external review, PHS Act section 2719 provides a system for applicability of either a State external review process or a Federal external review process. These regulations provide rules for determining which process applies, as well as guidance regarding each process. Consistent with the statutory structure, these interim final regulations adopt an approach that builds on applicable State external review processes. For plans and issuers subject to existing State external review processes, the regulations include a transition period until July 1, 2011. During this period, the State process applies and the Departments will work individually with States on an ongoing basis to assist in making any necessary changes to incorporate additional consumer protections so that the State process will continue to apply after the end of the transition period. For plans and issuers not subject to an existing State external review process (including self-insured plans), a Federal process

will apply for plan years (in the individual market, policy years) beginning on or after September 23, 2010. The Departments will be issuing more guidance in the near future on the Federal external review process.

These interim final regulations also set forth rules related to the form and manner of providing notices in connection with internal claims and appeals and external review processes. The regulations also reiterate and preserve the Departments' authority, pursuant to PHS Act section 2719(c), to deem external review processes in operation on March 23, 2010, to be in compliance with the requirements of PHS Act section 2719, either permanently or temporarily.

Paragraph (a)(2) of 26 CFR 54.9815–2719T, 29 CFR 2590.715–2719, 45 CFR 147.136 sets forth definitions relevant for these interim final regulations, including the definitions of an adverse benefit determination and a final internal adverse benefit determination. An adverse benefit determination is defined by incorporating the definition under the Department of Labor's regulations governing claims procedures at 29 CFR 2560.503–1 (DOL claims procedure regulation), and also includes a rescission of coverage. A final internal adverse benefit determination is the upholding of an adverse benefit determination at the conclusion of the internal appeals process or an adverse benefit determination with respect to which the internal appeals process has been deemed exhausted.

b. Internal Claims and Appeals Process

Paragraph (b) of 26 CFR 54.9815–2719T, 29 CFR 2590.715–2719, 45 CFR 147.136 requires group health plans and health insurance issuers offering group or individual health insurance coverage to implement an effective internal claims and appeals process. The regulations set forth separate rules for group health coverage and individual health insurance coverage.

1. Group Health Plans and Health Insurance Issuers Offering Group Health Insurance Coverage

A group health plan and a health insurance issuer offering group health insurance coverage must comply with all the requirements applicable to group health plans under the DOL claims procedure regulation. Therefore, for purposes of compliance with these interim final regulations, a health insurance issuer offering health insurance coverage in connection with a group health plan is subject to the DOL claims procedure regulation to the same extent as if it were a group health plan.

These interim final regulations also set forth six new requirements in addition to those in the DOL claims procedure regulation.

First, for purposes of these interim final regulations, the definition of an adverse benefit determination is broader than the definition in the DOL claims procedure regulation, in that an adverse benefit determination for purposes of these interim final regulations also includes a rescission of coverage. By referencing the DOL claims procedure regulation, an adverse benefit determination eligible for internal claims and appeals processes under these interim final regulations includes a denial, reduction, or termination of, or a failure to provide or make a payment (in whole or in part) for a benefit, including any such denial, reduction, termination, or failure to provide or make a payment that is based on:

• A determination of an individual's eligibility to participate in a plan or health insurance coverage;

• A determination that a benefit is not a covered benefit;

• The imposition of a preexisting condition exclusion, source-of-injury exclusion, network exclusion, or other limitation on otherwise covered benefits; or

• A determination that a benefit is experimental, investigational, or not medically necessary or appropriate.

A denial, reduction, or termination of, or a failure to provide or make a payment (in whole or in part) for a benefit can include both pre-service claims (for example, a claim resulting from the application of any utilization review), as well as post-service claims. Failure to make a payment in whole or in part includes any instance where a plan pays less than the total amount of expenses submitted with regard to a claim, including a denial of part of the claim due to the terms of a plan or health insurance coverage regarding copayments, deductibles, or other cost-sharing requirements.[3] Under these interim final regulations, an adverse benefit determination also includes any rescission of coverage as defined in the regulations restricting rescissions (26 CFR 54.9815–2712T(a)(2), 29 CFR 2590.715–2712(a)(2), and 45 CFR 147.128(a)(2)), whether or not there is an adverse effect on any particular benefit at that time. The regulations restricting rescissions generally define a rescission as a cancellation or discontinuance of coverage that has

---

[3] *See* the Department of Labor's Frequently Asked Questions (FAQs) About the Benefit Claims Procedure Regulations, FAQ C–12, at *http://www.dol.gov/ebsa*.

retroactive effect, except to the extent it is attributable to a failure to timely pay required premiums or contributions towards the cost of coverage. Rescissions of coverage must also comply with the requirements of the regulations restricting rescissions.[4]

Second, these interim final regulations provide that a plan or issuer must notify a claimant of a benefit determination (whether adverse or not) with respect to a claim involving urgent care (as defined in the DOL claims procedure regulation)[5] as soon as possible, taking into account the medical exigencies, but not later than 24 hours after the receipt of the claim by the plan or health insurance coverage, unless the claimant fails to provide sufficient information to determine whether, or to what extent, benefits are covered or payable under the plan or health insurance coverage.[6] This is a change from the requirements of the DOL claims procedure regulation, which generally requires a determination not later than 72 hours after receipt of the claim by a group health plan for urgent care claims. The Departments expect that electronic communication will enable faster decision-making today than in the year 2000, when the final DOL claims procedure regulation was issued.

Third, these interim final regulations provide additional criteria to ensure that a claimant receives a full and fair review. Specifically, in addition to complying with the requirements of the DOL claims procedure regulation, the plan or issuer must provide the claimant, free of charge, with any new or additional evidence considered, relied upon, or generated by the plan or issuer (or at the direction of the plan or issuer) in connection with the claim.[7] Such evidence must be provided as soon as possible and sufficiently in advance of the date on which the notice of adverse benefit determination on review is required to be provided to give the claimant a reasonable opportunity to respond prior to that date. Additionally, before the plan or issuer can issue an adverse benefit determination on review based on a new or additional rationale, the claimant must be provided, free of charge, with the rationale. The rationale must be provided as soon as possible and sufficiently in advance of the date on which the notice of adverse benefit determination on review is required to be provided to give the claimant a reasonable opportunity to respond prior to that date.

Fourth, these interim final regulations provide new criteria with respect to avoiding conflicts of interest. The plan or issuer must ensure that all claims and appeals are adjudicated in a manner designed to ensure the independence and impartiality of the persons involved in making the decision. Accordingly, decisions regarding hiring, compensation, termination, promotion, or other similar matters with respect to any individual (such as a claims adjudicator or medical expert) must not be made based upon the likelihood that the individual will support a denial of benefits. For example, a plan or issuer cannot provide bonuses based on the number of denials made by a claims adjudicator. Similarly, a plan or issuer cannot contract with a medical expert based on the expert's reputation for outcomes in contested cases, rather than based on the expert's professional qualifications.

Fifth, these interim final regulations provide new standards regarding notice to enrollees. Specifically, the statute and these interim final regulations require a plan or issuer to provide notice to enrollees, in a culturally and linguistically appropriate manner (standards for which are described later in this preamble). Plans and issuers must comply with the requirements of paragraphs (g) and (j) of the DOL claims procedure regulation, which detail

requirements regarding the issuance of a notice of adverse benefit determination.[8] Moreover, for purposes of these interim final regulations, additional content requirements apply for these notices. A plan or issuer must ensure that any notice of adverse benefit determination or final internal adverse benefit determination includes information sufficient to identify the claim involved. This includes the date of service, the health care provider, and the claim amount (if applicable)[9], as well as the diagnosis code (such as an ICD–9 code, ICD–10 code, or DSM–IV code)[10], the treatment code (such as a CPT code)[11], and the corresponding meanings of these codes. A plan or issuer must also ensure that the reason or reasons for the adverse benefit determination or final internal adverse benefit determination includes the denial code (such as a CARC and RARC)[12] and its corresponding meaning. It must also include a description of the plan's or issuer's standard, if any, that was used in denying the claim (for example, if a plan applies a medical necessity standard in denying a claim, the notice must include a description of the medical necessity standard). In the case of a notice of final internal adverse benefit determination, this description must include a discussion of the decision. Additionally, the plan or issuer must provide a description of available internal appeals and external review processes, including information regarding how to initiate an appeal. Finally, the plan or issuer must disclose the availability of, and contact information for, any applicable office of health insurance consumer assistance or ombudsman established under PHS Act section 2793 to assist enrollees with the

---

[4] These regulations generally provide that a plan or issuer must not rescind coverage with respect to an individual once the individual is covered, except in the case of an act, practice, or omission that constitutes fraud, or an intentional misrepresentation of material fact, as prohibited by the terms of the plan or coverage.

[5] Under the DOL claims procedure regulation, a "claim involving urgent care" is a claim for medical care or treatment with respect to which the application of the time periods for making non-urgent care determinations could seriously jeopardize the life or health of the claimant or the ability of the claimant to regain maximum function; or, in the opinion of a physician with knowledge of the claimant's medical condition, would subject the claimant to severe pain that cannot be adequately managed without the care or treatment that is the subject of the claim.

[6] In the case of a failure to provide sufficient information, under the DOL claims procedure regulation the claimant must be notified as soon as possible, but not later than 24 hours after receipt of the claim, of the specific information necessary to complete the claim. The claimant must be afforded a reasonable amount of time, taking into account the circumstances, but not less than 48 hours, to provide the specified information.

[7] This language underscores and is not inconsistent with the scope of the disclosure requirement under the existing Department of Labor claims procedure regulation. That is, the Department of Labor interprets 29 USC 1133 and the DOL claims procedure regulation as already requiring that plans provide claimants with new or additional evidence or rationales upon request and an opportunity to respond in certain circumstances. See Brief of amicus curiae Secretary of the United States Department of Labor. Midgett v. Washington Group International Long Term Disability Plan, 561 F.3d 887 (8th Cir. 2009) (No.08–2523) (expressing disagreement with cases holding that there is no such requirement).

[8] Paragraph (g) of the DOL claims procedure regulation requires that the notice must be written in a manner calculated to be understood by the claimant and generally must include any specific reasons for the adverse determination, reference to the specific provision on which the determination is based, a description of any additional information required to perfect the claim, and a description of the internal appeal process. Paragraph (i) of the DOL claims procedure regulation requires that the notice must also be provided in accordance with specified timeframes for urgent care claims, pre-service claims, and post-service claims.

[9] The amount of the claim may not be knowable or available at the time, such as in a case of preauthorization, or there may be no specific claim, such as in a case of rescission.

[10] ICD–9 and ICD–10 codes refer to the International Classification of Diseases, 9th revision and 10th revision, respectively. The DSM–IV codes refer to the Diagnostic and Statistical Manual of Mental Disorders, Fourth Edition.

[11] CPT refers to Current Procedural Terminology.

[12] CARC refers to Claim Adjustment Reason Code and RARC refers to Remittance Advice Remark Code.

internal claims and appeals and external review processes. The Departments intend to issue model notices that could be used to satisfy all the notice requirements under these interim final regulations in the very near future. These notices will be made available at *http://www.dol.gov/ebsa* and *http://www.hhs.gov/ociio/*.

Sixth, these interim final regulations provide that, in the case of a plan or issuer that fails to strictly adhere to all the requirements of the internal claims and appeals process with respect to a claim, the claimant is deemed to have exhausted the internal claims and appeals process, regardless of whether the plan or issuer asserts that it substantially complied with these requirements or that any error it committed was de minimis. Accordingly, upon such a failure, the claimant may initiate an external review and pursue any available remedies under applicable law, such as judicial review.

In addition to the six new requirements, the statute and these interim final regulations require a plan and issuer to provide continued coverage pending the outcome of an internal appeal. For this purpose, the plan or issuer must comply with the requirements of the DOL claims procedure regulation, which, as applied under these interim final regulations, generally prohibits a plan or issuer from reducing or terminating an ongoing course of treatment without providing advance notice and an opportunity for advance review. Additionally, individuals in urgent care situations and individuals receiving an ongoing course of treatment may be allowed to proceed with expedited external review at the same time as the internal appeals process, under either a State external review process or the Federal external review process, in accordance with the Uniform Health Carrier External Review Model Act promulgated by the National Association of Insurance Commissioners (NAIC Uniform Model Act). The provision of the NAIC Uniform Model Act requiring simultaneous internal appeals and external review is discussed later in this preamble.

2. Health Insurance Issuers Offering Individual Health Insurance Coverage

The statute requires the Secretary of Health and Human Services to set forth processes for internal claims and appeals in the individual market. Under these interim final regulations, the Secretary of Health and Human Services has determined that a health insurance issuer offering individual health insurance coverage must generally

comply with all the requirements for the internal claims and appeals process that apply to group health coverage.[13] The process and protections of the group health coverage standards are also pertinent to the individual health insurance market. Furthermore, many issuers in the individual market also provide coverage in the group market. To facilitate compliance, it is preferable to have similar processes in the group and individual markets. Accordingly, an individual health insurance issuer is subject to the DOL claims procedure regulation as if the issuer were a group health plan. Moreover, an individual health insurance issuer must also comply with the additional standards in these interim final regulations imposed on group health insurance coverage.

To address certain relevant differences in the group and individual markets, health insurance issuers offering individual health insurance coverage must comply with three additional requirements. First, these interim final regulations expand the scope of the group health coverage internal claims and appeals process to cover initial eligibility determinations for individual health insurance coverage. This protection is important because eligibility determinations in the individual market are frequently based on the health status of the applicant, including preexisting conditions. With the prohibition against preexisting condition exclusions taking effect for policy years beginning on or after September 23, 2010 for children under 19 and for all others for policy years beginning on or after January 1, 2014, applicants in the individual market should have the opportunity for a review of a denial of eligibility of coverage to determine whether the issuer is complying with the new provisions in making the determination.

Second, although the DOL claims procedure regulation permits plans to have a second level of internal appeals, these interim final regulations require that health insurance issuers offering individual health insurance coverage have only one level of internal appeals. This allows the claimant to seek either external review or judicial review immediately after an adverse benefit determination is upheld in the first level of the internal appeals process. There is no need for a second level of an internal appeal in the individual market since

the issuer conducts all levels of the internal appeal, unlike in the group market, where a third party administrator may conduct the first level of the internal appeal and the employer may conduct a second level of the internal appeal. Accordingly, after an issuer has reviewed an adverse benefit determination once, the claimant should be allowed to seek external review of the determination by an outside entity.

Finally, these interim final regulations require health insurance issuers offering individual health insurance coverage to maintain records of all claims and notices associated with their internal claims and appeals processes. The records must be maintained for at least six years, which is the same requirement for group health plans under the ERISA recordkeeping requirements. An issuer must make such records available for examination upon request. Accordingly, a claimant or State or Federal agency official generally would be able to request and receive such documents free of charge. Other Federal and State law regarding disclosure of personally identifiable health information may apply, including the HIPAA privacy rule.[14]

c. State Standards for External Review

The statute and these interim final regulations provide that plans and issuers must comply with either a State external review process or the Federal external review process. These interim final regulations provide a basis for determining when plans and issuers must comply with an applicable State external review process and when they must comply with the Federal external review process.

For health insurance coverage, if a State external review process that applies to and is binding on an issuer includes, at a minimum, the consumer protections in the NAIC Uniform Model Act in place on July 23, 2010,[15] then the issuer must comply with the applicable State external review process and not with the Federal external review process. In such a case, to the extent that benefits under a group health plan are provided through health insurance

---

[13] The special rules in the DOL claims procedure regulation applicable only to multiemployer plans (generally defined in section 3(37) of ERISA as plans maintained pursuant to one or more collective bargaining agreements for the employees of two or more employers) do not apply to health insurance issuers in the individual market.

[14] *See* 45 CFR 164.500 *et seq.*

[15] These interim final regulations specify that the relevant NAIC Uniform Model Act is the version in place on the date these interim final regulations are published. If the NAIC Uniform Model Act is later modified, the Departments will review the changes and determine to what extent any additional requirements will be incorporated into the minimum standards for State external review processes by amending these regulations. This version of the NAIC Uniform Model Act is available at *http://www.dol.gov/ebsa* and *http://www.hhs.gov/ociio/*.

coverage, the issuer is required to satisfy the obligation to provide an external review process, so the plan itself is not required to comply with either the State external review process or the Federal external review process. The Departments encourage States to establish external review processes that meet the minimum consumer protections of the NAIC Uniform Model Act. The Departments prefer having States take the lead role in regulating health insurance issuers, with Federal enforcement only as a fallback measure.

These interim final regulations do not preclude a State external review process from applying to and being binding on a self-insured group health plan under some circumstances. While the preemption provisions of ERISA ordinarily would prevent a State external review process from applying directly to an ERISA plan, ERISA preemption does not prevent a State external review process from applying to some self-insured plans, such as nonfederal governmental plans and church plans not covered by ERISA preemption, and multiple employer welfare arrangements, which can be subject to both ERISA and State insurance laws. A State external review process could apply to such plans if the process includes, at a minimum, the consumer protections in the NAIC Uniform Model Act.

Under these interim final regulations, any plan or issuer not subject to a State external review process must comply with the Federal external review process. (However, to the extent a plan provides health insurance coverage that is subject to an applicable State external review process that provides the minimum consumer protections in the NAIC Uniform Model Act, the plan does not have to comply with the Federal external review process.) A plan or issuer is subject to the Federal external review process where the State external review process does not meet, at a minimum, the consumer protections in the NAIC Uniform Model Act, as well as where there is no applicable State external review process.

For a State external review process to apply instead of the Federal external review process, the Affordable Care Act provides that the State external review process must include, at a minimum, the consumer protections of the NAIC Uniform Model Act. Accordingly, the Departments have determined that the following elements from the NAIC Uniform Model Act are the minimum consumer protections that must be included for a State external review process to apply. The State process must:

• Provide for the external review of adverse benefit determinations (and final internal adverse benefit determinations) that are based on medical necessity, appropriateness, health care setting, level of care, or effectiveness of a covered benefit.

• Require issuers to provide effective written notice to claimants of their rights in connection with an external review for an adverse benefit determination.

• To the extent the State process requires exhaustion of an internal claims and appeals process, make exhaustion unnecessary if: the issuer has waived the exhaustion requirement, the claimant has exhausted (or is considered to have exhausted) the internal claims and appeals process under applicable law, or the claimant has applied for expedited external review at the same time as applying for an expedited internal appeal.

• Provide that the issuer against which a request for external review is filed must pay the cost of an independent review organization (IRO) for conducting the external review. While having the issuer pay the cost of the IRO's review is reflected in the NAIC Uniform Model Act, if the State pays this cost, the Departments would treat the State process as meeting this requirement; this alternative is just as protective to the consumer because the cost of the review is not imposed on the consumer. Notwithstanding this requirement that the issuer (or State) must pay the cost of the IRO's review, the State process may require a nominal filing fee from the claimant requesting an external review. For this purpose, to be considered nominal, a filing fee must not exceed $25, it must be refunded to the claimant if the adverse benefit determination is reversed through external review, it must be waived if payment of the fee would impose an undue financial hardship, and the annual limit on filing fees for any claimant within a single year must not exceed $75.

• Not impose a restriction on the minimum dollar amount of a claim for it to be eligible for external review (for example, a $500 minimum claims threshold).

• Allow at least four months after the receipt of a notice of an adverse benefit determination or final internal adverse benefit determination for a request for an external review to be filed.

• Provide that an IRO will be assigned on a random basis or another method of assignment that assures the independence and impartiality of the assignment process (for example, rotational assignment) by a State or

independent entity, and in no event selected by the issuer, plan, or individual.

• Provide for maintenance of a list of approved IROs qualified to conduct the review based on the nature of the health care service that is the subject of the review. The State process must provide for approval only of IROs that are accredited by a nationally recognized private accrediting organization.

• Provide that any approved IRO has no conflicts of interest that will influence its independence.

• Allow the claimant to submit to the IRO in writing additional information that the IRO must consider when conducting the external review and require that the claimant is notified of such right to do so. The process must also require that any additional information submitted by the claimant to the IRO must be forwarded to the issuer within one business day of receipt by the IRO.

• Provide that the decision is binding on the plan or issuer, as well as the claimant, except to the extent that other remedies are available under State or Federal law.

• Provide that, for standard external review, within no more than 45 days after the receipt of the request for external review by the IRO, the IRO must provide written notice to the issuer and the claimant of its decision to uphold or reverse the adverse benefit determination.

• Provide for an expedited external review in certain circumstances and, in such cases, the State process must provide notice of the decision as expeditiously as possible, but not later than 72 hours after the receipt of the request.

• Require that issuers include a description of the external review process in the summary plan description, policy, certificate, membership booklet, outline of coverage, or other evidence of coverage it provides to claimants, substantially similar to what is set forth in section 17 of the NAIC Uniform Model Act.

• Require that IROs maintain written records and make them available upon request to the State, substantially similar to what is set forth in section 15 of the NAIC Uniform Model Act.

• Follow procedures for external review of adverse benefit determinations involving experimental or investigational treatment, substantially similar to what is set forth in section 10 of the NAIC Uniform Model Act.

The Departments invite comments on this list of minimum consumer

43336   **Federal Register** / Vol. 75, No. 141 / Friday, July 23, 2010 / Rules and Regulations

protections and whether other elements of the NAIC Uniform Model Act should be included in the list.

The Department of Health and Human Services will determine whether a State external review process meets these requirements (and thus whether issuers (and, if applicable, plans) subject to the State external review process must comply with the State external review process rather than the Federal external review process). A transition period will be provided, however, during which existing State external review processes may be treated as satisfying these requirements.

Under PHS Act section 2719, if a State external review process does not provide the minimum consumer protections of the NAIC Uniform Model Act, health insurance issuers in the State must implement the Federal external review process. The Departments' initial review of existing State external review processes indicates that not all State external review processes provide the minimum consumer protections of the NAIC Uniform Model Act. Under PHS Act section 2719(c), the Departments are provided with discretion to consider an external review process in place on the date of enactment of the Affordable Care Act to be in compliance with the external review requirement under section 2719(b) "as determined appropriate." In order to allow States time to amend their laws to meet or go beyond the minimum consumer protections of the NAIC Uniform Model Act set forth in these interim final regulations, the Departments are using their authority under PHS Act section 2719(c) to treat existing State external review processes as meeting the minimum standards during a transition period for plan years (in the individual market, policy years) beginning before July 1, 2011.

Thus, for plan or policy years beginning before July 1, 2011, a health insurance issuer subject to an existing State external review process must comply with that State external review process and not the Federal external review process. The applicable external review process for plan or policy years beginning on or after July 1, 2011 depends on the type of coverage and whether the State external review process has been determined by the Department of Health and Human Services to satisfy the minimum standards of the NAIC Uniform Model Act.

The applicable external review process for any particular claim is based on the external review process applicable to the plan or issuer at the time a final internal adverse benefit determination (or, in the case of simultaneous internal appeals and external review, the adverse benefit determination) is provided. For this purpose, the final internal adverse benefit determination includes a deemed final internal adverse benefit determination in which the internal claims and appeals process is exhausted because of the failure by the plan or issuer to comply with the requirements of the internal claims and appeals process. Thus, for an issuer with a calendar year plan year in a State in which the State external review process fails to meet the minimum standards, external review of final internal adverse benefit determinations provided prior to the first day of the first calendar year on or after July 1, 2011 (that is, January 1, 2012) must comply with the State external review process, while external reviews of final internal adverse benefit determinations provided on or after January 1, 2012 must meet the alternative Federal external review requirements.

An additional provision of the NAIC Uniform Model Act not addressed in the interim final regulations is the required scope of an applicable State external review process. The NAIC Uniform Model Act applies to all issuers in a State. The Departments' initial review of existing State external review processes indicates that some States do not apply the State external review process to all issuers in the State. For example, some State external review processes only apply to HMOs and do not apply to other types of health coverage. The Departments believe that State external review processes are more effective, and thus more protective, where the external review process is market-wide and available to all claimants with insured coverage. As States with external review processes decide whether to enact legislation amending their laws to provide the consumer protections that would satisfy the requirements of these interim final regulations, the Departments encourage States to establish external review processes that are available for all insured health coverage. This is consistent with the Departments general approach of having States take a lead role in providing consumer protections, with Federal enforcement only as a fallback measure.

That said, these interim final regulations do not set a specific standard for availability of the State external review process that is considered to meet the minimum consumer protections of the NAIC Uniform Model Act. If it is determined that market-wide application of the State external review process is required, plans and issuers would be subject to the Federal external review process in States that do not apply the State external review process to all issuers in the State. Alternatively, if it is determined that universal availability is not required, those plans and issuers that are not subject to the State external review process would be, as are self-insured plans, subject to the Federal external review process. The Departments seek comments whether the Federal external review process should apply to all plans and issuers in a State if the State external review process does not apply to all issuers in the State. After reviewing the comments, the Departments expect to issue future guidance addressing the issue.

d. Federal External Review Process

PHS Act section 2719(b)(2) requires the Departments to establish standards, "through guidance," governing an external review process that is similar to the State external appeals process that meets the standards in these regulations. These interim final regulations set forth the scope of claims eligible for review under the Federal external review process. Specifically, under the Federal external review process, the terms "adverse benefit determination" and "final internal adverse benefit determination" are defined the same as they are for purposes of internal claims and appeals (and, thus, include rescissions of coverage). However, an adverse benefit determination or final internal adverse benefit determination that relates to a participant's or beneficiary's failure to meet the requirements for eligibility under the terms of a group health plan (i.e., worker classification and similar issues) is not within the scope of the Federal external review process.

These interim final regulations set forth the standards that would apply to claimants, plans, and issuers under this Federal external review process, and the substantive standards that would be applied under this process. They also reflect the statutory requirement that the process established through guidance from the Departments be similar to a State external review process that complies with the standards in these regulations. They also provide that the Federal external review process, like the State external review process, will provide for expedited external review and additional consumer protections with respect to external review for claims involving experimental or investigational treatment. The

Departments will address in sub-regulatory guidance how non-grandfathered self-insured group health plans that currently maintain an internal appeals process that otherwise meets the Federal external review standards may comply or be brought into compliance with the requirements of the new Federal external review process.

e. Culturally and Linguistically Appropriate

The statute and these interim final regulations require that notices of available internal claims and appeals and external review processes be provided in a culturally and linguistically appropriate manner. Plans and issuers are considered to provide relevant notices in a culturally and linguistically appropriate manner if notices are provided in a non-English language as described these interim final regulations.[16] Under these interim final regulations, the requirement to provide notices in a non-English language is based on thresholds of the number of people who are literate only in the same non-English language. In the group market, the threshold differs depending on the number of participants in the plan. For a plan that covers fewer than 100 participants at the beginning of a plan year, the threshold is 25 percent of all plan participants being literate only in the same non-English language. For a plan that covers 100 or more participants at the beginning of a plan year, the threshold is the lesser of 500 participants, or 10 percent of all plan participants, being literate only in the same non-English language. The thresholds are adapted from the Department of Labor's regulations regarding style and format for a summary plan description, at 29 CFR 2520.102–2(c). In the individual market, the threshold is 10 percent of the population residing in the county being literate only in the same non-English language.[17] The Department of Health and Human Services will publish guidance that issuers may consult to

---

[16] For internal claims involving urgent care (for which the claim is generally made by a health care provider), where paragraph (g) of the DOL claims procedure regulation permits an initial oral notice of determination must be made within 24 hours and follow-up in written or electronic notification within 3 days of the oral notification, it may not be reasonable, practicable, or appropriate to provide notice in a non-English language within 24 hours. In such situations, the requirement to provide notice in a culturally and linguistically appropriate manner is satisfied if the initial notice is provided in English and the follow-up notice is provided in the appropriate non-English language.

[17] The county-by-county approach is generally adapted from the approach used under the Medicare Advantage program.

establish these county level estimates on its Web site at *http://www.hhs.gov/ociio/* by September 23, 2010. The Department of Health and Human Services welcomes comments on whether the threshold should remain 10 percent and whether it should continue to be applied on a county-by-county basis.

If an applicable threshold is met, notice must be provided upon request in the non-English language with respect to which the threshold is met. In addition, the plan or issuer must also include a statement in the English versions of all notices, prominently displayed in the non-English language, offering the provision of such notices in the non-English language. Once a request has been made by a claimant, the plan or issuer must provide all subsequent notices to a claimant in the non-English language. In addition, to the extent the plan or issuer maintains a customer assistance process (such as a telephone hotline) that answers questions or provides assistance with filing claims and appeals, the plan or issuer must provide such assistance in the non-English language.

f. Secretarial Authority

The statute provides the Departments with the authority to deem an external review process of a group health plan or health insurance issuer, in operation as of March 23, 2010, to be in compliance with PHS Act section 2719. These interim final regulations provide the Departments may determine that the external review process of a plan or issuer, in operation as of March 23, 2010, is considered in compliance with a State external review process or the Federal external review process, as applicable.

g. Applicability Date

The requirements to implement effective internal and external claims and appeals processes apply for plan years (in the individual market, policy years) beginning on or after September 23, 2010. The statute and these interim final regulations do not apply to grandfathered health plans. *See* 26 CFR 54.9815–1251T, 29 CFR 2590.715–1251, and 45 CFR 147.140 (75 FR 34538, June 17, 2010).

III. Interim Final Regulations and Request for Comments

Section 9833 of the Code, section 734 of ERISA, and section 2792 of the PHS Act authorize the Secretaries of the Treasury, Labor, and HHS (collectively, the Secretaries) to promulgate any interim final rules that they determine are appropriate to carry out the

provisions of chapter 100 of the Code, part 7 of subtitle B of title I of ERISA, and part A of title XXVII of the PHS Act, which include PHS Act sections 2701 through 2728 and the incorporation of those sections into ERISA section 715 and Code section 9815.

In addition, under Section 553(b) of the Administrative Procedure Act (APA) (5 U.S.C. 551 *et seq.*) a general notice of proposed rulemaking is not required when an agency, for good cause, finds that notice and public comment thereon are impracticable, unnecessary, or contrary to the public interest. The provisions of the APA that ordinarily require a notice of proposed rulemaking do not apply here because of the specific authority granted by section 9833 of the Code, section 734 of ERISA, and section 2792 of the PHS Act. However, even if the APA were applicable, the Secretaries have determined that it would be impracticable and contrary to the public interest to delay putting the provisions in these interim final regulations in place until a full public notice and comment process was completed. As noted above, the internal claims and appeals and external review provisions of the Affordable Care Act are applicable for plan years (in the individual market, policy years) beginning on or after September 23, 2010, six months after date of enactment. Had the Departments published a notice of proposed rulemaking, provided for a 60-day comment period, and only then prepared final regulations, which would be subject to a 60-day delay in effective date, it is unlikely that it would have been possible to have final regulations in effect before late September, when these requirements could be in effect for some plans or policies. Moreover, the requirements in these interim final regulations require significant lead time in order to implement. These interim final regulations require plans and issuers to provide internal claims and appeals and external review processes and to notify participants, beneficiaries, and enrollees of their rights to such processes. Plans and issuers will presumably need to amend current internal claims and appeals procedures, adopt new external review processes, and notify participants, beneficiaries, and enrollees of these changes before they go into effect. Moreover, group health plans and health insurance issuers subject to these provisions will have to take these changes into account in establishing their premiums, and in making other changes to the designs of plan or policy benefits. In some cases, issuers will need time to secure approval for these changes in advance of the plan or policy year in question.

Accordingly, in order to allow plans and health insurance coverage to be designed and implemented on a timely basis, regulations must be published and available to the public well in advance of the effective date of the requirements of the Affordable Care Act. It is not possible to have a full notice and comment process and to publish final regulations in the brief time between enactment of the Affordable Care Act and the date regulations are needed.

The Secretaries further find that issuance of proposed regulations would not be sufficient because the provisions of the Affordable Care Act protect significant rights of plan participants and beneficiaries and individuals covered by individual health insurance policies and it is essential that participants, beneficiaries, insureds, plan sponsors, and issuers have certainty about their rights and responsibilities. Proposed regulations are not binding and cannot provide the necessary certainty. By contrast, the interim final regulations provide the public with an opportunity for comment, but without delaying the effective date of the regulations.

For the foregoing reasons, the Departments have determined that it is impracticable and contrary to the public interest to engage in full notice and comment rulemaking before putting these interim final regulations into effect, and that it is in the public interest to promulgate interim final regulations.

IV. Economic Impact and Paperwork Burden

A. Summary—Department of Labor and Department of Health and Human Services

As stated earlier in this preamble, these interim final regulations implement PHS Act section 2719, which sets forth rules with respect to internal claims and appeals and external appeals processes for group health plans and health insurance issuers that are not grandfathered health plans.[18] This provision generally is effective for plan years (in the individual market, policy years) beginning on or after September 23, 2010. which is six months after the March 23, 2010 date of enactment of the Affordable Care Act.

The Departments have crafted these interim final regulations to secure the protections intended by Congress in the most economically efficient manner possible. In accordance with OMB Circular A–4, the Departments have quantified the benefits and costs where possible and provided a qualitative discussion of some of the benefits and costs that may stem from these interim final regulations.

B. Executive Order 12866—Department of Labor and Department of Health and Human Services

Under Executive Order 12866 (58 FR 51735), "significant" regulatory actions are subject to review by the Office of Management and Budget (OMB). Section 3(f) of the Executive Order defines a "significant regulatory action" as an action that is likely to result in a rule (1) Having an annual effect on the economy of $100 million or more in any one year, or adversely and materially affecting a sector of the economy, productivity, competition, jobs, the environment, public health or safety, or State, local or tribal governments or communities (also referred to as "economically significant"); (2) creating a serious inconsistency or otherwise interfering with an action taken or planned by another agency; (3) materially altering the budgetary impacts of entitlement grants, user fees, or loan programs or the rights and obligations of recipients thereof; or (4) raising novel legal or policy issues arising out of legal mandates, the President's priorities, or the principles set forth in the Executive Order. OMB has determined that this rule is significant within the meaning of section 3(f)(1) of the Executive Order, because it is likely to have an effect on the economy of $100 million in any one year. Accordingly, OMB has reviewed these rules pursuant to the Executive Order. The Departments provide an assessment of the potential costs and benefits of each regulatory provision below, summarized in table 1.

TABLE 1—ACCOUNTING TABLE

Benefits:

Qualitative: A more uniform, rigorous, and consumer friendly system of claims and appeals processing will provide a broad range of direct and indirect benefits that will accrue to varying degrees to all of the affected parties. These interim final regulations could improve the extent to which employee benefit plans provide benefits consistent with the established terms of individual plans. While payment of these benefits will largely constitute transfers, the transfers will be welfare improving, because incorrectly denied benefits will be paid. Greater certainty and consistency in the handling of benefit claims and appeals and improved access to information about the manner in which claims and appeals are adjudicated should lead to efficiency gains in the system, both in terms of the allocation of spending across plans and enrollees as well as operational efficiencies among individual plans. This certainty and consistency can also be expected to benefit, to varying degrees, all parties within the system, particularly consumers, and to lead to broader social welfare gains.

	Estimate	Year dollar	Discount rate	Period covered
Costs:				
Annualized Monetized ($millions/year)	51.2	2010	7%	2011–2013
	51.6	2010	3%	2011–2013

Qualitative: The Departments have quantified the primary source of costs associated with these interim final regulations that will be incurred to (i) administer and conduct the internal and external review process, (ii) prepare and distribute required disclosures and notices, and (iii) bring plan and issuers' internal and external claims and appeals procedures into compliance with the new requirements. The Departments also have quantified the start-up costs for issuers in the individual market to bring themselves into compliance.

Reversals:				
Annualized Monetized ($millions/year)	24.4	2010	7%	2011–2013

---

[18] The Affordable Care Act adds Section 715 to the Employee Retirement Income Security Act (ERISA) and section 9815 to the Internal Revenue Code (the Code) to make the provisions of part A of title XXVII of the PHS Act applicable to group health plans, and health insurance issuers providing health insurance coverage in connection with group health plans, under ERISA and the Code as if those provisions of the PHS Act were included in ERISA and the Code.

	Estimate	Year dollar	Discount rate	Period covered
	24.7	2010	3%	2011–2013

Qualitative: The Departments estimated the dollar amount of claim denials reversed in the external review process. While this amount is a cost to plans, it represents a payment of benefits that should have previously been paid to participants, but was denied. Part of this amount is a transfer from plans and issuers to those now receiving payment for denied benefits. These transfers will improve equity, because incorrectly denied benefits will be paid. Part of the amount could also be a cost if the reversal leads to services and hence resources being utilized now that had been denied previously. The Departments are not able to distinguish between the two types, but believe that most reversals are associated with a transfer.

1. Need for Regulatory Action

Before the enactment of the Affordable Care Act, health plan sponsors and issuers were not uniformly required to implement claims and appeals processes. For example, ERISA-covered group health plan sponsors were required to implement internal claims and appeal processes that complied with the DOL claims procedure regulation,[19] while group health plans that were not covered by ERISA, such as plans sponsored by State and local governments were not. Health insurance issuers offering coverage in the individual insurance market were required to comply with various applicable State internal appeals laws but were not required to comply with the DOL claims procedure regulation.

With respect to external appeal processes, before the enactment of the Affordable Care Act, sponsors of fully-insured ERISA-covered group health plans, fully-insured State and local governmental plans, and fully-insured church plans were required to comply with State external review laws, while self-insured ERISA-covered group health plans were not subject to such laws due to ERISA preemption.[20] In the individual health insurance market, issuers in States with external review laws were required to comply with such laws. However, uniform external review standards did not apply, because State external review laws vary from State-to-State. Moreover, at least six States did not have external review laws when the Affordable Care Act was enacted; therefore, issuers in those States were not required to implement an external review process.

Under this regulatory system, inconsistent claims and appeals processes applied to plan sponsors and

issuers and a patchwork of consumer protections were provided to participants, beneficiaries, and enrollees. The applicable processes and protections depended on several factors including whether (i) Plans were subject to ERISA, (ii) benefits were self-funded or financed by the purchase of an insurance policy, (iii) issuers were subject to State internal claims and appeals laws, and (iv) issuers were subject to State external review laws, and if so, the scope of such laws (such as, whether the laws only apply to one segment of the health insurance market, e.g., managed care or HMO coverage). These uneven protections created an appearance of unfairness, increased cost for issuers and plans operating in multiple States, and may have led to confusion among consumers about their rights.

Congress enacted new PHS Act section 2719 to ensure that plans and issuers implemented more uniform internal and external claims and appeals processes and to set a minimum standard of consumer protections that are available to participants, beneficiaries, and enrollees. These interim final regulations are necessary to provide rules that plan sponsors and issuers can use to implement effective internal and external claims and appeals processes that meet the requirements of new PHS Act section 2719.

2. PHS Act Section 2719—Claims and Appeals Process (26 CFR 54.9815–2719T, 29 CFR 2590.715–2719, 45 CFR 147.136)

a. Summary

As discussed earlier in this preamble, section 1001 of the Affordable Care Act adds new PHS Act section 2719, which requires all non-grandfathered group health plans and health insurance issuers offering group or individual health coverage to implement uniform internal claims and appeals and external appeals processes. Under PHS Act section 2719 and these interim final regulations, all sponsors of non-grandfathered group health plans and health insurance issuers offering group or individual health insurance coverage

must comply with all requirements of the DOL claims procedures regulation[21] as well as the new standards that are established by the Secretary of Labor and the Secretary of Health and Human Services in paragraphs (b)(2) and (b)(3) of these interim final regulations.

On the external appeals side, all group health plans or health insurance issuers offering group or individual health insurance coverage that are not grandfathered must comply with an applicable State external review process that, at a minimum, includes the consumer protections set forth in the Uniform Heath Carrier External Review Model Act promulgated by the National Association of Insurance Commissioners (the "NAIC Uniform Model Act") and is binding on the plan or issuer. If the State has not established an external review process that meets the requirements of the NAIC Uniform Model Act or a plan is not subject to State insurance regulation, (including a State law that establishes an external review process) because it is a self-insured plan, the plan or issuer must comply with the requirements of a Federal external review process set forth in paragraph (d) of these interim final regulations.

b. Estimated Number of Affected Entities

For purposes of the new requirements in the Affordable Care Act that apply to group health plans and health insurance issuers in the group and individual markets, the Departments have defined a large group health plan as an employer plan with 100 or more workers and a small group plan as an employer plan with fewer than 100 workers. The Departments make the following estimates about plans and issuers affected by these interim final regulations: (1) There are approximately 72,000 large and 2.8 million small ERISA-covered group health plans with

---

[19] 29 CFR 2560.503–1.

[20] To the extent that the ERISA preemption provisions do not prevent a State external review process from applying to a self-insured plan (for example, for self-insured nonfederal governmental plans, self-insured church plans, and self-insured multiple employer welfare arrangements) the State could make its external review process applicable to them. The Departments are unaware of the number of these plans that are subject to State external review laws.

[21] Please note that under these interim final regulations, the individual health insurance market is not required to comply with the requirements of the Department of Labor's claims and appeals procedure regulation that apply to multiemployer plans.

an estimated 97.0 million participants in large group plans and 40.9 million participants in small group plans;[22] (2) there are 126,000 governmental plans with 36.1 million participants in large plans and 2.3 million participants in small plans;[23] and (3) there are 16.7 million individuals under age 65 covered by individual health insurance policies.[24]

As described in the Departments' interim final regulations relating to status as a grandfathered health plan,[25] the Affordable Care Act preserves the ability of individuals to retain coverage under a group health plan or health insurance coverage in which the individual was enrolled on March 23, 2010 (a grandfathered health plan). Group health plans and individual health insurance coverage that are grandfathered health plans do not have to meet the requirements of these interim final regulations. Therefore, only plans and issuers offering group and individual health insurance coverage that are not grandfathered health plans will be affected by these interim final regulations.

Plans can choose to make certain disqualifying changes and relinquish their grandfather status.[26] The Affordable Care Act provides plans with the ability to maintain grandfathered status in order to promote stability for consumers while allowing plans and sponsors to make reasonable adjustments to lower costs and encourage the efficient use of services. Based on an analysis of the changes plans have made over the past few years, the Departments expect that more plans will choose to make these changes over time and therefore the number of grandfathered health plans is expected to decrease. Correspondingly, the number of plans and policies affected by these interim final regulations is likely to increase over time. In addition, the number of individuals receiving the full benefits of the Affordable Care Act is likely to increase over time. The Departments estimate that 18 percent of large employer plans and 30 percent of small employer plans would relinquish grandfather status in 2011, increasing over time to 45 percent and 66 percent respectively by 2013, although there is

substantial uncertainty surrounding these estimates.[27] The Departments also estimate that in 2011, roughly 31 million people will be enrolled in group health plans subject to PHS Act section 2719 and these interim final regulations, growing to approximately 78 million in 2013.[28]

In the individual market, one study estimated that 40 percent to 67 percent of individual policies terminate each year.[29] Because newly purchased individual policies are not grandfathered, the Departments expect that a large proportion of individual policies will not be grandfathered, covering up to and perhaps exceeding 10 million individuals.

Not all potentially affected individuals will be affected equally by these interim final regulations. As stated in the Need for Regulatory Action section above, sponsors of ERISA-covered group health plans were required to implement an internal appeals process that complied with the DOL claims procedure regulation before the Affordable Care Act's enactment, and the Departments also understand that many non-Federal governmental plans and church plans that are not subject to ERISA nonetheless implement internal claims and appeals processes that comply with the DOL claims procedure regulation.[30] Therefore,

[27] See 75 FR 34538 (June 17, 2010) for a detailed description of the derivation of the estimates for the percentages of grandfathered health plans. In brief, the Departments used data from the 2008 and 2009 Kaiser Family Foundations/Health Research and Educational Trust survey of employers to estimate the proportion of plans that made changes in cost-sharing requirements that would have caused them to relinquish grandfather status if those same changes were made in 2011, and then applied a set of assumptions about how employer behavior might change in response to the incentives created by the grandfather regulations to estimate the proportion of plans likely to relinquish grandfather status. The estimates of changes in 2012 and 2013 were calculated by using the 2011 calculations and assuming that an identical percentage of plan sponsors will relinquish grandfather status in each year.

[28] To estimate the number of individuals covered in grandfathered health plans, the Departments extended the analysis described in 75 FR 34538, and estimated a weighted average of the number of employees in grandfathered health plans in the large employer and small employer markets separately, weighting by the number of employees in each employer's plan. Estimates for the large employer and small employer markets were then combined, using the estimates supplied above that there are 133.1 million covered lives in the large group market, and 43.2 million in the small group market.

[29] Adele M. Kirk. The Individual Insurance Market: A Building Block for Health Care Reform? *Health Care Financing Organization Research Synthesis.* May 2008.

[30] This understanding is based on the Departments' conversations with industry experts. In addition, the Departments understand that ERISA-covered plans, State and local government

participants and beneficiaries covered by such plans only will be affected by the new internal claims and appeals standards that are provided by the Secretary of Labor in paragraph (b)(2)(ii) of these interim final regulations.

These interim final regulations will have the largest impact on individuals covered in the individual health insurance market, because as discussed earlier in this preamble, for the first time, these issuers will be required to comply with the DOL claims procedure regulation for internal claims and appeals as well as the additional standards added by the Secretary of the Department of Health and Human Services in paragraph (b)(3) of these interim final regulations that are in some cases more protective than the ERISA standard.[31]

On the external appeals side, before the enactment of the Affordable Care Act, issuers offering coverage in the group and individual health insurance market already were required to comply with State external review laws. At that time, all States except Alabama, Mississippi, Nebraska, North Dakota, South Dakota, and Wyoming had external review laws, and thirteen States had external review laws that apply only to certain market segments (for example, managed care or HMOs). Therefore, the extent to which enrollees covered by policies issued by these issuers will be affected by these interim final regulations depends on whether the applicable State external review law complies with the minimum consumer protections set forth in the NAIC Uniform Model Act, because if it does not, the policies will become subject to the Federal external review process that applies to self-insured plans that are not subject to State regulation[32] and plans

plans, and non-ERISA covered church plans generally use the same insurance issuers and service providers who apply the ERISA claims and appeals requirements to all types of plans.

[31] To address certain relevant differences in the group and individual markets, health insurance issuers offering individual health insurance coverage must comply with the following three additional requirements: (1) Expand the scope of the claims and appeals process to cover initial eligibility determinations; (2) provide only one level of internal appeal (although the DOL claims procedure regulation permits group health plans to have a second level of internal appeals), which allows claimants to seek either an external appeal or judicial review immediately after an adverse determination is upheld in the first level of internal appeal; and (3) maintain records of all claims and notices associated with their internal claims and appeals processes and make such records available for examination upon request by claimants and Federal or State regulatory officials.

[32] To the extent that the ERISA preemption provisions do not prevent a State external review process from applying to a self-insured plan (for example, for self-insured nonfederal governmental plans, self-insured church plans, and self-insured

[22] All participant counts and the estimates of individual policies are from the U.S. Department of Labor, EBSA calculations using the March 2009 Current Population Survey Annual Social and Economic Supplement and the 2008 Medical Expenditure Panel Survey.

[23] Estimate is from the 2007 Census of Government.

[24] U.S. Census Bureau, Current Population Survey, March 2009.

[25] 75 FR 34538 (June 17, 2010).

[26] See 75 FR 34538 (June 17, 2010).

and policies in States that do not have external review laws that meet the minimum consumer protections set forth in the NAIC Uniform Model Act.

Individuals participating in ERISA-covered self-insured group health plans will be among those most affected by the external review requirements contained in these interim final regulations, because the preemption provisions of ERISA prevent a State's external review process from applying directly to an ERISA-covered self-insured plan.[33] These plans now will be required to comply with the Federal external review process set forth under paragraph (d) of these interim final regulations.

In summary, the number of affected individuals depends on several factors, including whether (i) a health plan retains its grandfather status, (ii) the plan is subject to ERISA, (iii) benefits provided under the plan are self-funded or financed by the purchase of an insurance policy, (iii) the applicable State has enacted an internal claims and appeals law, and (iv) the applicable State has enacted an external review law, and if so the scope of such law, and (v) the number of new plans and enrollees in such plans.

c. Benefits

In developing these interim final regulations, the Departments closely considered their potential economic effects, including both costs and benefits. Because of data limitations and a lack of effective measures, the Departments did not attempt to quantify expected benefits. Nonetheless, the Departments were able to identify with confidence several of the interim final regulation's major economic benefits.

These interim final regulations will help transform the current, highly variable health claims and appeals process into a more uniform and structured process. As stated in the Need for Regulatory Action above, before the enactment of the Affordable Care Act, inconsistent internal and external claims and appeals standards applied to plan sponsors and issuers, and a patchwork of consumer protections were provided to participants, beneficiaries, and enrollees that depended on several factors including whether (i) Plans were subject

to ERISA, (ii) benefits were self-funded or financed by the purchase of an insurance policy, (iii) issuers were subject to State internal claims and appeals laws, and (iv) issuers were subject to State external review laws, and if so, the scope of such laws (such as, whether the laws only apply to one segment of the health insurance market, e.g., managed care or HMO coverage).

A more uniform, rigorous, and consumer friendly system of claims and appeals processing will provide a broad range of direct and indirect benefits that will accrue to varying degrees to all of the affected parties. In general, the Departments expect that these interim final regulations will improve the extent to which employee benefit plans provide benefits consistent with the established terms of individual plans. This will cause some participants to receive benefits that, absent the fuller protections of the regulation, they might otherwise have been incorrectly denied. In other circumstances, expenditures by plans may be reduced as a fuller and fairer system of claims and appeals processing helps facilitate enrollee acceptance of cost management efforts. Greater certainty and consistency in the handling of benefit claims and appeals and improved access to information about the manner in which claims and appeals are adjudicated may lead to efficiency gains in the system, both in terms of the allocation of spending at a macro-economic level as well as operational efficiencies among individual plans. This certainty and consistency can also be expected to benefit, to varying degrees, all parties within the system and to lead to broader social welfare gains, particularly for consumers.

By making claims and appeals processes more uniform, these interim final regulations will increase efficiency in the operation of employee benefit plans and health care delivery as well as health insurance and labor markets. These interim final regulations are expected to increase efficiency by reducing complexity that arises when different market segments are subject to varying claims and appeals standards. Idiosyncratic requirements, time-frames, and procedures for claims processing impose substantial burdens on participants, their representatives, and service providers. By establishing a more uniform and complete set of minimum requirements and consumer protections, these interim final regulations will reduce the complexity of claims and appeals processing requirements, thereby increasing efficiency.

The Departments expect that these interim final regulations also will improve the efficiency of health plans by enhancing their transparency and fostering participants' confidence in their fairness. When information about the terms and conditions under which benefits will be provided is unavailable to enrollees, they could discount the value of benefits to compensate for the perceived risk. The enhanced disclosure and notice requirements of these interim final regulations will help participants, beneficiaries, and enrollees better understand the reasons underlying adverse benefit determinations and their appeal rights.

The Departments believe that excessive delays and inappropriate denials of health benefits are relatively rare. Most claims are approved in a timely fashion. Many claim denials and delays are appropriate given the plan's terms and the circumstances at hand. Nonetheless, to the extent that delays and inappropriate denials occur, substantial harm can be suffered by participants, beneficiaries, and enrollees, which can also lead to an associated loss of confidence in the fairness and benefits of the system. A more timely and complete review process required under these interim final rules regulations should reduce the levels of delay and error in the system and improve health outcomes.

The voluntary nature of the employment-based health benefit system in conjunction with the open and dynamic character of labor markets make explicit as well as implicit negotiations on compensation a key determinant of the prevalence of employee benefits coverage. The prevalence of benefits is therefore largely dependent on the efficacy of this exchange. If workers perceive that there is the potential for inappropriate denial of benefits or handling of appeals, they will discount the value of such benefits to adjust for this risk. This discount drives a wedge in compensation negotiation, limiting its efficiency. With workers unwilling to bear the full cost of the benefit, fewer benefits will be provided. To the extent that workers perceive that these interim final regulations, supported by enforcement authority, reduces the risk of inappropriate denials of benefits, the differential between the employers' costs and workers' willingness to accept wage offsets is minimized.

Effective claims procedures also can improve health care, health plan quality, and insurance market efficiency by serving as a communication channel, providing feedback from participants, beneficiaries, and providers to plans

multiple employer welfare arrangements) the State could make its external review process applicable to such plans if it includes, at a minimum, the consumer protections in the NAIC Uniform Model Act.

[33] While it is possible that some ERISA-covered self-insured plans may have adopted external review procedures as a matter of good business practice, the Departments are uncertain regarding the level to which this has occurred.

43342 **Federal Register**/Vol. 75, No. 141/Friday, July 23, 2010/Rules and Regulations

about quality issues. Aggrieved claimants are especially likely to disenroll if they do not understand their appeal rights, or if they believe that their plans' claims and appeals procedures will not effectively resolve their difficulties. Unlike appeals, however, disenrollments fail to alert plans to the difficulties that prompted them. More uniform and effective appeals procedures can give participants and beneficiaries an alternative way to respond to difficulties with their plans. Plans in turn can use the information gleaned from the appeals process to improve services.

The Departments also expect that these interim final regulations' higher standard for more uniform internal and external claims appeals adjudication will enhance some insurers' and group health plans' abilities to effectively control costs by limiting access to inappropriate care. Providing a more formally sanctioned framework for internal and external review and consultation on difficult claims facilitates the adoption of cost containment programs by employers who, in the absence of a regulation providing some guidance, may have opted to pay questionable claims rather than risk alienating participants or being deemed to have breached a fiduciary duty.

In summary, the interim final regulations' more uniform standards for handling health benefit claims and appeals will reduce the incidence of excessive delays and inappropriate denials, averting serious, avoidable lapses in health care quality and resultant injuries and losses to participant, beneficiaries and enrollees. They also will enhance enrollees' level of confidence in and satisfaction with their health care benefits and improve plans' awareness of participant, beneficiary, and provider concerns, prompting plan responses that improve health care quality. Finally, by helping to ensure prompt and precise adherence to contract terms and by improving the flow of information between plans and enrollees, the interim final regulations will bolster the efficiency of labor, health care, and insurance markets. The Departments therefore conclude that the economic benefits of these interim final regulations will justify their costs.

d. Costs and Transfers

The Departments have quantified the primary source of costs associated with these interim final regulations that will be incurred to (i) Administer and conduct the internal and external review process, (ii) prepare and distribute required disclosures and

notices, and (iii) bring plan and issuers' internal and external claims and appeals procedures into compliance with the new requirements. The Departments also have quantified the start-up costs for issuers in the individual market to bring themselves into compliance and the costs and the transfers associated with the reversal of denied claims during the external review process. These costs and the methodology used to estimate them are discussed below.

i. *Internal Claims and Appeals.* As discussed above, these interim final regulations require all group health plans and issuers offering coverage in the group and individual health insurance market to comply with the DOL claims procedure regulation. The ERISA-covered market, with an estimated 2.8 million plans and 138 million covered participants, already is required to comply with the DOL claims procedure regulation and is far larger than either the non-Federal governmental plan market, with an estimated 126,000 governmental plans and 30 million participants, or the individual market, with 16.7 million participants. As stated in the Estimated Number of Affected Entities section, the Departments understand that many non-Federal governmental plans comply with the DOL claims procedure regulation, because they use the same issuers and service providers as ERISA-covered plans, and these issuers and service providers implement the internal claims and appeals process for plans in both markets. Therefore, for purposes of this regulatory impact analysis, the Departments assume that 90 percent of the claims volume in the non-Federal governmental group health plan market already complies with the DOL claims procedure regulation.[34]

The Departments estimate that 170 issuers offer policies only in the individual market.[35] While the Departments believe that some issuers are subject to applicable state laws governing internal appeals processes, and have evidence that some issuers already comply with the DOL claims procedure regulation, some issuers will have to change their internal claims and

appeals processes to comply with these interim final regulations.[36] The Departments estimate that issuers would incur a start-up cost of $3.5 million in the first year to comply with these interim final regulations by revising processes, creating or revising forms, modifying systems, and training personnel. These costs are mitigated by the model notice of initial benefit determination the Departments will be issuing in subregulatory guidance. This notice will not require any data to be provided that cannot be automatically populated by plans and issuers.

ii. *Cost Required to Implement DOL Claims Procedure Regulation Requirements.* The Departments' estimates of the annual costs for plans and issuers to comply with the DOL claims procedure regulation are based on the methodology used for the Paperwork Reduction Act (PRA) hour and cost burden analysis of DOL claims procedure regulation.[37] The Department first estimated the number of individuals covered by non-grandfathered plans using the March 2009 Current Population Survey Annual Social and Economic Supplement and the 2008 Medical Expenditure Panel Survey. Each covered individual was estimated to generate 10.2 claims on average per year,[38] 82 percent of which were filed electronically.[39] The Departments then assumed that 15 percent of these claims were denied.[40] The Departments assume that three percent of these claims were pre-service with the remaining being post-service claims.[41] The number of post-service claims extended was based on the share

<hr/>

[34] The Departments are uncertain regarding the 90 percent compliance rate for State and local government plans. Therefore, to establish a range, the Departments estimated the cost assuming 75 percent State and local governmental plan compliance. Assuming 75 percent compliance, the cost of State and local plan internal review compliance would increase from $2 million to $5 million in 2011, $3.6 million to $9.1 million in 2012, and $5 million to $12.4 million in 2012.

[35] Source: Estimates are from NAIC 2007 financial statements data and the California Department of Managed Healthcare (2009) (*http:// wpso.dmhc.ca.gov/hpsearch/viewall.aspx*).

[36] Discussions with the National Association of Insurance Commissioners suggest that three States require issuers in the individual market to follow the NAIC internal grievance appeals model. Eleven States have no set procedures in place, while the rest have varying requirements. Some issuers voluntarily follow the ERISA claims and appeals procedures.

[37] The OMB Control Number for the DOL procedure regulation is 1210–0053. OMB approved the three-year renewal of the Control Number through May 31, 2013, on May 21, 2010.

[38] Research at the time of the Claims Regulation as well as responses to the Claims RFI reported a wide range of claims per participant—between 5 and 18. The Department eventually settled on 10.2.

[39] AHIP, "Update: A Survey of Health Care Claims Receipt and Processing Times, 2009," January 2010.

[40] Health Insurance Association of America (HIAA, which later merged with AHIP) reported a denial rate of 14 percent in "Results from an HIAA Survey on Claims Payment Process," March 2003. These included duplicate claims as well as denied claims that were appeals. RAND reported an increased trend in claim denials in, "Inside the Black Box of Managed Care Decisions," Research Brief, 2004 from 3 percent to between 8 and 10 percent.

[41] The assumption that 3 percent of claims are pre-service is based on comments the Department received in response to the proposed DOL claims procedure regulation in 2000.

of "clean" claims that took more than 30 days to complete processing.[42] The share of denials expected to be appealed, 0.2 percent, was based on a RAND study.[43] The Departments expect half of these appeals to be reversed,[44] and those not reversed were divided between "medical claims" (28.9 percent) and "administrative claims" (71.1 percent).

The Departments attributed costs to notifying individuals of denied claims and processing appeals. Initial denials were assumed to only take a few minutes for a clerical worker to draft and send an adverse benefit determination notice based on the model notice that will be issued by the Departments that does not require any information to be included that cannot be auto-populated. Appealed denials deemed "medical" are assumed to require a physician, with an estimated labor rate of $154.07 to review and was expected to take 4 ½ hours to decide and draft a response, regardless of outcome.[45] Appealed denials deemed "administrative" require a legal professional with an estimated labor rate of $119.03, and a decision and response was expected to take two minutes for a reversal and two hours for a denial.[46] Mailing costs for the notice of adverse determination and notice of decision of internal appeal is estimated at 54 cents a notice for material, printing, and postage costs.

Because ERISA-covered plans already are required to comply with the DOL claims procedure regulation, the Departments did not attribute any cost to these plans to comply with the rule. As stated above, the Departments understand from consulting with industry experts that a substantial majority of State and local government plans also currently comply with the existing DOL claims procedure regulation; therefore, the Departments assumed that only ten percent of the estimated claims of individuals covered by these plans would constitute a new expense. All claims in non-grandfathered plans in the individual market were assumed to bear the full cost of compliance, because these policies are being required to comply with the DOL claims procedure regulation for the first time. Table 2 shows the estimated number of claims.

TABLE 2—ESTIMATED CLAIMS AND APPEALS IN NON-GRANDFATHERED COVERAGE

	2011			2012			2013		
	Private sector ESI	Govern-ment sec-tor ESI	Individual market	Private sector ESI	Govern-ment sec-tor ESI	Individual market	Private sector ESI	Govern-ment sec-tor ESI	Individual market
Total Enrollees (millions)	138.0	39.0	15.1	138.0	39.0	15.1	138.0	39.0	15.1
Non-Grandfathered Enrollees	24.4	6.9	6.0	44.5	12.6	9.7	61.0	17.2	11.8
Total Claims (millions)	248.9	70.4	61.5	453.8	128.3	98.5	622.4	175.9	120.6
Pre-Service:									
Claim Approved	6.3	1.8	1.6	11.6	3.3	2.5	15.9	4.5	3.1
Claim Denied	1.1	0.3	0.3	2.0	0.6	0.4	2.8	0.8	0.5
Post-Service:									
Claims Approved	196.2	55.5	45.2	357.8	101.1	72.3	490.7	138.7	88.6
Claim Denied	36.2	10.2	9.0	66.0	18.7	14.3	90.6	25.6	17.6
Claim Extended	9.0	2.5	5.6	16.4	4.6	8.9	22.5	6.3	10.9
Total Internal Appeals (thousands)	85.4	24.1	52.8	155.7	44.0	84.5	213.6	60.4	103.5
Appeals Upheld	34.2	9.7	21.1	62.3	17.6	33.8	85.4	24.1	41.4
Appeals Denied	51.2	14.5	31.7	93.4	26.4	50.7	128.1	36.2	62.1
Medical subtotal	24.7	7.0	15.3	45.0	12.7	24.4	61.7	17.4	29.9
Appeals Upheld	9.9	2.8	6.1	18.0	5.1	9.8	24.7	7.0	12.0
Appeals Denied	14.8	4.2	9.2	27.0	7.6	14.6	37.0	10.5	17.9
Administrative subtotal	60.7	17.2	37.5	110.7	31.3	60.1	151.8	42.9	73.6
Appeals Upheld	24.3	6.9	15.0	44.3	12.5	24.0	60.7	17.2	29.4
Appeals Denied	36.4	10.3	22.5	66.4	18.8	36.0	91.1	25.8	44.1
Total New External Appeals (thousands)	2.0	0.6	0.2	3.7	1.1	0.3	5.0	1.5	0.4

As shown in Table 3 below, the Departments estimate that the cost of the internal process, including the costs of internal appeals and notice distribution, is $1.5 million in 2011 and rises to $3.8 million in 2013 as the number of non-grandfathered plans increases. The Departments estimate that the cost for the internal review process for the individual market is $28.8 million in 2011 and rises to $56.4 million in 2013.

iii. *Additional Requirements for Group Health Plans.* As discussed earlier in this preamble, paragraph (b)(2)(i) of these interim final regulations imposes additional requirements to the DOL claims procedure regulation that must be satisfied by group health plans and issuers offering group and individual coverage in the individual and group health insurance markets. The Departments believe that the additional requirements have modest costs associated with them, because they merely clarify provisions of the DOL claims procedure regulation. These requirements and their associated costs are discussed below.

Definition of adverse determination. These interim final regulations expand the definition of adverse benefit determination to include rescissions of coverage. While new, the methodology used to estimate the burden for the internal appeals process already captures this burden as most rescissions are associated with a claim and therefore would already be accounted for. The requirement allows for appeal of rescinded coverage that does not have

---

[42] AHIP, "Update: A Survey of Health Care Claims Receipt and Processing Times, 2009," January 2010.

[43] "Inside the Black Box of Managed Care Decisions," Research Brief, 2004.

[44] The Department based this assumption on the number of appealed Medicare pre-authorization denials. They received comments for the proposed regulation arguing this estimate was either too high or too low and so the Department chose to retain the assumption.

[45] The Department in its initial claims regulation assumed that an expert consultation would cost $500 which translated into roughly 5 hours of a physician's time. EBSA has revised this slightly downward based on the costs reported by IROs to review medical claims.

[46] The Departments' estimates of labor rates include wages, other benefits, and overhead based on the National Occupational Employment Survey (May 2008, Bureau of Labor Statistics) and the Employment Cost Index June 2009, Bureau of Labor Statistics).

an associated claim. While the Departments lack data to estimate the number of rescissions that occur without an associated claim for benefits, the Departments believe this number is small.

Expedited notification of benefit determination involving urgent care. The current DOL claims procedure regulation requires that a plan or issuer provide notification in the case of an urgent care claim as soon as possible taking into account the medical exigencies, but no later than 72 hours after receipt of the claim by the plan. These interim final regulations reduce the time limit to no later than 24 hours after the receipt of the claim by the plan or issuer. The Departments are not able to quantify the costs of this requirement. However, two factors could suggest this requirement does not impose substantial cost. First, the DOL claims procedure regulation requires urgent care notification to be made as soon as possible; therefore, it is likely that some claims currently are handled in less than the 24 hours. In addition, the technological developments that have occurred since the 72 hour standard was issued in the 2000 DOL claims procedure regulation should facilitate faster notification at reduced costs. However, plans and issuers would incur additional cost for urgent care notices that take longer than the required 24 hours to produce. Speeding up the notification process for these determinations might necessitate incurring additional cost to add more employees or find other ways to shorten the timeframe. Additional costs may be associated with this requirement if a shorter timeframe results in claims being denied that would not have been under a 72 hour standard or claims being approved that would have been denied under a longer notification period.

Full and fair review. These interim final regulations require the plan or issuer to provide the claimant, free of charge, with any new or additional evidence relied upon or generated by the plan or issuer and the rationale used for a determination during the appeals process sufficiently in advance of the due date of the response to an adverse benefit determination. This requirement increases the administrative burden on plans and issuers to prepare and deliver the new and additional information to the claimant. The Departments are not aware of data suggesting how often plans rely on new or additional evidence during the appeals process or the volume of materials that are received.

For purposes of this regulatory impact analysis, the Departments assume, as an upper bound, that all appealed claims will involve a reliance on additional evidence. The Departments assume that this requirement will impose a cost of just under $1 million in 2013, the year with the highest cost. The Departments estimated this cost by assuming that it will require medical office staff with a labor rate of $26.85 five minutes[47] to collect and distribute the additional evidence considered, relied on, or generated during the appeals process. The Departments estimate that on average, material, printing and postage costs will be $2.24 per mailing. The Departments further assume that 38 percent of all mailings will be distributed electronically with no associated material, printing or postage costs.[48]

Eliminating conflicts of interest. As discussed earlier in this preamble, these interim final regulations require plans and issuers to ensure that all claims and appeals are adjudicated in a manner designed to ensure the independence and impartiality of the persons involved in making the decision. Accordingly, decisions regarding hiring, compensation, termination, promotion, or other similar matters with respect to any individual (such as a claims adjudicator or medical expert) must not be made based upon the likelihood or perceived likelihood that the individual will support or tend to support the denial of benefits.

This requirement could require plans or issuers to change policies that currently create a conflict of interest and to discontinue practices that create such conflicts. The Departments believe that many plans and issuers already have such requirements in place as a matter of good business practice, but do not have sufficient data to provide an estimate. However, the Departments believe that the cost associated with this requirement will be minimal.

Enhanced notice. These interim final regulations provide new standards regarding notice to enrollees. Specifically, the statute and these interim final regulations require a plan or issuer to provide notice to enrollees, in a culturally and linguistically appropriate manner (standards for which are described later in this

---

[47] EBSA estimates of labor rates include wages, other benefits, and overhead based on the National Occupational Employment Survey (May 2008, Bureau of Labor Statistics) and the Employment Cost Index June 2009, Bureau of Labor Statistics).

[48] This estimate is based on the methodology used to analyze the cost burden for the DOL claims procedure regulation (OMB Control Number 1210–0053).

preamble). Plans and issuers must comply with the requirements of paragraphs (g) and (j) of the DOL claims procedure regulation, which detail requirements regarding the issuance of a notice of adverse benefit determination. Moreover, for purposes of these interim final regulations, additional content requirements apply for these notices. A plan or issuer must ensure that any notice of adverse benefit determination or final adverse benefit determination includes information sufficient to identify the claim involved. This includes the date of service, the health care provider, and the claim amount (if applicable), as well as the diagnosis code (such as an ICD–9 code, ICD–10 code, or DSM–IV code), the treatment code (such as a CPT code), and the corresponding meanings of these codes. A plan or issuer must also ensure that description of the reason or reasons for the denial includes a description of the standard that was used in denying the claim. In the case of a notice of final adverse benefit determination, this description must include a discussion of the decision. Additionally, the plan or issuer must provide a description of available internal appeals and external review processes, including information regarding how to initiate an appeal. Finally, the plan or issuer must disclose the availability of, and contact information for, any applicable office of health insurance consumer assistance or ombudsman established under PHS Act section 2793 to assist such enrollees with the internal claims and appeals and external review process. The Departments intend to issue model notices that could be used to satisfy all the notice requirements under these interim final regulations in the very near future that will mitigate the cost associated with providing them. These notices will be made available at *http://www.dol.gov/ebsa* and *http:// www.hhs.gov/ociio/*. The cost of sending the notices is included in the costs of the internal and external review process. The Departments were unable to estimate the cost of providing the model notices in a linguistically and culturally appropriate manner. However the Departments believe the overall costs to be small as only a small number of plans are believed to be affected. The Departments request comments that could help in estimating these costs, particularly with respect to the individual insurance market.

Deemed exhaustion of internal process. These interim final regulations provide that, in the case of a plan or issuer that fails to strictly adhere to all the requirements of the internal claims and appeals process with respect to a claim, the claimant is deemed to have exhausted the internal claims and appeals process, regardless of whether the plan or issuer asserts that it substantially complied with these requirements or that the error was de minimis. Accordingly, under such deemed exhaustion, the claimant may initiate an external review and pursue any available remedies under applicable law, such as judicial review. The Departments are unable to quantify the costs that are associated with this requirement. While this provision possibly could result in an increased number of external appeals it could reduce overall costs if costly litigation is avoided.

Continued coverage. Finally, the statute and these interim final regulations require a plan and issuer to provide continued coverage pending the outcome of an internal appeal. For this purpose, the plan or issuer must comply with the requirements of paragraph (f)(2)(ii) of the DOL claims procedure regulation, which generally provide that a plan or issuer cannot reduce or terminate an ongoing course of treatment without providing advance notice and an opportunity for advance review. Moreover, as described more fully earlier in this preamble, the plan or issuer must also provide simultaneous external review in advance of a reduction or termination of an ongoing course of treatment.

This provision would not impose any additional cost on plans and issuers that comply with the DOL claims procedure regulation; however, costs would be incurred by issuers in the individual market. The Departments are unable to quantify the cost associated with this requirement, because they lack sufficient data on the number of simultaneous reviews that are conducted.[49]

iv. *Additional Requirements for Issuers in the Individual Insurance Market.* To address certain relevant differences in the group and individual markets, health insurance issuers offering individual health insurance coverage must comply with three additional requirements. First, these interim final regulations expand the scope of the group health coverage internal claims and appeals process to cover initial eligibility determinations.

This protection is important since eligibility determinations in the individual market are frequently based on the health status of the applicant, including preexisting conditions. The Departments do not have sufficient data to quantify the costs associated with this requirement.[50]

Second, although the DOL claims procedure regulation permits group health plans to have a second level of internal appeals, these interim final regulations require health insurance issuers offering individual health insurance coverage to have only one level of internal appeals. This allows the claimant to seek either external review or judicial review immediately after an adverse determination is upheld in the first level of internal appeals. The Departments have factored this cost into their estimate of the cost for issuers offering coverage in the individual market to comply with requirement.

Finally, these interim final regulations require health insurance issuers offering individual health insurance coverage to maintain records of all claims and notices associated with their internal claims and appeals processes. An issuer must make such records available for examination upon request. Accordingly, a claimant or State or Federal agency official generally would be able to request and receive such documents free of charge. The Departments believe that minimal costs are associated with this requirement, because most issuers retain the required information in the normal course of their business operations.

v. *External Appeals.* The analysis of the cost associated with implementing an external review process under these interim final regulations focuses on the cost incurred by the following three groups that were not required to implement an external review process before the enactment of the Affordable Care Act: plans and participants in ERISA-covered self-insured plans; plans and participants in States with no external review laws, and plans and participants in States that have State laws only covering specific market segment (usually HMOs or managed care coverage).

The Departments estimate that there are about 76.9 million participants in self-insured ERISA-covered plans and approximately 13.8 million participants

in self-insured State and local governmental plans. In the States which currently have no external review laws there are an estimated 4.2 million participants (2.5 million participants in ERISA-covered plans, 1.2 million participants in governmental plans and 0.6 million in individual with policies in the individual market). In the States that currently have limited external review laws, there are 15.6 million participants (8.4 million participants in ERISA-covered plans, 4.2 million participants in governmental plans and 3.0 million individuals with individual health insurance in the individual market). These estimates lead to a total of 110.5 million participants, however, only the 44.2 million participants in non-grandfathered plans will be newly covered by the external review requirement in 2011. As plans relinquish their grandfather status in subsequent years, more individuals will be covered.

The Departments assume that there are an estimated 1.3 external appeals for every 10,000 participants,[51] and that there will be approximately 2,600 external appeals in 2011. As required by these interim final regulations or applicable State law, plans or issuers are required to pay for most of the cost of the external review while claimants may be charged a modest filing fee. A recent report finds that the average cost of a review was approximately $605.[52] While the actual cost per review will vary by state and also type of review (standard or expedited), an older study covering many States suggests this is a reasonable estimate.[53] These estimates lead to an estimated cost of the external review of $1.6 million (2,600 reviews * $605) in 2011. Using a similar method and adjusting for the number of non-grandfathered plans in subsequent years, the Departments estimate that the total cost for external review is $2.9 million in 2012 and $3.9 million in 2013.

On average, about 40 percent of denials are reversed on external appeal.[54] An estimate of the dollar

---

[49] The Departments do not have a basis to estimate this, because the Departments do not know how often this denial takes place or how often they are appealed. The costs should be minimal, because the decisions will be made quickly, and the period of coverage will be brief. The Departments expect the cost to be small relative to the cost of reversals, which the Departments have estimated.

[50] However, the Departments believe this number to be small. Approximately 10 to 15 percent of applicants are declined coverage in the individual market, while the Departments do not know how many of those denied coverage will appeal, using appeal rates for internal and external appeals would result in only a few thousand appeals. See "Fundamentals of Underwriting in the nongroup Health Insurance Market," pages 10–12, April 13, 2005.

[51] AHIP Center for Policy and Research, "An Update on State External Review Programs, 2006." July 2008.

[52] North Carolina Department of Insurance "Healthcare Review Program: Annual Report," 2008.

[53] Pollitz, Karen, Jeff Crowley, Kevin Lucia, and Eliza Bangit "Assessing State External Review Programs and the Effects of Pending Federal Patient's Rights Legislation." Kaiser Family Foundation (2002) page 27.

[54] AHIP Center for Policy and Research, "An Update on State External Review Programs, 2006," July 2008.

amount per claim reversed in $12,400.[55] This leads to $13.4 million in additional claims being reversed by the external review process in 2011, which increases to $33.1 million in 2013. While this amount is a cost to plans, it represents a payment of benefits that should have previously been paid to participants, but was denied. Part of this amount is a transfer from plans and issuers to those now receiving payment for denied benefits. Part of the amount could also be a cost if the reversal leads to services and hence resources being utilized now that had been denied previously. The Departments are not able to distinguish

between the two types but believe that most reversals are associated with a transfer.

These interim final regulations also require claimants to receive a notice informing them of the outcome of the appeal. The independent review organization that conducts the external review is required to prepare the notice; therefore, the cost of preparing and delivering this notice is included in the fee paid them by the insurer to conduct the review.

3. Summary

These interim final rules extend the protections of the DOL claims procedure

regulation to non-Federal governmental plans, and the market for individual coverage. Additional protections are added that cover these two markets and also the market for ERISA covered plans. These interim final regulations also extend the requirement to provide an independent external review. The Departments estimate that the total costs for these interim final regulations is $50.4 million in 2011, $78.8 million in 2012, and $101.1 million in 2013. The estimates are summarized in table 3, below.

TABLE 3—MONETIZED IMPACTS OF INTERIM FINAL REGULATIONS
[In millions]

	2011	2012	2013
ERISA Market	$1.4	$2.5	$3.5
External Review	1.2	2.2	3.1
Internal Review*	0.0	0.0	0.0
Fair and Full Review	0.2	0.3	0.4
State & Local Government Market	2.4	4.3	6.0
External Review	0.4	0.6	0.9
Internal Review**	2.0	3.6	5.0
Fair and Full Review	0.05	0.1	0.1
Individual Market	32.5	46.4	56.8
External Review	0.1	0.2	0.2
Internal Review	28.8	46.0	56.4
Fair and Full Review	0.1	0.2	0.2
Recordkeeping	0.1	0.1	0.1
Start-up Costs	3.5	0.0	0.0
Total Costs	36.2	53.2	66.2
Amount of Reversals***	14.2	25.6	34.9
ERISA Plans	10.3	18.7	25.7
State & Local Government Plans	3.0	5.4	7.4
Individual Market	0.9	1.5	1.9

*Assumes that ERISA plans already comply with ERISA claims and appeals regulations.
**Assumes that 90 percent of State and Local Government plans already comply with the ERISA claims and appeals regulation.
***This amount includes both transfers and costs with identical offsetting benefits.

C. Regulatory Flexibility Act—Department of Labor and Department of Health and Human Services

The Regulatory Flexibility Act (5 U.S.C. 601 et seq.) (RFA) imposes certain requirements with respect to Federal rules that are subject to the notice and comment requirements of section 553(b) of the APA (5 U.S.C. 551 et seq.) and that are likely to have a significant economic impact on a substantial number of small entities. Section 9833 of the Code, section 734 of ERISA, and section 2792 of the PHS Act authorize the Secretaries to promulgate any interim final rules that they determine are appropriate to carry out the provisions of chapter 100 of the Code, part 7 of subtitle B or title I of ERISA, and part A of title XXVII of the

PHS Act, which include PHS Act sections 2701 through 2728 and the incorporation of those sections into ERISA section 715 and Code section 9815.

Moreover, under Section 553(b) of the APA, a general notice of proposed rulemaking is not required when an agency, for good cause, finds that notice and public comment thereon are impracticable, unnecessary, or contrary to the public interest. These interim final regulations are exempt from APA, because the Departments made a good cause finding that a general notice of proposed rulemaking is not necessary earlier in this preamble. Therefore, the RFA does not apply and the Departments are not required to either certify that the rule would not have a

significant economic impact on a substantial number of small entities or conduct a regulatory flexibility analysis.

Nevertheless, the Departments carefully considered the likely impact of the rule on small entities in connection with their assessment under Executive Order 12866. Consistent with the policy of the RFA, the Departments encourage the public to submit comments that suggest alternative rules that accomplish the stated purpose of the Affordable Care Act and minimize the impact on small entities.

D. Special Analyses—Department of the Treasury

Notwithstanding the determinations of the Department of Labor and Department of Health and Human

[55] North Carolina Department of Insurance "Healthcare Review Program: Annual Report," 2008.

Services, for purposes of the Department of the Treasury, it has been determined that this Treasury decision is not a significant regulatory action for purposes of Executive Order 12866. Therefore, a regulatory assessment is not required. It has also been determined that section 553(b) of the APA (5 U.S.C. chapter 5) does not apply to these interim final regulations. For the applicability of the RFA, refer to the Special Analyses section in the preamble to the cross-referencing notice of proposed rulemaking published elsewhere in this issue of the **Federal Register**. Pursuant to section 7805(f) of the Code, these temporary regulations have been submitted to the Chief Counsel for Advocacy of the Small Business Administration for comment on their impact on small businesses.

E. Paperwork Reduction Act

1. Department of Labor and Department of the Treasury

As discussed above in the Department of Labor and Department of the Treasury PRA section, these interim final regulations require group health plans and health insurance issuers offering group or individual health insurance coverage to comply with the DOL claims procedure regulation with updated standards. They also require such plans and issuers to implement an external review process.

Currently, the Departments are soliciting 60 days of public comments concerning these disclosures. The Departments have submitted a copy of these interim final regulations to OMB in accordance with 44 U.S.C. 3507(d) for review of the information collections. The Departments and OMB are particularly interested in comments that:

• Evaluate whether the collection of information is necessary for the proper performance of the functions of the agency, including whether the information will have practical utility;

• Evaluate the accuracy of the agency's estimate of the burden of the collection of information, including the validity of the methodology and assumptions used;

• Enhance the quality, utility, and clarity of the information to be collected; and

• Minimize the burden of the collection of information on those who are to respond, including through the use of appropriate automated, electronic, mechanical, or other technological collection techniques or other forms of information technology, for example, by permitting electronic submission of responses.

Comments should be sent to the Office of Information and Regulatory Affairs, Attention: Desk Officer for the Employee Benefits Security Administration either by fax to (202) 395–7285 or by e-mail to *oira_submission@omb.eop.gov*. A copy of the ICR may be obtained by contacting the PRA addressee: G. Christopher Cosby, Office of Policy and Research, U.S. Department of Labor, Employee Benefits Security Administration, 200 Constitution Avenue, NW., Room N–5718, Washington, DC 20210. Telephone: (202) 693–8410; Fax: (202) 219–4745. These are not toll-free numbers. E-mail: *ebsa.opr@dol.gov*. ICRs submitted to OMB also are available at reginfo.gov (*http://www.reginfo.gov/public/do/PRAMain*).

a. Department of Labor and Department of the Treasury: Affordable Care Act Internal Claims and Appeals and External Review Disclosures for Non-Grandfathered Plans

As discussed earlier in this preamble, under PHS Act section 2719 and these interim final regulations, all sponsors of non-grandfathered group health plans and health insurance issuers offering group health insurance coverage must comply with all requirements of the DOL claims procedure regulation (29 CFR 2560.503–1) as well as the new standards in paragraph (b)(2)(ii) of these interim final regulations.

Before the enactment of the Affordable Care Act, ERISA-covered group health plans already were required to comply with the requirements of the DOL claims procedure regulation. The DOL claims procedure regulation requires, among other things, plans to provide a claimant who is denied a claim with a written or electronic notice that contains the specific reasons for denial, a reference to the relevant plan provisions on which the denial is based, a description of any additional information necessary to perfect the claim, and a description of steps to be taken if the participant or beneficiary wishes to appeal the denial. The regulation also requires that any adverse decision upon review be in writing (including electronic means) and include specific reasons for the decision, as well as references to relevant plan provisions. The Departments are not soliciting comments concerning an information collection request (ICR) pertaining to the requirement for ERISA-covered group health plans to meet the disclosure requirements of DOL's claims procedure regulation, because the costs and burdens associated with complying with

these previsions already are accounted for under the Department of Labor's Employee Benefit Plan Claims Procedure Under ERISA regulation (OMB Control Number 1210–0053).

Additional hour and cost burden is associated with paragraph (b)(2)(ii)(C) of these interim final regulations, which requires non-grandfathered ERISA-covered group health plans to provide the claimant, free of charge, with any new or additional evidence considered relied upon, or generated by the plan or issuer in connection with the claim.[56] This requirement increases the administrative burden on plans and issuers to prepare and deliver the additional information to the claimant.

Additional hour and cost burden also is associated with the requirement in paragraphs (c) and (d) of the regulations which set forth the external review requirements. The requirement for group health plans to implement an external review process will impose an hour and cost burden on plans that were not required to implement such a process before the enactment of the Affordable Care Act, such as self-insured plans, plans in states with no external review laws, and plans in states with limited scope external review laws (such as laws that only impact specific market segments like HMOs).

The Departments estimate that approximately 93 percent of large benefit and all small benefit plans administer claims using a third-party provider, or roughly 5 percent of covered individuals. In-house administration burdens are accounted for as hours, while purchased services are accounted for as dollar costs. Based on the foregoing, total burden hours are estimated at 300 hours in 2011, 500 hours in 2012, and 700 hours in 2013. Equivalent costs are $11,000, $19,000, and $26,000 respectively.

As stated in the preceding paragraph, the bulk of claims will be processed by third-party service providers. Total cost is estimated by multiplying the number of responses by the amount of time required to prepare the documents and then multiplying this by the appropriate hourly cost of either clerical workers

---

[56] Such evidence must be provided as soon as possible and sufficiently in advance of the date on which the notice of adverse benefit determination on review is required to be provided to give the claimant a reasonable opportunity to respond prior to that date. Additionally, before the plan or issuer can issue an adverse benefit determination on review based on a new or additional rationale, the claimant must be provided, free of charge, with the rationale. The rationale must be provided as soon as possible and sufficiently in advance of the date on which the notice of adverse benefit determination on review is required to be provided to give the claimant a reasonable opportunity to respond prior to that date.

($26.14) or doctors ($154.07),[57] and then adding the cost of copying and mailing responses ($0.54 each for those not sent electronically). Based on the foregoing, the Departments estimate that the total estimated cost burden for those plans that use service providers, including the cost of mailing all responses (including mailing costs for those prepared in-house listed in Table 2), is $243,000 in 2011, $443,000 in 2012, and $607,000 in 2013.

Type of Review: New collection.
Agencies: Employee Benefits Security Administration, Department of Labor; Internal Revenue Service, U.S. Department of the Treasury.
Title: Affordable Care Act Internal Claims and Appeals and External Review Disclosures for Non-Grandfathered Plans.
OMB Number: 1210–0144; 1545–2182.
Affected Public: Business or other for-profit; not-for-profit institutions.
Total Respondents: 607,000.
Total Responses: 62,000.
Frequency of Response: Occasionally.
Estimated Total Annual Burden Hours: 150 hours (Employee Benefits Security Administration); 150 hours (Internal Revenue Service).
Estimated Total Annual Burden Cost: $121,500 (Employee Benefits Security Administration); $121,500 (Internal Revenue Service).

2. Department of Health and Human Services

As discussed above in the Department of Labor and Department of the Treasury PRA section, these interim final regulations require group health plans and health insurance issuers offering group or individual health insurance coverage to comply with the DOL claims procedure regulation with updated standards. They also require such plans and issuers to implement an external review process.

a. ICR Regarding Affordable Care Act Internal Claims and Appeals and External Review Disclosures for Non-Grandfathered Plans

As discussed earlier in the preamble, paragraph (b)(2) and (b)(3) of these interim final regulations require all group health plan sponsors and health insurance issuers offering coverage in the group and individual health insurance markets to comply with the requirements of DOL's claims procedure regulation for their internal claims and appeals processes. Plan sponsors and issuers offering coverage in the group market also are required to satisfy the additional standards that are imposed on group health plans and issuers in paragraph (b)(2)(ii) of these interim final regulations, while issuers offering coverage in the individual health insurance market are required to satisfy the additional standards set forth in paragraph (b)(3)(ii) of these interim final regulations.

On the external review side, for purposes of this PRA analysis, the Department estimates the hour and cost burden for plans that were not previously subject to any external review requirements (self-insured plans, plans in states with no external review programs, and non-managed care plans in states that require external review only for managed care plans) to implement an external review process.

Based on the foregoing, the Department estimates that state and local governmental plans and issuers offering coverage in the individual market will incur a total hour burden hours of 566,000 hours in 2011, 989,000 hours in 2012, and 1.2 million hours in 2013 to comply with equivalent costs of $28.1 million in 2011, $57.1 million in 2012, and $70.1 million in 2013. The total estimated cost burden for those plans that use service providers, including the cost of mailing all responses is estimated to be $20.7 million in 2011, $37.4 million in 2012, and $51.1 million in 2013

The hour and cost burden is summarized below:
Type of Review: New collection.
Agency: Department of Health and Human Services.
Title: Affordable Care Act Internal Claims and Appeals and External Review Disclosures.
OMB Number: 0938–1098.

Affected Public: Business; State, Local, or Tribal Governments.
Respondents: 27,829.
Responses: 132,035,000.
Frequency of Response: Occasionally.
Estimated Total Annual Burden Hours: 566,000 hours.
Estimated Total Annual Burden Cost: $20,700,000.

b. ICR Regarding Affordable Care Act Recordkeeping Requirement for Non-Grandfathered Plans

As discussed earlier in this preamble, a health insurance issuer offering individual health insurance coverage must generally comply with all the requirements for the internal claims and appeals process that apply to group health coverage.[58] In addition to these standards, paragraph (b)(3)(ii)(H) of 45 CFR 147.136 requires health insurance issuers offering individual health insurance coverage to maintain records of all claims and notices associated with their internal claims and appeals processes. The records must be maintained for at least six years, which is the same requirement for group health plans under the ERISA recordkeeping requirements. An issuer must make such records available for examination upon request. Accordingly, a claimant or State or Federal agency official generally would be able to request and receive such documents free of charge.

The Department assumes that most of these records will be kept in the ordinary course of the issuers' business. Therefore, the Department estimates that the recordkeeping burden imposed by this ICR will require five minutes of a legal professional's time (with a rate of $119.03/hour) to determine the relevant documents that must be retained and ten minutes of clerical staff time (with a labor rate of $26.14/hour) to organize and file the required documents to ensure that they are accessible to claimants and Federal and State governmental agency officials. As shown in Table 4, below, overall, the Department estimates that there to be a total annual hour burden of 1,800 hours with an equivalent cost of $105,000.

TABLE 4—TOTAL HOUR BURDEN AND EQUIVALENT COST

	Number (A)	Hours (B)	Hourly labor cost (C)	Hour burden A*B	Equivalent cost A*B*C
Record Keeping (attorney): Individual	7,350	0.08	$119	613	$72,906

[57] EBSA estimates of labor rates include wages, other benefits, and overhead based on the National Occupational Employment Survey (May 2008, Bureau of Labor Statistics) and the Employment Cost Index June 2009, Bureau of Labor Statistics).
[58] The special rules in the DOL claims procedure regulation applicable only to multiemployer plans, as described earlier in this preamble, do not apply to health insurance issuers in the individual market.

TABLE 4—TOTAL HOUR BURDEN AND EQUIVALENT COST—Continued

	Number (A)	Hours (B)	Hourly labor cost (C)	Hour burden A*B	Equivalent cost A*B*C
Record Keeping (clerical): Individual	7,350	0.17	26	1,225	32,022
Total				1,838	104,927

Because this burden is borne solely by the insurers offering coverage in the individual health insurance market, and these issuers are assumed to process all claims in-house, there is no annual cost burden associated with this collection of information.

These paperwork burden estimates are summarized as follows:

Type of Review: New collection.

Agency: Department of Health and Human Services.

Title: Affordable Care Act Recordkeeping Requirements.

OMB Number: 0938–1098.

Affected Public: For Profit Business.

Respondents: 490.

Responses: 7,350.

Frequency of Response: Occasionally.

Estimated Total Annual Burden Hours: 1,800 hours.

Estimated Total Annual Burden Cost: $0.

If you comment on any of these information collection requirements, please do either of the following:

1. Submit your comments electronically as specified in the **ADDRESSES** section of this proposed rule; or

2. Submit your comments to the Office of Information and Regulatory Affairs, Office of Management and Budget:

Attention: CMS Desk Officer, OCIIO–9994–IFC.

Fax: (202) 395 6974; or

E-mail:

OIRA_submission@omb.eop.gov.

F. Congressional Review Act

These interim final regulations are subject to the Congressional Review Act provisions of the Small Business Regulatory Enforcement Fairness Act of 1996 (5 U.S.C. 801 *et seq.*) and have been transmitted to Congress and the Comptroller General for review.

G. Unfunded Mandates Reform Act

The Unfunded Mandates Reform Act of 1995 (Pub. L. 104–4) requires agencies to prepare several analytic statements before proposing any rules that may result in annual expenditures of $100 million (as adjusted for inflation) by State, local and tribal governments or the private sector. These interim final regulations are not subject to the Unfunded Mandates Reform Act because they are being issued as interim final regulations. However, consistent with the policy embodied in the Unfunded Mandates Reform Act, the regulation has been designed to be the least burdensome alternative for State, local and tribal governments, and the private sector, while achieving the objectives of the Affordable Care Act.

H. Federalism Statement—Department of Labor and Department of Health and Human Services

Executive Order 13132 outlines fundamental principles of federalism, and requires the adherence to specific criteria by Federal agencies in the process of their formulation and implementation of policies that have "substantial direct effects" on the States, the relationship between the national government and States, or on the distribution of power and responsibilities among the various levels of government. Federal agencies promulgating regulations that have federalism implications must consult with State and local officials, and describe the extent of their consultation and the nature of the concerns of State and local officials in the preamble to the regulation.

In the Departments' view, these interim final regulations have federalism implications, because they have direct effects on the States, the relationship between the national government and States, or on the distribution of power and responsibilities among various levels of government. However, in the Departments' view, the federalism implications of these interim final regulations are substantially mitigated because, with respect to health insurance issuers, the Departments expect that the majority of States will enact laws or take other appropriate action to implement an internal and external appeals process that will meet or exceed Federal standards.

In general, through section 514, ERISA supersedes State laws to the extent that they relate to any covered employee benefit plan, and preserves State laws that regulate insurance, banking, or securities. While ERISA prohibits States from regulating a plan as an insurance or investment company or bank, the preemption provisions of section 731 of ERISA and section 2724 of the PHS Act (implemented in 29 CFR 2590.731(a) and 45 CFR 146.143(a)) apply so that the HIPAA requirements (including those of the Affordable Care Act) are not to be "construed to supersede any provision of State law which establishes, implements, or continues in effect any standard or requirement solely relating to health insurance issuers in connection with group health insurance coverage except to the extent that such standard or requirement prevents the application of a requirement" of a Federal standard. The conference report accompanying HIPAA indicates that this is intended to be the "narrowest" preemption of State laws. (See House Conf. Rep. No. 104–736, at 205, reprinted in 1996 U.S. Code Cong. & Admin. News 2018.) States may continue to apply State law requirements except to the extent that such requirements prevent the application of the Affordable Care Act requirements that are the subject of this rulemaking. State insurance laws that are more stringent than the Federal requirements are unlikely to "prevent the application of" the Affordable Care Act, and be preempted. Accordingly, States have significant latitude to impose requirements on health insurance issuers that are more restrictive than the Federal law. Furthermore, the Departments have opined that, in the instance of a group health plan providing coverage through group health insurance, the issuer will be required to follow the external review procedures established in State law (assuming the State external review procedure meets the minimum standards set out in these interim final rules).

In compliance with the requirement of Executive Order 13132 that agencies examine closely any policies that may have federalism implications or limit the policy making discretion of the States, the Departments have engaged in efforts to consult with and work cooperatively with affected State and local officials, including attending conferences of the National Association of Insurance Commissioners, meeting with NAIC staff counsel on issues arising from these interim final regulations and consulting with State insurance officials on an individual basis. It is expected that the Departments will act in a similar fashion in enforcing the Affordable Care Act requirements, including the provisions of section 2719 of the PHS Act. Throughout the process of developing these interim final regulations, to the extent feasible within the specific preemption provisions of HIPAA as it applies to the Affordable Care Act, the Departments have attempted to balance the States' interests in regulating health insurance issuers, and Congress' intent to provide uniform minimum protections to consumers in every State. By doing so, it is the Departments' view that they have complied with the requirements of Executive Order 13132.

V. Statutory Authority

The Department of the Treasury temporary regulations are adopted pursuant to the authority contained in sections 7805 and 9833 of the Code.

The Department of Labor interim final regulations are adopted pursuant to the authority contained in 29 U.S.C. 1027, 1059, 1135, 1161–1168, 1169, 1181–1183, 1181 note, 1185, 1185a, 1185b, 1191, 1191a, 1191b, and 1191c; sec. 101(g), Public Law 104–191, 110 Stat. 1936; sec. 401(b), Public Law 105–200, 112 Stat. 645 (42 U.S.C. 651 note); sec. 512(d), Public Law 110–343, 122 Stat. 3881; sec. 1001, 1201, and 1562(e), Public Law 111–148, 124 Stat. 119, as amended by Public Law 111–152, 124 Stat. 1029; Secretary of Labor's Order 6–2009, 74 FR 21524 (May 7, 2009).

The Department of Health and Human Services interim final regulations are adopted pursuant to the authority contained in sections 2701 through 2763, 2791, and 2792 of the PHS Act (42 U.S.C. 300gg through 300gg–63, 300gg–91, and 300gg–92), as amended.

List of Subjects

26 CFR Part 54

Excise taxes, Health care, Health insurance, Pensions, Reporting and recordkeeping requirements.

29 CFR Part 2590

Continuation coverage, Disclosure, Employee benefit plans, Group health plans, Health care, Health insurance, Medical child support, Reporting and recordkeeping requirements.

45 CFR Part 147

Health care, Health insurance, Reporting and recordkeeping requirements, and State regulation of health insurance.

Steven T. Miller,
Deputy Commissioner for Services and Enforcement, Internal Revenue Service.
Approved: July 19, 2010.
Michael F. Mundaca,
Assistant Secretary of the Treasury (Tax Policy).
Signed this 16th day of July 2010.
Phyllis C. Borzi,
Assistant Secretary, Employee Benefits Security Administration, Department of Labor.
Dated: July 19, 2010.
Jay Angoff,
Director, Office of Consumer Information and Insurance Oversight.
Dated: July 19, 2010.
Kathleen Sebelius,
Secretary, Department of Health and Human Services.

DEPARTMENT OF THE TREASURY

Internal Revenue Service

26 CFR Chapter 1

■ Accordingly, 26 CFR parts 54 and 602 are amended as follows:

PART 54—PENSION EXCISE TAXES

■ **Paragraph 1.** The authority citation for part 54 is amended by adding an entry for § 54.9815–2719T in numerical order to read in part as follows:

> Authority: 26 U.S.C. 7805 * * *

> Section 54.9815–2719T also issued under 26 U.S.C. 9833.

■ **Par. 2.** Section 54.9815–2719T is added to read as follows:

§ 54.9815–2719T Internal claims and appeals and external review processes (temporary).

(a) *Scope and definitions*—(1) *Scope.* This section sets forth requirements with respect to internal claims and appeals and external review processes for group health plans and health insurance issuers that are not grandfathered health plans under § 54.9815–1251T. Paragraph (b) of this section provides requirements for internal claims and appeals processes. Paragraph (c) of this section sets forth rules governing the applicability of State external review processes. Paragraph (d) of this section sets forth a Federal external review process for plans and issuers not subject to an applicable State external review process. Paragraph (e) of this section prescribes requirements for ensuring that notices required to be

provided under this section are provided in a culturally and linguistically appropriate manner. Paragraph (f) of this section describes the authority of the Secretary to deem certain external review processes in existence on March 23, 2010 as in compliance with paragraph (c) or (d) of this section. Paragraph (g) of this section sets forth the applicability date for this section.

(2) *Definitions.* For purposes of this section, the following definitions apply—

(i) *Adverse benefit determination.* An *adverse benefit determination* means an adverse benefit determination as defined in 29 CFR 2560.503–1, as well as any rescission of coverage, as described in § 54.9815–2712T(a)(2) (whether or not, in connection with the rescission, there is an adverse effect on any particular benefit at that time).

(ii) *Appeal (or internal appeal).* An *appeal* or *internal appeal* means review by a plan or issuer of an adverse benefit determination, as required in paragraph (b) of this section.

(iii) *Claimant. Claimant* means an individual who makes a claim under this section. For purposes of this section, references to claimant include a claimant's authorized representative.

(iv) *External review. External review* means a review of an adverse benefit determination (including a final internal adverse benefit determination) conducted pursuant to an applicable State external review process described in paragraph (c) of this section or the Federal external review process of paragraph (d) of this section.

(v) *Final internal adverse benefit determination. A final internal adverse benefit determination* means an adverse benefit determination that has been upheld by a plan or issuer at the completion of the internal appeals process applicable under paragraph (b) of this section (or an adverse benefit determination with respect to which the internal appeals process has been exhausted under the deemed exhaustion rules of paragraph (b)(2)(ii)(F) of this section).

(vi) *Final external review decision. A final external review decision,* as used in paragraph (d) of this section, means a determination by an independent review organization at the conclusion of an external review.

(vii) *Independent review organization (or IRO). An independent review organization (or IRO)* means an entity that conducts independent external reviews of adverse benefit determinations and final internal adverse benefit determinations pursuant to paragraph (c) or (d) of this section.

(viii) *NAIC Uniform Model Act.* The *NAIC Uniform Model Act* means the Uniform Health Carrier External Review Model Act promulgated by the National Association of Insurance Commissioners in place on July 23, 2010.

(b) *Internal claims and appeals process*—(1) *In general.* A group health plan and a health insurance issuer offering group health insurance coverage must implement an effective internal claims and appeals process, as described in this paragraph (b).

(2) *Requirements for group health plans and group health insurance issuers.* A group health plan and a health insurance issuer offering group health insurance coverage must comply with all the requirements of this paragraph (b)(2). In the case of health insurance coverage offered in connection with a group health plan, if either the plan or the issuer complies with the internal claims and appeals process of this paragraph (b)(2), then the obligation to comply with this paragraph (b)(2) is satisfied for both the plan and the issuer with respect to the health insurance coverage.

(i) *Minimum internal claims and appeals standards.* A group health plan and a health insurance issuer offering group health insurance coverage must comply with all the requirements applicable to group health plans under 29 CFR 2560.503–1, except to the extent those requirements are modified by paragraph (b)(2)(ii) of this section. Accordingly, under this paragraph (b), with respect to health insurance coverage offered in connection with a group health plan, the group health insurance issuer is subject to the requirements in 29 CFR 2560.503–1 to the same extent as the group health plan.

(ii) *Additional standards.* In addition to the requirements in paragraph (b)(2)(i) of this section, the internal claims and appeals processes of a group health plan and a health insurance issuer offering group health insurance coverage must meet the requirements of this paragraph (b)(2)(ii).

(A) *Clarification of meaning of adverse benefit determination.* For purposes of this paragraph (b)(2), an "adverse benefit determination" includes an adverse benefit determination as defined in paragraph (a)(2)(i) of this section. Accordingly, in complying with 29 CFR 2560.503–1, as well as the other provisions of this paragraph (b)(2), a plan or issuer must treat a rescission of coverage (whether or not the rescission has an adverse effect on any particular benefit at that time) as an adverse benefit determination. (Rescissions of coverage

are subject to the requirements of § 54.9815–2712T.)

(B) *Expedited notification of benefit determinations involving urgent care.* Notwithstanding the rule of 29 CFR 2560.503–1(f)(2)(i) that provides for notification in the case of urgent care claims not later than 72 hours after the receipt of the claim, for purposes of this paragraph (b)(2), a plan and issuer must notify a claimant of a benefit determination (whether adverse or not) with respect to a claim involving urgent care as soon as possible, taking into account the medical exigencies, but not later than 24 hours after the receipt of the claim by the plan or issuer, unless the claimant fails to provide sufficient information to determine whether, or to what extent, benefits are covered or payable under the plan or health insurance coverage. The requirements of 29 CFR 2560.503–1(f)(2)(i) other than the rule for notification within 72 hours continue to apply to the plan and issuer. For purposes of this paragraph (b)(2)(ii)(B), a claim involving urgent care has the meaning given in 29 CFR 2560.503–1(m)(1).

(C) *Full and fair review.* A plan and issuer must allow a claimant to review the claim file and to present evidence and testimony as part of the internal claims and appeals process. Specifically, in addition to complying with the requirements of 29 CFR 2560.503–1(h)(2)—

(1) The plan or issuer must provide the claimant, free of charge, with any new or additional evidence considered, relied upon, or generated by the plan or issuer (or at the direction of the plan or issuer) in connection with the claim; such evidence must be provided as soon as possible and sufficiently in advance of the date on which the notice of final internal adverse benefit determination is required to be provided under 29 CFR 2560.503–1(i) to give the claimant a reasonable opportunity to respond prior to that date; and

(2) Before the plan or issuer can issue a final internal adverse benefit determination based on a new or additional rationale, the claimant must be provided, free of charge, with the rationale; the rationale must be provided as soon as possible and sufficiently in advance of the date on which the notice of final internal adverse benefit determination is required to be provided under 29 CFR 2560.503–1(i) to give the claimant a reasonable opportunity to respond prior to that date.

(D) *Avoiding conflicts of interest.* In addition to the requirements of 29 CFR 2560.503–1(b) and (h) regarding full and fair review, the plan and issuer must

ensure that all claims and appeals are adjudicated in a manner designed to ensure the independence and impartiality of the persons involved in making the decision. Accordingly, decisions regarding hiring, compensation, termination, promotion, or other similar matters with respect to any individual (such as a claims adjudicator or medical expert) must not be made based upon the likelihood that the individual will support the denial of benefits.

(E) *Notice.* A plan and issuer must provide notice to individuals, in a culturally and linguistically appropriate manner (as described in paragraph (e) of this section) that complies with the requirements of 29 CFR 2560.503–1(g) and (j). The plan and issuer must also comply with the additional requirements of this paragraph (b)(2)(ii)(E).

(1) The plan and issuer must ensure that any notice of adverse benefit determination or final internal adverse benefit determination includes information sufficient to identify the claim involved (including the date of service, the health care provider, the claim amount (if applicable), the diagnosis code and its corresponding meaning, and the treatment code and its corresponding meaning).

(2) The plan and issuer must ensure that the reason or reasons for the adverse benefit determination or final internal adverse benefit determination includes the denial code and its corresponding meaning, as well as a description of the plan's or issuer's standard, if any, that was used in denying the claim. In the case of a notice of final internal adverse benefit determination, this description must include a discussion of the decision.

(3) The plan and issuer must provide a description of available internal appeals and external review processes, including information regarding how to initiate an appeal.

(4) The plan and issuer must disclose the availability of, and contact information for, any applicable office of health insurance consumer assistance or ombudsman established under PHS Act section 2793 to assist individuals with the internal claims and appeals and external review processes.

(F) *Deemed exhaustion of internal claims and appeals processes.* In the case of a plan or issuer that fails to strictly adhere to all the requirements of this paragraph (b)(2) with respect to a claim, the claimant is deemed to have exhausted the internal claims and appeals process of this paragraph (b), regardless of whether the plan or issuer asserts that it substantially complied with the requirements of this paragraph (b)(2) or that any error it committed was de minimis. Accordingly the claimant may initiate an external review under paragraph (c) or (d) of this section, as applicable. The claimant is also entitled to pursue any available remedies under section 502(a) of ERISA or under State law, as applicable, on the basis that the plan or issuer has failed to provide a reasonable internal claims and appeals process that would yield a decision on the merits of the claim. If a claimant chooses to pursue remedies under section 502(a) of ERISA under such circumstances, the claim or appeal is deemed denied on review without the exercise of discretion by an appropriate fiduciary.

(iii) *Requirement to provide continued coverage pending the outcome of an appeal.* A plan and issuer subject to the requirements of this paragraph (b)(2) are required to provide continued coverage pending the outcome of an appeal. For this purpose, the plan and issuer must comply with the requirements of 29 CFR 2560.503–1(f)(2)(ii), which generally provides that benefits for an ongoing course of treatment cannot be reduced or terminated without providing advance notice and an opportunity for advance review.

(c) *State standards for external review*—(1) *In general.* (i) If a State external review process that applies to and is binding on a health insurance issuer offering group health insurance coverage includes at a minimum the consumer protections in the NAIC Uniform Model Act, then the issuer must comply with the applicable State external review process and is not required to comply with the Federal external review process of paragraph (d) of this section. In such a case, to the extent that benefits under a group health plan are provided through health insurance coverage, the group health plan is not required to comply with either this paragraph (c) or the Federal external review process of paragraph (d) of this section.

(ii) To the extent that a group health plan provides benefits other than through health insurance coverage (that is, the plan is self-insured) and is subject to a State external review process that applies to and is binding on the plan (for example, is not preempted by ERISA) and the State external review process includes at a minimum the consumer protections in the NAIC Uniform Model Act, then the plan must comply with the applicable State external review process and is not required to comply with the Federal external review process of paragraph (d) of this section.

(iii) If a plan or issuer is not required under paragraph (c)(1)(i) or (c)(1)(ii) of this section to comply with the requirements of this paragraph (c), then the plan or issuer must comply with the Federal external review process of paragraph (d) of this section, except to the extent, in the case of a plan, the plan is not required under paragraph (c)(1)(i) of this section to comply with paragraph (d) of this section.

(2) *Minimum standards for State external review processes.* An applicable State external review process must meet all the minimum consumer protections in this paragraph (c)(2). The Department of Health and Human Services will determine whether State external review processes meet these requirements.

(i) The State process must provide for the external review of adverse benefit determinations (including final internal adverse benefit determinations) by issuers (or, if applicable, plans) that are based on the issuer's (or plan's) requirements for medical necessity, appropriateness, health care setting, level of care, or effectiveness of a covered benefit.

(ii) The State process must require issuers (or, if applicable, plans) to provide effective written notice to claimants of their rights in connection with an external review for an adverse benefit determination.

(iii) To the extent the State process requires exhaustion of an internal claims and appeals process, exhaustion must be unnecessary where the issuer (or, if applicable, the plan) has waived the requirement, the issuer (or the plan) is considered to have exhausted the internal claims and appeals process under applicable law (including by failing to comply with any of the requirements for the internal appeal process, as outlined in paragraph (b)(2) of this section), or the claimant has applied for expedited external review at the same time as applying for an expedited internal appeal.

(iv) The State process provides that the issuer (or, if applicable, the plan) against which a request for external review is filed must pay the cost of the IRO for conducting the external review. Notwithstanding this requirement, the State external review process may require a nominal filing fee from the claimant requesting an external review. For this purpose, to be considered nominal, a filing fee must not exceed $25, it must be refunded to the claimant if the adverse benefit determination (or final internal adverse benefit determination) is reversed through external review, it must be waived if payment of the fee would impose an undue financial hardship, and the

annual limit on filing fees for any claimant within a single plan year must not exceed $75.

(v) The State process may not impose a restriction on the minimum dollar amount of a claim for it to be eligible for external review. Thus, the process may not impose, for example, a $500 minimum claims threshold.

(vi) The State process must allow at least four months after the receipt of a notice of an adverse benefit determination or final internal adverse benefit determination for a request for an external review to be filed.

(vii) The State process must provide that IROs will be assigned on a random basis or another method of assignment that assures the independence and impartiality of the assignment process (such as rotational assignment) by a State or independent entity, and in no event selected by the issuer, plan, or the individual.

(viii) The State process must provide for maintenance of a list of approved IROs qualified to conduct the external review based on the nature of the health care service that is the subject of the review. The State process must provide for approval only of IROs that are accredited by a nationally recognized private accrediting organization.

(ix) The State process must provide that any approved IRO has no conflicts of interest that will influence its independence. Thus, the IRO may not own or control, or be owned or controlled by a health insurance issuer, a group health plan, the sponsor of a group health plan, a trade association of plans or issuers, or a trade association of health care providers. The State process must further provide that the IRO and the clinical reviewer assigned to conduct an external review may not have a material professional, familial, or financial conflict of interest with the issuer or plan that is the subject of the external review; the claimant (and any related parties to the claimant) whose treatment is the subject of the external review; any officer, director, or management employee of the issuer; the plan administrator, plan fiduciaries, or plan employees; the health care provider, the health care provider's group, or practice association recommending the treatment that is subject to the external review; the facility at which the recommended treatment would be provided; or the developer or manufacturer of the principal drug, device, procedure, or other therapy being recommended.

(x) The State process allows the claimant at least five business days to submit to the IRO in writing additional information that the IRO must consider when conducting the external review and it requires that the claimant is notified of the right to do so. The process must also require that any additional information submitted by the claimant to the IRO must be forwarded to the issuer (or, if applicable, the plan) within one business day of receipt by the IRO.

(xi) The State process must provide that the decision is binding on the issuer (or, if applicable, the plan), as well as the claimant except to the extent that other remedies are available under State or Federal law.

(xii) The State process must require, for standard external review, that the IRO provide written notice to the claimant and the issuer (or, if applicable, the plan) of its decision to uphold or reverse the adverse benefit determination (or final internal adverse benefit determination) within no more than 45 days after the receipt of the request for external review by the IRO.

(xiii) The State process must provide for an expedited external review if the adverse benefit determination (or final internal adverse benefit determination) concerns an admission, availability of care, continued stay, or health care service for which the claimant received emergency services, but has not been discharged from a facility; or involves a medical condition for which the standard external review time frame would seriously jeopardize the life or health of the claimant or jeopardize the claimant's ability to regain maximum function. As expeditiously as possible but within no more than 72 hours after the receipt of the request for expedited external review by the IRO, the IRO must make its decision to uphold or reverse the adverse benefit determination (or final internal adverse benefit determination) and notify the claimant and the issuer (or, if applicable, the plan) of the determination. If the notice is not in writing, the IRO must provide written confirmation of the decision within 48 hours after the date of the notice of the decision.

(xiv) The State process must require that issuers (or, if applicable, plans) include a description of the external review process in or attached to the summary plan description, policy, certificate, membership booklet, outline of coverage, or other evidence of coverage it provides to participants, beneficiaries, or enrollees, substantially similar to what is set forth in section 17 of the NAIC Uniform Model Act.

(xv) The State process must require that IROs maintain written records and make them available upon request to the State, substantially similar to what is set forth in section 15 of the NAIC Uniform Model Act.

(xvi) The State process follows procedures for external review of adverse benefit determinations (or final internal adverse benefit determinations) involving experimental or investigational treatment, substantially similar to what is set forth in section 10 of the NAIC Uniform Model Act.

(3) *Transition period for existing external review processes*—(i) For plan years beginning before July 1, 2011, an applicable State external review process applicable to a health insurance issuer or group health plan is considered to meet the requirements of this paragraph (c). Accordingly, for plan years beginning before July 1, 2011, an applicable State external review process will be considered binding on the issuer or plan (in lieu of the requirements of the Federal external review process). If there is no applicable State external review process, the issuer or plan is required to comply with the requirements of the Federal external review process in paragraph (d) of this section.

(ii) For final internal adverse benefit determinations (or, in the case of simultaneous internal appeal and external review, adverse benefit determinations) provided after the first day of the first plan year beginning on or after July 1, 2011, the Federal external review process will apply unless the Department of Health and Human Services determines that a State law meets all the minimum standards of paragraph (c)(2) of this section as of the first day of the plan year.

(d) *Federal external review process.* A plan or issuer not subject to an applicable State external review process under paragraph (c) of this section must provide an effective Federal external review process in accordance with this paragraph (d) (except to the extent, in the case of a plan, the plan is described in paragraph (c)(1)(i) of this section as not having to comply with this paragraph (d)). In the case of health insurance coverage offered in connection with a group health plan, if either the plan or the issuer complies with the Federal external review process of this paragraph (d), then the obligation to comply with this paragraph (d) is satisfied for both the plan and the issuer with respect to the health insurance coverage.

(1) *Scope.* The Federal external review process established pursuant to this paragraph (d) applies to any adverse benefit determination or final internal adverse benefit determination as defined in paragraphs (a)(2)(i) and (a)(2)(v) of this section, except that a denial, reduction, termination, or a failure to provide payment for a benefit based on a determination that a participant or beneficiary fails to meet the requirements for eligibility under the terms of a group health plan is not eligible for the external review process under this paragraph (d).

(2) *External review process standards.* The Federal external review process established pursuant to this paragraph (d) will be similar to the process set forth in the NAIC Uniform Model Act and will meet standards issued by the Secretary. These standards will comply with all of the requirements described in this paragraph (d)(2).

(i) These standards will describe how a claimant initiates an external review, procedures for preliminary reviews to determine whether a claim is eligible for external review, minimum qualifications for IROs, a process for approving IROs eligible to be assigned to conduct external reviews, a process for random assignment of external reviews to approved IROs, standards for IRO decision-making, and rules for providing notice of a final external review decision.

(ii) These standards will provide an expedited external review process for—

(A) An adverse benefit determination, if the adverse benefit determination involves a medical condition of the claimant for which the timeframe for completion of an expedited internal appeal under paragraph (b) of this section would seriously jeopardize the life or health of the claimant, or would jeopardize the claimant's ability to regain maximum function and the claimant has filed a request for an expedited internal appeal under paragraph (b) of this section; or

(B) A final internal adverse benefit determination, if the claimant has a medical condition where the timeframe for completion of a standard external review pursuant to paragraph (d)(3) of this section would seriously jeopardize the life or health of the claimant or would jeopardize the claimant's ability to regain maximum function, or if the final internal adverse benefit determination concerns an admission, availability of care, continued stay, or health care service for which the claimant received emergency services, but has not been discharged from a facility.

(iii) With respect to claims involving experimental or investigational treatments, these standards will also provide additional consumer protections to ensure that adequate clinical and scientific experience and protocols are taken into account as part of the external review process.

(iv) These standards will provide that an external review decision is binding on the plan or issuer, as well as the claimant, except to the extent other remedies are available under State or Federal law.

(v) These standards may establish external review reporting requirements for IROs.

(vi) These standards will establish additional notice requirements for plans and issuers regarding disclosures to participants and beneficiaries describing the Federal external review procedures (including the right to file a request for an external review of an adverse benefit determination or a final internal adverse benefit determination in the summary plan description, policy, certificate, membership booklet, outline of coverage, or other evidence of coverage it provides to participants or beneficiaries).

(vii) These standards will require plans and issuers to provide information relevant to the processing of the external review, including, but not limited to, the information considered and relied on in making the adverse benefit determination or final internal adverse benefit determination.

(e) *Form and manner of notice.* (1) For purposes of this section, a group health plan and health insurance issuer offering group health insurance coverage are considered to provide relevant notices in a culturally and linguistically appropriate manner—

(i) For a plan that covers fewer than 100 participants at the beginning of a plan year, if the plan and issuer provide notices upon request in a non-English language in which 25 percent or more of all plan participants are literate only in the same non-English language; or

(ii) For a plan that covers 100 or more participants at the beginning of a plan year, if the plan and issuer provide notices upon request in a non-English language in which the lesser of 500 or more participants, or 10 percent or more of all plan participants, are literate only in the same non-English language.

(2) If an applicable threshold described in paragraph (e)(1) of this section is met, the plan and issuer must also—

(i) Include a statement in the English versions of all notices, prominently displayed in the non-English language, offering the provision of such notices in the non-English language;

(ii) Once a request has been made by a claimant, provide all subsequent notices to the claimant in the non-English language; and

(iii) To the extent the plan or issuer maintains a customer assistance process (such as a telephone hotline) that answers questions or provides assistance with filing claims and appeals, the plan or issuer must provide such assistance in the non-English language.

(f) *Secretarial authority.* The Secretary may determine that the external review process of a group health plan or health insurance issuer, in operation as of March 23, 2010, is considered in compliance with the applicable process established under paragraph (c) or (d) of this section if it substantially meets the requirements of paragraph (c) or (d) of this section, as applicable.

(g) *Applicability/effective date.* The provisions of this section apply for plan years beginning on or after September 23, 2010. See § 54.9815–1251T for determining the application of this section to grandfathered health plans (providing that these rules regarding internal claims and appeals and external review processes do not apply to grandfathered health plans).

(h) *Expiration date.* The applicability of this section expires on July 22, 2013 or on such earlier date as may be provided in final regulations or other action published in the **Federal Register.**

PART 602—OMB CONTROL NUMBERS UNDER THE PAPERWORK REDUCTION ACT

■ **Par. 3.** The authority citation for part 602 continues to read in part as follows:

Authority: 26 U.S.C. 7805.

■ **Par. 4.** Section 602.101(b) is amended by adding the following entry in numerical order to the table to read as follows:

§ 602.101   OMB Control numbers.

*   *   *   *   *

(b) * * *

CFR part or section where identified and described	Current OMB control No.
* * * * *	
54.9815–2719T	1545–2182
* * * * *	

DEPARTMENT OF LABOR

Employee Benefits Security Administration

29 CFR Chapter XXV

■ 29 CFR part 2590 is amended as follows:

PART 2590—RULES AND REGULATIONS FOR GROUP HEALTH PLANS

■ 1. The authority citation for part 2590 continues to read as follows:

Authority: 29 U.S.C. 1027, 1059, 1135, 1161–1168, 1169, 1181–1183, 1181 note, 1185, 1185a, 1185b, 1191, 1191a, 1191b, and 1191c; sec. 101(g), Pub. L. 104–191, 110 Stat. 1936; sec. 401(b), Pub. L. 105–200, 112 Stat. 645 (42 U.S.C. 651 note); sec. 512(d), Pub. L. 110–343, 122 Stat. 3881; sec. 1001, 1201, and 1562(e), Pub. L. 111–148, 124 Stat. 119, as amended by Pub. L. 111–152, 124 Stat. 1029; Secretary of Labor's Order 6–2009, 74 FR 21524 (May 7, 2009).

Subpart C—Other Requirements

■ 2. Section 2590.715–2719 is added to subpart C to read as follows:

§ 2590.715–2719   Internal claims and appeals and external review processes.

(a) *Scope and definitions*—(1) *Scope.* This section sets forth requirements with respect to internal claims and appeals and external review processes for group health plans and health insurance issuers that are not grandfathered health plans under § 2590.715–1251 of this part. Paragraph (b) of this section provides requirements for internal claims and appeals processes. Paragraph (c) of this section sets forth rules governing the applicability of State external review processes. Paragraph (d) of this section sets forth a Federal external review process for plans and issuers not subject to an applicable State external review process. Paragraph (e) of this section prescribes requirements for ensuring that notices required to be provided under this section are provided in a culturally and linguistically appropriate manner. Paragraph (f) of this section describes the authority of the Secretary to deem certain external review processes in existence on March 23, 2010 as in compliance with paragraph (c) or (d) of this section. Paragraph (g) of this section sets forth the applicability date for this section.

(2) *Definitions.* For purposes of this section, the following definitions apply—

(i) *Adverse benefit determination.* An *adverse benefit determination* means an adverse benefit determination as defined in 29 CFR 2560.503–1, as well as any rescission of coverage, as described in § 2590.715–2712(a)(2) of this part (whether or not, in connection with the rescission, there is an adverse effect on any particular benefit at that time).

(ii) *Appeal (or internal appeal).* An *appeal* or *internal appeal* means review by a plan or issuer of an adverse benefit determination, as required in paragraph (b) of this section.

(iii) *Claimant. Claimant* means an individual who makes a claim under this section. For purposes of this section, references to claimant include a claimant's authorized representative.

(iv) *External review. External review* means a review of an adverse benefit determination (including a final internal adverse benefit determination) conducted pursuant to an applicable State external review process described in paragraph (c) of this section or the Federal external review process of paragraph (d) of this section.

(v) *Final internal adverse benefit determination.* A *final internal adverse benefit determination* means an adverse benefit determination that has been upheld by a plan or issuer at the completion of the internal appeals process applicable under paragraph (b) of this section (or an adverse benefit determination with respect to which the internal appeals process has been exhausted under the deemed exhaustion rules of paragraph (b)(2)(ii)(F) of this section).

(vi) *Final external review decision.* A *final external review decision*, as used in paragraph (d) of this section, means a determination by an independent review organization at the conclusion of an external review.

(vii) *Independent review organization (or IRO).* An *independent review organization (or IRO)* means an entity that conducts independent external reviews of adverse benefit determinations and final internal adverse benefit determinations pursuant to paragraph (c) or (d) of this section.

(viii) *NAIC Uniform Model Act.* The *NAIC Uniform Model Act* means the Uniform Health Carrier External Review Model Act promulgated by the National Association of Insurance Commissioners in place on July 23, 2010.

(b) *Internal claims and appeals process*—(1) *In general.* A group health plan and a health insurance issuer offering group health insurance coverage must implement an effective internal claims and appeals process, as described in this paragraph (b).

(2) *Requirements for group health plans and group health insurance issuers.* A group health plan and a health insurance issuer offering group health insurance coverage must comply with all the requirements of this paragraph (b)(2). In the case of health insurance coverage offered in connection with a group health plan, if either the plan or the issuer complies with the internal claims and appeals process of this paragraph (b)(2), then the

obligation to comply with this paragraph (b)(2) is satisfied for both the plan and the issuer with respect to the health insurance coverage.

(i) *Minimum internal claims and appeals standards.* A group health plan and a health insurance issuer offering group health insurance coverage must comply with all the requirements applicable to group health plans under 29 CFR 2560.503–1, except to the extent those requirements are modified by paragraph (b)(2)(ii) of this section. Accordingly, under this paragraph (b), with respect to health insurance coverage offered in connection with a group health plan, the group health insurance issuer is subject to the requirements in 29 CFR 2560.503–1 to the same extent as the group health plan.

(ii) *Additional standards.* In addition to the requirements in paragraph (b)(2)(i) of this section, the internal claims and appeals processes of a group health plan and a health insurance issuer offering group health insurance coverage must meet the requirements of this paragraph (b)(2)(ii).

(A) *Clarification of meaning of adverse benefit determination.* For purposes of this paragraph (b)(2), an "adverse benefit determination" includes an adverse benefit determination as defined in paragraph (a)(2)(i) of this section. Accordingly, in complying with 29 CFR 2560.503–1, as well as the other provisions of this paragraph (b)(2), a plan or issuer must treat a rescission of coverage (whether or not the rescission has an adverse effect on any particular benefit at that time) as an adverse benefit determination. (Rescissions of coverage are subject to the requirements of § 2590.715–2712 of this part.)

(B) *Expedited notification of benefit determinations involving urgent care.* Notwithstanding the rule of 29 CFR 2560.503–1(f)(2)(i) that provides for notification in the case of urgent care claims not later than 72 hours after the receipt of the claim, for purposes of this paragraph (b)(2), a plan and issuer must notify a claimant of a benefit determination (whether adverse or not) with respect to a claim involving urgent care as soon as possible, taking into account the medical exigencies, but not later than 24 hours after the receipt of the claim by the plan or issuer, unless the claimant fails to provide sufficient information to determine whether, or to what extent, benefits are covered or payable under the plan or health insurance coverage. The requirements of 29 CFR 2560.503–1(f)(2)(i) other than the rule for notification within 72 hours continue to apply to the plan and issuer.

For purposes of this paragraph (b)(2)(ii)(B), a claim involving urgent care has the meaning given in 29 CFR 2560.503–1(m)(1).

(C) *Full and fair review.* A plan and issuer must allow a claimant to review the claim file and to present evidence and testimony as part of the internal claims and appeals process. Specifically, in addition to complying with the requirements of 29 CFR 2560.503–1(h)(2)—

(1) The plan or issuer must provide the claimant, free of charge, with any new or additional evidence considered, relied upon, or generated by the plan or issuer (or at the direction of the plan or issuer) in connection with the claim; such evidence must be provided as soon as possible and sufficiently in advance of the date on which the notice of final internal adverse benefit determination is required to be provided under 29 CFR 2560.503–1(i) to give the claimant a reasonable opportunity to respond prior to that date; and

(2) Before the plan or issuer can issue a final internal adverse benefit determination based on a new or additional rationale, the claimant must be provided, free of charge, with the rationale; the rationale must be provided as soon as possible and sufficiently in advance of the date on which the notice of final internal adverse benefit determination is required to be provided under 29 CFR 2560.503–1(i) to give the claimant a reasonable opportunity to respond prior to that date.

(D) *Avoiding conflicts of interest.* In addition to the requirements of 29 CFR 2560.503–1(b) and (h) regarding full and fair review, the plan and issuer must ensure that all claims and appeals are adjudicated in a manner designed to ensure the independence and impartiality of the persons involved in making the decision. Accordingly, decisions regarding hiring, compensation, termination, promotion, or other similar matters with respect to any individual (such as a claims adjudicator or medical expert) must not be made based upon the likelihood that the individual will support the denial of benefits.

(E) *Notice.* A plan and issuer must provide notice to individuals, in a culturally and linguistically appropriate manner (as described in paragraph (e) of this section) that complies with the requirements of 29 CFR 2560.503–1(g) and (j). The plan and issuer must also comply with the additional requirements of this paragraph (b)(2)(ii)(E).

(1) The plan and issuer must ensure that any notice of adverse benefit

43356   Federal Register / Vol. 75, No. 141 / Friday, July 23, 2010 / Rules and Regulations

determination or final internal adverse benefit determination includes information sufficient to identify the claim involved (including the date of service, the health care provider, the claim amount (if applicable), the diagnosis code and its corresponding meaning, and the treatment code and its corresponding meaning).

(2) The plan and issuer must ensure that the reason or reasons for the adverse benefit determination or final internal adverse benefit determination includes the denial code and its corresponding meaning, as well as a description of the plan's or issuer's standard, if any, that was used in denying the claim. In the case of a notice of final internal adverse benefit determination, this description must include a discussion of the decision.

(3) The plan and issuer must provide a description of available internal appeals and external review processes, including information regarding how to initiate an appeal.

(4) The plan and issuer must disclose the availability of, and contact information for, any applicable office of health insurance consumer assistance or ombudsman established under PHS Act section 2793 to assist individuals with the internal claims and appeals and external review processes.

(F) *Deemed exhaustion of internal claims and appeals processes.* In the case of a plan or issuer that fails to strictly adhere to all the requirements of this paragraph (b)(2) with respect to a claim, the claimant is deemed to have exhausted the internal claims and appeals process of this paragraph (b), regardless of whether the plan or issuer asserts that it substantially complied with the requirements of this paragraph (b)(2) or that any error it committed was de minimis. Accordingly the claimant may initiate an external review under paragraph (c) or (d) of this section, as applicable. The claimant is also entitled to pursue any available remedies under section 502(a) of ERISA or under State law, as applicable, on the basis that the plan or issuer has failed to provide a reasonable internal claims and appeals process that would yield a decision on the merits of the claim. If a claimant chooses to pursue remedies under section 502(a) of ERISA under such circumstances, the claim or appeal is deemed denied on review without the exercise of discretion by an appropriate fiduciary.

(iii) *Requirement to provide continued coverage pending the outcome of an appeal.* A plan and issuer subject to the requirements of this paragraph (b)(2) are required to provide continued coverage pending the outcome of an appeal. For

this purpose, the plan and issuer must comply with the requirements of 29 CFR 2560.503–1(f)(2)(ii), which generally provides that benefits for an ongoing course of treatment cannot be reduced or terminated without providing advance notice and an opportunity for advance review.

(c) *State standards for external review*—(1) *In general.* (i) If a State external review process that applies to and is binding on a health insurance issuer offering group health insurance coverage includes at a minimum the consumer protections in the NAIC Uniform Model Act, then the issuer must comply with the applicable State external review process and is not required to comply with the Federal external review process of paragraph (d) of this section. In such a case, to the extent that benefits under a group health plan are provided through health insurance coverage, the group health plan is not required to comply with either this paragraph (c) or the Federal external review process of paragraph (d) of this section.

(ii) To the extent that a group health plan provides benefits other than through health insurance coverage (that is, the plan is self-insured) and is subject to a State external review process that applies to and is binding on the plan (for example, is not preempted by ERISA) and the State external review process includes at a minimum the consumer protections in the NAIC Uniform Model Act, then the plan must comply with the applicable State external review process and is not required to comply with the Federal external review process of paragraph (d) of this section.

(iii) If a plan or issuer is not required under paragraph (c)(1)(i) or (c)(1)(ii) of this section to comply with the requirements of this paragraph (c), then the plan or issuer must comply with the Federal external review process of paragraph (d) of this section, except to the extent, in the case of a plan, the plan is not required under paragraph (c)(1)(i) of this section to comply with paragraph (d) of this section.

(2) *Minimum standards for State external review processes.* An applicable State external review process must meet all the minimum consumer protections in this paragraph (c)(2). The Department of Health and Human Services will determine whether State external review processes meet these requirements.

(i) The State process must provide for the external review of adverse benefit determinations (including final internal adverse benefit determinations) by issuers (or, if applicable, plans) that are based on the issuer's (or plan's)

requirements for medical necessity, appropriateness, health care setting, level of care, or effectiveness of a covered benefit.

(ii) The State process must require issuers (or, if applicable, plans) to provide effective written notice to claimants of their rights in connection with an external review for an adverse benefit determination.

(iii) To the extent the State process requires exhaustion of an internal claims and appeals process, exhaustion must be unnecessary where the issuer (or, if applicable, the plan) has waived the requirement, the issuer (or the plan) is considered to have exhausted the internal claims and appeals process under applicable law (including by failing to comply with any of the requirements for the internal appeal process, as outlined in paragraph (b)(2) of this section), or the claimant has applied for expedited external review at the same time as applying for an expedited internal appeal.

(iv) The State process provides that the issuer (or, if applicable, the plan) against which a request for external review is filed must pay the cost of the IRO for conducting the external review. Notwithstanding this requirement, the State external review process may require a nominal filing fee from the claimant requesting an external review. For this purpose, to be considered nominal, a filing fee must not exceed $25, it must be refunded to the claimant if the adverse benefit determination (or final internal adverse benefit determination) is reversed through external review, it must be waived if payment of the fee would impose an undue financial hardship, and the annual limit on filing fees for any claimant within a single plan year must not exceed $75.

(v) The State process may not impose a restriction on the minimum dollar amount of a claim for it to be eligible for external review. Thus, the process may not impose, for example, a $500 minimum claims threshold.

(vi) The State process must allow at least four months after the receipt of a notice of an adverse benefit determination or final internal adverse benefit determination for a request for an external review to be filed.

(vii) The State process must provide that IROs will be assigned on a random basis or another method of assignment that assures the independence and impartiality of the assignment process (such as rotational assignment) by a State or independent entity, and in no event selected by the issuer, plan, or the individual.

(viii) The State process must provide for maintenance of a list of approved IRO qualified to conduct the external review based on the nature of the health care service that is the subject of the review. The State process must provide for approval only of IROs that are accredited by a nationally recognized private accrediting organization.

(ix) The State process must provide that any approved IRO has no conflicts of interest that will influence its independence. Thus, the IRO may not own or control, or be owned or controlled by a health insurance issuer, a group health plan, the sponsor of a group health plan, a trade association of plans or issuers, or a trade association of health care providers. The State process must further provide that the IRO and the clinical reviewer assigned to conduct an external review may not have a material professional, familial, or financial conflict of interest with the issuer or plan that is the subject of the external review; the claimant (and any related parties to the claimant) whose treatment is the subject of the external review; any officer, director, or management employee of the issuer; the plan administrator, plan fiduciaries, or plan employees; the health care provider, the health care provider's group, or practice association recommending the treatment that is subject to the external review; the facility at which the recommended treatment would be provided; or the developer or manufacturer of the principal drug, device, procedure, or other therapy being recommended.

(x) The State process allows the claimant at least five business days to submit to the IRO in writing additional information that the IRO must consider when conducting the external review and it requires that the claimant is notified of the right to do so. The process must also require that any additional information submitted by the claimant to the IRO must be forwarded to the issuer (or, if applicable, the plan) within one business day of receipt by the IRO.

(xi) The State process must provide that the decision is binding on the issuer (or, if applicable, the plan), as well as the claimant except to the extent the other remedies are available under State or Federal law.

(xii) The State process must require, for standard external review, that the IRO provide written notice to the issuer (or, if applicable, the plan) and the claimant of its decision to uphold or reverse the adverse benefit determination (or final internal adverse benefit determination) within no more

than 45 days after the receipt of the request for external review by the IRO.

(xiii) The State process must provide for an expedited external review if the adverse benefit determination (or final internal adverse benefit determination) concerns an admission, availability of care, continued stay, or health care service for which the claimant received emergency services, but has not been discharged from a facility; or involves a medical condition for which the standard external review timeframe would seriously jeopardize the life or health of the claimant or jeopardize the claimant's ability to regain maximum function. As expeditiously as possible but within no more than 72 hours after the receipt of the request for expedited external review by the IRO, the IRO must make its decision to uphold or reverse the adverse benefit determination (or final internal adverse benefit determination) and notify the claimant and the issuer (or, if applicable, the plan) of the determination. If the notice is not in writing, the IRO must provide written confirmation of the decision within 48 hours after the date of the notice of the decision.

(xiv) The State process must require that issuers (or, if applicable, plans) include a description of the external review process in or attached to the summary plan description, policy, certificate, membership booklet, outline of coverage, or other evidence of coverage it provides to participants, beneficiaries, or enrollees, substantially similar to what is set forth in section 17 of the NAIC Uniform Model Act.

(xv) The State process must require that IROs maintain written records and make them available upon request to the State, substantially similar to what is set forth in section 15 of the NAIC Uniform Model Act.

(xvi) The State process follows procedures for external review of adverse benefit determinations (or final internal adverse benefit determinations) involving experimental or investigational treatment, substantially similar to what is set forth in section 10 of the NAIC Uniform Model Act.

(3) *Transition period for existing external review processes*—(i) For plan years beginning before July 1, 2011, an applicable State external review process applicable to a health insurance issuer or group health plan is considered to meet the requirements of this paragraph (c). Accordingly, for plan years beginning before July 1, 2011, an applicable State external review process will be considered binding on the issuer or plan (in lieu of the requirements of the Federal external review process). If

there is no applicable State external review process, the issuer or plan is required to comply with the requirements of the Federal external review process in paragraph (d) of this section.

(ii) For final internal adverse benefit determinations (or, in the case of simultaneous internal appeal and external review, adverse benefit determinations) provided after the first day of the first plan year beginning on or after July 1, 2011, the Federal external review process will apply unless the Department of Health and Human Services determines that a State law meets all the minimum standards of paragraph (c)(2) of this section as of the first day of the plan year.

(d) *Federal external review process.* A plan or issuer not subject to an applicable State external review process under paragraph (c) of this section must provide an effective Federal external review process in accordance with this paragraph (d) (except to the extent, in the case of a plan, the plan is described in paragraph (c)(1)(i) of this section as not having to comply with this paragraph (d)). In the case of health insurance coverage offered in connection with a group health plan, if either the plan or the issuer complies with the Federal external review process of this paragraph (d), then the obligation to comply with this paragraph (d) is satisfied for both the plan and the issuer with respect to the health insurance coverage.

(1) *Scope.* The Federal external review process established pursuant to this paragraph (d) applies to any adverse benefit determination or final internal adverse benefit determination as defined in paragraphs (a)(2)(i) and (a)(2)(v) of this section, except that a denial, reduction, termination, or a failure to provide payment for a benefit based on a determination that a participant or beneficiary fails to meet the requirements for eligibility under the terms of a group health plan is not eligible for the external review process under this paragraph (d).

(2) *External review process standards.* The Federal external review process established pursuant to this paragraph (d) will be similar to the process set forth in the NAIC Uniform Model Act and will meet standards issued by the Secretary. These standards will comply with all of the requirements described in this paragraph (d)(2).

(i) These standards will describe how a claimant initiates an external review, procedures for preliminary reviews to determine whether a claim is eligible for external review, minimum qualifications for IROs, a process for approving IROs eligible to be assigned to conduct external reviews, a process for random assignment of external reviews to approved IROs, standards for IRO decisionmaking, and rules for providing notice of a final external review decision.

(ii) These standards will provide an expedited external review process for—

(A) An adverse benefit determination. if the adverse benefit determination involves a medical condition of the claimant for which the timeframe for completion of an expedited internal appeal under paragraph (b) of this section would seriously jeopardize the life or health of the claimant, or would jeopardize the claimant's ability to regain maximum function and the claimant has filed a request for an expedited internal appeal under paragraph (b) of this section; or

(B) A final internal adverse benefit determination, if the claimant has a medical condition where the timeframe for completion of a standard external review pursuant to paragraph (d)(3) of this section would seriously jeopardize the life or health of the claimant or would jeopardize the claimant's ability to regain maximum function, or if the final internal adverse benefit determination concerns an admission, availability of care, continued stay or health care service for which the claimant received emergency services, but has not been discharged from a facility.

(iii) With respect to claims involving experimental or investigational treatments, these standards will also provide additional consumer protections to ensure that adequate clinical and scientific experience and protocols are taken into account as part of the external review process.

(iv) These standards will provide that an external review decision is binding on the plan or issuer, as well as the claimant, except to the extent other remedies are available under State or Federal law.

(v) These standards may establish external review reporting requirements for IROs.

(vi) These standards will establish additional notice requirements for plans and issuers regarding disclosures to participants and beneficiaries describing the Federal external review procedures (including the right to file a request for an external review of an adverse benefit determination or a final internal adverse benefit determination in the summary plan description, policy, certificate, membership booklet, outline of coverage, or other evidence of coverage it provides to participants or beneficiaries.

(vii) These standards will require plans and issuers to provide information relevant to the processing of the external review, including, but not limited to, the information considered and relied on in making the adverse benefit determination or final internal adverse benefit determination.

(e) *Form and manner of notice.* (1) For purposes of this section, a group health plan and health insurance issuer offering group health insurance coverage are considered to provide relevant notices in a culturally and linguistically appropriate manner—

(i) For a plan that covers fewer than 100 participants at the beginning of a plan year, if the plan and issuer provide notices upon request in a non-English language in which 25 percent or more of all plan participants are literate only in the same non-English language; or

(ii) For a plan that covers 100 or more participants at the beginning of a plan year, if the plan and issuer provide notices upon request in a non-English language in which the lesser of 500 or more participants, or 10 percent or more of all plan participants, are literate only in the same non-English language.

(2) If an applicable threshold described in paragraph (e)(1) of this section is met, the plan and issuer must also—

(i) Include a statement in the English versions of all notices, prominently displayed in the non-English language, offering the provision of such notices in the non-English language;

(ii) Once a request has been made by a claimant, provide all subsequent notices to the claimant in the non-English language; and

(iii) To the extent the plan or issuer maintains a customer assistance process (such as a telephone hotline) that answers questions or provides assistance with filing claims and appeals, the plan or issuer must provide such assistance in the non-English language.

(f) *Secretarial authority.* The Secretary may determine that the external review process of a group health plan or health insurance issuer, in operation as of March 23, 2010, is considered in compliance with the applicable process established under paragraph (c) or (d) of this section if it substantially meets the requirements of paragraph (c) or (d) of this section, as applicable.

(g) *Applicability date.* The provisions of this section apply for plan years beginning on or after September 23, 2010. See § 2590.715–1251 of this part for determining the application of this section to grandfathered health plans (providing that these rules regarding internal claims and appeals and external

review processes do not apply to grandfathered health plans).

DEPARTMENT OF HEALTH AND HUMAN SERVICES

45 CFR Subtitle A

■ For the reasons stated in the preamble, the Department of Health and Human Services amends 45 CFR part 147 as follows:

PART 147—HEALTH INSURANCE REFORM REQUIREMENTS FOR THE GROUP AND INDIVIDUAL HEALTH INSURANCE MARKETS

■ 1. The authority citation for part 147 continues to read as follows:

Authority: Sections 2701 through 2763, 2791, and 2792 of the Public Health Service Act (42 U.S.C. 300gg through 300gg–63, 300gg–91, and 300gg–92), as amended.

■ 2. Add § 147.136 to read as follows:

§ 147.136 Internal claims and appeals and external review processes.

(a) *Scope and definitions—*(1) *Scope.* This section sets forth requirements with respect to internal claims and appeals and external review processes for group health plans and health insurance issuers that are not grandfathered health plans under § 147.140 of this part. Paragraph (b) of this section provides requirements for internal claims and appeals processes. Paragraph (c) of this section sets forth rules governing the applicability of State external review processes. Paragraph (d) of this section sets forth a Federal external review process for plans and issuers not subject to an applicable State external review process. Paragraph (e) of this section prescribes requirements for ensuring that notices required to be provided under this section are provided in a culturally and linguistically appropriate manner. Paragraph (f) of this section describes the authority of the Secretary to deem certain external review processes in existence on March 23, 2010 as in compliance with paragraph (c) or (d) of this section. Paragraph (g) of this section sets forth the applicability date for this section.

(2) *Definitions.* For purposes of this section, the following definitions apply—

(i) *Adverse benefit determination.* An *adverse benefit determination* means an adverse benefit determination as defined in 29 CFR 2560.503–1, as well as any rescission of coverage, as described in § 147.128 (whether or not, in connection with the rescission, there is an adverse effect on any particular benefit at that time).

(ii) *Appeal (or internal appeal).* An *appeal* or *internal appeal* means review by a plan or issuer of an adverse benefit determination, as required in paragraph (b) of this section.

(iii) *Claimant. Claimant* means an individual who makes a claim under this section. For purposes of this section, references to claimant include a claimant's authorized representative.

(iv) *External review. External review* means a review of an adverse benefit determination (including a final internal adverse benefit determination) conducted pursuant to an applicable State external review process described in paragraph (c) of this section or the Federal external review process of paragraph (d) of this section.

(v) *Final internal adverse benefit determination.* A *final internal adverse benefit determination* means an adverse benefit determination that has been upheld by a plan or issuer at the completion of the internal appeals process applicable under paragraph (b) of this section (or an adverse benefit determination with respect to which the internal appeals process has been exhausted under the deemed exhaustion rules of paragraph (b)(2)(ii)(F) or (b)(3)(ii)(F) of this section).

(vi) *Final external review decision.* A *final external review decision*, as used in paragraph (d) of this section, means a determination by an independent review organization at the conclusion of an external review.

(vii) *Independent review organization (or IRO).* An *independent review organization* (or *IRO*) means an entity that conducts independent external reviews of adverse benefit determinations and final internal adverse benefit determinations pursuant to paragraph (c) or (d) of this section.

(viii) *NAIC Uniform Model Act.* The *NAIC Uniform Model Act* means the Uniform Health Carrier External Review Model Act promulgated by the National Association of Insurance Commissioners in place on July 23, 2010.

(b) *Internal claims and appeals process*—(1) *In general.* A group health plan and a health insurance issuer offering group or individual health insurance coverage must implement an effective internal claims and appeals process, as described in this paragraph (b).

(2) *Requirements for group health plans and group health insurance issuers.* A group health plan and a health insurance issuer offering group health insurance coverage must comply with all the requirements of this paragraph (b)(2). In the case of health insurance coverage offered in connection with a group health plan, if

either the plan or the issuer complies with the internal claims and appeals process of this paragraph (b)(2), then the obligation to comply with this paragraph (b)(2) is satisfied for both the plan and the issuer with respect to the health insurance coverage.

(i) *Minimum internal claims and appeals standards.* A group health plan and a health insurance issuer offering group health insurance coverage must comply with all the requirements applicable to group health plans under 29 CFR 2560.503–1, except to the extent those requirements are modified by paragraph (b)(2)(ii) of this section. Accordingly, under this paragraph (b), with respect to health insurance coverage offered in connection with a group health plan, the group health insurance issuer is subject to the requirements in 29 CFR 2560.503–1 to the same extent as the group health plan.

(ii) *Additional standards.* In addition to the requirements in paragraph (b)(2)(i) of this section, the internal claims and appeals processes of a group health plan and a health insurance issuer offering group health insurance coverage must meet the requirements of this paragraph (b)(2)(ii).

(A) *Clarification of meaning of adverse benefit determination.* For purposes of this paragraph (b)(2), an "adverse benefit determination" includes an adverse benefit determination as defined in paragraph (a)(2)(i) of this section. Accordingly, in complying with 29 CFR 2560.503–1, as well as the other provisions of this paragraph (b)(2), a plan or issuer must treat a rescission of coverage (whether or not the rescission has an adverse effect on any particular benefit at that time) as an adverse benefit determination. (Rescissions of coverage are subject to the requirements of § 147.128 of this part.)

(B) *Expedited notification of benefit determinations involving urgent care.* Notwithstanding the rule of 29 CFR 2560.503–1(f)(2)(i) that provides for notification in the case of urgent care claims not later than 72 hours after the receipt of the claim, for purposes of this paragraph (b)(2), a plan and issuer must notify a claimant of a benefit determination (whether adverse or not) with respect to a claim involving urgent care as soon as possible, taking into account the medical exigencies, but not later than 24 hours after the receipt of the claim by the plan or issuer, unless the claimant fails to provide sufficient information to determine whether, or to what extent, benefits are covered or payable under the plan or health insurance coverage. The requirements of

29 CFR 2560.503–1(f)(2)(i) other than the rule for notification within 72 hours continue to apply to the plan and issuer. For purposes of this paragraph (b)(2)(ii)(B), a claim involving urgent care has the meaning given in 29 CFR 2560.503–1(m)(1).

(C) *Full and fair review.* A plan and issuer must allow a claimant to review the claim file and to present evidence and testimony as part of the internal claims and appeals process. Specifically, in addition to complying with the requirements of 29 CFR 2560.503–1(h)(2)—

(*1*) The plan or issuer must provide the claimant, free of charge, with any new or additional evidence considered, relied upon, or generated by the plan or issuer (or at the direction of the plan or issuer) in connection with the claim; such evidence must be provided as soon as possible and sufficiently in advance of the date on which the notice of final internal adverse benefit determination is required to be provided under 29 CFR 2560.503–1(i) to give the claimant a reasonable opportunity to respond prior to that date; and

(*2*) Before the plan or issuer can issue a final internal adverse benefit determination based on a new or additional rationale, the claimant must be provided, free of charge, with the rationale; the rationale must be provided as soon as possible and sufficiently in advance of the date on which the notice of final internal adverse benefit determination is required to be provided under 29 CFR 2560.503–1(i) to give the claimant a reasonable opportunity to respond prior to that date.

(D) *Avoiding conflicts of interest.* In addition to the requirements of 29 CFR 2560.503–1(b) and (h) regarding full and fair review, the plan and issuer must ensure that all claims and appeals are adjudicated in a manner designed to ensure the independence and impartiality of the persons involved in making the decision. Accordingly, decisions regarding hiring, compensation, termination, promotion, or other similar matters with respect to any individual (such as a claims adjudicator or medical expert) must not be made based upon the likelihood that the individual will support the denial of benefits.

(E) *Notice.* A plan and issuer must provide notice to individuals, in a culturally and linguistically appropriate manner (as described in paragraph (e) of this section) that complies with the requirements of 29 CFR 2560.503–1(g) and (j). The plan and issuer must also comply with the additional requirements of this paragraph (b)(2)(ii)(E).

(1) The plan and issuer must ensure that any notice of adverse benefit determination or final internal adverse benefit determination includes information sufficient to identify the claim involved (including the date of service, the health care provider, the claim amount (if applicable), the diagnosis code and its corresponding meaning, and the treatment code and its corresponding meaning).

(2) The plan and issuer must ensure that the reason or reasons for the adverse benefit determination or final internal adverse benefit determination includes the denial code and its corresponding meaning, as well as a description of the plan's or issuer's standard, if any, that was used in denying the claim. In the case of a notice of final internal adverse benefit determination, this description must include a discussion of the decision.

(3) The plan and issuer must provide a description of available internal appeals and external review processes, including information regarding how to initiate an appeal.

(4) The plan and issuer must disclose the availability of, and contact information for, any applicable office of health insurance consumer assistance or ombudsman established under PHS Act section 2793 to assist individuals with the internal claims and appeals and external review processes.

(F) *Deemed exhaustion of internal claims and appeals processes.* In the case of a plan or issuer that fails to strictly adhere to all the requirements of this paragraph (b)(2) with respect to a claim, the claimant is deemed to have exhausted the internal claims and appeals process of this paragraph (b), regardless of whether the plan or issuer asserts that it substantially complied with the requirements of this paragraph (b)(2) or that any error it committed was de minimis. Accordingly the claimant may initiate an external review under paragraph (c) or (d) of this section, as applicable. The claimant is also entitled to pursue any available remedies under section 502(a) of ERISA or under State law, as applicable, on the basis that the plan or issuer has failed to provide a reasonable internal claims and appeals process that would yield a decision on the merits of the claim. If a claimant chooses to pursue remedies under section 502(a) of ERISA under such circumstances, the claim or appeal is deemed denied on review without the exercise of discretion by an appropriate fiduciary.

(iii) *Requirement to provide continued coverage pending the outcome of an appeal.* A plan and issuer subject to the requirements of this paragraph (b)(2) are required to provide continued coverage pending the outcome of an appeal. For this purpose, the plan and issuer must comply with the requirements of 29 CFR 2560.503–1(f)(2)(ii), which generally provides that benefits for an ongoing course of treatment cannot be reduced or terminated without providing advance notice and an opportunity for advance review.

(3) *Requirements for individual health insurance issuers.* A health insurance issuer offering individual health insurance coverage must comply with all the requirements of this paragraph (b)(3).

(i) *Minimum internal claims and appeals standards.* A health insurance issuer offering individual health insurance coverage must comply with all the requirements of the ERISA internal claims and appeals procedures applicable to group health plans under 29 CFR 2560.503–1 except for the requirements with respect to multiemployer plans, and except to the extent those requirements are modified by paragraph (b)(3)(ii) of this section. Accordingly, under this paragraph (b), with respect to individual health insurance coverage, the issuer is subject to the requirements in 29 CFR 2560.503–1 as if the issuer were a group health plan.

(ii) *Additional standards.* In addition to the requirements in paragraph (b)(3)(i) of this section, the internal claims and appeals processes of a health insurance issuer offering individual health insurance coverage must meet the requirements of this paragraph (b)(3)(ii).

(A) *Clarification of meaning of adverse benefit determination.* For purposes of this paragraph (b)(3), an adverse benefit determination includes an adverse benefit determination as defined in paragraph (a)(2)(i) of this section. Accordingly, in complying with 29 CFR 2560.503–1, as well as other provisions of this paragraph (b)(3), an issuer must treat a rescission of coverage (whether or not the rescission has an adverse effect on any particular benefit at that time) and any decision to deny coverage in an initial eligibility determination as an adverse benefit determination. (Rescissions of coverage are subject to the requirements of 45 CFR 147.128.)

(B) *Expedited notification of benefit determinations involving urgent care.* Notwithstanding the rule of 29 CFR 2560.503–1(f)(2)(i) that provides for notification in the case of urgent care claims not later than 72 hours after the receipt of the claim, for purposes of this paragraph (b)(3), an issuer must notify a claimant of a benefit determination (whether adverse or not) with respect to a claim involving urgent care as soon as possible, taking into account the medical exigencies, but not later than 24 hours after the receipt of the claim by the issuer, unless the claimant fails to provide sufficient information to determine whether, or to what extent, benefits are covered or payable under the health insurance coverage. The requirements of 29 CFR 2560.503–1(f)(2)(i) other than the rule for notification within 72 hours continue to apply to the issuer. For purposes of this paragraph (b)(3)(ii)(B), a claim involving urgent care has the meaning given in 29 CFR 2560.503–1(m)(1).

(C) *Full and fair review.* An issuer must allow a claimant to review the claim file and to present evidence and testimony as part of the internal claims and appeals process. Specifically, in addition to complying with the requirements of 29 CFR 2560.503–1(h)(2)—

(1) The issuer must provide the claimant, free of charge, with any new or additional evidence considered, relied upon, or generated by the issuer (or at the direction of the issuer) in connection with the claim; such evidence must be provided as soon as possible and sufficiently in advance of the date on which the notice of final internal adverse benefit determination is required to be provided under 29 CFR 2560.503–1(i) to give the claimant a reasonable opportunity to respond prior to that date; and

(2) Before the issuer can issue a final internal adverse benefit determination based on a new or additional rationale, the claimant must be provided, free of charge, with the rationale; the rationale must be provided as soon as possible and sufficiently in advance of the date on which the notice of final internal adverse benefit determination is required to be provided under 29 CFR 2560.503–1(i) to give the claimant a reasonable opportunity to respond prior to that date.

(D) *Avoiding conflicts of interest.* In addition to the requirements of 29 CFR 2560.503–1(b) and (h) regarding full and fair review, the issuer must ensure that all claims and appeals are adjudicated in a manner designed to ensure the independence and impartiality of the persons involved in making the decision. Accordingly, decisions regarding hiring, compensation, termination, promotion, or other similar matters with respect to any individual (such as a claims adjudicator or medical expert) must not be made based upon the likelihood that the individual will support the denial of benefits.

(E) *Notice.* An issuer must provide notice to individuals, in a culturally and linguistically appropriate manner (as described in paragraph (e) of this section) that complies with the requirements of 29 CFR 2560.503–1(g) and (j). The issuer must also comply with the additional requirements of this paragraph (b)(2)(ii)(E).

(*1*) The issuer must ensure that any notice of adverse benefit determination or final internal adverse benefit determination includes information sufficient to identify the claim involved (including the date of service, the health care provider, the claim amount (if applicable), the diagnosis code and its corresponding meaning, and the treatment code and its corresponding meaning).

(*2*) The issuer must ensure that the reason or reasons for the adverse benefit determination or final internal adverse benefit determination includes the denial code and its corresponding meaning, as well as a description of the issuer's standard, if any, that was used in denying the claim. In the case of a notice of final internal adverse benefit determination, this description must include a discussion of the decision.

(*3*) The issuer must provide a description of available internal appeals and external review processes, including information regarding how to initiate an appeal.

(*4*) The issuer must disclose the availability of, and contact information for, any applicable office of health insurance consumer assistance or ombudsman established under PHS Act section 2793 to assist individuals with the internal claims and appeals and external review processes.

(F) *Deemed exhaustion of internal claims and appeals processes.* In the case of an issuer that fails to strictly adhere to all the requirements of this paragraph (b)(3) with respect to a claim, the claimant is deemed to have exhausted the internal claims and appeals process of this paragraph (b), regardless of whether the issuer asserts that it substantially complied with the requirements of this paragraph (b)(3) or that any error it committed was de minimis. Accordingly the claimant may initiate an external review under paragraph (c) or (d) of this section, as applicable. The claimant is also entitled to pursue any available remedies under applicable State law on the basis that the issuer has failed to provide a reasonable internal claims and appeals process that would yield a decision on the merits of the claim.

(G) *One level of internal appeal.* Notwithstanding the requirements in 29 CFR § 2560.503–1(c)(3), a health insurance issuer offering individual health insurance coverage must provide for only one level of internal appeal before issuing a final determination.

(H) *Recordkeeping requirements.* A health insurance issuer offering individual health insurance coverage must maintain for six years records of all claims and notices associated with the internal claims and appeals process, including the information detailed in paragraph (b)(3)(ii)(E) of this section and any other information specified by the Secretary. An issuer must make such records available for examination by the claimant or State or Federal oversight agency upon request.

(iii) *Requirement to provide continued coverage pending the outcome of an appeal.* An issuer subject to the requirements of this paragraph (b)(3) is required to provide continued coverage pending the outcome of an appeal. For this purpose, the issuer must comply with the requirements of 29 CFR 2560.503–1(f)(2)(ii) as if the issuer were a group health plan, so that the issuer cannot reduce or terminate an ongoing course of treatment without providing advance notice and an opportunity for advance review.

(c) *State standards for external review*—(1) *In general.* (i) If a State external review process that applies to and is binding on a health insurance issuer offering group or individual health insurance coverage includes at a minimum the consumer protections in the NAIC Uniform Model Act, then the issuer must comply with the applicable State external review process and is not required to comply with the Federal external review process of paragraph (d) of this section. In such a case, to the extent that benefits under a group health plan are provided through health insurance coverage, the group health plan is not required to comply with either this paragraph (c) or the Federal external review process of paragraph (d) of this section.

(ii) To the extent that a group health plan provides benefits other than through health insurance coverage (that is, the plan is self-insured) and is subject to a State external review process that applies to and is binding on the plan (for example, is not preempted by ERISA) and the State external review process includes at a minimum the consumer protections in the NAIC Uniform Model Act, then the plan must comply with the applicable State external review process and is not required to comply with the Federal

external review process of paragraph (d) of this section.

(iii) If a plan or issuer is not required under paragraph (c)(1)(i) or (c)(1)(ii) of this section to comply with the requirements of this paragraph (c), then the plan or issuer must comply with the Federal external review process of paragraph (d) of this section, except to the extent, in the case of a plan, the plan is not required under paragraph (c)(1)(i) of this section to comply with paragraph (d) of this section.

(2) *Minimum standards for State external review processes.* An applicable State external review process must meet all the minimum consumer protections in this paragraph (c)(2). The Department of Health and Human Services will determine whether State external review processes meet these requirements.

(i) The State process must provide for the external review of adverse benefit determinations (including final internal adverse benefit determinations) by issuers (or, if applicable, plans) that are based on the issuer's (or plan's) requirements for medical necessity, appropriateness, health care setting, level of care, or effectiveness of a covered benefit.

(ii) The State process must require issuers (or, if applicable, plans) to provide effective written notice to claimants of their rights in connection with an external review for an adverse benefit determination.

(iii) To the extent the State process requires exhaustion of an internal claims and appeals process, exhaustion must be unnecessary where the issuer (or, if applicable, the plan) has waived the requirement, the issuer (or the plan) is considered to have exhausted the internal claims and appeals process under applicable law (including by failing to comply with any of the requirements for the internal appeal process, as outlined in paragraph (b)(2) or (b)(3) of this section), or the claimant has applied for expedited external review at the same time as applying for an expedited internal appeal.

(iv) The State process provides that the issuer (or, if applicable, the plan) against which a request for external review is filed must pay the cost of the IRO for conducting the external review. Notwithstanding this requirement, the State external review process may require a nominal filing fee from the claimant requesting an external review. For this purpose, to be considered nominal, a filing fee must not exceed $25, it must be refunded to the claimant if the adverse benefit determination (or final internal adverse benefit determination) is reversed through external review, it must be waived if payment of the fee would impose an undue financial hardship, and the annual limit on filing fees for any claimant within a single plan year (in the individual market, policy year) must not exceed $75.

(v) The State process may not impose a restriction on the minimum dollar amount of a claim for it to be eligible for external review. Thus, the process may not impose, for example, a $500 minimum claims threshold.

(vi) The State process must allow at least four months after the receipt of a notice of an adverse benefit determination or final internal adverse benefit determination for a request for an external review to be filed.

(vii) The State process must provide that IROs will be assigned on a random basis or another method of assignment that assures the independence and impartiality of the assignment process (such as rotational assignment) by a State or independent entity, and in no event selected by the issuer, plan, or the individual.

(viii) The State process must provide for maintenance of a list of approved IRO qualified to conduct the external review based on the nature of the health care service that is the subject of the review. The State process must provide for approval only of IROs that are accredited by a nationally recognized private accrediting organization.

(ix) The State process must provide that any approved IRO has no conflicts of interest that will influence its independence. Thus, the IRO may not own or control, or be owned or controlled by a health insurance issuer, a group health plan, the sponsor of a group health plan, a trade association of plans or issuers, or a trade association of health care providers. The State process must further provide that the IRO and the clinical reviewer assigned to conduct an external review may not have a material professional, familial, or financial conflict of interest with the issuer or plan that is the subject of the external review; the claimant (and any related parties to the claimant) whose treatment is the subject of the external review; any officer, director, or management employee of the issuer; the plan administrator, plan fiduciaries, or plan employees; the health care provider, the health care provider's group, or practice association recommending the treatment that is subject to the external review; the facility at which the recommended treatment would be provided; or the developer or manufacturer of the principal drug, device, procedure, or other therapy being recommended.

(x) The State process allows the claimant at least five business days to submit to the IRO in writing additional information that the IRO must consider when conducting the external review and it requires that the claimant is notified of the right to do so. The process must also require that any additional information submitted by the claimant to the IRO must be forwarded to the issuer (or, if applicable, the plan) within one business day of receipt by the IRO.

(xi) The State process must provide that the decision is binding on the issuer (or, if applicable, the plan), as well as the claimant except to the extent the other remedies are available under State or Federal law.

(xii) The State process must require, for standard external review, that the IRO provide written notice to the claimant and the issuer (or, if applicable, the plan) of its decision to uphold or reverse the adverse benefit determination (or final internal adverse benefit determination) within no more than 45 days after the receipt of the request for external review by the IRO.

(xiii) The State process must provide for an expedited external review if the adverse benefit determination (or final internal adverse benefit determination) concerns an admission, availability of care, continued stay, or health care service for which the claimant received emergency services, but has not been discharged from a facility; or involves a medical condition for which the standard external review time frame would seriously jeopardize the life or health of the claimant or jeopardize the claimant's ability to regain maximum function. As expeditiously as possible but within no more than 72 hours after the receipt of the request for expedited external review by the IRO, the IRO must make its decision to uphold or reverse the adverse benefit determination (or final internal adverse benefit determination) and notify the claimant and the issuer (or, if applicable, the plan) of the determination. If the notice is not in writing, the IRO must provide written confirmation of the decision within 48 hours after the date of the notice of the decision.

(xiv) The State process must require that issuers (or, if applicable, plans) include a description of the external review process in or attached to the summary plan description, policy, certificate, membership booklet, outline of coverage, or other evidence of coverage it provides to participants, beneficiaries, or enrollees, substantially similar to what is set forth in section 17 of the NAIC Uniform Model Act.

(xv) The State process must require that IROs maintain written records and make them available upon request to the State, substantially similar to what is set forth in section 15 of the NAIC Uniform Model Act.

(xvi) The State process follows procedures for external review of adverse benefit determinations (or final internal adverse benefit determinations) involving experimental or investigational treatment, substantially similar to what is set forth in section 10 of the NAIC Uniform Model Act.

(3) *Transition period for existing external review processes*—(i) For plan years (in the individual market, policy years) beginning before July 1, 2011, an applicable State external review process applicable to a health insurance issuer or group health plan is considered to meet the requirements of this paragraph (c). Accordingly, for plan years (in the individual market, policy years) beginning before July 1, 2011, an applicable State external review process will be considered binding on the issuer or plan (in lieu of the requirements of the Federal external review process). If there is no applicable State external review process, the issuer or plan is required to comply with the requirements of the Federal external review process in paragraph (d) of this section.

(ii) For final internal adverse benefit determinations (or, in the case of simultaneous internal appeal and external review, adverse benefit determinations) provided after the first day of the first plan year (in the individual market, policy year) beginning on or after July 1, 2011, the Federal external review process will apply unless the Department of Health and Human Services determines that a State law meets all the minimum standards of paragraph (c)(2) of this section as of the first day of the plan year (in the individual market, policy year).

(d) *Federal external review process*— A plan or issuer not subject to an applicable State external review process under paragraph (c) of this section must provide an effective Federal external review process in accordance with this paragraph (d) (except to the extent, in the case of a plan, the plan is described in paragraph (c)(1)(i) of this section as not having to comply with this paragraph (d)). In the case of health insurance coverage offered in connection with a group health plan, if either the plan or the issuer complies with the Federal external review process of this paragraph (d), then the obligation to comply with this paragraph (d) is satisfied for both the plan and the issuer with respect to the health insurance coverage.

(1) *Scope.* The Federal external review process established pursuant to this paragraph (d) applies to any adverse benefit determination or final internal adverse benefit determination as defined in paragraphs (a)(2)(i) and (a)(2)(v) of this section, except that a denial, reduction, termination or, or a failure to provide payment for a benefit based on a determination that a participant or beneficiary fails to meet the requirements for eligibility under the terms of a group health plan is not eligible for the external review process under this paragraph (d).

(2) *External review process standards.* The Federal external review process established pursuant to this paragraph (d) will be similar to the process set forth in the NAIC Uniform Model Act and will meet standards issued by the Secretary. These standards will comply with all of the requirements described in this paragraph (d)(2).

(i) These standards will describe how a claimant initiates an external review, procedures for preliminary reviews to determine whether a claim is eligible for external review, minimum qualifications for IROs, a process for approving IROs eligible to be assigned to conduct external reviews, a process for random assignment of external reviews to approved IROs, standards for IRO decision-making, and rules for providing notice of a final external review decision.

(ii) These standards will provide an expedited external review process for—

(A) An adverse benefit determination, if the adverse benefit determination involves a medical condition of the claimant for which the timeframe for completion of an expedited internal appeal under paragraph (b) of this section would seriously jeopardize the life or health of the claimant, or would jeopardize the claimant's ability to regain maximum function and the claimant has filed a request for an expedited internal appeal under paragraph (b) of this section; or

(B) A final internal adverse benefit determination, if the claimant has a medical condition where the timeframe for completion of a standard external review pursuant to paragraph (d)(3) of this section would seriously jeopardize the life or health of the claimant or would jeopardize the claimant's ability to regain maximum function, or if the final internal adverse benefit determination concerns an admission, availability of care, continued stay or

health care service for which the claimant received emergency services, but has not been discharged from a facility.

(iii) With respect to claims involving experimental or investigational treatments, these standards will also provide additional consumer protections to ensure that adequate clinical and scientific experience and protocols are taken into account as part of the external review process.

(iv) These standards will provide that an external review decision is binding on the plan or issuer, as well as the claimant, except to the extent other remedies are available under State or Federal law.

(v) These standards may establish external review reporting requirements for IROs.

(vi) These standards will establish additional notice requirements for plans and issuers regarding disclosures to participants, beneficiaries, and enrollees describing the Federal external review procedures (including the right to file a request for an external review of an adverse benefit determination or a final internal adverse benefit determination in the summary plan description, policy, certificate, membership booklet, outline of coverage, or other evidence of coverage it provides to participants, beneficiaries, or enrollees.

(vii) These standards will require plans and issuers to provide information relevant to the processing of the external review, including, but not limited to, the information considered and relied on in making the adverse benefit determination or final internal adverse benefit determination.

(e) *Form and manner of notice*—(1) *Group health coverage*—(i) For purposes of this section, a group health plan and health insurance issuer offering group health insurance coverage are considered to provide relevant notices in a culturally and linguistically appropriate manner—

(A) For a plan that covers fewer than 100 participants at the beginning of a plan year, if the plan and issuer provide notices upon request in a non-English language in which 25 percent or more of all plan participants are literate only in the same non-English language; or

(B) For a plan that covers 100 or more participants at the beginning of a plan year, if the plan and issuer provides notices upon request in a non-English language in which the lesser of 500 or more participants, or 10 percent or more of all plan participants, are literate only in the same non-English language.

(ii) If an applicable threshold described in paragraph (e)(1)(i) of this section is met, the plan and issuer must also—

(A) Include a statement in the English versions of all notices, prominently displayed in the non-English language, offering the provision of such notices in the non-English language;

(B) Once a request has been made by a claimant, provide all subsequent notices to the claimant in the non-English language; and

(C) To the extent the plan or issuer maintains a customer assistance process (such as a telephone hotline) that answers questions or provides assistance with filing claims and appeals, the plan or issuer must provide such assistance in the non-English language.

(2) *Individual health insurance coverage*—(i) For purposes of this section, a health insurance issuer offering individual health insurance coverage is considered to provide relevant notices in a culturally and linguistically appropriate manner if the issuer provides notices upon request in a non-English language in which 10 percent or more of the population residing in the claimant's county are literate only in the same non-English language, determined in guidance published by the Secretary of Health and Human Services.

(ii) If the threshold described in paragraph (e)(2)(i) of this section is met, the issuer must also—

(A) Include a statement in the English versions of all notices, prominently displayed in the non-English language, offering the provision of such notices in the non-English language;

(B) Once a request has been made by a claimant, provide all subsequent notices to the claimant in the non-English language; and

(C) To the extent the issuer maintains a customer assistance process (such as a telephone hotline) that answers questions or provides assistance with filing claims and appeals, the issuer must provide such assistance in the non-English language.

(f) *Secretarial authority.* The Secretary may determine that the external review process of a group health plan or health insurance issuer, in operation as of March 23, 2010, is considered in compliance with the applicable process established under paragraph (c) or (d) of this section if it substantially meets the requirements of paragraph (c) or (d) of this section, as applicable.

43364   **Federal Register**/Vol. 75, No. 141/Friday, July 23, 2010/Rules and Regulations

(g) *Applicability date.* The provisions of this section apply for plan years (in the individual market, policy years) beginning on or after September 23, 2010. See § 147.140 of this part for determining the application of this section to grandfathered health plans (providing that these rules regarding internal claims and appeals and external review processes do not apply to grandfathered health plans).

[FR Doc. 2010–18043 Filed 7–22–10; 8:45 am]

BILLING CODE 4830–01–P, 4510–29–P, 4120–01–P

Core concept	Knowledge	Action/behavior
Protect	Act now to protect yourself from potential catastrophe later.	Choose appropriate insurance. Build up an emergency fund. Shop around.
	Identity theft/fraud/scams	Protect your identity. Avoid fraud and scams. Review your credit report.

Dated: August 18, 2010.

Alistair Fitzpayne,

Executive Secretary.

[FR Doc. 2010–21305 Filed 8–25–10; 8:45 am]

BILLING CODE 4810–25–P

DEPARTMENT OF THE TREASURY

Internal Revenue Service

Proposed Collection; Comment Request for Form 8809

AGENCY: Internal Revenue Service (IRS), Treasury.

ACTION: Notice and request for comments.

SUMMARY: The Department of the Treasury, as part of its continuing effort to reduce paperwork and respondent burden, invites the general public and other Federal agencies to take this opportunity to comment on proposed and/or continuing information collections, as required by the Paperwork Reduction Act of 1995, Public Law 104–13 (44 U.S.C. 3506(c)(2)(A)). Currently, the IRS is soliciting comments concerning Form 8809, Application for Extension of Time To File Information Returns.

DATES: Written comments should be received on or before October 25, 2010 to be assured of consideration.

ADDRESSES: Direct all written comments to Gerald Shields, Internal Revenue Service, room 6129, 1111 Constitution Avenue, NW., Washington, DC 20224.

FOR FURTHER INFORMATION CONTACT: Requests for additional information or copies of the form and instructions should be directed to Joel Goldberger at Internal Revenue Service, room 6129, 1111 Constitution Avenue, NW., Washington, DC 20224, or at (202) 927–9368, or through the Internet at *Joel.P.Goldberger@irs.gov.*

SUPPLEMENTARY INFORMATION:

Title: Application for Extension of Time To File Information Returns.

OMB Number: 1545–1081.

Form Number: Form 8809.

Abstract: Form 8809 is used to request an extension of time to file Forms W–2, W–2G, 1042–S, 1098, 1099, 5498, or 8027. The IRS reviews the information contained on the form to determine whether an extension should be granted.

Current Actions: There are no changes being made to the form at this time.

Type of Review: Extension of a currently approved collection.

Affected Public: Business or other for-profit organizations, individuals, not-for-profit institutions, farms, and Federal, State, local or tribal governments.

Estimated Number of Respondents: 50,000.

Estimated Time per Respondents: Three (3) hours, 15 minutes.

Estimated Total Annual Burden Hours: 162,500.

The following paragraph applies to all of the collections of information covered by this notice:

An agency may not conduct or sponsor, and a person is not required to respond to, a collection of information unless the collection of information displays a valid OMB control number. Books or records relating to a collection of information must be retained as long as their contents may become material in the administration of any internal revenue law. Generally, tax returns and tax return information are confidential, as required by 26 U.S.C. 6103.

Request for Comments: Comments submitted in response to this notice will be summarized and/or included in the request for OMB approval. All comments will become a matter of public record.

Comments are invited on: (a) Whether the collection of information is necessary for the proper performance of the functions of the agency, including whether the information shall have practical utility; (b) the accuracy of the agency's estimate of the burden of the collection of information; (c) ways to enhance the quality, utility, and clarity of the information to be collected; (d) ways to minimize the burden of the collection of information on respondents, including through the use of automated collection techniques or other forms of information technology; and (e) estimates of capital or start-up costs and costs of operation, maintenance, and purchase of services to provide information.

Approved: August 18, 2010.

Gerald Shields,

IRS Supervisory Tax Analyst.

[FR Doc. 2010–21207 Filed 8–25–10; 8:45 am]

BILLING CODE 4830–01–P

DEPARTMENT OF THE TREASURY

Internal Revenue Service

RIN 1545–BJ63

DEPARTMENT OF LABOR

Employee Benefits Security Administration

RIN 1210–AB45

DEPARTMENT OF HEALTH AND HUMAN SERVICES

RIN 0991–AB70

Availability of Interim Procedures for Federal External Review and Model Notices Relating to Internal Claims and Appeals and External Review Under the Patient Protection and Affordable Care Act; Notice

AGENCY: Internal Revenue Service, Department of the Treasury; Employee Benefits Security Administration, Department of Labor; Office of Consumer Information and Insurance Oversight, Department of Health and Human Services.

ACTION: Notice.

SUMMARY: This document announces the availability of guidance detailing interim procedures for the Federal external review process and model notices both for internal claims and appeals and for external review processes under the Patient Protection and Affordable Care Act.

FOR FURTHER INFORMATION CONTACT: Amy Turner or Beth Baum, Employee Benefits Security Administration, Department of Labor, at (202) 693–8335; Karen Levin, Internal Revenue Service, Department of the Treasury, at (202) 622–6080; Ellen Kuhn, Office of Consumer Information and Insurance Oversight, Department of Health and Human Services, at (301) 492–4100.

Customer Service Information: Individuals interested in obtaining

52598   Federal Register / Vol. 75, No. 165 / Thursday, August 26, 2010 / Notices

information from the Department of Labor concerning employment-based health coverage laws may call the EBSA Toll-Free Hotline at 1–866–444–EBSA (3272) or visit the Department of Labor's Web site (*http://www.dol.gov/ebsa*). In addition, information from HHS on private health insurance for consumers can be found on the Centers for Medicare & Medicaid Services (CMS) Web site (*http://www.cms.hhs.gov/ HealthInsReformforConsume/ 01_Overview.asp*) and information on health reform can be found at *http:// www.hhs.gov/ociio/* and *http:// www.healthcare.gov.*

SUPPLEMENTARY INFORMATION:

I. Background

The Patient Protection and Affordable Care Act (the Affordable Care Act), Public Law 111–148, was enacted on March 23, 2010; the Health Care and Education Reconciliation Act (the Reconciliation Act), Public Law 111– 152, was enacted on March 30, 2010. The Affordable Care Act and the Reconciliation Act reorganize, amend, and add to the provisions of part A of title XXVII of the Public Health Service Act (PHS Act) relating to group health plans and health insurance issuers in the group and individual markets. The Affordable Care Act adds section 715(a)(1) to the Employee Retirement Income Security Act (ERISA) and section 9815(a)(1) to the Internal Revenue Code (the Code) to incorporate the provisions of part A of title XXVII of the PHS Act into ERISA and the Code, and make them applicable to group health plans, and health insurance issuers providing health insurance coverage in connection with group health plans. The Departments of Labor, Health and Human Services, and the Treasury (the Departments) have been issuing regulations in several phases to implement the revised PHS Act sections 2701 through 2719A and related provisions of the Affordable Care Act.

Section 2719 of the PHS Act applies to group health plans and health insurance coverage that are not grandfathered health plans within the meaning of section 1251 of the Affordable Care Act.[1] It sets forth standards for plans and issuers regarding both internal claims and appeals and external review. The Departments published interim final regulations implementing PHS Act section 2719 on July 23, 2010, at 75 FR

43330 (the interim final regulations). In general, the interim final regulations require plans and issuers to comply with the requirements of 29 CFR 2560.503–1 (the DOL claims procedure regulation) and impose specified additional standards for internal claims and appeals.

Section 2719 of the PHS Act provides that plans and issuers in States without an applicable State external review process shall implement an effective external review process that meets minimum standards established by the Secretary through guidance and that is similar to a State external review process described in PHS Act Section 2719(b)(1). The statute and the interim final regulations also provide a basis for determining when plans and issuers must comply with an applicable State external review process and when they must comply with the Federal external review process. Generally, if a State has an external review process that meets, at a minimum, the consumer protections set forth in the interim final regulations, an issuer (or a plan) subject to the State process must comply with the State process. The regulations include a transition period for plan years (in the individual market, policy years) beginning before July 1, 2011, during which the Department of Health and Human Services (HHS) will work individually with States on an ongoing basis to assist in making any necessary changes to incorporate additional consumer protections so that the State process will continue to apply after the end of the transition period. For plans and issuers not subject to an existing State external review process (including self-insured plans), a Federal process is to apply for plan years (in the individual market, policy years) beginning on or after September 23, 2010.

The preamble to the interim final regulations provided that the Departments would issue additional guidance on the Federal external review process. In addition, the preamble stated that the Departments would issue model notices that could be used to satisfy the notice requirements under the interim final regulations. This notice announces the availability of and provides links to guidance on the interim Federal external review process, as well as links to the model notices.

II. Interim Federal External Review Process for Self-Insured Group Health Plans

This notice announces the availability of EBSA Technical Release No. 2010– 01, which provides an interim enforcement safe harbor for non-

grandfathered self-insured group health plans not subject to a State external review process, and therefore subject to the Federal external review process. (In the case of health insurance coverage offered in connection with a group health plan, the issuer has primary responsibility to comply with the interim final regulations.) This interim enforcement safe harbor applies for plan years beginning on or after September 23, 2010 and until superseded by future guidance on the Federal external review process that is being developed and that will apply after this interim period. During the period that this interim enforcement safe harbor is in effect, the Department of Labor and the Internal Revenue Service will not take any enforcement action against a self-insured group health plan that complies with either of the following interim compliance methods (and if a plan complies with one of the interim compliance methods of this notice, no excise tax liability should be reported on IRS Form 8928 with respect to PHS Act section 2719(b)):

• *Compliance with the procedures outlined in Technical Release 2010–01.* The Department of Labor and the Internal Revenue Service will not take enforcement action against any plan that complies with the procedures set forth in Technical Release No. 2010–01. These procedures are based on the Uniform Health Carrier External Review Model Act promulgated by the National Association of Insurance Commissioners (NAIC Model Act) in place on July 23, 2010.[2] The Technical Release is available today on the Department of Labor's Web site at: *http://www.dol.gov/ ebsa.*

• *Voluntary compliance with State external review processes.* Alternatively, States may choose to expand access to their State external review process to plans that are not subject to the applicable State laws, such as self-insured plans, and such plans may choose to voluntarily comply with the provisions of that State external review process. In such circumstances, while the interim enforcement safe harbor is in effect, the Department of Labor and

---

[1] The Departments published interim final regulations implementing section 1251 of the Affordable Care Act on June 17, 2010, at 75 FR 34538.

[2] Even though these procedures are based on the NAIC Model Act, they do not include all the consumer protections of the NAIC Model Act. For example, the procedures set forth in this notice do not include the special provisions for claims relating to experimental or investigational treatment and do not include a government agency certifying and assigning independent review organizations. The NAIC Model Act is available at *http:// www.dol.gov/ebsa* and *http://www.hhs.gov/ociio/.* Future guidance will address the minimum consumer protections required under the Federal external review process after the interim enforcement safe harbor period.

the Internal Revenue Service also will not take enforcement action against a plan that voluntarily complies with the provisions of a State external review process that would not otherwise be applicable or available.

The Departments will issue guidance regarding what process will apply under 26 CFR 54.9815–2719T(d), 29 CFR 2590.715–2719(d), and 45 CFR 147.136(d) no later than July 1, 2011 to replace the interim process.

III. Interim Federal External Review Process for Issuers

For issuers in the individual market and the small group and large group health insurance markets (including fully-insured group health plans), there will be an interim enforcement safe harbor which will apply only for plan years (in the individual market, policy years) beginning on or after September 23, 2010 and until superseded by future guidance on the Federal external review process that is being developed and that will apply after this interim period. During this limited interim enforcement safe harbor period, HHS will not take any enforcement action against an issuer that complies with the interim compliance method that will be detailed by HHS on the Office of Consumer Information and Insurance Oversight Web site (*http://www.hhs.gov/ociio/*). This method will either involve use of a State external appeals process or a temporary process established by HHS.

Prior to July 1, 2011, HHS will issue further guidance as to which State external review laws have been determined to satisfy the minimum standards of the NAIC Model Act as identified in 45 CFR 147.136(c). The Departments will issue guidance regarding what process will apply under 26 CFR 54.9815–2719T(d), 29 CFR 2590.715–2719(d), and 45 CFR 147.136(d) no later than July 1, 2011 to replace the interim process.

IV. Model Notices

Model notices that can be used to satisfy the disclosure requirements of the interim final regulations [3] are being posted on the Department of Labor's Web site at *http://www.dol.gov/ebsa* and the Department of HHS/Office of Consumer Information and Insurance Oversight Web site at *http://www.hhs.gov/ociio/*. These models include:

(1) A notice of adverse benefit determination;

(2) A notice of final internal adverse benefit determination; and

(3) A notice of final external review decision.

Model language for the description of the internal claims and appeals and external review procedures in the summary plan description provided to participants and beneficiaries will be posted on these websites in the future.

Please note that the Departments accounted for the actual costs of the external appeal process taking into account the model notices when the interim final regulations were issued.

Signed: August 19, 2010.

Sarah Hall Ingram,

Acting Deputy Commissioner for Services and Enforcement, Internal Revenue Service.

Signed: August 20, 2010.

Michael L. Davis,

Deputy Assistant Secretary, Employee Benefits Security Administration, Department of Labor.

Dated: August 20. 2010.

Jay Angoff,

Director, Office of Consumer Information and Insurance Oversight.

[FR Doc. 2010–21206 Filed 8–23–10; 11:15 am]

BILLING CODE 4830–01–P; 4510–29–P; 4120–01–P

DEPARTMENT OF THE TREASURY

Internal Revenue Service

Members of Senior Executive Service Performance Review Boards; Correction

AGENCY: Internal Revenue Service (IRS), Treasury.

[3] For rules regarding the form and manner of notice, see 26 CFR 54.9815–2719T(e), 29 CFR 2590.715–2719(e), and 45 CFR 147.136(e).

ACTION: Correction to notice.

SUMMARY: This document contains a correction to a notice that was published in the **Federal Register** on Wednesday, August 18, 2010 (75 FR 51168) providing the list of names of those IRS employees who will serve as members on IRS' Fiscal Year 2010 Senior Executive Service (SES) Performance Review Boards.

DATES: This notice is effective on September 1, 2010.

FOR FURTHER INFORMATION CONTACT: Sharnetta Walton, 1111 Constitution Avenue, NW., Room 2403, Washington, DC 20224, (202) 283–6246.

SUPPLEMENTARY INFORMATION:

Background

The notice that is the subject of this correction is pursuant to 5 U.S.C. 4314(c)(4) and announces the appointment of members to the Internal Revenue Service's SES Performance Review Boards.

Need for Correction

As published, the notice for Members of Senior Executive Service Performance Review Boards contains an error that may prove to be misleading and is in need of clarification.

Correction of Publication

Accordingly, the publication of the notice for Members of Senior Executive Service Performance Review Boards, which was the subject of FR Doc. 2010–20331, is corrected as follows:

On page 51169, column 1, in the preamble, under the caption **SUPPLEMENTARY INFORMATION,** the language "Charles Hunter, Director of Field Operations (CI)" is inserted between lines 16 and 17 of the column.

LaNita Van Dyke,

Chief, Publications and Regulations Branch, Legal Processing Division, Associate Chief Counsel, (Procedure and Administration).

[FR Doc. 2010–21272 Filed 8–25–10; 8:45 am]

BILLING CODE 4830–01–P

N. Amendment to Tri-Agency Regulations on Claims and Appeals Process

37208   Federal Register / Vol. 76, No. 122 / Friday, June 24, 2011 / Rules and Regulations

DEPARTMENT OF THE TREASURY

Internal Revenue Service

26 CFR Part 54

[TD 9532]

RIN 1545–BK30

DEPARTMENT OF LABOR

Employee Benefits Security Administration

29 CFR Part 2590

RIN 1210–AB45

DEPARTMENT OF HEALTH AND HUMAN SERVICES

[CMS–9993–IFC2]

45 CFR Part 147

RIN 0938–AQ66

Group Health Plans and Health Insurance Issuers: Rules Relating to Internal Claims and Appeals and External Review Processes

AGENCIES: Internal Revenue Service, Department of the Treasury; Employee Benefits Security Administration, Department of Labor; Centers for Medicare & Medicaid Services, Department of Health and Human Services.

ACTION: Amendment to interim final rules with request for comments.

SUMMARY: This document contains amendments to interim final regulations implementing the requirements regarding internal claims and appeals and external review processes for group health plans and health insurance coverage in the group and individual markets under provisions of the Affordable Care Act. These rules are intended to respond to feedback from a wide range of stakeholders on the interim final regulations and to assist plans and issuers in coming into full compliance with the law through an orderly and expeditious implementation process.

DATES: *Effective date.* This amendment to the interim final regulations is effective on July 22, 2011.

Comment date. Comments are due on or before July 25, 2011.

ADDRESSES: Written comments may be submitted to any of the addresses specified below. Any comment that is submitted to any Department will be shared with the other Departments. Please do not submit duplicates.

All comments will be made available to the public. *Warning:* Do not include any personally identifiable information (such as name, address, or other contact information) or confidential business information that you do not want publicly disclosed. All comments may be posted on the Internet and can be retrieved by most Internet search engines. Comments may be submitted anonymously.

Department of Labor. Comments to the Department of Labor, identified by RIN 1210–AB45, by one of the following methods:

• *Federal eRulemaking Portal: http:// www.regulations.gov.* Follow the instructions for submitting comments.

• *E-mail: E-OHPSCA2719amend.EBSA@dol.gov.*

• *Mail or Hand Delivery:* Office of Health Plan Standards and Compliance Assistance, Employee Benefits Security Administration, Room N–5653, U.S. Department of Labor, 200 Constitution Avenue, NW., Washington, DC 20210, *Attention:* RIN 1210–AB45.

Comments received by the Department of Labor will be posted without change to *http:// www.regulations.gov* and *http:// www.dol.gov/ebsa,* and available for public inspection at the Public Disclosure Room, N–1513, Employee Benefits Security Administration, 200 Constitution Avenue, NW., Washington, DC 20210.

Department of Health and Human Services. In commenting, please refer to file code CMS–9993–IFC2. Because of staff and resource limitations, we cannot accept comments by facsimile (FAX) transmission.

You may submit comments in one of four ways (please choose only one of the ways listed):

1. *Electronically.* You may submit electronic comments on this regulation to *http://www.regulations.gov.* Follow the instructions under the "More Search Options" tab.

2. *By regular mail.* You may mail written comments to the following address ONLY: Centers for Medicare & Medicaid Services, Department of Health and Human Services, Attention: CMS–9993–IFC2, P.O. Box 8010, Baltimore, MD 21244–8010.

Please allow sufficient time for mailed comments to be received before the close of the comment period.

3. *By express or overnight mail.* You may send written comments to the following address ONLY: Centers for Medicare & Medicaid Services, Department of Health and Human Services, Attention: CMS–9993–IFC2, Mail Stop C4–26–05, 7500 Security Boulevard, Baltimore, MD 21244–1850.

4. *By hand or courier.* If you prefer, you may deliver (by hand or courier) your written comments before the close of the comment period to either of the following addresses:

a. For delivery in Washington, DC— Centers for Medicare & Medicaid Services, Department of Health and Human Services, Room 445–G, Hubert H. Humphrey Building, 200 Independence Avenue, SW., Washington, DC 20201.

(Because access to the interior of the Hubert H. Humphrey Building is not readily available to persons without Federal government identification, commenters are encouraged to leave their comments in the CMS drop slots located in the main lobby of the building. A stamp-in clock is available for persons wishing to retain a proof of filing by stamping in and retaining an extra copy of the comments being filed.)

b. For delivery in Baltimore, MD— Centers for Medicare & Medicaid Services, Department of Health and Human Services, 7500 Security Boulevard, Baltimore, MD 21244–1850.

If you intend to deliver your comments to the Baltimore address, please call telephone number (410) 786–9994 in advance to schedule your arrival with one of our staff members.

Comments mailed to the addresses indicated as appropriate for hand or courier delivery may be delayed and received after the comment period.

Internal Revenue Service. Comments to the IRS, identified by REG–125592–10, by one of the following methods:

• *Federal eRulemaking Portal: http:// www.regulations.gov.* Follow the instructions for submitting comments.

• *Mail:* CC:PA:LPD:PR (REG–125592–10), Room 5205, Internal Revenue Service, P.O. Box 7604, Ben Franklin Station, Washington, DC 20044.

• *Hand or courier delivery:* Monday through Friday between the hours of 8 a.m. and 4 p.m. to: CC:PA:LPD:PR (REG–125592–10), Courier's Desk, Internal Revenue Service, 1111 Constitution Avenue, NW., Washington, DC 20224.

All submissions to the IRS will be open to public inspection and copying in Room 1621, 1111 Constitution Avenue, NW., Washington, DC from 9 a.m. to 4 p.m.

FOR FURTHER INFORMATION CONTACT: Amy Turner or Beth Baum, Employee Benefits Security Administration, Department of Labor, at (202) 693–8335; Karen Levin, Internal Revenue Service, Department of the Treasury, at (202) 622–6080; Ellen Kuhn, Centers for Medicare & Medicaid Services, Department of Health and Human Services, at (301) 492–4100.

Customer Service Information: Individuals interested in obtaining information from the Department of Labor concerning employment-based health coverage laws may call the EBSA Toll-Free Hotline at 1–866–444–EBSA (3272) or visit the Department of Labor's Web site (*http://www.dol.gov/ebsa*). In addition, information from HHS on private health insurance for consumers can be found on the Centers for Medicare & Medicaid Services (CMS) Web site (*http://www.cms.hhs.gov/ HealthInsReformforConsume/ 01_Overview.asp*). Information on health reform can be found at *http:// www.healthcare.gov.*

SUPPLEMENTARY INFORMATION:

I. Background

The Patient Protection and Affordable Care Act, Public Law 111–148, was enacted on March 23, 2010; the Health Care and Education Reconciliation Act, Public Law 111–152, was enacted on March 30, 2010 (collectively known as the "Affordable Care Act"). The Affordable Care Act reorganizes, amends, and adds to the provisions in part A of title XXVII of the Public Health Service Act (PHS Act) relating to group health plans and health insurance issuers in the group and individual markets. The term "group health plan" includes both insured and self-insured group health plans.[1] The Affordable Care Act adds section 715(a)(1) to the Employee Retirement Income Security Act (ERISA) and section 9815(a)(1) to the Internal Revenue Code (the Code) to incorporate the provisions of part A of title XXVII of the PHS Act into ERISA and the Code, and make them applicable to group health plans, and health insurance issuers providing health insurance coverage in connection with group health plans. The PHS Act sections incorporated by this reference are sections 2701 through 2728. PHS Act sections 2701 through 2719A are substantially new, though they incorporate some provisions of prior law. PHS Act sections 2722 through 2728 are sections of prior law renumbered, with some, mostly minor, changes.

On July 23, 2010, the Departments of Health and Human Services (HHS), Labor, and the Treasury (the Departments) issued interim final regulations implementing PHS Act section 2719 at 75 FR 43330 (July 2010 regulations), regarding internal claims and appeals and external review

processes for group health plans and health insurance issuers offering coverage in the group and individual markets. The requirements of PHS Act section 2719 and the July 2010 regulations do not apply to grandfathered health plans under section 1251 of the Affordable Care Act.[2]

A. Internal Claims and Appeals

With respect to internal claims and appeals processes for group health plans and health insurance issuers offering group health insurance coverage, PHS Act section 2719 provides that plans and issuers must initially incorporate the internal claims and appeals processes set forth in regulations promulgated by the Department of Labor (DOL) at 29 CFR 2560.503–1 (the DOL claims procedure regulation) and update such processes in accordance with standards established by the Secretary of Labor. Similarly, with respect to internal claims and appeals processes for individual health insurance coverage, issuers must initially incorporate the internal claims and appeals processes set forth in applicable State law and update such processes in accordance with standards established by the Secretary of HHS.

The July 2010 regulations provided such updated standards for compliance and invited comment on the updated standards. In particular, the July 2010 regulations provided the following additional standards[3] for internal claims and appeals processes:

1. The scope of adverse benefit determinations eligible for internal claims and appeals includes a rescission of coverage (whether or not the rescission has an adverse effect on any particular benefit at the time).[4]

---

[2] The Departments published interim final regulations implementing section 1251 of the Affordable Care Act on June 17, 2010, at 75 FR 34538, as amended on November 17, 2010 at 75 FR 70114.

[3] To address certain relevant differences in the group and individual markets, the July 2010 regulations provided that health insurance issuers offering individual health insurance coverage must comply with three additional requirements for internal claims and appeals processes. First, the July 2010 regulations include initial eligibility determinations in the individual market within the scope of claims eligible for internal appeals. Second, health insurance issuers offering individual health insurance coverage are permitted only one level of internal appeal. Third, health insurance issuers offering individual health insurance coverage must maintain all records of claims and notices associated with internal claims and appeals for six years and must make these records available for examination by the claimant, State or Federal oversight agency. 75 FR 43330, 43334 (July 23, 2010).

[4] This definition is broader than the definition in the DOL claims procedure regulation, which provides that a denial, reduction, or termination of,

2. Notwithstanding the rule in the DOL claims procedure regulation that provides for notification in the case of urgent care claims[5] not later than 72 hours after the receipt of the claim, a plan or issuer must notify a claimant of a benefit determination (whether adverse or not) with respect to a claim involving urgent care as soon as possible, taking into account the medical exigencies, but not later than 24 hours after the receipt of the claim by the plan or issuer.[6]

3. Clarifications with respect to full and fair review, such that plans and issuers are clearly required to provide the claimant (free of charge) with new or additional evidence considered, relied upon, or generated by (or at the direction of) the plan or issuer in connection with the claim, as well as any new or additional rationale for a denial at the internal appeals stage, and a reasonable opportunity for the claimant to respond to such new evidence or rationale.

4. Clarifications regarding conflicts of interest, such that decisions regarding hiring, compensation, termination, promotion, or other similar matters with respect to an individual, such as a claims adjudicator or medical expert, must not be based upon the likelihood that the individual will support the denial of benefits.

5. Notices must be provided in a culturally and linguistically appropriate manner, as required by the statute, and as set forth in paragraph (e) of the July 2010 regulations.

6. Notices to claimants must provide additional content. Specifically:

a. Any notice of adverse benefit determination or final internal adverse benefit determination must include information sufficient to identify the claim involved, including the date of the service, the health care provider, the claim amount (if applicable), the diagnosis code and its corresponding meaning, and the treatment code and its corresponding meaning.

---

or a failure to provide payment (in whole or in part) for a benefit is an adverse benefit determination eligible for internal claims and appeals processes.

[5] A claim involving urgent care is generally a claim for medical care or treatment with respect to which the application of the time periods for making non-urgent care determinations could seriously jeopardize the life or health of the claimant or the ability of the claimant to regain maximum function; or, in the opinion of the physician with knowledge of the claimant's medical condition, would subject the claimant to severe pain that cannot be adequately managed without the care or treatment that is the subject of the claim.

[6] Under the July 2010 regulations, there is a special exception if the claimant fails to provide sufficient information to determine whether, or to what extent, benefits are covered or payable under the plan.

---

[1] The term "group health plan" is used in title XXVII of the PHS Act, part 7 of ERISA, and chapter 100 of the Code, and is distinct from the term "health plan", as used in other provisions of title I of the Affordable Care Act. The term "health plan", as used in those provisions, does not include self-insured group health plans.

37210   Federal Register / Vol. 76, No. 122 / Friday, June 24, 2011 / Rules and Regulations

b. The plan or issuer must ensure that the reason or reasons for an adverse benefit determination or final internal adverse benefit determination includes the denial code and its corresponding meaning, as well as a description of the plan's or issuer's standard, if any, that was used in denying the claim. In the case of a final internal adverse benefit determination, this description must also include a discussion of the decision.

c. The plan or issuer must provide a description of available internal appeals and external review processes, including information regarding how to initiate an appeal.

d. The plan or issuer must disclose the availability of, and contact information for, an applicable office of health insurance consumer assistance or ombudsman established under PHS Act section 2793.

7. If a plan or issuer fails to strictly adhere to all the requirements of the July 2010 regulations, the claimant is deemed to have exhausted the plan's or issuer's internal claims and appeals process, regardless of whether the plan or issuer asserts that it has substantially complied, and the claimant may initiate any available external review process or remedies available under ERISA or under State law.

On September 20, 2010, based on a preliminary review of comments from stakeholders which indicated that they believed more time was needed to come into compliance with PHS Act section 2719 and the additional internal claims and appeal standards in the July 2010 regulations, the Department of Labor issued Technical Release 2010–02 (T.R. 2010–02), which set forth an enforcement grace period until July 1, 2011 for compliance with certain new provisions with respect to internal claims and appeals.[7]

Specifically, T.R. 2010–02 set forth an enforcement grace period until July 1, 2011 with respect to standard #2 above (regarding the timeframe for making urgent care claims decisions), standard #5 above (regarding providing notices in a culturally and linguistically appropriate manner), standard #6 above (requiring broader content and specificity in notices), and standard #7 above (regarding exhaustion). T.R. 2010–02 also stated that, during that period, the Department of Labor and the Internal Revenue Service (IRS) would

not take any enforcement action against a group health plan, and HHS would not take any enforcement action against a self-funded nonfederal governmental health plan that is working in good faith to implement such additional standards but does not yet have them in place.[8]

Based on further review of the comments received on the July 2010 regulations and T.R. 2010–02, and other feedback from interested stakeholders, on March 18, 2011, the Department of Labor issued Technical Release 2011–01 [9] (T.R. 2011–01), which modified and extended the enforcement grace period set forth in T.R. 2010–02. Specifically, T.R. 2011–01 extended the enforcement grace period until plan years beginning on or after January 1, 2012 with respect to standard #2 above (regarding the timeframe for making urgent care claims decisions), standard #5 above (regarding providing notices in a culturally and linguistically appropriate manner), and standard #7 above (regarding exhaustion). Moreover, whereas T.R. 2010–02 required plans to be working in good faith to implement such standards for the enforcement grace period to apply, T.R. 2011–01 stated that no such requirement would apply for either the extended or the original enforcement grace period.

With respect to standard #6 above (requiring broader content and specificity in notices), T.R. 2011–01 extended the enforcement grace period only in part. Specifically, with respect to the requirement to disclose diagnosis codes and treatment codes (and their corresponding meanings), T.R. 2011–01 extended the enforcement grace period until plan years beginning on or after January 1, 2012.[10] With respect to the other disclosure requirements of standard #6, the enforcement grace period was extended from July 1, 2011 until the first day of the first plan year beginning on or after July 1, 2011 (which is January 1, 2012 for calendar year plans), affecting: (a) The disclosure

of information sufficient to identify a claim (other than the diagnosis and treatment information), (b) the reasons for an adverse benefit determination, (c) the description of available internal appeals and external review processes, and (d) for plans and issuers in States in which an office of health consumer assistance program or ombudsman is operational, the disclosure of the availability of, and contact information for, such program.[11]

T.R. 2011–01 also stated the Departments' intent to issue an amendment to the July 2010 regulations that would take into account comments and other feedback received from stakeholders and make modifications to certain provisions of the July 2010 regulations. T.R. 2011–01 went on to state that the relief was intended to act as a bridge until an amendment to the July 2010 regulations was issued.

This amendment to the July 2010 regulations makes changes with respect to the provisions subject to the enforcement grace period under T.R. 2011–01. At the expiration of the enforcement grace period, the Departments will begin enforcing the relevant requirements of the July 2010 regulations, as amended by this rulemaking.

B. External Review

1. Applicability of Federal and State External Review Processes

PHS Act section 2719, the July 2010 regulations, and technical guidance issued by the Departments [12] provide a system with respect to applicability of either a State external review process or a Federal external review process for non-grandfathered plans and issuers. How this impacts plans and issuers varies, depending on the type of coverage:

a. Self-insured plans subject to ERISA and/or the Code.

In the case of self-insured plans subject to ERISA and/or the Code, a

---

[7] Technical Release 2010–02 is available at *http://www.dol.gov/ebsa/pdf/ACATechnicalRelease 2010-02.pdf.* HHS published a corresponding guidance document, available at: *http:// cciio.cms.gov/resources/files/ interim_procedures_for_internal_claims_and _appeals.pdf.*

[8] T.R. 2010–02 also stated that HHS was encouraging States to provide similar grace periods with respect to issuers and HHS would not cite a State for failing to substantially enforce the provisions of part A of title XXVII of the PHS Act in these situations.

[9] T.R. 2011–01 is available at *http://www.dol.gov/ ebsa/pdf/tr11-01.pdf.*

[10] Information related to diagnosis and treatment codes (and/or their meanings) is, however, generally required to be provided to claimants upon request under existing DOL claims procedures. *See* 29 CFR 2560.503–1(h)(2)(iii), which is also applicable to plans (whether or not they are ERISA plans) and issuers that are not grandfathered health plans pursuant to paragraph (b)(2)(i) of the July 2010 regulations. Nevertheless, a request for such information, in itself, should not be considered to be a request for (and therefore trigger the start of) an internal appeal or external review.

[11] Any enforcement grace period with respect to disclosure requirements that has been provided under T.R. 2010–02 or T.R. 2011–01 does not affect disclosure requirements still in effect for ERISA plans under the DOL claims procedure regulation and/or Part 1 of ERISA.

[12] See DOL Technical Release 2010–01, available at *http://www.dol.gov/ebsa/pdf/ ACATechnicalRelease2010-01.pdf;* HHS Technical Guidance issued August 26, 2010, available at *http://cciio.cms.gov/resources/files/interim_appeals _guidance.pdf;* and HHS Technical Guidance issued September 23, 2010, available at *http:// cciio.cms.gov/resources/files/technical_guidance _for_self_funded_non_fed_plans.pdf.* Additional clarifications were provided in the form of frequently-asked questions (FAQs), available at *http://www.dol.gov/ebsa/faqs/faq-aca.html* and *http://cciio.cms.gov/resources/factsheets/ aca_implementation_faqs.html#claims.*

Federal external review process supervised by DOL and Treasury applies (the "private accredited IRO process"[13]). On August 23, 2010, the Department of Labor issued Technical Release 2010–01 (T.R. 2010–01), which set forth an interim enforcement safe harbor for self-insured plans not subject to a State external review process or to the HHS-supervised process (the "HHS-administered process").[14] This interim enforcement safe harbor essentially permits a private contract process under which plans contract with accredited independent review organizations (IROs) to perform reviews. Separate guidance being issued contemporaneous with the publication of this amendment makes adjustments to, and provides clarifications regarding, the operation of the private accredited IRO process.

b. *Insured coverage.*

In the case of health insurance issuers in the group and individual market, the July 2010 regulations set forth 16 minimum consumer protections based on the Uniform External Review Model Act promulgated by the National Association of Insurance Commissioners (NAIC) that, if provided by a State external review process, will result in the State's process applying in lieu of a Federal external review process. Moreover, for insured group health plans, as provided under paragraph (c)(1) of the July 2010 regulations, if a State external review process applies to and is binding on the plan's health insurance issuer under paragraph (c) of the July 2010 regulations (regarding State standards for external review), then the insured group health plan is not required to comply with either the State external review process or the Federal external review process. The July 2010 regulations provided a transition period for plan years (in the individual market, policy years) beginning before July 1, 2011, during which any existing State external review process will be considered sufficient (and will apply to health insurance

issuers in that State). During the transition period, in States and territories without an existing State external review process (Alabama, Mississippi, Nebraska, Guam, American Samoa, U.S. Virgin Islands and the Northern Mariana Islands), HHS guidance generally provided that health insurance issuers will participate in the HHS-administered process. As explained later in this preamble, this amendment to the July 2010 regulations modifies the transition period originally issued as part of the July 2010 regulations so that the last day of the transition period for all health insurance issuers offering group and individual health insurance coverage is December 31, 2011.

In addition, the July 2010 regulations provided that, following the conclusion of the transition period, health insurance issuers in a State that does not meet the minimum consumer protection standards set forth in paragraph (c) of the July 2010 regulations will participate in an external review process under Federal standards similar to the process under the NAIC Uniform Model Act, such as the HHS-administered process. Separate guidance being issued contemporaneous with the publication of this amendment announces standards under which, until January 1, 2014, a State may also operate such an external review process under Federal standards similar to the process under the NAIC Uniform Model Act (an "NAIC-similar process"). Accordingly, if HHS determines that a State has neither implemented the minimum consumer protections required under paragraph (c) of the July 2010 regulations, nor an NAIC-similar process, issuers in the State will have the choice of participating in either the HHS-administered process or the private accredited IRO process. HHS is adopting this approach to permit States to operate their external review processes under standards established by the Secretary until January 1, 2014, avoiding unnecessary disruption, while States work to adopt an "NAIC-parallel process," consistent with the consumer protections set forth in paragraph (c) of the July 2010 regulations.

c. Self-insured, nonfederal governmental plans.

For self-insured, nonfederal governmental plans (which are subject to the PHS Act, but not ERISA or the Code), previous HHS guidance generally provided that they follow the private accredited IRO process.[15] (In States and territories that did not have an existing

external review process (Alabama, Mississippi, Nebraska, Guam, American Samoa, U.S. Virgin Islands and the Northern Mariana Islands), previous HHS guidance generally provided that such plans may choose to follow the HHS-administered process or follow the private accredited IRO process.) Separate guidance being issued contemporaneous with the publication of this amendment generally treats self-insured nonfederal governmental plans the same as health insurance issuers. That is, a State may temporarily operate such an external review process applicable to a self-insured nonfederal governmental plan under Federal standards similar to the process under the NAIC Uniform Model Act. If no such State-operated process exists, self-insured nonfederal governmental plans have the choice of participating in either the HHS-administered process or the private accredited IRO process.

2. Scope of Claims Eligible for External Review

While the process varies depending on the type of coverage, so does the scope of claims eligible for external review. That is, for insurance coverage and self-insured nonfederal governmental plans subject to a State external review process (either an NAIC-parallel process or an NAIC-similar process), the State determines the scope of claims eligible for external review.[16] For coverage subject to either the HHS-administered process or the private accredited IRO process, the July 2010 regulations provided that any adverse benefit determination (or final internal adverse benefit determination) could be reviewed unless it is related to a participant's or beneficiary's failure to meet the requirements for eligibility under the terms of a group health plan. As explained later in this preamble, this amendment to the July 2010 regulations modifies the scope of claims eligible for

---

[13] For simplicity, the Federal external review process for self-insured plans subject to ERISA and/or the Code supervised by DOL and Treasury is referred to as the "private accredited IRO process" throughout this preamble. However, the interim procedures for Federal external review issued as DOL Technical Release 2010–01 also recognizes that States may choose to expand access to their State external review process to plans not subject to applicable State laws (such as self-insured ERISA plans) and allows those plans to meet their responsibilities to provide external review under PHS Act section 2719(b) by voluntarily complying with the provisions of that State external review process.

[14] HHS Technical Guidance issued August 26, 2010 provided that, for insured coverage, the Federal external review process would be fulfilled through the HHS-administered process.

[15] See HHS Technical Guidance issued September 23, 2010.

[16] Under paragraphs (c)(2)(i) and (c)(2)(xvi) of the July 2010 regulations, State processes must provide external review for adverse benefit determinations (including final internal adverse benefit determinations) that are based on issuer's (or plan's) requirements for medical necessity, appropriateness, health care setting, level of care, or effectiveness of a covered benefit; or that involve experimental or investigational treatment. (A State external review process may also provide for external review of a broader scope of adverse benefit determinations.) At the same time, paragraph (c)(3) of the July 2010 regulations provides a transition period during which a State external review process will be considered binding on an issuer (or a plan), in lieu of the requirements of any Federal external review process, even if the State process does not meet all the requirements of paragraph (c)(2) of the July 2010 regulations. That transition period is being modified by this amendment, as described below.

external review under the Federal external review process.

II. Overview of Amendments to the Interim Final Regulations

A. Internal Claims and Appeals

1. Expedited Notification of Benefit Determinations Involving Urgent Care (Paragraph (b)(2)(ii)(B) of the July 2010 Regulations)

The July 2010 regulations provided that a plan or issuer must notify a claimant of a benefit determination (whether adverse or not) with respect to a claim involving urgent care (as defined in the DOL claims procedure regulation) [17] as soon as possible, taking into account the medical exigencies, but not later than 24 hours after the receipt of the claim by the plan or issuer, unless the claimant fails to provide sufficient information to determine whether, or to what extent, benefits are covered or payable under the plan or health insurance coverage. This was a change from the DOL claims procedure regulation, which generally requires a determination not later than 72 hours after receipt of the claim by a group health plan for urgent care claims. The preamble to the July 2010 regulations stated that the Departments expected electronic communication would enable faster decision-making than in the year 2000, when the DOL claims procedure regulation was issued. [18]

While some commenters supported the 24-hour rule (particularly consumer advocates and medical associations, including mental health providers who noted the 24-hour standard was especially important for people in psychiatric crisis), concerns were raised by many plans and issuers regarding the burden of a 24-hour turnaround. Some commenters argued that some of the claims constituting "urgent care" and thus qualifying for the expedited timeframe really do not need to be made within 24 hours. Moreover, a number of commenters highlighted that the 72-hour provision was intended only to serve as a "backstop"; as the general rule under both the July 2010 regulations and the DOL claims procedure regulation requires a decision

as soon as possible consistent with the medical exigencies involved, making the change to a 24-hour timeframe unnecessary for the most serious medical cases. Some commenters cited the Emergency Medical Treatment and Labor Act (EMTALA), [19] which generally requires hospitals to provide emergency care to individuals with or without insurance or preauthorization and, therefore, mitigates the need for expedited pre-service emergency claims determinations in many situations. Finally, some commenters stated that a firm 24-hour turnaround for urgent care claims will adversely affect claimants, as plans and issuers will not have sufficient time to properly review a claim, adversely affecting the quality of the review process in cases where the provider cannot be consulted in time, and leading to unnecessary denials of claims.

After considering the comments, and the costs and benefits of an absolute 24-hour decision-making deadline for pre-service urgent care claims, this amendment permits plans and issuers to follow the original rule in the DOL claims procedure regulation (requiring decision-making in the context of pre-service urgent care claims as soon as possible consistent with the medical exigencies involved but in no event later than 72 hours), *provided* that the plan or issuer defers to the attending provider with respect to the decision as to whether a claim constitutes "urgent care." At the same time, the Departments underscore that the 72-hour timeframe remains only an outside limit and that, in cases where a decision must be made more quickly based on the medical exigencies involved, the requirement remains that the decision should be made sooner than 72 hours after receipt of the claim.

2. Additional Notice Requirements for Internal Claims and Appeals (Paragraph (b)(2)(ii)(E) of the July 2010 Regulations)

The July 2010 regulations also provided additional content requirements for any notice of adverse benefit determination or final internal adverse benefit determination. The July 2010 regulations required a plan or issuer to:

(a) Ensure that any notice of adverse benefit determination or final internal adverse benefit determination includes information sufficient to identify the claim involved. Under the July 2010 regulations, this information included the date of service, the health care provider, and the claim amount (if

applicable), [20] as well as the diagnosis code (such as an ICD–9 code, ICD–10 code, or DSM–IV code), [21] the treatment code (such as a CPT code), [22] and the corresponding meanings of these codes.

(b) Ensure that the description of the reason or reasons for the adverse benefit determination or final internal adverse benefit determination includes the denial code (such as a CARC and RARC) [23] and its corresponding meaning. It must also include a description of the plan's or issuer's standard, if any, that was used in denying the claim (for example, if a plan applies a medical necessity standard in denying a claim, the notice must include a description of the medical necessity standard). In the case of a notice of final internal adverse benefit determination, this description must include a discussion of the decision.

(c) Provide a description of available internal appeals and external review processes, including information regarding how to initiate an appeal.

(d) Disclose the availability of, and contact information for, any applicable office of health insurance consumer assistance or ombudsman established under PHS Act section 2793 to assist enrollees with the internal claims and appeals and external review processes. [24]

Many comments received on the July 2010 regulations raised concerns about the additional content required to be included in the notices. Comments by a range of stakeholders, including plans, issuers, and consumer advocacy organizations focused heavily on the automatic provision of the diagnosis

---

[17] Under the DOL claims procedure regulation, a "claim involving urgent care" is a claim for medical care or treatment with respect to which the application of the time periods for making non-urgent care determinations could seriously jeopardize the life or health of the claimant or the ability of the claimant to regain maximum function; or, in the opinion of a physician with knowledge of the claimant's medical condition, would subject the claimant to severe pain that cannot be adequately managed without the care or treatment that is the subject of the claim.

[18] 75 FR 43330, 43333 (July 23, 2010).

[19] 42 U.S.C. 1395dd.

[20] The amount of the claim may not be knowable or available at the time, such as in a case of preauthorization, or there may be no specific claim, such as in a case of rescission that is not connected to a claim.

[21] ICD–9 and ICD–10 codes refer to the International Classification of Diseases, 9th revision and 10th revision, respectively. The DSM–IV codes refer to the Diagnostic and Statistical Manual of Mental Disorders, Fourth Edition.

[22] CPT refers to Current Procedural Terminology.

[23] CARC refers to Claim Adjustment Reason Code and RARC refers to Remittance Advice Remark Code.

[24] To assist plans and issuers in making these disclosures, the Departments provided a current list of relevant consumer assistance programs and ombudsmen in the Appendix to T.R. 2011–01. Plans and issuers with July 1 plan years may rely upon the list in that Appendix when developing their notices of adverse benefit determination and final internal adverse benefit determination for plan years beginning on July 1, 2011. The Departments are committed to reviewing and updating this list. The first update is being made available contemporaneous with publication of this amendment. The first update is available (and any future updates will be made available) at http://www.dol.gov/ebsa/healthreform and http://cciio.cms.gov/programs/consumer/capgrants/index.html.

and treatment codes (and their meanings). Concerns were raised about privacy (because explanations of benefits (EOBs) often are sent to an individual who is not the patient, such as an employee who is the patient's spouse or parent), interference with the doctor-patient relationship,[25] and high costs.[26] More specifically, commenters highlighted that sensitive issues such as mental health treatments would be identified by specific treatment or diagnosis codes and that privacy concerns are magnified for adult dependents under age 26 who may be covered by their parent's health plan. Others pointed out that there are over 20,000 treatment and diagnosis codes in use today, presenting a costly administrative and operational challenge for plans and issuers. Comments also questioned the efficacy of providing the codes, which some argued are often very difficult for the average patient to understand.[27]

Other comments were received in support of the coding provisions. Consumer advocates commented positively on the requirement that denial notices include information for consumers about their right to appeal denials and the availability of state consumer assistance programs (CAPs) that will help consumers file appeals. There were also positive comments on the requirement to provide a rationale for the denial (including a description of the plan's or issuer's standard (such as "medical necessity"), if any, that was used denying the claim). With respect to the provision of coding information, some commented that this would be helpful to consumers because coding errors and missing coding information often are the basis for denying claims.

After considering all of the comments, and the costs and benefits of the

additional disclosure, this amendment eliminates the requirement to automatically provide the diagnosis and treatment codes as part of a notice of adverse benefit determination (or final internal adverse benefit determination) and instead substitutes a requirement that the plan or issuer must provide notification of the opportunity to request the diagnosis and treatment codes (and their meanings) in all notices of adverse benefit determination (and notices of final internal adverse benefit determination), and a requirement to provide this information upon request.[28] This amendment also clarifies that, in any case, a plan or issuer must not consider a request for such diagnosis and treatment information, in itself, to be a request for (and therefore trigger the start of) an internal appeal or external review.

3. Deemed Exhaustion of Internal Claims and Appeals Processes (Paragraph (b)(2)(ii)(F) of the July 2010 Regulations)

The courts generally require claimants to exhaust administrative proceedings before going to court or seeking external review. When plans and issuers offer full and fair internal procedures for resolving claims, it is reasonable to insist that claimants first turn to those procedures before seeking judicial or external review of benefit denials. There is less justification, however, for insisting that a claimant exhaust administrative procedures that do not comply with the law. Accordingly, the July 2010 regulations permitted claimants to immediately seek review if a plan or issuer failed to "strictly adhere" to all of the July 2010 regulations' requirements for internal claims and appeals processes, regardless of whether the plan or issuer asserted that it "substantially complied" with the July 2010 regulations. The July 2010 regulations also clarified that, in such circumstances, the reviewing tribunal should not give special deference to the plan's or issuer's decision, but rather should resolve the dispute *de novo*. Consumer groups generally supported this "strict adherence" approach, but the approach received a number of negative comments from some issuers and plan sponsors, who advocate a "substantial compliance" approach.

The Departments continue to believe that claimants should not have to follow an internal claims and appeals procedure that is less than full, fair, and timely, as set forth in the July 2010 regulations. In response to comments, the Departments are retaining the general approach to this requirement, but this amendment also adds a new paragraph (b)(2)(ii)(F)(2) to the July 2010 regulations to provide an exception to the strict compliance standard for errors that are minor and meet certain other specified conditions. The new paragraph will also protect claimants whose attempts to pursue other remedies under paragraph (b)(2)(ii)(F)(1) of the interim final regulations are rejected by a reviewing tribunal. Under the amended approach, any violation of the procedural rules of the July 2010 regulations pertaining to internal claims and appeals would permit a claimant to seek immediate external review or court action, as applicable, unless the violation was:

(1) De minimis;
(2) Non-prejudicial;
(3) Attributable to good cause or matters beyond the plan's or issuer's control;
(4) In the context of an ongoing good-faith exchange of information; and
(5) Not reflective of a pattern or practice of non-compliance.

In addition, the claimant would be entitled, upon written request, to an explanation of the plan's or issuer's basis for asserting that it meets this standard, so that the claimant could make an informed judgment about whether to seek immediate review. Finally, if the external reviewer or the court rejects the claimant's request for immediate review on the basis that the plan met this standard, this amendment would give the claimant the right to resubmit and pursue the internal appeal of the claim.

4. Form and Manner of Notice (Paragraph (e) of the July 2010 Regulations)

PHS Act section 2719 requires group health plans and health insurance issuers to provide relevant notices in a culturally and linguistically appropriate manner. The July 2010 regulations set forth a requirement to provide notices in a non-English language based on separate thresholds of the number of people who are literate in the same non-English language. In the group market, the threshold set forth in the July 2010 regulations differs depending on the number of participants in the plan:

• For a plan that covers fewer than 100 participants at the beginning of a plan year, the threshold is 25 percent of

---

[25] Several commenters raised concerns that providers' initial or suspected diagnosis may not match the ultimate diagnosis or patients' perception of their diagnosis. One commenter gave the example of a patient who has a biopsy procedure. In that case, the patient would receive an EOB with an initial diagnosis code of cancer, however the results of the biopsy may rule out cancer. In that situation, the EOB can result in confusion and unnecessary mental anguish.

[26] In particular, comment letters cited concerns with respect to programming aspects of providing diagnosis codes at a time when plans and issuers are changing over from ICD–9 diagnosis codes to more extensive and technical ICD–10 codes.

[27] Several commenters noted that technical ICD–9 and/or ICD–10 codes can be confusing and/or cause worry. One commenter gave the example of a patient presenting with a white coating on his tongue, who is told not to worry and to brush the tongue with a toothbrush. The diagnosis code is 529.3, hypertrophy of tongue papillae, a term not used by the patient's doctor during the office visit and, therefore, prone to cause confusion and/or concern.

[28] As discussed earlier, in footnote 9, information related to diagnosis and treatment codes (and/or their meanings) is, however, generally required to be provided to claimants upon request under existing DOL claims procedures, which is also incorporated in the July 2010 regulations. See 29 CFR 2560.503–1(h)(2)(iii) and paragraph (b)(2)(i) of the July 2010 regulations.

all plan participants being literate only in the same non-English language.

• For a plan that covers 100 or more participants at the beginning of a plan year, the threshold is the lesser of 500 participants, or 10 percent of all plan participants, being literate only in the same non-English language.

These thresholds were adapted from the DOL regulations regarding style and format for a summary plan description, at 29 CFR 2520.102–2(c) for participants who are not literate in English. For the individual market, the threshold is 10 percent of the population residing in the county being literate only in the same non-English language. The individual market threshold was generally adapted from the approach used under the Medicare Advantage program, which required translation of materials in languages spoken by more than 10 percent of the general population in a service area at the time the threshold was established.

Under the July 2010 regulations, if an applicable threshold is met with respect to a non-English language, the plan or issuer must provide the notice upon request in the non-English language. Additionally, the plan or issuer must include a statement in the English versions of all notices, prominently displayed in the non-English language, offering the provision of such notices in the non-English language. Finally, to the extent the plan or issuer maintains a customer assistance process (such as a telephone hotline) that answers questions or provides assistance with filing claims and appeals, the plan or issuer must provide such assistance in the non-English language.

Comments received in response to the July 2010 regulations raised several concerns about this requirement. One group of commenters stated that the thresholds for the group market were difficult to comply with, especially for small plans (where an individual or a small number of individuals could cause a plan to change status with respect to the threshold) and insured plans (where the issuer may be in a very difficult position to determine the English literacy of an employer's workforce). Some commenters stated that the threshold requirements for the group and individual markets should be consistent.

Other commenters were concerned with the high costs of compliance with this rule, particularly the "tagging and tracking requirement" to the extent that individuals who request a document in a non-English language would need to be "tagged" and "tracked" so that any future notices would be provided automatically in the non-English

language. Some of these commenters cited the high costs associated with implementing translation requirements pursuant to California State law and the low take-up rates of translated materials in California. Some commenters also cited the importance of having written translation of documents available (at a minimum, upon request), as well as having oral language services for customer assistance.

Following review of the comments submitted on this issue and further review and consideration of the provisions of PHS Act section 2719, the Departments have determined it is appropriate to amend the provisions of the July 2010 regulations related to the provision of notices in a culturally and linguistically appropriate manner. This amendment establishes a single threshold with respect to the percentage of people who are literate only in the same non-English language for both the group and individual markets. With respect to group health plans and health insurance issuers offering group or individual health insurance coverage, the threshold percentage of people who are literate only in the same non-English language will be set at 10 percent or more of the population residing in the claimant's county, as determined based on American Community Survey data published by the United States Census Bureau.[29] The Departments will update this guidance annually on their Web site if there are changes to the list of the counties determined to meet this 10 percent threshold for the county's population being literate only in the same non-English language.[30]

This amendment to the July 2010 regulations requires that each notice sent by a plan or issuer to an address in a county that meets this threshold include a one-sentence statement in the relevant non-English language about the availability of language services. The Departments have provided guidance with sample sentences in the relevant languages in separate guidance being issued contemporaneous with the publication of this amendment. For ease of administration, some plans and issuers may choose to use a one-sentence statement for all notices within

_____

[29] At the time of publication of this amendment, 255 U.S. counties (78 of which are in Puerto Rico) meet this threshold. The overwhelming majority of these are Spanish; however, Chinese, Tagalog, and Navajo are present in a few counties, affecting five states (specifically, Alaska, Arizona, California, New Mexico, and Utah). A full list of the affected U.S. counties in 2011 is included in Table 2 later in this preamble, under the heading, "IV. Economic Impact and Paperwork Burden."

[30] This information will be made available at http://www.dol.gov/ebsa/healthreform and http://cciio.cms.gov/.

an entire State (or for a particular service area) that reflects the threshold language or languages in any county within the State or service area. For example, statewide notices in California could include the relevant one-sentence statement in Spanish and Chinese because, using the data from Table 2, Spanish meets the 10 percent threshold in Los Angeles County and 22 other counties and Chinese meets the 10 percent threshold in San Francisco County. This would be a permissible approach to meeting the rule under this amendment.

In addition to including a statement in all notices in the relevant non-English language, this amendment requires a plan or issuer to provide a customer assistance process (such as a telephone hotline) with oral language services in the non-English language and provide written notices in the non-English language upon request. For this purpose, plans and issuers are permitted to direct claimants to the same customer service telephone number where representatives can first attempt to address the consumer's questions with an oral discussion, but also provide a written translation upon request in the threshold non-English language. Finally, this amendment removes any "tagging and tracking" requirement that would have otherwise applied under the July 2010 regulations.

This amendment to the July 2010 regulations provides standards for providing culturally and linguistically appropriate notices that balance the objective of protecting consumers by providing understandable notices to individuals who speak primary languages other than English with the goal of simplifying information collection burdens on plans and issuers. (Note, nothing in these regulations should be construed as limiting an individual's rights under Federal or State civil rights statutes, such as Title VI of the Civil Rights Act of 1964 (Title VI) which prohibits recipients of Federal financial assistance, including issuers participating in Medicare Advantage, from discriminating on the basis of race, color, or national origin. To ensure non-discrimination on the basis of national origin, recipients are required to take reasonable steps to ensure meaningful access to their programs and activities by limited English proficient persons. For more information, see, "Guidance to Federal Financial Assistance Recipients Regarding Title VI Prohibition Against National Origin Discrimination Affecting Limited English Proficient Persons," available at http://www.hhs.gov/ocr/civilrights/resources/

specialtopics/lep/
policyguidancedocument.html.)

The Departments welcome comments on this amendment, including whether it would be appropriate to include a provision in the final rules requiring health insurance issuers providing group health insurance coverage to provide language services in languages that do not meet the requisite threshold for an applicable non-English language, if requested by the administrator or sponsor of the group health plan to which the coverage relates. For example, if Chinese does not meet the 10 percent threshold in New York County, but an employer with a large Chinese-speaking population asks the health insurance issuer providing its group health insurance coverage to provide language services in Chinese (as described in the amendment), the Departments invite comment on what obligations should be imposed on the issuer, if any, to provide language services in Chinese.

B. External Review

1. Duration of Transition Period for State External Review Processes

In general, if State laws do not meet the minimum consumer protections of the NAIC Uniform Model Act,[31] as set forth in paragraph (c)(2) of the July 2010 regulations, insurance coverage (as well as self-insured nonfederal governmental plan and church plan coverage) is subject to the requirements of an external review process under Federal standards similar to the process under the NAIC Uniform Model Act, such as the HHS-administered process. Paragraph (c)(3) of the July 2010 regulations provided a transition period for plan years (in the individual market, policy years) beginning before July 1, 2011 in order to allow States time to amend their laws to meet or go beyond the minimum consumer protections of the NAIC Uniform Model Act set forth in paragraph (c)(2) of the July 2010 regulations. HHS has been working closely with States regarding enactment of laws to conform to paragraph (c)(2) and much progress has been made. However, enacting State legislation and regulations can often be a complex and time-consuming process. Accordingly, the Departments are modifying the transition period under paragraph (c)(3) of the July 2010 regulations so that the last day of the transition period is

---

[31] The NAIC Uniform Model Act in place on July 23, 2010 provides external review for claims involving medical necessity, appropriateness, health care setting, level of care, effectiveness (of a covered benefit), whether a treatment is experimental, and whether a treatment is investigational.

December 31, 2011 to give States, which are making substantial progress in implementing State external review processes that conform to paragraph (c)(2), the requisite time to complete that process. Because the July 2010 regulations would have ended the transition period for plan years (in the individual market, policy years) beginning on or after July 1, 2011, the Departments note that ending the transition period on December 31, 2011 will reduce the length of the transition period for plans and policies with plan years (in the individual market, policy years) beginning after January 1 but before July 1. When the July 2010 regulations were published, the Departments anticipated that issuers in every State that had not enacted laws to conform to paragraph (c)(2) of the July 2010 regulations would need to participate in the HHS-administered process. Now, the Departments have decided that issuers may continue to participate in a State external review process under Federal standards similar to the process under the NAIC Uniform Model Act (an NAIC-similar process), which the Departments anticipate will reduce market disruption when the transition period ends. Therefore, based on the Departments' concerns for making the consumer protections of the Affordable Care Act available without undue delay and for ensuring as much uniformity as possible in the availability of those protections regardless of the form of a consumer's health coverage, the Departments have decided to end the transition period on December 31, 2011. Therefore, this amendment to the July 2010 regulations provides that, before January 1, 2012, an applicable State external process will apply in lieu of the requirements of the Federal external review process. PHS Act section 2719(c) authorizes the Departments to deem an external review process "in operation as of the date of enactment" of the Affordable Care Act as compliant with the external review requirements of PHS Act section 2719(b). Through December 31, 2011, any currently effective State external review process satisfies the requirements of either PHS Act section 2719(c) or section 2719(b)(2). If there is no applicable State external review process, separate guidance being issued contemporaneous with the publication of this amendment generally provides a choice between the HHS-administered process or the private accredited IRO process.

2. Scope of the Federal External Review Process

Paragraph (d)(1) of the July 2010 regulations sets forth the scope of claims eligible for external review under the Federal external review process. Specifically, any adverse benefit determination (including a final internal adverse benefit determination) could be reviewed unless it related to a participant's or beneficiary's failure to meet the requirements for eligibility under the terms of a group health plan (i.e., worker classification and similar issues were not within the scope of the Federal external review process).

Comments received in response to the July 2010 regulations were mixed on the scope of claims eligible for external review. Some commenters argued that PHS Act section 2719 requires the Federal external review process to be "similar to" the NAIC Uniform Model Act and that the broader scope of claims eligible for the Federal external review process is a major departure from the NAIC Uniform Model Act. In addition, some comments from plans and issuers stated that the IROs that are used in the private accredited IRO process traditionally have expertise in adjudicating medical claims, and questioned IROs' experience and expertise with legal and contractual claims. Other comments from IROs and the IRO industry stated that these organizations do currently conduct reviews that involve both medical judgment issues and legal and contractual issues, and that there is sufficient capacity for conducting reviews of such disputes.

Some plan and issuer comments highlighted that, with a limited number of accredited IROs and increased demand for their services, the cost of external review for self-insured group health plans will likely increase. By contrast, an IRO association group commented that member organizations are not at capacity with regard to the volume of work they can perform, and that they are confident that the number of accredited IROs can adequately handle the volume of reviews anticipated for the Federal external review process.

Some plans and issuers stated that handing plan document interpretation and legal interpretation issues over to an IRO may raise issues of consistency of interpretations within a plan, unwarranted consistency across plans that have unique standards, ERISA fiduciary responsibility concerns, and possible conflicts. At the same time, other comments generally supported the broad scope of claims eligible for the

Federal external review process as set forth in the July 2010 regulations. These commenters argued very strongly that it is nearly impossible to adjudicate contractual claims through traditional ERISA enforcement (which generally relies on Federal court adjudication), leaving plan participants and beneficiaries with no effective means of enforcing their rights to benefits under a plan. Consumer organizations further commented that external review finally provides the free, independent means of enforcement to level the playing field of claims adjudication and, therefore, the scope of claims eligible for the Federal external review process should be as broad as possible.

After considering all the comments, with respect to claims for which external review has not been initiated before September 20, 2011, the amendment suspends the original rule in the July 2010 regulations regarding the scope of claims eligible for external review for plans using a Federal external review process (regardless of which type of Federal process), temporarily replacing it with a different scope. Specifically, this amendment suspends the broad scope of claims eligible for the Federal external review process and narrows the scope to claims that involve (1) medical judgment (excluding those that involve only contractual or legal interpretation without any use of medical judgment), as determined by the external reviewer; or (2) a rescission of coverage. The more narrow scope under this amendment is more similar to the scope of claims eligible for external review under the NAIC Uniform Model Act. This amendment provides an example describing a plan that generally only provides 30 physical therapy visits but will provide more with an approved treatment plan. The plan's rejection of a treatment plan submitted by a provider for the 31st visit based on a failure to meet the plan's standard for medical necessity involves medical judgment and, therefore, the claim is eligible for external review. Similarly, another example describes a plan that generally does not provide coverage for services provided on an out-of-network basis, but will provide coverage if the service cannot effectively be provided in network. In this example, again, the plan's rejection of a claim for out-of-network services involves medical judgment. Additional examples of situations in which a claim is considered to involve medical judgment include adverse benefit determinations based on:

• The appropriate health care setting for providing medical care to an

individual (such as outpatient versus inpatient care or home care versus rehabilitation facility);

• Whether treatment by a specialist is medically necessary or appropriate (pursuant to the plan's standard for medical necessity or appropriateness);

• Whether treatment involved "emergency care" or "urgent care", affecting coverage or the level of coinsurance;

• A determination that a medical condition is a preexisting condition;

• A plan's general exclusion of an item or service (such as speech therapy), if the plan covers the item or service in certain circumstances based on a medical condition (such as, to aid in the restoration of speech loss or impairment of speech resulting from a medical condition);

• Whether a participant or beneficiary is entitled to a reasonable alternative standard for a reward under the plan's wellness program;[32]

• The frequency, method, treatment, or setting for a recommended preventive service, to the extent not specified, in the recommendation or guideline of the U.S. Preventive Services Task Force, the Advisory Committee on Immunization Practices of the Centers for Disease Control and Prevention, or the Health Resources and Services Administration (as described in PHS Act section 2713 and its implementing regulations);[33] and

• Whether a plan is complying with the nonquantitative treatment limitation provisions of the Mental Health Parity and Addiction Equity Act and its implementing regulations, which generally require, among other things, parity in the application of medical management techniques.[34]

The suspension is intended to give the marketplace time to adjust to providing external review. It will also

---

[32] See 26 CFR 54.9802–1(f)(2)(iv)(A), 29 CFR 2590.702(f)(2)(iv)(A), and 45 CFR 146.121(f)(2)(iv)(A), requiring that wellness programs that require individuals to satisfy a standard related to a health factor in order to obtain a reward allow a reasonable alternative standard (or waiver of the otherwise applicable standard) for obtaining the reward for any individual for whom, for that period, it is either unreasonably difficult due to a medical condition to satisfy the otherwise applicable standard, or medically inadvisable to attempt to satisfy the otherwise applicable standard.

[33] See 26 CFR 54.9815–2713T, 29 CFR 2590.715–2713, and 45 CFR 147.130; see also FAQ 8. FAQs About the Affordable Care Act Implementation Part II, regarding the scope, setting, or frequency of the items or services to be covered under the preventive health services recommendations and guidelines (available at http://www.dol.gov/ebsa/faqs/faq-aca2.html and http://cciio.cms.gov/resources/factsheets/aca_implementation_faqs2.html).

[34] See Code section 9812 and 26 CFR 54.9812–1T, ERISA section 712 and 29 CFR 2590.712, and PHS Act section 2726 and 45 CFR 146.136.

allow the Departments time to evaluate IROs' capacity for handling external reviews; to consider whether current accreditation standards are sufficient to ensure that IROs are capable of making accurate and consistent decisions (both across different plans and across different IROs) regarding legal and contractual issues that do not involve medical judgment or rescissions; and to assess the mechanics of the Federal external review process (and any potential adjustments). The Departments solicit comments on these issues, including on whether limiting the scope of claims during the suspension period will impose administrative costs in determining whether a claim is eligible for external review. The Departments also welcome any data on external review claims actually performed to date under private contracts pursuant to the private accredited IRO process for implementing PHS Act § 2719(b), including number of claims reviewed, type of review (such as whether it involved any medical judgment or not), and costs associated with the review. The Departments expect that the suspension will be lifted by January 1, 2014, when other consumer protections under the Affordable Care Act take effect. Moreover, if, after taking into account all the relevant information, including public comments, the Departments decide to return to the original rule providing for a broad scope of claims or permanently modify the scope of claims through rulemaking, the Departments will give sufficient advance notice to enable plans, their service providers, IROs, and other affected parties sufficient time to comply with a new rule.

Separate guidance being issued contemporaneous with the publication of this amendment announces standards under which, until January 1, 2014, a State may operate an external review process under Federal standards similar to the process under the NAIC Uniform Model Act (an NAIC-similar process). The Departments are adopting this approach to permit States to operate their external review processes under standards established by the Departments until January 1, 2014, avoiding unnecessary disruption, while States work to adopt the consumer protections set forth in paragraph (c) of the July 2010 regulations. Paragraph (d)(1) of the July 2010 regulations, as amended, will govern the scope of a State external review process under Federal standards similar to the process under the NAIC Uniform Model Act. Because the amended paragraph (d)(1) creates a broader scope of external review than is required under the NAIC Uniform Model Act, and because it would be illogical to require States to make changes to their process to encompass the broader scope of paragraph (d)(1) in their external review process while they work to adopt the consumer protections of the NAIC Uniform Model Act (which has a narrower scope), the Departments are also amending paragraph (d)(1) to permit the Secretaries to modify the scope of the Federal external review process in future guidance to permit State external review processes (both NAIC-similar processes and NAIC-parallel processes) to the scope that applies under the NAIC Uniform Model Act.

3. Clarification Regarding Requirement That External Review Decision Be Binding

The Departments have received a number of comments on the requirement that an IRO decision be binding on parties. Specifically, the July 2010 regulations provided that an external review decision by an IRO is binding on the plan or issuer, as well as the claimant, except to the extent that other remedies are available under State or Federal law.[35] This binding requirement is also one of the minimum consumer protections set forth in paragraph (c) of the July 2010 regulations.[36]

Some comments received in response to the July 2010 regulations highlighted the importance of this consumer protection and expressed approval that this requirement would minimize delays that could further hurt claimants, as the plan or issuer must provide coverage or payment for the claim immediately upon receipt of a notice of a final external review decision. Other commenters questioned whether the requirement that external review is binding eliminates the plan's or issuer's option to choose to pay a claim at any time during or after the external review process.

Nothing in PHS Act section 2719(b), the July 2010 regulations, or related guidance precludes a plan or issuer from choosing to provide coverage or payment for a benefit. Instead, the Departments read the requirement of the NAIC Uniform Model Act, which is incorporated into the July 2010 regulations, to require plans and issuers

to provide a benefit if that is the decision of the IRO. A plan or issuer may not delay payment because the plan disagrees and intends to seek judicial review. Instead, while the plan may be entitled to seek judicial review, it must act in accordance with the IRO's decision (including by making payment on the claim) unless or until there is a judicial decision otherwise. However, the requirement that the IRO's decision be binding does not preclude the plan or issuer from making payment on the claim or otherwise providing benefits at any time, including following a final external review decision that denies the claim or otherwise fails to require such payment or benefits.

After considering all the comments on the requirement that an IRO decision be binding on the plan and issuer, as well as the claimant, this amendment clarifies the language in paragraphs (c)(2)(xi) (regarding the minimum standards for State external review processes) and (d)(2)(iv) (regarding Federal external review process standards). Specifically, these two provisions are amended to add language stating that, for purposes of the binding provision, the plan or issuer must provide benefits (including by making payment on the claim) pursuant to the final external review decision without delay, regardless of whether the plan or issuer intends to seek judicial review of the external review decision and unless or until there is a judicial decision otherwise. The Departments welcome comments as to whether any additional clarifications about the binding provision would be helpful.

C. Separate, Contemporaneous Technical Guidance

Separate technical guidance is being issued by the Departments contemporaneous with the publication of this amendment. This technical guidance addresses both State- and Federally-administered external review processes. An appendix to this technical guidance contains revised versions of the three model notices issued by the Departments in connection with the July 2010 regulations. The updated versions of the model notice of adverse benefit determination, model notice of final internal adverse benefit determination, and model notice of final external review decision reflect the requirements contained in the provisions of this amendment and the guidance. This technical guidance will be available at *http://www.dol.gov/ebsa/healthreform* and *http://cciio.cms.gov.*

HHS is issuing also two additional technical guidance documents. The first provides instructions for self-insured

nonfederal governmental plans and health insurance issuers with respect to election of a Federal external review process. The second provides, for transparency purposes, updated information on how the county-level estimates pertaining to the 10 percent threshold were calculated for the rules related to culturally and linguistically appropriate notices. Both of these documents will be available at *http://cciio.cms.gov.*

III. Interim Final Rules

Section 9833 of the Code, section 734 of ERISA, and section 2792 of the PHS Act authorize the Secretaries of the Treasury, Labor, and HHS (collectively, the Secretaries) to promulgate any interim final rules that they determine are appropriate to carry out the provisions of chapter 100 of the Code, part 7 of subtitle B of title I of ERISA, and part A of title XXVII of the PHS Act, which include PHS Act sections 2701 through 2728 and the incorporation of those sections into ERISA section 715 and Code section 9815. The amendments promulgated in this rulemaking carry out the provisions of these statutes. Therefore, the foregoing interim final rule authority applies to these amendments.

Under the Administrative Procedure Act (APA) (5 U.S.C. 551 *et seq.*), while a general notice of proposed rulemaking and an opportunity for public comment is generally required before promulgation of regulations, this is not required when an agency, for good cause, finds that notice and public comment thereon are impracticable, unnecessary, or contrary to the public interest. The provisions of the APA that ordinarily require a notice of proposed rulemaking do not apply here because of the specific authority to issue interim final rules granted by section 9833 of the Code, section 734 of ERISA, and section 2792 of the PHS Act. Moreover, even if the APA requirements for notice and comment were applicable to this regulation, they have been satisfied. This is because the matters that are the subject of these amendments have already been subjected to public notice and comment, as they were addressed in the July 2010 regulations, and are a logical outgrowth of that document. The amendments made in this interim final rule are being made in response to public comments received on the July 2010 regulations. While the Departments have determined that, even if the APA were applicable, an additional opportunity for public comment is unnecessary in the case of these amendments, the Departments are issuing these amendments as an interim

---

[35] See 26 CFR 54.9815–2719T(d)(2)(iv), 29 CFR 2590.715–2719(d)(2)(iv), and 45 CFR 147.136(d)(2)(iv).

[36] See 26 CFR 54.9815–2719T(c)(2)(xi), 29 CFR 2590.715–2719(c)(2)(xi), and 45 CFR 147.136(c)(2)(xi).

final rule so as to provide the public with an opportunity for public comment on these modifications.

IV. Economic Impact and Paperwork Burden

A. Summary and Need for Regulatory Action—Department of Labor and Department of Health and Human Services

As stated earlier in this preamble, the Departments previously issued the July 2010 regulations implementing PHS Act section 2719, which were published in the **Federal Register** on July 23, 2010 (75 FR 43330). The July 2010 regulations set forth rules with respect to internal claims and appeals and external appeals processes for group health plans and health insurance issuers that are not grandfathered health plans.

As described in detail in Section II of this preamble, after the July 2010 regulations were issued, the Departments received public comments expressing concerns about the burdens associated with several of the regulations' provisions. In response to such comments, the Departments are hereby amending the following provisions of the July 2010 regulations:

• Expedited notification of benefit determinations involving urgent care (paragraph (b)(2)((ii)(B) of the July 2010 regulations);

• Additional notice requirements with respect to notice of adverse benefit determinations or final internal adverse benefit determination (paragraph (b)(2)(ii)(E) of the July 2010 regulations);[37]

• Deemed exhaustion of internal claims and appeals processes (paragraph (b)(2)(ii)(F) of the July 2010 regulations);

• Providing notices in a culturally and linguistically appropriate manner (paragraph (e) of the July 2010 regulations);

• The duration of the transition period for State external review processes (paragraph (c)(3) of the July 2010 regulations); and

• The scope of claims eligible for external review under the Federal external appeals process (paragraph (d)(1) of the July 2010 regulations).

The Departments crafted these amendments to the July 2010 regulations to secure the protections intended by Congress. In accordance with OMB Circular A–4, the Departments have quantified the costs of these amendments where feasible and provided a qualitative discussion of some of the benefits and costs that may stem from them.

The Departments believe that (i) the costs associated with the amended rules are less than the costs associated with the July 2010 regulations, (ii) the amended rules adequately protect the

rights of participants, beneficiaries, and policyholders, and (iii) the benefits of the amended rules justify their costs relative to the pre-Affordable Care Act baseline and the July 2010 regulations.

B. Executive Orders 12866 and 13563—Department of Labor and Department of Health and Human Services

Executive Orders 13563 and 12866 direct agencies to assess all costs and benefits of available regulatory alternatives and, if regulation is necessary, to select regulatory approaches that maximize net benefits (including potential economic, environmental, public health and safety effects, distributive impacts, and equity). Executive Order 13563 emphasizes the importance of quantifying both costs and benefits, of reducing costs, of harmonizing rules, and of promoting flexibility. This rule has been designated a "significant regulatory action" although not economically significant, under section 3(f) of Executive Order 12866. Accordingly, the rule has been reviewed by the Office of Management and Budget.

The Departments provide an assessment of the potential costs and benefits associated with each amended regulatory provision below, as summarized in Table 1.

TABLE 1—ACCOUNTING TABLE

Benefits
Qualitative: Amendments to the interim final regulations ensure urgent care benefit determinations are made in a timely manner, increase patient privacy, ensure non-English speakers understand their rights, and provide that claimants will be deemed to have exhausted their administrative proceedings and can proceed to court or external review if a plan or issuer fails to strictly adhere to the regulatory requirements with the exception of the requirements that are described in the amendment. These amendments are expected to reduce compliance costs while still ensuring patient protections.

Cost	Estimate	Year dollar	Discount rate	Period covered
Annualized Monetized ($millions/year)	1.7	2011	7 percent	2012–2014
	1.7	2011	3 percent	2012–2014

Qualitative: Monetized costs are for providing notices upon request in a culturally and linguistically appropriate manner. Non-monetized costs include costs for plans and issuers to respond to requests for diagnostic and treatment codes, and costs incurred by claimants to resolve whether a plan or insurer's failure to strictly adhere to the regulatory requirements is sufficient for a claimant to proceed directly to an external or court review.

1. Estimated Number of Affected Entities

For purposes of estimating the entities affected by these amendments to the July 2010 regulations, the Departments have defined a large group health plan

as an employer plan with 100 or more workers and a small group plan as an employer plan with fewer than 100 workers. The Departments make the following estimates about plans and issuers affected by these amendments:

(1) There are approximately 72,000 large and 2.8 million small ERISA-covered group health plans with an estimated 97.0 million participants in large group plans and 40.9 million participants in small group plans;[38] (2) there are

---

[37] Under the July 2010 regulations, this included the date of service, the health care provider, and the claim amount (if applicable), as well as the diagnosis code (such as an ICD–9 code, ICD–10 code, or DSM–IV code), the treatment code (such

as a CPT code), and the corresponding meanings of these codes.

[38] All participant counts and the estimates of individual policies are from the U.S. Department of

Labor, EBSA calculations using the March 2009 Current Population Survey Annual Social and Economic Supplement and the 2008 Medical Expenditure Panel Survey.

126,000 governmental plans with 36.1 million participants in large plans and 2.3 million participants in small plans;[39] and (3) there are 16.7 million individuals under age 65 covered by individual health insurance policies.[40]

The actual number of affected individuals depends on several factors, including whether (i) a health plan retains its grandfather status, (ii) the plan is subject to ERISA, (iii) benefits provided under the plan are self-funded or financed by the purchase of an insurance policy, (iii) the applicable State has enacted an internal claims and appeals law, and (iv) the applicable State has enacted an external review law, and if so the scope of such law, and (v) the number of new plans and enrollees in such plans.

2. Benefits and Costs

The benefits and costs of the amendments to the July 2010 regulations are discussed together under this section, because the primary effect of the amendments is to reduce the cost of compliance.

a. *Expedited notification of benefit determination involving urgent care.* As discussed in detail above, the July 2010 regulations generally provide that a plan or issuer must notify a claimant of a benefit determination with respect to an urgent care claim as soon as possible taking into account the medical exigencies, but no later than 24 hours after the receipt of the claim by the plan or issuer. This was a change from the DOL claims procedure regulation, which requires an urgent care determination to be made not later than 72 hours after receipt of the claim by a group health plan. The Departments received several comments regarding the burdens associated with meeting the 24-hour turnaround. Some commenters argued that some of the claims constituting "urgent care" and thus qualifying for the expedited timeframe really do not need to be decided within 24 hours. Moreover, a number of commenters highlighted that the 72-hour provision was never anything more than a "backstop"; the general rule under both the July 2010 regulations and the DOL claims procedure regulation is for a decision as soon as possible consistent with the medical exigencies involved, making the change to a 24-hour timeframe unnecessary for the most serious medical cases. Finally, some commenters cited the Emergency Medical Treatment and Labor Act

(EMTALA)[41], which generally requires emergency room care to be treated with or without insurance or preauthorization and, therefore, mitigates much of the need for expedited pre-service emergency claims determinations in many situations.

After considering the comments, and the costs and benefits of an absolute 24-hour decision-making deadline, the amendment permits plans and issuers to follow the original rule in the DOL claims procedure regulation (requiring decision-making in the context of pre-service urgent care claims as soon as possible consistent with the medical exigencies involved but in no event no later than 72 hours), *provided* the plan or issuer defers to the attending provider with respect to the decision as to whether a claim constitutes "urgent care."

The Departments expect that this amendment will ensure urgent care benefit determinations are made in a timely manner while reducing burden on plans and issuers for several reasons. ERISA-covered plans were already subject to this requirement; therefore, there is no additional burden imposed on such plans from the pre-Affordable Care Act baseline. For self-insured nonfederal governmental plans and issuers in the individual market, the 72-hour requirement would increase burden from a pre-Affordable Care Act baseline to the extent that such plans and issuers are not already meeting this standard. The Departments do not have sufficient data to estimate the fraction of plans and issuers that were not already in compliance with this standard. Many claims filed with self-insured nonfederal governmental plans and individual market issuers already could have been meeting this requirement for urgent care claims, because ERISA claims constitute a large portion of health claims, and the Departments understand that, in general, issuers and service providers apply the same claims and appeals standards to ERISA-covered and non-ERISA-covered plans.

Plans and issuers that previously were not subject to the DOL claims procedure regulation and that are not already meeting the claims and appeals standard under the DOL claims procedure regulation, could incur additional costs to become compliant with the 72-hour standard, but the Departments expect these costs to be less than those associated with a 24-hour standard. Speeding up the notification process for these determinations to meet the 72-hour standard could necessitate incurring

additional cost to add more employees or find other ways to shorten the timeframe, but again such costs are expected to be less than the costs associated with meeting the 24-hour standard provided in the July 2010 regulations. Additional costs for claimants may be associated with this requirement if meeting the 72-hour timeframe results in more claims being denied than would have been denied under a longer notification period, but again such costs are expected to be less than the costs associated with meeting the 24-hour standard provided in the July 2010 regulations. The Departments do not have sufficient data to estimate such costs.

b. *Additional notice requirements for internal claims and appeals.* As discussed above, the July 2010 regulations had additional content requirements for the required notices. The Departments received comments addressing the requirements to include the diagnosis code (such as an ICD–9 code, ICD–10 code, or DSM–IV code), the treatment code (such as a CPT code), and the corresponding meanings of these codes. Concerns were raised about patient privacy, interference with the doctor-patient relationship, and high costs. Commenters also pointed out that there are currently over 20,000 treatment and diagnosis codes in use today, presenting a costly administrative and operational challenge for plans and issuers. Comments also questioned the efficacy of providing codes which some argued are often very difficult for the average patient to understand.

After considering all the comments, and the costs and benefits of the additional disclosure, the amendment to the July 2010 regulations eliminates the requirement to automatically provide the diagnosis and treatment codes as part of a notice of adverse benefit determination (or final internal adverse benefit determination) and instead requires plans and issuers to provide notification of the opportunity to request the diagnosis and treatment codes (and their meanings) in all notices of adverse benefit determination (and notices of final internal adverse benefit determination) and to provide this information upon request.

Making the codes only available upon request protects patients' privacy while reducing the burden for plans and issuers to redesign notices. However, plans and issuers will still incur costs to establish procedures to receive, process, and mail the requests. The Departments do not have a basis to estimate the net cost associated with this amendment, because they do not have sufficient data available to estimate

---

[39] Estimate is from the 2007 Census of Government.

[40] US Census Bureau, Current Population Survey. March 2009.

[41] 42 U.S.C. 1395dd.

the savings that will result from plans and issuers not needing to redesign notices or calculate the number of future requests.

c. *Deemed exhaustion of internal claims and appeals process.* The July 2010 regulations provide that claimants can immediately seek judicial or external review if a plan or issuer failed to "strictly adhere" to all of the July 2010 regulations' requirements for internal claims and appeals processes, regardless of whether the plan or issuer asserted that it "substantially complied" with the July 2010 regulations. This approach received a number of negative comments from some issuers and plan sponsors, who prefer a "substantial compliance" approach, especially in cases where deviations from the regulatory standards were minor.

In response to these comments, the Departments are retaining the approach to this requirement, but this amendment also adds a new paragraph (b)(2)(ii)(F)(2) to the July 2010 regulations to provide an exception to the strict compliance standard for errors that are minor and meet certain other specified conditions. The new paragraph will also protect claimants whose attempts to pursue other remedies under paragraph (b)(2)(ii)(F)(1) of the interim final regulations are rejected by a reviewing tribunal. Under the amended approach, any violation of the procedural rules of July 2010 regulations pertaining to internal claims and appeals would permit a claimant to seek immediate external review or court action, as applicable, unless the violation was:

(1) De minimis;

(2) Non-prejudicial;

(3) Attributable to good cause or matters beyond the plan's or issuer's control;

(4) In the context of an ongoing good-faith exchange of information; and

(5) Not reflective of a pattern or practice of non-compliance.[42]

---

[42] In addition, the claimant would be entitled, upon written request, to an explanation of the plan's or issuer's basis for asserting that it meets this standard, so that the claimant could make an informed judgment about whether to seek immediate review. Finally, if the external reviewer or the court rejects the claimant's request for immediate review on the basis that the plan met this standard, this amendment would give the claimant the right to resubmit and pursue the internal appeal of the claim.

The Departments expect that this amendment will protect patients' right to proceed to external review while lowering costs based on the assumption that internal appeals are less expensive than external reviews or litigation. However, the amendment may add some costs, because participants and policyholders now may face uncertainty regarding whether a particular violation is minor. Many claimants may incur a cost to seek professional advice, because they will not be able to make this judgment on their own behalf. Alternatively, some claimants might seek immediate external review or judicial review and be denied it. The Departments do not have a sufficient basis to estimate these costs.

d. *Culturally and Linguistically Appropriate Notices.* PHS Act section 2719 requires group health plans and health insurance issuers to provide relevant notices in a culturally and linguistically appropriate manner. The July 2010 regulations set forth a requirement to provide notices in a non-English language based on separate thresholds of the number of people who are literate in the same non-English language. In the group market, the threshold set forth in the July 2010 regulations differs depending on the number of participants in the plan as follows:

• For a plan that covers fewer than 100 participants at the beginning of a plan year, the threshold is 25 percent of all plan participants being literate only in the same non-English language.

• For a plan that covers 100 or more participants at the beginning of a plan year, the threshold is the lesser of 500 participants, or 10 percent of all plan participants, being literate only in the same non-English language.[43]

For the individual market, the threshold is 10 percent of the population residing in the county being literate only in the same non-English language.[44]

---

[43] These thresholds were adapted from the DOL regulations regarding style and format for a summary plan description, at 29 CFR 2520.102–2(c) for participants who are not literate in English.

[44] The individual market threshold was generally adapted from the approach used under the Medicare Advantage program, which required translation of materials in languages spoken by more than 10 percent of the general population in a service area at the time the threshold was established.

Under the July 2010 regulations, if an applicable threshold is met with respect to a non-English language, the plan or issuer must provide the notice upon request in the non-English language. Additionally, the plan or issuer must include a statement in the English versions of all notices, prominently displayed in the non-English language, offering the provision of such notices in the non-English language. Finally, to the extent the plan or issuer maintains a customer assistance process (such as a telephone hotline) that answers questions or provides assistance with filing claims and appeals, the plan or issuer must provide such assistance in the non-English language.

As discussed earlier in this preamble, the Departments received comments that raised concerns regarding the burdens imposed by this provision. In response to these comments, the Departments have decided to amend the July 2010 regulations' provisions related to the provision of notices in a culturally and linguistically appropriate manner to establish a single threshold with respect to the number of people who are literate only in the same non-English language for both the group and individual markets. Under the amended provision, for group health plans and health insurance issuers offering group or individual health insurance coverage, the threshold percentage of people who are literate only in the same non-English language will be set at 10 percent or more of the population residing in the claimant's county, as determined based on American Community Survey (ACS) data published by the United States Census Bureau. Table 2, below provides a chart listing those 255 U.S. counties (78/255 are in Puerto Rico) in which at least 10 percent of the population speak a particular non-English language and speak English less than "very well." These data are applicable for 2011 and are calculated using 2005–2009 ACS data. The Departments will update this guidance annually on their Web site if there are changes to the list of the counties determined to meet this 10 percent threshold for the county's population being literate only in the same non-English language.

TABLE 2—PERCENT OF THE COUNTY POPULATION THAT SPEAK A PARTICULAR NON-ENGLISH LANGUAGE AND SPEAK ENGLISH LESS THAN "VERY WELL", BY U.S. COUNTY [45]

State	County	Non-English language			
		Spanish %	Chinese %	Tagalog %	Navajo %
AK	Aleutians West Census Area	13		16	
AK	Aleutians East Borough			35	
AR	Sevier County	17			
AZ	Apache County				12
AZ	Maricopa County	11			
AZ	Yuma County	22			
AZ	Santa Cruz County	39			
CA	Colusa County	27			
CA	Fresno County	15			
CA	Glenn County	14			
CA	Imperial County	32			
CA	Kern County	16			
CA	Kings County	18			
CA	Los Angeles County	19			
CA	Madera County	18			
CA	Merced County	20			
CA	Monterey County	25			
CA	Napa County	14			
CA	Orange County	14			
CA	Riverside County	15			
CA	San Benito County	21			
CA	San Bernardino County	15			
CA	San Diego County	11			
CA	San Francisco County		12		
CA	San Joaquin County	12			
CA	Santa Barbara County	15			
CA	Santa Cruz County	12			
CA	Stanislaus County	13			
CA	Sutter County	12			
CA	Tulare County	21			
CA	Ventura County	14			
CO	Adams County	12			
CO	Costilla County	11			
CO	Denver County	12			
CO	Eagle County	16			
CO	Garfield County	12			
CO	Lake County	11			
CO	Phillips County	12			
CO	Prowers County	12			
CO	Saguache County	15			
CO	Yuma County	10			
FL	Collier County	13			
FL	DeSoto County	21			
FL	Glades County	10			
FL	Hardee County	22			
FL	Hendry County	26			
FL	Miami-Dade County	31			
FL	Okeechobee County	12			
FL	Osceola County	16			
GA	Atkinson County	12			
GA	Echols County	20			
GA	Hall County	16			
GA	Telfair County	10			
GA	Whitfield County	18			
IA	Buena Vista County	12			
ID	Clark County	22			
ID	Minidoka County	11			
ID	Owyhee County	12			
ID	Power County	13			
IL	Kane County	15			
KS	Finney County	16			
KS	Ford County	23			
KS	Grant County	16			
KS	Hamilton County	11			
KS	Seward County	26			
KS	Stanton County	19			
KS	Stevens County	11			
KS	Wichita County	12			

37222   Federal Register / Vol. 76, No. 122 / Friday, June 24, 2011 / Rules and Regulations

TABLE 2—PERCENT OF THE COUNTY POPULATION THAT SPEAK A PARTICULAR NON-ENGLISH LANGUAGE AND SPEAK ENGLISH LESS THAN "VERY WELL", BY U.S. COUNTY [45]—Continued

State	County	Non-English language			
		Spanish %	Chinese %	Tagalog %	Navajo %
KS	Wyandotte County	10			
NC	Alleghany County	14			
NC	Duplin County	14			
NE	Colfax County	23			
NE	Dakota County	14			
NE	Dawson County	15			
NJ	Hudson County	18			
NJ	Passaic County	16			
NJ	Union County	13			
NM	Chaves County	11			
NM	Dona Ana County	18			
NM	Hidalgo County	12			
NM	Lea County	11			
NM	Luna County	18			
NM	McKinley County				15
NM	Mora County	11			
NM	Santa Fe County	12			
NM	Chaves County	11			
NV	Clark County,	11			
NY	Bronx County	20			
NY	New York County	10			
NY	Queens County	12			
OK	Texas County	18			
OR	Hood River County	15			
OR	Marion County	11			
OR	Morrow County	14			
TX	Andrews County	11			
TX	Atascosa County	11			
TX	Bailey County	18			
TX	Bexar County	12			
TX	Brooks County	18			
TX	Calhoun County	12			
TX	Cameron County	30			
TX	Camp County	11			
TX	Castro County	20			
TX	Cochran County	18			
TX	Concho County	29			
TX	Crane County	10			
TX	Crockett County	20			
TX	Crosby County	11			
TX	Culberson County	15			
TX	Dallam County	12			
TX	Dallas County	18			
TX	Dawson County	12			
TX	Deaf Smith County	20			
TX	Dimmit County	33			
TX	Duval County	26			
TX	Ector County	12			
TX	Edwards County	10			
TX	El Paso County	29			
TX	Frio County	16			
TX	Garza County	35			
TX	Gonzales County	14			
TX	Hale County	12			
TX	Hall County	14			
TX	Hansford County	16			
TX	Harris County	18			
TX	Hidalgo County	35			
TX	Howard County	16			
TX	Hudspeth County	31			
TX	Jim Hogg County	26			
TX	Jim Wells County	13			
TX	Karnes County	17			
TX	Kenedy County	14			
TX	Kinney County	15			
TX	Kleberg County	11			
TX	La Salle County	22			
TX	Lamb County	15			

TABLE 2—PERCENT OF THE COUNTY POPULATION THAT SPEAK A PARTICULAR NON-ENGLISH LANGUAGE AND SPEAK ENGLISH LESS THAN "VERY WELL", BY U.S. COUNTY [45]—Continued

State	County	Non-English language			
		Spanish %	Chinese %	Tagalog %	Navajo %
TX	Lipscomb County	14			
TX	Lynn County	12			
TX	Maverick County	48			
TX	Midland County	11			
TX	Moore County	19			
TX	Nueces County	12			
TX	Ochiltree County	17			
TX	Parmer County	22			
TX	Pecos County	18			
TX	Presidio County	36			
TX	Reagan County	21			
TX	Reeves County	27			
TX	San Patricio County	12			
TX	Schleicher County	12			
TX	Sherman County	14			
TX	Starr County	43			
TX	Sterling County	11			
TX	Sutton County	18			
TX	Tarrant County	10			
TX	Terrell County	12			
TX	Terry County	11			
TX	Titus County	20			
TX	Travis County	12			
TX	Upton County	11			
TX	Uvalde County	15			
TX	Val Verde County	29			
TX	Ward County	12			
TX	Webb County	49			
TX	Willacy County	20			
TX	Winkler County	13			
TX	Yoakum County	23			
TX	Zapata County	36			
TX	Zavala County	33			
UT	San Juan County				12
VA	Manassas city	17			
VA	Manassas Park city	18			
WA	Adams County	23			
WA	Douglas County	11			
WA	Franklin County	27			
WA	Grant County	16			
WA	Yakima County	17			
PR	Anasco Municipio	85			
PR	Adjuntas Municipio	86			
PR	Aguada Municipio	81			
PR	Aguadilla Municipio	78			
PR	Aguas Buenas Municipio	90			
PR	Aibonito Municipio	82			
PR	Arecibo Municipio	83			
PR	Arroyo Municipio	84			
PR	Barceloneta Municipio	78			
PR	Barranquitas Municipio	87			
PR	Bayamon Municipio	78			
PR	Cabo Rojo Municipio	82			
PR	Caguas Municipio	80			
PR	Camuy Municipio	88			
PR	Canovanas Municipio	83			
PR	Carolina Municipio	77			
PR	Catano Municipio	82			
PR	Cayey Municipio	86			
PR	Ceiba Municipio	73			
PR	Ciales Municipio	88			
PR	Cidra Municipio	86			
PR	Coamo Municipio	84			
PR	Comero Municipio	93			
PR	Corozal Municipio	88			
PR	Culebra Municipio	76			
PR	Dorado Municipio	77			
PR	Fajardo Municipio	78			

37224   Federal Register / Vol. 76, No. 122 / Friday, June 24, 2011 / Rules and Regulations

TABLE 2—PERCENT OF THE COUNTY POPULATION THAT SPEAK A PARTICULAR NON-ENGLISH LANGUAGE AND SPEAK ENGLISH LESS THAN "VERY WELL", BY U.S. COUNTY [45]—Continued

State	County	Non-English language			
		Spanish %	Chinese %	Tagalog %	Navajo %
PR	Florida Municipio	81			
PR	Guayama Municipio	80			
PR	Guayanilla Municipio	85			
PR	Guaynabo Municipio	69			
PR	Gurabo Municipio	81			
PR	Guánica Municipio	83			
PR	Hatillo Municipio	86			
PR	Hormigueros Municipio	74			
PR	Humacao Municipio	83			
PR	Isabela Municipio	85			
PR	Jayuya Municipio	91			
PR	Juana Diaz Municipio	86			
PR	Juncos Municipio	85			
PR	Lajas Municipio	83			
PR	Lares Municipio	87			
PR	Las Marias Municipio	91			
PR	Las Piedras Municipio	85			
PR	Loiza Municipio	89			
PR	Luquillo Municipio	79			
PR	Manati Municipio	84			
PR	Maricao Municipio	95			
PR	Maunabo Municipio	88			
PR	Mayaguez Municipio	77			
PR	Moca Municipio	86			
PR	Morovis Municipio	87			
PR	Naguabo Municipio	83			
PR	Naranjito Municipio	91			
PR	Orocovis Municipio	91			
PR	Patillas Municipio	84			
PR	Penuelas Municipio	86			
PR	Ponce Municipio	80			
PR	Quebradillas Municipio	83			
PR	Rincon Municipio	73			
PR	Rio Grande Municipio	85			
PR	Sabana Grande Municipio	83			
PR	Salinas Municipio	86			
PR	San German Municipio	85			
PR	San Juan Municipio	73			
PR	San Lorenzo Municipio	83			
PR	San Sebastian Municipio	84			
PR	Santa Isabel Municipio	86			
PR	Toa Alta Municipio	80			
PR	Toa Baja Municipio	80			
PR	Trujillo Alto Municipio	79			
PR	Utuado Municipio	83			
PR	Vega Alta Municipio	83			
PR	Vega Baja Municipio	76			
PR	Vieques Municipio	83			
PR	Villalba Municipio	88			
PR	Yabucoa Municipio	86			
PR	Yauco Municipio	85			

These amendments also require each notice sent by a plan or issuer to an address in a county that meets this threshold to include a one-sentence statement in the relevant non-English language about the availability of language services to be provided by the Departments. The Departments have provided guidance with sample sentences in the relevant languages in separate guidance being issued contemporaneous with the publication of this amendment.

In addition to including a statement in all notices in the relevant non-English language, a plan or issuer would be required to provide a customer assistance process (such as a telephone hotline) with oral language services in the non-English language and provide written notices in the non-English language upon request.

The Departments expect that the largest cost associated with the amended rules for culturally and linguistically appropriate notices will be for plans and issuers to provide notices in the applicable non-English language upon request. Based on the ACS data, the Departments estimate that there are about 12 million individuals living in

[45] Data are from the 2005–2009 ACS available at http://www.census.gov/acs. Only those counties where at least 10% of the county speak a particular non-English language and speak English less than "very well" are listed.

covered counties that are literate in a non-English Language. The ACS did not start collecting insurance coverage information until 2008. Therefore, to estimate the percentage of the 12 million affected individuals that were insured, the Departments used the percentage of the population in the State that reported being insured by private or public employer insurance or in the individual market from the 2009 Current Population Survey (CPS).[46] This results in an estimate of approximately seven million individuals who are eligible to request translation services.

In discussions with the regulated community, the Departments found that experience in California, which has a State law requirement for providing translation services, indicates that requests for translations of written documents averages 0.098 requests per 1,000 members. While the California law is not identical to the amendment to the July 2010 regulations, and the demographics for California do not match other counties, for purposes of this analysis, the Departments used this percentage to estimate of the number of translation service requests that plan and issuers can expect to receive. Industry experts also told the Departments that while the cost of translation services varies, $500 per document is a reasonable approximation of translation cost.

Using the ACS and the CPS, the Departments estimate 34 million insured lives in the affected counties. Based on the foregoing, the Departments estimate that the cost to provide translation services will be approximately $1.7 million annually (34,087,000 lives * 0.098/1000 * $500).

e. *Duration of the transition period for State external review processes.* These amendments to the July 2010 regulations modify the transition period under paragraph (c)(3) so that the last day of the transition period is December 31, 2011. Modifying the transition period gives states additional time to implement State external review processes that conform to paragraph (c)(2). This modification produces benefits and costs to participants and beneficiaries depending upon which state they live in and the timing of the beginning of the plan year. HHS is working closely with states to help them have external review processes that meet the requirements of paragraph (c)(2). The July 2010 regulations would have participants living in states with

laws that do not meet the minimum consumer protections in paragraph (c)(2) entering the Federal external review process that would provide more consumer protections. However, this requirement to enter the Federal external review process would take effect upon the start of a new plan year beginning on or after July 1, 2011.

This modification delays coverage of external review for participants whose plan year would have started between July 1, 2011 and December 31, 2011, but provides coverage sooner for participants in plans with plan years beginning after January 1, 2012, and has no change for participants in plans with plan years beginning on January 1, 2012.

The annual reporting form for certain ERISA covered health plans, the Form 5500, has information on health plan year end dates and also the number of participants in health plans. While most health plans with less than 100 participants are not required to file the Form 5500, the Departments are able to observe the plan year end dates and hence the plan year start dates for large plans. The Departments looked at the dispersion of plan year start dates for plans that filed the Form 5500 and found that nearly 76 percent of participants are in plans with a plan year start date of January 1, 2012 and hence will not be effected by the change in the rule; nearly 13 percent of participants are in plans that could possibly see a delay in receiving the protections of external review, while just over 10 percent of participants will be able to access the protections sooner. These estimates did not take into account the state in which the plan was located. The Departments do not have data on the start date of policies in the individual market. While on net about 2.4 percent of participants in affected plans could see a delay in receiving the protections, these costs are offset by giving states, and issuers additional time, and hence lower costs, to prepare for complying with the rule.

f. *Scope of Federal External Review.* Paragraph (d)(1) of the July 2010 regulations provides that any adverse benefit determination (including a final internal adverse benefit determination) could be brought to the Federal external review process unless it related to a participant's or beneficiary's failure to meet the requirements for eligibility under the terms of a group health plan (*i.e.*, worker classification and similar issues were not within the scope of the Federal external review process). As discussed earlier in this preamble, comments received in response to the July 2010 regulations indicate that the

scope of external review claims was too broad.

After considering all the comments, with respect to plans subject to the Federal external review process, for claims for which external review has not been initiated before September 20, 2011, the amendment suspends the original rule in the July 2010 regulations regarding the scope of claims eligible for external review for plans using the Federal process, temporarily replacing it with a different scope. Specifically, this amendment suspends the broad scope of claims eligible for external review and narrows the scope to those that involve (1) medical judgment (excluding those that involve only contractual or legal interpretation without any use of medical judgment), as determined by the external reviewer; or (2) a rescission of coverage. The suspension is intended to give the marketplace time to adjust to providing external review. The Departments believe that, once the market has so adjusted, it will become clear that the benefits of the July 2010 regulations' broader scope would be likely to justify its costs.

C. Regulatory Flexibility Act—Department of Labor and Department of Health and Human Services

The Regulatory Flexibility Act (5 U.S.C. 601 *et seq.*) (RFA) imposes certain requirements with respect to Federal rules that are subject to the notice and comment requirements of section 553(b) of the APA (5 U.S.C. 551 *et seq.*) and that are likely to have a significant economic impact on a substantial number of small entities. Under Section 553(b) of the APA, a general notice of proposed rulemaking is not required when an agency, for good cause, finds that notice and public comment thereon are impracticable, unnecessary, or contrary to the public interest. The interim final regulations were exempt from the APA, because the Departments made a good cause finding that a general notice of proposed rulemaking is not necessary earlier in this preamble. Therefore, the RFA did not apply and the Departments were not required to either certify that the regulations or this amendment would not have a significant economic impact on a substantial number of small entities or conduct a regulatory flexibility analysis.

Nevertheless, the Departments carefully considered the likely impact of the rule on small entities in connection with their assessment under Executive Order 12866. Consistent with the policy of the RFA, the Departments encourage the public to submit comments that suggest alternative rules that accomplish

---

[46] Please note that using state estimates of insurance coverage could lead to an over estimate if those reporting in the ACS survey that they speak English less than "very well" are less likely to be insured than the state average.

the stated purpose of the Affordable Care Act and minimize the impact on small entities.

D. Special Analyses—Department of the Treasury

Notwithstanding the determinations of the Department of Labor and Department of Health and Human Services, for purposes of the Department of the Treasury, it has been determined that this Treasury decision is not a significant regulatory action for purposes of Executive Order 12866. Therefore, a regulatory assessment is not required. It has also been determined that section 553(b) of the APA (5 U.S.C. chapter 5) does not apply to these temporary regulations. For the applicability of the RFA, refer to the Special Analyses section in the preamble to the cross-referencing notice of proposed rulemaking published elsewhere in this issue of the **Federal Register**. Pursuant to section 7805(f) of the Code, these temporary regulations have been submitted to the Chief Counsel for Advocacy of the Small Business Administration for comment on their impact on small businesses.

E. Paperwork Reduction Act

1. Department of Labor and Department of the Treasury

Currently, the Departments are soliciting 60 days of public comments concerning these disclosures. The Departments have submitted a copy of these interim final regulations to OMB in accordance with 44 U.S.C. 3507(d) for review of the information collections. The Departments and OMB are particularly interested in comments that:
• Evaluate whether the collection of information is necessary for the proper performance of the functions of the agency, including whether the information will have practical utility;
• Evaluate the accuracy of the agency's estimate of the burden of the collection of information, including the validity of the methodology and assumptions used;
• Enhance the quality, utility, and clarity of the information to be collected; and
• Minimize the burden of the collection of information on those who are to respond, including through the use of appropriate automated, electronic, mechanical, or other technological collection techniques or other forms of information technology, for example, by permitting electronic submission of responses.
Comments should be sent to the Office of Information and Regulatory Affairs, Attention: Desk Officer for the Employee Benefits Security Administration either by fax to (202) 395–7285 or by e-mail to *oira_submission@omb.eop.gov*. A copy of the ICR may be obtained by contacting the PRA addressee: G. Christopher Cosby, Office of Policy and Research, U.S. Department of Labor, Employee Benefits Security Administration, 200 Constitution Avenue, NW., Room N–5718, Washington, DC 20210. Telephone: (202) 693–8410; Fax: (202) 219–4745. These are not toll-free numbers. E-mail: *ebsa.opr@dol.gov*. ICRs submitted to OMB also are available at reginfo.gov (*http://www.reginfo.gov/public/do/PRAMain*).

a. Department of Labor and Department of the Treasury: Affordable Care Act Internal Claims and Appeals and External Review Disclosures for Non-Grandfathered Plans

These amendments make two changes to the interim final regulations that affect the paperwork burden. The first is an amendment no longer requiring that diagnosis and treatment codes be included on notices of adverse benefit determination and final internal adverse benefit determination. Instead, they must notify claimants of the opportunity to receive the codes on request and plans and issuers must provide the codes upon request. The Departments expect that this change will lower costs, because plans and issuers no longer will have to provide the codes on the notices. Plans and issuers will incur a cost to establish procedures for receive, process, and mail the codes upon request; however, the Departments are unable to estimate such cost due to a lack of a basis for an estimate of the number of requests that will be made for the codes.
The amendments also change the method for determining who is eligible to receive a notice in a culturally and linguistically appropriate manner, and the information that must be provided to such persons. The previous rule was based on the number of employees at a firm. The new rule is based on whether a participant or beneficiary resides in a county where ten percent or more of the population residing in the county is literate only in the same non-English language.
Participants and beneficiaries residing in an affected county and speaking an applicable non-English language will now receive a one-sentence statement in all notices written in the applicable non-English language about the availability of language services. In addition to including the statement, plan and issuers are required to provide a customer assistance process (such as a telephone hotline) with oral language services in the non-English language and provide written notices in the non-English language upon requests.
The Departments understand that oral translation services are already provided for nearly all covered participants and beneficiaries. Therefore, no additional burden is associated with this requirement of the amendment. The Departments estimate that plans will incur an annual cost burden of $1.2 million to translate written notices into the relevant non-English language.[47]
Based on the foregoing, the Departments have adjusted the total estimated cost burden for this information collection. The cost burden is $243,000 in 2011, $1.7 million in 2012, and $1.8 million in 2013.
Type of Review: Revised collection.
Agencies: Employee Benefits Security Administration, Department of Labor; Internal Revenue Service, U.S. Department of the Treasury,
Title: Affordable Care Act Internal Claims and Appeals and External Review Disclosures for Non-Grandfathered Plans.
OMB Number: 1210–0144; 1545–2182.
Affected Public: Business or other for profit; not-for-profit institutions.
Total Respondents: 1,020,000 (three-year average).
Total Responses: 111,000 (three-year average).
Frequency of Response: Occasionally.
Estimated Total Annual Burden Hours: 233 hours (Employee Benefits Security Administration); 233 hours (Internal Revenue Service) (three-year average).
Estimated Total Annual Burden Cost: $628,900 (Employee Benefits Security Administration); $628,900 (Internal Revenue Service) (three-year average).

2. Department of Health and Human Services

a. ICR Regarding Affordable Care Act Internal Claims and Appeals and External Review Disclosures for Non-grandfathered Plans

As discussed above in the Department of Labor and Department of the Treasury PRA section, these amendments make two changes to the interim final regulations that affect the paperwork burden. The first is an amendment no longer requiring that diagnosis and treatment codes be included on notices of adverse benefit determination and final internal adverse benefit

---

[47] The Department's methodology for this estimate is explained in IV, B, 2, d, above.

determination. Instead these codes are available upon request. The Departments expect that this change will lower costs compared to the July 2010 regulations because plans and issuers no longer will have to provide the codes on the notices. Plans and issuers will incur a cost to establish procedures for receiving, processing, and mailing the codes upon request; however, the Departments are unable to estimate such cost due to lack of a basis for an estimate of the number of requests that will be made for the codes. Second, the amendments also changes who is eligible to receive a notice in a culturally or linguistically appropriate manner.

The Departments estimated the new cost burden of providing the translation of requested notices into the applicable non-English language. The annual cost burden is estimated to be $430,000 annually starting in 2012. The derivation of this estimate was discussed above in the Economic Impact section.

Due to the amendments, the Department has adjusted the total estimated costs of this information collection. The Department estimates that State and local governmental plans and issuers offering coverage in the individual market will incur a total hour burden of 570,804 hours in 2011, 998,807 hours in 2012, and 1.22 million hours in 2013 to comply with equivalent costs of $28.2 million in 2011, $57.4 million in 2012, and $70.5 million in 2013. The total cost burden for those plans that use service providers, including the cost of mailing all responses is estimated to be $20.7 million in 2011, $37.9 million in 2012, and $51.7 million in 2013.

The hour and cost burden is summarized below:

Type of Review: Revised collection.
Agency: Department of Health and Human Services.
Title: Affordable Care Act Internal Claims and Appeals and External Review Disclosures
OMB Number: 0938–1099.
Affected Public: Business; State, Local, or Tribal Governments.
Respondents: 46,773 (three-year average).
Responses: 218,650,000 (three-year average).
Frequency of Response: Occasionally.
Estimated Total Annual Burden Hours: 929,870 hours (three-year average).
Estimated Total Annual Burden Cost: $36,600,000 (three-year average).

We have requested emergency OMB review and approval of the aforementioned information collection requirements by July 1, 2011. To obtain copies of the supporting statement and any related forms for the proposed paperwork collections referenced above, access CMS' Web site at *http:// www.cms.gov/ PaperworkReductionActof1995/PRAL/ list.asp#TopOfPage* or e-mail your request, including your address, phone number, OMB number, and CMS document identifier, to *Paperwork@cms.hhs.gov,* or call the Reports Clearance Office at 410–786–1326.

If you comment on any of these information collection requirements, please do either of the following:

1. Submit your comments electronically as specified in the **ADDRESSES** section of this proposed rule; or

2. Submit your comments to the Office of Information and Regulatory Affairs, Office of Management and Budget,

Attention: CMS Desk Officer, CMS–9993–IFC2

Fax: (202) 395–6974; or
E-mail:
OIRA_submission@omb.eop.gov

F. Congressional Review Act

These amendments to the interim final regulations are subject to the Congressional Review Act provisions of the Small Business Regulatory Enforcement Fairness Act of 1996 (5 U.S.C. 801 *et seq.*) and have been transmitted to Congress and the Comptroller General for review.

G. Unfunded Mandates Reform Act

The Unfunded Mandates Reform Act of 1995 (Pub. L. 104–4) requires agencies to prepare several analytic statements before proposing any rules that may result in annual expenditures of $100 million (as adjusted for inflation) by State, local and tribal governments or the private sector. These amendments to the interim final regulations are not subject to the Unfunded Mandates Reform Act because they are being issued as interim final regulations. However, consistent with the policy embodied in the Unfunded Mandates Reform Act, the regulation has been designed to be the least burdensome alternative for State, local and tribal governments, and the private sector, while achieving the objectives of the Affordable Care Act.

H. Federalism Statement—Department of Labor and Department of Health and Human Services

Executive Order 13132 outlines fundamental principles of federalism, and requires the adherence to specific criteria by Federal agencies in the process of their formulation and implementation of policies that have "substantial direct effects" on the States, the relationship between the national government and States, or on the distribution of power and responsibilities among the various levels of government. Federal agencies promulgating regulations that have federalism implications must consult with State and local officials, and describe the extent of their consultation and the nature of the concerns of State and local officials in the preamble to the regulation.

In the Departments' view, these amendments to the interim final regulations have federalism implications, because they have direct effects on the States, the relationship between the national government and States, or on the distribution of power and responsibilities among various levels of government. However, in the Departments' view, the federalism implications of these interim final regulations are substantially mitigated because, with respect to health insurance issuers, the Departments expect that the majority of States will enact laws or take other appropriate action to implement an internal and external appeals process that will meet or exceed federal standards.

In general, through section 514, ERISA supersedes State laws to the extent that they relate to any covered employee benefit plan, and preserves State laws that regulate insurance, banking, or securities. While ERISA prohibits States from regulating a plan as an insurance or investment company or bank, the preemption provisions of section 731 of ERISA and section 2724 of the PHS Act (implemented in 29 CFR 2590.731(a) and 45 CFR 146.143(a)) apply so that the HIPAA requirements (including those of the Affordable Care Act) are not to be "construed to supersede any provision of State law which establishes, implements, or continues in effect any standard or requirement solely relating to health insurance issuers in connection with group health insurance coverage except to the extent that such standard or requirement prevents the application of a requirement" of a Federal standard. The conference report accompanying HIPAA indicates that this is intended to be the "narrowest" preemption of State laws. (See House Conf. Rep. No. 104–736, at 205, reprinted in 1996 U.S. Code Cong. & Admin. News 2018.) States may continue to apply State law requirements except to the extent that such requirements prevent the application of the Affordable Care Act

37228   Federal Register / Vol. 76, No. 122 / Friday, June 24, 2011 / Rules and Regulations

requirements that are the subject of this rulemaking. State insurance laws that are more stringent than the Federal requirements are unlikely to "prevent the application of" the Affordable Care Act, and be preempted. Accordingly, States have significant latitude to impose requirements on health insurance issuers that are more restrictive than the Federal law. Furthermore, the Departments have opined that, in the instance of a group health plan providing coverage through group health insurance, the issuer will be required to follow the external review procedures established in State law (assuming the State external review procedure meets the minimum standards set out in these interim final rules).

In compliance with the requirement of Executive Order 13132 that agencies examine closely any policies that may have federalism implications or limit the policy making discretion of the States, the Departments have engaged in efforts to consult with and work cooperatively with affected State and local officials, including attending conferences of the National Association of Insurance Commissioners (NAIC), meeting with NAIC staff counsel on issues arising from the interim final regulations and consulting with State insurance officials on an individual basis. It is expected that the Departments will act in a similar fashion in enforcing the Affordable Care Act requirements, including the provisions of section 2719 of the PHS Act. Throughout the process of developing these amendments to the interim final regulations, to the extent feasible within the specific preemption provisions of HIPAA as it applies to the Affordable Care Act, the Departments have attempted to balance the States' interests in regulating health insurance issuers, and Congress' intent to provide uniform minimum protections to consumers in every State. By doing so, it is the Departments' view that they have complied with the requirements of Executive Order 13132.

Pursuant to the requirements set forth in section 8(a) of Executive Order 13132, and by the signatures affixed to these regulations, the Departments certify that the Employee Benefits Security Administration and the Centers for Medicare and Medicaid Services have complied with the requirements of Executive Order 13132 for the attached amendment to the interim final regulations in a meaningful and timely manner.

V. Statutory Authority

The Department of the Treasury temporary regulations are adopted pursuant to the authority contained in sections 7805 and 9833 of the Code.

The Department of Labor interim final regulations are adopted pursuant to the authority contained in 29 U.S.C. 1027, 1059, 1135, 1161–1168, 1169, 1181–1183, 1181 note, 1185, 1185a, 1185b, 1191, 1191a, 1191b, and 1191c; sec. 101(g), Pub. L. 104–191, 110 Stat. 1936; sec. 401(b), Pub. L. 105–200, 112 Stat. 645 (42 U.S.C. 651 note); sec. 512(d), Pub. L. 110–343, 122 Stat. 3881; sec. 1001, 1201, and 1562(e), Pub. L. 111–148, 124 Stat. 119, as amended by Pub. L. 111–152, 124 Stat. 1029; Secretary of Labor's Order 6–2009, 74 FR 21524 (May 7, 2009).

The Department of Health and Human Services interim final regulations are adopted pursuant to the authority contained in sections 2701 through 2763, 2791, and 2792 of the PHS Act (42 U.S.C. 300gg through 300gg–63, 300gg–91, and 300gg–92), as amended.

List of Subjects

26 CFR Part 54

Excise taxes, Health care, Health insurance, Pensions, Reporting and recordkeeping requirements.

29 CFR Part 2590

Continuation coverage, Disclosure, Employee benefit plans, Group health plans, Health care, Health insurance, Medical child support, Reporting and recordkeeping requirements.

45 CFR Part 147

Health care, Health insurance, Reporting and recordkeeping requirements, and State regulation of health insurance.

Steven T. Miller,
Deputy Commissioner for Services and Enforcement, Internal Revenue Service.

Approved: June 21, 2011.

Emily S. McMahon,
Acting Assistant Secretary of the Treasury (Tax Policy).

Signed this 20th day of June 2011.

Phyllis C. Borzi,
Assistant Secretary, Employee Benefits Security Administration, Department of Labor.

CMS–9993–IFC2

Approved: June 16, 2011.
Donald Berwick,
Administrator, Centers for Medicare & Medicaid Services.

Approved: June 17, 2011.
Kathleen Sebelius,
Secretary, Department of Health and Human Services.

Department of the Treasury

Internal Revenue Service

26 CFR Chapter I

Accordingly, 26 CFR part 54 is amended as follows:

PART 54—PENSION EXCISE TAXES

■ **Paragraph 1.** The general authority citation for part 54 continues to read as follows:

Authority: 26 U.S.C. 7805 * * *

■ **Par. 2.** Section 54.9815–2719T is amended by:
■ 1. Revising paragraphs (b)(2)(ii)(B), (b)(2)(ii)(E)(*1*), (b)(2)(ii)(F), (c)(2)(xi), (c)(3), (d)(1), (d)(2)(iv) and (e).
■ 2. Redesignating (b)(2)(ii)(E)(*2*), (b)(2)(ii)(E)(*3*), and (b)(2)(ii)(E)(*4*) as (b)(2)(ii)(E)(*3*), (b)(2)(ii)(E)(*4*), and (b)(2)(ii)(E)(*5*), respectively.
■ 3. Adding new paragraph (b)(2)(ii)(E)(*2*).

The revisions and addition read as follows:

§ 54.9815–2719T   Internal claims and appeals and external review processes (temporary).

*   *   *   *   *

(b) * * *
(2) * * *
(ii) * * *

(B) *Expedited notification of benefit determinations involving urgent care.* The requirements of 29 CFR 2560.503–1(f)(2)(i) (which generally provide, among other things, in the case of urgent care claims for notification of the plan's benefit determination (whether adverse or not) as soon as possible, taking into account the medical exigencies, but not later than 72 hours after receipt of the claim) continue to apply to the plan and issuer. For purposes of this paragraph (b)(2)(ii)(B), a claim involving urgent care has the meaning given in 29 CFR 2560.503–1(m)(1), as determined by the attending provider, and the plan or issuer shall defer to such determination of the attending provider.

*   *   *   *   *

(E) * * *
(*1*) The plan and issuer must ensure that any notice of adverse benefit determination or final internal adverse benefit determination includes information sufficient to identify the

claim involved (including the date of service, the health care provider, the claim amount (if applicable), and a statement describing the availability, upon request, of the diagnosis code and its corresponding meaning, and the treatment code and its corresponding meaning).

(2) The plan and issuer must provide to participants and beneficiaries, as soon as practicable, upon request, the diagnosis code and its corresponding meaning, and the treatment code and its corresponding meaning, associated with any adverse benefit determination or final internal adverse benefit determination. The plan or issuer must not consider a request for such diagnosis and treatment information, in itself, to be a request for an internal appeal under this paragraph (b) or an external review under paragraphs (c) and (d) of this section.

*   *   *   *   *

(F) *Deemed exhaustion of internal claims and appeals processes*—(1) In the case of a plan or issuer that fails to adhere to all the requirements of this paragraph (b)(2) with respect to a claim, the claimant is deemed to have exhausted the internal claims and appeals process of this paragraph (b), except as provided in paragraph (b)(2)(ii)(F)(2) of this section. Accordingly, the claimant may initiate an external review under paragraph (c) or (d) of this section, as applicable. The claimant is also entitled to pursue any available remedies under section 502(a) of ERISA or under State law, as applicable, on the basis that the plan or issuer has failed to provide a reasonable internal claims and appeals process that would yield a decision on the merits of the claim. If a claimant chooses to pursue remedies under section 502(a) of ERISA under such circumstances, the claim or appeal is deemed denied on review without the exercise of discretion by an appropriate fiduciary.

(2) Notwithstanding paragraph (b)(2)(ii)(F)(1) of this section, the internal claims and appeals process of this paragraph (b) will not be deemed exhausted based on *de minimis* violations that do not cause, and are not likely to cause, prejudice or harm to the claimant so long as the plan or issuer demonstrates that the violation was for good cause or due to matters beyond the control of the plan or issuer and that the violation occurred in the context of an ongoing, good faith exchange of information between the plan and the claimant. This exception is not available if the violation is part of a pattern or practice of violations by the plan or issuer. The claimant may request a

written explanation of the violation from the plan or issuer, and the plan or issuer must provide such explanation within 10 days, including a specific description of its bases, if any, for asserting that the violation should not cause the internal claims and appeals process of this paragraph (b) to be deemed exhausted. If an external reviewer or a court rejects the claimant's request for immediate review under paragraph (b)(2)(ii)(F)(1) of this section on the basis that the plan met the standards for the exception under this paragraph (b)(2)(ii)(F)(2), the claimant has the right to resubmit and pursue the internal appeal of the claim. In such a case, within a reasonable time after the external reviewer or court rejects the claim for immediate review (not to exceed 10 days), the plan shall provide the claimant with notice of the opportunity to resubmit and pursue the internal appeal of the claim. Time periods for re-filing the claim shall begin to run upon claimant's receipt of such notice.

*   *   *   *   *

(c) * * *
(2) * * *
(xi) The State process must provide that the decision is binding on the plan or issuer, as well as the claimant, except to the extent other remedies are available under State or Federal law, and except that the requirement that the decision be binding shall not preclude the plan or issuer from making payment on the claim or otherwise providing benefits at any time, including after a final external review decision that denies the claim or otherwise fails to require such payment or benefits. For this purpose, the plan or issuer must provide benefits (including by making payment on the claim) pursuant to the final external review decision without delay, regardless of whether the plan or issuer intends to seek judicial review of the external review decision and unless or until there is a judicial decision otherwise.

*   *   *   *   *

(3) *Transition period for external review processes*. (i) Through December 31, 2011, an applicable State external review process applicable to a health insurance issuer or group health plan is considered to meet the requirements of PHS Act section 2719(b). Accordingly, through December 31, 2011, an applicable State external review process will be considered binding on the issuer or plan (in lieu of the requirements of the Federal external review process). If there is no applicable State external review process, the issuer or plan is required to comply with the

requirements of the Federal external review process in paragraph (d) of this section.

(ii) For final internal adverse benefit determinations (or, in the case of simultaneous internal appeal and external review, adverse benefit determinations) provided on or after January 1, 2012, the Federal external review process will apply unless the Department of Health and Human Services determines that a State law meets all the minimum standards of paragraph (c)(2) of this section.

(d) * * *
(1) *Scope*—(i) *In general*. Subject to the suspension provision in paragraph (d)(1)(ii) of this section and except to the extent provided otherwise by the Secretary in guidance, the Federal external review process established pursuant to this paragraph (d) applies to any adverse benefit determination or final internal adverse benefit determination (as defined in paragraphs (a)(2)(i) and (a)(2)(v) of this section), except that a denial, reduction, termination, or a failure to provide payment for a benefit based on a determination that a participant or beneficiary fails to meet the requirements for eligibility under the terms of a group health plan is not eligible for the Federal external review process under this paragraph (d).

(ii) *Suspension of general rule*. Unless or until this suspension is revoked in guidance by the Secretary, with respect to claims for which external review has not been initiated before September 20, 2011, the Federal external review process established pursuant to this paragraph (d) applies only to:

(A) An adverse benefit determination (including a final internal adverse benefit determination) by a plan or issuer that involves medical judgment (including, but not limited to, those based on the plan's or issuer's requirements for medical necessity, appropriateness, health care setting, level of care, or effectiveness of a covered benefit; or its determination that a treatment is experimental or investigational), as determined by the external reviewer; and

(B) A rescission of coverage (whether or not the rescission has any effect on any particular benefit at that time).

(iii) *Examples*. The rules of paragraph (d)(1)(ii) of this section are illustrated by the following examples:

Example 1. (i) *Facts*. A group health plan provides coverage for 30 physical therapy visits generally. After the 30th visit, coverage is provided only if the service is preauthorized pursuant to an approved treatment plan that takes into account medical necessity using the plan's definition of the term. Individual *A* seeks coverage for a 31st physical therapy visit. *A*'s health care provider submits a treatment plan for approval, but it is not approved by the plan, so coverage for the 31st visit is not preauthorized. With respect to the 31st visit, *A* receives a notice of final internal adverse benefit determination stating that the maximum visit limit is exceeded.

(ii) *Conclusion.* In this *Example 1*, the plan's denial of benefits is based on medical necessity and involves medical judgment. Accordingly, the claim is eligible for external review during the suspension period under paragraph (d)(1)(ii) of this section. Moreover, the plan's notification of final internal adverse benefit determination is inadequate under paragraphs (b)(2)(i) and (b)(2)(ii)(E)(*3*) of this section because it fails to make clear that the plan will pay for more than 30 visits if the service is preauthorized pursuant to an approved treatment plan that takes into account medical necessity using the plan's definition of the term. Accordingly, the notice of final internal adverse benefit determination should refer to the plan provision governing the 31st visit and should describe the plan's standard for medical necessity, as well as how the treatment fails to meet the plan's standard.

Example 2. (i) *Facts.* A group health plan does not provide coverage for services provided out of network, unless the service cannot effectively be provided in network. Individual *B* seeks coverage for a specialized medical procedure from an out-of-network provider because *B* believes that the procedure cannot be effectively provided in network. *B* receives a notice of final internal adverse benefit determination stating that the claim is denied because the provider is out-of-network.

(ii) *Conclusion.* In this *Example 2*, the plan's denial of benefits is based on whether a service can effectively be provided in network and, therefore, involves medical judgment. Accordingly, the claim is eligible for external review during the suspension period under paragraph (d)(1)(ii) of this section. Moreover, the plan's notice of final internal adverse benefit determination is inadequate under paragraphs (b)(2)(i) and (b)(2)(ii)(E)(*3*) of this section because the plan does provide benefits for services on an out-of-network basis if the services cannot effectively be provided in network. Accordingly, the notice of final internal adverse benefit determination is required to refer to the exception to the out-of-network exclusion and should describe the plan's standards for determining effectiveness of services, as well as how services available to the claimant within the plan's network meet the plan's standard for effectiveness of services.

*   *   *   *   *

(2) * * *

(iv) These standards will provide that an external review decision is binding on the plan or issuer, as well as the claimant, except to the extent other remedies are available under State or Federal law, and except that the requirement that the decision be binding shall not preclude the plan or issuer from making payment on the claim or otherwise providing benefits at any time, including after a final external review decision that denies the claim or otherwise fails to require such payment or benefits. For this purpose, the plan or issuer must provide any benefits (including by making payment on the claim) pursuant to the final external review decision without delay, regardless of whether the plan or issuer intends to seek judicial review of the external review decision and unless or until there is a judicial decision otherwise.

*   *   *   *   *

(e) *Form and manner of notice*—(1) *In general.* For purposes of this section, a group health plan and a health insurance issuer offering group health insurance coverage are considered to provide relevant notices in a culturally and linguistically appropriate manner if the plan or issuer meets all the requirements of paragraph (e)(2) of this section with respect to the applicable non-English languages described in paragraph (e)(3) of this section.

(2) *Requirements*—(i) The plan or issuer must provide oral language services (such as a telephone customer assistance hotline) that include answering questions in any applicable non-English language and providing assistance with filing claims and appeals (including external review) in any applicable non-English language;

(ii) The plan or issuer must provide, upon request, a notice in any applicable non-English language; and

(iii) The plan or issuer must include in the English versions of all notices, a statement prominently displayed in any applicable non-English language clearly indicating how to access the language services provided by the plan or issuer.

(3) *Applicable non-English language.* With respect to an address in any United States county to which a notice is sent, a non-English language is an applicable non-English language if ten percent or more of the population residing in the county is literate only in the same non-English language, as determined in guidance published by the Secretary.

*   *   *   *   *

Department of Labor

Employee Benefits Security Administration

29 CFR Chapter XXV

29 CFR part 2590 is amended as follows:

PART 2590—RULES AND REGULATIONS FOR GROUP HEALTH PLANS

■ 1. The authority citation for part 2590 continues to read as follows:

Authority: 29 U.S.C. 1027, 1059, 1135, 1161–1168, 1169, 1181–1183, 1181 note, 1185, 1185a, 1185b, 1191, 1191a, 1191b, and 1191c; sec. 101(g), Pub. L. 104–191, 110 Stat. 1936; sec. 401(b), Pub. L. 105–200, 112 Stat. 645 (42 U.S.C. 651 note); sec. 512(d), Pub. L. 110–343, 122 Stat. 3881; sec. 1001, 1201, and 1562(e), Pub. L. 111–148, 124 Stat. 119, as amended by Pub. L. 111–152, 124 Stat. 1029; Secretary of Labor's Order 6–2009, 74 FR 21524 (May 7, 2009).

■ 2. Section 2590.715–2719 is amended by:

■ 1. Revising paragraphs (b)(2)(ii)(B), (b)(2)(ii)(E)(*1*), (b)(2)(ii)(F), (c)(2)(xi), (c)(3), (d)(1), (d)(2)(iv), and (e).

■ 2. Redesignating (b)(2)(ii)(E)(*2*), (b)(2)(ii)(E)(*3*), and (b)(2)(ii)(E)(*4*) as (b)(2)(ii)(E)(*3*), (b)(2)(ii)(E)(*4*), and (b)(2)(ii)(E)(*5*), respectively.

■ 3. Adding new paragraph (b)(2)(ii)(E)(*2*).

The revisions and addition read as follows:

§ 2590.715–2719   Internal claims and appeals and external review processes.

*   *   *   *   *

(b) * * *

(2) * * *

(ii) * * *

(B) *Expedited notification of benefit determinations involving urgent care.* The requirements of 29 CFR 2560.503–1(f)(2)(i) (which generally provide, among other things, in the case of urgent care claims for notification of the plan's benefit determination (whether adverse or not) as soon as possible, taking into account the medical exigencies, but not later than 72 hours after receipt of the claim) continue to apply to the plan and issuer. For purposes of this paragraph (b)(2)(ii)(B), a claim involving urgent care has the meaning given in 29 CFR 2560.503–1(m)(1), as determined by the attending provider, and the plan or issuer shall defer to such determination of the attending provider.

*   *   *   *   *

(E) * * *

(*1*) The plan and issuer must ensure that any notice of adverse benefit determination or final internal adverse benefit determination includes information sufficient to identify the claim involved (including the date of service, the health care provider, the claim amount (if applicable), and a statement describing the availability, upon request, of the diagnosis code and its corresponding meaning, and the treatment code and its corresponding meaning).

Federal Register / Vol. 76, No. 122 / Friday, June 24, 2011 / Rules and Regulations 37231

(2) The plan and issuer must provide to participants and beneficiaries, as soon as practicable, upon request, the diagnosis code and its corresponding meaning, and the treatment code and its corresponding meaning, associated with any adverse benefit determination or final internal adverse benefit determination. The plan or issuer must not consider a request for such diagnosis and treatment information, in itself, to be a request for an internal appeal under this paragraph (b) or an external review under paragraphs (c) and (d) of this section.

*   *   *   *   *

(F) *Deemed exhaustion of internal claims and appeals processes*—(*1*) In the case of a plan or issuer that fails to adhere to all the requirements of this paragraph (b)(2) with respect to a claim, the claimant is deemed to have exhausted the internal claims and appeals process of this paragraph (b), except as provided in paragraph (b)(2)(ii)(F)(*2*) of this section. Accordingly, the claimant may initiate an external review under paragraph (c) or (d) of this section, as applicable. The claimant is also entitled to pursue any available remedies under section 502(a) of ERISA or under State law, as applicable, on the basis that the plan or issuer has failed to provide a reasonable internal claims and appeals process that would yield a decision on the merits of the claim. If a claimant chooses to pursue remedies under section 502(a) of ERISA under such circumstances, the claim or appeal is deemed denied on review without the exercise of discretion by an appropriate fiduciary.

(*2*) Notwithstanding paragraph (b)(2)(ii)(F)(*1*) of this section, the internal claims and appeals process of this paragraph (b) will not be deemed exhausted based on *de minimis* violations that do not cause, and are not likely to cause, prejudice or harm to the claimant so long as the plan or issuer demonstrates that the violation was for good cause or due to matters beyond the control of the plan or issuer and that the violation occurred in the context of an ongoing, good faith exchange of information between the plan and the claimant. This exception is not available if the violation is part of a pattern or practice of violations by the plan or issuer. The claimant may request a written explanation of the violation from the plan or issuer, and the plan or issuer must provide such explanation within 10 days, including a specific description of its bases, if any, for asserting that the violation should not cause the internal claims and appeals process of this paragraph (b) to be

deemed exhausted. If an external reviewer or a court rejects the claimant's request for immediate review under paragraph (b)(2)(ii)(F)(*1*) of this section on the basis that the plan met the standards for the exception under this paragraph (b)(2)(ii)(F)(*2*), the claimant has the right to resubmit and pursue the internal appeal of the claim. In such a case, within a reasonable time after the external reviewer or court rejects the claim for immediate review (not to exceed 10 days), the plan shall provide the claimant with notice of the opportunity to resubmit and pursue the internal appeal of the claim. Time periods for re-filing the claim shall begin to run upon claimant's receipt of such notice.

*   *   *   *   *

(c) * * *

(2) * * *

(xi) The State process must provide that the decision is binding on the plan or issuer, as well as the claimant, except to the extent other remedies are available under State or Federal law, and except that the requirement that the decision be binding shall not preclude the plan or issuer from making payment on the claim or otherwise providing benefits at any time, including after a final external review decision that denies the claim or otherwise fails to require such payment or benefits. For this purpose, the plan or issuer must provide benefits (including by making payment on the claim) pursuant to the final external review decision without delay, regardless of whether the plan or issuer intends to seek judicial review of the external review decision and unless or until there is a judicial decision otherwise.

*   *   *   *   *

(3) *Transition period for external review processes.* (i) Through December 31, 2011, an applicable State external review process applicable to a health insurance issuer or group health plan is considered to meet the requirements of PHS Act section 2719(b). Accordingly, through December 31, 2011, an applicable State external review process will be considered binding on the issuer or plan (in lieu of the requirements of the Federal external review process). If there is no applicable State external review process, the issuer or plan is required to comply with the requirements of the Federal external review process in paragraph (d) of this section.

(ii) For final internal adverse benefit determinations (or, in the case of simultaneous internal appeal and external review, adverse benefit determinations) provided on or after

January 1, 2012, the Federal external review process will apply unless the Department of Health and Human Services determines that a State law meets all the minimum standards of paragraph (c)(2) of this section.

(d) * * *

(1) *Scope*—(i) *In general.* Subject to the suspension provision in paragraph (d)(1)(ii) of this section and except to the extent provided otherwise by the Secretary in guidance, the Federal external review process established pursuant to this paragraph (d) applies to any adverse benefit determination or final internal adverse benefit determination (as defined in paragraphs (a)(2)(i) and (a)(2)(v) of this section), except that a denial, reduction, termination, or a failure to provide payment for a benefit based on a determination that a participant or beneficiary fails to meet the requirements for eligibility under the terms of a group health plan is not eligible for the Federal external review process under this paragraph (d).

(ii) *Suspension of general rule.* Unless or until this suspension is revoked in guidance by the Secretary, with respect to claims for which external review has not been initiated before the effective date of this paragraph (d)(1) (September 20, 2011), the Federal external review process established pursuant to this paragraph (d) applies only to:

(A) An adverse benefit determination (including a final internal adverse benefit determination) by a plan or issuer that involves medical judgment (including, but not limited to, those based on the plan's or issuer's requirements for medical necessity, appropriateness, health care setting, level of care, or effectiveness of a covered benefit; or its determination that a treatment is experimental or investigational), as determined by the external reviewer; and

(B) A rescission of coverage (whether or not the rescission has any effect on any particular benefit at that time).

(iii) *Examples.* This rules of paragraph (d)(1)(ii) of this section are illustrated by the following examples:

Example 1. (i) *Facts.* A group health plan provides coverage for 30 physical therapy visits generally. After the 30th visit, coverage is provided only if the service is preauthorized pursuant to an approved treatment plan that takes into account medical necessity using the plan's definition of the term. Individual *A* seeks coverage for a 31st physical therapy visit. *A*'s health care provider submits a treatment plan for approval, but it is not approved by the plan, so coverage for the 31st visit is not preauthorized. With respect to the 31st visit, *A* receives a notice of final internal adverse benefit determination stating that the maximum visit limit is exceeded.

(ii) *Conclusion.* In this *Example 1*, the plan's denial of benefits is based on medical necessity and involves medical judgment. Accordingly, the claim is eligible for external review during the suspension period under paragraph (d)(1)(ii) of this section. Moreover, the plan's notification of final internal adverse benefit determination is inadequate under paragraphs (b)(2)(i) and (b)(2)(ii)(E)(*3*) of this section because it fails to make clear that the plan will pay for more than 30 visits if the service is preauthorized pursuant to an approved treatment plan that takes into account medical necessity using the plan's definition of the term. Accordingly, the notice of final internal adverse benefit determination should refer to the plan provision governing the 31st visit and should describe the plan's standard for medical necessity, as well as how the treatment fails to meet the plan's standard.

Example 2. (i) *Facts.* A group health plan does not provide coverage for services provided out of network, unless the service cannot effectively be provided in network. Individual *B* seeks coverage for a specialized medical procedure from an out-of-network provider because *B* believes that the procedure cannot be effectively provided in network. *B* receives a notice of final internal adverse benefit determination stating that the claim is denied because the provider is out-of-network.

(ii) *Conclusion.* In this *Example 2*, the plan's denial of benefits is based on whether a service can effectively be provided in network and, therefore, involves medical judgment. Accordingly, the claim is eligible for external review during the suspension period under paragraph (d)(1)(ii) of this section. Moreover, the plan's notice of final internal adverse benefit determination is inadequate under paragraphs (b)(2)(i) and (b)(2)(ii)(E)(*3*) of this section because the plan does provide benefits for services on an out-of-network basis if the services cannot effectively be provided in network. Accordingly, the notice of final internal adverse benefit determination is required to refer to the exception to the out-of-network exclusion and should describe the plan's standards for determining effectiveness of services, as well as how services available to the claimant within the plan's network meet the plan's standard for effectiveness of services.

*   *   *   *   *

(2) * * *

(iv) These standards will provide that an external review decision is binding on the plan or issuer, as well as the claimant, except to the extent other remedies are available under State or Federal law, and except that the requirement that the decision be binding shall not preclude the plan or issuer from making payment on the claim or otherwise providing benefits at any time, including after a final external review decision that denies the claim or otherwise fails to require such payment or benefits. For this purpose, the plan or issuer must provide any benefits (including by making payment on the

claim) pursuant to the final external review decision without delay, regardless of whether the plan or issuer intends to seek judicial review of the external review decision and unless or until there is a judicial decision otherwise.

*   *   *   *   *

(e) *Form and manner of notice*—(1) *In general.* For purposes of this section, a group health plan and a health insurance issuer offering group health insurance coverage are considered to provide relevant notices in a culturally and linguistically appropriate manner if the plan or issuer meets all the requirements of paragraph (e)(2) of this section with respect to the applicable non-English languages described in paragraph (e)(3) of this section.

(2) *Requirements*—(i) The plan or issuer must provide oral language services (such as a telephone customer assistance hotline) that include answering questions in any applicable non-English language and providing assistance with filing claims and appeals (including external review) in any applicable non-English language;

(ii) The plan or issuer must provide, upon request, a notice in any applicable non-English language; and

(iii) The plan or issuer must include in the English versions of all notices, a statement prominently displayed in any applicable non-English language clearly indicating how to access the language services provided by the plan or issuer.

(3) *Applicable non-English language.* With respect to an address in any United States county to which a notice is sent, a non-English language is an applicable non-English language if ten percent or more of the population residing in the county is literate only in the same non-English language, as determined in guidance published by the Secretary.

*   *   *   *   *

Department of Health and Human Services

45 CFR Subtitle A

For the reasons stated in the preamble, the Department of Health and Human Services amends 45 CFR part 147 as follows:

PART 147—HEALTH INSURANCE REFORM REQUIREMENTS FOR THE GROUP AND INDIVIDUAL HEALTH INSURANCE MARKETS

■ 1. The authority citation for part 147 continues to read as follows:

Authority: Sections 2701 through 2763, 2791, and 2792 of the Public Health Service Act (42 U.S.C. 300gg through 300gg–63, 300gg–91, and 300gg–92), as amended.

■ 2. Section 147.136 is amended by:
■ 1. Revising paragraphs (b)(2)(ii)(B), (b)(2)(ii)(E)(*1*), (b)(2)(ii)(F), (c)(2)(xi), (c)(3), (d)(1), (d)(2)(iv), and (e).
■ 2. Redesignating (b)(2)(ii)(E)(*2*), (b)(2)(ii)(E)(*3*), and (b)(2)(ii)(E)(*4*) as (b)(2)(ii)(E)(*3*), (b)(2)(ii)(E)(*4*), and (b)(2)(ii)(E)(*5*), respectively.
■ 3. Adding new paragraph (b)(2)(ii)(E)(*2*).

The revisions and addition read as follows:

§ 147.136   Internal claims and appeals and external review processes.

*   *   *   *   *

(b) * * *

(2) * * *

(ii) * * *

(B) *Expedited notification of benefit determinations involving urgent care.* The requirements of 29 CFR 2560.503–1(f)(2)(i) (which generally provide, among other things, in the case of urgent care claims for notification of the plan's benefit determination (whether adverse or not) as soon as possible, taking into account the medical exigencies, but not later than 72 hours after receipt of the claim) continue to apply to the plan and issuer. For purposes of this paragraph (b)(2)(ii)(B), a claim involving urgent care has the meaning given in 29 CFR 2560.503–1(m)(1), as determined by the attending provider, and the plan or issuer shall defer to such determination of the attending provider.

*   *   *   *   *

(E) * * *

(*1*) The plan and issuer must ensure that any notice of adverse benefit determination or final internal adverse benefit determination includes information sufficient to identify the claim involved (including the date of service, the health care provider, the claim amount (if applicable), and a statement describing the availability, upon request, of the diagnosis code and its corresponding meaning, and the treatment code and its corresponding meaning).

(*2*) The plan and issuer must provide to participants and beneficiaries, as soon as practicable, upon request, the diagnosis code and its corresponding meaning, and the treatment code and its corresponding meaning, associated with any adverse benefit determination or final internal adverse benefit determination. The plan or issuer must not consider a request for such diagnosis and treatment information, in itself, to be a request for an internal appeal under this paragraph (b) or an external review under paragraphs (c) and (d) of this section.

*   *   *   *   *

(F) *Deemed exhaustion of internal claims and appeals processes—(1)* In the case of a plan or issuer that fails to adhere to all the requirements of this paragraph (b)(2) with respect to a claim, the claimant is deemed to have exhausted the internal claims and appeals process of this paragraph (b), except as provided in paragraph (b)(2)(ii)(F)(*2*) of this section. Accordingly, the claimant may initiate an external review under paragraph (c) or (d) of this section, as applicable. The claimant is also entitled to pursue any available remedies under section 502(a) of ERISA or under State law, as applicable, on the basis that the plan or issuer has failed to provide a reasonable internal claims and appeals process that would yield a decision on the merits of the claim. If a claimant chooses to pursue remedies under section 502(a) of ERISA under such circumstances, the claim or appeal is deemed denied on review without the exercise of discretion by an appropriate fiduciary.

(*2*) Notwithstanding paragraph (b)(2)(ii)(F)(*1*) of this section, the internal claims and appeals process of this paragraph (b) will not be deemed exhausted based on *de minimis* violations that do not cause, and are not likely to cause, prejudice or harm to the claimant so long as the plan or issuer demonstrates that the violation was for good cause or due to matters beyond the control of the plan or issuer and that the violation occurred in the context of an ongoing, good faith exchange of information between the plan and the claimant. This exception is not available if the violation is part of a pattern or practice of violations by the plan or issuer. The claimant may request a written explanation of the violation from the plan or issuer, and the plan or issuer must provide such explanation within 10 days, including a specific description of its bases, if any, for asserting that the violation should not cause the internal claims and appeals process of this paragraph (b) to be deemed exhausted. If an external reviewer or a court rejects the claimant's request for immediate review under paragraph (b)(2)(ii)(F)(*1*) of this section on the basis that the plan met the standards for the exception under this paragraph (b)(2)(ii)(F)(*2*), the claimant has the right to resubmit and pursue the internal appeal of the claim. In such a case, within a reasonable time after the external reviewer or court rejects the claim for immediate review (not to exceed 10 days), the plan shall provide the claimant with notice of the opportunity to resubmit and pursue the internal appeal of the claim. Time

periods for re-filing the claim shall begin to run upon claimant's receipt of such notice.

*   *   *   *   *

(c) * * *

(2) * * *

(xi) The State process must provide that the decision is binding on the plan or issuer, as well as the claimant, except to the extent other remedies are available under State or Federal law, and except that the requirement that the decision be binding shall not preclude the plan or issuer from making payment on the claim or otherwise providing benefits at any time, including after a final external review decision that denies the claim or otherwise fails to require such payment or benefits. For this purpose, the plan or issuer must provide benefits (including by making payment on the claim) pursuant to the final external review decision without delay, regardless of whether the plan or issuer intends to seek judicial review of the external review decision and unless or until there is a judicial decision otherwise.

*   *   *   *   *

(3) *Transition period for external review processes.* (i) Through December 31, 2011, an applicable State external review process applicable to a health insurance issuer or group health plan is considered to meet the requirements of PHS Act section 2719(b). Accordingly, through December 31, 2011, an applicable State external review process will be considered binding on the issuer or plan (in lieu of the requirements of the Federal external review process). If there is no applicable State external review process, the issuer or plan is required to comply with the requirements of the Federal external review process in paragraph (d) of this section.

(ii) For final internal adverse benefit determinations (or, in the case of simultaneous internal appeal and external review, adverse benefit determinations) provided on or after January 1, 2012, the Federal external review process will apply unless the Department of Health and Human Services determines that a State law meets all the minimum standards of paragraph (c)(2) of this section.

(d) * * *

(1) *Scope—*(i) *In general.* Subject to the suspension provision in paragraph (d)(1)(ii) of this section and except to the extent provided otherwise by the Secretary in guidance, the Federal external review process established pursuant to this paragraph (d) applies to any adverse benefit determination or final internal adverse benefit

determination (as defined in paragraphs (a)(2)(i) and (a)(2)(v) of this section), except that a denial, reduction, termination, or a failure to provide payment for a benefit based on a determination that a participant or beneficiary fails to meet the requirements for eligibility under the terms of a group health plan is not eligible for the Federal external review process under this paragraph (d).

(ii) *Suspension of general rule.* Unless or until this suspension is revoked in guidance by the Secretary, with respect to claims for which external review has not been initiated before September 20, 2011, the Federal external review process established pursuant to this paragraph (d) applies only to:

(A) An adverse benefit determination (including a final internal adverse benefit determination) by a plan or issuer that involves medical judgment (including, but not limited to, those based on the plan's or issuer's requirements for medical necessity, appropriateness, health care setting, level of care, or effectiveness of a covered benefit; or its determination that a treatment is experimental or investigational), as determined by the external reviewer; and

(B) A rescission of coverage (whether or not the rescission has any effect on any particular benefit at that time).

(iii) *Examples.* This rules of paragraph (d)(1)(ii) of this section are illustrated by the following examples:

Example 1. (i) *Facts.* A group health plan provides coverage for 30 physical therapy visits generally. After the 30th visit, coverage is provided only if the service is preauthorized pursuant to an approved treatment plan that takes into account medical necessity using the plan's definition of the term. Individual *A* seeks coverage for a 31st physical therapy visit. *A*'s health care provider submits a treatment plan for approval, but it is not approved by the plan, so coverage for the 31st visit is not preauthorized. With respect to the 31st visit, *A* receives a notice of final internal adverse benefit determination stating that the maximum visit limit is exceeded.

(ii) *Conclusion.* In this *Example 1,* the plan's denial of benefits is based on medical necessity and involves medical judgment. Accordingly, the claim is eligible for external review during the suspension period under paragraph (d)(1)(ii) of this section. Moreover, the plan's notification of final internal adverse benefit determination is inadequate under paragraphs (b)(2)(i) and (b)(2)(ii)(E)(*3*) of this section because it fails to make clear that the plan will pay for more than 30 visits if the service is preauthorized pursuant to an approved treatment plan that takes into account medical necessity using the plan's definition of the term. Accordingly, the notice of final internal adverse benefit determination should refer to the plan provision governing the 31st visit and should

37234 Federal Register / Vol. 76, No. 122 / Friday, June 24, 2011 / Rules and Regulations

describe the plan's standard for medical necessity, as well as how the treatment fails to meet the plan's standard.

Example 2. (i) *Facts.* A group health plan does not provide coverage for services provided out of network, unless the service cannot effectively be provided in network. Individual *B* seeks coverage for a specialized medical procedure from an out-of-network provider because *B* believes that the procedure cannot be effectively provided in network. *B* receives a notice of final internal adverse benefit determination stating that the claim is denied because the provider is out-of-network.

(ii) *Conclusion.* In this *Example 2*, the plan's denial of benefits is based on whether a service can effectively be provided in network and, therefore, involves medical judgment. Accordingly, the claim is eligible for external review during the suspension period under paragraph (d)(1)(ii) of this section. Moreover, the plan's notice of final internal adverse benefit determination is inadequate under paragraphs (b)(2)(i) and (b)(2)(ii)(E)(*3*) of this section because the plan does provide benefits for services on an out-of-network basis if the services cannot effectively be provided in network. Accordingly, the notice of final internal adverse benefit determination is required to refer to the exception to the out-of-network exclusion and should describe the plan's standards for determining effectiveness of services, as well as how services available to the claimant within the plan's network meet the plan's standard for effectiveness of services.

* * * * *

(2) * * *

(iv) These standards will provide that an external review decision is binding on the plan or issuer, as well as the claimant, except to the extent other remedies are available under State or Federal law, and except that the requirement that the decision be binding shall not preclude the plan or issuer from making payment on the claim or otherwise providing benefits at any time, including after a final external review decision that denies the claim or otherwise fails to require such payment or benefits. For this purpose, the plan or issuer must provide any benefits (including by making payment on the claim) pursuant to the final external review decision without delay, regardless of whether the plan or issuer intends to seek judicial review of the external review decision and unless or until there is a judicial decision otherwise.

* * * * *

(e) *Form and manner of notice*—(1) *In general.* For purposes of this section, a group health plan and a health insurance issuer offering group or individual health insurance coverage are considered to provide relevant notices in a culturally and linguistically appropriate manner if the plan or issuer meets all the requirements of paragraph (e)(2) of this section with respect to the applicable non-English languages described in paragraph (e)(3) of this section.

(2) *Requirements*—(i) The plan or issuer must provide oral language services (such as a telephone customer assistance hotline) that include answering questions in any applicable non-English language and providing assistance with filing claims and appeals (including external review) in any applicable non-English language;

(ii) The plan or issuer must provide, upon request, a notice in any applicable non-English language; and

(iii) The plan or issuer must include in the English versions of all notices, a statement prominently displayed in any applicable non-English language clearly indicating how to access the language services provided by the plan or issuer.

(3) *Applicable non-English language.* With respect to an address in any United States county to which a notice is sent, a non-English language is an applicable non-English language if ten percent or more of the population residing in the county is literate only in the same non-English language, as determined in guidance published by the Secretary.

* * * * *

[FR Doc. 2011–15900 Filed 6–22–11; 4:15 pm]
BILLING CODE 4830–01–P

O. Model Notices for Claims and Appeals Decisions

Model Notice of Adverse Benefit Determination – Revised as of June 22, 2011

Date of Notice
Name of Plan
Address

Telephone/Fax
Website/Email Address

This document contains important information that you should retain for your records.
This document serves as notice of an adverse benefit determination. We have declined to provide benefits, in whole or in part, for the requested treatment or service described below. If you think this determination was made in error, you have the right to appeal (see the back of this page for information about your appeal rights).

Case Details:

Patient Name:	ID Number:
Address: (street, county, state, zip)	
Claim #:	Date of Service:
Provider:	

Reason for Denial (in whole or in part):

Amt. Charged	Allowed Amt.	Other Insurance	Deductible	Co-pay	Coinsurance	Other Amts. Not Covered	Amt. Paid

YTD Credit toward Deductible:	YTD Credit toward Out-of-Pocket Maximum:
Description of service:	Denial Codes:

[If denial is not related to a specific claim, only name and ID number need to be included in the box. The reason for the denial would need to be clear in the narrative below.]

Explanation of Basis for Determination:
If the claim is denied (in whole or in part) and there is more explanation for the basis of the denial, such as the definition of a plan or policy term, include that information here.

[Insert language assistance disclosure here, if applicable.
SPANISH (Español): Para obtener asistencia en Español, llame al [insert telephone number].
TAGALOG (Tagalog): Kung kailangan ninyo ang tulong sa Tagalog tumawag sa [insert telephone number].
CHINESE (中文): 如果需要中文的帮助，请拨打这个号码 [insert telephone number]。
NAVAJO (Dine): Dinek'ehgo shika at'ohwol ninisingo, kwiijigo holne' [insert telephone number].]

OMB Control Number 1210-0144 (expires 04/30/2014)

Model Notice of Adverse Benefit Determination – Revised as of June 22, 2011

Important Information about Your Appeal Rights

What if I need help understanding this denial?
Contact us at [insert contact information] if you need assistance understanding this notice or our decision to deny you a service or coverage.

What if I don't agree with this decision? You have a right to appeal any decision not to provide or pay for an item or service (in whole or in part).

How do I file an appeal? [Complete the bottom of this page, make a copy, and send this document to {insert address}.] [or] [insert alternative instructions] See also the "Other resources to help you" section of this form for assistance filing a request for an appeal.

What if my situation is urgent? If your situation meets the definition of urgent under the law, your review will generally be conducted within 72 hours. Generally, an urgent situation is one in which your health may be in serious jeopardy or, in the opinion of your physician, you may experience pain that cannot be adequately controlled while you wait for a decision on your appeal. If you believe your situation is urgent, you may request an expedited appeal by following the instructions above for filing an internal appeal and also [insert instructions for filing request for simultaneous external review)].

Who may file an appeal? You or someone you name to act for you (your authorized representative) may file an appeal. [Insert information on how to designate an authorized representative.]

Can I provide additional information about my claim? Yes, you may supply additional information. [Insert any applicable procedures for submission of additional information.]

Can I request copies of information relevant to my claim? Yes, you may request copies (free of charge). If you think a coding error may have caused this claim to be denied, you have the right to have billing and diagnosis codes sent to you, as well. You can request copies of this information by contacting us at [insert contact information].

What happens next? If you appeal, we will review our decision and provide you with a written determination. If we continue to deny the payment, coverage, or service requested or you do not receive a timely decision, you may be able to request an external review of your claim by an independent third party, who will review the denial and issue a final decision.

Other resources to help you: For questions about your rights, this notice, or for assistance, you can contact: [if coverage is group health plan coverage, insert: the Employee Benefits Security Administration at 1-866-444-EBSA (3272)] [and/or] [if coverage is insured, insert State Department of Insurance contact information]. [Insert, if applicable in your state: Additionally, a consumer assistance program can help you file your appeal. Contact [insert contact information].]

Appeal Filing Form

NAME OF PERSON FILING APPEAL: _____
Circle one: ☐Covered person ☐ Patient ☐ Authorized Representative
Contact information of person filing appeal (if different from patient)
Address: _____ **Daytime phone:** _____ **Email:** _____

If person filing appeal is other than patient, patient must indicate authorization by signing here:
_____

Are you requesting an urgent appeal? ☐Yes ☐ No

Briefly describe why you disagree with this decision (you may attach additional information, such as a physician's letter, bills, medical records, or other documents to support your claim):
_____
_____

Send this form and your denial notice to: [Insert name and contact information]
Be certain to keep copies of this form, your denial notice, and all documents and correspondence related to this claim.

Model Notice of Final Internal Adverse Benefit Determination – Revised as of June 22, 2011

Date of Notice
Name of Plan   Telephone/Fax
Address   Website/Email Address

This document contains important information that you should retain for your records.
This document serves as notice of a final internal adverse benefit determination. We have declined to provide benefits, in whole or in part, for the requested treatment or service described below. If you think this determination was made in error, you may have the right to appeal (see the back of this page for information about your appeal rights).

Internal Appeal Case Details:

Patient Name:				ID Number:				
Address: (street, county, state, zip)								
Claim #:				Date of Service:				
Provider:								
Reason for Upholding Denial (in whole or in part):								
Amt. Charged	Allowed Amt.	Other Insurance	Deductible	Co-pay	Coinsurance	Other Amts. Not Covered	Amt. Paid	
YTD Credit toward Deductible:				YTD Credit toward Out-of-Pocket Maximum:				
Description of Service:				Denial Codes:				

[If denial is not related to a specific claim, only name and ID number need to be included in the box. The reason for the denial would need to be clear in the narrative below.]

Background Information: *Describe facts of the case including type of appeal and date appeal filed.*

Final Internal Adverse Benefit Determination: *State that adverse benefit determination has been upheld. List all documents and statements that were reviewed to make this final internal adverse benefit determination.*

Findings: *Discuss the reason or reasons for the final internal adverse benefit determination.*

[Insert language assistance disclosure here, if applicable.
SPANISH (Español): Para obtener asistencia en Español, llame al [insert telephone number].
TAGALOG (Tagalog): Kung kailangan ninyo ang tulong sa Tagalog tumawag sa [insert telephone number].
CHINESE (中文): 如果需要中文的帮助，请拨打这个号码 [insert telephone number]。
NAVAJO (Dine): Dinek'ehgo shika at'ohwol ninisingo, kwiijigo holne' [insert telephone number].]

OMB Control Number 1210-0144 (expires 04/30/2014)

Model Notice of Final Internal Adverse Benefit Determination – Revised as of June 22, 2011

Important Information about Your Rights to External Review

What if I need help understanding this denial?
Contact us [insert contact information] if you need assistance understanding this notice or our decision to deny you a service or coverage.

What if I don't agree with this decision? For certain types of claims, you are entitled to request an independent, external review of our decision. Contact [insert external review contact information] with any questions on your rights to external review. [For insured coverage, insert: If your claim is not eligible for independent external review but you still disagree with the denial, your state insurance regulator may be able to help to resolve the dispute.] See the "Other resources section" of this form for help filing a request for external review.

How do I file a request for external review?
Complete the bottom of this page, make a copy, and send this document to {insert address}.] [or] [insert alternative instructions.] See also the "Other resources to help you" section of this form for assistance filing a request for external review.

What if my situation is urgent? If your situation meets the definition of urgent under the law, the external review of your claim will be conducted as expeditiously as possible. Generally, an urgent situation is one in which your health may be in serious jeopardy or, in the opinion of your physician, you may experience pain that cannot be adequately controlled while you wait for a decision on the external review of your claim. If you believe your situation is urgent, you may request an expedited external review by [insert instructions to begin the process (such as by phone, fax, electronic submission, etc.)].

Who may file a request for external review?
You or someone you name to act for you (your authorized representative) may file a request for external review. [Insert information on how to designate an authorized representative.]

Can I provide additional information about my claim? Yes, once your external review is initiated, you will receive instructions on how to supply additional information.

Can I request copies of information relevant to my claim? Yes, you may request copies (free of charge) by contacting us at [insert contact information].

What happens next? If you request an external review, an independent organization will review our decision and provide you with a written determination. If this organization decides to overturn our decision, we will provide coverage or payment for your health care item or service.

Other resources to help you: For questions about your rights, this notice, or for assistance, you can contact: [if coverage is group health plan coverage, insert: the Employee Benefits Security Administration at 1-866-444-EBSA (3272)] [and/or] [if coverage is insured, insert State Department of Insurance contact information]. [Insert, if applicable in your state: Additionally, a consumer assistance program can help you file your appeal. Contact:[insert contact information].]

NAME OF PERSON FILING REQUEST FOR EXTERNAL REVIEW: _____

Circle one:☐Covered person   ☐ Patient   ☐ Authorized Representative
Contact information of person filing request for external review (if different from patient)
Address:_____**Daytime phone:**_____**Email:**_____

If person filing request for external review is other than patient, patient must indicate authorization by signing here:_____

Are you requesting an urgent review? ☐Yes   ☐ No

Briefly describe why you disagree with this decision (you may attach additional information, such as a physician's letter, bills, medical records, or other documents to support your claim):

_____

_____

Send this form and your denial notice to: [Insert name and contact information]
Be certain to keep copies of this form, your denial notice, and all documents and correspondence related to this claim.

Model Notice of Final External Review Decision – Revised June 22, 2011

Date of Notice
Name of Plan   **Telephone/Fax**
Address   **Website/Email Address**

This document contains important information that you should retain for your records.
This document serves as notice of a final external review decision. We have
[upheld/overturned/modified] the denial of your request for the provision of, or payment for, a
health care service or course of treatment.

Historical Case Details:

Patient Name:	ID Number:						
Address: (street, county, state, zip)							
Claim #:	Date of Service:						
Provider:							
Reason for Denial (in whole or in part):							
Amt. Charged	Allowed Amt.	Other Insurance	Deductible	Co-pay	Coinsurance	Other Amts. Not Covered	Amt. Paid
YTD Credit toward Deductible:			YTD Credit toward Out-of-Pocket Maximum:				
Description of Service:			Denial Codes:				

[If denial is not related to a specific claim, only name and ID number need to be included in the box. The reason for the denial would need to be clear in the narrative below.]

Background Information: *Describe facts of the case including type of appeal, date appeal filed, date appeal was received by IRO and date IRO decision was made.*

Final External Review Decision: *State decision. List all documents and statements that were reviewed to make this final external review decision.*

Findings: *Discuss the principal reason or reasons for IRO decision, including the rationale and any evidence-based standards or coverage provisions that were relied on in making this decision.*

OMB Control Number 1210-0144 (expires 04/30/2014)

Model Notice of Final External Review Decision – Revised June 22, 2011

Important Information about Your Appeal Rights

What if I need help understanding this decision?

Contact us [insert IRO contact information] if you need assistance understanding this notice.

What happens now? If we have overturned the denial, your plan or health insurance issuer will now provide service or payment.

If we have upheld the denial, there is no further review available under the appeals process. However, you may have other remedies available under State or Federal law, such as filing a lawsuit.

Other resources to help you: For questions about your appeal rights, this notice, or for assistance, you can contact [if coverage is group health plan coverage, insert: the Employee Benefits Security Administration at 1-866-444-EBSA (3272)] [and/or] [if coverage is insured, insert State Department of Insurance contact information]. [Insert, if applicable in your state: Additionally, you can contact your consumer assistance program at [insert contact information].]

P. Blank and Completed Template Summaries of Benefits and Coverage

Summary of Benefits and Coverage: What this Plan Covers & What it Costs

Coverage Period: [See Instructions]

Coverage for: _____ | Plan Type: _____

⚠️ **This is only a summary.** If you want more detail about your coverage and costs, you can get the complete terms in the policy or plan document at www.[insert] or by calling 1-800-[insert].

Important Questions	Answers	Why this Matters:
What is the overall deductible?	$	
Are there other deductibles for specific services?	$	
Is there an out-of-pocket limit on my expenses?	$	
What is not included in the out-of-pocket limit?		
Is there an overall annual limit on what the plan pays?		
Does this plan use a network of providers?		
Do I need a referral to see a specialist?		
Are there services this plan doesn't cover?		

OMB Control Numbers 1545-2229, 1210-0147, and 0938-1146

Questions: Call 1-800-[insert] or visit us at www.[insert].com.
If you aren't clear about any of the bolded terms used in this form, see the Glossary. You can view the Glossary at www.[insert] or call 1-800-[insert] to request a copy.

1 of 6

Summary of Benefits and Coverage: What this Plan Covers & What it Costs

Coverage Period: [See Instructions]

Coverage for: _____ | **Plan Type:** _____

⚠
- Co-payments are fixed dollar amounts (for example, $15) you pay for covered health care, usually when you receive the service.
- Co-insurance is *your* share of the costs of a covered service, calculated as a percent of the allowed amount for the service. For example, if the plan's allowed amount for an overnight hospital stay is $1,000, your co-insurance payment of 20% would be $200. This may change if you haven't met your deductible.
- The amount the plan pays for covered services is based on the allowed amount. If an out-of-network provider charges more than the allowed amount, you may have to pay the difference. For example, if an out-of-network hospital charges $1,500 for an overnight stay and the allowed amount is $1,000, you may have to pay the $500 difference. (This is called balance billing.)
- This plan may encourage you to use _____ providers by charging you lower deductibles, co-payments and co-insurance amounts.

Common Medical Event	Services You May Need	Your cost if you use an		Limitations & Exceptions
		In-network Provider	Out-of-network Provider	
If you visit a health care provider's office or clinic	Primary care visit to treat an injury or illness			
	Specialist visit			
	Other practitioner office visit			
	Preventive care/screening/immunization			
If you have a test	Diagnostic test (x-ray, blood work)			
	Imaging (CT/PET scans, MRIs)			
If you need drugs to treat your illness or condition	Generic drugs			
	Preferred brand drugs			
	Non-preferred brand drugs			
More information about prescription drug coverage is available at www.[insert].	Specialty drugs			
If you have outpatient surgery	Facility fee (e.g., ambulatory surgery center)			
	Physician/surgeon fees			
If you need	Emergency room services			

Questions: Call 1-800-[insert] or visit us at www.[insert].com.
If you aren't clear about any of the bolded terms used in this form, see the Glossary. You can view the Glossary at www.[insert] or call 1-800-**[insert]** to request a copy.

2 of 6

Summary of Benefits and Coverage: What this Plan Covers & What it Costs

Coverage Period: [See Instructions]

Coverage for: _____ | Plan Type: _____

Common Medical Event	Services You May Need	Your cost if you use an		Limitations & Exceptions
		In-network Provider	Out-of-network Provider	
immediate medical attention	Emergency medical transportation			
	Urgent care			
If you have a hospital stay	Facility fee (e.g., hospital room)			
	Physician/surgeon fee			
If you have mental health, behavioral health, or substance abuse needs	Mental/Behavioral health outpatient services			
	Mental/Behavioral health inpatient services			
	Substance use disorder outpatient services			
	Substance use disorder inpatient services			
If you are pregnant	Prenatal and postnatal care			
	Delivery and all inpatient services			
If you need help recovering or have other special health needs	Home health care			
	Rehabilitation services			
	Habilitation services			
	Skilled nursing care			
	Durable medical equipment			
	Hospice service			
If your child needs dental or eye care	Eye exam			
	Glasses			
	Dental check-up			

Excluded Services & Other Covered Services:

Services Your Plan Does NOT Cover (This isn't a complete list. Check your policy or plan document for other excluded services.)
• •

Questions: Call 1-800-[insert] or visit us at www.[insert].com.
If you aren't clear about any of the bolded terms used in this form, see the Glossary. You can view the Glossary at www.[insert] or call 1-800-[insert] to request a copy.

3 of 6

Summary of Benefits and Coverage: What this Plan Covers & What it Costs	Coverage Period: [See Instructions]
	Coverage for: _____ | Plan Type: _____

Other Covered Services (This isn't a complete list. Check your policy or plan document for other covered services and your costs for these services.)

-

Your Rights to Continue Coverage:

[insert applicable information from instructions]

Your Grievance and Appeals Rights:

If you have a complaint or are dissatisfied with a denial of coverage for claims under your plan, you may be able to appeal or file a grievance. For questions about your rights, this notice, or assistance, you can contact: [insert applicable contact information from instructions].

To see examples of how this plan might cover costs for a sample medical situation, see the next page.

Questions: Call 1-800-[insert] or visit us at www.[insert].com.
If you aren't clear about any of the bolded terms used in this form, see the Glossary. You can view the Glossary at www.[insert] or call 1-800-**[insert]** to request a copy.

Coverage Examples	: _____	Coverage Period: [See instructions]
		Coverage for: _____	Plan Type: _____

About these Coverage Examples:

These examples show how this plan might cover medical care in given situations. Use these examples to see, in general, how much financial protection a sample patient might get if they are covered under different plans.

This is not a cost estimator.

Don't use these examples to estimate your actual costs under this plan. The actual care you receive will be different from these examples, and the cost of that care will also be different.

See the next page for important information about these examples.

Having a baby
(normal delivery)

- **Amount owed to providers: $7,540**
- **Plan pays $**
- **Patient pays $**

Sample care costs:

Hospital charges (mother)	$2,700
Routine obstetric care	$2,100
Hospital charges (baby)	$900
Anesthesia	$900
Laboratory tests	$500
Prescriptions	$200
Radiology	$200
Vaccines, other preventive	$40
Total	$7,540

Patient pays:

Deductibles	$
Co-pays	$
Co-insurance	$
Limits or exclusions	$
Total	$

Managing type 2 diabetes
(routine maintenance of a well-controlled condition)

- **Amount owed to providers: $4,100**
- **Plan pays $**
- **Patient pays $**

Sample care costs:

Prescriptions	$1,500
Medical Equipment and Supplies	$1,300
Office Visits and Procedures	$730
Education	$290
Laboratory tests	$140
Vaccines, other preventive	$140
Total	$4,100

Patient pays:

Deductibles	$
Co-pays	$
Co-insurance	$
Limits or exclusions	$
Total	$

Questions: Call 1-800-[insert] or visit us at www.[insert].com.
If you aren't clear about any of the bolded terms used in this form, see the Glossary. You can view the Glossary at www.[insert] or call 1-800-[insert] to request a copy.

5 of 6

Coverage Examples _____ : _____ Coverage Period: [See instructions]

Coverage for: _____ | Plan Type: _____

Questions and answers about the Coverage Examples:

What are some of the assumptions behind the Coverage Examples?

- Costs don't include premiums.
- Sample care costs are based on national averages supplied by the U.S. Department of Health and Human Services, and aren't specific to a particular geographic area or health plan.
- The patient's condition was not an excluded or preexisting condition.
- All services and treatments started and ended in the same coverage period.
- There are no other medical expenses for any member covered under this plan.
- Out-of-pocket expenses are based only on treating the condition in the example.
- The patient received all care from in-network providers. If the patient had received care from out-of-network providers, costs would have been higher.

What does a Coverage Example show?

For each treatment situation, the Coverage Example helps you see how deductibles, co-payments, and co-insurance can add up. It also helps you see what expenses might be left up to you to pay because the service or treatment isn't covered or payment is limited.

Does the Coverage Example predict my own care needs?

✖ **No.** Treatments shown are just examples. The care you would receive for this condition could be different based on your doctor's advice, your age, how serious your condition is, and many other factors.

Does the Coverage Example predict my future expenses?

✖ **No.** Coverage Examples are **not** cost estimators. You can't use the examples to estimate costs for an actual condition. They are for comparative purposes only. Your own costs will be different depending on the care you receive, the prices your providers charge, and the reimbursement your health plan allows.

Can I use Coverage Examples to compare plans?

✓ **Yes.** When you look at the Summary of Benefits and Coverage for other plans, you'll find the same Coverage Examples. When you compare plans, check the "Patient Pays" box in each example. The smaller that number, the more coverage the plan provides.

Are there other costs I should consider when comparing plans?

✓ **Yes.** An important cost is the premium you pay. Generally, the lower your premium, the more you'll pay in out-of-pocket costs, such as co-payments, deductibles, and co-insurance. You should also consider contributions to accounts such as health savings accounts (HSAs), flexible spending arrangements (FSAs) or health reimbursement accounts (HRAs) that help you pay out-of-pocket expenses.

Questions: Call 1-800-[insert] or visit us at www.[insert].com.
If you aren't clear about any of the bolded terms used in this form, see the Glossary. You can view the Glossary at www.[insert] or call 1-800-[insert] to request a copy.

Q. DOL Technical Release 2011-04—Guidance on Rebates for Group Health Plans Paid Pursuant to the Medical Loss Ratio Requirements of the Public Health Service Act

U.S. Department of Labor   Employee Benefits Security Administration
Washington, DC 20210

TECHNICAL RELEASE 2011-04

DATE: DECEMBER 2, 2011

SUBJECT: GUIDANCE ON REBATES FOR GROUP HEALTH PLANS PAID PURSUANT TO THE
             MEDICAL LOSS RATIO REQUIREMENTS OF THE PUBLIC HEALTH SERVICE ACT

BACKGROUND

Section 2718 of the Public Health Service Act (PHSA), 42 U.S.C. 300gg-18, as added by the
Patient Protection and Affordable Care Act (Affordable Care Act) (Pub.L. 111-148, 124 Stat.
119), enacted on March 23, 2010, requires that health insurance issuers publicly report on major
categories of spending of policyholder premium dollars, such as clinical services provided to
enrollees and activities that will improve health care quality. The law establishes medical loss
ratio (MLR) standards for issuers. Issuers are required to provide rebates to enrollees when their
spending for the benefit of policyholders on reimbursement for clinical services and health care
quality improving activities, in relation to the premiums charged (as adjusted for taxes), is less
than the MLR standards established pursuant to the statute. Rebates are based upon aggregated
market data in each State and not upon a particular group health plan's experience.

The Department of Health and Human Services (HHS) has promulgated regulations interpreting
and implementing the requirements of section 2718 of the PHSA (75 FR 74864, December 1,
2010 (Interim Final Rule); 75 FR 82277, December 30, 2010 (Technical Correction); and 45
CFR Part 158 (Final Rule with comment period made available to the public on December 2,
2011, and scheduled to be published in the Federal Register on December 7, 2011).[1] In order to
reduce burdens on issuers and to minimize the tax impacts on participants in and sponsors of
group health plans, the regulations provide that issuers must pay to the policyholder any rebates
owed to persons covered under a group health plan. The regulations do not give specific
instructions to policyholders who are group health plans covered by the Employee Retirement
Income Security Act of 1974 (ERISA) or the sponsors of such plans regarding their
responsibilities under ERISA concerning rebates. However, when rebates are issued to such
policyholders, issues concerning the status of such funds under ERISA and how such funds must
be handled necessarily arise.

DISCUSSION

Distributions from health insurance issuers, such as insurance companies, to their policyholders,
including employee benefit plans, take a variety of forms, including refunds, dividends,

---

[1] Regulations published by HHS pertaining to health insurance issuers implementing MLR requirements under the
Affordable Care Act are being issued contemporaneously with this Technical Release. Subpart B of the regulation
addresses the requirements for health insurance issuers in the group or individual market, including grandfathered
health plans, to provide an annual rebate to enrollees, if the issuer's MLR fails to meet minimum requirements.

demutualization payments, rebates, and excess surplus distributions. To the extent that distributions, such as premium rebates, are considered to be plan assets, they become subject to the requirements of Title I of ERISA. Anyone with authority or control over plan assets is a "fiduciary," as defined in section 3(21), and subject to, among other things, the fiduciary responsibility provisions of ERISA section 404 and the prohibited transaction provisions of ERISA section 406. Further, under section 403 of ERISA, plan assets generally must be held in trust, may not inure to the benefit of any employer, and must be held for the exclusive purpose of providing benefits to participants in the plan and their beneficiaries and defraying reasonable expenses of administering the plan. However, the trust requirement does not apply to any assets of a plan which consist of insurance contracts or policies issued by an insurance company qualified to do business in a State or to any assets of a plan which are held by such an insurance company. *See* ERISA sections 401(b)(2) and 403(b).

ERISA does not expressly define plan assets. The Department has issued regulations describing what constitutes plan assets with respect to a plan's investment in other entities and with respect to participant contributions. *See* 29 C.F.R. §2510.3-101 and 29 C.F.R. §2510.3-102. In other situations, the Department has indicated that the assets of an employee benefit plan generally are to be identified on the basis of ordinary notions of property rights.

For group health plans, a distribution such as the rebate will be a plan asset if a plan has a beneficial interest in the distribution under ordinary notions of property rights. Under ERISA section 401(b)(2), if the plan or its trust is the policyholder, the policy would be an asset of the plan, and in the absence of specific plan or policy language to the contrary, the employer would have no interest in the distribution. On the other hand, if the employer is the policyholder and the insurance policy or contract, together with other instruments governing the plan, can fairly be read to provide that some part or all of a distribution belongs to the employer, then that language will generally govern, and the employer may retain distributions.

In the Department's view, however, the fact that the employer is the policyholder or the owner of the policy would not, by itself, indicate that the employer may retain the distributions. In determining who is entitled to the distribution, one would need to carefully analyze the terms of the governing plan documents and the parties' understandings and representations.

Under ordinary notions of property rights, if a contract is ambiguous, other evidence may be used to determine the intent of the parties. In the absence of more direct evidence, the Department has looked to the sources of the insurance policies' premium payments.[2] For example, where the premium is paid entirely out of trust assets, it is the view of the Department that the entire amount received from the insurer by the policyholder constitutes plan assets.[3]

Similarly, assuming the plan documents and other extrinsic evidence do not resolve the allocation issue, the portion of a rebate that is attributable to participant contributions would be

---

[2] *See, e.g.,* Advisory Opinions 2001-02A (Feb. 15, 2001); 99-08A (May 20, 1999); 94-31A (Sept. 9, 1994); and 92-02A (Jan. 17, 1992).
[3] *See id.* and DOL Information Letter to Theodore Groom (Feb. 15, 2001).

2

considered plan assets. Thus, if the employer paid the entire cost of the insurance coverage, then no part of the rebate with respect to this particular policy would be attributable to participant contributions. However, if participants paid the entire cost of the insurance coverage, then the entire amount of the rebate would be attributable to participant contributions and considered to be plan assets. If the participants and the employer each paid a fixed percentage of the cost, a percentage of the rebate equal to the percentage of the cost paid by participants would be attributable to participant contributions. If the employer was required to pay a fixed amount and participants were responsible for paying any additional costs, then the portion of the rebate under such a policy that does not exceed the participants' total amount of prior contributions during the relevant period would be attributable to participant contributions. Finally, if participants paid a fixed amount and the employer was responsible for paying any additional costs, then the portion of the rebate under such a policy that did not exceed the employer's total amount of prior contributions during the relevant period would not be attributable to participant contributions.

In any case, employers that sponsor group health plans that use insurance policies to provide benefits would be prohibited by ERISA section 403(c)(1) from receiving a rebate amount greater than the total amount of premiums and other plan expenses paid by the employer. To the extent that an employer's portion of the rebate exceeds the amount of such employer's total amount of premiums and other plan expenses paid, that excess amount must be held in trust for the exclusive benefit of participants and beneficiaries.

Decisions on how to apply or expend the plan's portion of a rebate are subject to ERISA's general standards of fiduciary conduct. Under section 404(a)(1) of ERISA, the responsible plan fiduciaries must act prudently, solely in the interest of the plan participants and beneficiaries, and in accordance with the terms of the plan to the extent consistent with the provisions of ERISA. With respect to these duties, the Department notes that a fiduciary also has a duty of impartiality to the plan's participants. A selection of an allocation method that benefits the fiduciary, as a participant in the plan, at the expense of other participants in the plan would be inconsistent with this duty. See Restatement (Second) of Trusts § 183 (requiring fiduciaries to "deal impartially with beneficiaries"). An allocation does not fail to be impartial or "solely in the interest of participants," for purposes of ERISA section 404(a)(1), merely because it does not exactly reflect the premium activity of policy subscribers. In deciding on an allocation method, the plan fiduciary may properly weigh the costs to the plan and the ultimate plan benefit as well as the competing interests of participants or classes of participants provided such method is reasonable, fair and objective. For example, if a fiduciary finds that the cost of distributing shares of a rebate to former participants approximates the amount of the proceeds, the fiduciary may properly decide to allocate the proceeds to current participants based upon a reasonable, fair and objective allocation method.[4] Similarly, if distributing payments to any participants is not cost-effective (e.g., payments to participants are of de minimis amounts, or would give rise to tax consequences to participants or the plan), the fiduciary may utilize the rebate for other permissible plan purposes including applying the rebate toward future participant premium payments or toward benefit enhancements.

---

[4] See Field Assistance Bulletin 2006-01 (April 19, 2006); ERISA Advisory Opinion 2005-08A (May 11, 2005); and DOL Information Letter to Theodore Groom (Feb. 15, 2001).

3

Where a plan provides benefits under multiple policies, the fiduciary should allocate or apply the plan's portion of a rebate for the benefit of participants and beneficiaries who are covered by the policy to which the rebate relates provided doing so would be prudent and solely in the interests of the plan according to the above analysis. However, the use of a rebate generated by one plan to benefit the participants of another plan would be a breach of the duty of loyalty to a plan's participants.

Under ERISA section 403(a), plan assets generally must be held in trust until appropriately expended. However, many group health plans receiving premium rebates do not maintain trusts because their premiums are paid from the general assets of the employer (including employee payroll deductions) and all benefits are paid by the policy issuers. In ERISA Technical Release 92-01 (TR 92-01, May 28, 1992), the Department stated that in the case of cafeteria plans established under section 125 of the Internal Revenue Code and certain other contributory welfare plans, it would not assert a violation solely for a failure to hold participant contributions to the plan in trust. In the case of these types of plans, with respect to which a trust is not established in reliance on TR 92-01, the Department would treat the trust relief under TR 92-01 and the limited reporting exemptions in 29 CFR §§2520.104-20 and 104-44 as available for premium rebates that are plan assets if they are used within three months of receipt by the policyholder to pay premiums or refunds as provided in §§2520.104-20 and 2520.104-44. For other plans not otherwise subject to the trust requirements of section 403(a) of ERISA, fiduciaries may take into account the cost of creating a trust when deciding how to expend rebates. For example, directing insurers to apply the rebate toward future participant premium payments or toward benefit enhancements adopted by the plan sponsor would avoid the need for a trust, and may, in some circumstances, be consistent with fiduciary responsibilities.

In some cases, the plan involved may have terminated before the rebate is paid to the policyholder. The HHS regulation at §158.242(b)(4) describes the issuer's obligations in the event that it cannot, despite reasonable efforts, locate the policyholder with respect to a terminated plan. In cases where the issuer is able to locate the policyholder with respect to a terminated ERISA-covered plan, we believe that the policyholder must comply with ERISA's fiduciary provisions in the handling of rebates that it receives, including looking to the plan document to determine how assets of the plan are to be allocated upon termination. Under ERISA section 403(d)(2), the assets of an employee welfare benefit plan that terminates must be distributed in accordance with the terms of the plan to the extent the plan terms are consistent with the provisions of Title I of ERISA and following the terms of the plan would not violate any other applicable federal law or regulation. If the plan document does not provide direction, the policyholder may need to determine if it is cost effective to distribute the plan's portion of the rebate to the relevant former participants in the plan.

CONCLUSION

Rebates paid pursuant to section 2718 of the PHSA, in connection with group health plans covered by ERISA, may constitute plan assets. If the plan or its trust is the policyholder, in the absence of specific plan or policy language to the contrary, the entire rebate would constitute plan assets, and the policyholder would be required to comply with ERISA's fiduciary provisions

4

in the handling of rebates that it receives. If the plan sponsor is the policyholder, determining the plan's portion, if any, may depend on provisions in the plan or the policy or on the manner in which the plan sponsor and the plan participants have shared in the cost of the policy. Any portion of a rebate constituting plan assets must be handled in accordance with the fiduciary responsibility provisions of Title I of ERISA.

The Department expresses no view concerning the tax consequences of any action taken by a policyholder with regard to the receipt, holding, or distribution of the rebate. Such issues are exclusively within the jurisdiction of the Internal Revenue Service.

For Further Information Contact: Office of Regulations and Interpretations, Employee Benefits Security Administration, Department of Labor, at (202) 693-8510.

5

R. HHS Center for Consumer Information and Insurance Oversight—Essential Health Benefits Bulletin and Corresponding Frequently Asked Questions

ESSENTIAL HEALTH BENEFITS BULLETIN

Center for Consumer Information and Insurance Oversight

December 16, 2011

Contents

ii

ESSENTIAL HEALTH BENEFITS BULLETIN

Purpose

The purpose of this bulletin is to provide information and solicit comments on the regulatory approach that the Department of Health and Human Services (HHS) plans to propose to define essential health benefits (EHB) under section 1302 of the Affordable Care Act. This bulletin begins with an overview of the relevant statutory provisions and other background information, reviews research on health care services covered by employers today, and then describes the approach HHS plans to propose. This bulletin only relates to covered services. Plan cost sharing and the calculation of actuarial value are not addressed in this bulletin. We plan to release guidance on calculating actuarial value and the provision of minimum value by employer-sponsored coverage in the near future. In addition, we plan to issue future guidance on essential health benefit implementation in the Medicaid program.

The intended regulatory approach utilizes a reference plan based on employer-sponsored coverage in the marketplace today, supplemented as necessary to ensure that plans cover each of the 10 statutory categories of EHB. In developing this intended approach, HHS sought to balance comprehensiveness, affordability, and State flexibility and to reflect public input received to date.

Public input is welcome on this intended approach. Please send comments on the bulletin by January 31, 2012 to: EssentialHealthBenefits@cms.hhs.gov.

Defining Essential Health Benefits

A. Introduction and Background

Statutory Provisions

Section 1302(b) of the Affordable Care Act directs the Secretary of Health and Human Services (the Secretary) to define essential health benefits (EHB). Non-grandfathered plans in the individual and small group markets both inside and outside of the Exchanges, Medicaid benchmark and benchmark-equivalent, and Basic Health Programs must cover the EHB beginning in 2014.[1] Section 1302(b)(1) provides that EHB include items and services within the following 10 benefit categories: (1) ambulatory patient services, (2) emergency services (3) hospitalization, (4) maternity and newborn care, (5) mental health and substance use disorder services, including behavioral health treatment, (6) prescription drugs, (7) rehabilitative and habilitative services and devices, (8) laboratory services, (9) preventive and wellness services and chronic disease management, and (10) pediatric services, including oral and vision care.

---

[1] Self-insured group health plans, health insurance coverage offered in the large group market, and grandfathered health plans are not required to cover the essential health benefits.

1

Section 1302(b)(2) of the Affordable Care Act instructs the Secretary that the scope of EHB shall equal the scope of benefits provided under a typical employer plan. In defining EHB, section 1302(b)(4) directs the Secretary to establish an appropriate balance among the benefit categories. Further, under this provision, the Secretary must not make coverage decisions, determine reimbursement rates, or establish incentive programs. Benefits must not be designed in ways that discriminate based on age, disability, or expected length of life, but must consider the health care needs of diverse segments of the population. The Secretary must submit a report to the appropriate committees of Congress along with a certification from the Chief Actuary of the Centers for Medicare & Medicaid Services that the scope of the EHB is equal to the scope of benefits provided under a typical employer plan, as determined by the Secretary.

In addition, section 1311(d)(3) of the Affordable Care Act requires States to defray the cost of any benefits required by State law to be covered by qualified health plans beyond the EHB.

The statute distinguishes between a plan's covered services and the plan's cost-sharing features, such as deductibles, copayments, and coinsurance. The cost-sharing features will determine the level of actuarial value of the plan, expressed as a "metal level" as specified in statute: bronze at 60 percent actuarial value, silver at 70 percent actuarial value, gold at 80 percent actuarial value, and platinum at 90 percent actuarial value.[2]

Public and Other Input

To inform the Department's understanding of the benefits provided by employer plans, HHS has considered a report on employer plans submitted by the Department of Labor (DOL), recommendations on the process for defining and updating EHB from the Institute of Medicine (IOM), and input from the public and other interested stakeholders during a series of public listening sessions detailed below.

Section 1302(b)(2)(A) requires the Secretary of Labor to inform the determination of EHB with a survey of employer-sponsored plans. On April 15, 2011, the DOL issued its report, in satisfaction of section 1302(b)(2)(A) of the Affordable Care Act, providing results on the scope of benefits offered under employer-sponsored insurance to HHS.[3] The DOL survey provided a broad overview of benefits available to employees enrolled in employer sponsored plans. The report drew on data from the 2008 and 2009 National Compensation Survey (which includes large and small employers), as well as DOL's supplemental review of health plan Summary Plan Documents, and provided information on the extent to which employees have coverage for approximately 25 services within the 10 categories of EHB outlined in the Affordable Care Act (e.g., a certain percentage of plan participants have coverage for a certain benefit).

In order to receive independent guidance, HHS also commissioned the IOM to recommend a process that would help HHS define the benefits that should be included in the EHB and update the benefits to take into account advances in science, gaps in access,

---

[2] As noted, these will be the subject of forthcoming guidance.

[3] Available at http://www.bls.gov/ncs/ebs/sp/selmedbensreport.pdf

2

and the effect of any benefit changes on cost. The IOM submitted its consensus recommendations in a report entitled "Essential Health Benefits: Balancing Coverage and Cost" on October 7, 2011.[4] In order to balance the cost and comprehensiveness of EHB, the IOM recommended that EHB reflect plans in the small employer market and that the establishment of an EHB package should be guided by a national premium target. The IOM also recommended the development of a framework for updating EHB that would take into account new evidence about effective interventions and changes in provider and consumer preferences while ensuring that the cost of the revised package of benefits remains within predetermined limits as the benefit standards become more specific. The IOM recommended flexibility across States and suggested that States operating their own Exchanges be allowed to substitute a plan that is actuarially equivalent to the national EHB package. The IOM also recommended continued public input throughout the process.

Following the release of the IOM's recommendations, HHS held a series of sessions with stakeholders, including consumers, providers, employers, plans, and State representatives, in both Washington, D.C. and around the nation to gather public input. Several key themes emerged. Consumer groups and some provider groups expressed concern at the IOM's emphasis on cost over the comprehensiveness of benefits. Some consumer groups expressed a belief that small group plans may not represent the typical employer plan envisioned by the statute, while employers and health insurance issuers generally supported the IOM conclusion that EHB should be based on small employer plans. Consumer and provider groups commented that specific benefits should be spelled out by the Secretary, while health insurance issuers and employers commented that they prefer more general guidance, allowing for greater flexibility. Both provider and consumer groups expressed concern about discrimination against individuals with particular conditions. Employers and health insurance issuers stressed concern about resources and urged the Secretary to adopt a more moderate benefit package. Consumers generally favored a uniform benefits package, and many consumers requested that State mandates be included in the benefits package. Some requested a uniform benefit package so that consumer choice of plan could focus on other plan features such as premium, provider network, and quality improvement. Some employer, health insurance issuer, and State representatives focused on the need for flexibility across the country to reflect local preferences and practices. States, health insurance issuers, and employers emphasized the need for timely guidance in preparing for implementation around EHB.

B. Summary of Research on Employer Sponsored Plan Benefits and State Benefit Mandates

While the Affordable Care Act directs the Secretary to define the scope of EHB as being equal to a typical employer plan, the statute does not provide a definition of "typical." Therefore, HHS gathered benefit information on large employer plans (which account for

---

[4] Available at http://www.iom.edu/Reports/2011/Essential-Health-Benefits-Balancing-Coverage-and-Cost.aspx

3

the majority of employer plan enrollees), small employer products (which account for the majority of employer plans), and plans offered to public employees.5

There is not yet a national standard for plan reporting of benefits.6 While the DOL collects information on benefits offered by employer plans, no single data set includes comprehensive data on coverage of each of the 10 statutory essential health benefit categories. Consequently, to supplement information available from the DOL, Mercer,7 and Kaiser Family Foundation/Health Research & Educational Trust (KFF/HRET)8 surveys of employer plans, HHS gathered information on employer plan benefits from the IOM's survey of three small group issuers and supplemented this information with an internal analysis of publicly available information on State employee plans and Federal employee plans,9 and information on benefits submitted to HealthCare.gov by small group health insurance issuers. To inform our understanding of the category of pediatric oral and vision care, HHS staff also analyzed dental and vision plans in the Federal Employees Dental/Vision Insurance Program (FEDVIP).10 The FEDVIP program is a standalone vision and dental program where eligible Federal enrollees pay the full cost of their coverage.

Similarities and Differences in Benefit Coverage Across Markets

Generally, according to this analysis, products in the small group market, State employee plans, and the Federal Employees Health Benefits Program (FEHBP) Blue Cross Blue Shield (BCBS) Standard Option and Government Employees Health Association (GEHA) plans do not differ significantly in the range of services they cover. They differ mainly in cost-sharing provisions, but cost-sharing is not taken into account in determining EHB. Similarly, these plans and products and the small group issuers surveyed by the IOM appear to generally cover health care services in virtually all of the 10 statutory categories.

For example, across the markets and plans examined, it appears that the following benefits are consistently covered: physician and specialist office visits, inpatient and

---

[5] Nomenclature used in HealthCare.gov describes "products" as the services covered as a package by an issuer, which may have several cost-sharing options and riders as options. A "plan" refers to the specific benefits and cost-sharing provisions available to an enrolled consumer. For example, multiple plans with different cost-sharing structures and rider options may derive from a single product.

[6] Section 2715 of the Public Health Service Act (PHS Act) requires group health plans and health insurance issuers in the group and individual markets to provide a Summary of Benefits and Coverage in a uniform format to consumers. HHS, DOL, and the Department of the Treasury issued proposed rules for PHS Act section 2715 at 76 FR 52442 (August 22, 2011). Further information is available at http://www.gpo.gov/fdsys/pkg/FR-2011-08-22/pdf/2011-21193.pdf and http://www.dol.gov/ebsa/faqs/faq-aca7.html.

[7] Available at http://www.mercer.com/survey-reports/2009-US-national-health-plan-survey

[8] Available at http://ehbs.kff.org

[9] HHS staff analyzed the Federal Employees Health Benefits Program (FEHBP) Blue Cross Blue Shield (BCBS) Standard Option and Government Employees Health Association Benefit plan booklets.

[10] Further information is available at https://www.benefeds.com/Portal/jsp/LoginPage.jsp

4

outpatient surgery, hospitalization, organ transplants, emergency services, maternity care, inpatient and outpatient mental health and substance use disorder services, generic and brand prescription drugs, physical, occupational and speech therapy, durable medical equipment, prosthetics and orthotics, laboratory and imaging services, preventive care and nutritional counseling services for patients with diabetes, and well child and pediatric services such as immunizations. As noted in a previous HHS analysis, variation appears to be much greater for cost-sharing than for covered services.[11]

While the plans and products in all the markets studied appear to cover a similar general scope of services, there was some variation in coverage of a few specific services among markets and among plans and products within markets, although there is no systematic difference noted in the breadth of services among these markets. For example, the FEHBP BCBS Standard Option plan covers preventive and basic dental care, acupuncture, bariatric surgery, hearing aids, and smoking cessation programs and medications. These benefits are not all consistently covered by small employer health plans. Coverage of these benefits in State employee plans varies between States. However, in some cases, small group products cover some benefits that are not included in the FEHBP plans examined and may not be included in State employee plans, especially in States for which benefits such as in-vitro fertilization or applied behavior analysis (ABA) for children with autism are mandated by State law.[12] Finally, there is a subset of benefits including mental health and substance use disorder services, pediatric oral and vision services, and habilitative services – where there is variation in coverage among plans, products, and markets. These service categories are examined in more detail below.

Mental Health and Substance Use Disorder Services

In general, the plans and products studied appear to cover inpatient and outpatient mental health and substance use disorder services; however, coverage in the small group market often has limits. As discussed later in this document, coverage will have to be consistent with the Mental Health Parity and Addiction Equity Act (MHPAEA).[13]

The extent to which plans and products cover behavioral health treatment, a component of the mental health and substance use disorder EHB category, is unclear. In general, plans do not mention behavioral health treatment as a category of services in summary

---

[11] ASPE Research Brief, "Actuarial Value and Employer Sponsored Insurance," November 2011. Available at: http://aspe.hhs.gov/health/reports/2011/AV-ESI/rb.pdf.

[12] In addition to mandated benefits, it appears that the small group issuers the IOM surveyed also generally cover residential treatment centers, which the FEHBP BCBS Standard Option plan excludes. However, as this analysis compares three small group issuers to one FEHBP plan, it is unclear if this finding can be generalized to other plans.

[13] See Affordable Care Act § 1311(j); see also PHS Act § 2726, ERISA § 712, Internal Revenue Code § 9812. See also interim final regulations at 75 FR 5410 (February 2, 2010) and guidance published on June 30, 2010 (http://www.dol.gov/ebsa/faqs/faq-mhpaea.html), December 22, 2010 (http://www.dol.gov/ebsa/faqs/faq-aca5.html), and November 17, 2011 (http://www.dol.gov/ebsa/faqs/faq-aca7.html).

5

plan documents. The exception is behavioral treatment for autism, which small group issuers in the IOM survey indicated is usually covered only when mandated by States.

Pediatric Oral and Vision Care

Coverage of dental and vision care services are provided through a mix of comprehensive health coverage plans and stand-alone coverage separate from the major medical coverage, which may be excepted benefits under PHS Act section 2722.[14] The FEDVIP vision plan with the highest enrollment in 2010 covers routine eye examinations with refraction, corrective lenses and contact lenses, and the FEDVIP dental plan covers preventive and basic dental services such as cleanings and fillings, as well as advanced dental services such as root canals, crowns and medically necessary orthodontia. In some cases, dental or vision services may be covered by a medical plan. For example, the FEHBP BCBS Standard Option plan covers basic and preventive dental services.

Habilitative Services

There is no generally accepted definition of habilitative services among health plans, and in general, health insurance plans do not identify habilitative services as a distinct group of services. However, many States, consumer groups, and other organizations have suggested definitions of habilitative services which focus on: learning new skills or functions – as distinguished from rehabilitation which focuses on relearning existing skills or functions, or defining "habilitative services" as the term is used in the Medicaid program.[15,16,17] An example of habilitative services is speech therapy for a child who is not talking at the expected age.

Two of the three small group issuers surveyed by the IOM indicated that they do not cover habilitative services. However, data submitted by small group issuers for display on HealthCare.gov indicates that about 70 percent of small group products offer at least limited coverage of habilitative services.[18] Physical therapy (PT), occupational therapy (OT), and speech therapy (ST) for habilitative purposes may be covered under the rehabilitation benefit of health insurance plans, which often includes visit limits. All three issuers reporting to the IOM covered PT, OT, and ST, though one issuer did not cover these services for patients with an autism diagnosis. The FEHBP BCBS Standard Option plan also covers PT, OT, and ST. State employee plans examined appear to generally cover PT, OT, and ST.

---

[14] When dental or vision coverage is provided in plan that is separate from or otherwise not an integral part of a major medical plan, that separate coverage is not subject to the insurance market reforms in title XXVII of the PHS Act. See PHS Act §§ 2722(c)(1), 2791(c)(2).

[15] For State definitions, see Md. Code Ins. § 15-835(a)(3); D.C. Code § 31-3271(3); 215 Ill. Comp. Stat. 5/356z.14(i).

[16] See 76 Fed. Reg. 52,442 and 76 Fed. Reg. 52,475.

[17] For Medicaid definition, see Social Security Act, § 1915(c)(5)(A).

[18] Data submitted in October 2011.

6

Comparison to Other Employer Plan Surveys

These findings are generally consistent with other surveys of employer sponsored health coverage conducted by DOL, Mercer, and KFF/HRET. The Department of Labor survey found that employees had widespread coverage for medical services such as inpatient hospital services, hospital room and board, emergency room visits, ambulance service, maternity, durable medical equipment, and physical therapy. Similarly, Mercer found employers provided widespread coverage for medical services such as durable medical equipment, outpatient facility charges, and physical, occupational, and speech therapy. The KFF/HRET survey also found widespread coverage of prescription drugs among employees with employer-sponsored coverage.

State Benefit Mandates

State laws regarding required coverage of benefits vary widely in number, scope, and topic, so that generalizing about mandates and their impact on typical employer plans is difficult. All States have adopted at least one health insurance mandate, and there are more than 1,600 specific service and provider coverage requirements across the 50 States and the District of Columbia.[19]

Almost all State mandated services are typically included in benefit packages in States without the mandate – such as immunizations and emergency services. In order to better understand the variation in State mandates, their impact on the benefits covered by plans, and their cost, HHS analyzed 150 categories of benefit and provider mandates across all 50 States and the District of Columbia. The FEHBP BCBS Standard and Basic Options are not subject to any State mandates, but our analysis indicates that they cover nearly all of the benefit and provider mandate categories required under State mandates. The FEHBP BCBS Standard Option is not subject to any State mandates, but our analysis indicates that it covers about 95 percent of the benefit and provider mandate categories required under State mandates. The primary exceptions are mandates requiring coverage of in-vitro fertilization and ABA therapy for autism, which are not covered by the FEHBP BCBS Standard Option plan but are required in 8 and 29 States, respectively.

These two mandates commonly permit annual dollar limits, annual lifetime or frequency limits, and/or age limits. Research by States with these two mandates indicates that the cost of covering in-vitro fertilization benefits raises average premiums by about one percent[20,21] and the cost of covering ABA therapy for autism raises average premiums by approximately 0.3 percent.[22] Approximately 10 percent of people covered by small

---

[19] Of these 1,600 mandates, about 1,150 are benefit mandates and 450 are provider mandates.

[20] Maryland Health Care Commission. Study of Mandated Health Insurance Services: A Comparative Evaluation. January 1, 2008. Available at: http://mhcc.maryland.gov/health_insurance/mandated_1207.pdf

[21] University of Connecticut Center for Public Health and Health Policy. Connecticut Mandated Health Insurance Benefit Reviews. January, 2011. Available at: http://www.ct.gov/cid/lib/cid/2010_CT_Mandated_Health_Insurance_Benefits_Reviews_-_General_Overview.pdf

[22] California Health Benefits Review Program. Analysis of Senate Bill TBD 1: Autism. March 20, 2011. Available at: http://www.chbrp.org/docs/index.php?action=read&bill_id=113&doc_type=3.

7

group policies live in a State requiring coverage of in-vitro fertilization, and approximately 50 percent live in a State requiring coverage of ABA.

The small group issuers surveyed by the IOM indicated they cover ABA only when required by State benefit mandates. The FEHBP BCBS Standard Option does not cover ABA. The extent to which these services are covered by State employee plans is unclear, as there is variation between States in whether benefit mandates apply (either by statute or voluntarily) to State employee plans.

C. Intended Regulatory Approach

As noted in the introduction, the Affordable Care Act authorizes the Secretary to define EHB. In response to the research and recommendations described above, as a general matter, our goal is to pursue an approach that will:

- Encompass the 10 categories of services identified in the statute;
- Reflect typical employer health benefit plans;
- Reflect balance among the categories;
- Account for diverse health needs across many populations;
- Ensure there are no incentives for coverage decisions, cost sharing or reimbursement rates to discriminate impermissibly against individuals because of their age, disability, or expected length of life;
- Ensure compliance with the Mental Health Parity and Addiction Equity Act of 2008 (MHPAEA);
- Provide States a role in defining EHB; and
- Balance comprehensiveness and affordability for those purchasing coverage.

As recommended by the IOM, HHS aims to balance comprehensiveness, affordability, and State flexibility while taking into account public input throughout the process of establishing and implementing EHB.[23] Our intended approach to EHB incorporates plans typically offered by small employers and benefits that are covered across the current employer marketplace.

We intend to propose that EHB be defined by a benchmark plan selected by each State. The selected benchmark plan would serve as a reference plan, reflecting both the scope of services and any limits offered by a "typical employer plan" in that State as required by section 1302(b)(2)(A) of the Affordable Care Act. This approach is based on the approach established by Congress for the Children's Health Insurance Program (CHIP), created in 1997, and for certain Medicaid populations.[24,25] A major advantage of the benchmark approach is that it recognizes that issuers make a holistic decision in constructing a package of benefits and adopt packages they believe balance consumers' needs for comprehensiveness and affordability. As described below, health insurance

[23] Available at http://www.iom.edu/Reports/2011/Essential-Health-Benefits-Balancing-Coverage-and-Cost.aspx.

[24] Balanced Budget Act of 1997; Public Law 105-33

[25] Section 42 CFR 457.410 and 457.420

8

issuers could adopt the scope of services and limits of the State benchmark, or vary it within the parameters described below.

Four Benchmark Plan Types

Our analysis of offerings that exist today suggests that the following four benchmark plan types for 2014 and 2015 best reflect the statutory standards for EHB in the Affordable Care Act:

(1) the largest plan by enrollment in any of the three largest small group insurance products in the State's small group market;[26]
(2) any of the largest three State employee health benefit plans by enrollment;
(3) any of the largest three national FEHBP plan options by enrollment; or
(4) the largest insured commercial non-Medicaid Health Maintenance Organization (HMO) operating in the State.

HHS intends to assess the benchmark process for the year 2016 and beyond based on evaluation and feedback.

To reflect the State flexibility recommended by the IOM, under our intended approach, States are permitted to select a single benchmark to serve as the standard for qualified health plans inside the Exchange operating in their State and plans offered in the individual and small group markets in their State. To determine enrollment in plans for specifying the benchmark options, we intend to propose to use enrollment data from the first quarter two years prior to the coverage year and that States select a benchmark in the third quarter two years prior to the coverage year. For example, enrollment data from HealthCare.gov for the first quarter of calendar year 2012 could be used to determine which plans would be potential benchmarks for State selection and the benchmark plan specified during the third quarter of 2012 for coverage year 2014. If a State does not exercise the option to select a benchmark health plan, we intend to propose that the default benchmark plan for that State would be the largest plan by enrollment in the largest product in the State's small group market.

Defraying the Cost of Additional Benefits

Section 1311(d)(3)(B) of the Affordable Care Act requires States to defray the costs of State-mandated benefits in excess of EHB for individuals enrolled in any qualified health plan either in the individual market or in the small group market. Similar to other Exchange decisions, the State may select the benchmark plan. The approach for 2014 and 2015 would provide a transition period for States to coordinate their benefit mandates while minimizing the likelihood the State would be required to defray the costs of these mandates in excess of EHB. In the transitional years of 2014 and 2015, if a State chooses a benchmark subject to State mandates – such as a small group market plan – that benchmark would include those mandates in the State EHB package. Alternatively,

---

[26] Nomenclature used in HealthCare.gov describes "products" as the services covered as a package by an issuer, which may have several cost-sharing options and riders as options. A "plan" refers to the specific benefits and cost-sharing provisions available to an enrolled consumer. For example, multiple plans with different cost-sharing structures and rider options may derive from a single product.

9

under our intended approach a State could also select a benchmark such as an FEHBP plan that may not include some or all of the State's benefit mandates, and therefore under Section 1311(d)(3)(B), the State would be required to cover the cost of those mandates outside the State EHB package. HHS intends to evaluate the benchmark approach for the calendar year 2016 and will develop an approach that may exclude some State benefit mandates from inclusion in the State EHB package.

Benchmark Plan Approach and the 10 Benefit Categories

One of the challenges with the described benchmark plan approach to defining EHB is meeting both the test of a "typical employer plan" and ensuring coverage of all 10 categories of services set forth in section 1302(b)(1) of the Affordable Care Act. Not every benchmark plan includes coverage of all 10 categories of benefits identified in the Affordable Care Act (e.g., some of the benchmark plans do not routinely cover habilitative services or pediatric oral or vision services). The Affordable Care Act requires all issuers subject to the EHB standard in section 1302(a) to cover each of the 10 benefit categories.[27] If a category is missing in the benchmark plan, it must nevertheless be covered by health plans required to offer EHB. In selecting a benchmark plan, a State may need to supplement the benchmark plan to cover each of the 10 categories. We are considering policy options for how a State supplements its benchmark benefits if the selected benchmark is missing a category of benefits. The most commonly non-covered categories of benefits among typical employer plans are habilitative services, pediatric oral services, and pediatric vision services.

Below, we discuss several specific options for habilitative services, pediatric oral care and pediatric vision care. Generally, we intend to propose that if a benchmark is missing other categories of benefits, the State must supplement the missing categories using the benefits from any other benchmark option. In a State with a default benchmark with missing categories, the benchmark plan would be supplemented using the largest plan in the benchmark type (e.g. small group plans or State employee plans or FEHBP) by enrollment offering the benefit. If none of the benchmark options in that benchmark type offer the benefit, the benefit will be supplemented using the FEHBP plan with the largest enrollment. For example, in a State where the default benchmark is in place but that default plan did not offer prescription drug benefits, the benchmark would be supplemented using the prescription drug benefits offered in the largest small group benchmark plan option with coverage for prescription drugs. If none of the three small group market benchmark options offer prescription drug benefits, that category would be based on the largest plan offering prescription drug benefits in FEHBP. We are continuing to consider options for supplementing missing categories such as habilitative care, pediatric oral care and pediatric vision care if States do not select one of the options discussed below.

---

[27] A qualified health plan may choose to not offer coverage for pediatric oral services provided that a standalone dental benefit plan which covers pediatric oral services as defined by EHB is offered through the same Exchange.

10

Habilitation

Because habilitative services are a less well defined area of care, there is uncertainty on what is included in it. The NAIC has proposed a definition of habilitation in materials transmitted to the Department as required under Section 2715 of the PHSA, and Medicaid has also adopted a definition of habilitative services.[28],[29] These definitions include the concept of "keeping" or "maintaining" function, but this concept is virtually unknown in commercial insurance, which focuses on creating skills and functions (in habilitation) or restoring skills and function (for rehabilitation). Private insurance and Medicare may use different definitions when relating to coverage of these services.[30] We seek comment on the advantages and disadvantages of including maintenance of function as part of the definition of habilitative services. We are considering two options if a benchmark plan does not include coverage for habilitative services:

1) Habilitative services would be offered at parity with rehabilitative services -- a plan covering services such as PT, OT, and ST for rehabilitation must also cover those services in similar scope, amount, and duration for habilitation; or
2) As a transitional approach, plans would decide which habilitative services to cover, and would report on that coverage to HHS. HHS would evaluate those decisions, and further define habilitative services in the future.

Pediatric Oral and Vision

For pediatric oral services, we are considering two options for supplementing benchmarks that do not include these categories. The State may select supplemental benefits from either:

1) The Federal Employees Dental and Vision Insurance Program (FEDVIP) dental plan with the largest national enrollment; or
2) The State's separate CHIP program.[31]

We intend to propose the EHB definition would not include non-medically necessary orthodontic benefits.

For pediatric vision services we intend to propose the plan must supplement with the benefits covered by the FEDVIP vision plan with the largest enrollment. The rationale for a different treatment of this category is that CHIP does not require vision services. As with habilitative services, we also seek comment on an approach that lets plans define the pediatric oral and vision services with required reporting as a transition policy.

---

[28] See 76Fed. Reg. 52,442 and 76 Fed. Reg. 52,475.

[29] For Medicaid definition, see Social Security Act, Section 1915(c)(5)(A).

[30] See section 220.2(c) and (d) in the Medicare Benefits Policy Manual available here:
http://www.cms.gov/manuals/Downloads/bp102c15.pdf

[31] If a State does not have a separate CHIP program, it may establish a benchmark that is consistent with the applicable CHIP standards.
http://www.cms.gov/SMDL/downloads/CHIPRA%20Dental%20SHO%20Final%20100709revised.pdf

11

Mental Health and Substance Use Disorder Services and Parity

The MHPAEA expanded on previous Federal parity legislation addressing the potential for discrimination in mental health and substance use disorder benefits to occur by generally requiring that the financial requirements or treatment limitations for mental health and substance use disorder benefits be no more restrictive than those for medical and surgical benefits. However, although parity was applied for covered mental health and substance use disorder benefits, there was no requirement to offer such a benefit in the first instance. Also, prior to the Affordable Care Act, MHPAEA parity requirements did not apply to the individual market or group health coverage sponsored by employers with 50 or fewer employees.

The Affordable Care Act identifies coverage of mental health and substance use disorder benefits as one of the 10 categories and therefore as an EHB in both the individual and small group markets. The Affordable Care Act also specifically extends MHPAEA to the individual market. Because the Affordable Care Act requires any issuer that must meet the coverage standard set in section 1302(a) to cover each of the 10 categories, all such plans must include coverage for mental health and substance use disorder services, including behavioral health treatment. Consistent with Congressional intent, we intend to propose that parity applies in the context of EHB.

Benefit Design Flexibility

To meet the EHB coverage standard, HHS intends to require that a health plan offer benefits that are "substantially equal" to the benefits of the benchmark plan selected by the State and modified as necessary to reflect the 10 coverage categories. This is the same equivalency standard that applies to plans under CHIP.[32] Similar to CHIP, we intend to propose that a health insurance issuer have some flexibility to adjust benefits, including both the specific services covered and any quantitative limits provided they continue to offer coverage for all 10 statutory EHB categories. Any flexibility provided would be subject to a baseline set of relevant benefits, reflected in the benchmark plan as modified. Permitting flexibility would provide greater choice to consumers, promoting plan innovation through coverage and design options, while ensuring that plans providing EHB offer a certain level of benefits. We are considering permitting substitutions that may occur only within each of the 10 categories specified by the Affordable Care Act. However, we are also considering whether to allow substitution across the benefit categories. If such flexibility is permitted, we seek input on whether substitution across categories should be subject to a higher level of scrutiny in order to mitigate the potential for eliminating important services or benefits in particular categories. In addition, we intend to require that the substitution be actuarially equivalent, using the same measures defined in CHIP.[33]

To ensure competition within pharmacy benefits, we intend to propose a standard that reflects the flexibility permitted in Medicare Part D in which plans must cover the

---

[32] 42 CFR 457.420.

[33] 42 CFR 457.431

12

categories and classes set forth in the benchmark, but may choose the specific drugs that are covered within categories and classes.[34] If a benchmark plan offers a drug in a certain category or class, all plans must offer at least one drug in that same category or class, even though the specific drugs on the formulary may vary.

The Affordable Care Act also directs the Secretary to consider balance in defining benefits and to ensure that health insurance issuers do not discriminate against enrollees or applicants with health conditions. Providing guidelines for substitution will ensure that health insurance issuers meet these standards.

Updating Essential Health Benefits

Section 1302(b)(4)(G) and (H) direct the Secretary to periodically review and update EHB. As required by the Affordable Care Act, we will assess whether enrollees have difficulties with access for reasons of coverage or cost, changes in medical evidence or scientific advancement, market changes not reflected in the benchmarks and the affordability of coverage as it relates to EHB. We invite comment on approaches to gathering information and making this assessment. Under the benchmark framework, we note that the provision of a "substantially equal" standard would allow health insurance issuers to update their benefits on an annual basis and they would be expected on an ongoing basis to reflect improvements in the quality and practice of medicine. We also intend to propose a process to evaluate the benchmark approach.

---

[34] Drug category and class lists would be provided by the U.S. Pharmacopoeia, AHMS, or through a similar standard. Note: we do not intend to adopt the protected class of drug policy in Part D.

13

INDEX

References are to chapters, section numbers, and appendices.

A

Abortion, federal funding prohibited, 2.03[A]

Access to information. *See* Information accessibility

Account-based plans, 8.01[D]

Accountability requirements, Ch. 10. *See also* Transparency and accountability requirements

Acupuncture, 9.04

AD&D coverage, excepted benefits, 5.04

Administrative fees for self-funded and insured plans, 13.04
    background, 13.04[A]
    funding research into outcomes and clinical effectiveness, 13.04[A]. *See also* Patient-Centered Outcomes Research Institute (PCORI)
    PCORI fees, 13.04[B]
      covered lives, determination of, 13.04[D]
      exceptions for certain plans and programs, 13.04[C], 13.04[F]
      multiple plans, sponsor of, 13.04[C]
      payment of fees, 13.04[E]
      plans subject to PCORI fees, 13.04[C]
      reporting of fees, 13.04[E]
    temporary transitional reinsurance fee, 13.04[A], 13.04[F]

Adult children, extended coverage for. *See* Children

Affordability and accessibility, Ch. 6
    employment-based changes (effective January 2014), 6.03
    group plans, transition changes (effective September 2010), 6.02
    immediate provisions (effective March 2010), 6.01
    transparency and accountability requirements, Ch. 10. *See also* Transparency and accountability requirements

Affordable Care Act. *See* Health Care and Education Reconciliation Act of 2010 (HCERA); Patient Protection and Affordable Care Act of 2010 (PPACA)

Affordable Health Care for America Act (House passed 2009), 2.03[A]

Affordable Health Choices Act (Senate Committee 2009), 2.03[A]

Age limits. *See* Children

American Health Benefit Exchange. *See* Exchanges

American Indians. *See* headings starting with "Indian"

America's Affordable Health Care Choices Act (House Committees 2009), 2.03[A]

Annual dollar limits on benefits, 8.01[B]
    essential vs. non-essential benefits, 8.01[B][1]
    grandfathered health plans, 5.01[C], 5.01[D][4], 8.01
    HRAs, exemption for certain plans, 8.01[D]
    non-essential benefits, 8.01[B][2]
    restricted limits on essential benefits, 8.01[B][1]
    waiver of annual dollar limit restriction, 8.01[B][1]
      Annual Notice requirement, 8.01[B][1]
      "annual update" information, 8.01[B][1]
      extension of waiver, 8.01[B][1]

      revised procedure, 8.01[B][1]

Anti-dumping rule, 7.02

Appeals process, 6.02, 8.05
    adverse benefit determination, 8.05[A]
    amendment to tri-agency regulations on, App. N
    external claims, 8.05, 8.05[B]
      expedited external review, eligibility for, 8.05[B][2][a], 8.05[B][2][b]
      federal external review requirement, compliance with, 8.05[B][2]
      state external review law, compliance with, 8.05[B][1]
    grandfathered health plans, exemption for, 5.01[C]
    internal claims, 8.05, 8.05[A]
    model notices for claims and appeals decisions, App. O
    non-English language, communication in, 8.05[A]
    office of health insurance consumer assistance or ombudsman, 8.05[C]
    tri-agency regulations, App. M
      amendment to, App. N

Archer MSAs, 2.02[B]

Automatic enrollment arrangements, 12.03, 14.01[E]

B

Benefits summary. *See* Uniform summary of benefits and coverage

Brand-name prescription drugs
    cost-sharing, changes in level of, 5.01[D][2][d]

Breast Cancer EARLY Act, 2.03[B]

Breast cancer screening, 8.03

C

"Cadillac" health coverage, taxation of, 13.01

Cafeteria plans, 2.02[B]
    background, 12.07[A]
    definition of cafeteria plan, 12.07[A]
    exempt from nondiscrimination requirements, 12.07[B]
    small employers, 12.07

Calculation of employees
    Exchange eligibility, 11.04[A]
    large employers, 11.02[B]
    small employers, 7.03[E]

Cancellation of coverage. *See* Rescissions of plan coverage

Catalyst to Better Diabetes Care Act of 2009, 2.03[B]

Catastrophic plans offered through Exchange, 11.04[D]

Catastrophic policies, 11.04

Challenges to health care reform, Ch. 3

Change of benefits. *See* Grandfathered health plans

Children
    extension of coverage until age 26, 2.02[E], 6.02, 8.04
      exclusions from income for adult children coverage, App. L

U

V

W

Y